SUPPLEMENTS TO
NOVUM TESTAMENTUM

THE AUTHENTICITY
OF EPHESIANS

SUPPLEMENTS TO
NOVUM TESTAMENTUM

VOLUME XXXIX

LEIDEN
E. J. BRILL
1974

THE AUTHENTICITY
OF EPHESIANS

BY

A. VAN ROON

LEIDEN
E. J. BRILL
1974

Originally published in The Netherlands under the title of
Een onderzoek naar de authenticiteit van de Brief aan de Epheziërs

Translated from the Dutch by S. Prescod-Jokel

The translation of this book was fully subsidized by the Netherlands
Organisation for the Advancement of Pure Research (Z.W.O.)

ISBN 90 04 03971 6

CONTENTS

AUTHOR'S NOTE

This book is a translation of a theological dissertation submitted to the Leiden University in 1969. The promoter was Professor Dr. G. Sevenster.

I would like to express my sincere thanks to the Netherlands Origanisation for the Advancement of Pure Research (Z.W.O.), whose financial assistance has made this translation possible. In addition, I would like to give a word of thanks to Mrs. Prescod-Jokel who undertook the translation.

Hebrew and Greek biblical texts quoted in this book are numbered according to R. Kittel, Biblia Hebraica, Stuttgart ²1925 and E. Nestle-K. Aland, Novum Testamentum Graece, Stuttgart ²⁵1963. For the works of Philo, I have consulted Philo Alexandrinus, Opera quae supersunt ed. L. Cohn et P. Wendland Vol. I-VIII (Berolini 1896-1930). Insofar as this book concerns the Dead Sea Scrolls I have made use of Die Texte aus Qumran, Hebräisch und deutsch, München 1964, by E. Lohse.

When using abbreviations I have tried to follow as closely as possible the appendix entitled "Abkürzungs-Verzeichnis", added in 1960 to G. Kittel's Theologisches Wörterbuch zum Neuen Testament.

Other abbreviations include:

Abbott, Eph.-Col. for T. K. Abbott, A Critical and Exegetical Commentary on the Epistles to the Ephesians and to the Colossians, Edinburgh, 1897.

BZNW for Beihefte zur Zeitschrift für die neutestamentliche Wissenschaft, Gieszen bzw. Berlin, 1923ss.

CP for all epistles in the N.T. which record Paul as the sender.

CP min or CP minus for all the above with the exception of the pastorals.

HP for the homologoumena of the Corpus Paulinum.

Dib., Gefbr. for M. Dibelius, An die Kolosser, Epheser—an Philemon (Handbuch z. N.T. 12), ²1927.

Reitzenstein, HMR for R. Reitzenstein, Die hellenistischen Mysterienreligionen, Leipzig und Berlin, ³1927 and Reitzenstein, IEM for R. Reitzenstein, Das Iranische Erlösungsmysterium, Bonn 1921.

Schlier, Eph. for H. Schlier, Der Brief an die Epheser, Düsseldorf 1962.

Schürer, Gesch. J. V. for E. Schürer, Geschichte des jüdischen Volkes im Zeitalter Jesu Christi (Leipzig, ⁴1901-1909).

LXX for the Septuagint (ed. A. Rahlfs, Stuttgart 1935).

ἐν τ. δ. for ἐν τῷ δεῖνι, an expression used to replace an unknown geographical indication.

INTRODUCTION

Since the last decades of the eighteenth century the authenticity of the Epistle to the Ephesians has been a matter of considerable controversy. Up to the present, the question of whether or not the apostle Paul was the author of this work, has never found a definitive answer. This is a question which must, therefore, be raised again and again. Indeed, our knowledge and understanding of Paul and his theology is in part dependent on a satisfactory solution to the problem.

In coming to an assessment of that great spiritual driving force called Paul, it makes an important difference if this epistle is to be regarded as an original source. As it stands, Ephesians is too individual in content and character not to influence any picture we form of Paul and it would not be overstating the case to say that an erroneous appraisal in this respect would lead to a distorted image in general.

Nobody who chooses to embark upon this particular problem which has now engaged scholars for something over a century and a half, can expect his conclusions to be accepted as the final word. At the most, one can hope to rectify faulty arguments of the past, introduce some new and valid lines of reasoning and help to strengthen one or the other tenet, be it on the side of those contending or those disputing the authenticity of the work.

Furthermore, one may hope that such research, in this case partly aimed at the form and content of the work, will contribute towards the further exegesis of the epistle. For these results are also significant. It would be accurate to say that since the Second World War, a number of Christian churches have evinced special interest in the Epistle to the Ephesians. Impelled by the ecumenical struggle as well as ecclesiological considerations, these churches have studied this epistle in particular with marked attention. In addition, a renewed interest in the Jewish nation has been developing and theologians who were re-evaluating their views on the relationship of the Christian church with repsect to Israel, could not fail to turn towards this document. For these reasons, all research that promotes increased understanding of this epistle is of immediate relevance.

One thing which is of vital importance is that the position of one or the other of the protagonists in the controversy should be strengthened. As far as many theologians are concerned, the verdict of scholarship will decide the allotted place of the epistle within the framework of the New Testament as a whole. If the final verdict is that the work is not authentic, the fact will be that although the Christian church has always invested the epistle with canonical authority, it will nevertheless have to be relegated to the periphery of the New Testament. But if the contrary emerges and the authenticity of Ephesians becomes an increasingly likely proposition, the result will be a developing tendency to recognise it as a central source of information.

The first chapter of the present study describes the history of research and study that has already gone into the Epistle to the Ephesians, together with an outline of the surrounding problems. In so doing, I have tried to do justice to all concerned and mention all aspects involved.

In this book, I have specialised in an investigation into the disposition of the epistle and some details of style. I have also devoted particular attention to testing words and expressions used in this epistle against images and conceptions they were connected with in contemporary literature. This procedure was eddential since the defenders of the epistle on the one hand, generally tend to pay little attention to the religio-historical background of these words and expressions, whilst those, on the other hand, who dispute the authenticity of the epistle, often incorrectly relate this kind of material with syncretism and Gnosticism.

As a matter of course, the question of the relationship of this epistle to that addressed to the Colossians had to be dealt with. The consequences of this very special relationship have meant that in many a study, the Epistle to the Ephesians has tended to fall in the shadow of Colossians. To arrive at a just appraisal when determining the authenticity of Ephesians, the epistle must, to begin with, be looked at in its own right rather than in conjunction with Colossians, All the same, our epistle will constantly be subjected to comparison with the latter in the course of this book. The problem of corresponding fragments will not be treated until the final chapter.

CHAPTER ONE

INSTANCES FROM THE HISTORY
OF PROBLEMS SURROUNDING THE
EPISTLE TO THE EPHESIANS

1. THE ADDRESSEES

Already within the ancient church some surprise existed that the
Ephesians should have been named as the addressees of this epistle.
It was known that Paul, prior to his imprisonment, had accomplished
much work in Ephesus and the fact was remarked upon that in this
epistle, written during his imprisonment, he approaches the Christians
of Ephesus in such a manner as to suggest that they are not personally
known to him.[1]

Later, Beza put forward the explanation that the epistle was not
intended for the Ephesians alone but also for other communities in
Asia Minor.[2] Grotius recalled Marcion who described the epistle in
question as the epistle to the Laodiceans and believed that it had been
sent to the community in Laodicea as well as that of Ephesus.[3] J. Mill
held Laodicea to have been the original destination of the epistle,
maintainig that a combination of Eph. 6:21 and 2 Tim. 4:12 would have
had the result that Ephesus subsequently replaced Laodicea.[4] J. Ussher
supported the idea of an original text without indications concerning
the address, holding that Paul had meant the epistle to reach a number of communities in Asia Minor, leaving a space after the words τοῖς

---

[1] Theodori Episcopi Mopsuestiensis in ep. B. Pauli commentarii, ed. H. B. Swete I
(Cambridge 1880), p. 112 ss.; cf. J. Schmid, Der Epheserbrief des Apostels Paulus
(Freiburg i. Br. 1928), p. 49 s.

[2] Theodorus Beza, Nov. Testamentum greace et latine (Genevae 1598) p. 288.

[3] Hugonis Grotii Annotationes in Nov. Testamentum denuo emendatius editae
(Groningae 1829), 11. 4 and 147 (first edition Paris, 1646).

[4] J. Mill, Nov. Testamentum graecum (Roteodami 1710) : Prolegomena n. 71

[5] J. Ussher, Annales Veteris et Novi Testamenti (Londini 1654). C. J. Huth came to
similar conclusions in his Epistola ex Laodicea in Encyclica ad Ephesios adservata (diss.
Erlangen 1751), p. 54ss. L. Bertholdt wanted to prove in his Historisch-kritische Einleitung in sämmtliche canon. u. apokr. Schriften d. A. u. N.T., (Erlangen 1819), p. 2802,

οὖσιν (Eph. 1:1).[5] Thus. to whatever community the epistle was brought to be read, the appropriate name could be inserted.

When the rise of deism favoured the development of a Unitarian movement of free theological research in England, this problem surrounding the destination of the epistle was considered of sufficient magnitude by the Unitarian scholar E. Evanson, to altogether doubt its authenticity. He thought that an epistle in which Paul expressed himself in such a fashion could not possibly be genuine. This occasion (1792) was the first time that the non-genuineness of the epistle was put forward.[1] The problem however, remained an issue.

Later, A. von Harnack once again contended that Laodicea had been the originally designated recipient of the epistle, backing his tenet with a curious hypothesis. The name of Laodicea was to have disappeared from the text of the manuscript as the result of a collective measure of discipline, conceived by the Christendom of Asia Minor in the nature of a damnatio memoriae, in accordance with Apc. 3:16.[2] Nowadays, not a single defender of the authenticity of Eph. would still subscribe to the idea that Ephesus was to have been the sole intended recipient of the epistle.

2. The particular affinity between Eph. and Col.

A long time was to pass before the extraordinary resemblance between Eph. and Col. was considered in the light of a problem although it had already been remarked upon previously. A younger contemporary of Erasmus, Hyperius who sided with Luther, pointed out the resemblance and provided a psychological explanation. Paul had first of all dictated Eph. and shortly afterwards, Col. Both letters treated the same area. Involuntarily, the same formulations recurred. The difference between the two epistles lay in a certain brevity of tone in Col. and allowances for the particular conditions prevailing in Colossae.[3]

---

that Tychicus had had a number of copies of Eph. with a space (for adding the name of a place) as well as a number of copies with a place-name already filled in. He argued that the route the messenger was to take had been only partly fixed before he set off.

[1] E. Evanson, The dissonance of the four generally received Evangelists and the Evidence of their respective Authenticity examined (Ipswich 1792), p. 26.

[2] A. von Harnack, "Die Adresse des Epheserbriefes des Paulus" in SAB 1910, IIer Halbband, p. 696s.

[3] Andreas Hyperius, Commentarii in ep. Pauli ad Philipp., Coloss. ac Thessalonic ambas (ed. I. Mylius, Turici 1582), p. 69.

By 1790 the affinity had not as yet reached the proportions of a problem. W. Paley, the Latitudinarian, whose theories had in former years now and then clashed with tradition, now defended the authenticity of Paul's epistles on the basis of their inner testimony. Eph. and Col. were exactly that which they purported to be: the products of "a mind revolving a second time the same ideas". He rejected the possibility that either of the two letters could be a forgery, one being an imitation of the other, on the serious basis that this theory would have attributed to a forger more than possible refinement.[1]

During the course of subsequent years the resemblance between the two epistles was the subject of intensive study. The exegetical significance was recognised and the two epistles were found to elucidate each other.[2] J. G. Eichhorn gave a new explanation for this affinity; after Paul had himself completed Eph., he was thought to have dictated the basic draft of Col. to his pupil Timothy, also named as the co-sender in the opening to the epistle, who then worked out the draft independently.[3] Fr. Schleiermacher regarded Eph. as secondary and assumed that the epistle had, with Paul's consent, been completed by Tychicus following the example set by Col.[4]

L. Usteri found that the matter of the resemblance between the two epistles had really become a problem. The imagery and style of Eph. did not give him the slightest difficulty but on the grounds of the affinity which the epistle bore to Col., he doubted the authenticity of Eph.[5]

W. M. L. de Wette moreover, thought that even the style and imagery of Eph. were suspect. After some initial hesitation, he finally came to question the authenticity of the epistle which he held to be but a moderately successful imitation of Col.[6]

---

[1] W. Paley, Horae Paulinae or the Truth of the scripture history of St. Paul evinced (London 1823), p. 131-150 (1st. edition 1790).

[2] H. K. A. Haenlein in his Handbuch der Einleitung i.d. Schriften des N.T., IIIer Theil (Erlangen ²1794), p. 414, began by giving a detailed list of parallel fragments. A. van Bemmelen gave even more parallels in his Dissertatio exegetico critica de ep. Pauli ad Ephes. et Colloss. inter se collatis (L.B. 1803). He was the first to narrowly describe both the doth the corresponding and differing aspects of both epistles.

[3] J. G. Eichhorn, Einleitung i.d. N.T., IIIer Bd., le Hälfte (Leipzig 1812), p. 278ss.

[4] Fr. Schleiermacher, Einleitung i. N.T., Literarischer Nachlasz zur Theologie, IIIer Bd. (herausg. van G. Wolde, Berlin 1845), p. 163-166.

[5] L. Usteri, Entwickelung des paulinischen Lehrbegriffes mit Hinsicht auf die übrigen Schriften des N.T. (Zürich 1824), p. 2.

[6] W. M. L. de Wette, Lehrbuch der historisch-kritische Einleitung i.d. kanonischen

Around 1870 some new views arose concerning the relationship between the two epistles. S. Hoekstra regarded Eph. not as an imitation but a correction on Col. The author of Eph. had wanted to replace the inauthentic Col.[1] which diverged too far from Paul's thoughts, by a missive which corresponded more closely with the concepts of the apostle.[2] From C. H. Weisse,[3] F. Hitzig adopted the theory that Col. contained authentic and interpolated material. He now put forward that a pseudographer had conceived Eph. independently of the original Col. and had subsequently furnished the original Col. with interpolations to correspond with his own work.[4]

H. J. Holzmann presented a combination of different opinions. Eph. was not authentic and an imitation of Col. Col. in its turn, was a mixture of authentic and interpolated material. The author of Eph. who had imitated the original Col., later interpolated Col. with material from Eph.[5] In the fragments which Eph. has in common with Col., Eph. is thus occasionally dependent upon Col. but at other times, Eph. served as a model for Col.[6]

Bücher des N.T., 1842, p. 254ss. In this edition his judgement is still hesitant. In the following year he first declared himself to be definitely persuaded of the inauthenticity of Eph. in his Kurze Erklärung der Briefe a.d. Koloss., an Philem., a.d. Ephes. und Philipp., Kurzgefasztes exegetisches Handbuch z. N.T., Bd. II, Theil 4, p. 55ss. Before that, E. Th. Mayerhoff, in his Der Brief a.d. Kolosser mit vornehmlicher Berücksichtigung der drei Pastoralbriefe kritisch geprüft (Berlin 1838) had compared Col. on the one hand with the HP and on the other, with 1 and 2 Tim and Tit. He adjudged that it was precisely Col. which diverged in form and content from the H.P. whilst Eph. corresponded with it. His conclusion was that Col. was a pseudographical imitation of Eph.

[1] F. C. Bauer, Paulus der Apostel Jesu Christi, sein Leben und Wirken, seine Briefe und Lehre (Stuttgart 1845), pp. 417-436 and 455ss., shared De Wette's opinion on the relationship of Eph. to Col. but also declared Col. to be inauthentic.

[2] S. Hoekstra, "Vergelijking van de brieven aan de Efez. en de Coloss. vooral uit het oogpunt van beider leerstellige inhoud" in Theol. Tijdschrift 2, 1868, p. 559ss.

[3] C. H. Weisse, Beiträge zur Kritik der paulinischen Briefe a.d. Gl., R., Eph. und Kol. (herausg. von E. Sulze, Leipzig 1867), p. 59.

[4] F. Hitzig, Zur Kritik paulinischer Briefe (Leipzig 1870), p. 22-26.

[5] H. J. Holtzmann, Kritik der Epheser und Kolosserbriefe (Leipzig 1872); id., Lehrbuch der historisch. kritischen Einleitung i.d. N.T. (Freiburg i. Br. 1855), pp. 262ss. and 269ss.

[6] Mayerhoff (see p. 5 note 6) had defended the anteriority of Eph. with respect to Col. W. Hönig, with a thoroughness to match Mayerhoff's, studied the parallels between Eph. and Col. and, contrary to Mayerhoff, vindicated the priority of Col, in his article "Ueber das Verhältnis des Epheserbriefes zum Briefe an die Kolosser" in Z.w.Th. 15, 1872, p. 63-87. Thus Holtzmann also reconciled these two views.

Although Holtzmann gained widespread agreement, none of the New Testament scholars who were inspired under his influence to undertake intensive research on the subject of the relationship between Eph. and Col., adopted his views without modification. Emendations were put forward because a greater degree of independence was discovered in Eph.[1] and also because the hypothesis of interdependence did not do justice to the individual character of both epistles.[2] Furthermore, it was also thought wrong to explain all the identical features of the two epistles exclusively through the hypothesis of literary dependence.[3]

Some time later, W. Ochel came back to the opinion of Usteri and de Wette that the author of the non-authentic Eph. had copied Col. However, he recognised much material in Eph. which had not been derived from Col. and believed that the author of Eph. had made use of an already existing hymn and of traditional liturgical and paraenetical material. Nevertheless, even whilst drawing upon these other sources, the author was still held to have used Col. as an example again and again.[4]

---

[1] Thus Herm. von Soden. He held Col. to be authentic and found but few interpolations (later only one) in the epistle. The interpolator was not identical with the author of Eph. but was well-acquainted with Eph. ("Der Kolosserbrief", Jbch. pr. Th. 1885, pp. 320ss. and 497ss.; "Der Epheserbrief", Jbch. pr. Th. 1887, pp. 103ss. and 423ss.; Die Briefe a.d. Kolosser, Epheser, Philemon und die Pastoralbriefe, Hdktr. z. N.T. van H. J. Holtzmann, IIIer Bd., 1893, pp. 15, 28 and 33; cf. also Jbch. pr. Th. 1883. p. 482ss.).

[2] P. W. Schmiedel came to the conclusion that Col. had been interpolated twice; first independently from Eph. and then once more but dependent on Eph. In his view, Eph. also contained interpolations. See his article, Kolossae II in the Allgemeine Encyclopädie d. Wissensch. u. Künste, herausg. v. J. S. Ersch u. J. G. Gruber, IIe Section, 37er Theil (Leipzig 1885), p. 139s.

[3] Thus W. Soltau, "Die ursprüngliche Gestalt des Kolosserbriefes", Th. St. Kr. 1905, p. 521ss. Soltau arrived at a very complicated solution. Both Eph. and Col. contained original material. The epistle intended for Laodicea mentioned in Col. 4:16 had been lost. Material from that epistle was preserved in Col. 1:21-29 and 3:5-4:9. The original material of Col. was to be found in Col. 2:1-3:4. The author of Eph. was to have compiled his epistle from the already lost epistle to Laodicea, using excerpts and fragments. He was not thought to have been familiar with our complete Col. Occasionally he had in mind the form of Col. as known to him.

[4] W. Ochel, Die Annahme einer Bearbeitung des Kolosser-Briefes im Epheser-Brief in einer Analyse des Epheser-Briefes untersucht (Diss. Marburg 1934). Eph. 1:3-14 is the hymn. The liturgical material is to be found in Eph. 1:19-2:10; for the most part independent in his view., is Eph. 2:11-22. In Eph. 3:2-7 he thinks Col. 3 has been used intensively. The "Haustafel" in Eph. 5:22-6:9 is in his opinion an adaptation of the one found in Col. in a form even more suited to Christianity.

J. Schmid came to entirely different conclusions. His view is that the in every respect complicated affinities in Eph. and Col. do not admit the consideration of literary interdependence.[1]

3. The relationship to the other epistles of Paul

In the meantime, the relationship of Eph. to the other epistles of Paul became yet another problem. Ochel pointed out features in Eph. reminiscent of those other epistles.[2] Prior to that, J. Weiss had already propounded the possibility that the author of Eph. had really been the collector of the epistles of Paul.[3]

E. J. Goodspeed demonstrated that Eph. possesses an exceptionally large number of affinities with the HP and drew up a conspectus of these parallels in which he omitted not the slightest or least significant corresponding fragment. He tried to prove that the author of Eph. had long been familiar with Col. and Phlm. and had later collected the remaining HP. Wanting to make this collection more widely known, the author had added Eph., in which he tried to make Paul speak for himself as much as possible, as an introduction. Thus this epistle had come to be: "a mosaic of Pauline materials ... almost a Pauline anthology". Most of the material was to have come from Col. the words and thoughts of which had already been known to the author (probably Onesimus) for so long.[4]

C. L. Mitton, correcting and completing this interpretation, agreed with Goodspeed. Mitton regarded the creation of Eph. essentially in the light of a mnemo-technical process and not as the compilation of a kind of synopsis. In the course of years, Col. and Phlm. had more or less become the mental property of the author of Eph. As a result of reading and re-reading, he had subsequently also partially absorbed the remaining HP into his mental system. "Some of the outstanding passages he read again and again. Striking phrases expressing important

---

[1] J. Schmid, Der Epheserbrief des Apostels Paulus (B. St., 22er Bd., Heft 3 u. 4, 1928).

[2] Op. cit., p. 14.

[3] J. Weiss, Das Urchristentum (herausg. v. R. Knopf. Göttingen 1917), pp. 108 and 534.

[4] E. J. Goodspeed, The Meaning of Ephesians, a study of the origin of the Epistle (Chicago 1933). Id., The key to the Ephesians (Chicago ²1957).

truths resounded in his thoughts". He was thus able to accomplish the writing of Eph. without resorting to copying.[1] He wished to be nothing but a mouth-piece for Paul but he did make adaptations to cater for a specific circle of readers of his own time. Expressions deriving from Judaism which Paul had used and which by the author's time had more or less become technical terms, he replaced with more comprehensible words. He fitted the style of his work to suit the liturgical practises of the Christians of the communities in Asia Minor for whom he was writing.

Presumably—we are still quoting the opinion of Mitton—Tychicus, the former messenger of Paul had given his approval to the work, being hence mentioned in Eph. 6:21.

4. The relationship to 1 Pt.

The relationship of Eph. to 1 Pt. had already previously come under discussion. A. Schwegler, a follower of F. C. Bauer, dated both epistles in the second century, attributing to 1 Pt. an earlier date than Eph.[2] B. Weiss, a conservative scholar who considered both epistles to be authentic, also conceded anteriority to 1 Pt. In his opinion, it was clearly noticeable that in Eph. Paul was relying heavily on 1 Pt. and that this dependence was even more striking in R.[3]

But Hoekstra and Holtzmann adopted the contrary position: 1 Pt. was dependent on Eph. This view, namely, that 1 Pt. relies on Eph. was subsequently more or less generally accepted.[4]

W. Seufert saw so much affinity in style and material between the two epistles that he ascribed them to the same pseudographer. He iden-

---

[1] C. L. Mitton, The Epistle to the Ephesians (Oxford 1951); cf. p. 264-269.

[2] A. Schwegler, Das nachapostolische Zeitalter in den Hauptmomenten seiner Ent-wickelung (Tübingen 1846), cf. Bd. II, pp. 1ss. and 58ss.

[3] B. Weiss, Der petrinische Lehrbegriff (1855), p. 374ss. O. Pfleiderer, Der Paulinis-mus, Ein Beitrag zur Geschichte der urchristliche Theologie (Leipzig 1873), p. 434 note**, referred to Weiss respecting the anteriority of 1 Pt. to Eph. He held both epistles to be inauthentic. W. Brückner had the same opinion as Pfleiderer and gave a detailed list of parallel fragments in his article "Die Zeitlage der Briefe an die Kolosser und Epheser", Pr. M. 18, 1922, p. 164ss. (cf. also his Die Chronologische Reihenfolge, in welcher die Briefe des N.T. verfaszt sind (Haarlem 1890), pp. 41-56 and 256-275.)

[4] Hoekstra op. cit., p. 650 s., Holtzmann, Kritik, p. 259-266 and Einleitung, p. 276. Cf. F. W. Beare, The first epistle of Peter (Oxford 1947), p. 9: "all critics are now agreed, that the dependence is on the side of First Peter".

tified the forger as the author of the speeches which are attributed to
the apostles Peter and Paul in Acts.[1]

Ph. Carrington retraced the relationship between Eph. and 1 Pt.
to a catechistic tradition which had its roots in Judaism. Nevertheless,
he did leave open the possibility that the author of 1 Pt. had been
inspired to write his epistle through Eph. and had based the structure
of his work on that of Eph.[2] E. G. Selwyn followed Carrington and
moreover thought that besides this catechistic tradition, there existed
additional common sources of available material. These were to be
found in the liturgy of the young Christian communities and in a
homiletic and paraenetical tract which was put together to help the
evangelists and teachers in strengthening the faith of those communities at a time when the expansion of Christianity was accompanied
by a correspondingly developing hostility against it.[3]

Mitton disputed Selwyn. He thought that he could prove that material for 1 Pt., Eph. and Col. had not been gathered from common
sources but that Eph. is obviously dependent on Col. and 1 Pt.obviously
dependent on Eph.[4]

5. The style

Erasmus was the first to make the observation that Eph. is peculiar
in character. He thought that Paul had expressed himself somewhat
clumsily in this epistle; its stylistic inadequacies even caused him to
doubt the epistle's apostolic authorship.[5] Beza realized that there is

---

[1] W. Seufert, "Das Verwandtschaftsverhältnis des ersten Petrus und Epheserbriefes",
Z. w. Th. 24, 1881, pp. 178-197, 332-379.

[2] Ph. Carrington, The primitive Christian Catechism, A study in the Epistles (Cambridge 1940); cf. pp. 178-197, 332-379.

[3] E. G. Selwyn, The first epistle of St. Peter (London [3]1949), p. 17-19; see also
pp. 285, 297, 365-366 and especially pp. 262ss., 289 and 462.

[4] C. L. Mitton, "The Relationship between 1 Peter and Ephesians" in J. Th. St.
N.S. I 1950, p. 67-73.

[5] See Desiderius Erasmus, Annotationes of Aanteekeningen op 't N.T., van J. H.
Glazenmaker uit het Latijn vertaald (Amsterdam 1663) : "de voorreden op de brief aan
de Efezers" and the note ad. Eph. 1:18. (The original edition of the Annotationes appeared in 1519 in Basel.) Erasmus particularly objected to the construction of many
sentences. In his opinion the style of Ephesians differs greatly form that of the other
epistles. The spiritual content of the epistle, removed his doubts respecting its authenticity.

a remarkable similarity between the style of our epistle and that of Col.[1] In later times, this resemblance escaped the attention of many scholars. Thus Eichhorn asserted that these two epistles differ in the manner of expressing thought. His appreciation of Eph. diverged sharply from Erasmus' assessment. He thought that Paul had devoted a special amount of care to this epistle in particular. With de Wette however, the objection of the great humanist, be it in another form, was re-introduced with renewed vigour. On the basis of style and language, de Wette raised many arguments to question the authenticity of Eph.[2] Many shared his view. Nevertheless, when at a later period the style of Paul's epistles were subjected to intensive research, it took a long time before more specific attention was given to Eph. and a stylistic analysis of the work was undertaken.

J. Weiss,[3] Ed. Norden[4] and R. Bultmann[5] more or less ignored Eph. in their studies of the epistles.

Th. Innitzer accomplished the first systematic work on the style of Eph. Eph. 1:3-14, the "hymn", he classified as strongly rhythmical prose.[6] Some considerable time later, E. Lohmeyer and J. de Zwaan gave an analysis of the same pericope. Lohmeyer thought that he had in that passage discovered a certain type of rhythm which bears a Jewish liturgical character.[7] De Zwaan spoke of a typically pauline

[1] Novum Testamentum gr. et lat., ad Kol. 1:24. Viz. Beza, the affinity rests on a very special form of the oratio perpetua, the πτωτικός. Van Bemmelen in the Dissertatio (see p. 5 n. 2), p. 19s. supported Beza and pointed out the use of this form in the other CP and 1 and 2 Pt. He saw typical paulinic idiosyncracies in the language and style of Eph. and Col. and especially in the former.

[2] See for Eichhorn and de Wette p. 5.

[3] J. Weiss, "Beiträge zur paulinischen Rhetorik", in Thelogischen Studien Prof. Dr. Bernhard Weiss zu seinem 70. Geburtstag dargebracht (Göttingen 1897), p. 168ss.; id., Die Aufgabe der neutestamentliche Wissenschaft in der Gegenwart (Göttingen 1908), p. 15s.

[4] Ed. Norden, Agnostos theos (Leipzig-Berlin 1913), p. 253 and note 1; id.; Die antike Kunstproza II (Leipzig-Berlin [4]1923), p. 506, note 2.

[5] R. Bultmann, Der Stil der paulinischen Predigt und die kynisch-stoische Diatribe (Göttingen 1910), F. R. L. Heft 13, p. 73 note 1.

[6] Th. Innitzer, "Der Hymnus im Epheserbriefe" in Z. f. kath. Theologie (Innsbrück 1904), p. 612-620.

[7] E. Lohmeyer, "Das Proömium des Epheserbriefes", in Th. Bl. 5, 1926 pp. 120ss. and 233ss. A. Debrunner, "Grundsätzliches über Kolometrie im N.T.", Th. Bl. 5, 1926, p. 231ss., criticised Lohmeyer's colometric arrangement of Eph. Lohmeyer replied in a Replik, Th. Bl. 5, 1926, p. 233ss.

poetic style which is based on the principle of thought-rhyming. He encountered this style also in other places in Eph. as well as examples of it throughout the entire HP. For the style of Eph., de Zwaan entertained an appreciation as great as Eichhorn's, believing that in this epistle he had found the very grande dicendi genus of Paul of which Augustine had written so long before.[1] He even found that the quality of Eph. is such that Paul can be called a great literary artist. Upon comparing Eph. with Col., he came almost to the same conclusion as E. Th. Mayerhoff (the sole advocate for the anteriority of an absolutely authentic Eph. to an absolutely inauthentic Col.)[2] for de Zwaan thought als follows: "Het onderzoek van Paulus' stijl op woordenkeus en taaleigen geeft aan Efezen, zooals telkens weder bleek den voorrang op Colossenzen". (However, in contrast to Meyerhoff, he added: "voor beide brieven spreekt het positief ten gunste van Paulus als auteur").[3] Ochel too, analysed Eph. 1:3-14. From the elements he isolated, he attempted to reconstruct a liturgical hymn, rhythmical in character.[4] Ochel's ideas met with little response.[5]

An analysis which was more cautious than Ochel's and well-argued on the basis of similar material, was published by N. A. Dahl in 1951. His conclusion was that Eph. 1:3-14 came from a Jewish background and like Lohmeyer, he typified the pericope as a benediction (a בְּרָכָה) which was originally part of a liturgy (baptism) but—in accordance with the custom of placing a benediction at the beginning of a letter—used as an opening in the case of Eph.[6]

The "formgeschichtliche" method as followed by Dahl had already been applied to Eph. 1:15ss. by P. Schubert. Schubert investigated the formulas of thanksgiving and intercession with which the pauline

---

[1] Cf. Aug., De doctrina christiana IV, (7-) 20.

[2] See p. 5 note 6.

[3] J. de Zwaan, "Le Rhythme logique" dans l'épître aux Ephésiens", Rev. H. Ph. R. 6, 1927, p. 554-565; id., De Efezenbrief van Paulus togelicht en colometrisch vertaald (Haarlem 1927), p. 17-22. De Zwaan too, gave a colometric arrangement of Eph. (Quotation : an investigation into Paul's style in vocabulary and idiom speaks, as was proved again and again, for the anteriority of Eph. with regard to Col. .... in both letters it speaks in favour of Paul as the author.)

[4] See p. 26ss. of the work mentioned on p. 5 note 6.

[5] Cf. E. Percy, Die Probleme der Kolosser- und Epheserbriefe (Lund 1946) p. 373 note 18.

[6] N. A. Dahl, "Adresse und Proömium des Epheserbriefes", Th. Z. 7, 1951 IV, p. 241-64.

epistles, following the praescript, usually begin.[1] In his opinion Eph. 1:15ss. demonstrates most of the characteristics of the typically pauline formula and shows particular affinities with the corresponding section in Col. After the opening benediction at the beginning, this formula was relatively superfluous in Eph., but the author of Eph. had borrowed it from Col. in order to make his inauthentic letter appear genuine.[2]

Contrasting with the views of Ochel and Dahl, stands the opinion of Chr. Maurer. He again designates Eph. 1:3-14 as a hymn, regarding it as the key to an understanding of the epistle as a whole. He did not think that the passage can be split into component parts deriving from different sources; nor that there is any detectable dividing-line between this section and the remainder of the epistle. The theme of the epistle is summed up in the hymn. Most probably, the author of this inauthentic epistle had formed the hymn ad hoc.[3]

E. Percy was the first to present a thoroughly detailed analysis of the language and style of the whole epistle. He established all the characteristic features of this language and style and then demonstrated that practically without exception—be it to a greater or lesser degree—these also occur in Col. Percy convincingly showed that the language and style of Eph. and Col. can also be found in the HP. Moreover, he demonstrated that certain linguistic aspects of Eph. are not only typical of the HP but that some occur in on other literature.[4] If we overlook de Zwaans's predilection for the style of Eph. as against that

---

[1] The praescript is formed from the preceding lines of the real epistle with the name(s) of the sender(s), the recipient(s) and the greeting from the former to the latter.

[2] P. Schubert, "Form and function of the pauline Thanksgiving", ZNW, Beiheft 20. 1939; cf. pp. 37 and 44.

[3] Chr. Maurer, "Der Hymnus von Epheser I als Schlüssel zum ganzen Briefe", Ev. Theol. 11, 1951/52, p. 151ss. Maurer goes deeply into the content of the pericope and the historical religious interpretation of Eph. Ochel's view that Eph. 1:3-14 as an existing hymn can be separated from the whole epistle is also questioned by Percy (Die Probleme p. 373 note 18).

[4] Die Probleme der Kolosser-und Epheserbriefe, pp. 179-252, 481. E. Gaugler, after becoming acquainted with Percy's investigations, came to the conclusion that the problem of the authenticity of Eph. must be re-appraised. He thought that Percy had increased the likelihood of authenticity although he was unable to prove this. Through Percy, he came to the conclusion that the supporter of an authentic Eph. need not be an "unexakter Forscher" (loose inquirer) and that "allerdings auch die Unechtheitshypothese nicht zu sichern ist" (after all, the hypothesis of inauthenticity cannot be proved). See E. Gaugler, Der Epheserbrief (Auslegung neutestamentlicher Schriften Bd. 6—Aus dem Nachlass herausgeg. v. M. Geiger und K. Stalder, Zürich 1966), p. 13.

of Col., it may be said that Percy corroborated de Zwaan in his analysis. This also applies to Beza (and A. van Bemmelen) who were already alive to the corresponding nature of the styles of Eph. and Col.

Furthermore, Percy pointed out the influence of the LXX (particularly in the poetic sections) and other traditions based on ancient Hebrew or Aramaic prototypes and drew attention to a certain affinity with old synagogic liturgies.[1]

The manuscripts which have been found in the Judean desert since 1947, generally denoted as the Qumran scrolls, have brought to light clearly the Hebrew aspect of the style of Eph. K. G. Kuhn explored the similarities in language and style between Eph. and these writings and came to the conclusion that the author of Eph. and the community of Qumran had drawn upon the same tradition. To him it appears as inconceivable that both the author of Eph. and the sect, independently of one another and merely observing the customs of Old Testament language, should have arrived at a comparable language and style.[2]

Of a more general nature but nevertheless still pertinent to the authenticity of Eph., were the researches of Ed. Sievers [3] and H. J. Rose.[4] The methods of Sievers [5] and Rose [6] were too subjective to become

---

[1] Op. cit., pp. 29 note 19; 32s. note 21; 39 note 33; 41 note 37; 62s. note 79; 195, 222ss. and 252. For Van Bemmelen, see p. 5 note 2.

[2] K. G. Kuhn, "Der Epheserbrief im Lichte der Qumrantexte", N.T. St. 7, 1960/61, p. 334-346.

[3] Ed. Sievers, Die paulinischen Briefe klänglich untersucht u. herausg., Heft Epheser bis Philemon (Leipzig 1929). It is not so that Sievers separates the non-authentic from the authentic material in the CP. He does believe that he is able to distinguish those fragments in the epistle which, as it were, express the ipsissima vox of Paul from those which are formulated by Paul's helpers. An auditive "Schallanalyse" was to have enabled him to make these assessments.

[4] H. J. Rose, "The Clausulae of the Pauline Corpus", J. Th. St. 24, 1923, p. 12-23 and 25, 1924, p. 17-172. Rose divided the epistle into commata and thought that Paul had deliberately ended each comma with a clausula (For comma and colon, see H. Lausberg, Handbuch der literarischen Rhetorik, München 1960, par. 928-940 and for clausula, par. 985ss.). He thought Paul had an unconscious preference for clausulae with a very definite rhythm. For Rose, only epistles which contain clausulae with this specific rhythm with satisfactory frequency, were authentic.

[5] See A. Debrunner, "Literaturberichte" in Jahresbericht ü. d. Fortschritte der klassischen Altertumswissenschaft 236er Bd., 58, 1932, p. 212s. and 261er Bd., 64, 1938, p. 184.

[6] See the statement in the article mentioned in Note 45 by Debrunner: "Also alle Kolometrie an gegebene Texten ist subjektiv" (Therefore all colometry applied to a given text is subjective) Not only was Rose's commatic arrangement highly subjective,

popular. Ed. Schweizer thought that he had discovered a definitive criterion for establishing the authenticity of the Pauline epistles on the basis of the use of the vocative ἀδελφοί (resp. ἀδελφέ). The absence of this form of the vocative in Eph., he reagarded as conclusive evidence of its inauthenticity.[1]

Statistical methods which have been applied to the latest research into the CP are objective and form a broader basis. Because this type of analysis is still relatively unfamiliar it is to the purpose to elaborate upon the system in some detail.

In 1959 K. Grayston and G. Herdan established several criteria which must be credited with a large measure of objectiveness. To begin with, they devoted their attention to those words in the epistles of Paul which appear exclusively in one epistle. For methodological reasons they reject the usual denotation of hapax legomena to describe these words; instead, they write about "one-sample words" or "one-epistle words". Through a new statistical methodology, these words have become a new criterion.

The new feature in their method was that in comparing the number of "one-epistle words" used in the epistles of Paul, they simultaneously worked out the relationship to the number of different words used in each individual epistle as well as the relationship to the total number of words which appear in all the epistles collectively.

For every epistle they took the factor C which is defined as follows:

$$C = \frac{I + II}{III},$$

where: I = the number of one-epistle words
II = the number of words that appear in the epistles collectively
III = the vocabulary or the number of different words that appear in the epistle under disussions.

In R., 1 C., 2 C., Gal., Eph., Phil., Col. the factor C is respectively:

---

but on top of that the special method of scanning the clausulae which he had devised for Paul, gave him some possibilities for manoeuvring. His conclusions regarding the authenticity of the various epistles are not verified by any consensus of opinion.

[1] Ed. Schweizer, "Zur Frage der Echtheit des Kolosser- und Epheserbriefes", ZNW 1956, 47er Bd., p. 287.

33.9; 33.8; 32.6; 32.8; 31.0; 34.8; 34.6%. There are no significant differences.[1]

They also worked with a so-called double-logarithmic "type-token" ratio whereby the vocabulary or the number of different words in an epistle and the total number of words in that epistle were compared. The number of different words is in this case characterised as the factor V and the total number of words as N. For each epistle they took the factor γ which is calculated as follows:

$$\gamma = \frac{\log V}{\log N}$$

Also in this respect there are no significant differences between Eph. and the other epistles. In R., 1 C., 2 C., Gal., Eph., Phil., Col., 1 Th., 2 Th. the factor is respectively: 0.7864; 0.7788; 0.7944; 0.8131; 0.8046; 0.8257; 0.8238; 0.8092; 0.8223.[2]

Although Grayston and Herdan did not undertake their project with the authenticity of Eph. in mind, an argument in its favour can certainly be drawn from their results. Nevertheless, a conclusive proof for the authenticity of the epistle must not be sought from that work. According to the authors, the corresponding value of the respecitive factors C and γ in two different epistles does not necessarily indicate that the two works are by the same author but leaves open the possibility that this may be the case. Significant differences would practically eliminate this possibility, in their opinion.

Some time later, A. Q. Morton produced a criterion which he himself thought was infallible and which in his opinion, amongst other results established the inauthenticity of Eph. for once and all. His thesis is that each individual person in speech and writing uses a characteristic combination of mannerisms that are exclusive and distinguishing .These characteristics are in the first place the lengths of sentences used and the internal proportion of sentences of different lengths as well as the frequency with which certain very common words are employed. He believes that a detailed statistical survey of these data provides evidence as irrefutable as a fingerprint.[3]

---

[1] K. Grayston and G. Herdan, "The authorship of the Pastorals in the light of statistical linguistics", in N.T. St. 6, 1959, p. 8-11.

[2] Op. cit. p. 12-14.

[3] A. Q. Morton, "A computer challenges the Church", in "The Observer" (weekend review), 3 Nov. 1963, p. 21.

As a result of investigating the work of forty Greek writers, Morton learned that each of them as far as sentence-length is concerned, was invariably consistent. From this he deduced with assurance that every Greek writer of prose had by definition to remain constant in the length of his sentences.[1] A statistical analysis of the sixty-one works that are listed under the name of Demosthenes showed a considerable amount of variation in sentence-length and the internal relationship between sentences of different lengths. Next, he isolated a large group of works which were statistically homogeneous from a smaller group of statistically inconsistent works. The homogeneous works, in Morton's opinion, satisfied certain norms (i.e. with respect to sentence-length and the inter-relationship between sentences of different lengths). These norms he regarded as a criterion for authenticity.[2] The fact that he, Morton, on the basis of such criteria arrived at conclusions concerning the authenticity and inauthenticity of the works of Demosthenes which happened to coincide with the general consensus of opinion amongst classical scholars, was further evidence for him that he was on the right track.[3]

Along similar lines, he examined the frequency with which the words καί, ἐν, αὐτός, εἶναι and δέ appear in the works of various Greek authors. In the case of these frequencies, he also recognised that the authors were always constant in character. Amongst the works attributed to Demosthenes, he again found discrepancies. Once again, Morton believed that he had established criteria for determining the authenticity of a work.[4]

Next, he applied the same techniques to the epistles which are ascribed to Paul, including Hb., and there he found (statistically) one homogeneous group comprising R., 1 and 2 C. and Gal. from which the other (statistically) group of variating epistles was clearly distinguished. Because the authenticity of Gal. had always been so favourably regarded, Morton was sure that the authenticity of the epistle could now be

---

[1] Id., "The Authorship of Greek Prose" in Journal of the Royal Statistical Society, Series A (General) vol. 128, 1965, part 2, p. 170. in collaboration with others Morton continued his investigation. In "Paul, the Man and the Myth" (London 1966), A. Q. Morton and J. McLeman wrote on p. 63 that the writings of Leontius of Byzantine were being investigated and that by the end of 1965 all the prose writers in The Loeb Classical Library would have been investigated.

[2] Journal, pp. 171, 175-180.

[3] Journal, pp. 217 sub 9.2.

[4] Journal, p. 184-217.

vouchsaved beyond any doubt. On the basis of his statistical investigation, he now also declared R. and 1 and 2 C. to be as authentic as Gal., pronouncing the remaining epistles and thus also Eph., to be inauthentic.[1]

When Morton made his report before the Royal Statistical Society, on 20th. January 1965, he encountered as much derogatory criticism as approbation. It was pointed out that Paul could have employed the services of one or more secretaries,[2] and remarked that Morton had based his confident conclusions upon a comparatively scant number of Greek authors.[3]

Herdan, a statistician by profession, delivered an extensive and searingly-worded written criticism. Referring to previous linguistic research by other statisticians, he called a criterion which depends upon sentence-lenght "the most unsuitable of all available tests".[4] And on the basis of his own earlier research, he likewise rejected as unsuitable a criterion dependent on the frequency of some common words.[5]

T. Corlett pointed out that Morton did not strictly adhere to his own statistical method. Whilst Morton dismisses literary analysis of style at the beginning of his report, he later takes recourse in it when he

---

[1] Journal, p. 217-224. See also his Authorship of the Pauline Epistles (University Lectures No. 3, University of Saskatchewan, 1965) especially p. 15 and his article in The Observer, 3 Nov. 1963.

[2] Journal, p. 226, 227.

[3] Cf. the critique by G. A. Barnard, Journal, p. 227. Also see above, p. 000, note 0

[4] Journal, p. 229, 230 or G. U. Yule, "On sentence-length as a statistical characteristic of style in prose", Biometrika 30, 1939, p. 363ss. G. Herdan, Type-Token Mathematics ('s-Gravenhage 1960), para. 2.4 "Sentence- length as a style characteristic".

M. P. Brown, The authentic Writings of Ignatius (Durham 1963), p. 139. Defending himself against Herdan's criticism and his references to Yule, Morton—without mentioning Herdan by name—in his Authorship or the Pauline Epistles remarks that Yule had made a simple error in his calculation of the "standard errors", which was later discovered by W. C. Wake (op. cit., p. 11s.).

On the problematics of establishing sentence-length which his critics had brought forward, (cf. Journal, pp. 225, 229, 230) Morton has little to say (cf. Journal, p. 232s.). In Paul, the Man and the Myth, the authors examine the difficulty more closely. They define a sentences as follows : "the group of words which end with a full stop(.) a colon(.) or an interrogation mark(;) and maintain that the difference between various editions of a text lapses when the colon and full stop are equated (p. 54). But they do seem to be aware that even then, some differences remain, after all (p. 77s.).

[5] Journal, p. 229 refers to Chap. 6 of Herdan's Language as Choice and Chance (Groningen 1956).

seeks to neutralise statistical evidence of inauthenticity in the case of an otherwise accepted work of Demosthenes; he does the same with respect to some of the four authentic Pauline epistles in question.[1]

And indeed, it is so that Morton makes use of literary analysis, in contradiction to his own point of departure, when he discovers statistical data in a work he considers to be genuine which, according to his own rules, would cast a doubt on this authenticity. When that happens, he dispels this doubt through a reasoning process which is more related to literary analysis and historical criticism than to his statistical method.

For example, the frequency of the word $\alpha\vec{v}\tau\acute{o}s$ in R. differs greatly from the frequency of the same word in 1 and 2 C. and Gal. Morton reduces this disparity to insignificance by pointing out a strong Old Testamentarian influence in R.[2] In the statistical surveys attached to the lecture given before the University of Saskatchewan, he even completely omits to include a survey on the frequency of $\alpha\vec{v}\tau\acute{o}s$ in the CP.[3]

When in R. and 2 C. he determines a frequency of $\epsilon\tilde{\iota}\nu\alpha\iota$ which aberrates significantly from the frequency of this word in 1 C. and Gal., he does not hesitate to once more take refuge in the literary method and writes : "The differences are due to passages of direct address and rhetorical question ...".[4]

More can be added to this criticism of Morton. Thus it could be commented that he sometimes pays no further attention to some differences. Without further reservation he states that the four epistles in question do not make a corresponding use of $\acute{\epsilon}\nu$.[5] He does not even say in so many words that in the use of $\delta\acute{\epsilon}$ as the second or third word of a sentence, there is a strong discrepancy between R. and 2 C. on one hand and 1 C. and Gal. on the other. In the University of Saskatchewan lecture, Morton does draw attention to this; by way of explanation, he pointed out an Old Testamentarian influence on R again.[6]

---

[1] Journal, p. 228.

[2] Journal, p. 223.

[3] See p. 18 note 1

[4] Journal, p. 223.

[5] "The occurences of *en* show the first four epistles as inconsistent in their usage" (p. 223).

[6] The Authorship of the Pauline Epistles, p. 15. Statistical data on the usage of $\delta\acute{\epsilon}$ in journal, p. 222; University Lectures, p. 19, and Paul, the Man and the Myth, p. 92s.

2 C. diverges from Gal. not only with respect to the above-mentioned points but also as regards sentence-length. In explaining these differences, Morton repeatedly mentions the fact that the statistical picture of this epistle undergoes a complete change when the first fifty sentences of the epistle are deleted. They form "a section which has been questioned by many scholars".[1]

Morton almost completely ignores the fact that there are some remarkable affinities between the works of different authors.[2] Moreover, there is much to be argued against Morton's contended affinity between his assessment concerning the authenticity and inauthenticity of certain classical works and that of the general consensus of opinion.[3]

---

[1] Journal, p. 223 and University Lecture, p. 15. In Paul, the Man and the Myth, there are clearer explanations as in M-Levison, A. Q. Morton and W. C. Wake, "On Certain Statistical Features of the Pauline Epistles", The Philosophical Journal, Vol. 3, No. 2 (Edinburgh 1966), p. 129-148. In Paul, the Man and the Myth, only secondary importance is given to the investigation into δέ (as second or third word of a sentence), ἐν, αὐτός and εἶναι (pp. 88 and 93). Here is stated that the first 150 sentences or R. are non-pauline material. There is an inconsistency in the use of long sentences and also of the tiny word καί (p. 91 and 92). The same is said about the first section of 2 C. (p. 91 and 92). Concerning the last part of 2 C. they say that there is a somewhat inconsitent use of the particle δέ (p. 93). In "On Certain Statistical Features" they remark that the first part of 2 C. corresponds to Eph. in the usage of καί (p. 147) and —as distinct from Eph.—contains ἐν but rarely (pp. 142 and 144). Here is also mentioned that the use of ἐν in 1 C. varies from section to section (p. 144) and that the last part of R. (not counting Chap. 16) has some peculiarities. These disappear when Chap. 15 is also eliminated (p. 143s.). In A. Q. Morton, "The Integrity of the Pauline Epistles", Manchester Statistical Society, 10th. March 1965, p. 6 and Paul, the Man and the Myth, p. 90, the authenticity of Phlm. is considered possible.

[2] In Journal, table 39, p. 219 it appears from the different statistical measurements : mean, median, first and second quartile; that 2 C. and 2 Tm., which Morton ascribes to different authors, correspond in sentence-length. The statistical measurements : mean, median, third quartile and ninth decile, show that Phil. and Hb. correspond. Table 42, p. 222 shows a consistent usage of δέ in R., 2 C., Phil., 2 Tm, and Hb. On p. 223 Morton himself states that in the use of εἶναι R. and 2 C. correspond with Hb., whilst they differ with 1 C. and Gal. It is interesting to read that on p. 229, Herdan observes that according to the method of de Wake which Morton praises, the works of Xenophon and Aristoteles would, on the basis of sentence-length, have had to be the work of one author.

[3] Journal, p. 217 sub 9.2 : "The agreement between the statistical evidence and the consensus of literary opinion is good". In reality however, the works of Demosthenes denoted as nos. 7, 10, 13, 25, 35, 43 and 53 are authentic according to the statistical investigation into sentence-length, whereas the consensus of literary opinion, as quoted by Rose, rejects these works; cf. Journal, pp. 171 and 179. Consensus holds work no. 23

Besides, the question arises whether the statistical data, taking into account the small handful of epistles which form the Pauline body, provide a sufficiency of information to justify statements as uncompromising as those of Morton. His criteria would only be methodologically valid if they indicated averages drawn from (the averages of) an extensive corpus of literature of an already established authenticity. Criteria thus extracted, could be used to test extraneous literature of doubtful authenticity.

Open to attack in Morton's work is the fact that he sometimes leaves more and sometimes leaves less room for allowance around the norms he has set up.[1]

All in all, it is obvious that Morton has not yet hit upon the statistical-linguistic equivalent of a fingerprint. His conclusions on a number of non-coherent and sometimes conflicting data, which he is not able to fit into the framework of a relative connection [2] and which are essentially the result of some very elementary methods, are scarcely to be preferred to the more sophisticated statistical methods by which Grayston and Herdan arrived at their conclusions.[3]

---

to be authentic but the median and first quartile in the statistical survey indicate inauthenticity; cf. Journal, p. 171 and 179. The frequency of the tiny work καί indicates the inauthenticity of work 18, held to be authentic by consensus. It confirms the inauthenticity of only 3 out of 27 works, rejected by consensus; cf. Journal, p. 192, Tb. 11. The frequency of the word ἐν only confirms inauthenticity in the case of 6 out of 27 works rejected by consensus; cf. Journal, p. 209, Table 30. A statistical survey of sentences with δέ at the beginning only indicates the inauthenticity of 14 out of 20 works which can be controlled and are rejected as not authentic Demosthenes by consensus; cf. Journal, p. 200s. and p. 202 Table 22 and University Lectures, p. 24.

[1] Cf. Journal, p. 171 on Demosthenes : "If a range of three standard errors is accepted as the populations limits ..."; p. 217, on Paul : "A range of three standard errors of the population limits ..."; p. 223, on Paul : "All the other epistles lie more than two standards from the mean ...".

[2] There is a connection between sentence-length and the use of καί. An investigation into this connection as found in the CP is in "On Certain Statistical Features ...", pp. 129, 132-135. Sentence-length and the use of καί indicate the same trend. This is not so in the case of δέ. Although there is a correlation between the frequencies of καί and δέ if these frequencies are expressed as percentages of the total number of words used in the Pauline epistles, it becomes clear that investigating the use of δέ repeatedly pointed to a different direction than the investigation into the use of καί and sentence-length. (On Certain Statistical Features ..., p. 139-141).

[3] For critical reactions to Morton's notorious article in The Observer see p. 21 of The Observer (Weekend review) 10th. Nov. 1963 and the article by R. Schippers in Elsevier's Weekblad, 7 Dec. 1963, p. 7. I was grateful to accept the help of Ir. A. G. Noordam who was at the time attached to the University of Utrecht, in reading the article by

6. THE CONTENT

The content of Eph. has given rise to as many doubts as have its style and use of language. As we have already seen, De Wette's first and foremost objection against the authenticity of Eph. was based upon the content of the epistel.[1]

Bauer shared the doubts of De Wette. Not only disputing its authenticity, he moreover gave a clear alternative source of origin for the epistle from within the history of ancient Christendom. Bauer, with W. G. Kümmel, must be esteemed for at least one aspect of his historical-critical work on the New Testament. He established for once and for all that the task of historical criticism will only then have been completed when the origins of a work have been placed within the historical framework. In the history of ancient Christendom, Bauer saw an antithesis between a pauline Christianity (heathen converts) and a petrinic Christianity (Jewish converts) which was later succeeded by striving towards synthesis from both sides. He placed Eph. within a period when the antithesis was still dominant but attempts towards synthesis were already developing. With Col., Eph. was an expression of synthesis from the pauline side. Both epistles had been written by a single author; Eph. was a wordy repetition of Col. and had been dispatched into the world simultaneously with Col. The repetition served to heighten the effect. This particular period was also the period when gnosticism was beginning to develop and gnostic ideas were just coming into circulation; these gnostic ideas often still passed as unsuspected Christian speculations. In the unity of Christ and the ecclesia, which is found in the pericope Eph. 5 : 22-23, Bauer recognised the suzugia of Valentinian gnosis. He regarded the words $\pi\lambda\acute{\eta}\rho\omega\mu\alpha$, $\sigma\hat{\omega}\mu\alpha$, $\mu\upsilon\sigma\tau\acute{\eta}\rho\iota o\nu$, $\sigma o\phi\acute{\iota}\alpha$ $\gamma\nu\hat{\omega}\sigma\iota\varsigma$ and $\alpha\grave{\iota}\acute{\omega}\nu$ which appear in both epistles, as gnostic terms.[2]

Grayson and Herdan in the N.T. St. and the for me, as a non-mathematician and non-statistician, very difficult article by Morton in the Journal of the Royal Stat. Soc.

[1] See p. 5, De Wette (Lehrbuch, p. 254ss.) objected to the apostles being put on one single level with the Old Testament prophets in 2:20 and 3:5 and against the pretentious manner with which 3:4 describes Paul's revelation into the mystery of Christ and against the demonological concepts of the epistle.

[2] See the Bauer work mentioned in n. 15 on p. 6 and the references there listed. See also W. G. Kümmel, Das Neue Testament, Geschichte der Erforschung seiner Probleme (Freiburg/München 1958), pp. 162, 167 and 168.

Hoekstra, O. Pfleiderer (one of Bauer's last students) and P. W. Schmiedel have all disputed the view of Bauer that Eph. and Col. were by the same hand. All three thought that there was a theological difference between the two epistles and were agreed that the idea of pleroma in Eph. is different from that in Col.[1] Hoekstra felt that the author of Eph. had transformed ideas from Col which were foreing to Paul and adapted them to Pauline mentality.[2] Pfleiderer thought of Eph. as an improvement on Col.; the author of Eph. had been concerned to reinstate the narrow relationship between Christ, who in Col. has already been elevated to a cosmic deity so easily conceived as divorced from all that is earthly, and the ecclesia on earth.[3] Schmiedel saw a temporisation in Eph. which is not present in Col. In his opinion, the community has already come to fullnes of life in Col. 2 : 10 whereas in Eph. 3 : 19 this objective has still to be achieved. In Col. 2 : 15, the wicked angels have been vanquished whilst in Eph. 6 : 12 they have still to be fought. In Col. 2 : 10 and 1 : 16, Christ has his sovereignty from everlasting whilst in Eph. 1 : 21 as in Phil. 2 : 10, his resurrection

---

[1] According to Hoekstra, $\pi\lambda\acute{\eta}\rho\omega\mu\alpha$ represents a standing expression in Col. But not in Eph. In his opinion, the pleroma concept does not admit allowance for Paul's conception of the pneuma whilst in Eph., to the contrary, there is abundant indication of this. Pfleiderer sees the pleroma in Col. as a dogmatic concept which expresses the totality of the godly powers of salvation and the majesty of Christ. He thinks that in Eph. the word has a less clear meaning and has therefore been misunderstood as a varying ethical proposition. Schmiedel thinks that $\pi\lambda\acute{\eta}\rho\omega\mu\alpha$ in Eph. 1:23 and 4:13 has an entirely new meaning; holding that the ecclesia is there representative of an enhancement or complement to Christ. His interpretation is that the thought expressed is that Christ, the head, is not complete without this pleroma, his body.

[2] Hoekstra's view is expounded in an article in the Theol. Tijdschrift 2, 1868, p. 559ss. and especially on pp. 616, 605 and 623 ss. (cf. also p. 3 of this thesis). He thought that the more Pauline character of Eph. is evident from the following : whereas in Col. the Redeemer stands in a relationship of universality with everything in heaven and on earth, in Eph. as in the HP, it is only the salvation of mankind that is envisaged. From the verses Eph. 1:10, 2:15 and 16, which have been borrowed from Col. 1:20 and 2:15, the author omits the reconciliation of the angles.

[3] See pp. 431-457 of the work mentioned on p. 9 in n. 3. In his opinion, Eph. expresses an identification of the heavenly Christ with the community on earth. The preexistence which the HP attributes to Christ, is here extended to the community which is exclusive in him. In order to in truth become one in flesh with the ecclesia, the preexistent Christ has in actual fact entered into the flesh (Eph. 5:31ss.). Christ can fulfil the world completely only when the ecclesia has attained full growth. His activity is directed directly towards the community and only indirectly towards the universe.

is the commencement of this sovereignity.[1] Hoekstra and Holtzmann both rejected Bauer's gnostic interpretation of Eph. Hoekstra drew attention to the Old Testamentian and Jewish background of Eph. 5 : 22-23 and would not acknowledge any relationship between this pericope and the suzugia of the Valentinians. Holtzmann drew a negative relationship between Eph. and gnosticism and thought that the activities of the gnostic schools were, on the contrary, condemned in this epistle.[2] However, where Bauer did meet with more or less general agreement is, that according to its content, Eph. does not fit in with Paul and his times.

Holtzmann saw Eph. more in the nature of a sermon than an epistle. He thought the work had originated at a time when the apostles had become figures of reverence and untouchability from the past and Catholicism was beginning to develop. The apostles are conceived as a single body and have the same views regarding the mystery of the equal position of Jews and heathens, whilst it is evident from the HP that there existed some differences between Paul and the original apostles on that score. In Eph., the ecclesia is the universal church and in the HP it represents the local community. In Eph., the ecclesia which is the body of Christ, is inspired by Christ who is the head; in the HP, the body is inspired by the pneuma. The gifts that are peculiar to the pneuma as encountered in 1 C. 12:28 are no longer found in Eph. where everything in the church is functioning in a normal manner and there is an increasing interest in ecclesiastical offices.[3]

E. Renan found that the conception of marriage in Eph. diverged sharply from that in 1 C. 7.[4] Pfleiderer saw the situation pictured in Eph. as entirely different from that in the HP. The HP postulates the right of heathens to be Christians but Eph. encourages the Christians of heathen origin towards a continued co-operation with the Jewish Christians. The author of the epistle who is himself a Jew by birth, here stresses the prerogatives of Israel. He does this to circumvent that the Christians of heathen extraction should look down on the Jewish Christians. But by that time, the prerogatives of Israel were

---

[1] See the article mentioned in p. 7 note 2.

[2] Pfleiderer saw a rejection of the dualistic docetism in Eph. 4:10, 20 and 21 that divides the heavenly Christ from the historical Jesus (Der Paulinismus, p. 441ss.).

[3] Lehrbuch, p. 274-276; Kritik, pp. 7, 276-271, 272ss.

[4] E. Renan, Histoire des origines du Christianisme III, St. Paul (Paris 1869), p. XI-XXII.

no longer the same as they had been for Paul, namely, circumcision and birth from the seed of Abraham; these were unimportant in the eyes of the author. What did matter to him, were the prerogatives that were the typically Christian attribute of Israel; i.e., the promises.[1]

All these reflections upon the content of Eph. provoked reactions.[2] Pure commentaries were published in which this criticism was questioned.[3]

T, K. Abbott ascribed the differences to a development in Paul's thinking. Thoughts which were still in the process of formation in the HP, had developed to fruition in Eph. The absence of parousia had prompted the thoughts of the apostle towards another direction.[4] He now took into account a series of $\alpha i\hat{\omega}\nu\epsilon s\ \dot{\epsilon}\pi\epsilon\rho\chi\acute{o}\mu\epsilon\nu\sigma\iota$.[5]

Th. Zahn also defended the authenticity of Eph. in his introduction to the N.T. but refuted the notion that the idea of parousia had diminished in Eph.[6] The idea that the history of the world will long endure is as little expressed by the $\tau\sigma\hat{\imath}s\ \alpha i\hat{\omega}\sigma\iota\nu\ \tau\sigma\hat{\imath}s\ \dot{\epsilon}\pi\epsilon\rho\chi\sigma\mu\acute{\epsilon}\nu\sigma\iota s$ of Eph. 2 : 7

---

[1] Der Paulinismus, p. 433-436.

[2] J. J. Koster, De echtheid van de brieven aan de Kolossers en Epheziërs met het oog op de nieuwste bezwaren onderzocht (diss, Utrecht 1877), p. 129-193, was especially directed against Holtzmann. Koster demonstrated the kindred nature of the thoughts in Eph. and Col. on the one hand and the remaining epistles of Paul on the other. He explained the internal differences between Eph. and Col. as arising from the fact that Col. had served a very special purpose—the combatting of heterodoxy. Other supporters of the epistle's authenticity are also mentioned by Holtzmann, Lehrbuch, p. 273s.

[3] H. Oltramare, Commentaire sur les épîtres de S. Paul aux Colossiens, aux Ephésiens et à Philemon, Tome Deuxième (Paris 1892), p. 71-156. E. Haupt, Die Gefangenschaftsbriefe (Kritisch-exegetischer Kommentar über d. N.T. VIII u. IX, [7-8]1902), pp. 57-65, 81, 82. Oltramare's work is apologetic in character. Haupt saw many objections against the epistle's authenticity, but nevertheless came to the conclusion that the differences between Eph. and the HP were more superficial than the affinities. In his opinion there is an agreement between Eph. and the HP in "die inneren Denkformen" (the inner thought forms) and "die individuelle Art des Denkens" (the individual way of thinking).

[4] C. H. Dodd in the article "The Mind of Paul : Change and Development" in the Bulletin of the John Rylands Library Vol. XVIII, 1934, p. 69-110 (particularly p. 93-101) suggested that the epistles of Paul show a constantly decreasing interest for strictly eschatological matters.

[5] T. K. Abbott, A critical and exegetical commentary on the epistles to the Ephesians and to the Colossians (ICC 1897), p. XIXs.

[6] F. Barth, Einleitung in das N.T., 1921, p. 79s., also rejected the idea that the parousie should have been lost in Eph. He drew attention to the Christian hope expressed in the epistle (1:18; 4:4), the day of Deliverance (4:30; 1:14), the future restitution (6:8) and the coming wrath of God for the disobedient (5:6).

as by the εἰς τοὺς αἰῶνας of R. 1 : 25 and 9 : 5 or the εἰς τοὺς αἰῶνας τῶν αἰώνων of Gal. 1 : 5. The aiones eperchomenoi do specifically not belong to this dispensation but form part of the coming age.

Furthermore, in his opinion by no means everything that was regarded as specific to Eph. is in reality so a novel. The HP also intimated (1 C. 8 : 6) that Christ is significant for the whole of creation and the world of the spirits. In the HP, all is condemned to mortality through the sin of man (R. 5 : 12 ; 8 : 18s.) and the creation of the second Adam has meaning for the entire world (1 C. 15 : 22, 24-28 ; R. 8 : 19-21). The world of spirits also partakes of this universal apocatastis (1 C. 6 : 2s. ; 15 : 24). Eph. (1 : 10,20,21 ; 2 : 14-16 ; 3 : 10) is on exactly the same level just as Col. 2 : 15 has a bearing identical to that of 1 C. 8 : 5 (the spiritual forces that surround God have been "abgestreift" (cancelled out)).

Nor does Zahn believe that the epithet ἅγιοι in 3 : 5 or the offices mentioned in 4 : 11 place Eph. within the post-apostolic period. During the post-apostolic period, the appellation εὐαγγελιστής is not used as a denotation of function. The idea of the unity of the universal ecclesia is also discounted in 1 C. Zahn thought that merely the fact that Eph. in addition contains some ideas that are new, can scarcely count as a disqualification for authenticity.[1]

Thus, the fiercest battle has raged concerning the authenticity of Eph. and two camps remain ; one in defense of its authenticity and one which refutes it. A. Jülicher and M. Dibelius adopt an intermediate position and hold the answer to be non liquet.[2]

But the theological content of Eph. does remain in the focus of interest. Since the Nineties of the past century, the religious influence of the surrounding heathen environment upon the beginnings of Christendom have been the subject of intensive study. The indirect influence of these religious factors which penetrated into the N.T. by way of

---

[1] Th. Zahn, Einleitung in das N.T. ³1906, I, p. 358s.

[2] A. Jülicher, "Epistles to the Colossians and Ephesians". Encyclopaedia Biblica Vol. I, 1899, p. 864ss. A. Jülicher-E. Fascher, Einleitung i.d. N.T. (Tübingen 1931), p. 138ss. M. Dibelius, An die Kolosser, Epheser an Philemon (Handbuch z. N.T. 12), ²1927, p. 63ss. M. Dibelius-H. Greeven, An die Kolosser, Epheser an Philemon (Handbuch z. N.T. 12) 1953, p. 83ss. A similar point of view in H. Windisch, "The Case against the Tradition", Jackson-Lake I. 2, 1922, p. 306.

hellenistic and syncretic forms of Judaisms has been discussed.[1]
The possibilities of a direct influence were also debated.[2]

The theory of Bauer that the newly circulating ideas of a developing
gnosticism are reflected in the N.T.[3] returned in an altered form.
It was recognised that an older gnosticism, before the Christian era,
had preceded the gnosticism which had Christian characteristics and
both a pre-Christian heathen and a pre-Christian Jewish gnosticism
were discovered. A conviction developed that the oriental myth of the
godly archetypal man and the descent of the heavenly redeemer, had
occupied a central place in this older gnosticism. The myth, which
was also found in the writings of the Mandeans, was thought to have
been taken over into Christian gnosticism.

Names which should be particularly pointed out in this connection,
are those of W. Bousset[4] and R. Reitzenstein[5]. Bultmann has accom-

---

[1] Cf. Kümmel, Das Neue Testament, Geschichte der Erforschung seiner Probleme,
p. 325-332, where the views of H. Gunkel (Zum religionsgeschichtlichen Verständnis
des N.T., 1903) and W. Bousset (Religion des Judentums im neutestamentlichen Zeitalter,
1903 and Die jüdische Apokalyptik, ihre religionsgeschichtliche Herkunft und ihre
Bedeutung für das N.T., 1903) are quoted.

[2] Kümmel, op. cit. pp. 332 and 340, speaks of an adaptation begun by Bousset
(Hauptprobleme der Gnosis, 1907) of Paul to heathen hellenism which is continued in
a consistent manner by R. Reitzenstein, (Die hellenistische Mysterienreligionen, 1910).

[3] Cf. p. 22.

[4] Bousset, Hauptproblemen der Gnosis, pp. 160-203 and 238ss. In Kyrios Christos
([4]1935; first edition in 1913), p. 201-206, Bousset clearly explains that it is a question
of a number of different myths. He differentiates between the myth of the archetypal man
and the descending redeemer (cf. once again Kümmel, op. cit., p. 453). In Kyrios Christos,
Eph. is mentioned in another connection, namely the fading-out of pauline admonish-
ments on the enthusiastic kurioscult which was prevalent amongst the hellenistic communities. In his opinion, Col. and Eph. date from a post-apostolic period when once again
the ritual connections of the Christian religion and Jesus as the ritual head of his community come to the forefront. He thought that the author of Eph. had worked with
material from Col. Eph. represents a phase after Col. of the development of the pneumatic
and enthusiastic community into the organised Church (pp. 216 and 285-287).

[5] On Reitzenstein, see : C. Colpe, Die religionsgeschichtliche Schule Darstellung und
Kritik ihres Bildes vom gnostischen Erlösermythus (Göttingen 1961), p. 10-57. Reitzenstein devoted repeated casual attention to Eph. In Eph. he saw a plenitude of formulae
drawn from the hellenistic mystery-religions, partly tracing back to Iranian traditions
(Die Hellenistischen Mysterienreligionen [3]1927, p. 214). He sees the encouragement of
the sleeping soul to wakefulness which comes into the myth repeated in the anonymous quotation used in Eph. 5:14 but in a Jewish or early Christian form. (Das Iranische Erlösungsmysterium 1921, p. 5-9 and HMR, pp. 64 and 314). In his opinion,
the summing-up of the dimensions in Eph. 3:18, is a formula from an Egyptian mys-

plished an imposing synthesis of the various data and drawn up the pattern of the gnostic redeemer myth.[1] As do Bousset and Reitzenstein, Bultmann also recognised a usage of gnostic ideas and language in the N.T. Behind these ideas and language, lies concealed this myth. Nevertheless, Butlmann did not think that the N.T. contained any real gnosticism. Even when gnostic images and language are employed, the New Testament texts have an ulterior meaning which is not gnostic. When ancient Christianity sees the situation of man in the world in the light of an enslavement to the enimical cosmic forces and a subjection to a dark fate brought upon it by the fall of the first man, there is a close relationship between Christianity and gnosticism. But beside this, there is an essential difference. The New Testament revelation understands the human "self" in an entirely other sense than the gnostic myth. Paul and John deliberately made use of the myth to express the antithesis.[2]

The inauthentic epistles to the Col. and Eph. which were written by different authors-which clearly reflect Pauline theology, although the theme of justification through the faith resounds but faintly[3]—also remain within the framework of Paul in the use of gnostic ideas and language. The tradition of gnostic mythology and tradition which was already present in Paul's work, is merely developed more strongly in these epistles. The central themes of christiology, ecclesiology and eschatology are developed by means of material which is based on gnostic expressions. This application of gnostic ideas does not bear witness to a gnostic way of thinking. The same contradisposition to gnosticism is found in Eph. and the HP.

Cosmological ideas with gnostic features appear in Eph. and in Col.

---

tery relating to the godly light (Poimandres, Studien zur griechisch-ägyptischen und frühchristlichen Literatur, 1904, p. 24s. and IEM, p. 235). The $\alpha\iota\acute{\omega}\nu$ of Eph, 2:2 and the $\alpha\iota\acute{\omega}\nu\varepsilon\varsigma$ of Eph. 2:7 and 3:9 he regards as personalized beings. The author was thought to have used 1 C. 2:6 where an affinitive thought is present although the $\alpha\iota\acute{\omega}\nu$ does not appear as a personalized being (IEM, p. 235-237).

[1] See Colpe, Die Religionsgeschichtliche Schule, pp. 57s. and 171s. and also, eg.. R. Bultmann, Das Urschristentum im Rahmen der antiken Religionen (Zürich [2]1954), p. 177ss.

[2] See Bultmann, Das Urchristentum, p. 208; Colpe, p. 58 and E. Käsemann, Exegetische Versuche und Besinnungen II (Göttingen 1964), p. 258.

[3] See R. Bultmann, Theologie des Neuen Testaments (Tübingen [3]1958), p. 528s. Bultmann also misses the radical character of the renewal which God's mercy bestows and the Pauline antithesis of $\sigma\acute{\alpha}\rho\xi$ and $\pi\nu\varepsilon\tilde{\upsilon}\mu\alpha$ in Eph. and Col. (Theologie, p. 553-557).

Yet there is a difference in this respect between the two epistles. In Eph., the cosmological conceptions have more consistently than in Col. been subject to reinterpretation so that the history of salvation has replaced the cosmology. Eph. stands close in thought to Paul for whom the struggle against the cosmic forces has not yet come to an end. The conception of Col., where the resurrection or more precisely, the ascension of Christ constitutes a triumph over these forces, is more approximate to the gnostic way of thinking.[1]

In coming to his conclusions on Col. and Eph., Bultmann also made use of the investigations which his pupils H. Schlier and E. Käsemann had made. For Schlier, Eph. clearly bore witness to the myth of the heavenly anthropos and the gnostic allegory. The limbs of Christ's body are the limbs of that anthropos who is as great as the cosmos. When Eph. mentions οἰκοδομή, this represents the gnostic allegory of the heavenly edifice.[2]

Käsemann also found traces of the cosmic body of the heavenly anthropos in the HP, but he differentiated between the concept of the σῶμα Χριστοῦ in the HP and its counterpart in Col. and Eph. In the HP the idea of the cosmic body is modified by the idea of the body as an organism. The image of the church as the body of Christ is of a paraenetical and passing nature. In Col. and Eph. the body of Christ occupies a more central position. And there too, the anthropological aspect recedes into the background.[3]

Schlier later gave an explanation for the whole epistle to the Ephesians in which he made full use of the material provided by religio-historical research.[4] In this epxlanation he maintains a difference between the HP and Eph. Eph., as opposed to the HP, not only uses the language of gnosticism but has gnostic motives. The epistle also differs from the other epistles in that it is heavily ecclesiological in character; the ecclesia which is built up from a combination of Jews and heathens is the central theme of the epistle. Yet, this epistle was also written by Paul. Schlier now strenuously defends the authenticity of Eph. which he had previously refuted. In his opinion a mental continuation links the HP and Eph. Whatever Paul writes about

---

[1] Theologie, pp. 494-497, 502-504 and 526-530.

[2] See Colpe, Die religiongeschichtliche Schule, p. 62.

[3] E. Käsemann. Leib und Leib Christi (Beiträge zur historischen Theologie 9, Tübingen 1933), p. 118ss. Id., Exeg. Versuche und Besinnungen II, pp. 257s. and 245-247.

[4] H. Schlier, Der Brief an die Epheser (Düsseldorf ³1962).

the ecclesia in Eph. was already present in the HP by implication and had always been the background to his thinking. The difference with the other epistles is to be attributed to the very particular nature of Eph.; one should not search it for the "kerugma" of 1 C. 1 : 18ss. but for the "sophia" of 1 C. 2 : 6ss. "Unser Brief ist eine "Weisheits-rede", ein Sophiarede, ein σοφίαν λαλεῖν".[1] Schlier also wishes to bring into consideration that Paul has become older and that his thinking has undergone a process of maturation and development. The reason for the gnostic language and ideas in Eph. is that Paul had become acquainted with the manner of speaking and thinking in the Jewish-Christian movement in Asia Minor which was threatening the faith of the West Phrygian communities for whom the epistle was intended.[2] The apostle interprets the gnostic themes in his own way and subordinates them to his gospel. He himself has not in the least become a gnostic. He maintains the identity of the redeeming and creative God, refutes docetism and teaches that salvation has become a reality through the historical fact of the crucifiction. His "Uminterpretation" (re-interpretation) enables him to reveal the cosmic significance of the law which came to an end though Christ and to show the cosmic character of Christ's deed. He confronts his readers with the metaphysical basis of salvation. The statements which have a gnostic tinge are of ontological relevance.[3]

Thus Paul's conception of the ecclesia as understood by Schlier from Eph., may be defined as follows: the ecclesia is a preexistent reality. The preexistent Christ has loved her before. Now the crucified Christ is present in the world through her after bringing her about in the world through His death. The ecclesia is his body which is cosmic in its extent and reaches out through all dimensions. This body goes through a process of growth and development in which the cosmos is itself involved. When the process reaches completion, with the eccle-sia the cosmos will also attain the goal, which is Christ.[4]

By interpreting Eph. in such a way and attributing the epistle to Paul Schlier, who had meanwhile become a convert to R.C., not only adopted another attitude to Paul but an entirely different approach to the N.T. from that of his old teacher, Bultmann.

---

[1] "Our epistle is a "lesson in wisdom", a Sophia speech, a σοφίαν λαλεῖν".

[2] Op. cit., p. 16-22.

[3] Op. cit., pp. 126-133.

[4] Op. cit., pp. 99, 194, 196, 205-207, 258, 259, 279 and 280.

Because Bultmann sees every ruling of pauline theology on God also as a statement about man, Paul's theology is for him at the same time anthropology. In Bultmann's view, Paul is not concerned with the relationship between cosmic powers but the actions of God in history. Nor does he think that Paul speculates upon the metaphysical nature of Christ, but that he speaks of him as the one through whom God works his salvation for man and the world.[1]

Paul sees the relationship of man to God primarily as one of an individual kind. The acceptance of God's message reveals to man a new existential understanding of himself. It is true that in belonging to Christ, he becomes part of His body and is as such linked with the other members of this body in the unity of the community; but before God, he stands first and foremost in radical isolation. Although Paul—still according to Bultmann—expresses his ideas on the body of Christ in cosmological categories, the cosmological aspect is for him transposed into the historical. The decisive aspect is that membership of the body is attained through the faith, thus through "echte geschichtliche Entscheidung" (true historical decision). In that way, Paul can reconcile the gnostic conception of the body with the familiar image of the body as an organism.[2]

In the work of Schlier, not much remains of the anthropological interests and the individual character of the relationship to God, which Bultmann sees in Paul. A man decides, "sich entscheiden" between the various cosmic powers that represent time, space and spirit. Since the ascension of Christ, he can also make the choice and "sich entscheiden" for the might of Christ which, transcending and encompassing all other cosmic forces, is the body of Christ. Because he is and as long as he is on earth, the act of entering into this might means a struggle with the other forces. Accepted into the body of Christ through baptism, he must again and again reaffirm and "sich entscheiden" (choose for himself) for this space. This act of self-determination or "sich entscheiden", is a transcending of the self. Through the everlasting realization of his being in this space, "in guten Entscheidungen", (by good decisions), he will achieve a true and new existence.[3]

---

[1] Bultmann, Theol., p. 192.

[2] Bultmann, Das Urchristentum, pp. 205, 220 and 221.

[3] Der Brief an der Epheser, pp. 46-48, 117 and 118.

Käsemann's critique on the above commentary deserves particular attention.[1] In this work he again questioned the authenticity of Eph.[2] He maintained that the ecclesiastical situation from which this epistle springs is not the situation as it was known to Paul. The epistle emanated from a pauline community and demonstrates that from this direction there is also a path leading to early Catholicism.[3] Käsemann holds the epistle to be the most important document from the inheritance left by the pauline communities.

He concurs with Schlier that in Eph. the church has become the central objective of the gospel and the faith. Soteriology and eschatology are systematically regarded as ecclesiological incidentals. Christology is also interpreted almost exclusively from an ecclesiological point of view.[4]

Käsemann is however surprised that Schlier should so unhesitatingly represent this reduced kerugma as the essential core of Paul's theology and identify it with the gospel.[5] He expresses grave doubts on the way in which Schlier has interpreted the epistle and has obtained his ecclesiology.

He finds that Schlier has an excellent grasp of the religio-historical material that he brings in the commentary. Schlier is mistaken however, in acceptioning the quotations from other sources that are found in Eph. in their original sense and is wrong to be satisfied with Gnostic space-terminology as adequately expressive for the purpose in hand. Thoughts which are ontologically expressed, he gives an ontological interpretation. Schlier, according to Käseman, misses their functional meaning as used in the epistle.

The eschatological event of Christ penetrating the depths of the cosmos through the actions of his people whilst filling its breadths through missionary activities accomplished among the pagans becomes for Schlier—still quoting Käsemann—an ecclesiastical and cosmic process of maturation.

For Schlier, the church is not the body of Christ by virtue of her function but through her existence. The fact that the church can

---

[1] Exeg. Versuche und Besinnungen II, p. 253ss. : "Das Interpretations-problem des Epheserbriefes".

[2] He did this previously in RGG II ³1958, p. 518ss. s.v. Epheserbrief.

[3] Exeg. Versuche und Besinnungen II, p. 256.

[4] Op. cit., p. 254s.

[5] Op. cit., p. 256.

only function as the body of Christ through the path of obedience and that Christ as its head and lord remains independent, was overlooked by Schlier.[1]

For the purposes of our investigation, the critical commentaries which have recently been published on the school of Reitzenstein, Bousset, Bultmann, Schlier and Käsemann by C. Colpe [2] and H. M. Schenke,[3] are very important. They have criticised the concept of this school of thought and its ideas on the genesis of the myth of the godly anthropos and the descent of the heavenly redeemer.

Amongst the religio-historical school there have also been researchers who saw a lesser degree of syncretic influence upon Eph. than Reitzenstein, Bousset, Bultmann, Käsemann and Schlier. Of these, C. Clemen [4] and Dibelius [5] were especially prominent. Others have regarded Eph. above all, as a rejection of the gnostic influence. The (post-pauline) author of the epistle had not been simply and unwittingly exposed to this influence but had recognised and forsworn the dangers and pitfalls of gnostic thinking. Thus Maurer [6] for example. M. Goguel sees this defensive attitude expressed in only a few interpolations in Eph., which have to that purpose been inserted into the original and authentic Eph. In the authentic parts of Eph., there is in his opinion no evidence of gnosticism.[7]

Other researches totally refuted the religio-historical interpretation of Eph. and the entire HP. A. Schweitzer sought to understand the CP as part of the tradition of Jewish apocalyptic literature. He adopted a position of reserve concerning the doubts surrounding the authenticity of Eph. (and Col.), but admitted to a lack of comprehension of Paul's Jewish eschatological conception of the church as the body of Christ.[8]

---

[1] Op. cit., p. 257-261.

[2] Die religionsgeschichtliche Schule (see p. 27 note 5).

[3] H. M. Schenke, Der Gott "Mensch" in der Gnosis, Ein religionsgeschichtlicher Beitrag zur Diskussion über die paulinische Anschauung von der Kirche als Leib Christi (Göttingen 1962).

[4] C. Clemen, Religionsgeschichtliche Erklärung des N.T. Berlin ²1924), pp. 333, 343-345.

[5] An die Kolosser, Epheser an Philemon, p. 64s.

[6] Maurer, "Der Hymnus von Epheser I als Schlüssel zum ganzen Briefe", Ev. Theol. 11, p. 151ss.; cf. also K. L. Schmid, Th. W. III, p. 512-516, s.v. ἐκκλησία and J. Horst, Th. W. IV, p. 570-573, s.v. μέλος.

[7] M. Goguel, "Esquisse d'une solution nouvelle du problème de l'épître aux Éphésiens", RHR 56, 1935, t. III, p. 255s.

[8] A. Schweitze, Die Mystik des Apostels Paulus (Tübingen 1930), pp. 43, 121, 336.

P. Benoit was strongly opposed to the religio-historical and gnostic interpretation of Eph. (and Col) preferring an interpretation of the epistles on the basis of the Stoa and old testementarian Chokma literature.[1]

J. Dupont saw a mutual infiltration of religion and philosophy in the hellenistic world. The cosmological pronouncements of the Stoics were simultaneously religious statemtents which were familiar to Paul in their popular form. In Eph. and Col. he made use of the monistic formulas of this school of philosophy, to resist speculations over a multitude of heavenly powers which were circulating amongst the Jewish-christians of Asia Minor. In these epistles also, his thoughts continued to go back to the O.T. and were defined by contemporary Jewish orthodoxy. When he speaks of knowledge, he means an Old Testament and Jewish knowledge, modified by Christianity.[2] L. Cerfaux likewise regarded Eph. and Col. as a reaction against speculations which were current in the churches of Asia Minor.[4]

F. Mussner gave a lucid analysis of gnostic philosophy and demonstrated to what great extent the content of Eph. diverged from this in its way of thinking. However, he did attempt to give a highly one-sided Old Testament interpretation to Eph.[5] J. J. Meuzelaar, tried to explain Eph. more or less excusively from the point of view of rabbinical literature.[6]

Percy also rejects the religio-historical interpretation. His view goes back to the conception of the "corporative personality" which C. H. Dodd borrowed from the Old Testament scholar, H. W. Robinson and adapted to the Adam-Christ antithesis in R. 5.[7]

This conception enables Percy, besides rejecting the religio-historical

---

[1] P. Benoit, "L'Horizon Paulinien de l'Epître aux Ephésiens", Rev. Bibl. 46, 1937, p. 342ss. He contested the article by Goguel mentioned Nt. 131.

[2] D. J. Dupont, Gnosis, La connaissance réligieuse dans les Epîtres de Saint Paul (Louvain et Paris 1949).

[3] L. Cerfaux, La Théologie de l'eglise suivant Saint Paul (²1948).

[4] Fr. Mussner, Christus, das All und die Kirche, Studien zur Theologie des Epheserbriefes (Trierer Theolog. Studien V), 1955 (²1968).

[5] J. J. Meuzelaar, Der Leib des Messias, eine exegetische Studie über den Gedanken vom Leib Christi in den Paulusbriefen (Assen 1961).

[6] Cf. H. Wheeler Robinson, The People and the Book, Essays on the Old Testament (Oxford 1925), p. 353-382, "Hebrew Psychology" (especially p. 375-378) and C. H. Dodd, The Epistle of Paul to the Romans (MNTC-London 1932), ad R. 5.

interpretation of Eph. and Col., to give a well-argued explanation of the expression σῶμα in the HP, Eph. and Col. In his opinion the soma-idea is the same in these epistles as in the HP. Not the sole, but certainly the primary aspect of the soma conception is that Christ is the representative and substitute for the faithful who have a part in everything that befalls Christ and therefore also share in his death and crucifiction because they have been taken into his (own) body.[1]

St. Hanson makes more subtle distinctions. Christ is the representative of a collective corps. The representative and the collective body stand in the relationship of head and body; together they form a single whole. Everything which happens to the representative and everything that the representative possesses, happens also to the the aggregate and is also the possession of the aggregate. Christ is one; therefore the aggregate is also a unity. Unity is an attribute of its structure. Of necessity, the members of the collective aggregate in turn form a reciprocal unity.

Although Hanson is not concerned with defending the authenticity of Eph., he does establish that Paul's conception of unity finds its clearest and most eloquent voice in Eph. He furthermore believes that the conception of the "corporate personality" is not easily extracted from the O.T. This can be done only by taking into account rabbinical speculations concerning Adam and these may have been strongly under the influence of Iranian gnosticism.[2]

Since the discovery of the Qumran writings, the affinity between Eph. and these texts has been stressed. Kuhn demonstrated that especially the paraenetical aspect of Eph. is related to the Qumran texts.[3]

Käsemann and Schlier use the Qumran documents within the framework of their religio-historical interpretation. Schlier sees a correlation between these writings and the Jewish-Christian gnosticism which forms the background to Eph. The same mythological syncretism is

---

[1] E. Percy, Der Leib Christi in den paulinischen homologumena und antilegomena Lunds universitets årsskrift N. F. Avd. I, Bd. 38:1, 1942) and E. Percy, Die Probleme cf. note 47).

[2] St. Hanson, The Unity of the Church in the N.T., Colossians and Ephesians (Acta Sem. Neotest. Upsaliensis XIV, Uppsala-København 1926); especially p. 61s. On the lines of Scandinavian New Testament scholars, also I.J. du Plessis, Christus als hoofd van kerk en kosmos (diss. Kampen 1962) accepts the conception of the corporate personality as the key.

[3] "Der Epheserbrief im Licht der Qumrantexte" (see p. 000 note 00).

present in both streams of thought.[1] The ontological dualism, the cosmic-soteriological myth of the archetypal man and the accentuation of the identity of gnostic and redeemer, are nevertheless absent in the Qumran texts.[2]

---

[1] See article mentioned on p. 32 in note 2.

[2] This view of Schlier's in Der Brief an die Epheser, p. 19 Note 1. In his commentary he repeatedly refers to the Qumran texts.

CHAPTER TWO

THE OUTWARD TESTIMONY

1. Doubtful testimony

The outward testimony of Eph. has never been in question. It is a matter of general consent that a number of places in ancient Christian literature bear witness to a familiarity with Eph.

Now it is not so that each and every resemblance must of necessity indicate an acquaintance with Eph. Neither the writers of the New Testament epistles nor the apostolic Fathers were individualists who dwelt in spiritual isolation. All of them lived in a spiritual milieu which was partly responsible for their utterings and formulations. Sometimes a close relationship existed between the environment of several so that there was a greater or lesser source of common expressions and formulations upon which different authors could base their work. Especially when the subject concerns liturgical formulations or exhortations to a Christian way of life, such a source which may be common to two or more authors should be taken into account.

For that reason there are not sufficient grounds to warrant the assumption of an interdependent relationship between Barnabas and/or the Didache and Ephesians merely because the paraenetical material of Did. 4 : 10 11 and Bar. 19 : 7 are reminiscent of Eph. 6 : 5, 9. Nor should such words as ἀνακαινίζειν (6 : 11), κατοικεῖν, ναὸς ἅγιος, κατοικητήριον τῆς καρδίας (6 : 14, 15) and the combination of οἰκοδομεῖν, κτίζειν, κατοικητήριον, (πνευματικὸς) ναός (16 : 8, 9, 10) in Barnabas, necessarily be identified with καινός or ἀνανεοῦσθαι (2 : 15; 4 : 23, 24), κτίζειν (2 : 10, 15), the combination of ναὸς ἅγιος, συνοικοδομεῖν, κατοικητήριον ἐν πνεύματι (2 : 21, 22) and κατοικῆσαι ἐν ταῖς καρδίαις (3 : 17) in Eph., and perforce indicate a familiarity with Eph. on the part of the author of Barnabas.

Without doubt, there is a strong correlation; apart from Apoc. 18 : 2, the word κατοικητήριον occurs nowhere else in new testament and ancient Christian literature. As against that, the expressions καινός or ἀνανεοῦσθαι and κτίζειν in Eph. do not lie in the immediate proximity of expressions intimating to build and temple. Besides, it must be borne in mind that an allegorical use of the expressions to build an temple was fairly common.

Although the thought that Christ or the kurios, dwells in the heart is mutual to Barn. 6 : 14, 15 and Eph. 3 : 17, there is a clear differentiation. In Barnabas, the words ναός and κατοικητήριον appertain to the heart of the individual believer, whereas in Eph. they reflect upon the ecclesia as a whole. In Barn. τὸ κατοικητήριον is a typical signification for the heart of man and can even be used without the gen. epexeg. τῆς καρδίας (16 : 8). "Die Vorstellung unseres Herzengemaches als eines Tempels Gottes ist bei Barn. fast formelhaft und festgeprägt".[1]

That this use of κατοικητήριον (with a different connotation) as a standing expression should trace its origin in Eph. particularly, is scarcely probable. The more likely inference is that in Eph. and Barn. we are confronted with two versions of an already extant tradition.

2. ACCEPTABLE TESTIMONY

It is possible that the affinities between 1 Cl. 59 : 3; 36 : 2 and Eph. 1 : 18; 4 : 18 could originate from a traditional metaphor in which lack of knowledge or insight is equated with darkness and blindness and knowledge and insight are identified with light and well functioning eyes. A. J. Carlyle ascribed the corresponding nature of 1 Cl. 46 : 6 and Eph. 4 : 4-6 to already existing liturgical formulas.[2] As for 1 Cl. 32 : 3, 4 this could equally well be based on other places in the CP as on Eph. 2 : 8.

Nevertheless, the ὅτι μέλη ἐσμὲν ἀλλήλων of 1 Cl. 46 : 7 bears a remarkable resemblance to the ὅτι ἐσμὲν ἀλλήλων μέλη of Eph. 4 : 25. When Clement warns his readers against forgetfulness, he assumes that the truth of his message is already known to them. This is in connection with the comparison of the ecclesia with a body and the believers with the members of this body. This analogy was already previously treated in 1 Cl. 37 : 5.[3]

---

[1] O. Michel, Th. W. V, p. 158 r. 23s. "The image of the realms of our heart being like a temple of God is almost formal and sealed in Barn."

[2] A. J. Carlyle in : The N.T. in the Apostolic Fathers (by a committee of the Oxford Society of historical theology—Oxford 1905), p. 53 : "We must remember, that the passages both in Eph. and in 1 Cl. are very possibly founded upon some liturgical forms."

[3] Horst, Th. W. IV, p. 572r. 19s. and note 96 and Schmid, Der Epheserbrief des Apostels Paulus, p. 24 both regard 1 Cl. as dependent on 1 C. 8.

This likeness of a human community to a body was known to the Greek and Roman world, nor was it foreign to rabbinical literature.[1] The invariable emphasis was that each individual as a component part has a vested interest in the well-being of the whole and must, on his part, serve the whole.

Paul has the same idea but over and beyond that he accentuates the importance of mutual care and reciprocity (1 C. 12 : 25; R. 12 : 5)[2] Eph. is in the very same position. After Eph. 4 : 16 has expressed on the part of each individual, a strongly-worded admonition concerning mutual care and reciprocity follows in Eph. 4 : 25. The fact that 1 Cl. gave an almost identical rendering of this pauline truth leads to the assumption that Clement had borrowed from Eph. 4:25.

The possibility therefore exists that in other passages which bear a strong resemblance to Eph., the author was also dependent upon the same source. Such is the case with the immediately preceding correspondence between 1 Cl. 46:5, 6 and Eph. 4:2-6. The fact that the sequences in Eph. and 1 Cl. are identical, would bear this out. Thus we can agree with Harnack who wrote about Eph. as an epistle "den bereits um das Jahr 96 Klemens in Rom gelesen hat, der sich also weiter Verbreitung erfreute".[3]

The Ignitiana also betray a cognizance of Eph. Corresponding features in Ign. Pol. 6:2 and Eph. 6:11,17 and Ign. Eph. 9:1 and Eph. 2:20-22 could be based on the use of traditional material. The same applies to Ign. Eph. 1:1 and Eph. 5:1.

The idea of $\mu\iota\mu\epsilon\hat{\iota}\sigma\theta\alpha\iota$, sequi or imitari of the godhead is familiar in Greek, or more specifically Stoic, philosophy.[4] Eph. 5:1 however, distinguishes itself particularly from the general philosophical conception in one respect. Namely, the motivations for the imitation as based on the fact that the faithful are God's beloved children and the

---

[1] Dupont, Gnosis, p. 435ss. Horst, Th. W. IV, pp. 560 s., 572 Note 97. Midr. Ps. 39 par. 2 (128a); cf. Str.-B. III, 447 and Horst, Th. W. IV, 563.

[2] At first the Stoics compared the cosmos to a body (cf. Dupont, op. cit., 431ss.). Within this application there is a certain ($\sigma\upsilon\mu\pi\alpha\sigma\chi\epsilon\iota$ $\tau\grave{\alpha}$ $\mu\acute{\epsilon}\rho\eta$ $\grave{\alpha}\lambda\lambda\acute{\eta}\lambda\omicron\iota\varsigma$) solidarity and sense of mutual fate (cf. Meuzelaar, Der Leib des Messias, p. 159, note 3).

[3] Von Harnack "Die Adresse des Epheserbriefes", p. 706 ("which has been read by Clement in Rome circa 96, being widespread at the time"); cf. also Mitton, The epistle to the Ephesians, p. 167-169.

[4] Dupont. Gnosis, p. 352. W. Michaelis, Th. W. IV, pp. 663, 665.

concretion of the imitation through the love and example of Christ. This is lacking in Ign. 1:1. Abbott and Schmid confuted the theory that Eph. 3:4 underlies Ign. Eph. 12:2.[1]

Within a short stretch however, the proemial words of Ign. Eph. contain a number of resemblances to Eph. 1:1-14. But these are merely weak echos, no more but also no less. In Ign, Eph. 19:1 there is a throwback to 1 C, 2:7, 8 and in 19:2 a reminder of Eph. 3:9, Ign. 20:1 must almost certainly be a reflection of Eph. 2:15 and Eph. 4:24, for in no other instance is the phraseology of Ign. τὸν καινὸν ἄνθρωπον Ἰησοῦν Χριστόν so obvious. Ign. Pol. 5:1 contains paraeneses with reference to marriage. The example of the kurios and the ecclesia which is used there must find its roots in Eph. 5. The thoroughness with which Eph. defines the Christ-ecclesia relationship and the explicit ἐγὼ δὲ λέγω εἰς Χριστὸν καὶ τὴν ἐκκλησίαν suggest that this material is original and not drawn from a general source.[2]

Polycarp was evidently quoting from Eph. in his epistle.[3]

Likewise was Hermas, the author of the Pastor work, familiar with Eph. His declaration in praise of truth and against falsehood in mandatum III, 1-4 shows some affinity with the paraenesis which occurs in Eph. 4:25-30 and is introduced by a warning concerning lying and truth. The phrase ἐκ τοῦ στόματος (σου or) ὑμῶν ἐκπορευέσθω comes into both passages and there is also a caution in both instances against causing grief to the Holy Ghost which is, incidentally, differently formulated. However, in another connection in mandatum X, 2,4 the formulation λυπεῖν τὸ πνεῦμα (τὸ ἅγιον) of Eph. 4:30 is used. These consistencies in paraenetical material are too frequent to find a satisfactory explanation in mutual tradition.[4]

---

[1] Abbott, The epistles to the Ephesians and to the Collossians, p. XI. Schmid, Der Epheserbrief, p. 26ss.

[2] K. Heussi, Kompendium der Kirchengeschichte (Tübingen [8]1933), p. 35 places the death of Ignatius between the years 110-115 but also leaves open the possibility of inauthenticity and gives the year 150 as terminus ante quem. See also B. Altaner-A. Stuiber, Patrologie/Leben, Schriften und Lehre der Kirchenväter (Freiburg-Basel-Wien [7]1966), p. 48.

[3] Pol. 1:3 and 12:1 respectively contain quotations from Eph. 2:8 and 4:26. Heussi, l.c. gives as term. ante q. 155/156. Mitton, The Epistle to the Ephesians, p. 126 dates the epistle ± 140 and admits the possibility of an earlier date. Altaner-Stuiber, op. cit., p. 51 date (after P. N. Harrison, Polycarp's Two Epistles to the Philippians, 1936) the de capita 1-12 around the year 135.

[4] Holtzmann, Einleitung, p. 276 and Abbott, p. XII, also regard Herm. m. III,

The so-called second epistle of Clement has a difficult passage which is elucidated by Eph. 5:31, 32 and dependent on this text. In 2 Cl. 14:2, Genesis 1:27 is quoted as follows : ἐποίησεν ὁ θεὸς τον ἄνθρωπον ἄρσεν καὶ θῆ λυ. To this is appended τὸ ἄρσεν ἐστὶν ὁ Χριστός, τὸ θῆλυ ἡ ἐκκλησία. The author takes for granted that the ecclesia existed from the beginning (ἄνωθεν), was pneumatological in character and says (14:3) that she was recently manifest in the flesh of Christ (ἐφανερώθη τῇ σαρκὶ Χριστοῦ). This explanation of the masculine and feminine in Gen. 1:27 through Christ and the ecclesia is explicable on the basis of the exegesis which is found in Eph. 5:31, 32.

If it is assumed that the author of 2 Cl. was acquainted with Eph. 5:31, 32 it also becomes clear how he could have come to the declaration that the ecclesia became manifest in the flesh of Christ.

It was the word "καὶ ἔσονται οἱ δύο εἰς σάρκα μίαν" as applied to Christ and the ecclesia in Eph. 5:31, 32 which enabled the writer to express himself in such a manner. He does moreover emphasize that he has not gained his knowledge that the ecclesia has existed from the beginning from the O.T. alone (τὰ βιβλία τῶν προφητῶν), but is also indebted to the apostles (οἱ ἀπόστολοι) in 14:2.

The context of Eph. 5:31, 32 also expresses the thought found in 2 Cl. 14:2 that the ecclesia is σῶμα Χριστοῦ, as well as the association

---

4 as dependent on Eph. 4:30. On the dependence of s. IX, 13, 5-7; IX, 17, 4; IX, 18,4 upon Eph. 4:3-6, see Abbott, p. XII; Schmid, der Epheserbrief, p. 33s. (Schmid speaks abusively about m. IX) and Mitton, p. 165.

For the dependence of s. IX, 15,4 on Eph. 2:20 and s. IX, 18,4 on Eph. 5:25 see Schmid, op. cit. p. 33s. H. Weinel, Hennecke ²1924, p. 332 does not venture in Herm. "eine einzige wirkliche Benutzung zu behaupten" (to allege a definite usage). J. Drummond in The N.T. in the Apostolic Fathers, p. 106 says respecting the small measure of correspondence between Herm. and Eph. : "It is in the way of Hermas not to quote but to take suggestions and alter to suit his own purposes" and, regarding s. IX, 13,5; IX, 17,4; IX, 18,4 and Eph. 4:3-6 : "These passages have all the appearance of being imitated from Ephesians".

For myself, I would like to leave open the possibility in the case of all the places quoted from the s. IX, of a common tradition of εἰς formulations and allegorical expressions based on architecture. (For formulas characterised by the numeral one, cf. Dibelius, Gefbr. ²1927, p. 60).

The resemblance between Eph. 5:25 and s. IX, 18,4, noticed by Schmid, is too abstruse to have any independent significance.

P. Vielhauer, Hennecke II, ³1964, p. 454 thinks that Herm. cannot be dated after 140 and B. H. Streeter dates the manuscript between 97 and 110 (The Primitive Church, London ³1930, p. 98). Altaner-Stuiber, op. cit. p. 55, settle for the years 140-149. See also F. L. Cross, The Early Christian Fathers (London, 1960), p. 23s.

of σῶμα with σῳζειν which also occurs in 2 Cl. 14:1 (cf. Eph. 5:23 σωτὴρ τοῦ σώματος),besides a counterpart to the idea of the τηρῆσαι τὴν σάρκα in 14:3 (cf. Eph. 5:29). Probably the author of 2 Cl. understood Eph. 5:29 in such a way as to think that the ecclesia was being equated with the flesh of Christ; he was presumably familiar with the western version (μέλη ἐσμὲν τοῦ σώματος αὐτοῦ ἐκ τῆς σαρκὸς αὐτοῦ καὶ ἐκ τῶν ὀστέων αὐτοῦ of Eph. 5:30.[1]

A number of apocryphal writers bear witness of the widespread fame which the epistle enjoyed during the second century.[2]

In the 9th. decade of the 2nd. Century, Irenaeus quoted Eph. and explicitly mentioned Paul's epistle to the Ephesians as his source.[3] Tertullian was also familiar with the epistle as such,[4] as were the Canon of Muratori [5] and Clement of Alexandria.[6] Further proof that the epistle was universally known may be inferred from the fact that Marcion included Eph. as the epistle to the Laodiceans in his Apostolikon [7] and that the gnostic writers Basilides, Valentinus, Theodotus and Ptolemaeus quoted Eph. as γραφή and originating from Paul.[8]

---

[1] 2 Cl. is first mentioned by Eusebius, Hist. Eccl. III, 38, 4. The time and place of origin are difficult to determine, but thought to be in the region 135/140 and in Rome. (Thus Heussi, op. cit. par. 10. However, also see F. X. Funk, Patres apostolici Vol. I, Tübingen ²1901, p. LIs. and J. R. Harris, J. V. Bartlet and B. H. Streeter in The Oxford Dictionary of the Christian Church, London 1957, s.v. Clement of Rome.) That the author was familiar with the above-mentioned version of Eph. 5:30 becomes increasingly likely on recollecting that also Iren., Adv. Haer, V, 2, quotes Eph. 5:30 in this form. This is the oldest known quotation of the text, cf. Abbott, op. cit., pp. XII and 172.

Schmid, Der Epheserbrief, p. 35 defends the dependence of 2 Cl. 14:2 from Eph. 5:30, 31 and moreover of 2 Cl. 19:2 from Eph. 4:17, 18. Personally, I assume the possibility of a traditional paraenesis in the land instance. In 2 Cl. 12:2 there is a mention of unity and, as in 2 Cl. 14, of ἄρσεν and θῆλυ. There is no connection between the two chapters; unlike 14, chapter 12 refers neither to σῶμα, σάρξ and πνεῦμα, nor the relationship of Christ and the ecclesia. 12 concers σῶμα and ψυχή and the relations between the sexes. Unlike 14, the point of departure is not the books of the prophets and apostles but a statement of the kurios, thus a logion (for this logion cf. Hennecke I, ³1959, p. 110s.).

[2] A list of quotations in Schmid, Der Epheserbrief, p. 18 and p. 19, note 1.

[3] Adv. Haer. V, 2, 3; cf. also I, 8, 5 and furthermore Schmid, op. cit. p. 16 note 2.

[4] Adv. Marc. V, 17; cf. Schmid, p. 52.

[5] Das muratorische Fragment, Kl. T. n. 1, 1933, p. 6 and 7 line 51. Heussi, op. cit., para. 14f3 dates it circa 200.

[6] Strom. 4 para. 65 and Paed. 1 para. 18; cf. Abbott, p. XII and Schmid, p. 17 note 1.

[7] As apparent from Tertullianus, See note 3.

[8] Closer indications in Schmid, p. 17 Note 2. Cf. Holtzmann, Einl. 276 "Die Valentinianer beriefen sich mit unverkennbare Vorliebe auf ihn und zwar scheint es fast, als sei

Thus the epistle was generally attributed to Paul before matters came to a head between Marcion and the gnostics on the one hand and the church on the other.

When the controversy erupted, the epistle must already have been famous. That the letter could have been introduced at a later date is out of the question. Had the church been the first to accord a formerly unknown or at least little-known document with the dignity due to an apostolic epistle, this would never have been accepted by the opposing faction. Nor would the church have been prepared to accredit this epistle, which found much favour amongst the gnostics and was indeed used by them as an arsenal, as an authentic epistle by an apostle, had Marcion or one of the gnostics been the first to give it publicity.[1]

Taking into full consideration that a common source of expressions and formulations could perhaps have accounted for the affinity between a New Testament document and a work by an apostolic Father, we establish the following. 1 Cl. 46:7 is dependent upon Eph. 4:25 as is also likely in the case of 1 Cl. 46:5,6 and Eph. 4:2-6; Eph. 1:1-14 is echoed in the praescript of Ign. Eph.; there are traces of Eph. 3:9 in Ign. Eph. 19:2; Eph. 2:15 and 4:24 are reflected in Ign. Eph. 20:1 and Eph. 5 has been used in Ign. Pol. 5:1. We also came to the inference that Herm. m. III, 1-4 is dependent on Eph. 4:25-30; that 2 Cl. 14:2 has borrowed from Eph. 5:31,32 and that Polycarp quoted Eph.

All this evidence indicates that the epistle must have been written prior to the year 96. The multitude of quotations emanating from the years 96-140, prove that during that period the epistle must already have achieved the status of a well-known and esteemed document. The familiarity of 1 Cl. and Herm. with the epistle demonstrates that the epistle must have been available in Rome and was there considered to be of importance. The oldest trail in patristic literature leads to Rome (1 Cl.). The Ignitiana and Polycrap's letter indicates that the epistle must have been known to a wider circle (Antioch and Asia Minor).

Another factor which substantiates a general awareness of the epistle

---

derselbe in ihrer Schule förmlich commentirt worden" (The Valentinians quoted him with unparalleled preference and it would seem almost as if he was the subject of formal commentary amongst their school).

[1] Cf. F. Bleek, Vorlesungen über die Briefe an die Kolosser, den Philemon und die Epheser (hrsg. von Fr. Nitsch, Berlin 1865), p. 188 and Schmid, op. cit., p. 18.

at an early date, is the fact that both the Christian church as well as Marcion as well as the gnostics particularly associated with the east (Syria) and Egypt, were familiar with the epistle. That the epistle was not only known and esteemed at an early date but acknowledged as an authentic epistle by Paul during the period immediately preceding the conflict between the Christian church and the gnostics is strengthened by the fact that the church never questioned the high estimation in which Marcion and the gnostics held the epistle as authentically written by Paul and γραφή.

Our *conclusion* may therefore be that the epistle was written before 96, was subsequently widely read and had achieved an undisputed reputation as an authentic epistle by Paul, by the year 120.

CHAPTER THREE

THE DISPOSITION

1. TYPICAL ELEMENTS OF THE ANCIENT LETTER IN EPH.

In this chapter we wish to discuss some formal aspects of the epistle which will also serve to give us an insight into the nature of the work and therefore also affect our judgement concerning its authenticity. To begin with, we direct our attention towards the disposition of the epistle; for it is desirable that the structure and composition of the whole be reviewed before certain details and facets are subjected to closer scrutiny.

The disposition is as follows :

1 the praescript, naming sender and recipients and which furthermore contains a greeting   1:1,2

2 a eulogy or praising of God ending with a mention of the addressees as sharers in salvation   1:3-14

3 a eucharistia-formulation or expression of thanksgiving to God for reports received concerning the addressees, resolving into an intercession on their behalf and an avowal [1] of the rising and might of Christ   1:15-23

---

[1] In this work we wish to denote the formulations of the CP in which great things about Jesus Christ are stated as fact or great deeds which God has accomplished with respect to Jesus Christ as avowals or professions. For Paul and his communities, the declaration that Jesus (Christ) is Lord was of the outmost importance, cf. 1 C. 12:3; R. 10:9, 10 and Phil, 2:11.

I assume that also those conclusive statements regarding Jesus Christ were of great significance to him and his communities. They encompass the essence of that which had to handed down and formed intermediate stages on the path which led from the basic creed that Jesus is Lord to the later professions of the ancient church. Some, as we read them in the CP were probably formed ad hoc. Others, e.g., 1 C. 15:3ss. had already been formulated earlier. In using the qualification "avowal", we wish to indicate that the issues concerned were pronouncements which were of primary importance to the author and the first readers of the epistle, striking the very roots of the faith. Cf. also O. Cullmann, "Die ersten christlichen Glaubensbekenntnisse" (Theol. Studien, Heft 15, [2]1949).

4   an exposition in which the participation of the addressees
    in salvation is developed and Christ is professed as the
    peace in which circumcised and uncircumcised were
    united and reconciled with God   2:1-22
5   recapitulation of the intercession, containing a digression
    upon the sender, Paul, and the musterion entrusted to him
    and concluding with reflections on the immeasurable
    and all-transcending   3:1-19
6   a doxology or glorification of God   3:20,21
7   a paraenetical section. (This part is introduced with the
    words παρακαλῶ οὖν. At the beginning a number of
    formulations occur, all expressive of the thought of unity.
    The last of these formulations has reference to God and
    is characterised by the repeated use of the word πᾶς. An
    account of Christ and his gifts follows these formulations,
    in which the idea of unity once again comes to the
    fore. This is succeeded by a large number of admonitions.
    The section closes with an exhortation to prayer and a
    plea for intercession.)   4:1-6:20
8   a reference to the bearer who will convey news of the
    sender by word of mouth   6:21-22
9   a greeting   6:23-24

A number of elements present in this disposition are elements
common to the ancient letter.[1]

This applies in the first place to the *praescript*. The praescript of
Eph. bears the typically Jewish character of all the pauline praescripts.
The normal Greek counterpart is in the form of a single sentence,
containing the names of sender, recipient(s) as well as the greeting.
In the Jewish environment, the tradition was to write two sentences
of which the first, written in the third person, mentions the names

---

[1] Cf. O. Roller, Das Formular der paulinischen Briefe, BWANT Heft 58, Ve Folge 6
(Stuttgart 1933); F. X. J. Exler, The Form of the Ancient Greek Letter, a Study in
Greek Epistolography (Washington 1923); S. Witkowski, Epistulae privatae Graecae
(Bibl. Scr. Gr. et Lat. Teubneriana ²1911); D. Brooke, Private Letters Pagan and Chris-
tian (London 1929); A. Deissmann, Licht vom Osten, ⁴1923, p. 119ss.; G. Fitzer, Biblisch-
Historisches Handwörterbuch, herausg. v. B. Reicke u. L. Rost (Göttingen 1962-1966),
s.v. Brief. For the letter in antiquity and Paul, see also G. J. Bahr, "Paul and Letter
Writing in the First Century" in The Catholic Biblical Quarterly 28, 1966, p. 465ss.; id.,
"The Subscriptions in the Pauline Letters" in JBL 87, 1968, p. 27ss.

of the sender and the recipient(s), possibly embellished with a multitude of attributes. The second sentence calls a blessing upon the recipient(s), now indicated in the second person. This tradition has its roots in the Babylonian and Persian "Kurialstil" and falls within the framework of an official letter. This prescript arouses the impression that the Pauline epistles are official missives.[1] The *eulogy* or praising of God is not an element of the ancient letter in the Graeco-Roman world. It is rooted in eastern tradition and in Israel it was founded on ritual. Deliverance from peril is a reason to praise God in his sanctuary.[2] Tobit, after his son Tobias has returned upon escaping mortal danger and he himself has been healed, utters a eulogy (Tob. 11:13). When the angel Raphael has revealed the secret of God's acts of salvation, he writes a eulogy which is typified as a προσευχὴ εἰς ἀγαλλίασιν (Tob. 13:1ss.). We also find eulogies upon the receiving of good news: 1 Sam. 25:32,39; 1 Kings 1:48; Ezra 7:27. The good tidings themselves can also be introduced by means of a eulogy : 2 Sam. 18:28. In that case, the eulogy is also a response to the acts of deliverance of God; these are now expressed through the bringing of messages.

A letter forms a written message. A eulogy can thus equally well function in a letter. If a comparison is drawn between 2 Chron. 2:11s. and 1 Kings 5:7, the development of a panegyric at the intimation of a message can be traced out to the placing of a eulogy at the beginning of a letter.[3] In Dan. 3:28,29, a eulogy is declaimed after an act of deliverance by God but the spoken word evidently pertains to an imperial decree intended for publication. Dahl correctly observes that the shift from the spoken word in 1 Kings 5:7 to a letter in 2 Chron. 2:11s. best becomes comprehensible if the use of a eulogy at the beginning of a letter was customary practise.[3] It naturally follows that the form of the edict in Dan. 3:28,29 reflects a form common to letters of the time.[4]

A parallel phenomenon to the Jewish eulogy at the beginning of a letter is manifest in the eucharistia-formulation or epistolatory thanksgiving which was found in the hellenistic worls long before

---

[1] Cf. E. Lohmeyer, Probleme paulinischer Theologie, ZNW 1927, 26er Bd., p. 158-163.

[2] Cf. Ps. 40:4 and H. J. Kraus, Psalmen (Bibl. Komm. A. T. XV), p. 308.

[3] Dahl, Adresse und Proömium des Epheserbriefes, p. 250s.

[4] Schubert, Form and function of the Pauline Thanksgivings, p. 171, speaks in such cases of "the generally valid principle, that the style and function of official edicts are in some respects closely akin to the form and function of private epistolary documents.".

Paul and was of pagan derivation. The most ancient extant example is presented in a papyrus dated 168 B.C.[1] in which an Egyptian lady (following the praescript and formulas of intercession with information concerning her own state and that of the household) informs her husband that upon receiving the letter in which he has reported his arrival in Memphis, she has given thanks to the gods for his well-being.

A letter addressed to her husband by his brother at the same time, corresponds closely with her letter and contains a similar formula of thanksgiving in the parallel position. This second letter makes clear that the spouse in question had himself written a letter describing how he had been delivered from great peril, whereupon he betook himself to Memphis to thank the god Serapis at the Serapeion.[2] There are but few papyri remaining, bearing examples of hellenistic letters containing such formulae of thanksgiving to the gods. Such a eucharistia-formulation presupposes a certain intimacy and was used exclusively when there existed very real grounds for thankfulness—and then, even, it was not always expressed.[3]

The eulogy commences with the word εὐλογητός, possesses a direct character and is a direct praising of God which readily develops into προσευχή or panegyric. The eucharistia-formulation begins with the finite form of the verb εὐχαριστεῖν and is indirect in character; the godhead is not here praised in so direct a fashion. The situation is more that the recipients are informed of the thankfulness which the writer harbours with respect to the godhead. In 2 Macc. 1:10ss., a combination form is found; at the beginning of the letter, deliverance from great peril through the intervention of God is recounted. The story commences in 1:11 with the words : ἐκ μεγάλων κινδύνων ὑπὸ τοῦ θεοῦ σεσωσμένοι μεγάλως εὐχαριστοῦμεν αὐτῷ and is concluded in 1:17 by a eulogy : κατὰ πάντα εὐλογητὸς ἡμῶν ὁ θεός, ὃς παρέδωκεν τοὺς ἀσεβήσαντας.

To the Jewish-hellenistic mind, familiar with the eulogy as such,

---

[1] Schubert, op. cit., p. 168.

[2] See Schubert, op. cit., p. 161-164. On p. 166 in Schubert and also on p. 145-150 of Deissmann, Licht v. O., may be read that in the second centure A.D. a seagoing soldier reports deliverance from great peril at sea in a letter (after praescript and expressing a wish that the recipients of the letter and all connected with him may be well) with a formula thanking the god Serapis.

[3] Cf. Schubert, op. cit., p. 161-173.

there is no distinction between this eulogy and the eucharistia-formula-tion that was native to hellenic culture.[1]

Another normal element of the ancient letter, is the intercession, or the expressed wish that all may fare well with the recipient(s). The letter already mentioned, written in 168 B.C., in which an Egyptian lady assures her husband that she continues to pray on his behalf, is example.[2] This intercession is followed by the information that she herself and the housefold as a whole are in good health to which afterwards—probably on re-reading—are added the words σοῦ διὰ παντὸς μνείαν ποιούμενοι. Her brother-in-law was satisfied to express only a wish.[3]

The letter written by the seagoing soldier Apion to his father in the second century A.D., contains, immediately after the praescript, a wish, introduced with the words πρὸ μὲν πάντων εὔχομαι concerning the well-being of his father and the rest of the household. In a letter written by the same soldier to his sister some time later, the same sentiments are expressed with the additional information that the sender himself is also well. This is followed by an assurance that he habitually offers prayers for his sister to the gods of his dwelling-place : μνίαν σου ποιούμενος παρὰ τοῖς [ἐν]θάδε θεοῖς. The praescript of a letter written by a second century A.D. Egyptian to his mother, is directly succeeded by a wish concerning her health, beginning with the words διὰ πάντων εὔχομαι whereupon the immediate assurance follows that he prays for her daily before the god Serapis.[4]

A Jewish-hellenistic equivalent to this type of blessing is found in the extended blessing which follows the praescript in the letter written by the Jewish community of Jeruzalem to the Jews of Egypt (2 Macc.

---

[1] For the greeks the expressions εὐλογεῖν and εὐχαριστεῖν were equal in value. This is evident from a 3rd. century B. C. Delphic inscription, cf. Schubert, op. cit., p. 147. The same applies to the Hellenic Jew; the final books of the LXX make liberal use of εὐχαριστεῖν and εὐχαριστία. 1 C. 14:16-19 shows that for Paul εὐλογεῖν and εὐχαριστεῖν are interchangeable expressions. This is also clear from the following : whereas in the LXX Ps. 71:19 εὐλογητός is connected with God and his glory. In R.2:21 and 2 C. 4:15 εὐχαριστεῖν and εὐχαριστία apply to these realities.

[2] εἰ ἐρρωμένοι σοι τἆλλα κατὰ λόγον ἀπανταῖ, εἴη ἂν ὡς τοῖς θεοῖς εὐχομένη διατελῶ.

[3] The εἴη ἂν ὡς τοῖς θεοῖς εὐχομένη διατελῶ from the above note here corresponds with εἴη ἂν ὡς βούλομαι; cf. P. Oxy. 1070r. 47ss. (p. 174ss. in Schubert op. cit.) which gives the impression that writing a letter was synonymous with μνησθῆναι τινὸς περὶ τῆς ἀσφαλείας τῆς οἰκίας αὐτοῦ.

[4] Cf. Deissmann, Licht v. O., p. 147-161 for more examples.

1:2-6). The narrow relationship between thanksgiving and intercession which we find in Eph., is in keeping with the mental framework of the pagan-hellenist world. Paul was not the only one to be aware that thanksgiving and prayer belonged together (Phil. 4:6) as is apparent from two magical papyri in which the magical prayer is preceded by an utterance of thankfulness for the appearance or manifestation of the deity. A Christian amulet bears an invocation to God which is immediately followed by the words εὐχαριστῶ ἐγώ after which the prayer proper then comes, introduced by certain formulae.[1]

A statue which the Achaeian Bond erected to the emperor Aelius Aurelius Verus ± 170 A.D., bears an inscription in which pagan thanksgiving and an intercession are closely allied.[2] In letters too, similar combinations must have been known. A specimen is left from either the period of Trajan or Hadrian. The expression of thanksgiving is addressed directly to the addressees, indirectly to the god Hermes and immediately connected with a formula of intercession : τοιοῦτο σοὶ μόνῳ εὐχαριστῶ παρὰ τῷ κυρίῳ ῾Ερμῇ καὶ οὐ διαλείπω τὸ προσκύνημα σου ποιῶν καθ᾽ ἑκάστην ἡμέραν.[3]

The *paraenetical section* of Eph. which is introduced by παρακαλῶ οὖν, is in essence a traditional element in the ancient letter. A basic function of the letter as such, is the conveying of a wish which may, according to the relationship between the sender of the letter and its recipients, be either an order or a request. The O.T. offers examples of ancient Hebrew or less ancient Aramaic letters in which such an order or request constitutes either the main part of the letter or, together with an announcement on the part of the senders, forms the essence of the letter.[4] The most ancient Greek letter which has been

---

[1] In Schubert, p. 157s.

[2] The inscription quoted by Schubert, p. 153 and CIG 1318 : εὐχαριστοῦντες τοῖς θεοῖς καὶ αἰτούμενοι τὰ ἀγαθὰ τῷ οἴκῳ (namely that of Aelius. Aelius was co-ruler with the emperor Marcus Aurelius).

[3] Cf. Schubert, p. 168 and P. Giess. 85.

[4] 2 Sam. 11:14, 15; 1 Ki. 21:8-10 and 2 Ki. 10:1-6 where the sender is a king, convey an order. In Ezra 4:17-22, a letter (with praescript) expresses a reaction to a report that has been received and subsequently contains an instruction from a Persian king to his officials which is pressed home threefold. Ezra 5:6-17 and 4:9-16 contain a request from servants to the king. The first letter, after the praescript, contains a report with extensive data and at the conslusion a request to instigate an investigation into the royal archives as well as a request for an opinion from the king. The second letter, after the praescript, gives a report of facts as well as in indirect request for an investigation into the royal archives and, indirectly, insistence that the monarch decide one way or another.

left to us contains, after the praescript in which the sender greets the addressees, expresses his wish for their well-being and informs them that he is well, a request to send him certain articles. He then adds a promise concerning the return of the articles at a future date.[1] To illustrate this, examples from the Jewish-hellenistic world are : a) the letter found in Macc. 1:1-10 in which, following the praescript and blessing, there is an account of events ending with a closing sentence in the form of an exhortation, expressing the desire of the senders; b) the letter of 2 Macc. 9:19-27 in which Antiochus Epiphanes informs the Jews that he has appointed Antiochus Eupator to succeed him after his death. With the introductory words παρακαλῶ οὖν ὑμᾶς καὶ ἀξιῶ, the last-mentioned letter concludes with a request to remember the beneficent acts of Epiphanes and to maintain a spirit of goodwill towards him and his son Eupator.

We also have some examples from the Egyptian-hellenistic world. In the year 1 B.C., the workman Hilarion writes from Alexandria to his wife in Oxyrhynchos; a statement concerning the writer's state follows the praescript after which comes a request opening with the words : ἐρωτῶ σε καὶ παρακαλῶ σε.

The letter by the soldier Apion which has already been mentioned, contains, subsequent to the praescript, intercession and thanksgiving for his own deliverance, a request, beginning with the words ἐρωτῶ σε οὖν κύριέ μου πατήρ for news from the parental home. The other letter, already mentioned, from the Egyptian in the second century A.D. to his mother, also expresses a plea introduced by παρακαλῶ σαι μῆτηρ. This formula in reiterated several times in the fragment of this letter which we possess.[2]

An equally traditional and normal custom was the placing of a *greeting* at the end of a letter. The vale en cura ut valeas at the conclusion of Roman letters is well known.[3] Letters written in hellenistic Egypt, from 258/257 B.C. until the third century A.D. invariably closed with the words εὐτύχει, ἔρρωσο or ἔρρωσθε in the case of official or business letters [4] and the formula εὖ πράττετε, ἐρρῶσθαί σε εὔχομαι,

---

[1] This letter from the beginning of the 4th. century B. C. in Deissmann, Licht v. O., p. 119-121.

[2] Deissmann, Licht v. O., resp. pp. 134, 148 and 154.

[3] See e.g. Deissmann, op. cit., p. 164, letter 17 line 34.

[4] Op. cit., pp. 121, 128, 131, 138, 139.

ἐρρωσό μοι ἡ κυρία μου διαπαντός,ἐρρωσό μοι ἀδελφέ of ἔρρωσο in
correspondence of a personal and intimate nature.[1]

We also encounter the greeting ἔρρωσθε in a letter of Lysias to the
Jews (2 Macc. 11:21), in the one from his brother, Antiochus Eupator
(2 Macc. 11:33) as well as in the letter which the apostles and elders
of the church address to the Christians (from heathendom) in Antioch,
Syria and Cilicia (Acts 15:29). The greeting ὑγιαίνετε occurs in a letter
to the Jews from two Roman ambassadors during the reign of the
emperor Antiochus Eupator (2 Macc. 11:38).

2. A NORMAL SEQUENCE OF THESE ELEMENTS.

Not only does Eph. contain the typical elements of the ancient letter,
but also the sequence of these (praescript, eulogy, eucharistia-formula,
intercession, a section introduced with παρακαλῶ οὖν and a greeting
at the end) corresponds with the customary sequence of ancient letters.
The fact that a eulogy as well as a eucharistia-formulation is used, is a
deviation from the normal pattern. But neither is this abnormal.
The two expressions are sufficiently allied to be combined. This is
demonstrated by the mixed form which we saw in 2 Macc. 1:10ss.
(On that occasion, the eucharistia-formulation made the transition
into a eulogy; here, in Eph., the eulogy comes first and then the eucharistia-formulation follows.)

In Eph. each part of this dual-unit has a sensible function. As in
Tob. 13:1ss., the background thought to the eulogy is the experience
of God's acts of deliverance; it is the public acclamation of the salvation of God and a proclamation of God's secret (cf. Tob. 12:6, 7).[2]
Furthermore, as in 2 Sam. 18:28, it forms the introduction to a message
of good tidings; the report of deliverance. It is a προσευχὴ εἰς ἀγαλλίασιν (Tob. 13:1) which functions as a prologue.[3] Essentially, the

---

[1] Op. cit., pp. 143, 144, 150, 160 (the κυρία is the mother of the writer of the letter),
168, 171.

[2] Cf. τὴν ἀπολύτρωσιν in 1:7 and τὸ μυστήριον in 1:9.

[3] Innitzer, Lohmeyer and Maurer also regarded the pericope which we characterise
as a eulogy, as a prologue to the content to follow. Lohmeyer spoke of a prooemium
and recognised in the pericope the blessing בְּרָכָה, which so often occurs in Jewish life
under the law. Previously, Innitzer had already called the pericope a hymn or a panegyrics
in a hidden form. Maurer spoke of a hymn, the content of which was entirely "ausgerich-

eulogy functioned as it did in Old Testament ritual and should, as in Ps. 40:4 and Ps. 51:17, be regarded as a Godgiven paean. The eucharistia-formulations has the function of a response on the part of the writer of the letter, to news received concerning the addressees.

Whoever has received news of deliverance concerning a loved one, can utter thanks to the gods through a ritual act and can also express his gratefulness in a letter to the saved.[1] In Eph. 1:16 a like occasion is at hand. The writer has heard reports about the faith of the addressees and the way in which they have accepted the gospel of "their salvation" and is now expressing his thankfulness.

The original placing of the intercession which originated in the pagan-hellenistic world, was before the thanksgiving. If both elements appear, the intercession or the blessing comes first. Thus is the case with the Egyptian lady, writing to her husband in the year 168 B.C.[2] Later, we see the intercession if—as in Eph.—it is narrowly combined with the thanksgiving, follow after the thanksgiving as on the statue erected $\pm$ 170 B.C. and the letter quoted above, written during the reign of Trajan or Hadrian.[3]

The repetition of the intercession in Eph. is not alien to the disposition of the ancient letter. Eph. 1:16 commences with an intercession which ends in Eph. 1:20-23 with an avowal of Christ. In Eph. 3:1-19 the intercession is recapitulated in totally different words. The intention behind both blessings is the same, namely the spiritual well-being of the addressees.

In the letters of hellenistic Egypt, we see a repetition of the blessing for health and well-being. In so doing, the writer indicates his attach-

---

tet" (aimed) at the theme of Eph. (for publications cf. p. 11, notes 6, 7: p. 13 note 3).

We think that the eulogy is a special prelude to the exposition of element 4 and the digression of element 5 and have, following Dahl, above indicated the normal epistolary function of the eulogy. This function, in our opinion goes back to the original function of the eulogy, namely, the glorification of God in his sanctuary for his acts of salvation.

[1] See the letter mentioned in para. 1 by the Egyptian lady to her husband in the year 168 B. C. More on this letter on p. 54 and in note 2.

[2] The sequence there is : praescript, assurance of intercession, information concerning personal health and that of the household with the addition that, after receiving her husband's letter, she has given thanks to the gods. Then follows the real purpose of the letter; an indignant demand for his return, cf. Schubert, op. cit., p. 161-164 or the letter (as well as that of her brother-in law) in P. Lond. 42 (also in A. Deissmann, Bible Studies, Edinburgh 1901, p. 204 and U. Wilcken, Urkunden d. Ptolemäerzeit I (1922-1927), p. 297ss. and p. 320ss.)

[3] Cf. p. 50.

ment and his affection. The Egyptian lady who was writing to her husband, indignant at his long absence, wanted to make clear that there was no lack of fidelity and attachment on her part or that of her household. After the praescript, she assures him that she continues to pray for him. Following the next statement, that she and her household are well, are added—not directly when the letter was being written, but later—the words σοῦ δία παντὸς μνείαν ποιούμενοι so that the intercessory blessing is echoed and the aggressive tone of the letter is mitigated.[1]

The seagoing soldier Apion, after the praescript, expresses his attachment to his father by a very intensive wish for the father's health through πρὸ μὲν πάντων εὔχομαί σε ὑγιαίνειν καὶ διὰ παντὸς ἐρρωμένον εὐτυχεῖν[2] and closing his letter with the words ἐρρῶσθαί σε εὔχομαι. Later, in a letter to his sister beginning with the obligatory praescript, he writes πρὸ μὲν πάντων εὔχομαί σε ὑγιαίνειν and, upon adding καὶ 'γὼ γὰρ αὐτὸς ὑγιαίν[ω] he once again expresses that he is wont to pray on her behalf μνίαν σου ποιούμενος παρὰ τοῖς [ἐν] θάδε θεοῖς.[3] In a letter from an Egyptian to his mother, we find a repetition in an immediate follow-up πρὸ τῶν ὅλων ἐρρῶσθέ σε εὔχομαι μετὰ καὶ τῶν ... ἀδελφῶν and ἅμα δὲ καὶ τὸ προσκύνημα ὑμῶν ποιοῦμε ἡμερησίως παρὰ τῷ κυρίῳ Σεράπιδι. Further on in the letter, he again says that her σωτηρία, her well-being and health are his constant wish and prayer : τοῦτό μοι γὰρ εὐκτέον ἐστὶν διαπαντός.[4]

The paraenetical section of Eph., introduced by παρακαλῶ οὖν, is in a suitable position. This element of the ancient letter never stood at the very beginning of the missive; there was indeed, a tendency to place it nearer the end of a letter—as was already made obvious in our earlier treatment of this element.[5]

We noted that Holtzmann regarded Eph. as more in the nature of a sermon than a letter.[6] He is not alone in this. Fairly recently, Käsemann wrote: "Mehr als jedes andere nt. Schreiben ist E. ein brieflich

---

[1] See p. 53 note 2.

[2] Cf. Deissmann, Licht v. O., p. 147 and p. 147, Note 2.

[3] Op. cit., p. 150.

[4] Op. cit., p. 160.

[5] Cf. again p. 53 note 2. In the brother-in-law's letter, matters are similarly arranged : praescript, an expressed wish for the health of the recipient, acknowledgement of the letter in which his brother describes his adventures and his deliverance, an assurance of thanksgiving to the gods and an exhortation for the brother's return.

[6] Cf. Chapter I, § 6 and Holtzmann, Einleitung p. 274 sub 1.

nur eingekleideter Traktat mit einheitlichem Thema und systematischer Gliederung".[1] When we study the disposition of the epistle with its traditional epistolary characteristics, it becomes impossible to subscribe to this view. Eph., according to its structure, is a complete letter. Admittedly, this letter is unusually prolonged in comparison with the letters listed n. 1 on p. 46. Nor, in contrast to those letters, does it contain precise instructions governing a concrete situation in which the recipients or the sender find themselves. However, exceptional length is also a trait of the HP. And even if these epistles generally deal to a greater extent with the concrete situation in the recipient community, they also possess a general character and are partly intended to be read before a wider circle.[2] Taking into account the typical epistolary elements and their sequence in the epistle, we may without further hesitation *conclude* that Eph. fulfills the formal requirements of an ancient letter.

It is possible that Eph. is a simulated letter which was constructed at a later date; but even so, there is no question of "ein brieflich nur eingekleideter Traktat". For that, the epistles bears too many of the characteristics of an ancient letter.

---

[1] Käsemann's remarks, in RGG 2er Bd., ²1958, p. 518 s.v. Epheserbrief. G. Schille in his article "Der Autor des Epheserbriefes" in the Theologische Literaturzeitung 28, 1957 No. 5, writes : "dass die Form des Eph. ... aus dem gewöhnlichen Briefschema nicht zu erklären ist ..." (p. 326—"that the form of Eph. cannot be explained on the basis of the normal epistolary pattern"). He also writes : "Man hat früher das unbriefliche am Eph. als Argument gegen dessen Echtheit ausgewertet" (p. 333—"formerly, the non-epistolary features of Eph. were used as an argument against its authenticity"). Schille does not consider this deviation from the normal epistolary patters in the light of an objection to the authenticity of Eph. He thinks that the epistle was written to correspond with the pattern of the baptismal paraenesis. With Percy (Die Probleme, p. 447), we believe that various details of Eph. become explicable only when the fact is taken into account that the writer is addressing newly-baptised Christians. We emphatically disagree with those who deny the epistolary character of Eph. and point out that a statement pertaining to a formal correspondence between Eph. and "das Schema der Taufparänese" (the pattern of the baptismal paraenesis) can be based only upon hypothesis and reconstruction.

Quotation; "Eph., more than any other N.T. writing, is merely a treatise in epistolary guise, with unity as the theme and a systematic arrangement".

[2] R. especially possesses a very general character which is epressed in the frequently doctrinal tone of the epistle. In this connection, we draw attention to the affinities with the diatribe which Bultmann recognised in the HP. (See the work mentioned on p. 11 in note 5.) The desire that an epistle be read to a wider circle is apparent in 2 C. 1:1. (For 1 C. 1:2, see p. 81).

In order to test the authenticity of Eph., it is now necessary in the first place to make a comparison with the other Pauline epistles with regard to the disposition and nature of the elements present. This we shall now proceed to do; the so-called pastoral epistles we shall not take into consideration since they are not addressed to communities collectively but to one person.[1] Philemon is not addressed to a single person but to different people as well as a community.[2] With the pastorals, there is moreover an additional difficulty. Most N.T. scholars who do not feel closely bound to a particular ecclesiastical tradition, regard these as non-authentic. If we were to involve ourselves with this problem, it would not be within the framework of this investigation.

---

[1] According to the greeting at the close of the Past., this must not be put with excessive certitude.

[2] Cf. the praescript.

CHAPTER FOUR

A COMPARISON OF THE DISPOSITION AND ELEMENTS WITH THOSE OF THE OTHER PAULINE EPISTLES ADDRESSED TO THE COMMUNITIES

1. THE POSSIBILITY THAT NOT ALL THESE EPISTLES ARE PRESERVED IN THEIR ORIGINAL FORM AND AUTHENTICITY

In a comparison between the disposition and elements of Eph. with those of the other epistles, it should be taken into account that the possibility exists that these epistles may not have been preserved in their original form. Thus, the authenticity of the doxology in R.16:25-27 are more or less generally rejected. Of equal doubtful nature is the preceding part, R. 15:1-16:24; although authentic Pauline material is recognised in this passage, it is not certain whether it constituted part of the original R.[1]

The homogeneity of the epistles 1 and 2 C. is also questioned. De Zwaan removed from 1 C. the section 6:12-20.[2] Jülicher distrusted the authenticity of 2 C. 6:14-7:1. De Zwaan was in agreement with him that this section was a strange element in 2 C. However, he thought that 2 C. 6:14-7:1 as well as 1 C. 6:12-20 were original material which— he supposed—had initially formed part of an epistle addressed to the Corinthians written prior to 1 C.[3] He also concurred with the old hypothesis that 2 C. 10-13 had not originally been part of 2 C. and that the content suggests an epistle from Paul to the Corinthians written after 1 C. and before 2 C.[4] Moreover he believed that he had discovered material from two epistles in 2 C., also from Paul to the Corinthians,

---

[1] Cf. H. Lietzmann. An die Römer (hndbch N.T. 8, [4]1933), p. 128ss. Jülicher-Fascher, Einleitung i. d. N.T., p. 105ss. A separation of R. 1:1-15:33 was recently proposed by J. Kinoshita in his article "Romans-Two Writings combined", Novum Testamentum VII 4, 1965, pp. 258-274.

[2] J. de Zwaan, Inleiding tot het N.T. II (Haarlem 1941), pp. 41, 56, 57.

[3] Jülicher, op. cit., p. 87, de Zwaan, op. cit., p. 46, 57.

[4] Cf. Jülicher, op. cit., pp. 89, 96ss.; de Zwaan, op. cit., p. 57.

which were to have been written shortly after 2 C. This material was contained in 2 C. 8:1-23 and 2 C. 9:1-15.1.

W. Schmithals and K. G. Eckhardt went even further. In 1960, Schmithals split Philemon into different epistles which were all to have emanated from Paul. In 1964 he redistributed 1 and 2 Th. into four epistles, namely : A combining 2 Th. 1:1-12 and 3:6-16; B composed of 1 Th. 1:1-2:12 and 4:3-5:28; C from 2 Th. 2:13-14, 2:1-12, 2:15, 2:16-3:5 and 3:17, 18 (apparently the praescript would have been lost); D comprising 1 Th. 2:13-4:2 (praescript, greeting and the end of the epistle were thought to have been lost).[2] Eckhardt tried to prove in 1961 that 1 Th. was a composite of two genuine Pauline epistles.[3]

Furthermore, the possibility exists that 2 Th. is not an authentic epistle. Confronting a number of scholars who reject the epistle's authenticity, stand some non-conservative researchers who argue its pedigree.[4]

An examination of all these opinions regarding the homogeneity and authenticity of the above-mentioned epistles falls outside the scope of our investigation. Where necessary, we shall take the negative views into account.

A question which is more closely related to our investigation is that concerning the authenticity of the epistle to the Colossians, which

---

[1] De Zwaan, op. cit., p. 57.

[2] For the division of Phil. see W. Schmithals "Die Irrlehre des Philipperbriefes" in Z. Th. K. 54, 1957, p. 297-341; id., "Zur Abfassung und ältesten Sammlung der paulinischen Hauptbriefe", ZNW 1960, 21 p. 225ss.; id., "Die Thessalonicherbriefe als Briefkompositionen" in Zeit und Geschichte (Dankesgabe an Rudolf Bultmann zum 80 Geburtstag—Tübingen 1964), pp. 295-315. Schmithals believes that an ecclesiastical organisation re-edited and compiled the epistles of Paul. The fact that the composition of 2 Th. so closely resembles that of 1 Th. is the haphazard and certainly not intended result of editing by the compiler. The καὶ διὰ τοῦτο καὶ ἡμεῖς in 1 Th. 2:13 and the ἡμεῖς δέ in 1 Th. 2:13 (two clauses which certainly do not gain in significance and lucidity through Schmithals' compilation-theory) are eliminated by S. as editorial "Floskeln" or "Klammern" (flourishes or parentheses). For reactions to Schmithals' division of Phil., see the statement on literature by A. F. J. Klijn, "Paul's Opponents in Phillipians III" in Novum Testamentum 1965, VII, 4, p. 278 note 1.

[3] K. G. Eckhardt, "Der zweite echte Brief des Apostels Paulus an die Thessalonicher", Z. Th. K. 58, 1961, p. 30ss. His view was disputed by W. G. Kümmel in, "Das literarische und geschichtliche Problem des ersten Thessalonicherbriefes in Neotestamentica et Patristica (Freundesgabe für Oscar Cullmann, Novum Testamentum 1962, Suppl. 6), p. 213ss.

[4] Cf. P. Feine, J. Behm, W. G. Kümmel, Einleitung i.d. N.T. ([14]1965), p. 186ss.

has such special connections with Eph.[1] There is a widespread consensus of opinion on this. Numerically, a greater number of sholars support the authenticity of Col. than maintain the authenticity of Eph. We shall take as our point of departure that consensus regarding Col. In the course of our investigation there will be opportunities to examine the justifications for this consensus.

2. The affinity of Eph. with the other Pauline epistles

When comparing Eph. with the other epistles of the CP proper, it transpired that as far as surveyability is concerned, there exists a great difference in disposition with 1 and 2 C., Phil. and 1 and 2 Th.

The disposition of 1 C. can still be overlooked :

a	praescript	1:1-3
b	thanksgiving with a formulation expressing the intent of prayer	1:4-9
c	a section introduced with $\pi\alpha\rho\alpha\kappa\alpha\lambda\hat{\omega}$ $\delta\acute{\epsilon}$ which has the dividedness of Corinth as its background motif	1:10-4:15
c[1]	a section introduced with $\pi\alpha\rho\alpha\kappa\alpha\lambda\hat{\omega}$ $o\mathring{v}\nu$ which has bearing on the paraenesis	4:16-21
c[2]	various instructions (partly of a punitative nature) which concern conduct (with a digression on Paul's own conduct) or gatherings of the communities (with a digression on the $\dot{\alpha}\gamma\acute{\alpha}\pi\eta$)	5:1-14:40
d	a lesson on the resurrection opening with a formulation of avowal of the gospel and ending with a peroration consisting of a thanksgiving ($\tau\hat{\omega}$ $\delta\grave{\epsilon}$ $\theta\epsilon\hat{\omega}$ $\chi\acute{\alpha}\rho\iota s\ldots$) which is followed by a paraenesis	15:1-58
e	instruction for a collection, linked with a statement on the coming of Paul, the coming of Timothy and the postponed arrival of Apollos	16:1-14
f	a request introduced with $\pi\alpha\rho\alpha\kappa\alpha\lambda\hat{\omega}$ $\delta\acute{\epsilon}$ to accept the leadership of particularly deserving persons	16:15-18
g	greetings from others	16:19,20
h	a complicated conclusion	16:21-24

---

[1] Cf. Chapter I, para. 2.

The form of Phil. is equally simple to survey :

α	praescript	1:1-2
β	thanksgiving and formula of intercession	1:3-11
γ	information about Paul	1:12-26
δ	paraenetical section	1:27-2:18
ε	statement on the coming of Timothy and the coming of Epaphroditus with an exhortation to hold in honour particularly meritorious persons	2:19-2:30
ζ	paraenetical section with a digression on Paul	3:1-4:1
ζ¹	admonition for certain persons to cooperate	4:2-3
ζ²	paraenetical section	4:4-9
η	profession of thanksgiving with a word of blessing and a doxology at the end	4:10-20
θ	greetings for others and from others	4:21-22
ι	greeting	4:23

Section ζ, ζ^1 and ζ^2 can in effect be regarded as one element. Section β is in itself a complicated element but is closely linked with part γ; for part γ ends with the desire of Paul to be amongst the recipients. This a typical manner of expressing an intent of prayer at the beginning of a letter; cf. R. 1:10.

It is difficult to compare 2 C. If we take into account the possibility that 2 C. 6:14-7:1 and 2 C. 10-13 are sections which have been inserted, the disposition of the remainder is insubstantial but subject to oversight.

A	praescript	1:1-2
B	eulogy with the report of a deliverance	1:3-11
C	exposition on the failure of plans for travelling, on the work of the senders and its value and on their relationship with the addressees	1:12-6:13 7:2-16
D	treatment concerning a collection of monies	8:1-9:15

The two epistles to the Thessalonians are both impossible to survey. If the hypothesis of Schmithals is taken into account, each of the two are reduced to two small epistles which readily lend themselves to analysis.

With the remaining epistles of Paul addressed to the communities, Eph. is in its disposition very similar—that is, to Col. and R. The resemblance to R. is heightened to an even greater extent if the suggestion of de Zwaan is followed and R. 16:1-20 and also R. 16:25-27 are not counted as part of the original epistle.[1] On p. 62 we show the disposition of the remaining epistles, Col., R., Gal. and Phlm. indicated in parallel columns which can be conveniently followed. A parallel column of figures refers to the elements of the disposition of Eph. listed at the beginning of Chapter III. Small letters, capital letters and Greek letters refer respectively to the elements of 1 C., 2 C. and Phil. which correspond with elements of Col., R., Gal., Phlm. and also Eph. In this, we take into account the sequences of the individual dispositions of 1 C., 2 C., and Phil.

We now see that as in Eph., the elements of the usual ancient letter, namely; praescript, eucharistia-formulation, intercession, section in which the sender(s) intimate requests or instructions and a greeting, also occur in the same order in R., 1. C., Phil., Col. and Phlm. To a certain extent, the disposition of Gal. also follows the same pattern.[2]

In 1 C., it is better not to include c under that part of the disposition in which the sender(s) express their wishes or demands. Since in this case the sender(s) give voice to great anxiety and the theological concepts of the Corinthians are being corrected, this section of 1 Cor. may be regarded as independent. Section c^1, c^2, e and f designate the element which indicates the requests and instructions. Such is also the case with Phil., where parts δ, ϵ, ζ, ζ^1 and ζ^2 represent this element.

Eph., R., Gal. and Col. have in common the feature that the element of request or giving instructions in homogeneous and of a paraenetical character. The word parkalo does not introduce this particular element in all the epistles mentioned; in Col. and Phil. it is otherwise. In 1 C. and Phlm. however, the word parkalo does feature in this element. Between R. and Eph. there is a strong resemblance in that the element in question is introduced by the same words παρακαλῶ οὖν ὑμᾶς.

It may be observed that in all the epistles of our survey, praescript, a possible eulogy and possible eucharistia-formulation with an intercession at the end are followed by one or more elements which precede the element dealing with requests or instructions. (In 2 C., after 2 C. 6:14-7:1 has been eliminated, C may be regarded as the preceding element and D that in which the requests and instructions occur.)

---

[1] De Zwaan, op. cit., p. 17-25.

[2] Gal. is the only epistle of the CP, lacking a eucharistia-formulation and intercession and not having a eulogy (Schubert, op. cit., 162 : the normal thanksgiving has been omitted because the situation did not admit it.).

Eph.	Col.	R.	Cal.	Phlm.	1C.	2C.	Phil.
1 praescript 1:1,2	praescript 1:1-7	praescript 1:1-7	praescript 1:1-5	praescript 1-3	a	A	α
2						B	
3 eucharistia-formulation + intercession formula 1:3-8 intercession 1:9-20	eucharistia-formulation + intercession 1:8-15			eucharistia-formulation + intercession 4-7	b		β
4 short exposition on the participation of the readers in salvation 1:21-23	exposition on the gospel as a salvation, in the first place for the Jew but also for the Greek 1:16-8:39		exposition on the gospel and Paul who brings it 1:6-2:21		(c)	C	
5 exposition on Paul 1:24-2:3 changing to warning against false belief 2:4,5	exposition on the Israelites 9:1-11:32		instruction on the gospel 3:1-5:12				γ
6		perotarion and doxology 11:33-36					
7 paraenesis (with plea for intercession) 2:6-4:6	paraenesis 12:1-15:4 (παρακαλῶ οὖν)		paraenesis 5:13-6:10	a request for obedience 8-21	c^1 c^2 e f	D	δ ε ζ $ζ^1$ $ζ^2$
8 reference to messengers for news of sender 4:7-9	actions and undertakings of sender 15:15-29 plea for intercession 15:30-32			announcement of his imminent arrival and allusion to intercession 22			
greetings from others, special greetings, instructions 4:10-17			final personal warnings with a certain greeting 6:11-17	greetings from others 23, 24	g		θ
9 greeting 4:18	greeting 15:33 special greetings 16:21-23		greeting 6:18	greeting 25	(h)		ι

Eph. has three such elements : element 4 (Eph. 2:1-22); 5 (Eph. 3:1-19); and 6 (Eph. 3:20,21). Element 4 is instructive in character and authoritative for the theological thinking of the addressees. Element 5 is a recapitulation of the intercession but consists for the most part of a digression on Paul which interrupts the intercession. Element 6 is a doxology.

R. also contains three of such elements. Two of these, R. 1:16-8:39 and R. 9:1-11:32 are extensive, instructive and authoritative for the theological tinking of the addressees. Furthermore, they are corrective. Thoughts which are also encountered in element 4 of Eph., are found here. The idea that the law has been abolished (Eph. 2:8, 9, 15) is the leading theme in R. 1:16-8:39. The prerogatives of Israel (Eph. 2:11-13) are extensively treated in R. 3:1-4 and 9:1-11:32. Ideas that not only the nations (τὰ ἔθνη) but all have sinned, that the nations have as much share in salvation as the circumcised, that there is peace through Christ and that a new humanity begins with him (passim in Eph. 2:1-22) are even more extensively developed in R. 2:16-8:39. The attention that is devoted to Paul in element 5 of Eph., is not lacking in R. 9:1-11:32 (R. 9:2, 3 ; 11:13, 14) but in Eph. 3:1-19, Paul is featured more centrally.

Element 6 of Eph., a doxology, corresponds strongly with the third element of R. 11:33-36), a peroration with a doxology. Both elements in the two epistles emphasise that God transcends human understanding. The conclusion of the preceding element 5 in Eph., a prayer, is exalted in character and contains the word βάθος. The same may be said of the peroration in R. 11:33-36.

Gal. has two preceding elements, Gal. 1:6-2:21 and 3:1-5:12. Both are detailed and—especially the latter—instructive, authoritative for the theological thinking of the addressees and corrective in character. The idea that the law has been abolished which was found in element 4 of Eph. (Eph. 2:8, 9, 15) is the theme of Gal. 3:1-5:12 as it is of R. 1:16-8:39. Paul is as much the subject of Gal. 1:16-2:21 as of element 5 in Eph.

Col. contains two or three preceding elements, namely : Col. 1:21-23 and 1:24-2:5 (which could be split into Col. 1:24-2:3 and 2:4, 5). The idea of element 4 in Eph., that the nations have a share in salvation, is also present in the short element Col. 1:21-23 and again in Col. 1:27. As with element 5 of Eph., Paul is also the focus of attention in Col. 1:24-2:5.

The preceding element c in 1 C. (1:10-4:15) sets out to correct the theological concepts of the Corinthians and, in 1:13-17 and 2:1-4:15, gives great attention to the work and task of Paul and others who work beside him. The preceding element C in 2 C. (1:12-6:13; 7:2-16) expounds comprehensively on the diakonia and the gospel which has been entrusted to Paul and others such as Silvanus and Timotheus who are named. The preceding element γ in Phil. (1:12-26) is an announcement concerning Paul. (Phil. 3:4-14, again contains a digression on Paul.)

In yet another epistle, that is in 1 Th., where the disposition is very unclear, we note that at the beginning, following the praescript and a section containing formulae of thanksgiving and intercession, attention is given to the work, suffering and efforts of Paul, Silvanus and Timotheus (1 Th. 2:1-12; cf. 2:2).

We may come to the conclusion that Eph., in disposition and the nature of the elements contained in it, corresponds largely with R., is close to Gal. and Col. and moreover shows frequent affinity with the remaining epistles.[1]

3. THE DISSIMILARITY OF EPH. WITH THE OTHER PAULINE EPISTLES

Meanwhile, there are also dissimilarities between the disposition of Eph. and that of the other epistles. In none of the epistles which have

---

[1] C. J. Bjerkelund, Parakalo-Form, Funktion und Sinn der parakalo-Sätze in den paulinischen Briefen (Oslo 1967), believes that the author of Eph. deviates from an epistolary tradition which Paul, in R. 12:1 and 1 Th. 4:1 does follow. Whereas Paul is familiar with παρακαλεῖν as a "Petitionsverb" in these passages, the author of Eph. had used this word in 4:1 as "einen seelsorgelichen Ermahnungsbegriff" (a term of spiritual warning). (See especially pp. 168 and 186.) We are of the opinion that the tradition in question has been followed equally in all three instances. In this particular case, it acquires a new content because it has been subordinated to the paraenesis in an original fashion which modifies the strong distinction drawn by Bjerkelund between a plea and a warning. Neither is the character of "ein indringliches Petitionsverb, mit dem sich Paulus bittend und beschwörend an seine Addressaten wendet" (a penetrating verb of petition with which Paul addresses his readers in pleaful beseechings) failing in Eph. 4:1. It is not so that the author wishes to give authority to his παρακαλῶ with the words ἐγὼ ὁ δέσμιος ἐν κυρίῳ. They express that the warning is the plea of a humble prisoner who does not himself command but who speaks in the name of the kurios for whose sake he is imprisoned and to whom he is wholly committed.

Bjerkelund refers for the pleading character of the 'parakalo-Sätze" in R. 12:1 and 1 Th. 4:1 to the obsecro of the older Latin translations (p. 167). We think that the corresponding sentence in Eph. 4:1 is no less possessed of this character than the translations in questions and point out that these too have the obsecro in this place. Apparently, Bjerkelund overlooked this.

a eucharistia-formulation is this (as in Eph.) preceded by a eulogy. Schubert saw an indication of inauthenticity in the succession of these two elements in Eph. He thought that the eucharistia was superfluous after the eulogy. The author had borrowed this from Col., finding that such a eucharistia-formulation was characteristic of the genuine pauline epistles, whilst not realizing that the placing of this eucharistia gave Eph. a bis in idem.[1]

It is curious that Schubert himself, elsewhere in the pauline epistles, senses something of a formal compulsion to place a eucharistia-formulation at the beginning of an epistle. On p. 46 of his study he points out that the syntactic elements of the usual thanksgiving which he has singled out as a result of a thorough analysis of the structure of thanksgivings, are also found at the conclusion of the eulogy of 2 C., i.e., in 2 C. 1:11. There he finds as it were, the normal thanksgiving which generally comes at the beginning of a pauline epistle, but in the form of a reflection. Subsequently, on p. 50, he remarks : "This strangely consistent structural inversion seems to lead to the conclusion, that Paul compelled by a strong habit of epistolary form, could not refrain from bringing the εὐχαριστῶ-clause into the proemium of II Corinthians". To us it appears somewhat far-fetched that he could add a eucharistia to a eulogy in the form of an inversion, as in 2 C. whereas this was not directly possible, as in Eph. In Chapter III, para. 2 and n. 1 on p. 49, we saw how easily the one form could merge into the other for the Jewish-hellenistic mind. The thanksgiving in reflected form of 2 C. 1:11 proves that for Paul also, thanksgiving and eulogy could well be combined.

The reason that in 2 C. Paul does not follow the eulogy with a direct thanksgiving but a thanksgiving in reflected form, is not that his epistolographical judgement would admit such an indirect thanksgiving but a direct thanksgiving would have been an inadmissible repetition. The case is different; the dramatic nature of the first

---

[1] Cf. Chapter I para. 5. Schubert, op. cit., p. 44 speaks of "a conscious imitation of the genuine Pauline thanksgiving, particularly influenced (as everything in Ephesians) by Colossians.". One asks why in that case, the supposed imitator did not wholly accommodate the beginning to the usual opening of Paul's epistles and especially to Col. Why was it absolutely necessary for an imitator to insert a eulogy between the praescript and the thanksgiving ? It seems to me that Schubert, as has also been the case more than once amongst scholars, has based himself to too great an extent on the inauthenticity of Eph. and its secondary importance with respect to Col. so that any recognition and confirmation of authentic Pauline material is initially already precluded.

seven chapters of 2 C. demand that the news received concerning the addressees should be discussed at a later stage. As soon as Paul mentions his meeting with Titus, the bearer of the good news that the Corinthians have yielded to the authority of Paul's gospel, his thankfulness towards God finds immediate expression (2 C. 2:13-17). Then, in accordance with the dramatic character of the whole, this thankfulness is given a direct voice and is not converted into an epistolographical eucharistia-formulation. This is so spontaneous, that the account of the actual meeting with Titus in Macedonia and the content of his message are even forgotten; this follows later, in 2 C. 7:5-7. But first of all, this feeling of thankfulness must find utterance and the glory and power of the gospel before which the Corinthians have bowed themselves, must be revealed.[1]

Thus, even if a direct eulogy-eucharistia sequence cannot be pointed out in the CP, excluding Eph., it is nevertheless probable that in an authentic pauline writing, such a similar sequence can be found. The view of Schubert, that a eucharistia-formulation following the eulogy is senseless, is certainly incorrect. At the commencement of para. 2 of the preceding chapter, I have indicated that each part of the two-fold unit of eulogy-eucharistia, has a function. The eulogy is based on the acts of salvation of God which the writer wished to describe. It is the prologue to glad tidings. The eucharistia is a response or reaction to a message that has been received.

The eulogy of 2 C. 1:3-11 also has the character of a prologue. The antithesis between death and life, the relationship between the mishaps of Paul and the salvation of the Corinthians are themes which appear more than once in the epistle, e.g., 2 C. 3:2, 3; 4:11-15; 7:3-7 and 13:4.

As in 2 Macc. 1:17 and Da. 3:28, 29, the eulogy of 2 C. refers to an incidental act of God. In 2 C. the act concerns the deliverance of Paul and Timothy from mortal peril; in 2 Macc., the Jews have been saved through the death of Antiochus and in Da., three friends have escaped

---

[1] This connection between thankfulness to God in 2 C. 2:14 and the meeting with Titus, the bearer of good news, has escaped Lietzmann in his commentary. Paul does not, as L. believes, "aus einem nur undurchsichtigen Motiv zum Lob seines Apostolats über" (launch into praise of his apostolate for some inexplicable reason). The motive is provided by Titus' account of the Corinthians' conversion to the power of Paul's gospel. Lietzmann's view in H. Lietzmann, An die Korinther (Hndbch. z. N.T. 9), [3]1931, p. 107s. or in H. Lietzmann-W. H. Kümmel, An die Korinther (Hndbch. z. N.T.) [4]1949, p. 107s.

from the fiery oven. In Eph., however, the eulogy reflects the all-encompassing salvation which God brought about through Christ. In principle, this is not different from the preceding examples. God's incidental intervention is seen in a wider context both in Da. and in 2 C. The eulogy in Da. 3:29s. concludes on a general note : "because there is no other God that can deliver after this sort."

The παράκλησις for which God is praised in 2 C. 1:3-11 is a specimen of πᾶσα παράκλησις and the total salvation which God works through Christ; cf. verses 3, 5 and 10.

The combination of eulogy and eucharistia, rare to the CP, which is found in Eph. demonstrates a certain excess in praise and thanksgiving. I would like to point out that even if this is not elsewhere expressed in the same way, there is a tendency throughout the other epistles addressed to the communities to praise and thank.

2 C. repeatedly gives utterance to thankfulness towards God : 2 C. 2:14; 8:16 and 9:15. Furthermore, in both 2 C. 1:11 and 2 C. 9:11 and 12, the hope and expectation is voiced that through the work and faith of Paul and the Corinthians, many others too, will thank God.[1]

In 1 and 2 Th., the spiritual well-being of the addressees frequently provides the motive for thanking God. In fact this is so oft-repeated that Schmithals regarded this as one of the reasons why each of the two epistles should be split into two smaller separate epistles. In epistle D which he reconstructed from 1 Th., a double thanksgiving for the faith of the addressees nevertheless remains intact.[2]

R. 6:17 does prove that when the issue concerned the conversion and faith of his audience, Paul was accustomed to thank God. In R. 1:8 thanksgiving for the faith of the Roman Christians has already been expressed. In R. 6:17 God is once again thanked when their conversion and obedience to the faith are again recorded. Therefore, we need not be surprised when following the account of the faith of the addressees at the end of the eulogy in Eph., Paul adds a eucharistia.

Another difference between the disposition of Eph. and that of the other epistles, is the occurrence of two important prayers. Not only does the epistle contain an extended intercession at the beginning (1:17-23) but after an exposition on the participation in salvation by the addressees, there follows another long prayer of intercession in

---

[1] Cf. Schubert, op. cit., p. 89.

[2] See para. 1 of this chapter and p. 58 note 2. Epistle D consists of 1 Th. 2:13-4:2. The thanksgiving occurs in 2:13 and 3:9.

3:(1)14-19. Such an abundance of prayer is found nowhere else in the epistles.

In para. 2 of the preceding chapter, we saw that a recapitulation of the intercession is a normal feature of the ancient letter. This phenomenon occurs also in other epistles of the CPminus. Phil, after an explicit intercession in 1:3, 4 contains a second intercession in 1:9-11. Col., after the intercession in 1:3, has another intercession in 1:9-20. R. contains an intercession in 1:10 and prayers that the addressees may be blessed in 15:5s. and 15:13. 2 C. has no intercession at the beginning but a prayer for blessing upon the addressees in 9:8-11 and two intercessions in 13:7 and 9.

If we examine the divisions which Schmithals has made in the epistles to the Thessalonians, we find that even the curtailed epistles contain repeated intercession. 1 and 2 Th. contain a substantial number of intercessions and blessings : 1 Th 1:2 ; 3:10 ; 3:11-13 ; 5:23 ; 2 Th. 1:11, 12, 1:16, 17 and 3:16. The striking aspect in Eph. is the extent of the two prayers.

As a comparison to these two prayers, Col. 1:9-20 stands alone. This last is even more comprehensive than the longest prayer in Eph.

As a point of fact, the remaining epistles of the CP minus do contain some statements which would make acceptable in Paul such an amplitude of prayer; for it appears that the prayer as such occupied a highly important position in his work.

Thus, in R. 10:1, he gives an account of his prayer for the Israelites. In 2 C. 11:28, he speaks about his inner difficulties and anxieties [1] after he has related his practical sufferings; he speaks of his daily care for all the communities. It would not have been feasible that Paul maintained daily contact with all his communities through letters and messengers. This contact must have existed through other channels. The most obvious solution is that Paul exercised his care and "watching"[2] over the communities through daily prayer. In this way he was "ἀπὼν τῷ σώματι, παρὼν δὲ τῷ πνεύματι" and made his decisions (cf. 1 C. 5:3). Such prayer was a matter of ἀγών (R. 15:30; Col. 2:1).[3]

---

[1] As a counterpart to the summing-up of 2 C. 11:23-27, stands v. 28—as apparent from v. 29—as an inner suffering, cf. the meaning Liddell-Scott gives to παρεκτός s.v.

[2] Cf. for ἐπίστασις and the narrow relationship with the function ἐπιστάτης Liddell-Scott, s.v.

[3] The οὐχ ἑόρακαν τὸ πρόσωπόν μου ἐν σαρκί (Col. 2:1) alludes to the same παρεῖναι τῷ πνεύματι as does 1 C. 5:3.

Others who were with him (Col. 4:12) or gathered with him (cf. 1 C. 5:4) in prayer could therein help and augment him (cf. R. 15:30).[1]

Intercession was an important part of the prophet's role.[2] Paul placed himself amongst the prophets [3] and particularly beside Jeremiah [4] and Moses.[5] His prayer for Israel which is mentioned in R. 10:1 reached, as we may see in R. 9:3, the proportions reached in the prayer of Moses as found in Ex. 32:32. The intensiveness of prayer as we encounter it in Eph. 1:17ss. and 3:16ss. on behalf of nations with whom the apostle has not yet established contact, is wholly compatible with the image which the apostle Paul conveys of himself in the other epistles. Certainly, it is very possible that his "ἱερουργοῦν" of the gospel of God and "εἶναι λειτουργὸν Χριστοῦ Ἰησοῦ εἰς τὰ ἔθνη (ἵνα γένηται ἡ προσφορὰ τῶν ἐθνῶν εὐπρόσδεκτος, ἡγιασμένη ἐν πνεύματι ἁγίῳ)" R. 15:16, inspired him to write these prayers in Eph.[6]

Also, it should be taken into account that the longest prayer in Eph. namely, Eph. 1:17-23 is in part an avowal of faith in Christ (1:20-23). In Col. too, the big prayer (Col. 1:9-20) declares Christ (1:15-20). Both epistles contain these professions near the beginning; in the remaining epistles there is likewise an avowal of Christ either at the very beginning or a little later on. R. and Gal. express the faith in Christ in the praescript which has contributed towards those sections being somewhat prolonged (cf. R. 1:3,4 and Gal. 1:2 and 4). Following the praescript, eucharistia and formula of thanksgiving, 1 Th. also has a similar declaration in 1:10.

If we now come to summarize the contents of this chapter, we may say that in disposition Eph. is distinguished from the other epistles by the combination of a eulogy and eucharistia-formulation and by the extended prayers it contains. However, statements and indications

---

[1] Cf. E. Stauffer, Th. W. I, p. 139 ad Col. 4 and R. 15 : "Paulus spricht von Kampf-bund der Beter" (Paul speaks of a brotherhood of prayer).

[2] Cf. W. Zimmerli, Ezechiel (Bibl. Kommentar z. A. T. XIII), p. 229.

[3] Cf. E. Lohmeyer, Grundlagen paulinischer Theologie (Beiträge z. Hist. Theol. 1929, I), p. 200ss.; K. H. Rengstorf, Th. W. I, p. 400ss. and Gal. 1:15; Jer. 1:5 and Is. 49:1.

[4] Cf. Dupont, Gnosis, p. 240ss.

[5] 2 C. 3:3, 6, 12 and 13.

[6] The fact that this intercessor should, towards the end of his epistle, also ask for intercession on behalf of himself and the other faithful (Eph. 6:18-20) corresponds with the image he presents of himself in R. 15:30 and with the disposition of other epistles, cf. Col. 4:2-4; Phlm. 22; 1 Th. 5:25 and 2 Th. 3:1.

can be found in those other epistles which could provide an explanation for this combination and for these expanded prayers.

Eph. follows an epistolary tradition which decrees that a letter begin with a praescript to be followed by a eucharistia-formulation with an intercession or alternatively, a eulogy, to be succeeded by a section containing the sender's requests or instructions and concluding with a greeting. Col., R. and Phlm. observe the same traditional form; Gal. does so partially and in 1 and 2 C. and Phil., traces of the same tradition can still be discerned.

There are more affinities. Eph., in common with R., Phlm. and 1 C., features the traditional word "parakalo" in the section dealing with requests or instructions. In Eph. as well as in R., the words παρακαλῶ οὖν ὑμᾶς are used to introduce this section. With regard to Col., R., and Gal., Eph. corresponds with these epistles in that this section is homogeneous and paraenetical in character.

None of the above-mentioned epistles are confined to the stated elements of that particular epistolary tradition. All of them contain more besides. Worthy of note are those elements which have been inserted at a specific place, namely, before the section containing requests or instructions and—if this is present—after the eucharistia-formulation. The three elements found in that position in Eph. are connected in character and contend with the elements occupying the same place in the other epistles. This relationship is especially pronounced in the case of the three elements which R. contains in the parallel instance. (See p. 63.)

Romans is indeed the epistle with which Eph. shares most both in disposition as well as in the nature of the various elements. If, as de Zwaan suggests, R. 16:1-20 is eliminated and R. 16:25-27 is also no longer counted as part of the original epistle, this resemblance is heightened to an increased degree. Furthermore, Eph. and Col. correspond greatly in disposition and in the elements present. Then, the affinity between Eph. and Gal. should also be mentioned.

Our *conclusion*, on a basis of comparison between the disposition and the elements of Eph. and the other pauline epistles addressed to the communities, can be that no objections can be raised against the authenticity of Eph. on that account and that on the contrary, the narrow relationship which Eph. demonstrates in this respect with the other epistles, must be regarded rather as an indication in favour of its authenticity.

To this conclusion may be added some further remarks. The very strong affinity with R. represents a direct weakening of the hypothesis that an imitator produced Eph. in imitation of Col. This hypothesis does neither justice to the formal affinity which we have discovered Eph. to have with R. nor to its relationship with Gal.

Goospeed and Mitton, who also devoted their attention to the material resemblance which Eph. bears to the various other Pauline epistles, also had their eyes closed to this formal affinity which Eph. has with R. and Gal. They regard Eph. as the work of an admirer of Paul who was initially only acquainted with Col. and Phlm. and but later saw the other epistles. There is too much affinity between the dispositions of Eph. and R. and too much relationship between the elements contained in the two epistles to warrant such a late familiarity with R. on the part of the author of Eph. If Eph. is not authentic, the formal affinity between Eph. and R. and the other epistles makes such a late awareness of those epistles improbable. It would seem more as if the author of Eph. had been witness to the genesis of those other epistles and in particular that of R.

CHAPTER FIVE

SOME PECULIARITIES IN THE PRAESCRIPT
AND ENDING OF THE EPISTLE

1. A CONJECTURE REGARDING THE ADDRESSEES

A contradiction exists between the tradititional reading of ἐν ᾿Εφέσῳ in the opening and the content of the epistle.[1] The impression the epistle makes is that it was written for Christians who had not been in direct contact with Paul and to whom he had not himself preached the gospel (1:15; 3:2-4; 4:21, 22). Yet, according to the Acts of the apostles, the community of Ephesus was one with which Paul was particularly closely acquainted.

The old solution of Theodorus of Mopsuestia[2], namely that Paul had written the epistle at a time when he had not yet met the Ephesians is not adequate in that it overlooks the fact nothing is known of any imprisonment as described in this epistle, prior to the period of Paul's activities in Ephesus.

Another solution whereby the traditional destination is considered of secondary consequence and the epistle is regarded as the work mentioned in Col. 4:16, with the community of Laodicea as the original addressees is also defective. Although Marcion may be quoted in support of this theory, a new problem now arises through the remarkable situation that Paul writes an epistle to both the Laodiceans and the Colossians and expresses his greetings to the former not in the epistle intended for them but in that to the Colossians (Col. 4:15, 17).[3]

The third and increasingly accepted explanation for the contradiction [4] is that originally the epistle contained a space in place of the

---

[1] Cf. Chapter I. para. 1.

[2] See the sources quoted in note 1 of Chap. I for this view.

[3] Cf. Schmid, Der Epheserbrief, p. 73-93.

[4] Cf. Schmid, op. cit., p. 94, 95 and p. 95, note 1. Percy (Die Probleme, p. 458-466) also strenuously supported this "Lückenhypothese". The derivative of this hypothesis, the "Enzyklikahypothese" as described according to Berthold on p. 3 in note 5, can be regard as unacceptable.

words ἐν Ἐφέσῳ and was in fact a writing intended for a number of communities at the same time (the name of the appropriate community being mentioned as the epistle was read). On the one hand, this explanation is borne out by evidence presented by several manuscripts but on the other, it presupposes a practise of which there is no other recorded instance.[1]

However, just as there are objections to be raised against reading ἐν Ἐφέσῳ in the passage, all the above mentioned explanations suffer from yet another drawback. Whatever geographical indications the reader may choose to read or add, the clause τοῖς ἁγίοις τοῖς οὖσιν ἐν τ. δ. καὶ πιστοῖς ἐν Χριστῷ Ἰησοῦ remains contorted and unclear and differently formulated from the other pauline praescripts. Both οὖσιν as well as πιστοῖς could be regarded as attributive to τοῖς ἁγίοις but then, in that case, one would similarly, also expect the article before πιστοῖς which would lend clarity to the sequence of the clause.

There is yet another possibility open, namely that ἐν τ. δ. and πιστοῖς are both taken as predicates of τοῖς οὖσιν. (With predicates, absence of the article is the general rule).[2] In that case, we are confronted with a type of "syllepse oratoire" or a semantically complicated zeugma where οὖσιν although occurring but once, applies equally to two little clauses of which the first is concrete and the second abstract.[3] But it is unlikely that we should be expected to find such finesses of rhetoric in a praescript.

A more probable solution is that the words ἁγίοις and πιστοῖς belong together and are indicative of the state which the addressees merit. Such is also the case in Col. 1:1 : τοῖς ... ἁγίοις καὶ πιστοῖς ἀδελφοῖς ...[4]

The fact that the two predicates should have been separated through the inclusion of an address of destination, in spite of the fact that they belong together, is no great objection. Nevertheless, a certain degree of obscurity is left and the whole remains contorted.

---

[1] Cf. Schmid, op. cit., p. 117 and Percy, op. cit., p. 459s. It is significant that Roller, Das Formular der paulinischen Briefe, p. 202-212, also refutes this hypothesis because during the course of his researches into ancient chancery procedures, he never fournd examples of such practises as the hypothesis puts formard.

[2] See Bl.-Debr. para. 273 and Radermacher para. 117.

[3] Cf. Lausberg, Handbuch der Literarischen Rhetorik, para. 707 and 708.

[4] In the N.T. πιστός is often combined with a second predicate, cf. Matt. 24:25; 25:21; 1 C. 4:17 and Rev. 3:14. In classical Greek, πιστός is often combined with another adjective, cf. Plato, Tim. 49b πιστῷ καὶ βεβαίῳ ... λογῷ and Liddell-Scott, s.v.

With regard to textual criticism, the following may be remarked
concerning the destination of the epistle. It is possible that Marcion
who regarded Eph. to be an epistle to the Laodiceans, gave the τοῖς
οὖσιν ἐν Λαοδικείᾳ .... version of Eph. 1:1 in his Apostolikon.

Tertullianus, Adv. Marc. V, 11, writes when introducing a quotation
from Eph. 2:12 "et de alia epistula, quam nos ad Ephesios praescriptam
habemus, haeretici (i.e. Marcion cum suis) vero ad Laodicenos". In
Adv. Marc. V, 5 Tertullianus uses the word "praescribit" to describe
the writing of the opening of 1 C., meaning the writing of the greeting
following the destined address. Thus, it is highly likely that "praescriptam" (Adv. Marc. V, 11) refers not to the superscription heading
the epistle but to the opening, the real praescript [1] of the epistle.

In Adv. Marc. V, 17, Tertullianus writes about Eph. : «Ecclesiae
quidem veritate epistulam istam ad Ephesios habemus emissam, non
ad Laodicenos, sed Marcion ei titulum aliquando interpolare gestiit
quasi et in isto diligentissimus explorator. Nihil autem de titulis
interest, cum ad omnes apostolus scripserit, dum ad quosdem." Tertullianus employs the word "titulus" in the most divergent contexts.
In the above-mentioned place, V, 5, Tertullianus also uses the word
titulus, quite clearly intending to denote the praescript of 1 C. and the
other epistles. The meaning of "interpolare" is not to weld in [2] but
to embellish or falsify. Thus Tertullianus accuses Marcion of altering
the titulus [3] of Eph. It could very well be that Tertullianus was thinking of the superscription which the epistle, amongst a collection of
copies of more letters, bore. But equally possible is that in taking
totum pro parte, he had in mind the address mentioned in the praescript
of the episte. [4]

---

[1] The original epistles were not headed by superscriptions. The official address was
not placed over a letter but on the outside cover of the folded missive. A copy of letter
could only contain directions if it was included in a collection of copies. Only then
would there be any purpose in placing the directions above the letter in order to record
whither it was sent; cf. Deissmann, Licht v. O., p. 120 note 3.

[2] This erroneous translation is found in H. U. Meyboom, Oud-Christelijke geschriften
in Nederlandsche vertaling XLI (Leiden 1927), p. 238. For the meanings of titulus in
Tertullianus, see v. Harnack, Die Adresse, p. 703, note 1.

[3] Although the word "alter" does not convey the emotional force of Tertullian's.
"interpolare", it does reproduce the essential meaning of the word, cf. Adv. Marc,
V, 21,1 "Affectavit opinor etiam numerum epistolarum interpolare" and IV, 1, 1,
"evangelium ... quod interpolando suum fecit." (CCh I, Tert. Opera I.)

[4] V. Harnack, "Die Adresse des Epheserbriefes des Paulus", p. 703 : "Titulus und
Adresse fallen für die ungelehrte Betrachtung bei einem Briefe zusammen." (To the

If the correct interpretation of the data given by Tertullianus is that Marcion gave the version τοῖς οὖσιν ἐν Λαοδικείᾳ at the opening of the epistle, then as far as Tertullianus himself is concerned, these data must be understood to mean that he preferred the τοῖς οὖσιν ἐν Ἐφέσῳ rendering.[1]

Nevertheless, even if Marcion only recorded the name Laodicea in the directions heading the epistle and mentioned neither Laodicea nor Ephesus in the text, it is still possible that Tertullianus took the τοῖς οὖσιν ἐν Ἐφέσῳ version as his point of departure. His reference to the veritas ecclesiae could very well embrace a version of ἐν Ἐφέσῳ which was familiar to him. Most copies of the epistle, the Latin tradition and the Syrian translations give or are cognizant of the τοῖς οὖσιν ἐν Ἐφέσῳ version.

Yet there also exists some important evidence in support of the omission of geographical indications. For the Chester Beatty papyrus (p[14], circa the year 200) gives the following rendering : τοῖς ἁγίοις οὖσιν καὶ πιστοῖς ἐν Χριστῷ Ἰησοῖ. The Sinaïticus (א, fourth century) originally contained the version τοῖς ἁγίοις τοῖς οὖσιν καὶ πιστοῖς ἐν Χριστῷ Ἰησοῦ. Later, another hand added the words ἐν Ἐφέσῳ to follow τοῖς ἁγίοις τοῖς οὖσιν. The Vaticanus (B, fourth century) gives the same version as the Sinaïticus prima manu (א*). In this case, the words ἐν Ἐφέσῳ are found in the margin of the manuscript. Apart from the examples quoted above, other manuscripts which would corroborate an original text without geographical directions could also be mentioned.[2]

Origen in his commentary, is familiar with our epistle as the epistle to the Ephesians although he had evidently not construed the direction

---

unschooled mind, the titulus and address of a letter are one and the same). Yet it is certain that in the titulus (in its wider sense) the names (i.e. the tituli in a narrower sense) form the essential part.

[1] Cf. Schmid, Der Epheserbrief, p. 59, line 13ss.

[2] 1. Minusc. 1739 (10th. Century); 2. Minusc. 424 (11th. Century), which originally contained the words ἐν Ἐφέσῳ which were later deleted (cf. F. J. A. Horst, Prologomena to St. Paul's Epistles to the Romans and the Ephesians, London 1895, p. 75s. : "The corrections of the corrector of MS 67 (= 424) are evidently taken from another quite different MS of great excellence now lost"; see Schmid, Der Epheserbrief, p. 51 note 4 and Abbott, p. I). See Abbott's comment (p. I) for the weight of the combined evidence presented by Sinaïcus, Vaticanus and the second version of the Minusc. 424 : "Lightfoot observes that a reading in St. Paul's Epistles supported by אB67[2] almost always represents the original text."

ἐν Ἐφέσῳ out the opening of the epistle. Since he bases his comments
on the words τοῖς ἁγίοις τοῖς οὖσιν, giving a very subtle explanation
for the words τοῖς οὖσιν.[1] Basil the Great who also knew the work
as the epistle to the Ephesians concurred with this interpretation
which he called the traditional one quoting, in support of this exgesis
τὰ παλαιὰ τῶν ἀντιγράφων. This proves that the ancient manuscripts
known to Basil contained the same version of the text as found in the
Chester Beatty papyrus.[2]

We are thus concerned with divergent data. Firstly, there is the
evidence of Marcion that the epistle was addressed to Laodicea;
moreover, it is possible that he gave the reading τοῖς ἁγίοις τοῖς οὖσιν
ἐν Λαοδικείᾳ in the praescript.

Beside this, an ancient tradition has it that the epistle was addressed
to the Ephesians. This tradition is maintained in the writings of Irenaeus,[3] Clement of Alexandria [4] and Tertullian as well as in the
Canon Muratorianus.[5]

The majority of manuscripts give the ἐν Ἐφέσῳ version for Eph.
1:1, which reading of the text was probably familiar to Tertullian,
Victorinus Afer, Jerome and Pseudo-Ignatius.[6]

A small number of manuscripts fail to record the words ἐν Ἐφέσῳ in

---

[1] Cf. Cramer, Cat. VI, 102; J. A. F. Gregg, "The commentary of Origen upon the
Epistle to the Ephesians", in JThSt 3, 1902, p. 233-244; Abbott, op. cit., p. II and Schmid
op. cit., p. 61s.

[2] Basil, C. Eunomium II, 19, MPG 29,611; Schmid, op. cit., p. 62 s. and Abbott, op.
cit., p. I.

[3] Ad. Haer. V, 2, 3; cf. Schmid, op. cit., p. 16 note 2 or Abbott, op. cit. p. XII.

[4] Paedag., I, 5, 18 de. Stählin I, p. 100; Stromata 4, 8 ed. Stählin II, p. 277; cf.
Schmid, op. cit., p. 17 note 1 or Abbott, op. cit., p. XII.

[5] H. Lietzmann, Das Muratorische Fragment, Kl. T. 1, 1933, p. 6(7), line 51.

[6] According to the introduction of his commentary, Jerome consulted Origen (Schmid,
op. cit., p. 64). In his commentary (Commentarii in epistolam ad Ephesios libri tres) he
refutes, without mentioning Origen, the latter's strange explanation for τοῖς οὖσιν.
Thus, Jerome was probably criticising Origen. He does not record that this extraordinary
explanation was due to the omission of a place name to follow τοῖς οὖσιν; in all probability
he overlooked this aspect since his Greek and Latin text did not contain this omission
(Schmid, op. cit., p. 65 note 1). Another possibility is that he did not see the necessity
of mentioning the existence of a version without ἐν Ἐφέσῳ because as far as he was
concerned, the Greek and Latin text used by himself eliminated any shadow of doubt
from the version with ἐν Ἐφέσῳ. (In Jülicher-Fascher, Einleitung, p. 603, there is an
analysis of the method of textual criticism followed by Jerome.) For Victorinus Afer,
MPL VIII. 1235 and Pseud-Ign. ad Eph. 9, see Schmid, op. cit., p. 66, note 1 and p. 67,
note 1.

the praescript. This minority comprises precisely those manuscripts that are important.[1] The assumption may be made that Origines was only acquainted with the text as presented in these manuscripts. Subsequently, the veracity of their evidence was strengthened by Basil who strenuously defended this version of the text.

From the point of view of textual criticism, the text as rendered in the τοῖς ἁγίοις τοῖς οὖσιν ἐν Λαοδικείᾳ καὶ πιστοῖς ἐν Χριστῷ Ἰησοῦ version stands in a weak position and if the authenticity of Eph. is accepted, gives rise to a problem. If the authenticity of Eph. is not accepted, this problem is of diminished proportions. History proves that forgers, in spite of the greetings for the community of Laodicea in Kol. 4:15, 17, were nevertheless intrigued by Col. 4:16 and, under cover of this text, drew up a forged epistle to the Laodiceans. The Canon Muratorianus mentions one such false epistle compiled at the behest of the Marcionites. Furthermore, we are acquainted with a Latin epistle to the Laodiceans and there is evidence that between the end of the fourth and eighth centuries there was in the East an epistle in circulation, addressed to the Laodiceans.[2]

The version τοῖς ἁγίοις τοῖς οὖσιν ἐν Ἐφέσῳ καὶ πιστοῖς ἐν Χριστῷ Ἰησοῦ is supported by many extant manuscripts and appears to have been known to several Christian writers of antiquity. If the authenticity of the epistle is accepted, this gives rise to even greater problematics than the version containing ἐν Λαοδικείᾳ. If the authenticity of the epistle is not accepted, the difficulty remains; for it is not obvious why a forger should have picked precisely on Ephesus as a fictitious destination. Surely, if either tradition or Acts had made him aware of the fact that Paul had worked for a long period in Ephesus, it is strange that the falsificator framed his text as if Paul had not been acquainted with the community.

Finally, there is the rendering τοῖς ἁγίοις τοῖς οὖσιν καὶ πιστοῖς ἐν Χριστῷ Ἰησοῦ. Submitted to textual criticism, this version is quite strong. Seen from the point of view that the epistle is inauthentic, it loses in credibility. Why, after all, should a forger have imitated the praescripts of the authentic epistles of Paul in such a mishappen and senseless manner?

---

[1] See p. 75 note 2.

[2] Cf. Lietzmann, Das Muratorische Fragment, p. 8 (and 9), line 63 s.; R. Knopf-G. Krüger, "Laodicenerbrief" in Hennecke[2], p. 150; W. Schneemelcher, "Der Laodicenerbrief" in Hennecke[3] II, p. 81 and Schmid, op. cit., p. 79 note 3.

If one accepts the authenticity of the epistle, this reading also treates problems. We were unable to give credence to the hypothesis that the author had left open a space following the words τοῖς οὖσιν to allow for geographical indications, for this theory is based on a practise which is not familiar to us from antiquity. Moreover, this leads to the same objection as does every version in which the words τοῖς οὖσιν are followed by the preposition ἐν and the name of a place; the passage sounds forced and unintelligible. Most interpreters of later times who are of the opinion that the words τοῖς ἁγίοις τοῖς οὖσιν καὶ πιστοῖς ἐν Χριστῷ Ἰησοῦ should form a consecutive uninterrupted sequence and are authentic, arrive at an exegesis as complicated as that of Origen which had been rejected already as early as Jerome.[1]

The most plausible exegesis is still that given by H. Lake and R. J. Cadbury in 1931. Their translation ran : "to the local saints and believers in Jesus Christ".[2] However, although the examples they quote

---

[1] Origen quotes the name ὁ ὤν which God uses of himself to Moses in Exodus 3:14 and says in explanation of τοῖς οὖσιν in the praescript of Eph., that οἱ μετέχοντες τοῦ ὄντος have themselves also become ὄντες and are therefore designated as τοῖς ἁγίοις τοῖς οὖσιν. (See p. 76 note 1 for the reference). Jerome questioned this exegesis : "Quidam curiosius quam necesse est, putant ex eo quod Moysi dictum sit "Haec dices filiis Israel : qui est misit me" etiam eos qui Ephesi sunt, sancti et fideles, essentiae vocabulo nuncupatos, ut quo modo a Sancto sancti, a Iusti iusti, a Sapient sapientes, ita ab eo qui est, hi "qui sunt" appellentur." (See note 20 for the reference).

C. St. Matthies, Erklärung des Briefes Pauli an die Epheser (Greifswald 1834), p. 7 translates : "sämtlich daseinden Heiligen und Gläubigen in Christo Jesu."

M. Schneckenburger, Beiträge zur Einleitung i.d. N.T. (Stuttgart 1932), p. 133s.; "Den Heiligen, die es in der Tat sind."

W. Milligan, "Ephesians", in Encycl. Britt. : "To the saint existing and faithful in Jesus."

J. G. Reiche, Commentarius criticus in N.T. II (Göttingen 1839), p. 122 : "sancti, qui sunt et (= etiam) credentes in Christum". B. Weisz, Lehrbuch der Einleitung i.d. N.T. (Berlin ³1897), p. 248, also supports this exegesis and adds that the intention was to differentiate between the saints of the New Covenant and those of the Old Covenant. Schmid, op. cit., p. 121, remarks : "Sicher ist bis jetzt, das jede Textgestalt, die nur ἐν Ἐφέσῳ streicht ohne einen andern Ortsnamen dafür einzufügen rein sprächlich beurteilt, eine unmöglichkeit ist."

[2] See their remark ad Acts 5:17 in the commentary The Acts of the Apostles (Jackson-Lake I 4), p. 56. N. Turner (J. H. Moulton, A Grammar of N.T. Greek, Vol. III, Edinburgh 1963 XI, para. 2, p. 151) does not find this version gramatically unacceptable. He thinks the point in question concerns a superfluous use of the participle ὤν as is characteristic of papyri of the Ptolemaic period and also in his opinion, the case in R. 13:1 (αἱ δὲ οὖσαι) and especially Acts 5:17 and 13:1. In my view, the participle in Acts 5:17; 13:1 and R. 13:1 is of a greater significance. Besides, in Acts 15:17 and 13:1, it occurs between

from papyri as supportive evidence do clearly indicate that the present participle of εἶναι was often employed in order to circumvent lengthier descriptions and unnecessary detail, this by no means supplies the proof that this participle, purely as a technical term when not modified by the textual context, at any time had the meaning "local".

Acts 13:1; 28:17 and R. 13:1 also fail to yield any such evidence. In the final analysis, this exegesis still leaves us with an unintelligible and forced construction; it is simply not comprehensible why the expressions ἅγιος and πιστός should have been separated in such a manner as to suggest that they are quite different. Furthermore, it is somewhat surprising that the participle of εἶναι should in this particular praescript be used in a manner so totally different from that in in the other pauline praescripts.

There is yet another possibility, namely that the text is impure as it stands in which case the original version should be identified. L. Grensted has called the theory that *EN ΕΦΕΣΩ* is a misrendering of *ΕΘΝΕΣΙΝ* "the most ingenious conjecture".[1] In my opinion, the resemblance between both groups of letters is not of such a nature that this interchange is very likely. In addition, this corruption lacks motive.

Schmid believes that the original version read τοῖς ἁγίοις καὶ πιστοῖς ἐν Χριστῷ 'Ιησοῦ and that τοῖς οὖσιν ἐν 'Εφέσῳ was a later addition and the subsequent deletion of ἐν 'Εφέσῳ resulted in the τοῖς ἁγίοις τοῖς οὖσιν καὶ πιστοῖς ἐν Χριστῷ 'Ιησοῦ version. One objection against this conjecture is that this epistle which, judging by the content, was written with a definite group of Christians in mind, should have borne such an unlimited and world-wide address. Another objections is that the—according to Schmid—last version in the codex Sinaïticus and the codex Vaticanus is more accurate and older than the — according to Schmid—second version and that Basil the Great explicitly records of the rendering τοῖς ἁγίοις τοῖς οὖσιν καὶ πιστοῖς ἐν Χριστῷ 'Ιησοῦ that this is the old version : οὕτω γὰρ καὶ οἱ πρὸ ἡμῶν

---

the article and the noun. The p[46] bears equally little resemblance to the pauline praescripts; this constitutes an objection whether the epistle is assumed to be inauthentic or authentic.

[1] L. W. Grensted DAC I, s.v. Ephesians. A. Kiene gave this suggestion in "Der Epheserbrief" ThStKr 1869, p. 316. R. Scott (The Pauline Epistles, Edinburgh 1909, p. 182) independently arrived at the same conjecture.

παραδεδώκασι καὶ ἡμεῖς ἐν τοῖς παλαιοῖς τῶν ἀντιγράφων εὑρήκαμεν.[1] Basil, who rejects a version containing ἐν ᾿Εφέσῳ, excludes any possibility that a version without τοῖς οὖσιν was of greater antiquity than any with τοῖς οὖσιν.

A more acceptable conjecture is that of P. Ewald who regards τοῖς ἀγαπητοῖς οὖσιν as the original. Nevertheless, here too objections may be made. It is odd that, contrary to all the pauline epistles, the recipients are not more precisely identified by name or by location.

What would be conceivable is that in the case of this epistle such indications were inscribed only on the outside covering of the document. But then another objection remains; the purpose of the superfluous οὖσιν after ἀγαπητοῖς.[2]

Since not one of the conjectures that have hitherto been put forward is in our opinion satisfactory, we shall now attempt to find a different solution. To do this, it is necessary to take into consideration two facts :

1st τοῖς οὖσιν demands some sort of geographical indication

2nd the result of a geographical indication is a distorted and obscure praescript.

The incorporation of a *double* geogrpahical indication presents a possible solution : τοῖς ἁγίοις τοῖς οὖσιν <ἐν τ. δ.> καὶ <ἐν τ. δ.> πιστοῖς ἐν Χριστῷ ᾿Ιησοῦ. Although we are not familiar with any instance in a pauline praescript where the names of two places, connected by καί occurs, we are accustomed to indications in the praescript that an epistle is directed at more than one community and the naming of more than one name or group.[3]

The assignation of an attribute to a dative construction which contains both a qualification and an indication of place introduced by the present participle of εἶναι, lends to the proposed reading of the

---

[1] For the exact place, see p. 76 note 2. For Schmid's conjecture, see Der Epheserbrief, p. 125-129.

[2] P. Ewald, NkZ XV, 1904, p. 506-568. For an additional number of less acceptable guesses, see Schmid, op. cit., p. 122-125.

[3] 2 C. 1:1   τῇ ἐκκλησίᾳ τοῦ θεοῦ τῇ οὔσῃ ἐν Κορίνδῳ σὺν τοῖς ἁγίοις πᾶσιν τοῖς οὖσιν ἐν ὅλῃ τῇ ᾿Αχαιᾳ.

    Gal. 1:2   ταῖς ἐκκλησίαις τῆς Ταλατίας.

    Phil. 1:1   πᾶσιν τοῖς ἁγίοις ἐν Χριστῷ ᾿Ιησοῦ τοῖς οὖσιν ἐν Φιλίπποις σὺν ἐπισκόποις καὶ διακόνοις.

    Phlm. 1,2   Φιλήμονι τῷ ἀγαπητῷ καὶ συνεργῷ ἡμῶν καὶ ᾿Απφίᾳ τῇ ἀδελφῇ καὶ ᾿Αρχίππῳ τῷ συστρατιῶ τῃ ἡμῶν καὶ τῇ κατ᾿ οἶκόν σου ἐκκλησίᾳ.

passage a great affinity with the praescripts of generally acknowledged pauline epistles :

cf. R. 1:7 dative construction : πᾶσιν τοῖς οὖσιν ἐν 'Ρώμῃ ἀγαπητοῖς
θεοῦ
attribute : κλητοῖς ἁγίοις,

1 C. 1:2 dative construction : τῇ ἐκκλησίᾳ τοῦ θεοῦ τῇ οὔσῃ ἐν
Κορίνθῳ
attribute : ἡγιασμένοις ἐν Χριστῳ 'Ιησοῦ
attribute : κλητοῖς ἁγίοις.

In the same way our reading of Eph. 1:1 contains

dative construction : τοῖς ἁγίοις τοῖς οὖσιν ἐν τ. δ. καὶ ἐν τ. δ.
attribute : πιστοῖς ἐν Χριστῷ 'Ιησοῦ.

Our theory is that the two names were subsequently scrapped in the same manner as, according to the Boernerianus, majuscule was the case with some copies of R. This codex records a text in which the words ἐν 'Ρώμῃ after τοῖς οὖσιν are missing from the praescript (1:7) and the words τοῖς ἐν 'Ρώμῃ are omitted (1:14) from the continuation of the epistle. If deletion of the place names in the praescript of Eph. occurred in as careful a fashion as in the case of R. so that after τοῖς οὖσιν only place names introduced by the preposition ἐν were omitted, the version that remained as τοῖς οὖσιν καὶ πιστοῖς ἐν Χριστῷ 'Ιησοῦ was the same one which Basil the Great regarded as the ancient text. Besides the τοῖς οὖσιν which in R. 1:7 of the Boernerianus occurs in an identical context, the word καί also remained as a vestige of a second place name.

There was a tendency in ancient Christianity to stress the ecumenical validity of the epistles of Paul; cf. Tertullian, Adv. Marc. V, 17 : "Nihil autem de titulis interest, cum ad omnes apostolus scripserit." This is no doubt the same tendency which prompted the omission of the geographical indications in R. 1:7 and 14. Perhaps the same attitude is also responsible for an extension of the praescript of 1 C. in which, according to the theory of J. Weiss, the words σὺν πᾶσιν τοῖς ἐπικαλουμένοις τὸ ὄνομα τοῦ κυρίου ἡμῶν 'Ιησοῦ Χριστοῦ ἐν παντὶ τόπῳ, αὐτῶν καὶ ἡμῶν were not part of the original text.[1]

---

[1] See von Harnack, Die Briefsammlung des Apostels Paulus und die anderen vorkonstantinischen Briefsammlungen (Leipzig 1926), p. 9.

The same explanation accounts for the omission in Eph. V. Harnack, whilst believing Laodicea to have been the original and subsequently deleted address on the epistle and seeking for different motives behind the deletion of this name,[1] yet declared : "An sich reicht das Motiv, den ökumenischen Character des Briefs zum Ausdruck zu bringen aus um die Streichung der partikularen Adresse ... zu erklären.[2]

But which were the two place names originally mentioned in the epistle ? If the epistle and also the passage 6:21, 22 is authentic, we must look for its intended readers in an area which the messenger Tychicus visited on his journey to Colossae and in places where Paul had not himself worked. The towns of Hierapolis and Laodicea which are named in Col. 4:13 come to mind in this connection. Thus the ancient speculation that the epistle is identical with the epistle to which there is a reference in Col. 4:16 comes once again to the fore.

In Col. 4:16 the term $\tau \grave{\eta} \nu$ $\dot{\epsilon} \kappa$ $\varLambda \alpha o \delta \iota \kappa \epsilon \acute{\iota} \alpha s$ could be a reference to an epistle which arrived first in Hierapolis and later in Laodicea. A closer definition would have been wordier. The singular fact that Paul should have conveyed his greetings to the community of Laodicea in Col. 4:16 rather than in the epistle intended for that particular community can be explained within the framework of the hypothesis that argues that Eph. was an epistle from Paul to Hierapolis and Laodicea and the one indicated in Col. 4:16. Paul himself has not worked in these communities. We observe in R. 1:11-13 and 15:14, 15 how tactfully and cautiously Paul approaches a community in which he himself has not worked. He approaches Hierapolis and Laodicea with equal circumspection.

As is apparent from Col. 2:1, these communities dwelt in some danger.[3] This danger was certainly that of heterodoxy. Nevertheless, in the epistle to Laodicea and Hierapolis, Paul refrains from direct polemics whereas in his epistle to the community of Colossae with which he identified himself he did not draw back from direct remonstrance.

---

[1] See Chapter L, para. 1.

[2] Die Briefsammlung, p. 74, note 26. "in itself the motive of stressing the ecumenical character of the epistle suffices to explain the deletion of individual addresses."

[3] The actual words are $\tau \hat{\omega} \nu$ $\dot{\epsilon} \nu$ $\varLambda \alpha o \delta \iota \kappa \epsilon \acute{\iota} \alpha$ $\kappa \alpha \grave{\iota}$ $\ddot{o} \sigma o \iota$ $o \dot{\upsilon} \chi$ $\dot{\epsilon} \acute{o} \rho \alpha \kappa \alpha \nu$ $\tau \grave{o}$ $\pi \rho \acute{o} \sigma \omega \pi \acute{o} \nu$ $\mu o \upsilon$ $\dot{\epsilon} \nu$ $\sigma \alpha \rho \kappa \acute{\iota}$.
Col. 4:13 suggests that this second category applies in the first place to the Christians of Hierapolis. Several minusculi and the revision of the Peshitto by Thomas of Heraclea confirm this.

The selfsame discretion was responsible for the fact that he did not include special greetings for Laodicea in an epistle addressed to both Laodicea and Hierapolis; Paul wanted to be "omnes idem". The lending or exchange of copies of epistles which is suggested in Col. 4:16 represents an attempt by Paul to tighten the bonds with Laodicea through internal relations between Colossae and Laodicea; the greetings to Laodicea which the Colossians were to convey were designed to strengthen these bonds.[1]

It is possible that the community of Hierapolis never gained possession of a copy of the epistle because Tychicus upon arrival either read the epistle out personally or, after having it read out, departed for Laodicea taking with him the epistle. Furthermore, it is fully conceivable that the community of Hierapolis which aroused the anxiety of Paul and Epaphras (Col. 2:1 and 4:12) did not take sufficient pains to preseve for posterity a record of the fact that Paul had to them addressed an epistle. (This community was subsequently to enjoy another honour which may have had more glamonr. The Philippus mentioned in Acts 6:5; 8:4-10 and 21:8, 9 was said to have worked in that city with a number of daughters who were prophetesses and been buried there.[2]) In a similar manner, the responce of Laodicea to receiving an epistle could account for the equal lack of pains taken to keep alive the memory of the honour bestowed by a missive from the apostle Paul.

With the subsequent dissemination of the epistle by way of Ephesus, ecumenical motives may have provided a contributory factor in the eradication of the earlier reminders of Hierapolis and Laodicea from the praescript. Still later, Ephesus, this metropolitan city of Asia where Paul had so long laboured, graced either itself or was by others graced with the distinction of a pauline writing, thus attaining to the same category of importance as Rome, the capital city of the Empire and Corinth, the capital city of Achaia.

---

[1] The Laodiceans who are first approached in Eph. are thus addressed a second time in Col. 4:15. The first instance is direct, the second indirect. The same method approach was adopted in the case of Archippus. In Phlm. 1, 2 Paul directly addresses him whilst in Col. 4:17, he does so through others.

[2] Eus. Hitst. Eccl. III, 39,9; III, 31,3 and V, 24,2 (cf. Heussi, Kompendium, p. 32, para. w.). It is worth noting that Papias, bishop of Hiërapolis 135-150 A.D., from whom Eusebius drew his information on Philippus, although greatly interested in gospel material, i.e. the words and deeds of Jesus, showed no interest in the epistles of Paul. (Incidentally, it is by no means certain that he meant the evangelist Philippus; he may have intended the apostle Philippus.)

This conjecture of ours harmonies with the explanation for the word ἀγών in Col. 2:1., where we related this word to Paul's prayer. Col. 2:1 concerns the praying of Paul for the Colossians; the emphasis placed upon intercession and the exhaustive nature of the intercession which we remark in Col. 2:1 reflect the agon of the apostle for the Colossians. Col. 2:1 also mentions a prayer for the faithful in Laodicea and for others of the faith whom Paul has not personally encountered. On the basis of Col. 4:13 we must count the faithful of Hierapolis as the third category. If Eph. was originally addressed to the communities of Laodicea and Hierapolis, then the intercession mentioned in Eph. 1:16 and the prayers which occur in Eph. 1:17-23 and 3:16ss. manifest to an equal degree the agon of the apostle for the faithful of Laodicea and Hierapolis which is expressed in Col. 2:1.

Furthermore, this conjecture has the great advantage of totally eliminating the tortuousness and lack of clarity of the construction τοῖς ἁγίοις τοῖς οὖσιν <ἐν ᾿Εφέσῳ> καὶ πιστοῖς ἐν Χριστῷ ᾿Ιησοῦ In this construction it is above all the tiny word καί that in so puzzling. Thus, by introducing the name of a place preceded by the word ἐν following καί, we gain a clear and coherent sequence. Also, since πιστοῖς stands in an adjectival relationship to ἁγίοις, the connected expressions of ἅγιοι and πιστοί are also more closely welded together.

On the basis of these reasons, we shall adopt this conjecture as our point of departure in further investigation and read the praescript as τοῖς ἁγίοις τοῖς οὖσιν ἐν ῾Ιεραπόλει καὶ ἐν Λαοδικείᾳ, πιστοῖς ἐν Χριστῷ ᾿Ιησοῦ.

Thus the opening of Eph. fits entirely within the framework of the praescripts of the other epistles. One common charecteristic of all these praescripts is that the name Παῦλος is immediately followed by an attribute in which the genitive Χριστοῦ ᾿Ιησοῦ occurs and sometimes a further διὰ θελήματος θεοῦ. (Gal. contains a corresponding formulation. In 1 and 2 Th. the attribute is missing. In Phil. Timotheus and Paul share a common attribute.) This attribute or a subsequent definition denotes Paul as ἀπόστολος. (Phil., Phlm. and 1 and 2 Th. form the exception.)

Usually the addressees are denoted in such a manner that a relationship to Christ or to God or to God and Christ is brought to expression. In the first instance this occurs through the use of ἐν with the dative, in the second through the genitive θεοῦ and in the third case again through ἐν accompanied by the dative. Often, they are denoted initially or by subsequent narrower qualification as ἅγιοι. The geographical delineation is described either by means of the substantive pres. part. of εἶναι followed by ἐν with the dative or through the use of a genitive.

2. The peculiar aspect that Paul alone is named as the sender

Another peculiarity of the praescript is that Paul alone is therein named as the sender of the epistle. This is also the case in R. In all other epistles addressed either to a community or more than one community we find, besides Paul's, one or more additional names. In Gal. these others, although not mentioned by name, are described as οἱ σὺν ἐμοι πάντες αδελφοί.

If Eph. is not authentic, it is difficult to find an explanation for this exclusive mention of Paul. A semblance of authenticity would have been better served by a correspondence between this praescript and the praescripts of the other epistles. Since Paul alone is named as sender, the praescript distinguished itself from praescripts which mention a number of senders. Moreover, Eph. differs much in form from the only other praescript in which Paul occurs as the sole sender, namely R.

The only reasonable assumption in this case is that the putative pseudographer followed the praescript of Col. which is related in form but omitted the name of Timotheus because he wished to create the impression that Paul alone was the author of the words of his epistle.

If however the assumption is made that Eph. is authentic, a more plausible explanation may be found for the fact that Paul is described as the sole sender of the epistle. The reason may be the same as that which governed in the case of R. In that case, R. and Eph. are both epistles to Christians with whom Paul has not as yet had personal contact and who, he might imagine, would not on their own initiative be yearning for contact with him or feel closely bound to the apostle.

The case is different with the Galations, the Philippians, the Thessalonians and the Corinthians. Those were the communities where Paul had himself laid the fundaments of the faith (1 C. 3:10). These Christians are his children (Gal. 4:19) and should follow his example (1 C. 4:16, Phil. 3:17). It is in the very nature of a letter that the absent are made to seem present.[1] In those epistles, Paul is present with

---

[1] Cf. Turpilus' definition of a letter : "sola res est, quae homines absentes praesentes facit." (See the fly-leaf of Witkowski's Epistulae privatae).

those Christians as he was formerly present with them in person, i.e. together with others.

This being together with others was an aspect of Paul's work not to be neglected. His speaking to these Christians was a word of truth, no mere word of yes or no (2 C. 1:18). According to the rule of Deut. 17:6 and 19:15 it was necessary that more than one person should speak to make valid a true word. John the Baptist, Jesus and the ancient community all respected this rule, (Matt. 11:2; Luke 7:19; Mark 6:7; Luke 10:1 and Matt. 18:16) and so did Paul (2 C. 13:1).[1] The firm word of truth in 2 C. 1:18 had been preached by Paul himself, Silvanus and Timotheus (2 C. 1:19). Very explicitly Paul here names, besides himself, these two other witnesses. To work and preach alone was unthinkable to him and to his contemporaries.[2]

The Christians of Rome and the recipients of Eph., Paul approaches completely alone in his epistles. To them, he does not present himself as the one who, together with others, hae worked amongst them.

The thoughts which Paul entertains about himself contain, besides the principle of working and bearing witness together in the company of others, a second principle : the consciousness of a special mission of a prophetic nature.[3] From his very birth, God has set him apart, called

---

[1] In his characteristic fashion, he gives a very remarkable application to the rule in 2 Cor. 13:1 (cf. H. Strathmann, Th. W. IV, p. 493, 494). From this it is also clearly manifest that he was well acquainted with the rule. For a further application of this rule in 2 C. 13:1 and the rest of the N.T. see H. van Vliet, No Single Testimony—A Study on the adoption of the law of Deut. 19:15 par. into the New Testament (diss. Utrecht 1958), spec. p. 88 sub 3 and p. 73.

[2] Cf. Acts 13:2; 15:36, 39 and 40. Acts 13:2 (as Acts 11:30) also concerns the custom that a community sends out two evoys together (cf. Rengstorf, Th. W I, p. 417, line 27ss.). Other facets of the common work of Paul and his associates in P. J. du Plessis, Τέλειος, The Idea of Perfection (diss. Kampen 1959), p. 180 ad 1 C. 2:6 : "The speakers adressing this religious community are Paul and his associate. Sosthenes. It would be doing the apostle an injustice to regard his use of the first person plural as a mere stylistic feature. By this aid he betrays his humble attitude of relegating his person to a modest equal amongst brethren" and in a sermon by Fr. Hood in Dome, The Magazine of the Friends of St. Paul's Cathedral, Oct. 1963, Nt. 1 p. 15s. : "The most eminent men, both in the old dispensation and the new, have been notable in three ways : dependence on God: passionate desire to serve their fellow men ; reliance on trusted friends ... We see the same characteristics in our Patron St. Paul ... He relied to a touching degree on his friends. He was bitterly disappointed when he arrived at Troas and ... "found not Titus" his brother. A separate sermon could be preached on his relations with Timothy, Barnabas, Luke and Mark." In this connection I also draw attention to 2 Tm. 4:9, 10.

[3] For this prophetic role, see p. 69 and note 2 of that page. Lohmeyer, Grundlagen

him through his grace and revealed to him his Son so that he, Paul, might preach the gospel amongst the heathens (εὐαγγελίζεσθαι). Paul has not learned the word of the gospel which he preaches through man but received it through the revelation of Jesus Christ.

The Galatians were right to receive him as an ἄγγελος θεοῦ, indeed as Christ Jesus (Gal. 1:15, 16, 12; 4:14). God has granted him the mercy of being a λειτουργὸς Χριστοῦ Ἰησοῦ εἰς τὰ ἔθνη, ἱερουργῶν τὸ εἰαγγέλιον τοῦ θεοῦ, so that the offering of the Gentiles might be acceptable to God and sanctified by the Holy Ghost (R. 15:15, 16). Paul himself is nothing but by the grace of God he is what he is and has he, the least of the apostles, laboured more than they. That is to say, not he but the grace of God which is with him (1 C. 15:9, 10) or Christ, who works through him (R. 15:18).

Paul approaches the Christians amongst whom he has not built the foundations of the faith with the outmost tact and modesty.[1] He even hesitates to address them in the first place and when finally, he does boldly write to them, he does so exclusively on the strength of the grace of God that enables him to be a minister of Jesus Christ to the nations (R. 15:15-21). Thus Paul, in the strong awareness of his exceptional calling addresses in R. the Christians of Rome as he does, in Eph., those of Hierapolis and Laodicea.

At this point the question may be raised why Paul did not address himself in a similar way to the Colossians but present himself to them together with Timotheus. The fact is that the Colossians occupy an intermediate position. Essentially, the roots amongst them were laid by Paul. For, prior to the time when the addressees of Col. heard and accepted the gospel preached to them by Epaphras, Colossians had already been converted by Paul and his associates : Epaphras himself, Philemon, Archippus and probably others too,[2] As far as Paul was concerned, those Christian Colossians whom he had not yet seen, would have been encompassed by the first fruits of Colossae. And although he personally had not visited Colossae, he had nevertheless made the beginnings and laid down the fundamentals.

---

p. 195-209 also drew a sharp picture of this second principle in Paul's ideas concerning himself. In Rengstorf, p. 440ss. it also comes to the fore with clarity.

[1] See previous paragraph.

[2] Col. 1:7; 4:12, 17; Phlm. 1, 2, 19 and 23 (cf. Jülicher-Fascher, Einleitung, pp. 129, 124).

3. Consequences of this peculiarity

We should now consider whether the fact that Paul addresses the recipients as the sole author of the epistle in the praescript has any consequences which have a bearing on our investigation. Such indeed is the case. To the ancient way of thinking, there was a decided distinction whether a letter had been sent by one alone or more senders. The latter event was unusual. In fact, amongst collections of ancient letters which I have consulted, examples of letters sent by more than one person where exceedingly rare.[1]

In the past, the slightly facile attitude was adopted that an authentic epistle of Paul contained nothing but thoughts and words emanating from Paul himself. However, the history of the ancient letter which we found reflected in the above-mentioned collections forbid us to ignore or minimize the fact that in most of the epistles other senders besides Paul are named. Thus the oft-quoted enthusiastic opinion of U. von Wilamowitz-Moellendorf should not be endorsed without qualification :

---

[1] Exler gives the praescripts of hundreds of letters (both private and official) and other documents written in the form of letters. These occur in papyri found in Egypt and covering a period from 300 B. C. to 300 A.D. He divides these writings into : 1. Familiar letters; 2. Business letters; 3. Petitions, complaints, applications; 4. Letters from and to officials. In the first category, letters from more than one sender are very scarce. In the remaining categories they are more frequent. The reason for this is that the common interests of several parties concerned are being dealt with simulatneously or that the senders form a closed group or college.

Witkowski who delves into other sources as well as those provided by the extensive body of papyri gives 72 letters out of which only nos. 20 and 49 come from more than one sender. In the first case this concerns a petition from a college of priests and in the latter, a private letter. Everything mentioned in this letter concerns both senders equally and because a promise of intervention with the king on both their behalf occurs, the document is slightly official in character. Deissmann, Licht v. O. has only one note from more than one sender in his collection of 26 missives written on papyrus or ostraca. This letter. written c. 600 A.D. in Coptic is from three candidates for the deaconry who make certain mutual pledges to their bishop.

Brooke covers a wider area and includes not a single letter deriving from more than one sender. (Her survey gives 202 letters from antiquity in Greek and Latin, dated between 500 B.C. and 500 A.D.) For these works, see p. 46, n. 1. Bahr, "Paul and Letter Writing in the First Century", p. 476 makes the following comment regarding letters mentioning more than one sender : "The solitary reference to this phenomenon which I have been able to find in other ancient literature is a notice in Cicero that his friend Atticus once wrote Cicero a letter together with others." (Ad. Att. XI, 5,1).

"Endlich, endlich redet wieder einer auf Griechisch von einer frischen inneren Lebenserfahrung, das ist sein Glaube ... Als einen Ersatz seiner persönlicher Wirkung schreibe er seine Briefe. Dieser Briefstil ist Paulus, niemand als Paulus ..."[1]

This assessment has failed to take into account a number of factors. For example, it should be borne in mind that "das Kerygma der hellenistischen Gemeinden vor und neben Paulus" exerted an influence upon the formulation of Paul's epistles.[2] Furthermore, it may be taken for granted that those who travelled around with Paul as participants in his work also exercised some influence upon the apostle which must have functioned in the writing of the epistles.[3] And, above all, the influence of those who are mentioned in the praescripts of the epistles as co-senders should be reckoned as an important force. They too were partly responsible for the content of those epistles; as in all ancient letters which named more than one sender in the praescript, the responsibility for that letter rested equally on each of those mentioned in the praescript.

Now it is true that Acts gives the impression that soon after the first missionary journey started Paul began to dominate amongst his travelling companions.[4] The content of the epistles always show

---

[1] U. von Wilamowitz-Moellendorf, Die griechische Literatur des Altertums, Die Kultur der Gegenwart I, 8³, p. 232. ("At last, at last some one once again speaks in Greek from a fresh and personal experience of life which is his faith ... he writes his letters to substitute for his personal presence. This style of letter is Paul, no-one but Paul"). Norden, Die Antike Kunstprosa I³, p. 11s., has exactly questioned that in antiquity the style is expressive of the individual. In his opinion, the style is to a much greater extent governed by the subject under discussion.

[2] For this influence, on Paul, see Bultmann, Theologie, p. 188ss. In the chapter entitled "Das Kerygma der Hellenistischen Gemeinde vor und neben Paulus", Bultmann extracts this kerugma to a major degree form the epistles of Paul. H. J. Schoeps, Paulus, die Theologie des Apostels im Lichte der jüdischen Religionsgeschichte (Tübingen 1959), p. 54-56 contradicts Bultmann's thesis that the hellenistic communities formed the definitive connection between Paul and the original community of Palestine and he defends the idea of a direct influence on Paul from the kerugma of the original Palestinic community.

[3] It can scarcely be supposed that in the course of the association between Paul and those who accompanied him, the only influence was that of Paul upon them and that this was in no way reciprocal, not even in the sense that they formed a linguistic environment.

[4] In Acts. 11:30; 13:2 and 13:7 Barnabas is first mentioned in connection with Paul. Whenever there is a subsequent reference to him together with Paul, the latter's name usually comes first.

Paul to be the dominant figure in the common work and also in the composition of the epistles, he was clearly the dominant personality amongst the senders.

It would however, have been contrary to all tradition if no responsibility whatsoever or, at the most, a mute responsibility were to have been the share of those who are mentioned as co-senders in the praescript of those epistles. The first person plural in those epistles is not used merely for stylistic purposes [1] or as an indication of persons mentioned in the contents of that epistle [2] but again and again to indicate the communal senders.

One letter found in Memphis, written in Greek and dating from 153 B.C., is the work of two Arabs.[3] They used the plural form. The letter is obviously the responsibility of both of them and continually refers to their mutual action.

The first epistle to the Thessalonians is a somewhat more complicated case. One of the three senders (Timotheus) was temporarily absent. Therefore, if the we-form concerns this period of absence, only the other two senders could be understood from the first person plural. Apart from this, the epistle is in essence of the same character as the note from the two Arabs. The first person plural form has reference to the common senders, is their common responsibility and concerns their common action. Paul does dominate in this epistle but that is once more made clear expressis verbis by an emphatic ἐγὼ μὲν Παῦλος in 2:18. The situation in 2 Th. is of a corresponding nature.

1 and 2 C. are epistles from two senders. Although the first person plural form is not there used so repeatedly as in 1 and 2 Th. as an indication of the unanimity of the two senders, this aspect does find frequent reference whilst Paul's own words are more than once distinguished by means of an unequivocal ἐγώ. As a matter of interest, Paul by no means uses this device invariably to distinguish himself from the other senders but in order to demonstrate that he is wholly for a particular statement and is prepared to maintain this before everybody.[4]

---

[1] Cf. Bl.-Debr., para. 280 and Stauffer, Th. W. II, p. 354.

[2] Eg. 1 C. 3:9.

[3] Witkowski, Epistulae priv. graec., no. 49, cf. note 41.

[4] Cf. Stauffer, Th. W. II, p. 354 line 18ss. Turner (Moulton, A Grammar of N.T. Greek, Vol. III Syntax, V. para. 2, p. 37) remarks that the nominatives ἐγώ, σύ, ἡμεῖς and ὑμεῖς are more often used in the N.T. and the papyri than in classical Greek. Classical Greek only uses these nominatives for emphasis or to indicate an alternative.

In Gal., Phil. and Phlm., the personality of Paul is strongly preponderant. A number of reasons were accounted for this. In the community
of Galatia the truth of Paul's gospel had come under the shadow of
doubt. To the Philippians, the apostle's testimony was of a highly
personal nature whilst in the epistle to Philemon, Paul urges a request
with the whole of his being. In each of the three epistles the other
senders remain in the background.[1]

Nevertheless, it would not be correct to assume that in all the epistles which record the names of other senders besides Paul, we are concerned with the ipsissima vox Pauli. For on the whole, we have to
take into account a definite contribution from those co-senders.[2]
Therefore, the fact that in R. and Eph. Paul alone is named as the
sender should be seriously evaluated and any correspondence or discrepancy between Eph. and R. should be carefully weighed if an
assessment concerning the authenticity of Eph. is to be pronounced.
In the matter of the disposition and certain elements of the epistles,
we have already been able to ascertain a remarkable affinity between
Eph. and R.

4. SECRETARIAL HELP

We would like to draw attention to one more incorrect opinion on the
subject of pauline praescripts. It has sometimes been maintained the
others besides Paul were named in the praescripts because they had
acted in a secretarial capacity[3]. This view is entirely without foundation.

Paul did make use of the services of a secretary or scribe. That was

---

[1] In Gal. they even remain anonymous : οἱ σὺν ἐμοὶ πάντες ἀδελφοί. (These are
Paul's associates and not the christians of the town in which Paul is staying; cf. the
distinction in Phil. 4:21 between οἱ σὺν ἐμοὶ ἀδελφοί, the associates and πάντες οἱ ἅγιοι,
the local christians.)

[2] Bahr, "Paul and Letter Writing in the First Century", p. 476s., rules "In either
case, the thought of all the senders might be adequately expressed, but the actual
vocabulary, style, and grammar must, of necessity, be that of only one person, either
one of the authors or the secretary". This view of Bahr's partly corroborates our view.
We feel that the influence of the co-senders need not have been restricted to the contents
of their minds. They could also have influenced the formulation of those thoughts.

[3] Cf. the hypothesis of Eichhorn concerning Tinotheus as the author of Col. in
Chapter I, para. 2 and cf. also de Zwaan, Inleiding tot het N.T. II, p. 170.

the frequent practice of his time. There is no evidence that a comprehensive system of abbreviated script or stenography existed in Paul's
time. However, what was customary was that people would entrust
either the whole or part of their correspondence to slaves or to freed
slaves.[1] It seems quite clear that Paul was not usually in the habit of
writing his own letters. Once, we find a scribe mentioned by name
(Tertius) in R. 16:22.[2] At the end of Gal., it becomes evident that Paul
has with his own hand written the close of the epistle (Gal. 6:11-18) after
another had written the previous part.[3] 2 Th. 3:17 declares that (in
accordance with epistolatory tradition) Paul was accustomed to complete his epistles in his own hand as a token of their authenticity.[4]
Although we are not in a position to consult the signatures on the
epistles, the emphatic statement ὁ ἀσπασμὸς τῇ ἐμῇ χειρὶ Παύλου
in 1 C. 16:21 and Col. 4:18 makes clear, even now to us, that Paul's
epistles were concluded in his own handwriting (in 1 C.: 1 C. 16:21-24
and in Col.: Col. 4:18).

Apart from the above quoted instance in R. 16:22, the name of the
secretary is mentioned nowhere else. The reason in this case may have
been that this scribe had a particular relationship with the addressees
and recorded his name as a greeting. In other cases, this was not necessary. To mention a secretary by name was not customary unless there
existed some legal matter which demanded such procedure. Only at a
later period did an absorption in titilature entail that the name and
quality of a secretary be included in a letter.[5]

---

[1] R.Y. Tyrell, The Correspondence of M. Tullius Cicero (Dublin-London, ²1885), p.
47s. : "for the handwriting was generally that of a slave, if the writer possessed sufficient
means to keep a servus a manu or ab epistolis."

K. Dziatzko in Pauly-W. 1889 III, s.v. Brief : "Vielbeschäftigte Personen, namentlich
solche in offentlicher Stellung, und Behörden liessen ihren Correspondenz ganz oder
zum Teil durch Sclaven oder Freigelassenen besorgen."

See also Deissmann, Licht v. O., p. 132s. Note 6 and H. Lietzmann, An die Galater
(Handbuch z. N.T. 10, 1932), p. 43.

[2] Cf. the remarks of Deissmann, o.c., p. 200.

[3] Cf. Fr. Sieffert, Der Brief an die Galater (Krit.-exeg. Ktr. ü. d. N.T. VII, ⁹1899);
Lietzmann, o.c. and P. A. van Stempvoort, Oud en Nieuw, De Brief aan de Galatiërs
(De Prediking v. h. N.T. VII, 1951), ad Gl. 6:11.

[4] See Deissmann, o.c., p. 132 note 6 and p. 137-139; cf. also Lietzmann, l.c.

[5] It was not necessary that the name of the secretary be mentioned. Letter no. 36
by Cicero of the letters collected by Brooke, was written by a secretary. His name is
not mentioned. Also letters nos. 118, 119 and 120 from the Emperor Julian testify to the
anonymity of the secretaries. Exler, o. c., p. 127 points out that many letters written

There are no examples to prove that in Paul's time the name of a secretary or, moreover, a secretary as co-sender, was ever given at the beginning of a letter. At that time, the normal place for this was at the conclusion of a letter, in which case the name was accompanied by a definite statement.[1] We thus see this in R. 16:22 and in 1 Pt. 5:12.

Percy has combatted the view that it was a general custom in antiquity that letters were partly or entirely written by employees.[2] He did admit to this possibility in the case of persons with a very busy life but not as far as Paul was concerned.

However, to counterbalance this view, it must be pointed out that the letters of Paul were of an exceptional length.[3]

We must reckon with the possibility that the final texts of Paul's epistles were partly determined by a secretary and that the activities of this scribe cannot have wholly and absolutely been restricted to the purely mechanical setting down of whatever was dictated.[4] We do not

---

on papyri must have been accomplished on behalf of the senders by those who made letter-writing their profession. "In purely private letters the scribe or whoever wrote the letter did not need to declare, that he and not the person, whose name was found on the document was the writer. In official communications, however, and in contractual and business letters, such a delcaration seems to have been required." A special formula at the end then named the scribe and recorded that the sender of the letter did not know how to write. In this case, the naming of the scribe had a legal significance. See also the end of the letter in which the candidates for the deaconry undertook an obligation in Deissmann, op. cit., p. 188s. In some 3rd. century letters which betray an interest in titulature in the praescript, the praescript contains an adverbial clause introduced by διά naming the secretary and his function(s); cf. Exler, op. cit., pp. 39, 55 and 56. Amongst his examples there is one which may even date from the second century A.D. (i.e. P. Tebt, II 1907, 370/207).

[1] See the previous note.

[2] Percy, Probleme, p. 10ss. note 62.

[3] Cf. de Zwaan, Inleiding I, p. 48: "Paulus' brieven zijn de langste, die wij uit de oudheid kennen." ("Paul's letters are the longest which are known to us from antiquity.")

[4] Roller, Das Formular der paulinischen Briefe, p. 69-88 has made it almost certain that a personally written greeting could in antiquity have had the same significance as a signiture in our time. 2 Th. 3:17 suggests the same. Furthermore Roller, op. cit., p. 187-191, gives a curious explanation for the formula ὁ ἀσπασμὸς τῇ ἐμῇ χειρὶ Παύλου. He thought this was to warn the reader that in the case of epistles in Paul's own hand, the foregoing had also been written by Paul himself and that therefore a change of hand writing was not to be expected. This explanation is based entirely on Roller's own reconstruction and is not corroborated by any other known examples. I myself see no evidence that, as distinct from the other epistles, 2 Th., Col., Gal. and Phlm. should have been written by Paul himself (cf. the discussion in Percy, Probleme, p. 10ss. note 62). See also the two papers by Bahr mentioned in note 2, Chapter III. Quite correct-

know whether Paul could always make use of the same secretarial assistance and must therefore take into account the possibility that different people were involved. Certainly, one does not get the impression that his financial circumstances would have permitted him to maintain the permanent services of a servus a manu or ab epistolis.

5. DIFFERENCE AND AFFINITY WITH OTHER EPISTLES IN THE ENDING OF EPH.

The greetings or blessings at the end of Eph. demand our attention because they do not display an obvious affinity with the greetings at the conclusion of the other epistles. This lack of a clear affinity need not necessarily per se be interpreted as an indication of inauthenticity. For the falsificator, there would have been nothing but advantage in making the ending of his epistle correspond with the ending of the genuine epistles. Indeed, the forger of the epistle of Paul to the Laodiceans which has remained in the Latin version, did see to it that the epistle contained an ending with the requisite affinities.[1]

When these greetings or blessings in Eph. are subjected to a narrower scrutiny, it emerges that a deeper affinity with the usages of the other epistles is by no means absent. The first greeting is an adaptation of the peace greeting with which letters could not only begin but also conclude.[2]

Gal. 6:16 is also an adaptation of this peace greeting. The peace greeting has been incorporated in a complete blessing at the first conclusion of the epistle to the Romans (R. 15:33), at the second conclusion (R.

---

ly, Bahr concludes from the circumstances that Paul sometimes had co-senders and was accustomed to use the services of a scribe : "... it would be well to speak with caution on topics such as Pauline terminology or Pauline theology. There may be less of Paul in the Pauline corpus than we have been assuming." (Paul and Letter Writing in the First Century", p. 477). In his essay on "The Subscriptions" however, he takes too little into account the position of dominance which Paul held amongst his associates.

[1] Cf. Hennecke II[3], p. 84. Incidentally, it is curious that he follows the greetings with an exhortation conforming to Col. 4:18, for nowhere in the authentic epistles does such a feature occur.

[2] The Aramaic letter from the Persian king, Artaxerxes, in Ezra 4:17 begins with the word peace. This could be in conformity with the traditions of the Aramaic chancelry. Aramaic letters from the rabbinical period could also begin with a peace greeting; cf. W. Foerster, Th. W. II. p. 407, line 25ss. That letters could also end with a peace greeting is demonstrated by 1 Pt. 5:14 and 3 J. 15 (op. cit., p. 409, line 44 s.).

16:20) and at the end of 2 Th. (3:16). In Phil., as the epistle is running quite close to its termination, two paraenetical passages are concluded by blessings which concern respectively, the peace of God and the God of peace (Phil. 4:7, 9).

In the first greeting of Eph., ἀγάπη and πίστις, connected in hebraicised fashion, are also mentioned.[1] We find the ἀγάπη τοῦ θεοῦ in the greeting at the end of 2 C. (13:13). This had already been preceded by a blessing in 2 C. 13:11 in which agape and eirene are linked. The fact that pistis also occurs in Eph. 6:23, fits within the framework of the blessing. As do eirene and agape (cf. 2 C. 13:11) the word is indicative of something which is God's own and which He bestows upon the blessed. God has pistis (R. 3:3).[2] He is pistos. He makes true his promises (2 C. 1 18) and will preserve them who are of Christ for the future in Christ (2 C. 1:18, 21; 1 C. 10:13; 1 C. 1:9 and 1 Th. 5:24). Likewise, he bestows pistis upon men (Eph. 2:8).

Πίστις is "die durch Gottes eschatologische Tat ermöglichte eschatologische Haltung des Menschen, die Haltung des "neuen" Menschen[3] ... wie sie ständig auf das zurückbezogen ist, was Gott in Christus getan hat, so ist sie andrerseits ständig auf die Zukunft gerichtet, auf das was Gott tun wird ... Unsere σωτηρία ist durch die πίστις nicht zum verfügbaren Besitz, sondern zur sichern Hoffnung geworden".[4]

In 1 C. 1:7-9, a eucharistia formulation assumes the character of a prayer in which the eschatological perseverance of the addressees is discussed, is then transformed into a blessing which concerns the same topic and resolves into an appeal to God's being pistis. 1 Th. 5:23, at the end of the epistle speaks in a prayerful manner of the God of peace who will preserve the addressees in blamelessness for the coming of Christ. This is again followed by an appeal to God who is pistos, who has called them and will bring about that they will so be preserved. A similar eschatological leaning also belongs to the pistis in the blessing of Eph. 6:23. It is a gift from God who is true and gives to them

---

[1] Cf. Kuhn, N.T. St. 7, p. 337.

[2] R. Bultmann, Th. W. VI, p. 204, note 227.

[3] Op. cit., p. 222 line 19, 20. (πίστις is "the eschatological attitude of man made possible by the eschatological act of God, the attitude of the "new" man ... as it is constantly linked to what God has done in Christ, so it is on the other hand constantly directed at the future and that which God will do ... Our σωτηρία has, through the πίστις become not an available possession but a certain hope.)

[4] Op. cit., p. 222 line 38-41 and p. 223 line 8-10.

who are of Christ, perseverance in being Christian. Only when it is thus interpreted, does this blessing become comprehensible.

In keeping with the greeting in the praescripts of the Pauline epistles, the concept of eirene combines with that of charis. The latter is found in the final greeting. After the ἀπὸ θεοῦ πατρὸς καὶ κυρίου Ἰησοῦ Χριστοῦ of 6:23, it was not necessary to repeat, as it is elsewhere repeated (in R. 16:20; 1 C. 16:23; 23; 2 C. 13:13; Gal. 6:18; Phil. 4:23; 1 Th. 5:28; 2 Th. 3:18 and Phlm. 25) that it concerns the χάρις τοῦ κυρίου ἡμῶν Ἰησοῦ (the χάρις τοῦ κυρίου Ἰησοῦ, the χάρις τοῦ κυρίου Ἰησοῦ Χριστοῦ or the χάρις τοῦ κυρίου ἡμῶν Ἰησοῦ Χριστοῦ).

Neither was there any point in repeating the formula ἀπὸ θεοῦ πατρὸς ἡμῶν καὶ κυριοῦ Ἰησοῦ Χριστοῦ [1] (which in the praescript greetings related both to εἰρήνη and to χάρις) in 6:24 after this had already been added to εἰρήνη ... καὶ ἀγάπη μετὰ πίστεως in 6:23.

In 6:23 we find the triad of concepts εἰρήνη ... ἀγάπη μετὰ πίστεως, and in 6:24 the twosome ἡ χάρις ... ἐν ἀφθαρσίᾳ· The latter are connected in a hebraicised fashion as are the last two ideas of the preceding vers. Both μετά + genitive as well as ἐν + dative come in place of καί and (in agreement with the first member) the nominative.[2] The ἐν ἐφθαρσίᾳ which stands in the place of καὶ ἀφθαρσία only then follows when, immediately after the first of the two concepts has been expressed, it is stated for whom the blessing is intended. Similarly, the earlier blessing concept, has already intimated, after the first concept of the triad, for whom the blessing is meant.

In the past this placing of ἐν ἀφθαρσίᾳ has often given rise to bewilderment and some scholars wanted to forge a connection there with ἀγαπώντων. However, now that Kuhn has demonstrated through the Qumran documents that μετά and ἐν virtually substitute for καί in these places, it evolves that the parallel construction of the two blessings entails this behindhand placing of ἐν ἀφθαρσίᾳ as a matter of course.[3]

---

[1] This formula occurs in the praescript greeting almost everywhere in the CPmin; only in 1 Th. is it absent. In Col. it is reduced to ἀπὸ θεοῦ πατρὸς ἡμῶν.

[2] See p. 95 note 1 and Chapter VI, para.5.

[3] As the pistis (the last thought in the triple of Eph. 6:23), the aphtharsia (the last of the two concepts expressed in Eph. 6:24) is of an eschatological nature; cf. 1 C. 15:42, 50, 53 and 54. The blessing which mentions the aphtharsia in effect promises participation in the basileia. (ἀφθαρσία is an identical and substitute term for βασιλεία; cf. Bultmann, Theologie, p. 79.) In contraposition to the aphtharsia or participation in the basileia, stands the idea of becoming the object of the wrath of God; cf. R. 2:7, 8.

Another feature which seems odd, is that they for whom both blessings are intended are not addressed in the second person but are mentioned in the third person.

In R. 16:20; 1 C. 16:23; 2 C. 13:13; Gal. 6:18; Phil. 4:25; 1 Th. 5:28;
2 Th. 3:18 and Phlm. 25, the second part of the greeting or formula
of blessing with charis, consists of $\mu\epsilon\theta$' $\dot{\upsilon}\mu\hat{\omega}\nu$, $\mu\epsilon\tau\grave{\alpha}$ $\pi\acute{\alpha}\nu\tau\omega\nu$ $\dot{\upsilon}\mu\hat{\omega}\nu$ or
$\mu\epsilon\tau\grave{\alpha}$ $\tau o\hat{\upsilon}$ $\pi\nu\epsilon\acute{\upsilon}\mu\alpha\tau o\varsigma$ $\dot{\upsilon}\mu\hat{\omega}\nu$. In Gal. 6:18 this is in addition followed by
the vocative $\dot{\alpha}\delta\epsilon\lambda\phi o\acute{\iota}$.

Such a directness is absent from Eph. However, the fact that there
is no use of the direct form of address is a phenomenon which is not
strange to the endings of some of the epistles of Paul. Such is the case
in Gal. where the blessing, which is given in the second person plural
in the vocative, has already been preceded (in 6:16) by another blessing
which is in the third person plural. The use of the third person plural
lends to this blessing the additional character of an exhortation and
a warning; it is clear that the blessing is conditional.

In C. 16:22, the blessing formula which, contains the word charis,
is also preceded by a declaration which serves the same purpose, being
an exhortation and a warning (the second predominating), expressed in
the third person singular. In this case, the formula conveys a malediction rather than a blessing. But again, as in Gal. 6:16, the condition
for the blessing is made clear.

Although the blessing of 2 C. 13:11 is in the second person plural,
a number of imperatives which indicate the conditions for the blessing,
have come before.

Thus it may be said that in Gal. as in 2 C. and 1 C., the blessing is
linked with an observance of discipline. (This connection with discipline
is also manifest in 2 Th. 3:13-16. This relationship between blessedness and discipline is compatible with the feature that in R. 16:19, 20
the obedience of the addressees is stated before the blessing which is
also preceded by an exhortation to the good.)

In Eph., the blessing is similarly coupled with instructions. The use
of the third person plural here too imbues the blessings with the character of an exhortation and a warning and the demands which must
be fulfilled in order to attain to the blessing can be clearly understood.
As in Gal. 6:16c it is conditional to the blessing of belonging to the
Israel of God, in Eph. 6:23, the condition for the blessing is to be adel-
phos. As in Gal. 6:16a it is necessary to adhere to a certain rule in
order to obtain the blessing and there is an exhortation to this path
and as in 1 C. 16:22 there is a warning against not loving the kurios, so

loving τὸν κύριον ἡμῶν 'Ιησοῦν Χριστόν in Eph. 6:24 is the condition
for the blessing to which is added an exhortation to this love. In 1 C.
16:22, the malediction (ἀνάθεμα) is the consequence of not loving
(οὐ φιλεῖν). In Eph. 6:24; grace and immortality (ἀφθαρσία) are the
rewards of loving (ἀγαπᾶν).[1]

Thus we are, in fact, presented with a remarkable affinity. This
affinity is far-reaching. We recognise it in the εἴ τις οὐ φιλεῖ τὸν κύριον
of 1 C. 16:22; the ὅσοι τῷ κανόνι τουτῳ στοιχήσουσιν of Gal. 6:16; the
χαίρετε, καταρτίζεσθε, παρακαλεῖσθε, τὸ αὐτὸ φρονεῖτε, εἰρηνεύετε
of 2 C. 13:11 and the πάντες οἱ ἀγαπῶντες τὸν κύριον ἡμῶν 'Ιησοῦν
Χριστόν of Eph. 6:24, being always concerned with the same phenomenon. Not only the subordinate clauses of 1 C. 16:2 and Gal. 6:16 but
also the series of imperatives of 2 C. 13:11 and the participle construction introduced by πάντες of Eph. 6:24 constitute, in a semiticised
Greek, perfect alternatives describing a condition.[2]

In effect therefore, at the end of Eph. and the endings of the epistle
of the HP the same trend of thought and the same concepts are present.
If the lack of a directly pronounced affinity with the greetings at the
ends of other epistles did not as such present any evidence for inauthenticity, then on the other hand the deeper affinities which become
manifest only upon further investigation, confirm the greetings at the
end of Eph. to be a valid indication of the authenticity of the epistle.

We shall now give a brief *summary* of the content of this chapter.
Of the versions of Eph. 1:1 which remain extant, the one containing
the words τοῖς ἁγίοις τοῖς οὖσιν καὶ πιστοῖς ἐν Χριστῷ 'Ιησοῦ is the
most plausible. This can scarcely be reconciled with the inauthenticity of the epistle. If the authenticity is accepted, there are other
problems. The words τοῖς οὖσιν demand a geographical indication.
Only a double geographical indication would eliminate the contorted
construction of the praescript and make it lucid. Evidence exists
which leads us to presume that the geographical indication in Eph.
has been deleted in order to lend general ecumenical significance to
the epistle. If Eph. in authentic, it may be recommended that Eph.
1:1 be read as τοῖς ἁγίοις τοῖς οὖσιν ἐν 'Ιεραπόλει καὶ ἐν Λαοδεκείᾳ,
πιστοῖς ἐν Χριστῷ 'Ιησοῦ.

---

[1] In note 3 on p. 96 we already saw that the wrath of God stands in contradistinction
to the aphtharsia. The same antithesis exists between aphtharsia and anathema.

[2] Cf. K. Beyer, Semitische Syntax im Neuen Testament (Studien zur Umwelt des
Neuen Testaments) I, 1 (1962), p. 142ss. and p. 239ss.

The fact that Paul alone is mentioned as the sender of the epistle can be explained in a most satisfactory way if the authenticity of Eph. is taken as a basic assumption. Communities amongst whom Paul has not personally laid the foundations of the faith are approached by him, both in Eph. as well as in R., entirely on the strength of the consciousness of an extraordinary and prophetic calling.

If Eph. really is authentic, the conclusion may be drawn from the fact that only Paul is named as the sender, that this epistle contains no contribution from others. This contribution is however, probable in the case of the epistles in which the praescript mentions one or more co-senders in addition to Paul. It cannot be expected that such associates merely existed silently in the shadow of Paul. Thus, even if they do not speak directly, whatever was written must have been previously discussed with them. In the case of Eph. and R. however, Paul speaks alone. For that reason, the affinities and differences between Eph. and R. are important if a definitive conclusion regarding the authenticity of Eph. is to be established.

In forming such a conclusion it should not be overlooked that all the epistles of Paul—thus also the epistles in which he is named as the sole sender—could be influenced by one or other of the scribes whose hand actually wrote the epistle. The secretary who wrote Eph. need not be the one who wrote R. It is conceivable that the work of such a secretary was not entirely restricted to the mechanical transcription of a dictation.

The greetings or blessings at the end of Eph. have not striking affinities with the greetings at the conclusions of the other epistles. There are, however, deeper affinities which become evident only upon closer investigation. These affinities constitute evidence for the authenticity of Eph.

Looking back on Chapters III-V in which the purely formal aspects of Eph. were considered, we elicit from these aspects—as well as from the early date from which the epistle was known in antiquity, as pointed out in Chapter II—some evidence favourable to the authenticity of the epistle. With regard to the significance of the affinities and discrepancies with R. in forming an opinion in favour of the authenticity of Eph., I would give a reminder of the strong affinity in the disposition and in the component elements between Eph. and R. as established in Chapter IV.

CHAPTER SIX

THE STYLE

1. Different styles in the epistles of Paul

Now that the disposition and elements of the epistle have been considered, it is time to examine the remaining formal aspects of the work i.e. the style, grammatical particularities and the vocabulary. These last aspects have in the past already been the subject of much attention.[1] More often than not, it was assumed that these aspects should feature identically in all authentic pauline epistles. This theory does not take into account the contributory factor of one or more co-senders who may have influenced the style, grammatical details and the vocabulary of the epistle; moreover, the secretary who wrote a particular epistle may have been another influence in these matters.[2] It is not to be expected that an authentic epistle of Paul invariably presents the ipsissima vox Pauli. In any event, critics of Paul during his lifetime still distinguished between the epistles and the spoken word of the apostle.[3]

Furhtermore, if it is considered that we have but a scant number of epistles by Paul at our disposal and that each of these epistles owes its existence to a concrete historical situation, there is every reason for reserve and caution when appraising the style, grammatical details and vocabulary of an epistle. The same is of relevance when the thought matter of the epistle is analysed. There is a vast difference whether the letters under discussion emanate from a litterator who wrote, either in person or through the medium of direct dictation, who had already developed and formulated his thoughts in previous writings and is now expanding certain ideas in a letter to a friend, or whether one is dealing with an epistle of Paul. For Paul's epistles may be expected to yield considerable less affinity in formulation and trend of

---

[1] See Chapter I. para. 5.
[2] See Chapter V, para. 3 and p. 99.
[3] 2 C. 10:10.

thought and it is always worth while keeping in mind the comment expressed by H. Oltramare : "Paul manque de l'habitude d'ecrire".[1]

If we are to discuss the style of Eph., it must first of all be pointed out that different styles are encountered in the epistles of Paul which are addressed to communities. (In this study we shall continue to exclude the pastoral epistles because few scholars hold these epistles, as a body, to be authentic and there would thus be little point in taking these epistles as a criterion for the authenticity of Eph.)

In the past, J. Weiss already commented on the to him enigmatic variation in style between major sections of R., 1 and 2 C. and Gal. on the one hand and, on the other, parts of 1 and 2 Th., Phil., Col. and Eph.[2] Later, Weiss was to remark that there are not two epistles found in the whole of the CP minus which are really written in the same style. His explanation was based on the assumption that Paul had used a number of scribes or amansuenses.[3]

Following in the footsteps of Weiss, Bultmann also drew attention to a great diversity of style within the HP. He recognised both an "eindrucksvoll beweglichen Predigtton" and a "Schwerfälligen Satzbau" ("impressively versatile preaching style" ... "awkward sentence structure").

Bultmann attributed this to different spiritual attitudes on the part of the apostle. The first style represented the apostle turned outwards; the second reflected a turning inwards of the apostle.[4]

At this point, it would be to the purpose to consider a remark made by Norden in another context : "Der Stil war damals eine erlernte Kunst, deren Regeln im allgemeinen keiner seiner Individualität zuliebe übertreten dürfte ... Erstens : die Individuen treten zurück hinter allgemeinen Richtungen der Zeit, deren Repräsentanten sie sind. Zweitens : ein und derselbe Schriftsteller konnte nebeneinander in ganz verschiedenen Stilarten schreiben, indem er bald diese, bald jene ἰδέα verwertete, je nachdem sie ihm für das vorliegende Werk zweckentsprechend schien ... Der Stil war im Altertum nicht der

---

[1] Oltramare, Commentaire sur les Epîtres de S. Paul aux Coloss., aux Ephes. et à Philem. I, p. 87.

[2] J. Weiss, Die Aufgaben der Neutest. Wissenschaft in der Gegenwart (Göttingen 1908), p. 15s.

[3] Das Urchristentum (1917), p. 316 (cf. Percy, Probleme, p. 46 note 43).

[4] Bultmann, Der Stil der paulinischen Predigt, p. 68ss.

Mensch selbst, sondern ein Gewand, das er nach Belieben wechseln konnte".[1]

Thus, two more lines of reasoning can be accepted:

Bultmann's argument that the spiritual state of the apostle was subject to change and Norden's observation in the works of other authors of a variable, non-individual style or rather, styles; these augmenting the explanations for the changes in style in the other epistles, which take into account a contribution from other senders in the formulation of several epistles of Paul and the fact that the major part of each epistle was put to paper by a secretary who, in all likelihood, was not always the same person.

The question is now whether the style of Eph. remains within the framework of variation in style encountered in the rest of the CP minus and whether the specific style of the epistle can be explained in the same way. The following analysis will demonstrate that the components which make up the particular style of Eph. do occur elsewhere in the epistles of Paul but that an accumulation of them (and thus, a completely identical style) is found in no other epistle. There is one single exception; the style of Col. showns a extraordinary affinity with that of Eph., being almost the same.

2. Characteristics of style in the other epistles not found in Eph.

In what way does the style of Eph. distinguish itself? In the first place there are some features present in the CP minus which are totally absent from Eph. In Eph. there is no rhetorical dialogue.[2] The vocative ἀδελφοί or ἀδελφέ does not occur. There are no rhetorical questions and syllogisms recede into the background. The testimony is seldom presented in the form of conclusions. Nor is any use made of the con-

---

[1] Norden, Die antike Kunstprosa I[3], p. 11s. "At that time, style was an acquired technique, the rules of which generally nobody could break for the sake of individuality ... Firstly : individuals recede behind the general trends of the time which they represent. Secondly : one and the same writer was able to write, side by side, in quite different styles in that he sometimes made use of one, sometimes another, depending upon which seemed suitable for the work in hand ... In ancient times, style represented not the individual man but a habit which he could change at will."

[2] Rhetorical dialogue in : R. 3:1-9; 3:27-4:11; 6:1-3; 8:31-37; 9:19-32; 10:18-11:21; 1 C. 6:15, 16; 7:18-22; 7:27, 28; 2C. 11:22, 23; 12:13, 15-17; Gal. 2:17 and 3:19-22.

junction εἰ to introduce a proposition from which a conclusion is then
drawn. The conjunction γάρ which may strengthen an inference which
has already been drawn, is rare. The particle μέν occurs but once and
the particle δέ but rarely. All the characteristics which are absent from
Eph., we do encounter in R., 1 and 2 C. and Gal.[1]

If on the other hand we turn to Phil., I and 2 Th. and Phlm., it
becomes clear that the stylistic phenomena which are rare or absent
in Eph., are likewise sparse or even wholly absent from these epistles.[2]
Thus, it may be said that there exists a remarkable degree of variation
in the style of the HP.

---

[1] R. Morgenthaler, Statistik des neutestamentlichen Wortschatzes (Zürich-Frankfurt
a/d M. 1958), gives us extensive information on the frequency of the various words
occuring in the CP. Some information is also found in Morton's article "The Authorship
of Greek Prose", p. 220ss. Since Morgenthaler and Morton do not follow the same edition
of the text of the N.T., they sometimes end up with different results. Even before the
work of Morgenthaler appeared, I personally investigated the frequency of certain phenomena and words in the CP with the aid of E. Nestle, Novum Testamentum Graece
Stuttgart, [17]1941 (and C. H. Bruder, Concordantiae omnium vocum Novi Testamenti
Graeci, Leipzig 1853). Whenever there is a discrepancy between Morgenthaler and Morton, I give the result of each counting. When it is not a question of statistics concerning
certain words but a matter respecting statistics in other regards, I follow my own figures.
When a certain phenomenon or word is under discussion, the indication 1/111 e.g.,
conveys that this phenomenon or word occurs in the epistle in question once in 111 lines
of Nestle.

For the length of epistles, see note 1 on p. 105. Below are listed the frequencies
of several words and phenomena occurring in the text. R. (vocative) ἀδελφοί 1/111;
interrogative sentence 1/12,5; εἰ 1/29 (since it is difficult to count the special use made
of εἰ to introduce a proposition from which a conclusion is drawn, these footnotes record merely the frequency of the common use of εἰ as described by Morgenthaler on p.
58); γάρ 1/7; μέν 1/53; δέ 1/7 (I myself counted δέ in R. 138 times, Morgenthaler
147 times (p. 86) and Morton 141 times, Journal p. 222).

1 C. ἀδελφοί 1/44; interrogative sentence 1/9; εἰ 1/35; γάρ 1/9; μέν 1/48; δέ 1/4 (author
202 times, Morgenthaler 209 times and Morton 194 times). 2 C. ἀδελφοί 1/211 : interrogative sentence 1/26; εἰ 1/30; γάρ 1/8; μέν 1/79; δέ 1/9 (author 76 times, Morgenthaler 73
and Morton 71). Gal. ἀδελφοί 1/35; interrogative sentence 1/16; εἰ 1/19,5; γάρ 1/9; μέν
1/104; δέ 1/5.

[2] Phil. no dialogue; ἀδελφοί 1/38; interrogative sentence 1/230; εἰ 1/57,5; γάρ 1/18;
μέν 1/36; δέ 1/8,5 (author 24 times, Morgenthaler 27 times and Morton 26 times).

1 Th. no dialogue; ἀδελφοί 1/15; interrogative sentence 1/105,5; εἰ 1/211; γάρ 1/9;
μέν 1/211; δέ 1/14 (author and Morgenthaler 15 times and Morton 13 times).

2 Th. no dialogue; ἀδελφοί 1/16; interrogative sentence 1/114; εἰ 0/114; γάρ 1/23;
μέν 0/114; δέ 1/10.

Phlm. no dialogue; ἀδελφέ 1/23; interrogative sentence 0/46; εἰ 1/46; γάρ 1/15;
μέν 0/46; δέ 1/8.

This same range of variation may sometimes be found even within a single epistle. In the case of R., for example in R. 1; R. 4:11-5:21 and R. 15:14-33, there are entire sections in which interrogative sentences, the conjunction εἰ or the particle μέν do not occur. In R. 2:1-6:23 (a section almost equal to Eph. in length), the vocative ἀδελφοί is not found. In the section R. 8:18-16:23 (far exceeding Eph. in length), the particle μέν is used but on one occasion. 1 C. contains a very small section, 1 C. 1:1-9 (the praescript and eucharistia formulation in which the intent of prayer is also expressed) which features not one of the missing or recessive characteristics of Eph.[1]

A great affinity exists between Eph. and Col.; in the latter all the stylistic features which are missing or recessive in Eph., are likewise missing or recessive. In this aspect, there is little to choose between the two epistles. In Col., the particles γάρ and δέ are even rarer than in Eph.[2] The fact that these characteristics are features either extremely infrequently or missing altogether from Eph. and Col., accounts for the fact that the style of these epistles is less lively and mobile than that of the pauline epistles in general.

A certain semiticising element is present in the omission or sparse use of the particle μέν, δέ, γάρ and εἰ, since a paucity of particles is a distinguishing mark of the semitic languages.[3] The infrequent appearance of the μέν - δέ correlative and also the diminished usage of the simple μέν bear witness that the writing in question was accomplished by a non-Greek or an individual of mixed ancestry.[4] Whereas a

---

[1] R. 1 (78 lines) no dialogue; ἀδελφοί 1/78; interrogative sentences 0/78; εἰ 0/78; γάρ 1/11; μέν 1/78; δέ 1/39 (1 additional instance in LXX citation).

R. 4:11-5:21 (95 lines) no dialogue: ἀδελφοί 0/95; interrogative sentences 0/95; εἰ 1/24; γάρ 1/6; μέν 0/95; δέ 1/8.

R. 15:13-33 (51 lines) no dialogue; ἀδελφοί 1/25; interrogative sentences 0/51; εἰ 1/51; γάρ 1/10; μέν 0/51; δέ 1/5.

R. 2:1-6:23 (± 300 lines) no ἀδελφοί.

R. 8:18-16:23 (±540 lines) one single μέν.

1 C. 1:1-9 (20 lines) no ἀδελφοί; no γάρ; no μέν; no δέ; no εἰ and of course, no interrogative sentenses or dialogue. See also note 3 on p. 104.

[2] Eph. (338 lines) no dialogue; ἀδελφοί 0/338; interrogative sentences 0/338; εἰ 1/169; γάρ 1/31; μέν 1/338; δέ 1/20.

Col. (222 lines) no dialogue; ἀδελφοί 0/222; interrogative sentences 1/222; εἰ 1/55,5; γάρ 1/44; μέν 1/222; δέ 1/44.

[3] Bl.-Debr., para. 438.

[4] Norden, Die antike Kunstprosa I[3], p. 25 note 3 "Wie spezifisch griechisch diese Partikeln sind, kann man überall da hübsch beobachten, wo Nichtgriechen oder Misch-

Greek would by preference choose to employ a conditional clause using εἰ, the semitic languages possessed alternative stylistic possibilities.[1]

It is worth remarking that there is some compensation for the diminished frequency of the above-mentioned particles in Eph. through the (in comparison with the other epistles) oft-repeated appearance of the particle διό and the single occurrence of the combined particles ἄρα οὖν, which appear in the N.T. only in R. and 1 and 2 Th.[2]

Keeping in mind this phenomenon of the diminished use or omssion of features which lend a certain liveliness and mobility to a style, it connot be asserted, when comparing Eph. and Col., that Eph. is further removed from the other epistles than is the case with Col. In fact, taking into account the compensatory feature in Eph. described above, the contrary is more true. Also with regard to the use of the conjunction ὅτι, Col. deviates more from the other epistles than does Eph. Eph. does have a low frequency incidence of this conjunction but there are sections in the other epistles (i.e. R. 1; R. 15:13-33 and 1 C. 1:1-9) where it is almost as or equally rare. Col., however, contains a particularly low incidence of the conjunction.[3]

3. SENTENCE-LENGTH IN EPH.

A second component in the style of Eph. is found in the length of its sentences. Now it is true that opinions may vary concerning the lengths of many sentences in the New Testament. There are other ways of punctuating the epistles of Paul than the interpunctuation given by Nestle. Moreover, Nestle's interpunctuation is, naturally, subjective. Yet this does not cancel out the fact that he does fully account for his results and that moreover, by using one single reliable system of

---

völker in griechischer Sprache schreiben". ("The extent to which these particles are specifically Greek can be neatly observed when non-Greeks or mixed races write Greek.") He established the omission in the work of a Jewish author; inscriptions executed by Romans and even in stylised letters and Senate decisions originating from Roman hands.

[1] Cf. Beyer, Semitische Syntax im N.T., p. 73s.

[2] διό occurs 6 times in R.; 2 times in 1 C.; 9 times in 2 C.; 1 time in Gal.; 5 times in Eph.; 1 time in Phil.; 0 times in Phlm. ἄρα οὖν occurs 8 times in R.; 1 time in Eph.; 1 time in 1 Th.; 1 time in 2 Th.

[3] ὅτι in R. 1/18; 1 C. 1/15,5; 2 C. 1/13; Gal. 1/11; Eph. 1/26; Phil. 1/11; Col. 1/37; 1 Th. 1/16; 2 Th. 1/10; Phlm. 1/11,5. In R. 1 the frequency is 1/26; in R. 15:13-33,1/25,5 and in 1 C. 1:1-9,1/20 (in R. 4:11-5:21 the frequency is 1/16).

interpunctation, (in our case, that of Nestle) we are enabled to attain a high measure of objectivity in a comparison of the various epistles.

Now it evolves that Eph. uses very many long sentences. The average length of the sentences is great. In. R., 1 and 2 C. and Gal., this average length is far shorter.

In this respect too, the style of the epistles of Paul is not consistent. The average sentence-length in Phil., 1 and 2 Th. and Phlm. is not all that much shorter than that in Eph. Furthermore, the three sections of R. and the small section of 1 C. which we discussed in para 2 (in connection with the affinity with Eph. in the matter of the first stylistic component) are more or less of the same contents as Eph. with regard to average sentence-length. Col. too, corresponds closely to Eph. in this respect.[1]

We may be agreed that sentences which occupy eight or more lines in the well-known edition of Nestle can be designated as long sentences. Of these, Eph. contains a total of 14. This figure exceeds that of any other epistle in the CP. If however, the shortness of 2 Th. is taken into account, it presently becomes clear that proportionately this epistle has just as many or even slightly more long sentences than Eph.[2] Phil., Phlm. and the relevant three sections of R. also contain a relatively large number, whilst 1 C. 1:1-9 and Phil. 1:1-2, 11 are even

---

[1] In the Nestle edition, Eph. has 338 lines and 59 sentences of an average length of 5.7 lines. Corresponding figures for the other epistles are :

R.	1000	ls.,	364	sen.,	av.1.2.75	Phil.	230	ls.,	58	sen.,	av.1.4
1C.	916	ls.,	406	sen.,	av.1.2.25	1 Th.	211	ls.,	50	sen.,	av.1.4.2
2C.	634	ls.,	197	sen.,	av.1.3.2	2 Th.	114	ls.,	26	sen.,	av.1.4.3
Gal.	313	ls.,	122	sen.,	av.1.2.5	Phlm.	46	ls.,	10	sen.,	av.1.4.6

In the relative sections of R. and 1 C. the situation is as follows :

R.1	78 ls.	15 sen.,	av.1.5.2
R.4:11-5:21	95 ls.,	16 sen.,	av.1.5.9
R.15:13-33	51 ls.	10 sen.	av.1.5.1
1C.1:1-9	20 ls.	3 sen.	av.1.6.6

In C. the position is : 222 ls., 40 sen., av.1.5.5. Data for the complete epistles have been taken from de Zwaan, De Efezerbrief, p. 24. Corrections have been made in the data concerning Eph.

[2] 1 Th. yields the frequency 1/23 and Eph. 1/24, For these long sentences see : 1 Th. 1:2-5; 1:8-10; 2:4-8; 2:14-16; 3:6-8; 3:11-13; 4:3-6; 5:7-10; 5:15-18; and Eph. 1:3-14; 1:15-23; 2:1-7; 2:14-18; 2:19-22; 3:1-7; 3:8-12; 3:14-19; 4:1-6; 4:11-16; 4:20-24; 5:7-13; 6:5-8; 6:14-20.

composed of a very high proportion of these long sentences.[1] Col.,
with 7 long sentences also has a relatively high proportion of them.[2]

Sentences which comprise more than 14 lines of the Nestle edition,
can properly be called exceedingly long sentences. Of this type of
sentence, Eph. contains more than any of the other epistles, i.e. 6.
The minute 2 Th., although in actual figures it has but one of these
sentences, this represents a high proportion. This is also true of one
of the three fragments of R., i.e. R. 4:11-5:21, which features one
exceedingly long sentence. Following immediately upon Eph. in statistical order, comes Col., with three such sentences. Col. also contains
the longest sentence found in the collective epistles. This sentence
occupies 29 lines of space and is closely followed by Eph. which features
a sentence of 28 lines.[3]

---

[1] Phil. has the frequency 1/38 (see Phil. 1:3-8; 1:12-14; 1:18-20; 1:27-30; 2:1-5 and
3:8-11); Philm. has the frequency 1/46 (see Phlm. 8-15); R. 1 has the frequency 1/26
(see R. 1:1-7; 26-28 and 28-32); R. 4:11-5:21 : 1/31.7 (see R. 4:11, 12; 16-21 and 5:12-15);
R. 15:13-33 : 1/25.5 (see R. 15:22-25 and 15:30-33); 1C. 1:1-9 : 1/7.6 (see 1C. 1:1-3 and
4-8).

In 90 lines of Nestle, we find in Phil. 1:1-2:11, 5 sentences which exceed 7 lines in
length, i.e.: 1:3-8; 1:12-14; 1:18-20; 1:27-30 and 2:1-4, whilst there are also two sentences
of 7 lines: 2:5-8 and 2:9-11. As far as sentencen in excess of 7 lines are concerned, this
section yields a frequency of 1/18.

[2] The frequency is 1/31.7. The sentences are : 1:3-8; 1:9-20; 1:21-23; 1:24-29; 2:1-3;
2:8-15; 3:5-11. The frequencies, not yet mentioned, in the other epistles are: R. 1/100
(for long sentences see R. 1:1-7; 1:26, 27; 1:28-32; 2:14-17; 3:21-26; 4:16-21; 5:12-14;
15:22-25; 15:30-32; 16:25-27); 1 C. 1/101 (1 C. 1:1-3; 1:4-8; 1:26-29; 2:6-9; 9:19-23;
10:1-4; 12:8-11; 12:21-24; 15:3-8); 2 C. 1/63 1:8-11; 4:7-11; 6:1-10; 8:1-7; 8:18-21; 9:10-14;
10:3-6; 10:14-16; 11:24-28; 12:20, 21); Gal. 1/104 (Gal. 1:1-5; 1:15-17; 2:6-10); 2 Th.
1/57 (2 Th. 1:3-14; 2:8-10).

[3] In Eph. sentences of more than 14 lines are : 1:3-14; 1:15-23; 2:1-7; 3:1-7; 4:11-16;
6:14-20, the frequency being 1/56. The sentence in question occurring in 2 Th. is 2 Th.
1:3-10, the frequency being 1/114. The sentence in R. 4:11-5:21 is R. 4:16-21, the frequency in this case being 1/95. The relevant sentences in Col. are : 1:9-20; 1:24-29; 2:8-15
with a frequency of 1/74. The longest sentence in Col. is Col. 1:9-20 and in Eph., Eph.
1:3-14.

Another method of determining sentence-length is by counting the no. of words in
a sentence. Morton, who had a computor at his disposal, used this method. He bases
himself on a different interpunction than the one given by Nestle. Whereas Nestle
divides Eph. into 59 sentences, Morton counts 100. For Morton, the longest sentence in
Eph. numbers 139 words, whilst Nestle counts 202 words in the same sentence (1:3-14).
In the longest sentence of Col. (Col. 1:9-20), Morton calculates 76-80 words, whereas
Nestle gives 218 words. (A survey of sentence-length in the pauline epistles calculated
according to the number of words, is found in "The Authorship of Greek Prose", Journal

We encounter the long sentences of Eph. :

a. in the eulogy which also contains a statement concerning the addressees (1:3-14);

b. in the eucharistia-formulation resolving into an intercession (1:15-23) and in the second intercession (3:14-19);

c. in statements concerning the addressees (2:1-7, 14-18 and 19-22);

d. in a digression upon Paul (3:1-7, 8-12);

e. in the paraenesis (4:1-6 which has the theme of unity and which contains an avowal; 4:11-16, a lesson on the charismata and the work of the diakonia; 4:20-24, a lesson on the new man; 5:7-13, paraenesis with the themes of light and darkness as antitheses; 6;5-8, paraenesis for slaves; 6:14-20, paraenesis concerning armour, ending with a plea for intercession).

When these fourteen sentences are compared with the fifty sentences of corresponding length in R., 1 and 2 C., Gal., Phil., 1 and 2 Th. and Phlm.[1], it becomes apparent that there is a certain correlation in the distribution of these sentences. In Eph. as well as in the other epistles, the long or exceedingly long sentences (which we shall henceforth designate as long, without differentiating) occur in the most diverse places, but never at the conclusion of an epistle. Thanksgiving to God, praise of God and prayer to God may all be expressed through the medium of long sentences. In Eph. this is demonstrated in the eulogy, the eucharistia and in the intercessions. In the other epistles, in no less than seven instances, such sentences are features in eucharistia-formulations, intercessions, blessings and in a doxology.[2] In Eph. we observe that long sentences are used in a digression on the subject of Paul; a remarkable number of long sentences are used in precisely the same way in the other epistles.[3]

---

p. 218). Morton's comparison of the lengths of sentences in Eph. with those in the other epistles must be credited with a high degree of objectivity, but his assumption that he attained an absolute measure of objectiveness is an illusion. For criticism of his neglect of differences in interpunctation, see Journal, pp. 225, 229, 230 (cf. also note 4 on p. 18).

[1] For the long sentences in R., 1 and 2 C. and Gal., see p. 106 note 2; for those in Phil., note 1; for those in 1 Th., note 2 on p. 105; for those in 2 Th., note 2 and for those in Phlm., note 1 on p. 106.

[2] 1 C. 1:4-8; Phil. 1:3-8; 1 Th. 1:2-5; 2 Th. 1:3-10; 2 C. 9:10-14; 1 Th. 3:11-13 and R. 16:25-27.

[3] This concerns no less than 12 of the 50 relevant sentences to which may be added two praescripts which describe Paul's position in greater detail : 1 C. 9:19-23; 2 C. 4:7-11;

Three complete long sentences and the end of the first long sentence in Eph. express statements concerning the addressees. This is more than is usual in the other epistles where long sentences are not generally used for such passages. Only in 1 Th. is there a comparable incidence but there it occurs on just two occasions.[1]

The fact is that these passages in Eph. 2 are strongly doctrinal in character. A similar mixture is found in the long 1 C. 1:26-29 sentence. In the other epistles, passages with a doctrinal bearing are usually formulated in long sentences. Consequently, the biggest group of long sentences are those of a doctrinal content.[2] Inasmuch as it concerns the contents, there is a strong affinity between the long sentences in Eph. 2 and the long sentences in the first five chapters of R.[3]

Moreover, as in the other epistles, we encounter long sentences in explicitly paraenetical sections.[4] As in the other epistles, these, on more than one occasion, are of a doctrinal tendency.[5] And, once more, there is a strong affinity with regard to the content matter. Both Eph. 4:1-6 and 4:11-16 as well as 1 C. 12:8-11; 21:24 and Phil. 1:27-20; 2:1-4 (5-8 and 9-11) have the common theme of unity. Eph. 4:1-6 and the complex of long sentences of seven to eleven lines in Phil. 1:27-2:11 both commence with an exhortation to unity which undergoes a

---

6:1-10; 10:3-6, 14-16; 11:24-28; Gal. 1:15-17; 2:6-10; Phil. 1:12-14; 18-20; 3:8-11; 1 Th. 2:5-8; R. 1:1-7 and Gal. 1:1-5. The subject in these cases is not always Paul alone. The often employed first person plural, can embrace more persons. Nevertheless, Paul is usually the centre of attention. (It is probable that all parts of the epistles we have mentioned which deal with Paul, we are concerned with the word of the apostle himself, irrespective of possible additions and corrections by his secretary. Furthermore, the very fact that there should be so many long sentences in precisely those sections of pauline literature with which Paul was especially concerned, should prevent us from regarding the great length of the sentences in Eph. as an indication of its inauthenticity).

[1] 1 Th. 1:8-10 and 2:14-16.

[2] Such sentences of a doctrinal trend are found in R. 1:26, 27, 28-32; 2:14-17; 3:21-26; 4:16-21; 5:12-21; 1 C. 1:26-29; 2:6-9; 1 C. 15;3-8: 1 Th. 4:15-18 and 2 Th. 2:8-10. They are also found in a paraenetical context. See 1 C. 10:1-4 (called a "Midrasch mit echt hellenistisch-jüdischen Mitteln" by Lietzmann, An die Korinther, p. 44); 1 C. 12:8-11 and 21 24.

[3] R. 1:26, 27, 28-32 and 2:14-17 deal with God's wrath over the corrupted gentiles; R. 5:12-14 concerns the dominion of death; R. 4:16-21 speaks of the gentiles' participation in salvation.

[4] Besides 1 C. 10:1-4; 12:8-11, 21-24, also 2 C. 12:20, 21; Phil. 1:27-30; 2:1-5 (with 2:5-8 and 9-11); 1 Th. 4:3-6 and 5:7-10 occur in paraenetical passages.

[5] Eph. 4:11-16 and 4:20-24 are doctrinal. For long doctrinal sentences in the other epistles, see note 2.

transition, becoming a series of professions doxological in character, in which the word πᾶς is repeatedly used. Eph. 4:11-16 contains a summing-up of δόματα for the ἔργον διακονίας and the analogy oft he ecclesia as a body. 1 C. 12:8-11 presents a summing-up of χαρίσματα, διακονίαι and ἐνεργήματα and 12:21-24 gives a comparison of the ecclesia with a body.

As against the paraenesis of Eph. 5:7-13 with its theme of the antithesis between darkness (or night) and light and the paraenesis which deals with the armour of God in Eph. 6:10-20, 1 Th. 5:7-10 contains a single long sentence which treats the themes of day and night and the taking up of arms.[1]

From our comparison of long sentences as used in the HP and in Eph., we learn that in the latter, lang sentences are used under the same epistolatory circumstances, to deal with the same material, and under the influence of the same association patterns as in the other epistles. It is unthinkable that this striking correspondence between Eph. and the HP should be the result of a painstaking pseudographical imitation of the long sentences form authentic epistles. For. particularly there, where we found a strong affinity between the long sentences of Eph. and those of the other epistles, even Goodspeed and Mitton who discern a copying from other epistles throughout practically the whole of Eph., could find almost nothing derivative.[2]

---

[1] In the paraenesis of R. 13:12, 13 day and night and the armour of light are treated in short sentences. For the rest, armour is treated only in sentences of 7 or more lines in the CP minus, i.e. : R. 6:13; 2 C. 6:7 and 10:4. Pendant to the plea for intercession at the end of the long sentence about the armour of God in Eph. 6:14-20 is the plea for intercession in R. 15:30-32, a long sentence in which the concept of the struggle in likewise present. (συναγωνίζεσθαι is a word for a real struggle, not a competition, cf. Liddell-Scott s.v.).

[2] We discovered an affinity between Eph. 2:1-7, 14-18 and 19-22 on the one hand and R. 1:26-27, 28-32; 2:14-17; R. 4:16-21 and R. 5:12-14 on the other. Mitton, in The Epistle to the Ephesians. p. 286ss., places not a single fragment from the sentences quoted in R. beside the sentences quoted from Eph. We furthermore saw an affinity between Eph. 4:1-6 and Phil. 1:27-2:11. Mitton, op. cit. p. 296ss., considers that only the words ἀξίως τοῦ εὐαγγελίου τοῦ Χριστοῦ ... ἐν ἑνὶ πνεύματι ... from Phil. 1:27 would have been suitable material for adaptation. Whilst there is an affinity between Eph. 4:11-16 and 1 C. 12:8-11 and 21-24, Mitton (op. cit. p. 298ss.) cannot point out anything to suggest borrowing. As a comparison with Eph. 5:7-13 and 6:14-20, he only suggests from the so-related passage 1 Th. 5:7-10 the words of 1 Th. 5:8 ἐνδυσάμενοι θώρακα πίστεως ... καὶ περικεφαλαίαν σωτηρίας in connection with Eph. 6:14-17 (op. cit. p. 312s.).

The long sentences in Col. are surrounded by the same epistolatory circumstances as they are in Eph.[1] An affinity with Eph. is that here too, the digression on Paul is composed of two long sentences.

4. Use of the oratio perpetua

As elsewhere in the CP, use is made of oratio perpetua or λέξις εἰρομένη in the long sentences of Eph. This construction is formed by stringing together a series of sentences in a coordinated fashion, following the natural order suggested by their meaning. For the most part these are principal sentences but subordinates may likewise be used in the construction.

The string of sentences can be extended by means of relative clauses, sentences introduced with ὅτι or another conjunction or by a participial construction.[2] In Eph., the subordinate element in the oratio perpetua is sometimes very strong. The consequence is that in such cases the construction of a sentence becomes far less intelligible than when a certain balance is imparted through the coordination of principal sentences and an internal coordination of subordinate clauses.

A lucid and balanced construction is found in 1 C, 10:1-4 (5) :
1. principal sentence — subordinate clause + subordinate clause + subordinate clause + subordinate clause
2. principal sentence + principal sentence

---

[1] We find the sentences of Col. in :
a. the eucharistia-formulation (Col. 1:3-8);
b. the intercession (Col. 1:9-20);
c. the statement concerning the addressees (Col. 1:21-23);
d. the digression on Paul (Col. 1:24-29 and 2:1-3);
e. the paraenesis (Col. 2:8-15 and 3:5-11).

[2] For oratio perpetua see : A.v. Veldhuizen, Het taaleigen des N.T. (Utrecht 1906), p. 253s.; Bl.-Debr. para. 459 and Lausberg, Handbuch der literarischen Rhetorik, para. 921. J. Weiss, Aufgaben der neutestamentl. Wissenschaft, p. 15s., spoke of "lange Sätze, die mit dem Mittel von Relativsätzen und Participia coniuncta sich weiter schleppen". Similarly, Bultmann wrote in Der Stil der paulinischen Predigt, p. 68; of : "lange schwerfällige Sätze, die sich in übermässigen Aneinanderreihungen von Relativsätzen und Participia coniuncta fortspinnen." See also p. 11 note 1. (Quoatations : "long sentences with drag themselves on by means of relative clauses and participia coniuncta". Bultmann : "long, heavy-going sentences which weave on in the form of excessively prolonged series of linked relative clauses and participia coniuncta.")

3. (principal sentence + principal sentence).[1] [2]

An unintelligible construction is that found in Eph. 1:3-14 :

1. ellipt. principal sentence — attributive participle — subordinate
   clause — participium coniunctum — subordinate clause — subordinate clause — subordinate clause — participium coniunctum
   (— subordinate clause)
2. ellipt. principal sentence — subordinate clause --- participium
   coniunctum — ellipt. subordinate clause (participium coniunctum)
   + subordinate clause (— subordinate clause)

or that of Eph. 1:15-23 :

1. principal sentence (participium coniunctum) — participium coniunctum — subordinate clause — subordinate clause + subordinate
   clause + subordinate clause — attributive participium — subordinate clause — participium coniunctum + participium coniunctum
   — attributive participium +
2. principal sentence +
3. principal sentence — subordinate clause

This form of oratio perpetua is also remarked in Eph. 2:19-22;
3:1-7, 8-13; 4:11-16. In the rest of the CP it is used more sparingly,
being found in R. 1:1-7; 4:16-21; 1 C. 1:4-8; 2 C. 1:8-11; Phil. 1:27-30;
3:8-11 and 2 Th. 1:3-10. In Col. however, it is used as exhaustively
as in Eph. when the number of long sentences are taken into consideration. It is found in Col. 1:3-8, 9-20; 2:1-3 and partly in 2:8-15.

Both the unusual and usual form in which the lexis eiromene is
used in Eph. as well as in general throughout the other epistles, must
be explained in terms of a certain lack of formative education in the
traditions of Greek literature. This applies to the xriter(s) of the
epistles as it does to many who belonged to the hellenistic world.

Nevertheless, this was not the sole cause. Kuhn has pointed out the

---

[1] We use the symbol—to indicate that a subordinate clause or an equivalent member
is subordinate to the preceding principal sentence or subordinate clause or member
equivalent to a subordinate clause. The sign + is used to denote coordination. A subordinate clause or an equivalent member is placed in parenthesis when another sentence
or a member equivalent to a sentence is only interrupted by it.

[2] The words of 1 C. 10:1-5 are expressed as one single sentence in the 15th. edition
of Nestle's Novum Testamentum Graece (1932) but in the 17th. impression (1941) it is
divided into two sentences.

"unendlich sich hinziehenden locker-gereihten Bandwurmsätze" which occur with frequency in the Qumran scrolls, particularly in the hymns, but also in several passages of the other writings.[1] Besides an absence of grounding in Greek literature therefore, another factor to be taken into account when making a stylistic assessment, is a Jewish religious and cultural influence.

5. THE ADVERBIAL ADJUNCT INTRODUCED BY A PREPOSITION

A very characteristic component in the style of Eph. is the use of adverbial adjuncts introduced by a preposition. This is syntactically superfluous, since they do not form a necessary extension to the verb or predicate and are placed at the end of a principal sentence, subordinate clause or part of a sentence equivalent to a clause.

Very often the proposition used to introduce such an adjunct is ἐν. The formula ἐν Χριστῷ Ἰησοῦ and its counterparts occurs with frequency.[2] Other prepositions are also used.

However, strangest of all are the accumulations of such adjuncts (not those in the form of an enumeration as in Eph. 6:12 [3]) in the form of a (partly) asyndetically coordinated and / or a (partly) subordinate connection, e.g. Eph. 1:5 εἰς υἱοθεσίαν διὰ Ἰησοῦ Χριστοῦ εἰς αὐτόν, κατὰ τὴν εὐδοκίαν τοῦ θελήματος αὐτοῦ, εἰς ἔπαινον ... τῆς χάριτος αὐτοῦ 4:12 πρὸς τὸν καταρτισμὸν τῶν ἁγίων εἰς ἔργον διακονίας, εἰς οἰκοδομὴν τοῦ σώματος τοῦ Χριστοῦ. Sometimes adjuncts. introduced by the same preposition are welded together, e.g. Eph. 2:2 : κατὰ τὸν αἰῶνα τοῦ κόσμου τούτου, κατὰ τὸν ἄρχοντα τῆς ἐξουσίας τοῦ ἀέρος.

Percy wrote about the occurrence of adverbial adjuncts introduced by ἐν. This construction also occurs frequently in the other epistles of Paul but in Eph. and Col. there is a greater incidence. Likewise, it is found in the remainder of the N.T. and other ancient Christian literature. In the rest of Greek literature, it is rare.

The LXX, the Test. XII and old synagogic liturgies also feature this adjunct or its Hebrew equivalent. For that reason Percy ascribed

---

[1] "Der Epheserbrief im Lichte der Qumrantexte", N.T. St. 7, 1960/61, p. 335. ("endless tapeworm-like sentences which drag on, loosely strung together").

[2] Cf. Schmid, Der Epheserbrief, p. 196.

[3] Such enumerationes are also found in 2 C. 6:4-8 and 12:10.

its occurrence in the CP minus, the rest of the N.T. and ancient Christian literature, to the influence of the LXX and other writings based
on a Hebrew or Aramaic original text.[1]

For myself, I would prefer to attribute this frequent appearance
of the preposition ἐν in Eph. (and in Col. [2]) and the adverbial adjuncts
introduced by ἐν partly to a direct Hebrew influence. For ancient synagogic liturgies cited by Percy are not the only writings to contain
sentences or parts of sentences ending with adverbial adjuncts introduced by the prefix בְּ. Nor are they common only to the originally Hebrew
or Aramaic forms of the LXX and other Jewish literature since they
also occur in the Qumran scrolls.[3]

The use of the adverbial adjunct was also stimulated by a certain
peculiarity inherent in Hebrew, namely the custom of connecting two
substantives with בְּ. Thus, in Ex. 31:3, the words רוּחַ אֱלֹהִים and חָכְמָה
are linked by בְּ, whereupon a whole enumeration of synonyms follows
which are likewise connected with רוּחַ אֱלֹהִים by בְּ.[4] This formulation
is also found in Ex. 35:31.

In Eph. 1:17, the words πνεῦμα σοφίας καὶ ἀποκαλύψεως are
similarly linked with ἐπιγνώσει αὐτοῦ through the preposition ἐν.
The same type of connection occurs in Eph. 4:19; 5:26; 6:24 and R. 5:15

---

[1] Percy, Probleme, p. 27-31 and p. 29ss. note 19.

[2] The prepostition ἐν is very frequent in Eph. and Col. and somewhat higher in the
latter. In the CP minus, the frequency is as follows : R. 1/6; 1 C. 1/5; 2 C. 1/4; Gal. 1/8;
Eph. 1/3; Phil. 1/3.5; Col. 1/2.5; 1 Th. 1/4; 2 Th. 1/4; Phlm. 1/5. (In R., the author
counted 166 times, Morgenthaler 172 and Morton 168 times; in 1 C., author 162 times,
Morgenthaler and Morton 169 times; in 2 C., author 164 times, Morgenthaler 159 and
Morton 174 times; in Gal., author and Morgenthaler 41 and Morton 42 times; in Eph.,
author 122 times, Morgenthaler 117 and Morton 121 times; in Phil., author 63 times,
Morgenthaler 64 and Morton 65 times; in Col., author 86 times, Morgenthaler 87 and
Morton 80 times; in 1 Th., author 53 times Morgenthaler 51 and Morton 52 times; in
author and Morgenthaler 26 times; in Philm., author 10 and Morgenthaler 9 times.)

[3] See 1 QH2,7; 9,31 and 1 QpHab 7,13. From Kuhn, "Der Epheserbrief im Lichte
der Qumrantexte", N.T. St. 7, p. 335s., it is seen that the expression ἐνδυναμοῦσθε
... ἐν τῷ κράτει τῆς ἰσχύος αὐτοῦ (Eph. 6:10) probably derives from a Hebrew background.

[4] B. Baentsch, Exodus-Leviticus (Handkommentar z. A.T.I, 2, 1, 1900, p. 265)
on this point, remarks that בְּחָכְמָה is not dependent on the verb but that the text is
saying that the godly spirit manifests itself in wisdom. E. F. C. Rosemüller, Scholia in
Pentateuchum (Scholia in Vet. Test. I, Lipsiae 1828), p. 462; "Per hanc nominum
synonymorum congeriem maxima dotum, quibus a Deo instructus fuit Bazaleel, copia
significatur.". The LXX likewise connects the words רוּחַ אֱלֹוהִים by translating
them as πνεῦμα θεῖον σοφίας.

in the respective formulations ἀκαθαρσίας πάσης ἐν πλεονεξίᾳ/τῷ λουτρῷ τοῦ ὕδατος ἐν ῥήματι/ἡ χάρις ... ἐν ἀφθαρσίᾳ en ἡ δωρεὰ εν χάριτι. The Qumran scrolls occasionally feature precisely such a connection.[1]

Percy also writes of the welding together of adverbial adjuncts introduced by a preposition and considers the cumulations of this form, although it is also found in the rest of the N.T., in the works of the most ancient Christian writiers and liturgical texts,[2] characteristic of the HP. Especially typical of Paul, he finds the way in which these culmulations are added to the end of an already complete sentence, a subordinate clause or equivalent part of a sentence. (In such cases, Percy speaks of "nachhinken" — limping behind.) He does not therefore regard the high frequency of prepositional adjuncts in Eph. and Col.—in Eph. the frequency in highest—as an objection against authenticity.[3]

The use of adjuncts introduced by a preposition could have been stimulated by a general tendency in the Greek of the hellenistic period towards the use of an increasing number of prepositions. The old cases were losing ground and prepositions took their place. Moreover, adverbial adjuncts introduced by a preposition (often in a substantiated form) were conducive to completeness and clarity of expression. Writers of official letters and documents could avoid lengthy description by means of this device.[4]

A Hebrew influence could also have contributed to the use of these adjuncts. There are parts of the O.T. in which an intensive use of prepositions—by which we mean prefixe such as עִם, עַל, מִן, לְ, כִּי, בְּ, אֶת, אֶל and their possible variants—occur. Is. 47:9 has three adjuncts at he end with respectively, כִּי עַל and בְּ. In Is 63:7-9, the prepositions לְ and כְּ together with the word כְּ־ל confirm the sense of the whole

---

[1] 1 QH 4,32; 1 QS 4,7 and Damask. 2,5 (see Kuhn, "Der Ephesebrief im Lichte der Qumrantexte", p. 337).

[2] In a letter written by a fourth century Egyptian Christian, a cumulation occurs : ἐπὶ μέγιστον χρόνον ἐν κυρίῳ Χριστῷ. This is the letter of a simple person, no litterator. From the abbreviation, ἐν κυρίῳ Χριστῷ appears to be a stereotype expression (cf. Deissmann, L. v. O., p. 183, line 27s.)

[3] Percy, Probleme, pp. 185, 186, 191, 192, 211-214, 497, 480, especially p. 213/214.

[4] Cf. Radermacher, p. 137; E. Mayser, Gramm. d. griech. Pap. 1.d. Ptzt 112 (1934), p. 336, 337 and the examples quoted there; P. Petr. (Para 63), p. 18ss. and the circular issued by Herod's Minister of Justice in 165 B.C., col. 1, 16s., 2, 34ss. (Wilcken, Urkunden d. Ptzt I, 110).

connection. Jer. 44:5 contains four prepositions at the end of the passage.

At the end of Ez. 31:14 (according to W. Zimmerli, a paraenetical additions by a later hand[1]) we find four adjuncts, parallel in meaning, introduced respectively by לְ אֶל׳ בְּ and אֶל. In the subsequent verses, adjuncts with prepositions are also found in succession. In the middle of v. 16, at the end of the sentence, are two adjuncts with respectively בְּ and אֶת. V. 17 has two adjuncts at the end with בְּ. Vs. 18 has one sentence beginning with אֶל and ending with coordinated adjuncts introduced by בְּ and in addition, a subordinate adjunct introduced by בְּ. Then follows a sentence which ends with two adjuncts which are introduced respectively by אֶת and אֶל. This is succeeded by a sentence beginning with an adjunct introduced by בְּ and ending with an adjunct introduced by אֶת.[2] In the case of Ez. 31:14-18, one could speak of an interplay of prepositions.

This is certainly so in Ps. 18:16-27. In verses 16-18, the preposition מִן plays a part. In verses 19-21, the the prepositions כִּי׳ בְּ and לְ feature repeatedly. Then, in verses 22-24, we find לְ once, מִן three times and עַם on one occasion. In verse 25, we find the sequence לְ׳ כִּי׳ כִּי׳ לְ. Verses 26 and 27 are composed of four little sentences, each beginning with an adjunct introduced by עִם.

A similar play with prepositions is found in Eph. 1:1-14. They occur partly in a series of adverbial adjuncts, strung together. The scheme is as follows :

vs. 1	διά		ἐν		καὶ ἐν				ἐν [3]
vs. 2	ἀπό								
vs. 3	ἐν	◡	ἐν	◡	ἐν				
vs. 4	ἐν	◡	πρό						
	κατενώπιον	◡	ἐν						
vs. 5, 6	εἰς	◡	διά	◡	εἰς	◡	κατά	◡	εἰς
	ἐν								

---

[1] Ezechiel, p. 760.

[2] Also see Ez. 32:6 in which two rather superfluous adjuncts with מִן and אֶל occur —the text is considered as impure—and Ez. 32:9 in which בְּ with a subordinated עַל and עַל is found.

[3] We follow the version τοῖς οὖσιν ἐν Ἱεραπόλει καὶ ἐν Λαοδικείᾳ, πιστοῖς ἐν Χριστῷ Ἰησοῦ, cf. Chapter V para. 1.

vs. 7	ἐν ᾧ		διά		
	κατά				
vs. 8	εἰς	◡	ἐν		
vs. 9, 10	κατά				
	ἐν	◡	εἰς		
	ἐν				
	τὰ ἐπί		καὶ τὰ ἐπί		ἐν
vs. 11	ἐν ᾧ		κατά		κατά
vs. 12	εἰς		εἰς		
	ἐν				
vs. 13	ἐν ᾧ				
	ἐν ᾧ				
vs. 14	εἰς	◡	εἰς [1]		

The prepositions lend a certain unity to the otherwise unintelligible mass. Particularly the adjuncts ἐν ᾧ in verses 7, 11, 13 and 13 strengthen and support the construction of the entire.

The same type of play with prepositions is encountered in the praescript and eucharistia-formulation of R. (1:1-10) :

vs. 1	εἰς						
vs. 2, 3	διά	◡	ἐν	◡	περί		
	ἐκ	◡	κατά				
vs. 4	ἐν	◡	κατά	◡	ἐξ		
vs. 5	δι(ά)		εἰς	◡	ἐν	◡	ὑπέρ
vs. 6	ἐν						
vs. 7	ἐν						
	ἀπό						
vs. 8	διά	◡	περί				
	ἐν						
vs. 9	ἐν	◡	ἐν				
vs. 10	ἐπί						
	ἐν						
	πρός						

---

[1] When an adverbial adjunct with a preposition is connected to a preceding adverbial adjunct with a preposition, this is indicated by the sign ◡.

When two adverbial adjuncts, whether substantiated or not, are coordinated by καί, this is indicated by καί.

From this use of prepositions as a stylistic device, a practise which coincides with Hebrew usage, it may be deduced that the style of Eph. has been stimulated not so much by the LXX as by a direct influence from the Hebrew in the use of prepositions. Also the cumulation of prepositions in strung-together adverbial adjuncts which goes side by side with a frequent use of prepositions, appears to me to be the result of Hebrew literary influences. The Old Testament examples we have quoted corroborate this. In the O.T. we also saw the preposition used as a stylistic device in combination with cumulations of prepositions featuring in strung-together adverbial adjuncts.

The special advantage of the preposition as a stylistic device is that adverbial adjuncts introduced by a prepositions can mark the end and sometimes the beginning of a particular section within a greater whole. In Hebrew, the sequence of words ensures that a preposition can easily be placed at the end or the beginning of a sentence. In Ez. 31:14-18 and Ps. 18:16-25, the prepositions at the end of the minor sentences within the major framework, occupy a usual and normal place. And indeed, it is quite normal that the sentence of Ez. 31:14 should commence with לְ (לְמַעַן) just as the first sentence of verse 18 begins with אֶל (אֶל–מִי) and the third sentence of that verse with בּ (בְּתוֹךְ). To the ear, however, they form an automatic signal that the end (or the beginning) of a sentence is near.

In Gen. 24:7, a formula linked with an oath (one of the few long sentences in the Hebrew O.T.) and in Gen. 28:20s., a vow, adverbial adjuncts introduced by a preposition (and especially double adjuncts coordinated by וְ or two parallel adjuncts or two strung-together adjuncts) indicate unmistakeably to the ear where the smaller sentences, which make up the whole, end. The entire structure and arrangement of the passage depends on this device.[1]

In Eph. 1:1-14, the prepositions are intended to have a like effect. The quadruple appearance of ἐν ᾧ. in each case marks the beginning of a sentence whilst the other adverbial adjuncts introduced by a preposition (and especially the strung-together adjuncts) indicate

---

[1] In Gen. 24:7 there are respectively the adjuncts מִבֵּית אָבִי וּמֵאֶרֶץ מוֹלַדְתִּי; לְפָנֶיךָ; לִי; לְי. לִבְנֵי מִשָּׁם en. On one occasion the beginning of a small sentence is indicated by לֵאמ׳ר לְדַרְעֲךָ. In Gen. 28:20, 21 the endings of small sentences are demarcated by respectively. בְּשָׁלוֹם אֶל–בֵּית אָבִי; לִלְבֹּשׁ; לֶאֱכ׳ל; בְּדֶרֶךְ הַזֶּה; עִמָּדִי; and לִי לֵאלֹהִים.

where the sentence or phrase equivalent to a sentence, ends. In R. 1:1-10, the end of a phrase is on each occasion characterised in a similar fashion.

The desired effect was not achieved because the Greek-speaking Hellenist automatically expected the end of a sentence (or an equivalent phrase) whenever an adverbial adjunct introduced by a preposition occurred in the text. The reason for the success of the device was that the prepositions, due to their frequency and repetitiveness, are so manifestly obvious and because the adjuncts with a preposition are so unusually placed (pre-eminently characterised by Percy as a "nachhinken"—limping behind) that they function as a break in the flow; they involuntarily produce a momentary pause in the stream of words. What the Greek orator strove to gain by means of long-syllabled clausulae, extended or striking clausulae, i.e. a check in the wordstream,[1] is in Eph. 1:1-14 and R. 1:1-10 achieved through adverbial adjuncts with prepositions.

Further on in Eph., adjuncts with preposition are used fairly intensively to the same purpose. In the remaining part of R. as well as in the rest of the CP minus, these adjuncts, in cumulations or not as the case may be, are also found, in the guise of a type of clausulae. Evidently, as in the case of the rhetorical clausulae,[2] these are also used to satisfy an aesthetic aim.[3]

The LXX does not punctiliously follow the example of the Hebrew in the use of adverbial adjuncts introduced by a preposition and does not do justice to the stylistic play on prepositions. When dealing with the integration of adverbial adjuncts which are introduced by a preposition, the LXX sometimes gives way, where as in other places it surpasses the original.[4]

In Eph. the incidence of cumulations of adjuncts introduced by a preposition is very high. However, the most extended cumulation is found in the long sentence of R. 3:21-26. If all the non-enumerative cumulations of this type of adverbial adjunct in the CP minus are coun-

---

[1] See Lausberg, Handburch der literarischen Rhetorik, para. 990 and 997.

[2] See op. cit., para. 985, 990-994 for rhetorical clausulae.

[3] In my opinion an aesthetic objective is clearly present in R. 4:25 and Phil. 2:11.

[4] The inferiority of the LXX in comparison with the Hebrew original is apparent in the contrast between LXX Jer. 51:5 and Mas. Jer. 44:5. When comparing LXX Ez. 31:14-18 and Mas. Ez. 31:14-18, it can be observed that the LXX is superior to the Hebrew original.

ted, this particular point demonstrates the great extent to which the style of these epistles is subject to variation.

For example, 1 C. deviates much further from the average frequency in the CP minus than Eph. In 1 C. this deviation is manifested in an almost complete absence of this feature. 1 and 2 Th. are closest to Eph. in the use of this stylistic phenomenon. Col. comes next. In R., the praescript and eucharistia-formulation (R. 1:1-10) contain a particularly high frequency. Curiously enough, the praescript and the eucharistia-formulation of 1 C. (1 C. 1:1-9) also displays a fairly high incidence. Each epistle has parts in which few or no cumulations occur. In this respect Eph. is no exception, Eph. 4:20-6:4 contains but one single cumulation and that comes in the middle of a prhase (Eph. 5:20).[1]

Percy has meticulously treated cumulations of adverbial adjuncts in Eph. which are introduced by one and the same preposition with special reference to those cumulations in which the adjuncts have an identical or narrowly-related meaning (Eph. 2:2; 4:13, 18).[2] He demonstrates that such cumulations also occur in the HP and are more or less an exclusively pauline phenomenon.

Real analogies are not found in the ancient Christian literature of the first two centuries. However, analogies are found in old liturgical texts. In these, its occurrence is mainly restiricted to descriptions of salvation after death, the desired outcome of certain ritual acts and heaven as the dwelling-place of God. Usually, these take the form of stereotype expressions. An equivalent description to that used for expressing the desired outcome of ritual acts, is found in the syncretic magical papyri for the desired result of a magical ritual.

In non-Christian literature this type of cumulation is almost unknown; one or two examples are all we have. Later Christian writers (third and fourth centuries), under the influence of the LXX and the Christian traditions it furthered, did use the stylistic device in question. Amongst these Christian traditions, handed on and defined by the LXX, Percy in the first place counts the Pauline epistles themselves. In his opinion, subsequent Christian writers were urged to use these cumulations by "die Vorliebe der asianischen Prosa für asyndetisch parallele Kola".[3] For that reason they acquired the habit of using

---

[1] The frequency in the epistles is as follows : R. 1/19; 1 C. 1/83; 2 C. 1/16; Gal. 1/28; Eph. 1/7.6; Phil. 1/15; Col. 1/13.8; 1 Th. 1/11; 2 Th. 1/10 and Phlm. 1/46. In R. 1:1-10 the frequency is 1/3.6; in 1 C. 1:1-9 it is 1/10.

[2] He includes the enumeratio of Eph. 6:12 amongst these.

[3] "a predilection in Asian prose for asyndetically parallel colons".

three or more adjuncts whereas in the LXX, usually no more than two occur.

The fact that in Col., in 2:2, 8, 11, these selfsame cumulations are also found, is evidence that the two epistles emanate from a common author. Percy sees a blending of three stylistic tendencies in the use of the cumulations : predilection for words and expressions which are synonymous in meaning; the general tendency towards the use of cumulations of adverbial adjuncts introduced by prepositions; a leaning towards asyndetically parallel colons.[1]

To his observations we could further add that the use of these adjuncts possessing synonymous or closely-related meanings introduced by a single preposition in Eph. and the rest of the CP minus, could equally well have been the result of an influence exercised by the original Hebrew. In the Hebrew O.T. we remark them in e.g. Jer. 51:5; Jer. 31:40; Ez. 19:13; Hos. 13:5 (10:13); Micah 6:6; Ps. 18:16, 17, 18 and Is. 47:9.

There is even a case of three adjuncts parallel in meaning, namely in Ps. 88:7. (The LXX Ps. 87:7 adds a καί. The Hebrew original shows more affinity with Eph. 4:13 than with the LXX version.)

6. CONSECUTIVE GENITIVES, RHYTHM OF THE GENITIVES

Another component present in the style of Eph. is the repeated use of consecutive genitives. Firstly, there is a great number of cumulations of adnominal genitives.[2] Of these, there are 15 of which 2 are even composed of three consecutive substantives in the genitive case.[3] If the genitives of the pronomina personalia and the non-adnominal genitives are included, the total amounts to as many as 49 of these cumulations. In this respect there is some variation in the CP minus, Col. being on a par with Eph.[4]

---

[1] Percy, Probleme, pp. 21s., 25, 215-249, 280, 281. For the coincidence of the three stylistic tendencies, see p. 240.

[2] For the adnominal genitive, cf. Bl.-Debr., para. 162-168.

[3] Amongst these 15, we have not included those cumulations in which the second genitive is that of a pron. pers. Cumulations of three genitives are found in R. 2:5; 8:21; 11:17 and Eph. 4:13, 13. The frequency of all cumulations of adnominal genitives without pron. pers. is : R. 1/77: 1 C. 1/152; 2 C. 1/317; Gal. 1/313; Eph. 1/26.5; Phil. 1/57.5; Col. 1/25; 1 Th. 1/211; 2 Th. 1/38 and Phlm. 0/46.

[4] The frequency of cumulations of all kinds of genitives is : R. 1/13.5; 1 C. 1/34; 2 C. 1/19; Gal. 1/14; Eph. 1/7; Phil. 1/13; Col. 1/9; 1 Th. 1/14; 2 Th. 1/7 and Phlm.

Besides the cumulations of genitives, the relationship in which some genitives stand in relation to the nomen regens in also noteworthy. Again and again, words which are either synonymous or related in meaning are linked by means of a genitive construction.[1] More than once, the nomen regens expresses the majesty or glory of what has been indicated in the genitive.[2] In the other epistles, some instances are less frequent.[3] Col. on the other hand, does contain a good number of connections between words that are synonymous or related in meaning.[4]

Amongst the many genitives of Eph., is one which is highly remarkable, namely τοὺς ὀφθαλμοὺς τῆς καρδίας ὑμῶν (1:18). In this case, the primum comparationis is not indicated through the word in the genitive as occurs elsewhere in connections of this variety such as those of Eph. 6:14 τὸν θώρακα τῆς δικαιοσύνης; Eph. 6:17 τὴν μάχαιραν τοῦ πνεύματος or θώρακα πίστεως καὶ ἀγάπης in 1 Th. 5:8 (genitivus explicativus). In that construction the heart is not being likened to the eyes but to the heart is ascribed a talent for insight (whether or not it is exercised) which in its turn is likened to the capacity of eyes. In fact, it is a genitivus possessivus but is used in a metaphor.

An equally strange use of the genitive is found in R. 4:12 where it concerns τοῖς ἴχνεσιν τῆς ... πίστεως τοῦ πατρὸς ἡμῶν Ἀβραάμ. Here is a construction which is no less pregnant. The genitive expresses the concept of faith and in particular the faith of Abraham. This faithful Abraham acted in a particular way in life and deed which was exam-

---

1/15. Excluding the genitives of pron. pers., the frequencies are : R. 1/22; 1 C. 1/61; 2 C. 1/49; Gal. 1/24; Eph. 1/20; Phil. 1/25.5; Col. 1/16; 1 Th. 1/70; 2 Th. 1/13 and Phlm. 0/46.

[1] There are 14 (Eph. 1:5; 6, 11, 12, 19, 2:2, 14, 15; 3:7, 12, 21; 4:23 and 5:2).

[2] Cf. ... δόξης τῆς χάριτος ... or τὸ πλοῦτος τῆς χάριτος ... (1:6, 7), τὸ ὑπερβάλλον μέγεθος τῆς δυνάμεως (1:19) and τὸ πλοῦτος τῆς δόξης ... (3:16) and Percy, op. cit., p. 189.

[3] For the incidence of constructions in the genitive linking synonymous or related words in meaning, in the rest of the CP minus, cf. Percy, op. cit., p. 195-197. For the incidence of connections in which the nomens regens expresses the majesty or glory of the concept indicated in the genitive, see op. cit., p. 197 and p. 198s.

[4] Cf. Percy, p. 194-197 and p. 195, note 2. In my opinion, we are also concerned with connections between expressions related in meaning in Col. 1:12 and and 2:11 (τὸ σῶμα τῆς σαρκός ...); 1:5 (ὁ λόγος τῆς ἀληθείας τοῦ εὐαγγελίου) and 2:2 (πᾶν πλοῦτος τῆς πληροφορίας), in addition to the connected synonyms of Col. 1:12 and 3:12. πληροφορία is certainly not synonymous with πλοῦτος, but both words arouse similar associations. W. Bauer, Wörterbuch z. N.T., ⁴1952, s.v. considers the meaning "Fülle" ("abundance") very likely in Col. 3:2. Thus a total of five connections between words which are synonymous or related in meaning occurs in Col.

plary. By means of a metaphor, this exemplary way of life and beha-
viour are described as τοῖς ἴχνεσιν and ascribed to the faith. In both
Eph. 1:18 and R. 4:12, we are confronted with a directness and con-
ciseness of expression lacking in cases as Eph. 6:14 and 17 and 1 Th.
5:8.[1]

Percy sees the above-mentioned cumulations of genitives in Eph.
and Col. as another typically Pauline characteristic. They are very
rare in the works of profane authors and are scarce also in non-Pauline
ancient Christian writings.[2]

To the LXX, such comulations are familiar.[3] In the LXX, the use
of genitives has been stimulated by the text of the original Hebrew
version.

Hebrew is poor in adjectives and therefore often adds a second substantive to the preceding substantive (in the status constructus) as an
attribute. This is one of the reasons why the LXX utilized the genitivus qualitatis more than was customary in ordinary Greek.[4]. The
LXX reconstructed a Hebrew connection by means of this genitive
construction.

Moreover, there were certain factors inherent in Hebrew which
necessitated the use of the genitive. In many cases, the Hebrew suffix
possesivum had to be translated by the genitive of the pron. pers.
Translating Hebrew prefixes with Greek prepositions which demand
a genitive, also increased the number of genitives.[5] Furthermore,
the Hebrew stimulus towards a use of the genitive was so strong that
free translation and incorrect translation resulted in even more genitives than was necessary.[6] It would seem that the genitive as such

---

[1] In the case of Eph. 6:14 and 17, Percy rightly speaks of "metaphor erklärende
Genitive" ("metaphor-explaining genitives", op. cit., para. 198) but in the case of Eph. 1:18
this is unjust. In Eph. 1:18 and R. 4:12 we should speak of real metaphor. The criterion
for a real metaphor is that of brevity (cf. Lausberg, Handbuch I, para. 558). Percy also
discusses the genitives linking abstract concepts. He points out that these occur also
elsewhere in the CP minus and specifically in R., in plenty (op. cit., p. 188 and 197s.)
and gives an excursus on the incidence of such genitives in ancient Christian literature
(op. cit., pp. 250-252).

[2] Percy, op. cit., p. 62, p. 62s. note 79 and p. 214s. note 59.

[3] Op. cit., p. 62ss. notes 77 and 79.

[4] Cf. H. St. J. Thackeray, A Grammar of the O,T. in Greek I (Cambridge 1909),
p. 23 : "The extended use of the genitive of quality, equivalent to an adj. is partly but
not altogether due to literal translations." See also v. Veldhuizen, Het taaleigen des
N.T., p. 120 and Radermacher, p. 108s.

[5] Cf. LXX Is. 2:10; 25:12 and Ps. 17:16.

[6] Cf. LXX Is. 2:8; 3:20 and 49:7 with the original Hebrew.

was considered to be an element in keeping with the style of these religious writings.

This had its reasons. The connection by means of the status constructus was sometimes applied to Hebrew poetry. In Ps. 17:4, three such connections lend unity in a (slightly unintelligible) part of the psalm. In Ps. 1, the direct correspondence between the wordgroupings בַּעֲצַת רְשָׁעִים וּבְדֶרֶךְ חַטָּאִים at the beginning and the words וְדֶרֶךְ רְשָׁעִים. at the conclusion of the hymn give a sense of completion and the other connections, by means of the status constructus, consolidate and carry this unity. In Ps. 18; 74 and 145, these connections support the parallelismus membrorum and likewise continue the thread which unifies the whole. In Ps. 18:5, 6 and 16, they serve to strengthen the emphasis. In Is. 2:6-21, the reiterated combination of two certain connections (vs. 10, 19 and 21) intensify the emphatic formulation of the hymn's theme, by which means it is unified into a complete work.

In Eph., a LXX influence could have encouraged the use of genitives and cumulations of genitives. But the case is not such that every conspicuous genitive or each genitive connection can individually be regarded as a hebraism. An expression, as υἱοὶ τῆς ἀπειθείας is generally only too quickly labelled a hebraism.[1] F. W. Danker has demonstrated that this kind of expression could also be constructed in ordinary Greek.[2] An expression such as τέκνα φύσει ὀργῆς (Eph. 2:3) betrays a certain adeptness in Greek which is on a far higher level than the standard which the man on the street who happened to write a note, would command.

The fact that more genitives occur in Eph. than is usual in classical Greek, is no cause for astonishment. Frequent use of the genitive used as an attribute (adnominativus) is a tendency familiar in the koine.[3] Neither need connections by means of the genitive immediately suggest a semitism.[4] Nevertheless, the attributively placed (adnominal) genitivus qualitatis occurs so often in Eph. that in this case a semitic influence should be kept in mind. Throughout the rest of the CP minus

---

[1] Kuhn, "Der Epheserbrief im Lichte der Qurantexte", N.T. St. 7, p. 339 : "υἱοὶ τῆς ἀπειθείας ein Semitismus". Cf. also Vl.-Bebr. para 162,6.

[2] F. W. Danker, "The υἱός Phrases in the N.T.". N.T. St. 7, p. 94.

[3] Cf. Radermacher, p. 108 and 109.

[4] Cf. Bl.-Debr. para. 168.

the number of these genitives is mostly too considerable to exclude the probability of a semitic influence.[1]

The semitic influences present in Eph. cannot be exclusively attributed to the LXX, This is evident from the connections between synonyms or words related in meaning, by means of the genitive.

As early as 1932, W. Grundmann drew attention to expressions in the Targum which are equivalent to τὸ κράτος τῆς ἰσχύος αὐτοῦ and ἡ ἐνέργεια τοῦ κράτους τῆς ἰσχύος αὐτοῦ.[2] Since then, through the Qumran scrolls, late Hebrew equivalents for this expressions, the related expression ἡ ἐνέργεια τῆς δυνάμεως αὐτοῦ and the expressions ἡ εὐδοκία τοῦ θελήματος αὐτοῦ or ἡ βουλὴ τοῦ θελήματος αὐτοῦ which also feature in Eph. have become known.[3] These expressions lead us not so much in the direction of the O.T. and the LXX as towards the later Hebrew use of language. The same applies to the expression σπλάγχνα οἰκτιρμοῦ in Col. 3:12.[4]

In one single place in the O.T. we already see an intensive use of the connection between synonymous or related words by means of the status constructus. This occurs in Ps. 145. In Ps. 145:5, two substantives have been added to a substantive of similar meaning by means of the status constructus and in Ps. 145:12, two substantives have been connected with a substantive by means of the status constructus of which the first is related in meaning.

This psalm in which more substantives are strung together and in which prepositions also have a stylistic function [5] is chronologically already close to the Qumran scrolls. Unlike in other psalms, no obvious metre is manifest. It is not possible to establish a regular structure to the verses. We recognise an "Abgeschliffenheit der Formen" (H. Gunkel—"worn-out forms"). "Die klaren Formprägungen der

---

[1] Cf. Bl.-Debr., para 165 and Radermacher, p. 111.

[2] W. Grundmann, Der Begriff der Kraft in der neutestamentlichen Gedankwelt (Stuttgart 1932), p. 109s. note 2. See also idem, Th. W. III, p. 405 and also Percy, op. cit. p. 195s.

[3] E. g. 1 QH 4,32 בְּכֹחַ גְּבוּרָתוֹ and Damasc. 3.15 חֶפְצֵי רְצוֹנוֹ; cf. Kuhn, "Der Epheserbrief im Lichte der Quamrantexte", p. 335s.

[4] Cf. H. Köster, Th. W. VII, p. 552 and p. 552 note 28.

[5] See for the substantives the beginning of v.7—the word רָב here is probably a substantive; cf. LXX Ps. 144:7 and H. J. Kraus, Psalmen (Bibl. Komm. A.T. XV), p. 947, v. 5b and v. 6a. For prepositions, i.e. prefixes, v. 1b, v. 2a, v. 2b, v. 9, v. 12, v. 14, v. 15, v. 17 and v. 18.

hymnischen Gattung sind weithin verwischt" (H. J. Kraus—"the clear
stamp of the hymnic form has faded considerably"). "The psalm is one
of the latest in the Psalter" (W. O. E. Oesterley).[1]

I am for these reasons of the opinion that besides the influence of
the Hebrew O.T. or the LXX, later Hebrew must also play a part
in the many genitives and cumulations of genitives found in Eph.
The assessment of virtues and defects of 1 QS. 4, 2ss. makes apparent
the predilection inherent to later Hebrew for connecting substantives
through the status constructus (as well as by means of prepositions).

In Eph., the order of words where one or more genitives are employed,
is very simple. The dominant word always precedes the attributive
genitive by which it is followed. This phenomenon suggests a Jewish-
hellenistic or Hebrew influence.[2] Because of this simplicity of sequence,
it was not difficult for the original hearers to follow the meaning of the
epistle as it was read out to them, in spite of the high frequency of
genitives. The parallelism and symmetry which characterise the style
of the epistle, as we shall see presently, are accentuated by the genitives.
Through the introduction of two or more genitives at the end of the
adverbial adjuncts introduced by a preposition which had the function
of clausulae, the effect of staunching the speed of these so-called
clausulae, was enhanced. By this means, an even greater measure of
clarity was achieved,

One even has the impression that the ceaseless reverberation of
genitives and connections forged with genitives, were through the
variety of their number which could be one, two or three, designed to
please the ear, in which case it would not be inappropriate to speak
of a rhythm of genitives.

The following consecutive number of genitives are found in Eph.
1:3-14 :

    vs. 3: 2   (at the end of a principal sentence)
    vs. 4: 2   (in clausula)
    vs. 4: 1

---

[1] See Kraus, op. cit., p. 947s. (The opinions of Gunkel and Oesterley are quoted.)

[2] $\theta\epsilon o\hat{v}$ $\tau\grave{o}$ $\delta\hat{\omega}\rho o\nu$ in Eph. 2:8 is the only combination in which the dominant follows
the genitive. The usual pattern in Eph. coincides with the Hebrew rule that the dominant
substantive in the status constructus precedes the dependent substantive. In the Koine,
unlike Eph., the genitive does not always follow the nomen regens; cf. the $\acute{v}\pi\grave{o}$ $\tau\hat{\omega}\nu$ $\tauo\hat{v}$
$\beta\alpha\sigma\iota\lambda\acute{\epsilon}\omega\varsigma$ $\phi\acute{\iota}\lambda\omega\nu$ and the $\tau\hat{\omega}\nu$ $\phi\acute{\iota}\lambda\omega\nu$ $\grave{\epsilon}\mu\hat{\omega}\nu$ $\tau\grave{\alpha}$ $\grave{o}\nu\acute{o}\mu\alpha\tau\alpha$ quoted in Deissmann, L. v. O.,
pp. 121 and 141.

vs. 5: 2

vs. 5: 3   (in clausula)

vs. 7: 2

     1 + 2 (in clausula) } in a parallelismus membrorum

vs. 9: 2

     1   (in clausula)

     2   (in clausula)

vs. 10: 1

vs. 11: 2   (in clausula)

vs. 12: 2   (in clausula)

vs. 13: 1 }

     2 } in a parallelismus membrorum

vs. 14: 1

     2

     1 + 2 (in clausula)

There is a similar rhythm in Eph. 2:19, 20 :

vs. 19: 1 + 2

vs. 20: 1 + 1

vs. 20: a series of genitives in a genitivus absolutus.

In Eph. 4:12, 13, we find :

vs. 12: 1 }

     1 } (in clausula)

     2 }

vs. 13: 1 + 3

vs. 13: 3   (in clausula)

The importance of the genitive as a stylistic factor is manifest also elsewhere in the epistles of Paul, e.g. in R. 1:1-4; 3:21-26; 8:2; 1 Th. 1:2-4; 3:13; Gal. 1:1-5; 2 C. 1:3; 8:2, 23, 24 and Phil. 3:21. Where the general rule that a stronger membrorum must be placed at the end is followed (the so-called Gesetz der wachsenden Glieder)[1], the results has something of a genitive rhythm.

---

[1] For this rule of gradation see Lausberg, Handbuch, para. 451 and 710.

Such is the case in R. 1:23: 1

$$2+1+1+1$$
R. 8:19: 1+2
R. 8:21: 2+3
1 C. 4:1: 1+2
1 C. 2: 6: 1+2 (+1 in apposition)
and Col. 1:13: 1+3

7. THE TENDENCY TOWARDS PARALLELISM

We have already ascertained that in Eph., adverbial adjuncts introduced by the same preposition are welded together and that this
also happens in the case of genitives. In addition, the parts which are
joined are time and time again of a synonymous or related meaning.
This tendency to doubling is coupled with a particularly strong tendency towards parallelism which governs the style of Eph.

This tendency in also manifested in :

a. the often syndetical placing side by side of synonyms or words
   which are connected in meaning (e.g. σοφία καὶ φρονήσει Eph. 1:8)
b. the addition of a further elaboration (e.g. in Eph. 1:7, the addition
   of τὴν ἄφεσιν τῶν παραπτωμάτων to τὴν ἀπολύτρωσιν διὰ τοῦ αἵματος αὐτοῦ [1]
c. side by side placing of phrases which resemble each other (cf. Eph.
   1:15 τὴν καθ' ὑμᾶς πίστιν ἐν τῷ κυρίῳ Ἰησοῦ καὶ τὴν ἀγάπην τὴν
   εἰς πάντας τοὺς ἁγίους [2]
d. the connecting of adjuncts which are adjacent in meaning and
   governed by participles (e.g. Eph. 1:20 ἐγείρας αὐτὸν ἐκ νεκρῶν καὶ
   καθίσας ἐν δεξιᾷ αὐτοῦ ἐν τοῖς ἐπουρανίοις [3]

---

[1] Thus also Eph. 1:13 τὸ εὐαγγέλιον τῆς σωτηρίας ὑμῶν after τὸν λόγον τῆς ἀληθείας
and 1:23 τὸ πλήρωμα τοῦ τὰ πάντα ἐν πᾶσιν πληρουμένου after τὸ σῶμα αὐτοῦ.

[2] Thus also Eph. 2:12 ἀπηλλοτριωμένοι τῆς πολιτείας τοῦ Ἰσραὴλ καὶ ξένοι τῶν
διαθηκῶν τῆς ἐπαγγελίας. Here there is formal as well as material affinity.

[3] A similar welding occurs when the phrases quoted in note 2 are followed by
ἐλπίδα μὴ ἔχοντες καὶ ἄθεοι ἐν τῷ κόσμῳ. This is also the case in Eph.
2:14 ὁ ποιήσας ... καὶ ... λύσας ... καταργήσας

e. the connecting of constructions with an infinitive which are adjacent in meaning (see Eph. 3:18 καταλαβέσθαι σὺν πᾶσιν τοῖς ἁγίοις τὶ τὸ πλάτος κ.τ.λ. γνῶναί τε τὴν ὑπερβάλλουσαν κ.τ.λ.[1]

f. the parallelism of sentences and modal subordinate clauses (e.g. Eph. 5:25 οἱ ἄνδρες, ἀγαπᾶτε τὰς γυναῖκας, καθὼς καὶ ὁ Χριστὸς ἠγάπησεν τὴν ἐκκλησίαν.[2]

The characteristic described under point a is also found elsewhere in the CP minus; in Phil. almost as frequently as in Eph. and in Col. far more frequently than in Eph.[3] The syndetic character of the combinations of synonyms and words connected in meaning, suggests a Hebrew influence.[4] In general, the connecting of synonyms lends rhetorical power to the prose. The great predilection which the later Syrian writer Afrahates had for this particular combination shows how much combined synonyms were appreciated for their pleasing quality in the Semitic languages.[5]

The additional figure described under point b is also found in the

---

4: 3 ἀνεχόμενοι ... σπουδάζοντες.

4:18 ἐσκοτωμένοι ... ἀπηλλοτριωμένοι

5:19 λαλοῦντες ... ᾄδοντες καὶ ψάλλοντες ... εὐχαριστοῦντες

6:14-16 περιζωσάμενοι ... καὶ ἐνδυσάμενοι καὶ ὑποδησάμενοι ... ἐν πᾶσιν ἀναλάβοντες and

6:18 διὰ πάσης προσευχῆς καὶ δεήσεως προσευχόμενοι ἐν παντὶ καιρῷ ἐν πνεύματι καὶ εἰς αὐτὸ ἀγρυπνοῦντες ἐν πάσῃ προσκαρτερήσει καὶ δεήσει.

[1] A like connection in Eph. 4:22-24 ἀποθέσθαι ... τὸν παλαιὸν ἄνθρωπον ... ἀνανεοῦσθαι δὲ ... καὶ ἐνδύσασθαι τὸν καινὸν ἄνθρωπον.

[2] Parallelisms of this kind are also found in Eph. 3:5; 4:17, 32; 5:23 and 25.

[3] The frequency in Eph. 1/22.5, in Phil. 1/23 and in Col. 1/15.8.

Also see Percy, Probleme, p. 20s. Percy points out that the way in which in Eph. 4:17 a verbum dicendi is reinforced by a related verbum dicendi, is characteristic of Paul; op. cit., p. 240-242.

[4] The use of synonyms was highly rated in Greek rhetoric (cf. Bultmann, Der Stil d. paul. Predigt, p. 18s. on synonymity in the diatribe). There, synonyms usually took the asyndetic form (cf. Lausberg, Handbuch para. 563). Hebrew tended towards the syndeton (cf. Norden, Agnostos Theos, p. 263). J. Weiss in Beiträgen zur paul. Rhetorik, p. 7ss. and p. 169 as well as Ed. König, Stilistik, Rhetorik und Poetik i. Bezug a.d. biblische Literatur (Leipzig 1900), p. 157-161, remark on the hebraicising effect of these combinations. Weiss uses the term "hebraisierender Doppelausdruck" (hebraicising twin-expression).

[5] Afrahates generally uses two synonyms although he sometimes uses more. Cf. L. Haefeli, Stilmittel bei Afrahat dem persischen Weisen (Leipziger Semitische Studien NF Bd. IV, 1832), p. 12-18.

other epistles (e.g. R. 1:1 δοῦλος Χριστοῦ ᾿Ιησοῦ,κλητὸς ἀπόστολος[1]).
It is especially common in Col.[2]

The combination described under point c is sometimes featured
in the other epistles on a few occasions.[3] It also occurs in Col. but with
less use of parallelism.[4]

The phenomenon described in point d is vaguely reminiscent of the
parallelismus membrorum found in Hebrew.[5] In Hebrew parallelisms,
participles may also occupy a dominant position.[6] With respect ot
Eph. 2:12, J. Weiss commented : "Beispiel für hebräisierenden paral-
lelen Doppelausdruck, der noch nicht geradezu parallelismus membrorum ist."[7]

---

[1] Cf. also R. 1:7; 1 C. 1:2; 2 C. 1:3 and Phil. 2:15 (forming an elaboration on the
pair of synonyms ἄμεμπτοι καὶ ἀκέραιοι). Such elaborations are also found in R. 9:30;
1 C. 1:23 ; 3:9 ; 2 C. 5:1 and 2 C. 7:7. This however, is a better Greek. Two or more designations are placed not at the end of a completed phrase but before the verb, are interrupted
by the verb, are contrasted by means of the particles μέν and δέ (sometimes only by δέ)
or form a climax.

[2] Cf. Col. 1:14; 1:15; 1:18; 1:25.

[3] Cf. R. 15:30; 2 C. 1:3 and 2 C. 13:13.

[4] Col. 1:4 and 2:5.

[5] The parallelism of phrases or sentences is a general phenomenon (cf. Norden,
Die antike Kunstprosa, p. 814ss. and Agnostos Theos, p. 214). Similar formulations are
found in Greek parallelism. The Hebrew parallelismus membrorum is based on the affinity
of thought. These thoughts are variously formulated. The fact that in Hebrew sentences
the verbal expression is placed at the beginning, is a secondary distinguishing feature
of the Hebrew parallelismus membrorum. (Norden, Die ant. Kunstprosa, p. 817 and
Agn. Theos., pp. 256ss., 260 and 356). The difference in formulation in the Hebrew
parallelismus membrorum is, although a difference in the words, not so much in the order
and the character of the words used. This is described by R. Lowth, who discovered
the parallelismus membrorum in Hebrew. In De sacro poesi Ebraeorum (1753) he writes :
"Poetica sententiarum compositio maximam partem constat in aequalitate ac similitudi-
dine quadam sive parallelismo membrorum cuiusque periodi, ita ut in duobus plerumque
membris res rebus, verba verbis quasi demensa ac paria respondeant." This quotation
is found in König, Stilistik, Rhetorik, Poetik etc., p. 307s. König correctly speaks of
a "Gleichlauf" of membra. (The correspondence in the order and nature of the words in
the Hebrew parallelism does not come into its own in Norden.) The combinations in
Eph. are only remotely reminiscent of the Hebrew parallelism because they lack this
"Gleichlauf" (concurrence) and because they always appear in an isolated incidence.
A Hebrew parrallelism generally appears within a series of parrallelisms.

[6] Cf. Ps. 19:8-10; Ps. 111:7,8. These part show an affinity with the literature of the
Chokma. (In Ps. 119:130, one sole isolated participial member of the same type occurs.)
In addition, a "hymnischer Partizipialstil" (Kraus, Psalmen, pp. 449 and 451) is combined
with a parallellismus membrorum in Ps. 65:7,8.

[7] J. Weiss, Beiträge, p. 168. The order of the words in ἐλπίδα μὴ ἔχοντες καὶ ἄθεοι

The same may be said of Eph. 2:14. The syndetic combination of participles in ὁ ποιήσας τὰ ἀμφότερα ἓν καὶ τὸ μεσότοιχον τοῦ φραγμοῦ λύσας corresponds closely with Sap. 9:1 ὁ ποιήσας τὰ πάντα ἐν λόγῳ σου καὶ τῇ σοφίᾳ σου κατεσκεύασας ἄνθρωπον.[1] To the combination in Eph., is added a third participial construction : τὴν ἔχθραν ἐν τῇ σαρκὶ αὐτοῦ, τὸν νόμον τῶν ἐντολῶν ἐν δόγμασιν καταργήσας. As here, in Eph., a participium coniunctum follows a couple of attributive participles introduced by the article, in LXX Ps. 64:7, 8 one attributive participle introduced by the article follows a couple of participia coniuncta.[2]

Most in keeping with the real Hebrew parallelism, is Eph. 6:14-16, where there is a double sequence of parallel members. There is a special correspondence between the first members of the first couple περιξωσάμενοι κ.τ.λ. and of the second couple καὶ ὑποδησάμενοι κ.τ.λ. and the second members of the first couple καὶ ἐνδυσάμενοι κ.τ.λ. and of the second couple ἐν πᾶσιν ἀναλαβόντες κ.τ.λ.[3]

In all these combinations of adjuncts governed by participles, there is no reason to speak of direct Hebrew stimulation; it is sufficient to assume a Jewish-hellenistic influence. Such combinations are also found in the other epistles where they resemble the Hebrew parallelismus membrorum in an identical fashion, e.g. R. 1:3, 4 τοῦ γενομένου ἐκ σπέρματος Δαυὶδ κατὰ σάρκα, τοῦ ὁρισθέντος υἱοῦ θεοῦ ἐν δυνάμει

ἐν τῷ κόσμῳ is freer than in the Hebrew parallelism. ("Example of a hebraicising double-expression which is yet not quite a parallelismus membrorum")

[1] Both in Eph. 2:14 as well as in Sap. 9:1, the order is freer than in the Hebrew parallelism. Sap. has been written directly in Greek by a Jew. Jerome wrote of him : "graecam eloquentiam redolet" (quoted by Norden, Die ant. Kunstprosa I, p. 25, Note Note 3). J. Weiss, op. cit., p. 168, says that Sap. was not only known to Paul, but was "für ihn dedeutsam" (important to him).

[2] In Eph. 2:14, Sap. 9:1 and Ps. 64:7,8, we are concerned with the "hymnischer Partizipialstil". The use of the article with this kind of participle is indicative of a non-Greek derivation. Cf. Norden, Agnostos Theos, p. 202s. The participial construction without article in Eph. 2:14, satisfies the demands of Greek rhetoric, containing an uncomplicated zeugma and a homoeoteleuton. The last syllable of καταργήσας corresponds with that of λύσας (for zeugma and homoeoteleuton, cf. Lausberg, Handbuch, para. 687 and 725).

[3] In the one case, the correspondence rests upon the fact that the participle is followed by an accusative of the object and a description with ἐν which replaces the dativus instrumentalis. In the second case, it lies therein that the participle is followed by an accusative of the object with an attached genitive.

κατὰ πνεῦμα ἁγιωσύνης ἐξ ἀναστάσεως νεκρῶν.[1] In Col. the frequency
of such combinations is somewhat higher.[2]

We are once again slightly reminded of the Hebrew parallelismus
membrorum by the connections using an infinite construction, described in point e. In Eph. 3:18, there is a correspondence of thought
between the first and the second constructions. The τί in the first construction which precedes the enumeration, has the implication of a
concept exceeding all other [3] which is adequately echoed in the
ὑπερβάλλουσαν τῆς γνώσεως of the second construction.

In the other combination of constructions with an infinitive in Eph.,

---

[1] Similarly to Eph. 2:14, this construction is reminiscent of the "hymnische Partizipialstil" (see p. 130 n. 6 and p. 131 n. 2). Furthermore, there is 2 C. 3:2 ἐγγεγραμμένη ἐν
ταῖς καρδίαις ἡμῶν, γινωσκομένη καὶ ἀναγινωσκομένη ὑπὸ πάντων ἀνθρώπων (as in Eph. 2:14
there is parallelism between a single participial construction and a double participial
construction) : 2 C. 3:3 διακονηθεῖσα ὑφ᾽ ἡμῶν, ἐγγεγραμμένη οὐ κ.τ.λ. (in this instance,
the last member has been extended by means of several antitheses; as such, these antit-
theses are not Hebrew but their formulation is not truly Greek); Gal. 2:20 τοῦ ἀγαπήσαντός
με καὶ παραδόντος ἑαυτὸν ὑπὲρ ἐμοῦ (another example of the "hymnische Partizipialstil"
and, as Eph. 2:14, correspondent with Sap. 9:1); Gal. 4:4 γενόμενον ἐκ γυναικός, γενόμενον
ὑπὸ νόμον (the anteriority of the participle could be hebraic in disposition but in addition,
this like-worded opening, the anaphora, fulfills the requirements of Greek rhetoric
(cf. Lausberg, Handbuch, para. 629); Phil. 2:7 μορφὴν δούλου λαβών. ἐν ὁμοιώματι
ἀνθρώπων γενόμενος; Phil. 3:6 κατὰ ζῆλος διώκων τὴν ἐκκλησίαν, κατὰ ... γενόμενος and
Phil. 3:13 τὰ μὲν ὀπίσω ἐπιλανθανόμενος, τοῖς δὲ ἔμπροσθεν ἐπεκτεινόμενος (a Greek antithesis).

[2] Eph. has the frequency 1/42, Col., 1/32. In Col. the combinations are 1:10 ἐν παντὶ
ἔργῳ ἀγαθῷ καρποφοροῦντες καὶ αὐξανόμενοι τῇ ἐπιγνώσει τοῦ θεοῦ, ἐν πάσῃ δυνάμει δυναμούμενοι κατὰ ... (as in Eph. 2:14, a corresponcence is found between two participial
constructions and a single participial construction and there is an element of anaphorism);
1:28 νουθετοῦντες ... καὶ διδάσκοντες (the repeated πάντα ἄνθρωπον is reminiscent of the
Greek parallelism of the form); 2:7 ἐρριζωμένοι καὶ ἐποικοδομένοι ἐν αὐτῷ καὶ βεβαιού-
μενοι τῇ πίστει ... περισσεύοντες ἐν εὐχαριστίᾳ (two doubles but interrupted by a subordinate clause and without correspondence in the last member with regard to the
content); 2:13 χαρισάμενος ... ἐξαλείψας; 3:9 ἀπεκδυσάμενοι ... καὶ ἐνδυσάμενοι; 3:13
ἀνεχόμενοι ... καὶ χαριζομένοι (with respesct to "Gleichlauf", much resembling the
Hebrew parallelismus mentrorum); 3:16 (again two membra and one more separate
membrum).

[3] In essence, Eph. 3:18 is a rhetorical question in an indirect form. This rhetorical
question expresses wonderment. (It is an interrogative, serving the admiration, cf.
Lausberg, Handbuch, para. 768.) As in the verse Aen. 3,56 the "Quid non mortalia pectora
cogis, auri sacra fames" or in Ps. 31:20 the מָה רַב־טוּבְךָ, the pronomen interrogativum
in Eph. 3:18 seeks to express that a matter is not to be defined or described. Kraus,
Psalmen, comments with respect to Ps. 31:20 on a "Kennzeichen der Sprache des Hymnus" (a characteristic of the language of the hymn).

i.e. that of Eph. 4:22-24, there is in the manner of the Hebrew antithetic parallelismus membrorum, a contradistinction between the first
and the (in this case, third) last construction. Also the form of these
corresponding membra is reminiscent of the Hebrew figure.[1]

Combinations of parallel constructions using an infinitive are not
lacking in the rest of the CP minus. From time to time, we encounter
combinations of two double constructions with an infinitive. These
constructions are either shorter or further removed from Hebrew
parallelism.[2]

In the phenomenon mentioned under Point f, we remark the following : the modal subordinate clauses introduced by ὡς or καθώς which
are parallel to a principal sentence, subordinate clause or an equivalent phrase, have much correspondence, in form and content, with
the dominant sentence or dominant sentence-part and repeat the verb.
Only in Eph. 3:5 is another verb used. On the basis of the conclusions
reached by Norden, this far-reaching correspondence must be defined
as non-Greek; for it is Semitic in character.[3]

This type of Semiticism is typical of Paul. It is found in R. 15:7;
1 C. 15:49 and 1 C. 10:6-10 in an identical form.[4] Variations of the
phenomenon are likewise found. Just as in Eph. 5:25 the parallel modal
subordinate clause is followed by an additional καὶ ἑαυτὸν παρέδωκεν
ὑπὲρ αὐτῆς to reinforce the exhortation, in 1 C. 10:8, καὶ ἔπεσαν μιᾷ
ἡμέρᾳ εἴκοσι τρεῖς χιλιάδες follows the parallel modal subordinate
clause to intensify the warning.

8. Parallelisms which occur in the other Pauline epistles

In Eph. we observed certain phenomena which are indicative of
a predilection for parallelism and we also remarked that these pheno-

---

[1] There is a certain amount of "Gleichlauf".

[2] See R. 12:15; 2 C. 5:4,8; Phil. 4:12; 1 Th. 5:12, 13 and Col. 1:19, 20.

[3] Cf. Norden, Agnostos Theos, pp. 261ss., 354ss.

[4] In the modal subordinate clause of 1 C. 10:7, the verbal part is missing (εἰδωλολάτραι
ἐγενήθησαν), because a direct quotation from the LXX follows which explicitly renders
the thought expressed in the verbal part of the clause. In 1 C. 11:1 we see a modal subordinate clause, parallel to a principal sentence, in which the verbal part is totally absent.
This lesser correspondence lends a Greek aspect to the parallelism. A similar example of
Greek parallelism is found in Eph. namely in Eph. 5:29 where the verb or rather, verbs,
are also missing from the subordinate clause.

mena sometimes occur in the other epistles.[1] Moreover, in those other epistles are found yet other phenomena of parallelism which have been described by J. Weisz and Bultmann.[2] These phenomena which form an important stylistic component of the other epistles, are not lacking in Eph.

Thus the τὰ ἐπὶ τοῖς οὐρανοῖς καὶ τα ἐπὶ τῆς γῆς of 1:10, the ἐν οὐρανοῖς καὶ ἐπὶ γῆς of 3:15 and the εἴτε δοῦλος εἴτε ἐλεύθερος of 6:8 (cf. 1 C. 12:13) reflect "die Neigung... einen Begriff in seine Teile zu zerlegen" (the tendency... to divide an expression into its component parts), which Weiss remarked in Paul and of which he wrote : "Eine Zerlegung in die Teile verwertet er zuweilen rhetorisch recht wirksam." (Sometimes he turns a redistribution of the parts to really good rhetorical account.)[3] The rhetorical effectiveness of Eph. 1:10 and 3:15 is open to doubt. But in any event, the antithesis of 1:10 is somewhat rhetorical in character through the preposition ἐπί which stands both before οὐρανοῖς and γῆς.[4]

Good rhetorical antitheses are formed by μὴ ὡς ἄσοφοι ἀλλ 'ὡς σοφοί (5:15) and ἦτε γάρ ποτε σκότος, νῦν δὲ φῶς ἐν κυρίῳ (5:8).[5] The antitheses of Eph. 2:8, 13, 19; 4: 25 and 29[6] may also be regarded as comparable to the antitheses of the HP. In 4:14, 15 (ἐν πανουργίᾳ πρὸς τὴν μεθοδείαν τῆς πλάνης, ἀληθεύοντες δὲ ἐν ἀγάπῃ in which

---

[1] The predilection for parallelism in Eph. is also manifested in the parallel course of two consecutive final subordinat clauses with ἵνα of which the last is subordinate to the first. This phenomenon occurs also elsewhere in the CP minus. Percy discussed this in Die Probleme, p. 242s. For the cumulation of three indirect parallel interrogative sentences in Eph. 1:18ss. and the affinity between this cumulation and the cumulation of three participial constructions in Col. 1:9ss., I also refer to Percy, op. cit., p. 22.

[2] J. Weisz, Beiträge zur paulinischen Rhetorik, p. 170ss. and Bultmann, Der Stil der paulinischen Predigt, p. 76ss. Bultmann concentrated on the rhetorical antitheses and parallelisms which occur in those parts of Paul's epistles where a lively, mobile style and dialogue are in evidence. In his opinion, these figures of style were in keeping with and belonged to such passages. He adds : "Verständlich ist es aber wenn die Klangfiguren ... über diesen Grenzen hinausdringen und sich auch in anderen Partien finden." (p. 94ss.) "It becomes comprehensible when the patterns of sound ... transcend these limits and are carried over into other parts."

[3] Op. cit., p. 178-180.

[4] This is reminiscent of the anaphora; cf. Lausberg, Handbuch, para. 629.

[5] Cf. op. cit., para. 787ss.

[6] In Eph. 4:29, πᾶς λόγος σαπρός and εἴ τις ἀγαθός form parallel and equal phrases, the first is hebraicising in effect. (The Semitic languages do not have an adjective pronomen indefinitum. Hebrew bridges this lacuna with, e.g. כָּל־ = πᾶς; cf. Beyer, Semit. Syntax im N.T., p. 142).

ἀληθεύοντες sets off πρὸς τὴν μεθοδείαν τῆς πλάνης and ἐν ἀγάπῃ is in contrast with ἐν πανουργίᾳ) and in 4:28 (where the contrast lies between ἐργαζόμενος ταῖς ἰδίαις χερσὶν τὸ ἀγαθόν and ὁ κλέπτων; κοπιάτω and κλεπτέτω) we are dealing with antitheses which display a χιαστὸν σχῆμα (a crosswise contrapuntal placing of corresponding sentence-parts).[1]

Thus in my opinion the rhetorical sententia ὁ ἀγαπῶν τὴν ἑαυτοῦ γυναῖκα ἑαυτὸν ἀγαπᾷ (5:28) with its parallel character is analogous not only in content but also in form with 1 C. 7:12-14 and 1 C. 11:11 and 12. It is striking that in the matter of the marriage paraenesis and the relationship between man and wife, both epistles express statements using the same formal structure.

9. PARALLEL SENTENCES AND PARTS OF SENTENCES; THE RHYMING OF THOUGHTS

In Eph. there is a parallelism not only between sentences or equivalent sentence-parts which immediately follow each other, but also between sentences or equivalent sentence-parts, which are more widely separated. In such cases, correspondence between parallel membra is slighter; of the "Gleichlauf" treated on page 130 in note 5, there is no question. There is only a certain measure of correspondence.

In the eulogy, we find three membra which share the concept that God has chosen the faithful before the beginning or has predestined them for something, i.e. the modal subordinate clause 1:4 καθὼς ἐξελέξατο ἡμᾶς ἐν αὐτῷ πρὸ καταβολῆς κόσμου and the constructions with a participium coniunctum in 1:5 προορίσας ἡμᾶς εἰς υἱοθεσίαν διὰ Ἰησοῦ Χριστοῦ εἰς αὐτόν and in 1:11 προορισθέντες κατὰ πρόθεσιν κ.τ.λ.

The eulogy also contains three relative clauses, introduced by ἐν ᾧ, which have in common the idea that the faithful have inherited something in Christ, i.e. 1:7 ἐν ᾧ ἔχομεν τὴν ἀπολύτρωσιν διὰ τοῦ αἵματος αὐτοῦ, 1:11 ἐν ᾧ καὶ ἐκληρώθημεν and 1:13 ἐν ᾧ καὶ πιστεύσαντες ἐσφραγίσθητε τῷ πνεύματι τῆς ἐπαγγελίας τῷ ἁγίῳ.

Once again, we are reminded of Hebrew poetry where there is also a certain amount of parallelism between verses which follow each other at some distance.

---

[1] Cf. Lausberg, op. cit., para. 723 and p. 361 note 1 (subsequently paras. 787 and 793) and J. Jeremias, "Chiasmus in den Paulusbriefen", ZNW 1958, p. 45ss.

In Ps. 34 there is a correspondence between verses 5, 7, 18, 19, 20, 21 and 23 (A.V.4, 6, 17, 18, 19, 20, and 22) which share the concept that God delivers and redeems the righteous. In Ps. 5, there is a correspondence between verses 5 and 13 (A.V. 4 and 12) which stand in a relationship of antithesis.

In the eulogy of Eph. there is even more than this type of parallelism between separated sentences of sentence-parts. De Zwaan remarked that the long sentence of Eph. 1:3-14 is constituted of fragments which vary in character. He observed that fragments of a similar character reappear continuously and spoke of a logical rhythm or rhyming of thoughts. According to de Zwaan, Paul's thought rhyming was inspired by Hebrew poetry.[1]

As a matter of fact, there are instances in the Psalms of a constant recurring of certain thoughts. We have selected Ps. 1 for our purpose. When the character of the various sentences and phrases is characterised by code letters, features of difference and correspondence become obvious. For sentences or phrases which speak of blessing or malediction, we have chosen respectively the letters f and k. If the blessing or malediction is expressed in terms of a comparison, we have coded this as respectively f' and k'. When the sense concerns the rejection of that which is censurable in an ethical-religious context, we denote this by the letter a; when the sense concerns the choosing of that which is praiseworthy in an ethical-religious context, we use the letter b.

Thus, we find the following scheme in this psalm : [2]

f	Blessed is the man
a	that walketh not in the counsel of the ungodly,
a	nor standeth in the way of sinners,
a	nor sitteth in the seat of the scornful.
b	But his delight is in the law of the Lord;
b	and in his law doth he meditate day and night.
f'	And he shall be like a tree planted by the rivers of water,
f'	that bringeth forth his fruit in his season;
f'	his leaf also shall not wither;

---

[1] "Le Rhythme logique dans l'èpître aux Ephésiens", p. 554ss. and De Efezenbrief van Paulus, p. 17ss.

[2] We chose the A.V., because this corresponds closely with the structure of the Hebrew sentences.

f   and whatsoever he doeth shall prosper.

k   The ungodly are not so :

k'   but are like the chaff which the wind driveth away.

k   Therefore the ungodly shall not stand in the judgement,

k   nor sinners in the congregation of the righteous.

f   For the Lord knoweth the way of the righteous :

k   but the way of the ungodly shall perish.

The fragments of Eph. 1:3-14 can be similarly characterised, in which case a like scheme is revealed. One difference lies therein that the letters characterise the sentences and phrases of Psalm 1 according to their content, whereas in the eulogy the letters merely indicate the function of the fragments. Another difference is that the Hebrew parallelismus membrorum is present in Psalm 1, whereas in Eph. 1:3-14 we could find but a remote parallel between a few (separated) sentences or sentence-parts.

The way in which the great mass of words forming Eph. 1:3-14 should be broken into fragments we saw in section 5 of this chapter. The quadruple appearance of ἐν ᾧ marks the beginning of a sentence and the other adjuncts introduced by a preposition (especially the strung-together adjuncts) mark the ends of sentences or the equivalent sentence-parts. This method of arrangement circumvents the arbitrariness of de Zwaan's method of division. He occasionally regarded an adverbial adjunct introduced by a preposition as part of a fragment but would then use such an adjunct as an independent component fragment. Subordinate clauses, he treated in a similar fashion. Although de Zwaan described his system as colometric, no colometric arguments can be discerned to support his arrangement. For as it is, his fragments are not cola.[1]

---

[1] The colon is an independently complete component of the Greek period. De Zwaan saw in the long sentences of Paul, with their peculiar structure, a semiticising counterpart of the Greek period and spoke of the "Paulinische periode" (De Efezenbrief, p. 19). It was probably by way of a comparison that he called the component parts of the "Paulinische perioden", cola. His position is perhaps concordant with Lohmeyer's point of view. The latter presented a colometric dissection of the eulogy of Eph. a year before de Zwaan (with 45 cola) and answered Debrunner's criticism as follows : "Es ist völlig unmöglich das Proömium des Epheserbriefes von den Gesichtspunkten aus, die für antike Rhetorik masgebend sind, so zu gliedern, wie ich es vorgeschlagen habe ; bezeichnet man sie als kolometrisch, dann ist die vorgeschlagene Gliederung alles andere als kolometrische Einteilung"—it is wholly impossible to organise the proömium of the epistle to

The code which we have selected for the fragments of the eulogy is as follows : for fragments which indicate an aim or consequence, D; for fragments which deal with a course of action or deed of God, H; for fragments which record an action of God in the passive form, Hp [1] and for the remaining fragments, F. The corresponding fragments 1:4, 5 and 11 discussed previously, we designate by *, and the ditto fragments of verses 1:7, 11, 13 and 13 by **. We indicate the fragments by only the beginning and the end.

The scheme is as follows :

F	εὐλογητὸς ...	Ἰησοῦ Χριστοῦ	1 :3
H	ὁ εὐλογήσας ...	ἐν Χριστῷ	1 :3
H*	καθὼς ἐξελέξατο ...	κόσμου	1 :4
D	εἶναι ...	ἐν ἀγάπῃ	1 :4
H*	προορίσας ...	αὐτοῦ	1 :5, 6
H	ἧς ἐχαρίτωσεν ...	ἐν τῷ ἠγαπημένῳ	1 :6
F**	ἐν ᾧ ἔχομεν ...	αὐτοῦ	1 :7
H	ἧς ἐπερίσσευσεν ... ἐν πάσῃ σοφίᾳ καὶ φρονήσε ι	1 :8
H	γνωρίσας ...	αὐτοῦ	1 :9
H	ἣν προέθετο ...	τῶν καιρῶν	1 :9, 10
D	ἀνακεφαλαιώσασθαι ...	τῆς γῆς ἐν αὐτῷ	1 :10
Hp**	ἐν ᾧ καὶ ἐκληρώθημεν		1 :11
Hp*	προορισθέντες ...	αὐτοῦ	1 :11
D	εἰς τὸ εἶναι ...	ἐν τῷ Χριστῷ	1 :12[2]
F**	ἐν ᾧ καὶ ὑμεῖς ἀκούσαντες ...	ὑμῶν	1 :13
HP**	ἐν ᾧ καὶ ...	τῷ ἁγίῳ	1 :13
F	ὅς ἐστιν ...	αὐτοῦ	1 :14

---

the Ephesians in the way I suggested, when the aspects which formed the criteria for ancient rhetoric are taken into account; if these are designated as colometric, then the entire proposed arrangement becomes anything but colometric—(see Th. Bl. 5, 1926, pp. 120ss. and cf. p. 11 note 8 and p. 12 note 3). For definitions of the colon, see F. Blasz, Rhein. Mus. 1869, p. 258; R. Schütz. "Die Bedeutung der Kolometrie für das N.T." (ZNW 21, 1922, p. 174); Debrunner, Th. Bl. 1926, p. 232 and Lausberg, op. cit., paras. 925-934. The preponderance of long syllables at the end of de Zwaan's so-called cola are already in conflict with the requirements demanded of a colon; cf. Lausberg, op. cit., para. 997 sub 1 and paras. 994-996.

[1] In late Judaism there is a proneness for recording the action of God in the passive form; cf. G. Dalman, Die Worte Jesu I (Leipzig 1930), p. 183s.

[2] On account of their grammatical structure, the verses Eph. 1:11a are 12 are to be regarded as independent fragments.

The long sentence in Eph. 2:14-18 has a similar structure and although it contains only a few adverbial adjuncts introduced by a preposition, it is easily divided into fragments from a grammatical point of view.

In this sentence thought-rhyming approaches Hebrew poetry more closely than is the case with the eulogy. The fragments may be characterised according to their content (cf. Ps. 1).—In dealing with Eph. 1:3-14, we had to restrict ourselves to indicating the function of the fragments.—In the participles of 2:14 which are preceded by the article, we are reminded of the "hymnische Partizipialstil" of some psalms.[1] A Jewish-hellenistic parrallelism may also be remarked in this long sentence, particularly in the series with the participles of 2:14 and 15.[2]

We have coded this sentence as follows : fragments pertaining to peace V ; those which speak of destruction or enmity O and those dealing with unity, E.

The scheme of the sentence is as follows :

V	αὐτὸς γάρ ἐστιν ἡ εἰρήνη ἡμῶν	2 :14
E	ὁ ποιήσας τὰ ἀμφότερα ἓν καὶ τὸ μεσότοιχον τοῦ φραγμοῦ λύσας	2 :14
O	τὴν ἔχθραν ἐν τῇ σαρκὶ αὐτοῦ, τὸν νόμον τῶν ἐντολῶν ἐν δόγμασιν καταργήσας	2 :15
E	ἵνα τοὺς δύο κτίσῃ ἐν αὐτῷ εἰς ἕνα καινὸν ἄνθρωπον	2 :15
V	ποιῶν εἰρήνην	2 :15
E	καὶ ἀποκαταλλάξῃ τοὺς ἀμφοτέρους ἐν ἑνὶ σώματι τῷ θεῷ διὰ τοῦ σταυροῦ	2 :16
O	ἀποκτείνας τὴν ἔχθράν ἐν αὐτῷ	2 :16
V	καὶ ἐλθὼν εὐηγγελίσατο εἰρήνην ὑμῖν τοῖς μακρὰν καὶ εἰρήνην τοῖς ἐγγύς	2 :17
E	ὅτι δι᾽ αὐτοῦ ἔχομεν τὴν προσαγωγὴν οἱ ἀμφότεροι ἐν ἑνὶ πνεύματι πρὸς τὸν πατέρα	2 :18

---

[1] See para. 7 of this chapter and p. 130 n. 6 and p. 131 n. 2.

[2] See notes 1 and 2 on p. 131. There is furthermore a certain parallelism in form in 2:14, 15 between the two phrases τὴν ἔχθραν ἐν τῇ σαρκὶ αὐτο and τὸν νόμον τῶν ἐντολῶν ἐν δόγμασιν which both belong to the participle καταργήσας through a detractio (cf. Lausberg, op. cit., para. 693). There is an antithetical parallelism between the two constructions with a participium coniunctum ποιῶν εἰρήνην and ἀποκτείνας τὴν ἔχθραν ἐν αὐτῷ in 2:15 and 16. In 2:17 there is a non-Greek parallel doubling in the phrases (apposite to the verbal form εὐηγγελίσατο) εἰρήνην ὑμῖν τοῖς μακρὰν καὶ εἰρήνην τοῖς ἐγγύς.

Schemata of this nature which are reminscent of monotonous compositions, based on a limited scale, are also found in R. The sentence R. 1:1-7 can be broken into a number of fragments with corresponding and differing aspects from not only a grammatical point of view but also on the basis of the adverbial adjuncts introduced by a preposition which assume the function of clausulae. A proportion of the fragments are strongly qualificative in character. These relate to respectively Paul, Christ and the addressees.

We distinguish this type of fragment by respectively Q, Q^1 and Q^2. Three of the fragments are relative subordinate clauses: the last two of these concern persons and are also of a qualificative nature. We designate the latter by the letters RQ, whilst the first is distinguished by R. There is one fragment which is of local significance and this has been characterised as L. The remaining fragment has the Symbol F. We have characterised not the content of the fragments but their function.

The scheme is as follows :

Q	Παῦλος δοῦλος Χριστοῦ ᾿Ιησοῦ	1	:1
Q	κλητὸς ἀπόστολος	1	:1
Q	ἀφωρισμένος εἰς εὐαγγέλιον θεοῦ	1	:1
R	ὃ προεπηγγείλατο διὰ τῶν προφητῶν αὐτοῦ ἐν γραφαῖς ἁγίαις περὶ τοῦ υἱοῦ αὐτοῦ	1	:2
Q^1	τοῦ γενομένου ἐκ σπέρματος Δαυὶδ κατὰ σάρκα	1	:3
Q^1	τοῦ ὁρισθέντος υἱοῦ θεοῦ ἐν δυνάμει κατὰ πνεῦμα ἁγιωσύνης ἐξ ἀναστάσεως νεκρῶν	1	:4
Q^1	᾿Ιησοῦ Χριστοῦ τοῦ κυρίου ἡμῶν	1	:4
RQ	δι᾿ οὗ ἐλάβομεν χάριν καὶ ἀποστολὴν εἰς ὑπακοὴν πίστεως ἐν πᾶσιν τοῖς ἔθνεσιν ὑπὲρ τοῦ ὀνόματος αὐτοῦ	1	:5
RQ^2	ἐν οἷς ἐστε καὶ ὑμεῖς κλητοὶ ᾿Ιησοῦ Χριστοῦ	1	:6
L	πᾶσιν τοῖς οὖσιν ἐν ῾Ρώμῃ	1	:7
Q^2	ἀγαπητοῖς θεοῦ	1	:7
Q^2	κλητοῖς ἁγίοις	1	:7
F	χάρις ὑμῖν καὶ εἰρήνη ἀπὸ θεοῦ πατρὸς ἡμῶν καὶ κυρίου ᾿Ιησοῦ Χριστοῦ	1	:7

There is parallelism in the fragments Q^1 and Q^1 in 1:3 and 4.

The long sentence R. 3:21-26 may be divided in the same way.

For fragments relating to a deed of God, we use H; for fragments
recording the same but in the passive form, Hp; Q is used to characterise qualificatory fragments; D for final fragments and M for two
fragments indicating motive which feature the particle γάρ.

We indicate the fragments with the first and the last word and arrive
at the following scheme :

Hp	νῦνι ...	πεφανέρωται	3 :21
Q	μαρτυρουμένη ...	προφητῶν	3 :21
Q	δικαιοσύνη ...	πιστεύοντας	3 :22
M	οὐ ...	διαστολή	3 :22
M	πάντες ...	θεοῦ	3 :23
Hp	δικαιούμενοι ...	Ἰησοῦ	3 :24
H	ὃν ...	καιρῷ	3 :25, 26
D	εἰς ...	Ἰησοῦ	3 :26

The fragments of the long sentences Eph. 1:3-14, R. 1:1-7 and 3:21-26
may be further subdivided into still smaller fragments. De Zwaan
correctly observed that in Eph. 1:3-14 and R. 3:21-26, thought rhyming
also occurs in exceedingly small fragments. However, due to the arbitrariness of his system of arrangement, the individual character of
these little fragments does not always come to light. A more objective
arrangement is reached when the following parts of sentences are always
separated :

1. every adverbial adjunct introduced by a preposition (except ἐν ᾧ);
2. a verb and its direct subject when this is mentioned and possibly
   with its object;
3. a doubled verb with the substantive part of the sense.

For these smaller fragments into which the larger fragments may be
subdivided, we use the same letters as for the former, substituting small
letters for capitals. We add letter g for fragments which are modal
in character; 1 for fragments indicating a place or time; dr for fragments which convey a direction or relationship. It becomes apparent
that these little fragments too are varied and alternating in a rhythmic
pattern.

The scheme for Eph. 1:3-14 follows below :

F	εὐλογητὸς ὁ θεὸς καὶ πατὴρ τοῦ κυρίου ἡμῶν Ἰησοῦ Χριστοῦ	f	(1)
H	ὁ εὐλογήσας ἡμᾶς	h	(2)
	ἐν πάσῃ εὐλογίᾳ πνευματικῇ	g	(3)
	ἐν τοῖς ἐπουρανίοις	l	(4)
	ἐν Χριστῷ	g	(5)
H	καθὼς ἐξελέξατο ἡμᾶς	h	(6)
	ἐν αὐτῷ	g	(7)
	πρὸ καταβολῆς κόσμου	l	(8)
D	εἶναι ἡμᾶς ἁγίους καὶ ἀμώμους	d	(9)
	κατενώπιον αὐτοῦ	dr	(10)
	ἐν ἀγάπῃ	g	(11)
H	προορίσας ἡμᾶς	h	(12)
	εἰς υἱοθεσίαν	d	(13)
	διὰ Ἰησοῦ Χριστοῦ	g	(14)
	εἰς αὐτόν	dr	(15)
	κατὰ τὴν εὐδοκίαν τοῦ θελήματος αὐτοῦ	g	(16)
	εἰς ἔπαινον δόξης τῆς χάριτος αὐτοῦ	d	(17)
H	ἧς ἐχαρίτωσεν ἡμᾶς	h	(18)
	ἐν τῷ ἠγαπημένῳ	g	(19)
F	ἐν ᾧ ἔχομεν τὴν ἀπολύτρωσιν	f	(20)
	διὰ τοῦ αἵματος αὐτοῦ	g	(21)
	τὴν ἄφεσιν τῶν παραπτωμάτων	f	(22)
	κατὰ τὸ πλοῦτος τῆς χάριτος αὐτοῦ	g	(23)
H	ἧς ἐπερίσσευσεν	h	(24)
	εἰς ἡμᾶς	dr	(25)
	ἐν πάσῃ σοφίᾳ καὶ φρονήσει	g	(26)
H	γνωρίσας ἡμῖν τὸ μυστήριον τοῦ θελήματος αὐτοῦ	h	(27)
	κατὰ τὴν εὐδοκίαν αὐτοῦ	g	(28)
H	ἣν προέθετο	h	(29)
	ἐν αὐτῷ	g	(30)
	εἰς οἰκονομίαν τοῦ πληρώματος τῶν καιρῶν	l	(31)
D	ἀνακεφαλαιώσασθαι τὰ πάντα	d	(32)
	ἐν τῷ Χριστῷ	g	(33)
	τὰ ἐπὶ τοῖς οὐρανοῖς καὶ τὰ ἐπὶ τῆς γῆς	l	(34)
	ἐν αὐτῷ	g	(35)

Hp	ἐν ᾧ καὶ ἐκληρώθημεν	hp	(36)
Hp	προορισθέντες	hp	(37)
	κατὰ πρόθεσιν τοῦ τὰ πάντα ἐνεργοῦντος	g	(38)
	κατὰ τὴν βουλὴν τοῦ θελήματος αὐτοῦ	g	(39)
D	εἰς τὸ εἶναι ἡμᾶς	d	(40)
	εἰς ἔπαινον δόξης αὐτοῦ	d	(41)
	τοὺς προηλπικότας	f	(42)
	ἐν τῷ Χριστῷ	g	(43)
F	ἐν ᾧ καὶ ὑμεῖς ἀκούσαντες τὸν λόγον τῆς ἀληθείας	f	(44)
	τὸ εὐαγγέλιον τῆς σωτηρίας ὑμῶν	f	(45)
Hp	ἐν ᾧ καὶ πιστεύσαντες	f	(46)
	ἐσφραγίσθητε	hp	(47)
	τῷ πνεύματι τῆς ἐπαγγελίας τῷ ἁγίῳ	g	(48)
F	ὅς ἐστιν ἀρραβὼν τῆς κληρονομίας ὑμῶν	f	(49)
	εἰς ἀπολύτρωσιν τῆς περιποιήσεως	d	(50)
	εἰς ἔπαινον τῆς δόξης αὐτοῦ.	d	(51)

The scheme of R. 1:1-7 becomes :

Q	Παῦλος δοῦλος Χριστοῦ Ἰησοῦ	q	(1)
Q	κλητὸς ἀπόστολος	q	(2)
Q	ἀφωρισμένος	q	(3)
	εἰς εὐαγγέλιον θεοῦ	d	(4)
R	ὁ προεπηγγείλατο	r	(5)
	διὰ τῶν προφητῶν αὐτοῦ	g	(6)
	ἐν γραφαῖς ἁγίαις	g	(7)
	περὶ τοῦ υἱοῦ αὐτοῦ	dr	(8)
Q¹	τοῦ γενομένου	q	(9)
	ἐκ σπέρματος Δαυὶδ	g	(10)
	κατὰ σάρκα	g	(11)
Q¹	τοῦ ὁρισθέντος υἱοῦ θεοῦ	q	(12)
	ἐν δυνάμει	g	(13)
	κατὰ πνεῦμα ἁγιωσύνης	g	(14)
	ἐξ ἀναστάσεως νεκρῶν	g	(15)
Q¹	Ἰησοῦ Χριστοῦ τοῦ κυρίου ἡμῶν	q	(16)
RQ	δι' οὗ ἐλάβομεν χάριν καὶ ἀποστολὴν	rq	(17)

εἰς ὑπακοὴν πίστεως   d   (18)
ἐν πᾶσιν τοῖς ἔθνεσιν   l   (19)
ὑπὲρ τοῦ ὀνόματοσ αὐτοῦ   dr   (20)

RQ²   ἐν οἷς ἐστε καὶ ὑμεῖς κλητοὶ Ἰησοῦ Χριστοῦ   rq   (21)
L   πᾶσιν τοῖς οὖσιν ἐν Ῥώμῃ   l   (22)
Q²   ἀγαπητοῖς θεοῦ   q   (23)
Q²   κλητοῖς ἁγίοις   q   (24)
F   χάρις ὑμῖν καὶ εἰρήνη   f   (25)
      ἀπὸ θεοῦ πατρὸς ἡμῶν καὶ κυρίου Ἰησοῦ Χριστοῦ.   dr   (26)

The scheme for R. 3:21-26 becomes :

Hp   νυνὶ δὲ χωρὶς νόμου   g(l)   (1)
     δικαιοσύνη θεοῦ πεφανέρωται   hp   (2)

Q   μαρτυρουμένη   q   (3)
     ὑπὸ τοῦ νομου καὶ τῶν προφητῶν   q(l)   (4)

Q   δικαιοσύνη δὲ θεοῦ   q   (5)
     διὰ πίστεως Ἰησοῦ Χριστοῦ   g   (6)
     εἰς πάντας τοὺς πιστεύοντας   dr   (7)

M   οὐ γάρ ἐστιν διαστολή   m   (8)
M   πάντες γάρ ἥμαρτον καὶ ὑστεροῦνται τῆς δόξης   m   (9)
     τοῦ θεοῦ
Hp   δικαιούμενοι δωρεάν   hp   (10)
     τῇ αὐτοῦ χάριτι   g   (11)
     διὰ τῆς ἀπολυτρώσεως τῆς ἐν Χριστῷ Ἰησοῦ   g   (12)

H   ὃν προέθετο ὁ θεὸς ἱλαστήριον   h   (13)
     διὰ πίστεως   g   (14)
     ἐν τῷ αὐτοῦ αἵματι   g   (15)
     εἰς ἔνδειξιν τῆς δικαιοσύνης αὐτοῦ   d   (16)
     διὰ τὴν πάρεσιν τῶν προγεγονότων ἁμαρτημάτων   g   (17)
     ἐν τῇ ἀνοχῇ τοῦ θεοῦ   l   (18)
     πρὸς τὴν ἔνδειξιν τῆς δικαιοσύνης αὐτοῦ   d   (19)
     ἐν τῷ νῦν καιρῷ   l   (20)

D   εἰς τὸ εἶναι αὐτὸν δίκαιον καὶ δικαιοῦντα τὸν ἐκ   d   (21)
     πίστεως Ἰησοῦ.

Already from the schemata which form the structural basis of the

long sentences Eph. 1:3-14, R. 1:1-7 and 3:21-26, it became apparent
that there is a relationship in style. Thus compare :

Eph. 1:3-14   F H H D H H F H H H D Hp Hp D F Hp F
R. 1:1-7   Q Q Q R Q¹ Q¹ Q¹ RQ RQ² L Q² Q² F
R. 3:21-26   Hp Q Q M M Hp H D

The closeness of this relationship only becomes truly apparent
through a comparison of the detailed schemata. Taking into account
that the adverbial adjuncts introduced by a preposition assume the
place of clausulae, these schemata may be set out as follows :

Eph. 1:3-14
f h g l g   = F H
h g l   = H
d dr g   = D
h d g dr g d   = H
h g   = H
f g f g   = F
h dr g   = H
h g   = H
h g l   = H
d g l g   = D
hp hp g g   = Hp Hp
d d f g   = D
f f f hp g f d d   = F Hp F

R. 1:1-7
q q q d   = Q Q Q
r g g d r   = R
q g g   = Q¹
q g g g   = Q¹
q rq d l dr   = Q¹ RQ
rq l q q f d r   = RQ² L Q² Q² F

R. 3:21-26
g hp q q   = Hp Q
q g dr   = Q
m m hp g g   = M M Hp
h g g d g l d l   = H
d   = D

Somewhat related to the scheme of Eph. 2:14-18 is the scheme of
Phil. 2:5-8. J. Weiss has analysed the pericope Phil. 2:5-11 as an example of a cumulation of Greek-rhetorical parallelisms.[1] In following
his analysis, it becomes apparent that the fragments in this pericope
can also be characterised according to their content. For fragments
which are negatively inclined with regard to the glory of God, we use
N and for fragments which are positively inclined in the same matter,
P. We furthermore used letters D and F in the previous sense.

The sentence Phil. 2:5-8 has the following scheme :

F   τοῦτο φρονεῖτε ἐν ὑμῖν ὃ καὶ ἐν Χριστῷ ᾽Ιησοῦ

N   ὃς ἐν μορφῇ θεοῦ ὑπάρχων οὐχ ἁρπαγμὸν ἡγήατο τὸ εἶναι
     ἴσα θεῷ

N   ἀλλὰ ἑαυτὸν ἐκένωσεν μορφὴν δούλου λαβών

N   ἐν ὁμοιώματι ἀνθρωπῶν γενόμενος καὶ σχήματι εὑρεθεὶς
     ὡς ἄνθρωπος

N   ἐταπείνωσεν ἑαυτὸν γενόμενος ὑπήκοος μέχρι θανάτου,
     θανάτου δὲ σταυροῦ.

This is followed by Phil. 2:9-11 with the scheme ;

P   διὸ καὶ ὁ θεὸς αὐτὸν ὑπερύψωσεν

P   καὶ ἐχαρίσατο αὐτῷ τὸ ὄνομα τὸ ὑπὲρ πᾶν ὄνομα

D   ἵνα ἐν τῷ ὀνόματι ᾽Ιησοῦ πᾶν γόνυ κάμψῃ ἐπουρανίων καὶ
     ἐπιγείων καὶ καταχθονίων

D   καὶ πᾶσα γλῶσσα ἐξομολογήσηται ὅτι κύριος ᾽Ιησοῦς
     Χριστὸς εἰς δόξαν θεοῦ πατρός.

The pericope has the same christocentric character as Eph. 2:14-18
and likewise concludes with an assignation of God as πατήρ. With
reference to the fragment ἐν ὁμοιώματι ἀνθρώπων γενόμενος καὶ
σχήματι εὑρεθεὶς ὡς ἄνδρωπος (Phil. 2:7) J. Weisz speak of a syn-
thetic parallelism in miniature. Similarly, one could also speak of an
antithetic parallelism in miniature with respect to the fragment
ὁ ποιήσας τὰ ἀμφότερα ἓν καὶ τὸ μεσότοιχον τοῦ φραγμοῦ λύσας
(Eph. 2:15). Furthermore, as an example of synonymous parallelism,
the binary subordinate clause (ἵνα ... καί) in Phil. 2:10 and 11 could

---

[1] Beiträge zur Paulinischen Rhetorik, p. 190s.

be set beside the binary subordinate clause (ἵνα ... καί) from Eph.
2:15 and 16. In these last two fragments, Phil. 2:10 and Phil. 2:11,
J. Weisz sees a rhetorical expansion. The same remark may be applied
to Eph. 2:17 and Eph. 2:18, which are the last two fragments of the
corresponding piece in Ephesians. The difference between the scheme
of the long sentence Eph. 2:14-18 and the pericope, Phil. 2:5-11, is
that in Eph. fragments of a corresponding nature follow each other
not directly, but after an interval whereas in Phil. there are consecutive
sets of corresponding fragments. In Eph. 2:14-18 the scheme is V E O
E V E O V E and in Phil. 2:5-11 it is F N N N N P P D D.

But a closer examination reveals that there is nevertheless a fair
amount of variation in Phil. 2:5-11. The fragments characterised as
N may be split into :

a. parts which record a deed of Christ and have the verbum indicativus;
b. parts which record a circumstance surrounding Christ and contain
   a participle.

These last elements we characterise more precisely as O and, according
to their positive or negative mood, with P or N. Fragments which
record a deed of Christ, we designate as HN. These deeds—directly
negative in mood with regard to the glory of God—are in contradisposition to the in this respect positive deeds of God himself which we have
already designated by the letter P; in addition, we now also describe
these deeds of God with the letter H on account of their "character
of action".

As becomes apparent from the following analysis, the scheme F N
N N N P P D D changes into F OP HN HN ON ON HN ON HP HP
D D.

F	τοῦτο φρονεῖτε ἐν ὑμῖν ὃ καὶ ἐν Χριστῷ Ἰησοῦ
OP	ὃς ἐν μορφῇ θεοῦ ὑπάρχων
HN	οὐχ ἁρπαγμὸν ἡγήσατο τὸ εἶναι ἴσα θεῷ
HN	ἀλλὰ ἑαυτὸν ἐκένωσεν
ON	μορφὴν δούλου λαβών
ON	ἐν ὁμοιώματι ἀνθρώπων γενόμενος καὶ σχήματι εὑρεθεὶς ὡς ἄνθρωπος
HN	ἐταπείνωσεν ἑαυτὸν
ON	γενόμενος ὑπήκοος μέχρι θανάτου, θανάτου δὲ σταυροῦ.
HP	διὸ καὶ ὁ θεὸς αὐτὸν ὑπερύψωσεν
HP	καὶ ἐχαρίσατο αὐτῷ τὸ ὄνομα τὸ ὑπὲρ πᾶν ὄνομα

D   ἵνα ἐν τῷ ὀνόματι Ἰησοῦ πᾶν γόνυ κάμψῃ ἐπουρανίων καὶ
     ἐπιγείων καὶ καταχθονίων
D   καὶ πᾶσα γλῶσσα ἐξομολογήσηται ὅτι κύριος Ἰησοῦς
     Χριστὸς εἰς δόξαν θεοῦ πατρός.

Thus it may be seen that in Phil. 2:5-11 there is definitely also evidence of thought-rhyming.

Thought-rhyming is particularly characteristic of the Epistle to the Romans; we see this phenomenon not only in R. 1:1-7 and R. 3:21-26 but also in the pericope R. 1:18-31 which Bultmann regards as typical of Paul's preaching.[1] In R. 1:23 there is a sharp Greek contrast between ὁ ἄφθαρτος θεός and φθαρτὸς ἄνθρωπος but also a specimen of the combination of interdependent genitives which is so frequent in Eph. Towards the end (in R. 1:29-31), the pericope assumes an uncompromisingly Greek aspect.[2] If the adverbial adjuncts introduced by a preposition are treated as clausulae and grammatical indications are for the rest taken as a criterion, these sentences are amenable to fragmentation. We indicate these fragments by the number and opening of the verse.

The fragments may be characterised by their content. Some deal with the wrath of God or a punitory action by God, for these we have selected the letter T. When the fragments convey that God "gave over" the sinners to foolishness and dishonour, we indicate this in its turn by T[1]. On several occasions the text says that the holy truth of God is known; these we characterise with a W. A large number of fragments concern the concepts of untruth and blindness. This is indicated by L. Other fragments which may be characterised as dealing with the concepts of shame and corruption, are designated by an S. The remaining fragments are again indicated by the letter F.

The scheme is found to run as follows :

1 : 18	ἀποκαλύπτεται ...	T
1 : 18	ἐπὶ πᾶσαν ...	L
1 : 19	διότι τὸ γνωστὸν ...	W

---

[1] Der Stil der paulinischen Predigt, p. 71 : "So wie Röm. 1:18ff. wird Paulus seine Missionspredigt begonnen haben." (Paul will have begun his missionary word as decribed in R. 1:18ss.)

[2] Cf. Norden, Agnostos Theos., p. 260 and Bultmann, loc. cit.

1 : 19	ὁ θεὸς γάρ ...	W
1 : 20	τὰ γάρ ...	W
1 : 20	εἰς τὸ εἶναι ...	F
1 : 21	διότι γνόντες ...	L
1 : 21	ἀλλὰ ἐματαιώθησαν ...	L
1 : 21	καὶ ἐσκοτίσθη ...	L
1 : 22	φάσκοντες ...	L
1 : 23	καὶ ἤλλαξαν ...	L
1 : 24	διὸ παρέδωκεν ...	T¹
1 : 24	τοῦ ἀτιμάζεσθαι ...	S
1 : 25	οἵτινες μετήλλαξαν ...	L
1 : 25	καὶ ἐσεβάσθησαν ...	L
1 : 25	ὅς ἐστιν εὐλογητὸς ...	F
1 : 26	διὰ τοῦτο παρέδωκεν ...	T¹
1 : 26	αἵ τε γὰρ θήλειαι ...	S
1 : 27	ὁμοίως τε καὶ οἱ ἄρσενες ...	S
1 : 27	ἄρσενες ἐν ἄρσεσιν ...	S
1 : 27	καὶ τὴν ἀντιμισθίαν ...	T
1 : 28	καὶ καθὼς οὐκ ἐδοκίμασαν ...	L
1 : 28	παρέδωκεν ...	T¹
1 : 28	ποιεῖν ...	S
1 : 29-31	πεπληρωμένους πάσῃ ἀδικίᾳ ...	S
1 : 32	οἵτινες τὸ δικαίωμα ...	W
1 : 32	ὅτι οἱ τὰ τοιαῦτα πράσσοντες ...	T
1 : 32	οὐ μόνον αὐτὰ ποιοῦσιν ...	S
1 : 32	ἀλλὰ καὶ συνευδοκοῦσιν ...	S

A trace of thought-rhyming is also found in part of the paraenesis of Eph., in Eph. 4:25-6:9. Here we find three types of thought : negative exhortations or prohibitions (for which we select the letter a); positive exhortations or commands (letter b) and motives or arguments (letter m). Furthermore, there are parallel fragments and formal affinities.

Three different constructions recur constantly in the fragments designated as a :

1. the subject concerns one or more sins and the verb is in the third person singular of the imperativus medii or passivi (aᴵ);
2. the meaning is characterised by the imperative form μὴ γίνεσθε (aᴵᴵ);
3. the phrase is governed by another imperative in the second person plural with the negation μή (aᴵᴵᴵ).

In the fragments designated as b, three different types of construction also recur constantly :

1. the fragment is governed by a participium coniunctum in the no minative plural (bᴵ);
2. the verb of the sentence is the imperative γίνεσθε (bᴵᴵ);
3. the fragment is composed of a verbum cognoscendi (in the form of a participium or an imperativus), followed by an interrogative (bᴵᴵᴵ).

In the section treating family life, the case is sometimes that in the fragments designated as a and b, the category to which the exhortation applies is first named in the vocative. After that, the verb may follow. At the end is found an accusative or dative belonging to the verb or the implied verb. According to their negative or positive mood, these fragments are characterised as aˣ or bˣ.

The fragments designated as m repeatedly feature six different forms:

1. the fragments is a causal subordinate clause introduced by ὅτι (mᴵ);
2. the fragment is causal in mood and contains the conjunction γάρ (mᴵᴵ);
3. the fragment consists of a relative subordinate clause introduced by ἐν ᾧ (mᴵᴵᴵ);
4. the fragment is of a modal adverbial character and is introduced by the adverb ὡς (mᴵⱽ);
5. the fragment is a modal subordinate clause introduced by καθώς (mⱽ);
6. the fragment is a final subordinate clause introduced by ἵνα (mⱽᴵ).

Sometimes the motivation for an exhortation is complicated. In such cases, it consists of a compound sentence or a succession or sentences or subordinate clauses. The matter under consideration always concerns one single concept upon which is elaborated. We indicate this by placing the entire sequence in parentheses. These complicated motives interrupt the regularity of the framework as a whole.

The following survey which follows Nestle's sentence arrangements and gives the first word of each sentence, gives an impression of thought-rhyming in the paraenetical section of Eph.

4 : 25	διό ...	a = quotation b m^I	
4 : 26	ὀργίζεσθε ...	a^{iii} = quatotion a a^{III} [1]	
4 : 28	ὁ ...	a b m^{VI}	
4 : 29	πᾶς ...	a^1 b m^{VI}	
4 : 30	καὶ ...	a^{III} m^{III}	
4 : 31	πᾶσα ...	a^1	
4 : 32	γίνεσθε ...	b^{11} b^1 m^V	
5 : 1	γίνεσθε ...	b^{11} m^{IV} b m^V	
5 : 3	πορνεία ...	a^1 m^V a^1 m b	
5 : 5	τοῦτο ...	(m^{11} m m	
5 : 6	μηδεὶς ...	m m^{11}) [2]	
5 : 7	μή ...	a^{11} m^{11} b m^{11} b^{111}	
		a^{111} b (m^{11} m m m^{11}	
5 : 14	διό ...	m = ciaat)	
5 : 15	βλέπετε ...	b^{111} a b b^1 m^1	
5 : 17	διὰ ...	a^{11} b^{111}	
5 : 18	καὶ ...	a^{111} m^{111} b b^1 b^1 b^1 b^1	
5 : 22	αἱ ...	b^x (m^{IV} m^1 m^{VI})	
5 : 24	ἀλλὰ ...	m^{iv} b^x	
5 : 25	οἱ ...	b^x (m^V m^{VI} m^{VI} m^{VI})	
5 : 28	οὕτως ...	b (m^{IV}	
5 : 28	ὁ ...	m m^{11} m m^V m^1	
5 : 31	ἀντὶ ...	m = quotation	
5 : 32	τό ...	m m = exegessis)	
5 : 33	πλὴν ...	b m^{IV} b	
6 : 1	τὰ ...	b^x m^{11}	
6 : 2	τίμα ...	b = quotation m m^{VI} = quotation	
6 : 4	καὶ ...	a^{111} x b	
6 : 5	οἱ ...	b^x m^{IV} a^{111} m^{IV} m^{IV} b^1 b^1 (m^{VI} m)	
6 : 9	καὶ ...	b^x [3] b^1 (m m)	

---

[1] ὀργίζεσθε καὶ μὴ ἁμαρτάνετε is a negative exhortation : sin not in wrath. The subsequent negative exhortations clarify the first. There is sin in wrath if that wrath persists at the end of the day. By harbouring wrath also in the night, the devil is given a place. This last exhortation at the same time provides a motive. Possibly, the last two exhortations are renderings of a traditional explanation of the first which has been borrowed from an evening psalm.

[2] The μηδεὶς ὑμᾶς ἀπατάτω κενοῖς λόγοις is parallel to τοῦτο γὰρ ἴστε γινώσκοντες. The διὰ ταῦτα (sc. l. πορνεία, ἀκαθαρσία, πλεονεξία, αἰσχρότης κ.τ.λ.) γὰρ ἔρχεται ἡ ὀργὴ κ.τ.λ. is parallel to ὅτι πᾶς πόρνος ἢ ἀκάθαρτος κ.τ.λ. οὐκ ἔχει κληρονομίαν κ.τ.λ. These are not direct paraenetical exhortations but warnings against beliefs which lead to bad actions and are therefore corrupt.

[3] We equate πρὸς αὐτούς with a dative.

The same type of thought-rhyming is also found in the paraenetical section of Col. 3:18-4:1. Here again, the a-, b- and m- concepts and the interplay between them, recur. In Col., this section is short and only relates to family life. The a-, b- and m- fragments are not as varied in construction or form as in Eph. The typical b-form which is repeatedly used in Eph. when the family is under discussion is almost as frequent in Col. These b^x-fragments follow here in a more rapid succession than in Eph. The a^{III} x-form which is found in Eph. 6:4 is present in Col. 3:21.

The survey below reveals : these features

3 : 18	ai ...	b^x m^{Iv}
3 : 19	oi ...	b^x a^{III}
3 : 20	$\tau\grave{a}$ ...	b^x m^{II}
3 : 21	oi ...	a^{III} x m^{VI}
3 : 22	oi ...	b^x a^{III} m^{IV} b m
3 : 23	$\hat{o}$ ...	b (m^{IV} m)
3 : 25	$\tau\hat{\omega}$ ...	b m^{II}
4 : 1	oi ...	b^x [1] m

In the paraenetical passage R. 12:9-21, there is a rhyming with a quartet of thoughts. Besides the a-, b- and m-fragments, there are also a few conditional subordinate clauses which we indicate by v. The a-, b- and m-fragments are more restricted in the number of constructions or forms than is the case in Eph. New forms are here found in the negative exhortations in the form of a participial construction in the nominative plural which we indicate by a ^{IV} and in the positive exhortations in the form of an infinitive which are indicated by b^{IV}. Use is made in this passage of material from Proverbs. Furthermore, there is one explicit quotation from Deut. 32:35.

12 : 9	$\mathring{\eta}$	a
12 : 9	$\mathring{a}\pi o\sigma\tau\upsilon\gamma o\mathring{\upsilon}\nu\tau\epsilon\varsigma$ ...	a^{IV} b^1 b b^1 a b^1 b^1 b^1 b^1 b^1 b^1 b^1
12 : 14	$\epsilon\mathring{\upsilon}\lambda o\gamma\epsilon\mathring{\iota}\tau\epsilon$ ...	b b a^{III}
12 : 15	$\chi a\acute{\iota}\rho\epsilon\iota\nu$ ...	b^{IV} b^{IV}
12 : 16	$\tau\grave{o}$ ...	b^1 a^{IV} b^1
12 : 16	$\mu\grave{\eta}$ ...	a^{II} a^{IV} b^1

---

[1] The b^x-fragment in Col. 4:1 is deviating in order; the verbal element follows an accusative of the object and a dative belonging to the verb.

12 : 18	εἰ ...	v b¹ a^IV b m^II = quotation
12 : 20	ἀλλὰ ...	v b v b m^II
12 : 21	μή ...	a^III b

Thought-rhyming is also found in the paraenetical material of the Diache, i.e. in Did. 3:1-4:11. This section contains a-, b- and m-fragments and there is one example of a v-fragment. These a-, b- and m-fragments have fewer different forms or constructions than they have in Eph. but more than in either Col. or R. The b^x-form occurs once and, as elsewhere, the fragment pertains to family life. Apart from the last-mentioned instance, all other exhortations are expressed in the singular. In place of the fragments that are governed by γίνεσθε or μὴ γίνεσθε or μή with another imperative in the 2nd. person plural, the Didache fragments have γίνου, μὴ γίνου or μή and another imperative in the 2nd. person singular.

In the analysis below, we keep the designations b^II, a^II and a^III for these fragments.[1] Causal subordinate clauses introduced by ὅτι do not feature in Did. 3:1-4:11. Fragments introduced by ἐπεί or ἐπειδή are found and we designate these by m^I.

3 : 1	τέκνον ...	a
3 : 2	μή ...	a^II m^II a^II m^II
3 : 3	τέκνον ...	a^II m^II a^II m^II
3 : 4	τέκνον ...	a^II m^I a^II a^III m^II
3 : 5	τέκνον ...	a^II m^I a^II m^II
3 : 6	τέκνον ...	a^II m^I a^II m^II
3 : 7	ἴσθι ...	b m^I
3 : 8	γίνου ...	b^II
3 : 9	οὐχ ...	a
3 : 9	οὐ ...	a b
3 : 10	τὰ ...	b m
4 : 1	τέκνον ...	b b (m^II m)
4 : 2	ἐκζητήσεις ...	b m^VI
4 : 3	οὐ ...	a b b a
4 : 4	οὐ ...	a
4 : 5	μή ...	a^II a^II
4 : 6	ἐάν ...	v b

---

[1] We follow the text of F. X. Funk, Patres Apostolici, Vol. I (Tübingen ²1901), p. 8ss. and observe the sentence arrangements given by Funk.

4 : 7	οὐ ...	a m¹¹
4 : 8	οὐκ ...	a b a m¹¹
4 : 9	οὐκ ...	a b
4 : 10	οὐκ ...	a (m^{VI 1} m¹¹ m)
4 : 11	ὑμεῖς ...	bˣ m^{IV}

These four paraenetical sections remind us of the chokma literature of the O.T.; the affinities and differences between corresponding fragments are reminiscent of the parallelism and antithetic parallelism which is found in that literature. Another common feature is the substantiation of exhortations by the setting out of motives and arguments.[2]

Did. 3:1-4:11 is particularly closely related to this type of literature. The oft-repeated form of address τέκνον μου in this part of Did. calls to mind the frequent use of בְּנִי in Prov. [3] A considerable amount of "Gleichlauf" in the corresponding fragments of Did. lends to the section a strong measure of the character of Hebrew parallelism.

It is probable that the paraenesis with its patterns of thought-rhyming as found in these four sections, evolved under the influence of chokma literature. The impression is furthermore aroused that Eph. 5:22-6:9; Col. 3:18-4:1 and Did. 4:11 all trace back to a paraenetical composition which related to family relations and also had thought-rhyming. It is almost certain that such a whole must have existed; an instruction in which exhortations in a characteristic form were repeated again and again. This form identifies itself through the following pattern : the category to which the exhortation applied, was mentioned first; this was followed by a verbal element after which an accusative or dative

---

[1] The subordinate clause with μήποτε οὐ μὴ ... is equivalent to a final clause introduced by ἵνα.

[2] In Prov. 3:5-12, verses 6b, 8, 10 and 12 each state the motives for the preceding exhortations.

[3] Alongside the τέκνον μου of Did. stands the frequent τέκνον in Sir, It is generally accepted that in Did. 3:1-4:11 we are concerned with material which has been adapted from Jewish paraenetical material. Without directly accepting the hypothesis that this material sprung from a catechism for proselytes, it may be accepted that it originated from hellenistic Jewry in the diaspora which had such strong interests in Jewish propaganda material. See G. Klein, Der älteste christliche Katechismus und die Jüdische Propagandaliteratur (Berlin 1909), p. 157ss.; Michaelis, Th. W. V, p. 99; Bultmann, Theolog., pp. 496, 515 and 567 and Schoeps, Paulus, die Theologie des Apostels im Lichte der Jüdischen Religionsgeschichte, p. 236 and p. 236, note 1 and 2.

belonging to the verb came at the end. These typical exhortations we find again in the b^x and the a^{III} ^{x}-fragments of Eph. 5:22-6:9 and Col. 3:18-4:1 in which the verbal element is sometimes missing but can easily be reconstructed from the context.

In Did. 4:11, we find one single isolated b^x-fragment. After all the exhortations in the imperative singular, this exhortation with an imperative plural provides a heterogeneous element and its character makes it unlikely that we are concerned with an ad hoc formulation. The scant affinity with Eph. 6:5 or Col. 3:22, suggests that Did. 4:11 was not adapted from either of these places.

Several exhortations in the prototype form are also found in 1 P. 2:18; 3:1 and 7. In 1 P., the verbal form is not constituted of an imperative as in Eph., Col. and Did., but of a participle. The lack of affinity with Eph., Col. or Did. runs counter to any possibility of interdependence between the four passages. Most probably, the four works all derive from one ethical instruction in which a number of exhortations, expressed in this specific form, occurred.

Between Eph. 5:22-6:9 and Col. 3:18-4:1 there is a great affinity with regard to these exhortations. A possibility exists that there is an interdependence between these two pericopes.

If that is so, one of the pericopes must have been constructed first, drawing on material from the original paraenetical source, whilst the second pericope was compiled on the basis of the first.[1] Col. 3:18-4:1, where the characteristic exhortations come in closer succession than in Eph., probably has most in common with the older paraenesis which was Jewish-hellenistic in disposition.[2]

---

[1] K. Weidinger, Die Haustafeln, ein Stück unchristlicher Paränese (UNT 14, 1928), sees the family-paraenesis as an item of popular Greek ethic which was continually promoted through Stoa propaganda. Weidinger holds that this paraenesis was taken over into the moral propaganda of hellenistic Jewry in the diaspora and thus came into the N.T. and early Christian writings. In his view, it must be taken into account that it could be that in this N.T. and ancient Christian literary paraenesis "ein bis zu gewissem Grade fixierter Stoff vorliegen kann" (there could to a certain extent be standard material) and that there could be a multitude of possibilities in connection with this paraenesis which cannot be checked. (cf. pp. 13-18, 48-50, 4 and 49-51) Cf. also G. Narder, Bibl.-Hist. Handwörterbuch, s.v. Haustafel.)

[2] The opinion of Weidinger quoted in note 1 makes this probable. It is also demonstrated in the continually recurrent order in which the category addressed is first named, followed by the verbal component and then by the accusative or dative belonging to the verb. This is a Hebrew pattern which is also found in Ps. 135:19 and 20 (LXX 134:19 and 20).

When thought-rhyming in the four sections Eph. 4:25-6:9; Col. 3:18-4:1; R. 12:9-21 and Did. 3:1-4:11 is subjected to closer scrutiny, it evolves that this rhyming is based on a number of patterns. R. 12:9-21 has a simple scheme with a remarkable linking of b-fragments and the frequent combination of an a-fragment and a b-fragment. The scheme of Col. is equally uncomplicated; combinations of a b-fragment and an m-fragment, or an a-fragment and an m-fragment predominate. This last-named (a-m) combination very often occurs in Did. 3:1-4:11. Within the somewhat complicated scheme of the latter, there are even whole series of this combination. Usually, the a-fragment can be more precisely identified as a^{Π} and the m-fragment as m^{Π}. The b-m combination which we saw repeatedly in Col. and the a-b combination which was often encountered in R., also occur.

Even more complicated is the scheme of the Eph. section. Here are found the various combinations from R., Col and Did. as well as the linked b-fragments of R. whilst, as in Col., the b-m combination plays a dominant role. What is however a new phenomenon in Eph. is the joining of b-m and a-b fragments to form an a-b-m pattern. Moreover, there is again more variation within a single combination because of the independent character of individual fragments. Eph. is allied to R. and Col. and distinguished from Did. through the preponderance of b-fragments as against a-fragments.[1]

The style of the three Pauline paraenetical sections is more in accordance with the stylistic demands of Greek than is the case with Did. 3:1-4:11. In para. 8, we have already commented on the rhetorical sentence Eph. 5:28 and the antitheses of Eph. 4:25, 28, 29; 5:8 and 15, some of which form correct antitheses. The end of the Col. 3:18-4:1 section is less hebraic in character than the preceding part. The fragment τῷ κυρίῳ Χριστῷ δουλεύετε in Col. 3:25 has the verb not at the beginning but at the end, whilst the b^x -fragment in Col. 4:1 also has the verb at the conclusion.[2]

---

[1] The proportions are : Eph. 17a/34b; R. 9a/22b; Col. 3a/8b and Did. 24a/13b.

[2] For the b^x-fragment in Col. 4:1 see p. 152 n. 1. In Norden, Agnostos Theos., pp. 257 and 365 one may read that it is typical of the Semitic languages that the verbal element takes precedence (p. 257 : "Die Voranstellung der Verbalbegriffe ist für den semitischen Parallelismus, wie die semitischen Sprachen überhaupt, typisch gewesen."; p. 365: "Die Voranstellung des Verbums ist neben dem Satzparallelismus ... der sicherste Semitismus des N.T., besonders in den Fällen, wo diese Stellung serienweise auftritt." —"The anterior placing of the verb was typical of the Semitic parallelism as it was indeed, of all Semitic languages." / "The anteriority of the verb is, next to the parallelism of

In the section R. 12:9-21, the succession of cola in R. 12:11 and 12, all comprised of a substantive in the dative and a participle in the nominative plural, conforms to the rules of parallelism in Greek. Throughout the entire pericope runs something of the "kunstreiche Gestaltung im kleinen" which Norden regarded as characteristic of Greek parallelism.[1] But it is nevertheless not genuinely Greek in character. The passage R. 12:9-14 falls just slightly short of ideal Greek parallelism as envisaged by Norden; a parallelism which corresponds in form and in which sentences which correspond in form and almost word by word, are placed side by side.[2]

Although the section Eph. 4:25-6:9 never aspires to the beauty which is undeniably present in the pericope R. 12 :9-21,it must nevertheless be concluded that a familiarity with the rules of Greek rhetoric is equally present in Eph. 4:25-6:9 and R. 12:9-21.

When the two epistles Eph. and R. are compared, we see a clear affinity with respect to thought-rhyming. Eph. contains parts in 1:3-14; 2:14-18 and 4:25-6:9 which include thought-rhyming. In R. there is thought-rhyming in 1:1-7; 1:18-31; 3:21-26 and 12:9-21.

The character of thought-rhyming in Eph. 1:3-14 and R. 1:1-7 and 3:21-26, is of the same kind. The fragments that are rhymed, can be characterised according to their function. These fragments may furthermore be divided into still smaller fragments in which thought-rhyming also occurs.

In Eph. 4:25-6:9 and R. 12:9-21 there is once again a similar kind of thought-rhyming. This is different from the thought-rhyming in Eph. 1:3-14 and R. 1:1-7 and R. 3:21-26; less striking and entirely adapted to the paraenesis. The rhyming relates to the content of the fragments which can be characterised as either positive or negative, their function which can be of an argumentative or a conditional nature, and their form.[3] We discovered in Eph. 4:25-6:9, contrary to R. 12:9-21, a complicated scheme and many different forms. In the small pericope R. 12:9-21, a similarly complicated structure and variation in form would not be possible.

Then there are the sections Eph. 2:14-18 and R. 1:18-31. In both

---

sentences ... the most explicit semiticism in the N.T., especially when this occurs in series.")

[1] Op. cit., p. 260ss. (Quotation : "skilful form in miniature".)

[2] Antike Kunstprosa, p. 816-819.

[3] We indicate the individual character of the different forms by Roman numerals.

these passages, the rhymed fragments can be characterised by their content. For the rest, they differ. Between Eph. 2:14-18 and Phil. 2:5-8, there is more correspondence than between Eph. 2:14-18 and R. 1:18-31. Eph. 2:14-18 and Phil. 2:5-8 speak of avowal; R. 1:18-31. is more in the nature of a penitential sermon. In Eph. 2:14-18, we found a "hymnischer Partizipialstil" and a Jewish-hellenistic parallelism, whereas the pericope R. 1:18-31 assumes a truly Greek character towards the conclusion of the passage.

Taking into account the relative length of the two epistles, we must come to the conclusion that thought-rhyming has been more intensively utilised in Eph. than in R. Admittedly, the paraenetical passage R. 12:9-21 is very tiny as compared to the whole section Eph. 4:25-6:9 but on the other hand, to counterbalance this, the "penitential sermon" of R. 1:18-31, a pericope which is closely allied to the paraenesis, presents us with an additional extensive section in which thought-rhyming features.

10. MONOTONY AND REPETITION; CANTILENA

When repeated genitives and connected genitives are used within a restricted sphere in Eph., the variation in the number of genitives featured introduces a certain rhythmic element into the style of the epistle. For that reason we spoke of a rhythm of genitives (para. 6). With de Zwaan, one may also recognise a rhythmic element in the arrangement of thoughts in the thought-rhymes and it is not out of place to speak of a logical rhythm (para. 9). Innitzer and Lohmeyer discerned even more rhythmic elements in Eph. 1:3-14; they spoke in terms of rhythmic prose.

Innitzer divided Eph. 1:3-14 into 38 cola and thought that each of these cola ended rhythmically, that the beginning or middle part could also be rhythmic and that occasionally an entire colon was rhythmical.

Lohmeyer arranged Eph. 1:3-14 in 45 cola. He found whole series of cola ending with a word in which the accent falls on the last syllable; series of cola ending with a word in which the accent falls on the penultimate syllable and series of cola ending with a word in which the accent falls on the third before last syllable. He found moreover, that these three types of cola featured intermittently and that they alternated with greater or lesser regularity. Lohmeyer assumed that the accented syllables were stressed.

Innitzer gave the metre a very odd treatment indeed. It escaped his attention both that his cola are not cola within the terms of reference of Greek rhetoric and that the rhythm he discovered was not in accordance with the rules of the rhythmic prose of this rhetoric. Objectivity was lacking in the work of both these scholars because their cola suffered from the same arbitrariness as the arrangement laid down by de Zwaan.[1]

The analysis which we already gave (p. 137ss.) leads us to adopt a view which diverges from the conclusions of Innitzer and Lohmeyer. For when the 51 small fragments into which we objectively divided the eulogy are carefully examined, it becomes evident that there is something special about the alternation of long and short syllables and about the accents. The fact is that 21 of the fragments end with three or more long syllables. These fragments usually occur in direct succession or after a short interval. The fragments in question are : 1, 2, 5, 8, 12, 14, 15, 25, 28, 31, 33, 36, 37, 38, 40, 41, 43, 44, 45, 49 and 51. Of these, nos. 1, 41 and 51 have a large number of consecutive long syllables at the end. (There is also a preponderance of long syllables in fragments 46 and 47 which do not form part of the group of 21 fragments.)

---

[1] For the publications of Innitzer and Lohmeyer see p. 11 n. 6 and 7 (cf. p. 137 n. 1). Innitzer divides the eulogy into three larger units of cola or "Abschnitte", each composed of a number of smaller units or "Strophen". Although the eulogy evinces a certain regularity in the reccurrence of successions of long syllables, there is not "die Wiederkehr und das Entsprechen des Gleichen oder Ähnlichen" (the reccurrence and correlation of the identical and the similar) of which he speaks (op. cit., p. 618). He could do so because he gave the metre such singular treatment. On checking his data, however, it is seen that he is not consistent; sometimes he equates a long syllable with two short syllables, then again with one short syllable. On other occasions he equates a metrical unit with a like metrical unit plus a succeeding long syllable, or he equates a unit with preceding long syllable with the same unit followed by a long syllable. The arbitrary nature of his distribution into cola is demonstrated by the fact that he sometimes turns an adverbial adjunct introduced by a preposition into part of a large colon whereas at other times he turns a single or two consecutive adjuncts of that kind into an independent colon. Lohmeyer bundles his cola or "Glieder" into three strophes of 4 × 3 cola and one strope of 3 × 3 cola. He has given some reason for his attempt to take the number 3 as the guiding principle for his method of division in "Die Offenbarung des Johannes" (Hndbch. NT 16, 1929, pp. 9, 38 and 39). His application of this key to Eph., however, is entirely arbitrary. There seems to be no reason why the adjunct ἐν αὐτῷ should now be an independent colon and at other times part of a larger colon. Neither is it reasonable that an adverbial adjunct introduced by a preposition should sometimes be included with the sentence-part in which it occurs and at other times function as the second or third colon of a "Dreizeiler" (triad) whereas at other times again, they would not be

In addition there is a tendency throughout the entire eulogy to place a word at the end of a fragment in which the accent falls on the last syllable. In the case of 7 fragments, the last word has the accent on the antepenultimate syllable (20, 24, 29, 36, 46, 47 and 50). 14 fragments end in a word with the accent on the penultimate syllable (4, 8, 9, 11, 13, 19, 22, 26, 32, 37, 38, 42, 44 and 48) and no less than 30 fragments have the accent on the ultimate syllable of the last word. These are fragment nos. 1, 2, 3, 5, 6, 7, 10, 12, 14, 15, 16, 17, 18, 21, 23, 25, 27, 28, 30, 31, 33, 34, 35, 39, 40, 41, 43, 45, 49, and 51. (With the exception of fragment 15, the last word in each case is a perispomenon.)

These facts prompt us to consider the following points. A succession of long syllables has a slowing-down effect.[1] Through the repeated appearance of a series of long syllables at the conclusion of a fragment, the stream of words is periodically halted. This will undoubtedly have led to a resonant oration. Many fragments must have ended with a reverberant flourish during the recitation and the narrative may even have acquired a singing quality. After all, according to the ancient definition of Aristoxenus, the difference between speaking and singing is that in speech the voice continues without interruption whereas in singing the voice pauses on notes (and continues with intervals).[2]

Series of long syllables do not only occur at the ends of fragments but reappear with a certain regularity throughout the entire eulogy. This phenomenon imposes a highly monotonous character on the whole piece.

The stimulation to chant comes not only towards the ending of fragments but is continually reinforced.

The constant resurgence of a perispomenon at the end of fragments could have promoted this chant-like narration. Such was the case when an accent on the last syllable of a fragment caused this syllable to gain in emphasis. Even stronger was the effect when the ancient habit persisted, whereby the accent did not have an "expiratorisch-energisch" but a musical effect and caused a very slight variation in pitch.[3]

---

counted with the sentence-part to which they are attached, but would count as the first colon of a new "Dreizeiler".

[1] Cf. Lausberg, para. 997, 1.

[2] Cf. Norden, Die Antike Kunstprosa, p. 55-60. Norden here deals with the musical aspect of Greek rhetoric.

[3] Cf. Norden, op. cit. I, p. 4 and II, p. 867 note 1 and also A. J. Koster, The Greek Accent (Leiden 1962), p. LXs.

Innitzer regarded the succession of long syllables as "feierlich".[1]
The creator of Eph. must also have conceived of them as such; for it is
precisely fragments 1, 41 and 51, which are possessed of a strongly
doxological character, that end in the most extended series of long
syllables. Also the doxology of Eph. 3:21 ends with a succession of long
syllables.

Not only do series of long syllables or perispomena recur again and
again at the ends of fragments, but the endings return to the same
connection of words i.e. τοῦ θελήματος αὐτοῦ (fragments 16, 27 and
39) and τῆς χάριτος αὐτοῦ (fragments 17 and 23). Besides this, there
are a number of similar or resemblant fragments : ἐν Χριστῷ (5);
ἐν αὐτῷ (7); εἰς αὐτόν (15); εἰς ἡμᾶς (25); ἐν αὐτῷ (30); ἐν αὐτῷ (35);
ἐν τῷ Χριστῷ (33) and ἐν τῷ Χριστῷ (43).

The tendency to sing rather than speak the recitation will have
been strengthened by this repercussion of the same connections at the
ends of fragments and the reiteration of like or similarly-formed
fragments. All these repetitions are symptomatic of a predilection
for pauses. Hebrew poetry, with its parallelisms and repetitions,
displays the same tendency.[2]

That the author of Eph. had a cantillating form of recitation in mind
when he conceived the eulogy and that for him there was but a narrow
line of division between speaking and singing, is borne out by Eph.
5:19 where λαλεῖν, ᾄδειν and ψάλλειν are placed on one line and there
is reference to a λαλεῖν ψαλμοῖς καὶ ὕμνοις καὶ ᾠδαῖς.

All in all, there is a certain monotony inherent in the eulogy with
its everlasting harping on the same or similar elements which is in
sharp contrast with the requirements of Greek aesthetics governing
the ars rhetorica and rhythmic prose.[3]

Some aspects of the particular features of the eulogy described above,
are found again in the two sections of R. which have a structural
affinity with the eulogy of Eph. and can be separated into small
fragments along the same principle. R. 1:1-7 contains 26 fragments;
of these, 9 (1,6, 8, 10, 16, 21, 22, 25 and 26) have three or more long

---

[1] Op. cit., p. 617 ("solemn").

[2] The parallelism of Semitic poetry supports the lyrical character of the poetry.
The thought is often expressed in the style of a stagnant aria and is longer maintained
through the use of synonyms. Thus says Schütz, Der parallele Bau der Satzglieder im N.T.
(Göttingen 1920), p. 8.

[3] Cf. Lausberg, op. cit., para. 275,26; 1072; 961; 981 and 994-996.

syllables at the end. Of these, 4 are greatly distinguished by long syllables (1, 6, 21 and 26). Furthermore, the accent comes on the final
syllable of the ultimate word in 13 of the 26 fragments (1, 4, 6, 8, 10,
12, 15, 16, 17, 20, 21, 23 and 26).

R. 3:21-26 can be broken into 21 fragments. 7 of them (6, 9, 12, 16,
19, 20 and 21) end with three or more long syllables. A preponderance
of long syllables occurs in 4 fragments (7, 16, 19 and 20). 12 fragments
end in a word with the accent on the last syllable. There is also some
demonstration of the repetition of identical or similar connections of
words. Thus fragment 6 (διὰ πίστεως ᾽Ιησοῦ Χριστοῦ) is more or
less repeated in fragment 21 (ἐκ πίστεως ᾽Ιησοῦ). Likewise fragment
19 (πρὸς τὴν ἔνδειξιν τῆς δικαιοσύνης αὐτοῦ) can be seen as a repetition
of fragment 17 (εἰσ ἔνδειξιν τῆς δικαιοσύνησ αὐτοῦ).

R. corroborates the theory that a succession of long syllables must
be regarded as an indication of solemnity. The final part of the doxology R. 11:36 consists of a series of nine successive long syllables.

11. OTHER FORMS OF REPETITION

Even more types of repetition or recurrence of identical or similar
features are found in Eph. In the eulogy and in the remnant epistle
there are certain words which are repeated; words and expressions
which are related in meaning and content or belong together, are
placed at a certain distance from each other and maintain, as it were,
contact from afar.[1]

In Eph. 1:3-14, the repetition of the words εὐδοκία and θέλημα
and the internal correspondence between the words εὐδοκία, θέλημα,
βουλή, and μυστήριον form a constructive element.[2]

In Eph. 1:15-23 there is the correspondence between the words πίστις
and ἀγάπη in 15 and ἐλπίς in 18. These words belong together in the
CP minus as can be seen from the triad in 1 C. 13:13 and 1 Th. 1:3 and
the correspondence of words in R. 5:1-5; Gal. 5:5, 6 and Col. 1:4,5.
In addition, this sentence Eph. 1:15-23 also manifests correspondences
in the words σοφία, ἀποκάλυψις, ἐπίγνωσις, φωτίζειν and εἰδέναι;

---

[1] De Zwaan speaks of correspondences wihch underline the architecture (De Efezenbrief van Paulus, p. 22) and brought them out by means of larger or thickly printed
letters in his article "Le "Rhythme logique" dans l'épître aux Ephésiens".

[2] The word μυστήριον is associated with βουλή in Jdt. 2:2.

between the word ὁ πλοῦτος and the expression τὸ ὑπερβάλλον μέγεθος; between the words, δύναμις, ἐνέργεια, κράτος, ἰσχύς and ἐνεργεῖν and between the words πόδες, κεφαλή and σῶμα..

Eph. 2:1-7 contains numerous correspondences of this kind which hold the construction together. Correspondence exists between νεκροὺς τοῖς παραπτώμασιν (2×) and συνεζωοποίησεν; between τὸν αἰῶνα τοῦ κόσμου τούτου and τοῖς αἰῶσιν τοῖς ἐπερχομένοις; between υἱοὶ τῆς ἀπειθείας and τέκνα ὀργῆς; between the expressions πλούσιος ὢν ἐν ἐλέει διὰ τὴν πολλὴν ἀγάπην αὐτοῦ ἣν ἠγάπησεν and τὸ ὑπερβάλλον πλοῦτος τῆς χάριτος αὐτοῦ ἐν χρηστότητι and between the words συνεζωοποίησεν, συνήγειρεν and συνεκάθισεν.

In 2:10, there is correspondence between ποίημα, κτισθέντες and προητοίμασεν. In 2:18-22, there is an antithesis between the formulations ξένοι καὶ πάροικοι and συμπολῖται ... καὶ οἰκεῖοι. There is also correspondence between the various derivatives of the word οἶκος.

In Eph. 5:7-13, there is an antithesis between the words σκότος and φῶς (which are repeated); a correspondence between τέκνα φωτός and ὁ καρπὸς τοῦ φωτός; an antithesis between the expressions ὁ καρπὸς τοῦ φωτός and τοῖς ἔργοις τοῖς ἀκάρποις τοῦ σκότους and an antithesis between the word τὰ κρυφῇ and frequently recurrent combination of φῶς with φανεροῦν.

In 6:10 there is a correspondence between the words ἐνδυναμοῦσθαι, κράτος and ἰσχύς. The word combination δύνασθαι στῆναι at the beginning of the sentence 6:11, 12 reappears in the combination δυνηθῆτε ἀντιστῆναι ... καὶ στῆναι in the sentence 6:13 and the words στῆτε and δυνήσεσθε, which are featured separately in the sentence 6:14ss.

The purpose of these repetitions and combinations is that they introduce a unity into sentences which lack the well-formed construction of the Greek period.

An allied principle of unity is found in Hebrew poetry. For instance, in Ps. 71 the entire psalm revolves around the antithesis of youth and age and the combination of troubles (and enmity), deliverance and praise. The latter combination, together with the corresponding terms of calling (or prayer) and answering (or hearing), carries the weight of the construction in Ps. 69. Ps. 16 is built up around the antithetical combination of death (or sorrow) and life (or joy), whilst Ps. 12 is based on vain (or false) and pure words.

When we turn our attention to Col., we find the same phenomena as in Eph. In the long sentence Col. 1:9-20, there is the combination of ἐπίγνωσις (2×), σοφία and σύνεσις in 1:9, 10; δύναμει δυναμούμενοι and κράτος in 1:11; the antithesis of τῷ φωτί and τοῦ σκότους in 1:12, 13 and the internal correspondence of the expression πρὸ πάντων and the words πρωτότοκος (2×), κεφαλή, ἀρχή and πρωτεύων in 1:15-18.

Similar examples are also found in Romans. In the sentence R. 1:1-7, the κλητός of 1:1 returns twice, namely in 1:6 and 1:7, In the pericope 1:18-31, there is the correspondence between γνωστόν, φανερόν and ἐφανέρωσεν in 1:19 and that of ἤλλαξαν and μετήλλαξαν (2×) in 1:23-26. The construction of R. 3:21-26 is held together by the combination of δικαιοσύνη (4×), δικαιοῦν, δικαιοῦσθαι and δίκαιος, the combination of πεφανέρωται and μαρτυρουμένη and the repetition of the word πίστις (3×) which is combined with πιστεύοντας.

All this bespeaks the predilection for pauses which has already been discussed. This preference is also exemplified by the usage of directly linked verbs and substantives which derive from the same root. Often, it concerns the figura etymologica. The phenomenon has an aesthetic purpose and was probably intended to intensify a given expression. In Col., it appears less frequently and it is not alien to the HP.[1]

Equally intensive, aesthetic in nature and connected with the tendency for pauses are the exalted formulation τὸ ὑπερβάλλον μέγεθος τῆς δυνάμεως αὐτοῦ (1:19), τὸ ὑπερβάλλον πλοῦτος τῆς χάριτος αὐτοῦ (2:7) and τὸ ἀνεξιχνίαστον πλοῦτος τοῦ Χριστοῦ (3:8). The exalted character is in itself a normal Greek phenomenon, fully in keeping with the epideictic oration.[2] The prominence of genitives in the first two formulation suggests a Hebrew stimulus and is reminiscent of Ps. 145:7.

As is the case with Col. and Phil., Eph. makes a remarkably extensive use of the word πᾶς. This again serves to intensify and exalt. In addition, it helps to shape the epistle into a homogeneous unit just as sometimes in Hebrew poetry the word "all" contributes in consolidating the unity of a composition, cf. Ps. 145 and Ps. 34.[3]

---

[1] Cf. Percy, Probleme, p. 32. The relevant places in Eph. are 1:3, 6, 19s, 21, 23; 2:4; 4:1, 8 and 6:18. In Col. they are 1:11, 29; 2:11,19 and 3:16. Apart from the places quoted by Percy, the following may be mentioned : 1 C. 5:6; 10:4; 2 C. 11:7 and Gal. 5:1. For the aesthetic value, see Lausberg, para. 503, 604 and 648 and König, Stilistik, Rhetorik, Phetorik i. B. a.d. Bibl. Literatur, p. 287.

[2] Cf. Quintiliani Institutio oratio 3, 7, 6 ("proprium laudis est res amplificare et ornare"), in Lausberg, p. 55. Also see Lausberg, para. 503.

[3] According to Morgethaler's statistics, the frequency of πᾶς in the CP minus is : R. 1/14; 1 C. 1/8; 2 C. 1/12; Gal. 1/21; Eph. 1/7; Phil. 1/7; Col. 1/6; 1 Th. 1/12; 2 Th. 1/17; Phlm. 1/23.

12. AESTHETIC DEVICES

It is clear that the author of Eph. was also concerned with beauty. Thus the first fragment of the eulogy contains four words which end with the sound ου. This includes the last word. The ου sound recurs again at the end (and also within various fragments) of a number of fragments. Also the last fragment ends with this sound.

In Eph. 1:23 τὸ πλήρωμα τοῦ τὰ πάντα ἐν πᾶσιν πληρουμένου the combination of consonants π(λρμ)πππ(λρμ) captures the attention.[1]

In Eph. 5:15 βλέπετε οὖν ἀκριβῶς πῶς περιπατεῖτε μὴ ὡς ἄσοφοι ἀλλ' ὡς σοφοί the frequency of the consonant π in the first part is striking. The same applies to the ὡς sound which is reiterated throughout the entire sentence. In Eph. 4:9, the sound of η is constantly repeated, culminating with a climax ηη in μέρη τῆς γῆς.[2]

In Eph. 2:7, 8 the combination ρχ in ἐπερχομένοι precedes the quadrupled combination χρ in χάρις, χρηστότης, Χριστός. The identical χρ combination appears at larger intervals four times in Eph. 4:28, 29 and four times in Eph. 4:32.

In 3:12, four words begin with the consonant π. This consonant is reduplicated in one of the words. A little further on in 3:19, the π once again plays a part in πληρωθῆτε εἰς πᾶν τὸ πλήρωμα τοῦ θεοῦ just as it does in the words πάντα ποιῆσαι ὑπερεκπερισσοῦ at the beginning of the subsequent doxology, in Eph. 3:20.

Such aesthetic devices are not absent in the HP. In 1 C. 15:39-41 there are the recurrent sounds of αλλα and ἀλλη. In 2 C. 8:22 there is a repetition of the sound πολλ and the sound σπουδ. In 2 C. 7:4 the sound πολλ and the combination of consonants πρ recur whilst they

---

[1] Generally, such a cumulation of identical consonants is not desirable according to ancient rhetorical opinion (cf. Lausberg, para. 975), but this ending to a pericope deserves a positive rating on those terms (cf. op. cit., para. 637-639 and 800-803, annominatio and commutatio). Norden (Antike Kunstprosa I, pp. 57ss. and 29) reveals that the Greeks were sensitive to pleasant sounds. They had a preference for certain letters and were wont to place these at the beginning of a number of consecutive words. From his examples it appears that for example, π, πλ and πρ were desired. The σ was not desirable (cf. note 2 on p. 58).

[2] The reappearance of the same vowel or vowels could have something to do with a Semitic sensitivity for correspondence in vowels. König, Stilistik, gives examples of repetitions of the same vowel and vowels in the Hebrew O.T. (cf. p. 290 where he speaks of "Assonanz" or "vokalischer Gleichklang" (assonance or harmonious vowelization).

are strengthened by the combination ππλρ in the word πεπλήρωμα. In R. 1:29 the consonant π and the combination πλ come back in the beginning of the words πεπληρωμένους πάση (ἀδικία) πονηρία πλεονεξία. In the passage 1 C. 15 : 39 which has already been mentioned, the sounds η and ω play an important part.

The use of the isocolon also contributes to the mellifluence of Eph. Again and again there is a correspondence in the number of syllables in parallel sentences or parallel sentence-parts.[1] Thus the phrases ἐλπίδα μὴ ἔχοντες and ἄθεοι ἐν τῷ κόσμῳ in Eph. 2:12 which are connected by καί, each have 7 syllables. In Eph. 2:13, the antithetic phrases οἵ ποτε ὄντες μακράν and ἐγένηθητε ἐγγύς which, if not syntactically related are at least logycally of a like order, both contain 7 syllables.[2] In 2:14, each of the two phrases ὁ ποιήσας τὰ ἀμφότερα ἕν and τὸ μεσότοιχον τοῦ φραγμοῖ λυσᾶς which are again connected by καί, have 10 syllables.

If ἡ εἰρήνη is scanned with crasis, the preceding sentence is also composed of 10 syllables. The phrase ἀποκτείνας τὴν ἔχθραν ἐν αὐτῷ which concludes the complex of thoughts relating to peace at the end of 2:16 is likewise formed by 10 syllables.

In the phrases ἕν σῶμα and ἕν πνεῦμα connected by καί in Eph. 4:4 each has three syllables and the phrases εἷς κύριος, μία πίστις, and ἕν βάπτισμα all contain 4.

More or less isocolic are the closer definitions describing the path of the unbelievers in 4:17 (end) and 18 (resp. 11, 12, 13, 12 and 12 syllables) which, although differing in the matter of syntax are logically in agreement.

The sentences καθὼς καὶ ὁ Χριστὸς ἠγάπησεν ὑμᾶς — καὶ παρέδωκεν ἑαυτὸν ὑπὲρ ἡμῶν (5:2); ὑποτασσόμενοι ἀλλήλοις ἐν φόβῳ Χριστοῦ — αἱ γυναῖκες τοῖς ἰδίοις ἀνδράσιν ὡς τῷ κυρίῳ (5:21, 22) and ὅτι ἀνήρ ἐστιν κεφαλὴ τῆς γυναικός — ὡς καὶ ὁ Χριστὸς κεφαλὴ τῆς ἐκκλησίας (5:23) can be divided into like or similar fragments along the lines described.

---

[1] Is his work περὶ Ἑρμηνείας (par. 25), the retor Demetrius maintains that the cola of the isocolon have the same number of syllables (cf. K. Ohly, Stichometrische Untersuchungen, Zentralblatt für Bibliothekwesen, Beiheft 61, Leipzig 1928, p. 23). As a rule, isocola were merely formed by an identical number of words and an identical syntactical arrangement. That an equal munber of syllables was considered to be one of the ideals of mellifluence can be deduced from the frantic attempts of later theoreticians to discover syllabic identity in the isocolon (cf. Lausberg, para. 721 and para. 1246, s.v. macrocole).

[2] Cf. Lausberg, op. cit. para. 738.

Isocolism may also occur where there is no parallelism; thus it is found in Eph. 4:9, 10 τὸ δὲ ἀνέβη — τί ἐστιν εἰ μή — ὅτι καὶ κατέβη — εἰς τὰ κατώτερα μέρη τῆς γῆς — ὁ καταβὰς αὐτός ἐστιν καὶ ὁ ἀναβάς — ὑπεράνω πάντων τῶν οὐρανῶν (resp. 5, 5, 6, 10, 13 and 10 syllables) and in 4:15 ἀληθεύοντες δε ἐν ἀγάπη — αὐξήσωμεν εἰς αὐτὸν τὰ πάντα (each containing 10 syllables).

In 4:8 we meet an Old Testament quotation which diverges from both the Hebrew original and the LXX version.[1] Isocolism is there seen in the phrases ᾐχμαλώτευσεν αἰχμαλωσίαν and ἔδωκεν δόματα τοῖς ἀνθρώποις.

Isocoliom also occurs in the HP. In R. 13:7, 8 there is a series of successive cola with resp. 10, 7, 7, 7, 7, 9, 9 syllables: In R. 13:12, two exhortations in the first person plural follow one after another, each with 12 syllables and in R. 13:13, there are three characterisations defining bad conduct with respective lengths of 6, 8 and 7 syllables. In R. 14:3, the two commands are respectively 16 and 15 syllables long and in R. 14:18, the substantive part consists of two cola, connected by καί, of 7 syllables each. The R. 15:14 sentence ends in two participial constructions, each of 11 syllables. In Phil. 3:3s., we find a sentence which can be divided into five cola of a respective 10, 10, 10, 9 and 14 syllabic length. Examples of isocolism are also found in 1 and 2 C.[2]

13. GRAMMATICAL DETAILS

A number of grammatical details are deserving of attention. More often than is usual in the other epistles of the CPminus, the article is placed before the mere designation Χριστός in Eph.[3] Eph. as a general

---

[1] M. McNamara, "Targumic Studies", The Catholic Biblical Quarterly 28, 1966, p. 11s., cites a remark made by T. Walker (in his article "Targum", in Hastings' Dictionary of the Bible) which has been previously quoted with approval by J. Rendel Harris ("Traces of Targumism in the New Testament", Exp. T. 32, 1920/21, p. 374) : "We find in the N.T. traces of Aramaic renderings of Heb. verses in books like the Psalms." As an example, Walker named the rendering of Ps. 68:19 in Eph. 4:8.

[2] 1 C. 6:12, 13; 7:14; 10:4, 9, 16; 12:4-6, 13, 26, 28; 15:38, 41, 42, 43; 2 C. 4:8, 10 and 11.

[3] In the survey below, for each epistle is given first the number of times when the mere indication Χριστός is preceded by the article and then the munber of times when the indication is used without an article : R. 8-26; 1 C. 14-30; 2 C. 3-20; Gal. 4-14;

rule displays a strong tendency to use the article. This same tendency is found to some extent in Col. but in a lesser degree.[1]

The nominative $αὐτός$ is repeatedly used as the pron. pres. of the 3rd. pers. sing. This nominative is also used in the sole instance in the other epistles where a pron. pers. of the 3rd. pres. sing. is featured, i.e. in 2 C. 10:7, where $αὐτός$ corresponds with $ἡμεῖς$.[2] The nominative plural $αὐτοί$ is often used in the CP as a pronomen personale (R. 11:31; 2 C. 6:16; 10:12; 1 Th. 2:14).

There is a particular aspect to the use of the nominative singular $αὐτός$ in Eph. It is redolent of the use of the pronomen personale in the Semitic languages. In Eph. 4:10, the $αὐτος$ of $ὁ$ $καταβὰς$ $αὐτός$ $ἐστιν$ $καὶ$ $ὁ$ $ἀναβάς$ is reminiscent of the Hebrew or Aramaic הוא which is used to precipitate a substantive which has assumed the function of a subject even before the predicate is given and then intimates that the subject has remained unchanged.[3] The $αὐτός$ of $αὐτὸς$ $ἔδωκεν$ in Eph. 4:11 accentuates that the subject under discussion is still the the same paradoxical personality mentioned in Eph. 4:10. This device is as superfluous as the Hebrew הוא or אֲנִי before a verb or at the beginning of a sentence can be and its sole function is an aesthetic one.[4]

Eph. 21-7; Phil. 1-2; Col. 11-8; 1 Th. 1-2; 2 Th. 1-0; Phlm. 0-2. Turner in Moulton, A Grammar of N.T. Greek, Vol. III, XII, para. 1, p. 167 comments : "The epistles also usually omit the article with $Χριστός$; it is here regarded as a proper name rather than = Messiah, probably reflecting a development in Christology. But in Col. 2⁶ the author reverts to the earlier designation of $Χριστός$ as a title = Messiah.". If that is so, then Eph. reverts strongly to an older linguistic usage. However, it must be borne in mind that in one certain case there is also in the other epistles a preference for using this designation with the article, i.e. when it is expressed in the genitive. E.g., we find in R. 5 times $τοῦ$ $Χριστοῦ$ and 4 times $Χριστοῦ$; in 1 C. 8 times $τοῦ$ $Χριστοῦ$ as against 10 times $Χριστοῦ$ and in Col. 7 times $τοῦ$ $Χριστοῦ$ as against $Χριστοῦ$ but once.

[1] We give the frequency of the article in two decimals : R. 1/0.90; 1 C. 1/1,06; 2 C. 1/1.15; Gal. 1/1.10; Eph. 1/0.76; Phil. 1/1.19; Col. 1/0.85; 1 Th. 1/1.10; 2 Th. 1/1 and Phlm. 1/1.27. See Morgenthaler, Statistik, pp. 55 and 124 and the graph at the end.

[2] The $ἐκεῖνος$ in 2 C. 10:18 is not used as a pron. pers. but functions purely as a pron. demonstrativum. If the sentence were complete, $οὗτος$ would have to balance the $ἐκεῖνος$. In R. 8:9 and 1 C. 8:3, the $οὗτος$ is also a demonstrative and refers to the preceding $τις$.

[3] E.g. in Gen. 15:4 and 24:7; cf. Ges.-K., para. 135a Note 2. Beside from the words from Eph. 4:10, one could put the words עֵשָׂו הוּא אֱדֹום (LXX $Ησαν$ $αὐτός$ $ἐστιν$ $Εδωμ$) in Gen. 36:8. הוא or $αὐτός$ indicate that the expressions are identical.

[4] Essentially superfluous, הוא already occurs in the places in Gen. 15 and 24 quoted in note 3. Although the pronomen in Is. 53:5, 7 and 12 introduces a certain contrast, it is still more or less unnecessary. An overt unnecessary use of the pron. pers. אֲנִי occurs

The αὐτός in Eph. 2:14 is emphatic as becomes obvious through the subsequent γάρ. Comparable to the sentence with αὐτός in Eph. 2:14 are corresponding sentences (or clauses) with αὐτός in the LXX and the N.T., i.e. Da. 4:37; 6:27; Mat. 11:14; 16:20 and Acts 14:12. In Da. 6:27, αὐτὸς(γάρ ἐστι) corresponds to הוּא at the beginning of a nominal sentence. Probable is that the lost Aramaic text of Da. 4:37 used הוּא in the same way.[1] The statements in Da. are of a confessional nature and are doxological in character. Eph. 2:14 is also confessional in mood.[2]

In Col the nominative αὐτός is also repeatedly used as a pron. personale. If the καὶ αὐτός ἐστιν πρὸ πάντων of Col 1:17 were not followed directly by a second καὶ αὐτός ἐστιν in Col. 1:18, the nominative αὐτός in the sentence καὶ αὐτὸς ἐστιν πρὸ πάντων could be interpreted as determinative but through the repetition, an emphatic "he" is the probable meaning in both cases.[3] Here, therefore is an

---

in Is. 38:10 אֲנִי אָמַרְתִּי. Ges.-K., para. 135b note 1 : "Bisweilen scheint jedoch das Pron. sep. mehr aus rhytmischen Gründen (d.h. um an Stelle der nackten Verbalform einer voller tönende Aussage zu erhalten, analog dem Inf. abs.) dem Verb vorausgeschickt zu sein ... Aus demselben Grunde erklärt sich אֲנִי an der Spitze von Sätzen ..."

("However, it would seem that sometimes, for purposes connected with rhythm, (i.e. to achieve, instead of the naked verbal sound, a full, resounding declaration, analogous to the inf. abs.) the pron. sep. was nevertheless dispatched ahead of the verb ... The אֲנִי at the climax of sentences can be explained on the same grounds") Carl Brockelmann, Grundrisz der vergleichenden Grammatik der semitischen Sparchen II (Berlin 1913), para. 63b. comments on the tendency of the pron. pers. to become increasingly less important. Judging by Is. 38:10, this tendency is already present in Hebrew. It becomes stronger in Aramaic and especially striking in Syrian and the Aramaic of Christian Palestine.

[1] In late Aramaic such a הוּא is followed by a second הוּא as a copulative. See G, Dalman, Gr. ³1960, p. 107. Cf. also A. Ugnad, Syrische Grammatik (München ³1932), para. 9e (or Th. Nöldeke, Kurzgef. Syr. Gramm. para. 227) for the Syrian corresponding equivalent ܗܘ to הוּא הוּא.

[2] Percy, Probleme, p. 40s. sees a relationship between sentences featuring αὐτος with the οὗτος predicates on which Norden, Agnostos Theos., pp. 163ss. and 187s. commented. In as far as sentences with οὗτός ἐστι are derived from a Hebrew or Aramaic source of influence, in my opinion a demonstrative underlies this αὐτός; cf. the reiterated זֶה in Is. 15:9 and the דֵין הוּא and הַדֵין הוּא in Talmud and Targumim (see Dalman, Gr., pp. 107, 108, 111 and 112 and Jesus-Jeschua, Leipsig 1922, p. 129ss.).

[3] Turner, in Moulton, A Grammar of N.T. Greek III, Syntax, V para. 3, p. 40, thinks that in both these places αὐτός is pron. pers. and emphatic. He translated αὐτός in Col. 1:17 as "he and no other" and in Col. 1:18 (καὶ αὐτός ἐστιν ἡ κεφαλή) as "he himself (alone)".

αὐτός which is like the αὐτός in Eph. 2:14. The αὐτός in the sentence
ἵνα γένηται ἐν πᾶσιν αὐτὸς πρωτεύων (Col. 1:18) is like the αὐτός in
καὶ αὐτὸς ἔδωκεν (Eph. 4:11), it confirms that the person in question
is still the same as in the preceding and is rather redundant.

In both epistles, the casus obliqui of αὐτός are used to a remarkable
extent. This suggests a Semitic influence as well as a concession to
colloquial usage. The fact that there is a tendency in Eph. to use the
genitive αὐτοῦ with its ου sound at the end, is connected with an
aesthetic motivation.[1]

The adjunct ἐν αὐτῷ is used in an extraordinary way in Eph.
1:4, 9 and 2:16 where it more or less repeats the subject of the verbs
ἐξελέξατο, προέθετο and ἀποκτείνας. During the Hellenistic period,
writers were partial to the substitution of ἐν with a dative for the
simple dative. Sometimes this ἐν cum dativo replaced ὑπό with the
genitive and indicated the active party in a construction using a
passive verb. It is possible that it was used along similar lines in
the abovementioned constructions, being welded in to give a further
and unnecessary mention of the active person.

Another possibility is that we are here confronted with a Semitic
ethical dative which refers to the subject.[2]

---

[1] For this motivation see p. 165.

The frequency of the collected cases αὐτοῦ, αὐτῷ and αὐτόν are : R. 1/14; 1 C.
1/26, 2 C. 1/26; Gal. 1/28; Eph. 1/7; Phil. 1/12; Col. 1/17; 1 Th. 1/30; 2 Th. 1/10 and
Phlm. 1/15.

The frequency of αὐτοῦ is : R. 1/23; 1 C. 1/48; 2 C. 1/42; Gal. 1/63; Eph. 1/10; Phil.
1/33; Col. 1/15: 1 Th. 1/42; 2 Th. 1/19 and Phlm. 0/46.

The frequency of αὐτῷ is ; R. 1/71; 1 C. 1/114.5; 2 C. 90.5; Gal. 1/104; Eph. 1/37.5
Phil. 1/77; Col. 1/18.5; 1 Th. 1/105.5; 2Th. 1/57 and Phim. 0/46.

The frequency of αὐτόν is : R. 1/67; 1 C. 1/114.5; 2 C. 1/317; Gal. 1/104; Eph. 1/68;
Phil. 1/25.5; Col. 1/44; 1Th. 0/211; 2 Th. 1/38 and Phlm. 1/15.

Norden finds a high frequency of the casus obliqui of αὐτός typical of "Judengriechisch"
("Jewish Greek"; cf. Antike Kunstprosa, p. 484, p. 506 Note 2 and Nachträge, p. 2).

Blasz sees the repeated use of the possessive genitives μου, σου and αὐτοῦ as an adaptation to colloquial usage and the result of Semitic influences (cf. Bl.-Bebr. para. 278).
Frequencies have been established on the basis of Morgenthaler, Statistik, p. 158.

[2] For the substitution of ἐν cum dativo for a simple dative, see A. N. Iannaris, An
historical Greek Grammar (London 1897), para. 1562.

A. Pallis, To the Romans, A Commentary (London 1920), p. 43 and on R. 1:19 proposes
that a preference for this idiom (as a result of its frequency in the LXX) led to the use
of ἐν αὐτῷ instead of ὑπ' αὐτοῦ and even to the insertion of this ἐν αὐτῷ with active
verbs as a sort of reiteration of the subject. Turner, (Moulton, A Grammar of N.T. Greek
III, Syntax V, para. 2b, p. 41) believes that the ἐν αὐτῷ of Eph. 2:16 stands for ἐν ἑαυτῷ.

In Eph. 1:10 the preposition ἐπί is used with the dative to indicate precise the locality .Elsewhere in the CP ἐπί is not used in this way. In Eph. 1:10 this ἐπί is followed directly by another ἐπί with the genitive. For the sake of a variatio, quae delectat, the author has deliberately switched the cases.[1]

In Eph. 3:19 the verb πληροῦσθαι occurs in conjunction with an adverbial adjunct introduced by εἰς; if this adjunct serves to indicate the fulness which fills, we are here confronted with an exception in Pauline literature. In Eph. 5:18, the fulness which fills, using the same verb, is indicated by ἐν and the dative as in usual in the CP. This correspondence with current language lessens the likelihood of a deviation in Eph. 3:19. What is more probable is that in Eph. 3:19 πληροῦσθαι is used absolutely and that the adjunct introduced by εἰς indicates the measure of fulness. In that case at least one of the objections E. Haupt holds against the authenticity of Eph. is unfounded.[2]

The Nestle text gives the following reading in Eph. 1:17 ἵνα ὁ θεὸς ... δώῃ A final optative in a dependent clause is an atticism. It is found nowhere else in the CP or the rest of the N,T. If this reading of Eph. 1:17 is the correct one and if such an atticism really does occur, it would be astonishing. However, it could be that the conjunctive δώῃ. is intended by this δώῃ. It could also be that this is indeed a final optative in a dependent clause, using a contracted form of the stereotype formula δώῃ θεός. We find the formula in its direct form in the blessings of R. 15:5 ὁ δὲ θεὸς ... δώῃ and in 2 Th. 3:16 αὐτὸς δὲ ὁ κύριος ... δώῃ. If there is an optative in Eph. 1:17, it would be in accordance with CP linguistics that this optative should be an optativus aoristi; every optative in the CP is an optativus aoristi.[3]

He also thinks it possible that the ἐν αὐτῷ in Eph. 2:16 refers to τοῦ σταυροῦ. For the dativus ethicus referring to the subject, see Ugnad, Syrische Grammatik, para. 13b.

[1] In classical Greek ἐπί in this sense is generally used with a genitive, in prose. It can also be combined with the dative; poets use whatever case suits the metre (cf. Liddell-Scott, s.v. B, I). For the aesthetic motivation, cf. Abbott on Eph. 1:10 : "The variation in case after the same preposition has frequent parallels in classical writers.".

[2] The fulness that fills is indicated by, a dative in the CP (R. 1:29; 2 C. 7:4), an accusative (Phil. 1:11; Col. 1:9) or by ἐν with the dative (Gal. 5:14). Phil. 4:18 corroborates that πληροῦσθαι can be used absolutely. The fact that an adjunct introduced by εἰς indicates degree or intensity can also be seen in 2 C. 10:15 (εἰς περισσείαν) and 2 C. 4:17 (εἰς ὑπερβολὴν αἰώνιον βάρος δόξης; (cf. A. Oepke, Th. W. II, p. 25-41). For Haupt's objections, see his Gefbr., Einleitung, p. 54.

[3] In the margin in Nestle, we find the reading δῷ (B1739), For the possibility of

The independent ἵνα with a coniunctivus praesentis in Eph. 5:33 tallies completely with the linguistic practises of the HP.[1]

Eph. makes less use of the substantiated infinitive than the other epistles in the CPminus. Whenever an infinitive without article occurs in this epistle, it is more frequently than in the other epistles an infinitive of intention or result. Both these peculiarities also occur in Col. with an increased frequency.[2]

Eph. 5:5, like Col. 3:14, has an ἐστιν preceded by a relative in which, contrary to the rest of the CP, the relative element does not correspond in gender with the correlative or the predicate.[3]

Thus Eph. does have some grammatical idiosyncraries. Sometimes, these have a Semitic complexion. But it could not, however, be said that Eph. distinguishes itself strongly from the rest of the CPminus with respect to grammar. Moreover, there is a close affinity between Eph. and Col.

---

a confusion between the optative δῴη and the conjunctive δώῃ, see Bl.-Debr., para. 95,2. For the possiblility that δῴη θεός is a stereotype formula, see Radermacher, p. 97 ("Ein Opt. δῴη ist genügend bezeugt, ausserdem noch δοίη, δόῃ, δοῖ. In der Wunschformel δῴη θεός und Verwandtem haben sich diese Gebilde lebendig im Volsbewusstsein erhalten"—An opt. δῴη has been sufficiently attested, also δοίη, δόῃ, δοῖ. In the formula of request δῴη θεός and the like, these forms have remained vivid in the popular consciousness). For the optativus aoristi as used in the CP, see Moulton, Grammar of the N.T. Greek, Introd., p. 307 note 2. Turner, Moulton Grammar III, Syntax IX, para. 2c, p. 128s, thinks it impossible that the N.T. contains the atticism of a final optative in a dependent position. He comments on 1:17, e.g. "and in any case the ἵνα may be imperatival ..."

[1] An independent ἵνα with a conjunctive is found in the N.T. in Mk. 5:23; 2 C. 8:7; Gal. 2:10; Eph. 5:33 and Apoc. 14:13. In the CP places, the coniunctivus praes. is found and in the other places, the coniunctivus aoristi.

[2] I found the following frequencies of the substatiated infinitive : R. 1/29; 1 C. 1/62; 2 C. 1/35; Gal. 1/62; Eph. 1/113; Phil. 1/16; Col. 0/230; 1 Th. 1/21; 2 Th. 1/16 and Phlm. 0/46. It is not surprising that the tiny Phlm. work should not contain a substantiated infinitive. The infinitive of intent or result is different from the ordinary complementary inf. in that it states in an action which is already complete in itself, what the aim or result of that action is (cf. Bl.-Debr., para. 390-392 and J. de Zwaan, Syntaxis der wijzen en tijden in het Griekse N.T. (Haarlem 1906), para. 358, 360 and 361.). In the CP this inf. is found only in R. 1:28; 1 C. 1:17; 2 C. 9:5; 11:2,32; Gal. 1:18; Eph. 3:16, 19; Col. 1:10, 22 and 4:3. Eph. and Col. therefore have a higher frequency of this infinitive.

[3] Percy wrote about this (Probleme, p. 33s.).

14. WORDS USED IN A COMMON AND IN AN UNCOMMON WAY AND UNUSUAL EXPRESSIONS.

We shall now devote some attention to commonly and uncommonly used words in Eph. and to some unusual expressions. For a long time the number of words in Eph. which do not occur in the rest of the N.T. or the CP, the so-called hapax legomena, counted as an objection against the authenticity of the epistle. But a close comparison of the frequencies of hapax legomena in the various epistles of the CPminus reveals that their number in Eph. is in no way out of the ordinary.[1]

What is out of the ordinary is that Eph. has 10 or 11 words in common with Col. which occur nowhere else in the N.T. to which can be added another 10 or 11 words which occur nowhere else in the CP. No other pair of epistles in the CPminus has relatively so many words of this kind in common. In this large number of dis legomena, the close relationship between Eph. and Col once again manifests itself.[2]

This relationship also shows itself in the common tendency of both epistles to use words which are formed through combinations of different words wherein adjectives, substantives or the roots of verbs are conjoined. Col. has a greater number of these than Eph.[3]

---

[1] The most thorough comparison of hapax legomena is given by Grayston and Herdan (who use the more correct term "one sample words"). See the exhaustive account of their research in Chapter I, para. 5. I found the following incidence of N.T. hapax legomena : R. 1/10; 1 C. 1/10; 2 C. 1/7; Gal. 1/11; Eph. 1/8; Phil. 1/6.5; Col. 1/6.5; 1 Th. 1/14; 2 Th. 1/16 and Phlm. 1/9. The frequency of hapax legomena within the CP is according to Morgenthaler (Statistik, p. 173) : R. 1/3.5; (auth. 1/4); 1 C. 1/4; 2 C. 1/3.5 (auth. 1/3); Gal. 1/3 (auth. 1/4); Eph. 1/4 (auth. 1/3.5); Phil. 1/3; Col. 1/3 (auth. 1/4) 1 and 2 Th. together 1/6 (auth. 1/5 or 1 Th. 1/5.5 and 2 Th. 1/5); Phlm. 1/5 (auth. 1/6). Percy (Probleme, p. 179s.) added to the words in Eph. which do not occur in the rest of the N.T. also the words in Eph. which do occur in the N.T. but not in R., 1, 2 C., Gal., Phil., Col., 1 Th. and Phlm. and furthermore included words which are common to Eph. and Col. which do occur in the N.T. but not in R., 1 and 2 C., Gal., Phil., 1 Th. and Phlm. He thus arrived at 116 hapax legomena in Eph. The corresponding frequencies were established to be Phil. 73 and Col. 86. (The frequencies are then resp. 1/3, 1/3 and 1/2.5.)

[2] The 10 words which are common to Eph. and Col. which do not occur elsewhere in the N.T. are : ἀνθρωπάρεσκος, ἀπαλλοτριοῦσθαι, ἀποκαταλλάσσειν, αὔξησις, ἁφή, ὀφθαλμοδουλία, ῥιζοῦσθαι, συζωοποιεῖν, συνεγείρειν and ὕμνος.

[3] The frequencies are : R. 1/36; 1 C. 1/42; 2 C. 1/30: Gal. 1/26; Eph. 1/15; Phil. 1/33; Col. 1/10; 1 Th. 1/19; 2 Th. 1/57 and Phlm. 0/46. (These frequencies were established on the basis of Bruders concordantiae, ²1853 and Nestle's N.T. Graece, ¹⁷1941. The word ἀκροβυστία was not counted because the root βυστ had already long since fallen into disuse.)

The two epistles have an additional affinity in that both lack relatively many words which are frequently used in the rest of the CP. Col. has even slightly fewer of them than Eph. However, these words make an even more infrequent appearance in both 1 and 2 Th.[1] The fairly strong leaning towards the use of dicomposita in Col. is not present in Eph.[2]

It has been unjustly asserted that matters which are indicated through certain words in the HP have been reconstructed with different words in Eph. For example, instead of the hapax legomenon διάβολος in Eph., σατανᾶς is supposed to be the word always found in the HP. Now the fact is that the words διάβολος and σατανᾶς are used indiscriminately[3] and that the name σατανᾶς occurs only on eight occasions in the CPminus. Taking into account the low frequency of the word σατανᾶς in the CPminus, it does not seem a justified proposition to me that in a genuine Pauline work "the devil" cannot be indicated through the word διάβολος. 2 C. 6:15 and 1 Th. 3:5 moreover prove that in an authentic Pauline work other appellations for this creature definitely were used. In the above-mentioned cases, the names Βελίαρ and ὁ πειράζων are found.

Equally unobjectionable is the designation τὰ πνευματικὰ (τῆς πονηρίας) in Eph. 6:12 for τὰ πνεύματα. In the HP a neuter plural followed by a genitive is often used to indicate the categoric number of persons or things involved.[4] Furthermore, the plural πνεύματα occurs so rarely in the HP that it would be impossible to call this expression the usual one. This particular plural is found exclusively in 1 C. 12:10; 14:12 and 32 and then in a fairly narrow context and overwhelmingly in bono sensu. Finally, the various reading of 1 C. 14:12 suggesto that πνεύματα and πνευματικά can be used indiscriminately.[5]

---

[1] See Morgenthaler, Statistik, pp. 54 and 184. Morgenthaler calculates for Eph., Col., 1 and 2 Th. resp. 8, 9, 12 and 19 missing words.

[2] Cf. op. cit., p. 161s.

[3] For the objection see de Wette, Lehrbuch, p. 258ss. In Jn., Acts., 1 Tm. and Rev., σατανᾶς and διαβολος are used indiscriminately.

[4] See Bl.-Debr., para. 263,4. De Wette objected to τὰ πνευματικά.

[5] De Wette (loc. cit.) also objected to τὸ σωτήριον instead of ἡ σωτηρία in Eph. 6:17. The term ἡ περικεφαλαία τοῦ σωτηρίου in Eph. 6:17 is sufficiently explained by the περικεφαλαία σωτηρίου in LXX Is. 59:17. Besides, the words ἡ σωτηρία and τὸ σωτήριον are used promiscuously in Lk. and sometimes the neuter singular of an adjective is found in the HP in place of the corresponding abstract substantive. In that case, the neuter is somewhat more concrete in meaning (cf. A.v. Veldhuizen. Het taaleigen des

But it is true that a number of words are used differently in Eph. than in the rest of the CP. One instance of a word used in an unusual way is οἰκονομία in Eph. 1:10 and 3:9. It is indicative of a (godly) scheme or a (godly) dispensation. Elsewhere in the CPminus, the word is not used in that sense. However, the word is altogether so rare that no importance can be attached to this divergence. In the HP the word occurs only in 1 C. 9:17 where—as is generally assumed—it signifies the function of a οἰκονόμος (cf. 1. C. 4:1, 2). The word is also used in Col. 1:25 to describe a function which God has assigned to Paul. In this sense it is also found in Eph. 3:2. With respect to both these places, one has the impression that this designation carries overtones of an (godly) dispensation or a (godly) scheme. The apostle has been granted his function on the basis of that dispensation or scheme and must serve the realization of that plan. A transition can thus be seen in Col. 1:25 and Eph. 3:2 from the word οἰκονομία as it is intended in 1 C. 9:17 to οἰκονομία as it is intended in Eph. 1:10 and 3:9.[1]

N.T., Utrecht 1906, para. 43,8 and Bl.-Debr., para. 163,2). Herm. v. Soden, Der Epheser-brief, Jbch. pr. Th. 1887, p. 103ss. and Die Briefe an die Kol., Eph., Phlm. und die Pastoralbriefe, Hdktr. z. N.T., ²1893, p. 88s. raised objections to δέσμιος and μεθοδεία. δέσμιος however, occurs in Phlm. 1 and 9. One furthermore asks oneself what typical Pauline equivalent should have replaced μεθοδεία, since the word μέθοδος does not occur at all in the CP and the rest of the N.T. For the words τὰ ἐπουράνια and κοσμοκράτορες disputed by de Wette, see para. 3 of the next chapter.

[1] For οἰκονομία in Col. 1:25 the following interpretations have been given. Abbott, Eph.-Col. : "the office or function of a steward"; Haupt, Gefbr. : "von der Tätigkeit des Hausverwaltens, dem Haushalten" (concerning the activity of administrating the house, the household); Dib. Gefbr., ²1927 : "dem Ambt" (appertaining to the office). Another interpretation of οἰκονομία in Col. 1:25 is given by Chrysostomos who, according to Abbott, accepts the meaning "dispensation"; Grotius, who also gives the meaning "dispensatio" (Annotationes in N.T.) and Percy, who gives the translations "Haushal-tung" or "Anordnung" (to keep house or to arrange) and regards the command to the pagans to preach the gospel as the content of this "Anordnung" (Probleme, p. 344, note 9). With respect to Eph. 3:2, Erasmus (Annotationes of aantekeningen), Oltramare (Commentaire) and Dibelius (Gefbr.) think of the meaning "office or function" but the meaning "dispensatio" is found in Chrysostomos (cf. Abbott, a.1), Grotius op. cit., Abbott op. cit. ; Haupt ("Anstalt"—preparation) and Percy, (Probleme, p. 343s. : "Anordnung"—order). Here, in Eph. 3:2, Percy not only regards the command which has been given the apostle as the content of this "Anordnung" or dispensatio but also the revelation of the secret of salvation.

Michel makes it probable that there is a connotation of "dispensatio" in Col. 1:25 and Eph. 3:2 when οἰκονομία is there used to mean "office" or "function". In Th. W. V. p. 154, line 32ss., Michel writes : "Freilich ist es für die Gefbr. bezeichnend, dass ein Zweifel enstehen kann, ob οἰκονομία hier "Amt" oder "Heilsplan" Gottes meint, beides

The word περιποίησις in Eph. 1:14 also diverges in meaning from
the word περιποίησις in the rest of the CPminus; however it occurs
very seldom there (only in 1 Th. 5:9 and 2 Th. 2:14) and the difference in
meaning is, in my view, exceedingly slight.

Within the expression εἰς ἀπολύτρωσιν τῆς περιποιήσεως in Eph.,
περιποίησις is practically synonymous with ἀπολύτρωσις.[1] περιποίησις
can mean either salvation or deliverance and it is used in that sense
in Heb. 10:39. This corresponds with the meaning "to keep alive" of
the verb περιποιεῖσθαι in LXX Is. 31:5 and in Luke 17:33a (cf. Lk.
9:24 and Mk. 8:35).

In 1 Th. 5:9 and 2 Th. 2:14 περιποίησις has the literal meaning of
obtaining, but in both cases the word has an affinity with the idea
of redemption or salvation. In 2 Th. 2:14 the obtaining of the doxa
indirectly implies salvation and in the expression εἰς περιποίησιν σωτηρίας of 1 Th. 5:9 the word περιποίησις is only too clearly connected
with the concept of salvation. More often than not, the verb περιποιεῖσθαι
when it means to obtain directly, indirectly means redemption or
salvation (as in LXX Is. 43:21 and Acts. 20:28 where God is the subject.).

It is even possible that in the term εἰς περιποίησιν σωτερίας in
1 Th. we are dealing with a pendant of the expression εἰς ἀπολύτρωσιν
τῆς περιποιήσεως in Eph. 1:14. The words περιποίησις and σωτηρία can
be synonyms or words connected in meaning which have been linked

---

ist ja in den Gefbr. eng mit einander verbunden" (It is certainly characteristic of the
Capt. Epls that doubt could arise whether οἰκονομία here means "office" or "God's
design of salvation", since the two are closely connected in the Capt. Epls.)

The above-quoted opinion that both in Col. 1:25 and in Eph. 3:2 the idea of a (godly)
disposal or a (godly) plan is present, can also be found in J. Reumann, "οἰκονομία-Terms
in Paul in comparison with Lucan Heilsgeschichte" in N.T. St. 13, 1966/1967, pp. 161s.,
165 : ad Col. 1:25 "I do not see how the nuance of Gol's plan or administration can be
left out ..." and ad. Eph. 3:2 "Hence here, as at Col. 1:25, I incline to see a double refe-
reference : (1) to God's gospel-plan or μυστήριον and the divine administration there of;
and (2) to the role in this given to Paul as an apostle, to make this known". The Pauline
character of the expression οἰκονομία in Eph. can be elicited from Reumann's comment
(op. cit., p. 157) "Most example of οἰκονομία-terminology in Paul occur in the close
proximity to the word μυστήριον. The sole exception is 1 Cor. IX. 17 ... Μυστήριον
therefore seems an important term for understanding Paul's reference to οἰκονομία."

[1] Cf. Lake and Cadbury in Jackson-Lake I 4, p. 161s. : "the synonymous genitive
construction characteristic of Ephesians". The exegesis advocated by Percy (Probleme,
p. 188 note 15) whereby περιποίησις definitely means "God's possession" is too forced and
was already rejected by Abbott (op. cit., on Eph. 1:14) and confuted.

by a genitive construction. εἰς περεποίησιν σωτηρίας in 1 Th. corresponds to εἰς ὀργήν. It is conceivable that the subject of the sentence ὁ θεός which is also the subject of ὀργή is in the same manner the subject of περιποίησις. God has then redeemed and saved the faithful through Jesus Christ, who died. The redemption is salvation.[1]

In that case the genitive σωτηρίας is a genitivus qualitatis (as the genitive τῆς δικαιοσύνης in R. 5:17 in the expression τῆς δωρεᾶς τῆς δικαιοσύνης is a genitivus qualitatis and like the genitive τῆς ζωῆς in the expression τὸ πνεῦμα τῆς ζωῆς of R. 8:2).

Μανθάνειν with a person as the object never occurred in the Greek of pre-Christian times or in the CP. However, the pregnant expression μανθάνειν τὸν Χριστόν in Eph. 4:20 is pre-eminently in keeping with the pregnant expressions of the HP in which Christ is the object of verbs such as κερδαίνειν, γνῶναι (Phil. 3:8, 10); κηρύσσειν (1 C. 1:23; 15:12; 2 C. 1:19; 4:5; 11:4; Phil. 1:15) and προγράφειν (Gal. 3:1) A similar expression (παραλαμβάνειν τὸν Χριστὸν κ. τ. λ.) is also found in Col. 2:1.

Πράσσειν occurs in R., 1 and 2 C. and in Phil. with the sense of doing good or bad deeds. In 1 Th. 4:11, it has the meaning of "to occupy oneself with". Possibly it has the latter connotation in Eph. 6:21; but it could also be that τί πράσσω should be translated as "how I do" or "how it is with me". πράσσειν with this meaning does not occur in the rest of the CP. Nevertheless, it is a fairly widespread connotation of the word.[2]

In the past, the extent to which Eph. uses words in a different context from the rest of the CP[3] has not only been exaggerated, but

---

[1] The concept that the faithful, through the death of Jesus Christ and his —in the context of 1 Th. 5:9 even envisaged—resurrection have been made possession and that this being possession represents "redemption", is also present in R. 14:7-9 and 2 C. 5:15.

[2] Bauer, Wörterbuch zum N.T., s.v. πράσσω on 1 Th. 4:11 : "die eigenen Angelegenheiten (be)treiben"—to pursue one's own affairs. Dib. Gefbr., on Eph. 6:21 : "was ich schaffe"—what I do. Bauer, Wörterbuch, s.v. πράσσω on Eph. 6:21 : "wie ich mich befinde" — how I am. Liddell-Scott, s.v. πράσσω II : "experience certain fortunes, fare well or ill".

[3] De Wette, l c cit., mentioned besides οἰκονομία, περιποίησις and μανθάνειν also μυστήριον, πλήρωμα, αἰών, ἀφθαρσία, φωτίζειν and πληροῦσθαι ἐν or εἰς. The words μυστήριον, πλήρωμα and αἰών will be dealt with when we treat the content of the epistle. ἀφθαρσία has no different meaning in Eph. 6:24 than in R. 2:7 or 1 C. 15:42ss. (cf. Bauer, Wörterbuch, s.v. and Bultmann, theolog., p. 79, last but one line). φωτίζειν has the

scholars have also incorrectly taken the view that there is little variation in meaning to the words in the HP.

Nontheless, it repeatedly happens that a word has different meanings
within the HP. τελεῖν features in R. 13:6 with the unusual meaning, in
terms of the CP, of "to pay" and τέλος in R. 13:7 conveys the equally
unfamiliar connotation of "tribute". In R., Gal. and 1 Th., ἀκοή means
"that which is heard" whereas in 1 C. 12:17 it means "the hearing",
"hearing" (or simply "the ear").[1]

A number of unusual expressions occur in Eph. which are not
featured in the rest of the CPminus. These expressions have been
used to raise objections against the authenticity of the epistle. Examples of these are the connections ἀγαθὸς πρός τι (4:29); ἴστε γινώσκοντες (5:5); διδόναι τινά τι (1:22 and 4:11);[2] τὰ θελήματα τῆς σαρκὸς

---

same meaning in Eph. 3:9 as in 1 C. 4:5, i.e. to bring something to light that was hitherto
hidden. Apart from this φωτίζειν ὀφθαλμούς in Eph. 1:18, i.e. to grant sight to the eyes
and let them see; this is a hebrewism which is also encountered in LXX 2 Esdr. 9:8 and
Ps. 18:9. The occurrence of φωτίζειν, apart from Eph., is confined to 1 C. 4:5, πληροῦσθαι
has formally the same meaning in Eph. as in the rest of the CP minus; πληροῦσθαι ἐν
occurs in Gal. 5:14. We dealt with πληροῦσθαι εἰς in the preceding paragraph.

A. Klöpper, Der Brief an die Epheser, (Göttingen 1891), p. 27s. listed besides πράσσειν,
τὰ ἐπουράνια, σεσωσμένοι, ξένος, γενεά, ποιμήν, θυσία, προσφορά and σβεννύναι. In the CP
ξένος only occurs in R. 16:23 and Eph. 2:12, 19. The meaning of the word "host" in
R. 16:23 is secondary. γενεά is found in the CP only in Phil. 2:15, Col. 1:26 and Eph. 3:5,21.
In Phil. 2:15 γενεά in an expression deriving from the LXX, has the original meaning
of "generation". In Col. and Eph. the word is used in the plural and in the temporal sense
as also happens repeatedly in the LXX. ποιμήν is a hapax legomenon in the CP. θυσία,
προσφορά and σβεννύναι are used metaphorically not only in Eph. but also in the HP.

[1] Similarly, more could be quoted. ἰδιώτης which has a particular shade of meaning
in 1 C. 14:16, 23, 24 and indicates people who do not belong to the ἐκκλησία, lacks this
connotation in 2 C. 11:6 where it indicates a person who does not command a certain
craft or activity. φαίνεσθαι in R. 7:13 and 2 C. 13:7 means "appear" but in Phil. 2:15 it
means "shine" or "light". In R. 3:25, 26 and 2 C. 8:24 ἔνδειξις means manifestation;
the intended matter is shown. ἔνδειξις in Phil. 1:28 is "token" and the matter in question
is only hinted at.

[2] Holtzmann, Einleitung, p. 275 has reservations about these expressions. He also
objects to:

τὰ πνευματικὰ τῆς πονηρίας	(6 : 12)	ἀγαπᾶν τὴν ἐκκλησίαν	(5 : 25)
ἀγαπᾶν τὸν κύριον	(6 : 24)	ἡ ἁγία ἐκκλησία	(5 : 27)
τὰ κατώτερα μέρη τῆς γῆς	(4 : 9)	αἱ μεθοδείαι τοῦ διαβόλου	(6 : 11)
ἀγάπη μετὰ πίστεως	(6 : 23)	ἄνεμος τῆς διδασκαλίας	(4 : 14)
ἡμέρα ἀπολυτρώσεως	(4 : 30)	εἰς πάσας τὰς γενεὰς τοῦ	
αἰῶνες ἐπερχομένοι	(2 : 7)	αἰῶνος τῶν αἰώνων	(3 : 21)
τὰ ἔργα τὰ ἄκαρπα	(5 : 11)	τὸ πνεῦμα τοῦ νοός	(4 : 23).

It would be going too far to discurs all these combinations of words. We already remarked καὶ τῶν διανοιῶν (2:3);[1] διὸ λέγει (4:8 and 5:14); and αἷμα καὶ σάρξ (6:12).[2]

A closer examination reveals that some of these expressions are less unusual than would at first seem to be the case. They are fairly in keeping with the linguistic practises of the rest of the CPminus. The expression εἴ τις ἀγαθὸς πρὸς οἰκοδομὴν τῆς χρείας (Eph. 4:29) is comparable to the question καὶ πρὸς ταῦτα τίς ἱκανός (2 C. 2:16) and the expression δυνατὰ ... πρὸς καθαίρεσιν ὀχυρωμάτων (2 C. 10:4). In all three instances, the preposition πρός with the accusative is used to indicate the aim or objective in the same way as it is the case in ancient Greek, when adjectives are connected with πρός.[3]

In ἴστε γινώσκοντες we are dealing with the 2nd. person plural of the indicative.[4] G. Stählin has proved the likelihood that this expression is a specimen of the typically Pauline use of the "Beteuerungsformeln" (formalature of protestation) which entails an invocation to God, to Christ or to the knowledge of the readers.[5]

The verb διδόναι with its double accusative in Eph. 1:22 and 4:11 is a septuagintism.

It means : to make or put to. This verb, with the double accusative, is found with this meaning in the LXX as a translation of the Hebrew נתן with a double accusative. The same Hebrew verb is also translated as τιθέναι with a double accusative. The Hebrew construction is generally used when someone is acting in the fulness of might of when God acts, the latter being the most usual.

In Eph. 1:22 there is likewise question of an action of God.[6] In an

---

on the hebraic character of the combination ἀγάπη μετὰ πίστεως on p. 95. We shall revert to the connection εἰς πάσας τὰς γενεὰς τοῦ αἰῶνος τῶν αἰώνων later. The other expressions are not at all extraordinary from a grammatical point of view. It is incomprehensible why, within the small framework of the CP minus, such expressions which occur but once, should be immediately suspect.

[1] Cf. Abbott, Eph.-Col., p. XVI.

[2] Cf. Percy, Probleme, p. 184.

[3] Cf. Liddell-Scott, p. 1498 2nd. column III, 3.

[4] Liddell-Scott, s.v., εἴδω B, line 7 (p. 483 1st. column) gives ἴστε as indicative. Bauer, Wörterbuch, s.v., οἶδα (p. 1008) commented that ἴστε can be indicative or imperative. He gives 3 Macc. 3:14 as an example of the indicative.

[5] See G. Stählin, "Zum Gebrauch von Beteuerungsformeln im N.T.", Nov. Test. Vol. V, Fasc. 2/3, 1962, p. 138.

[6] נתן with a double accusative is used in Ps. 69:12 for an ordinary human action. We also find it when someone who is mighty or powerful takes action. (Moses : Deut. 1:15. A king : 1 Ki. 9:22; 1 Ch. 16;4 and 2 Ch. 8:9) Usually however, God is the subject

analogous fashion in 4:11 - following a quotation from the psalms which speaks of God and is applied to Christ—it is Christ who acts. This psalmic quotation with the words ἔδωκεν δόματα provides grounds for the repitition of ἔδωκεν in 4:11. It would seem that the idea of "giving" also persists in this ἔδωκεν with the double accusative.

In the rest of the CPminus διδόναι τινά τι does not occur, although τιθέναι τινά τι is found in R. 4:17; 1 C. 9:18 and 12:28. However, the circumstances in these passages are not quite the same. Reasons can be found why διδόναι should not have been used. R. 4:14 concerns a quotation from the LXX which has not διδόναι but τιθέναι in the relevant place. In 1 C. 12:28 which has affinities with Eph. 4:11, the ἔθετο of 12:18 returns in the ἔθετο with the double accusative in precisely the same way as a preceding ἔδωκεν is echoed in the ἔδωκεν of Eph. 4:11. In 1 C. 9:18 τιθέναι with a double accusative is used in a neutral sense and there is no question of an act of God or Christ,

The διὸ λέγει in Eph. 4:8 and 5:14 which introduced a quotation, does not occur elsewhere in the CP. Following Percy, I would like to point out that λέγει is quite often used in one way or another, with a quotation.[1] Sometimes, the words λέγει κύριος have been added to the quotation.[2]

The following expressions are less in keeping with linguistic usage in the rest of the CPminus. The combination αἷμα καὶ σάρξ in Eph. 6:12 distinguishes itself by another order from the ordinary Jewish formulation σάρξ καὶ αἷμα which appears on two occasions in the CP, i.e. in 1 C. 15:50 and Gal. 1:16. Now the usual Jewish expression is as a rule used to contrast man, the creature, with God.[3] In Eph.

---

of this נָתַן with a double accusative. (Gen. 17:5; Ex. 7:1; 23:27 and countless other places) Also, when נָתַן without double acc. is used in the sense of make or put to, God is always the subject (Gen. 17:20; 1 Ch. 17:22; Jer. 25:18; Ez. 25:5; 26:4,14; 29:10 and Mi. 6:16). נָתַן with a souble acc. is rendered as διδόναι τινά τι in LXX Ex. 7:1; 23:27 (paraphrasing); 1 Ki. 16:2; Is. 55:4; Thr. 1:13; Ez. 3:8, 17; 29:12; 30:12; 35:3; Ob. 2 and Mal. 2:9. God is always the subject. (A king as the subject is found with διδόναι τινά τι in 2 Ch. 25:16). The αὐτὸν ἔδωκεν κεφαλὴν (ὑπὲρ πάντα) τῇ ἐκκλησίᾳ of Eph. 1:22 corresponds strongly with the δέδωκά σε θεὸν Φαραω of Ex. 7:1.

[1] Percy, Probleme, p. 184 gives as examples : R. 15:10; 2 C. 6:2 and Gal. 3:16. Cf. Also R. 4:3,6; 9:15, 17, 25; 10:6, 8, 11, 16; 11:4, 9; 15:12 and Gal. 4:30.

[2] R. 12:19 and 1 C. 14:21. This is in imitation of O.T. and LXX; cf. R. 14:11 and esp. 2 C. 6:17, 18. Also in Eph. 4:8 and 5:14 κύριος could be thought of as the subject.

[3] J. Behm, Th. W. I, p. 172 line 1s. : "fester Jüdischer Begriff für den Menschen ... in seiner Kreatürlichkeit und seinem Abstand von Gott". (fixed Jewish expression for man ... in his creaturelikeness and in his distance from God.)

6:12 the point of issue is not this contradistinction, here man is placed against a non-human category. Perhaps for that reason, αἷμα has been placed first in order of succession. For according to a certain concept, humanity is connected by the same common blood.[1] The word αἷμα which is accentuated by its position, could indicate that the struggle is not against the fellow-men with whom one is joined by blood, but against a non-human category.[2] Both the plural θελήματα as well as the plural διάνοιαι which we encountered in the formulation τὰ θελήματα τῆς σαρκὸς καὶ τῶν διανοιῶν (Eph. 2:3), constitute exceptions within the CPmin in which θελήμα is otherwise always found in the singular. διάνοια is found only in Col. 1:21 and there appears in the singular form. In the LXX both words are sometimes found in the plural. However, apart from Eph. and the LXX, the singular form is the rule.[3]

There is not only discrepancy between Eph. and the other epistles of the CPminus. There is also an affinity between our epistle and those epistles. The discrepancy in terms of words and expressions is slight, the affinity is quite strong. Percy showed this affinity and devoted seven pages to the "lexicalische, semasiologische und phraseologische Berührungspunkte" (lexocographic, semasiological and phraseological points of contract) between the HP and Eph. He gives a number of words, meanings of words and expressions which occur in Eph. and are typical of the HP within the extended scope of the LXX, N.T. and ancient Christian writings.[4]

The hypotheses of Goodspeed and Mitton who deny the authenticity of Eph. and try to prove a dependence on the part of the author of Eph. upon Col. and the HP., give insufficient explanation for this striking affinity. Only a fraction of these words and expressions which are typical of the HP could automatically have found their way into the text of Eph. through imitation of fragments from the HP. The remaining typically Pauline words and expressions could not possibly have been included via this route of automatic reproduction. For we

---

[1] Loc. cit., 1. 18s. : "das Blut des Stammvaters ist das Band, das das ganze Menschengeschlecht zur Einheit zusammenschliesst." (the blood of the common ancestor is the bond which embraces the whole race of men in unity.)

[2] A different explanation in Percy, Probleme, p. 184.

[3] In Jer. 23:17 and 26 is found θελήματα and in Num. 15:39 and Jos. 5:1 διάνοιαι occurs.

[4] Percy, Probleme, p. 202-209.

find these other words and expressions in places in Eph. which, for the
rest, have no or almost no correspondence in form or content with the
places in the HP where these same words or expressions occur.

Thus the context of the word θάλπειν in Eph. (5:29) has no correspondence with the same word in 1 Th. (2:7). The same applies with regard to
the word ὑπερεκπερισσοῦ in Eph. 2:20 and 1 Th. 3:10 (5:13); the word
ὑπερβάλλων in Eph. 1:19; 2:7; 3:19 and 2 C. 3:10; 9:14 (11:23); the
connection εἴγε in Eph. 3:2; 4:21 and 2 C. 5:3; the expression ὁ ἔσω
ἄνθρωπος in Eph. 3:16 and R. 7:22 (2 C. 4:16) and the expression
ἐν ἑνὶ πνεύματι in Eph. 2:18 and 1 C. 12:13 or Phil. 1:27.

15. A new phase of a traditional jewish-hellenistic style

The study of the formal aspects of Eph. in this chapter make clear
that the Greek of Eph. does not fulfill the requirements of literary
Greek prose. The prolific use of oratio perpetua and especially the
use of a peculiar version of this form, bear witness to an inadequate
literary education (p. 112). The poverty in particles and conjunctions,
the many syntactically redundant adverbial adjuncts which are introduced by a preposition, the countless cumulations of genitives and the
repetitive element that is present in the connection of synonyms or
related words and in the parallel formulations, denude the style of all
liveliness and mobility (pp. 103, 111, 113, 122, 128). The element of
surprise is missing in the order of words. Genitives are strung together
without any inner tension. Again and again, the next genitive determines the last. One has the continuous impression of sluggishness
and verbosity.

Small wonder then that the great classicist, Norden, should have
contemplated the passages Eph. 1:3-14 and 3:1-14 with such disparagement.[1] Notwithstanding, Eph. is not entirely divorced from literary
feelings or an awareness of the demands or rhetoric. From time to time,
one encounters a sharp expression here, a few good antitheses there,
a sententia or intimations of isocolism (pp. 124; 135s.; 166s.).

---

[1] With regard to Eph. 1:3-14 he comments : "das monströseste Satzkonglomerat,
(denn von einer Periode kann man gar nicht mehr reden) das mir in griechischer Sprache
begegnet ist und dem das Anakoluth 3:1-14 würdig zur Seite steht." Agnostos Theos.,
p. 253 note 1. ("the most monstrous conglomeration of sentences (for there is no question
of a period any more) that I have encountered is in the Greek language from which the
anacoluthon of 3:1-14 stands out in splendid isolation.")

These indications, which point to education and eloquence, do suggest that the author of Eph. would have been capable of producing a somewhat superior style of Greek prose. Surely, the many cumulations of genitives and the many connected adverbial adjuncts introduced by a preposition, syntactically so totally superfluous, could have been avoided. Since therefore the author so flagrantly deviates from anything resembling a lively discourse with well-shaped sentences, one must assume that his interests lay elsewhere. In short, he was intent on offering something different.

There have always been different means of expression. Poetic language is familiar with the parallelismus membrorum which—to quote A. Jeremias—to begin with was certainly not a consciously artificial expression but "das natürliche Ergebnis schwungvoll gehobener Rede" (The natural result of buoyant, exalted oratory).[1] Hebrew poetry uses the parallelismus membrorum. According to R. Schütz, this Hebrew parallelism is not recitative but lyrical in character. Often, a thought stops to linger as is the case in a musical aria; the use of synonymy helps it to linger longer.[2] Then there are sacred incantations which play on the inner strength of the repetitions. I quote G. v. d. Leeuw : "Die Wiederholung der Worte steigert deren Macht in demselben Masze, wie die Erhöhung des Tons und der Rhythmus".[3]

Now there is in Eph. no direct rendering of the Hebrew parallelismus membrorum (p. 130s). Neither does one find an immediate repetition of the same word or words. Froms related to these two modes of expression are, however, found.

The apparent sluggishness and verbosity of style which the epistle displays, irreconcilably divorced from the requirements of Greek prose, are the result of the same predilection for pause which is characteristic of the parrallelism in Hebrew poetry. When synonymous words or words related in meaning are syndetically placed one after another (p. 128); are connected by means of the genitive (p. 122); an aleboration

---

[1] Norden wrote about the parallelismus membrorum in Die antike Kunstprosa II, p. 814ss. and in Agnostos Theos, p. 214 and 256s. He quotes the comment of A. Jeremias in Die antike Kunstprosa II, p. 815 note 3 and refers to that author's work, Die babylonysch-assyr. Vorstell. v. Leben nach dem Tode (Leipzig 1887), p. 9.

[2] See p. 161, note 2.

[3] (Quotation : The repetition of the words enhances their power to the same extent as the heightened pitch and the rhythm.) G. v. d. Leeuw, Phänomenologie der Religion (Tübingen 1933), p. 384.

is added (p. 128) and when an adverbial adjunct introduced by a preposition is followed by a similar adjunct using the same preposition with the same or a related meaning (pp. 113, 120), the intention, as in a Hebrew parallelism, is to prolong the thought.

Furthermore, there is an affinity with Hebrew poetry when a sense of unity is introduced by means of repeated words or combinations of certain words, into sentences which lack the concentrated structure of the Greek period. The identical device is used in some of the psalms to introduce some unity into a multitude of words and to prolong the thought (p. 163). Although we do not find a direct instance of the Hebrew parallelismus membrorum in Eph., we are sometimes strongly reminded of it (pp. 130s.; 139).

Granted that all these combinations betray an element of repetition, it may be said that a genuine predilection asserts itself when genitive is strung after genitive and one adjunct with a preposition is suceeded by the next (pp. 121, 113). Furthermore, the repetition of a certain connective tends to reappear after a few words. In the eulogy, the fragments ἐν αὐτῷ and ἐν Χριστῷ recur frequently and a number of fragments end with the connectives τοῦ θελήματος αὐτοῦ and τῆς χάριτος αὐτοῦ (p. 161).

All this repetition reveals the lyrical character of the style and expresses the tendency to pause and prolong the thought, as we mentioned above. However, a relationship must be recognised between this repetition and the above-mentioned sacred incantations which, through the immediate repetition of the same words, enhances the power of these words. Partly the purpose behind the repetitions in Eph. is to lend inner power to the words. This same purpose probably underlies the frequent use of a substantive and a verb with the same root, in conjunction (p. 164).

All this demonstrates that it is unfair to judge the Greek of Eph. by the criteria of Greek prose. The epistle is written in a lyrical style which has more in common with Hebrew poetry. At the same time, it is a style of powerful, intensive words.

Repetition is not the only factor which contributes to a heightened intensity of prose; we remarked above that rhythm and an increased pitch have the same effect (p. 183). In this connection I would like to comment on the number factor in Eph.; numbers play a part in thought-rhyming. Because fragments of a different character alternate, the substantial result is a rhythmic one. De Zwaan correctly spoke of a logical rhythm (pp. 158, 136). Moreover, there is a definite interplay

between short and long syllables in the thought-rhymes of Eph.
1:3-14. Some fragments have a preponderance of long syllables;
fragments with three or more long syllables at the end follow in direct
succession or after a short interval.

In addition to this, the majority of fragments end in a word with
the accent on the last syllable (p. 159s.). The number factor is also an
important factor in the constantly recurrent genitives and cumulations
of genitives. In fact, we spoke of a rhythm in genitives (p. 126).

Each of these idiosyncratic rhythmic phenomena are designed to
lend a heightened intensity and to augment the potency of the words.
Nor is there an absence of that other intensifying factor, the heightened
pitch of tone. For the rhythm of the eulogy asks for a song-like mode
of recitation (p. 160) It is indeed even conceivable that the many
perispomena at the end of fragments in Eph. 1:3-14 were intended to
bring about a heightening of pitch and thus stimulate a chant-like
oration (p. 160). And thus, again and again, we are made aware that
the prose of Eph. is no ordinary prose. The style of the epistle in lyrical,
poetic and intensive.

There is yet another aspect to the style. Eph. strives to achieve
beauty and mellifluence. The adjuncts introduced by a preposition
which have the function of clausulae, have been used partly in the
interests of aesthetics (p. 119). This interest is also served by the inter-
twinement of series of prepositions which we have called (p. 116) the
interplay of prepositions. In para. 12 of this chapter, we collated a
number of phenomena symptomatic of a striving towards beauty.

With this striving, goes the use of exalted formulations. We have
already mentioned some of these (p. 164). To this number may be added
the expresion found in 3:9 : τὴν ὑπερβάλλουσαν τῆς γνώσεως ἀγάπην.
Also the indirect interrogative clauses introduced by τίς or τί in 1:18
and 19 and 2:18 are elated in character. The same may be said of the
frequently used word πᾶς (p. 164). According to criteria of style in
ancient times, embellishment and the use of elative expressions
belonged to the epideictic, the panegyric style.[1]

"Proprium laudis est res amplificare et ornare".[2] A superabun-
dancy of words, within certain bounds, is in keeping with the epideictic
or panegyric oration.[3]

---

[1] Lausberg, Handbuch der literarischen Rhetorik, para. 61,3 (p. 55).

[2] See p. 164, note 2.

[3] Cf. Lausberg, para. 502 and 503 (p. 268s.).

With all the repetition concealed within the connections of words
that are synonymous or similar in meaning and within its parrallel
formulations, Eph. does embrace a superabundance of words. Nor
does this superabundance remain within bounds. Nevertheless, it
does lend an epideictic character to the style. Thus, the style of Eph.
is not only lyrical, poetic and intensive but also—be it not without
defects in this respect—epideictic.

The epideictic oration contains no arguments. The real epideictic
oration was a laudatory and acclamatory festive speech, to be delivered
before a festive audience. This style of speech was, however, also used
by the orators of antiquity to win the public over to a political party
or to encourage it to persevere in its choice.[1] In such cases, the acclamation became a commendation. The extolling of the good could go
side by side with disparagement and condemnation of the bad.[2]

All these strains are found in Eph. In the eulogy, the godhead is
praised and acclaimed in the presence of a festive congregation. The
laudatory tenor of the speech in addition serves to consolidate the
addressees in their chosen path.

Disparagement and condemnation are expressed when (in 2:1-3;
4:17-19 and 5:3, 4, 12-14) living in transgression and the gentiles are
discussed or when (as in 4:14) the malefic nature of heresy is expounded.

Thus, the style of Eph. transports us to the frontier dividing two
worlds. On the one hand, we have before us an acquaintance with
Greek rhetoric; on the other, a relationship with Hebrew poetry. Here,
the style of the Greek epideictic oration and the style of Hebrew lyric
poetry, are become one.

On the Semitic character of the style, we wish to expound. Further
to the already mentioned correspondences with Hebrew poetry, the
use of prepositions as a stylistic device and the interplay of prepositions
(p. 116ss.), other Semitic aspects must be brought to bear.

The prominence of genitives in a few elative formulations and the frequent use of the exaltive word $\pi\hat{a}s$ (p. 164) declare the Hebrew influence.
This influence is also manifest in the so-striking rhyming of thoughts
in Eph. It can be deduced from the psalms and the chokma of the O.T.
(pp. 136; 155s.).

The expression $\delta\iota\delta\acute{o}\nu\alpha\iota\ \tau\iota\nu\acute{a}\ \tau\iota$ and $\phi\omega\tau\acute{\iota}\zeta\epsilon\iota\nu\ \tau\sigma\grave{v}s\ \acute{o}\phi\theta\alpha\lambda\mu\sigma\upsilon s$; the two

---

[1] Cf. Lausberg, para. 61,3 and para. 538.
[2] Cf. Lausberg, para. 61,3.

plural forms $\theta\epsilon\lambda\dot{\eta}\mu\alpha\tau\alpha$ and $\delta\iota\alpha\nu\omega\hat{\omega}\nu$ and the plural $\gamma\epsilon\nu\epsilon\alpha\acute{\iota}$ as temporal concept are septuagintisms (pp. 179s.; 181).

Thought-rhyming in Eph. 4:25-6:9 resembles thought-rhyming in Did. 3:1-4:11 which contains paraenetical material based on missionary hellenistic Judaism.[1] The material of Did., with its less complicated scheme of thought rhyming is somewhat closer to Old Testamentarian chokma literature than Eph. 4:25-6:9 (p. 154ss.).

The Greek of Eph. is a semiticised Greek. Semitic phenomena are evident in the omission and regressive character of certain particles, the peculiar use of the nominative singular $\alpha\dot{\upsilon}\tau\acute{o}s$ and the frequency of the casus obliqui of $\alpha\dot{\upsilon}\tau\acute{o}s$ which is symptomatic of "Judengriechisch"[2] (pp. 103; 168ss.).

The correspondence between Eph. 4:25-6:9 and Did. 3:1-4:11 proves that in the thought-rhyming of the former, we are dealing with a traditional Jewish-hellenistic style. The manifestation of this style in Eph. 4:25-6:9 makes it probable that in the thought-rhymings of Eph. 1:3-14 and 2:14-18 we are again presented with the same traditions of the Jewish-hellenistic style. The above-mentioned septuagintisms and the further influence of the LXX upon the style of Eph., which Percy often mentions,[3] also help to typify the style of Eph. as Jewish-hellenistic.

This Jewish-hellenistic style does not exclusively owe its Jewish character to the LXX and other works derived from a Hebrew or Aramaic source. There is a direct Hebrew influence in the use of prepositions used as a stylistic device; in the interplay of prepositions, in the cumulations of adjuncts introduced by the same preposition and in the connection of synonyms or words related in meaning, through the genitive (pp. 114ss.; p. 129).

The Hebrew O,T. was not the only source of Semitic influence; the Semitic equivalent of the connected synonyms or words related in meaning is only found in Ps. 145, which is one of the later psalms, the Quamran scrolls and the Targum (p. 125s.).

The same late psalm contains equivalents for the elative formulations in Eph. and a high frequency of the equivalent of $\pi\hat{a}s$ (p. 164). Just as Eph. again and again takes a doxological turn at the end of a frag-

---

[1] See p. 154, note 3.

[2] See p. 170, note 1.

[3] See above, p. 113s., p. 120 and p. 123 as well as the Sachregister of Percy, Die Probleme der Kolosser- und Epheserbriefe, p. 514 s.v. Septuaginta.

ment with the words ἔπαινος and δόξα (Eph. 1:6, 12, 14), Ps. 145 repeatedly has words at the end of a verse which bespeak "the blessing of God's name for ever and ever" (Ps. 145:1,2 and 21).

Kuhn remarked on the correspondence between the long sentences of Eph. and those of (the hymns in) the Qumran scrolls (p. 111s.). The Hebrew equivalent for the connection of two substantives by means of ἐν also features in these manuscripts (p. 114). Finally, the semitic aspects of the style mentioned on p. 187 can best be explained in terms of a contemporary Hebrew and/or Aramaic influence.

We now find that Eph. is written in a traditional Jewish-hellenistic style. In our opinion it is likely that this style evolved in an evironment where Hebrew and Aramaic were also spoken. The development of this style could be envisaged as described below.

Originally, the psalms and the chokma of the O.T. inspired Hebrew and/or Aramaicspeaking Jews to a devotional and moralizing style of speech which was in conformity with the style of the O.T., especially the psalms, and the chokma. The Qumran writings and particularly the hymns, present us with this kind of devotional and moralizing tone, adopted by Hebrew or Aramaic-speaking Jews. The period during which these works were written lies close to the beginning of our first millenium.

As an intermediate link between this late Judaic devotional and moralizing trend in speech, and the psalms of the O.T., we could quote Psalm 145 which is one of the latest psalms.

Within a sphere where besides Hebrew (and Aramaic), Greek was also spoken, this devotional and moralizing style of speech could easily have translated itself into a corresponding Greek equivalent. In style, these Greek orations were also in keeping with the O.T. and particularly the psalms, and the chokma. Sometimes this happened through the medium of the LXX.

This reconstruction of the origins of the traditional Jewish-hellenistic style in which Eph. is written, gives us an acceptable explanation for the fact that the style of Eph. has so much in common with Psalm 145 and the Qumran scrolls.

Finally, we would like to turn our attention to Psalm 34. In this psalm, praise and chokma are united. G. Klein thought it probable that this psalm had provided the point of departure for the Palestinic-Jewish and hellenistic missionary paraenesis.[1] If this was the case, it

---

[1] Der älteste christliche Katechismus und die jüdische Propagandaliteratur, pp. 154 and 160.

may be expected that this psalm was one of the parts of the O.T. which exercised such a formative influence upon the devotional and moralizing figures of speech developed amongst Hebrew or Aramaic-speaking Jews and, consequently, upon the Greek-speaking Jews who dwelt in their midst.

Now it is noteworthy that Eph. too, corresponds remarkably with this psalm in some respects. Both in Eph. as well as in Ps. 34 we find the convergence between praise of God and chokma, a repeated use of the word "all" (p. 164), a certain measure of parallelism between verses which follow at a distance (p. 136) and the rhyming of thoughts. Equally noteworthy in this is that not only in Eph. but in Psalm 34 too, sentences can be characterised by their function.[1] This affinity between Eph. and Ps. 34 confirms our view that Eph. is a specimen of a traditional Jewish-hellenistic style which has its foundations in the psalms and the chokma of the O.T.

To us it seems as if the traditional Jewish-hellenistic style has undergone some changes in Eph. The style has been attuned to the ideals of Greek mellifluence and has also acquired the character of the epideictic oration (p. 185s.). In the paraenetical section 4:25-6:9, we found a rather complicated pattern of thought-rhyming. This paraenesis is further removed from the chokma of the O.T. than Did. 3:1-4:11 (p. 156).

The pattern of thought-rhymes in Eph. 4:25-6:9 is complicated because it is so full of variations. There is a combination of different possibilities. In general, the style of Eph. is characterised by the reconciliation of all kinds of details, by effusiveness and by verbosity. This richness of detail and this effusiveness suggest that the traditional Jewish-hellenistic style reached a late phase in Eph.

Käsemann called the style of Eph. "pathetisch" and "manieriert" (mannered).[2] This qualification is merited if Eph. is assessed by the same aesthetic standards as classical prose. But the author of Eph. was not concerned to write such prose. However, he was writing a

---

[1] In Ps. 34 there are alternate sentences in which the poet speaks of himself in the 1st. pers. sing. or in the 3rd. pers. sing. (vs. 2, 3a, 5a, 7-A.V. vs. 1, 2a, 4a, 6); sentences which speak of others in the 3rd. pers. plur. (vs. 3b, 6, 10b, 11b, 18a, 23b-A.V. vs. 2b, 5, 9b, 10b, 17a, 22b); sentences in which God is mentioned in the 3rd. pers. sing. (vs. 5b, 7b, 18b, 19, 20b, 21, 23a-A.V. vs. 4b: 6b, 17b, 18, 19b, 20, 22a) and imperative sentences (vs. 4, 9a, 10, 12, 14, 15-A.V. vs. 3, 8a, 9, 11, 13, 14).

[2] Exeget. Versuche und Besinnungen II, p. 255.

letter. (His work embodies the typical elements of the ancient letter
and the order in which these elements come conforms to the usual
order in the ancient letter.) In this letter, he expresses himself as
wholeheartedly as the speaker would before an assembled Christian
community. He praises God, he utters thanks, he prays, he warns.
And in so doing, he commits no outrage upon the nature of the (ancient)
letter. "Epistula sola res est, quae homines absentes praesentes facit".[1]
Through the medium of his epistle, he is as much present for the addressees as if he were in their midst and were praising, thanking, praying
and exhorting. (The form of the ancient letter allowed for thanksgiving,
prayer and exportation.)

The author made use of a traditional Jewish-hellenistic style which
was in keeping with the atmosphere of a religious gathering. We assume
that this style found its original home in the synagogues of Greek-
speaking Jews who lived in an environment where Hebrew and Aramaic
were also spoken. In Eph. however, we remark the heralding of a new
phase in this style. We were struck by the effusiveness and profuseness
of manner. Now, the author speaks repeatedly of "riches". Thus we
have the riches of grace, the riches of glory and the riches of Christ.
(We shall see later how the author speaks about the totality of God's
eschatological gifts.) Our assumption is that the author, through the
many exalted formulations, the constant recurrence of the elative $\pi\hat{a}s$,
the wealth of detail with which his style abounds, the superabundance
of words and all that is complicated and effusive in his style, wished
to express and demonstrate the riches of which he speaks in a to him
befitting manner.

The author also repeatedly speaks of power. Words such as $\delta\acute{v}\nu\alpha\mu\iota s$,
$\mathring{\iota}\sigma\chi\acute{v}s$ and $\kappa\rho\acute{a}\tau os$ occur repeatedly. Probably he also wanted to
manifest the strength of that power. We have already characterised
his style as intense, words of power (p. 184).

From his hearers, the author expects a $\lambda\alpha\lambda\epsilon\hat{\iota}\nu$ which flows from the
$\pi\lambda\eta\rho o\hat{v}\sigma\theta\alpha\iota$ $\mathring{\epsilon}\nu$ $\pi\nu\epsilon\acute{v}\mu\alpha\tau\iota$ (5:18,19). It is conceivable that he himself
should have incorporated a specimen of this pneumatological utterance
in his epistle; in 5:18, 19, it is intended that the bordelines between
prose and poetry, speech and song, be transcended. We read of a speaking in psalms and hymns and spiritual or pneumatological, songs.
Subsequently, this speaking is equated with singing and jubilating.

---

[1] See p. 85, note 1.

In the epistle itself too, the borderline between prose and poetry
is more or less transcended. The eulogy (1:3-14) could be seen in the
light of a psalm or a hymn and the section 2:14-18, as a song. The
dividing-line between speech and song is sometimes elided; we have
seen how the constant return of series of long syllables (and perispomena)
at the ends of the fragments of the eulogy, could have resulted in
a more or less singing recitation of this section (p. 160).

There are, in the epistle, no demonstrable joints welding together
possible material from older sources, and the original material of the
epistle. That does not necessarily mean that all pronouncements which
occur in the epistle, are ad hoc formulations. In Eph. 5:22-6:9, we
discerned a dependence upon a hellenistic-Jewish paraenetical source
(p. 154). The borrowed material has been adapted and integrated
completely. Similarly, other material such as the avowals of 1:7 and
1:20, could have derived from an older source which has been absorbed
and integrated.

This integration was probably facilitated by the fact that the style
of the older material was of the same Jewish-hellenistic mould as
that of Eph. It is possible that Ochel (pp. 7, 12) was to some extent
right and that the eulogy (Eph. 1:3-14) consists for a good part of
older and integrated material. However, it must be conceded to Maurer
that there is no detectable dividing-line between this section and the
remainder of the epistle (p. 13). Dahl's conclusion (p. 12) that this
section in its entirety is borrowed, is not acceptable; for that, it is
too interwoven with the rest of the epistle. We have already (p. 52s.)
established, how meaningful a function this section has within the
framework of the entire epistle.

G. Schille finds several non-original parts in Eph. According to
him, an "hymnische Vorlage" (hymnic model) was utilized for Eph.
1:3-12a; 2:4-10 was a piece borrowed from a confession or liturgy
which had obviously been touched-up by the author, whilst 2:14-18
was supposed to be "ein Erlöserlied" (a song on the deliverer) of the
hellenistic community with the addition of a few explanatory comments
which gave the song a connotation which was applicable to the author's
own theme.

Our own investigation into the style of Eph., led us to regard the
epistle as a homogeneous unit. We found no evidence of a divergent
style in the abovementioned three sections. Thus, we were unable
to yield to the persuasions of Schille's researches. We do think that it
is quite probable that the author did make use of "liturgisches Gut"

in 2:4-10 and 2:14-18, but it is impossible to deduce this liturgical
material from the style. Nor are we agreed with the view that the
article δέ in 2:4 and the particle γάρ in 2:14 clearly mark the opening
of a quotation.[1] It is furthermore our opinion that Schille, when
he points out interpolations which the author of Eph. was to have
introduced into the borrowed material of 2:4-10 and 2:14-18, is basing
his arguments on excessively subjective grounds.

16. Affinity in style between Eph., Col. and parts of the Homologoumena

The relationship in style between Eph. and the homologoumena

The style of Col. corresponds to a large extent whit that of Eph.
The peculiar form of oratio perpetua; the poverty in particles and
conjunctions; the many syntactically superfluous adverbial adjuncts
introduced by a preposition; cumulations of such adjuncts and the
cumulations of genitives; are all found in Col. (pp. 112; 104; 113s.;
121).

The syndetic adjacence of synonyms or words related in meaning
or their combination by means of the genitive; the addition of an
elaboration; combinations of adjuncts with the same or a similar
meaning introduced by the same preposition; the repetition of certain
words and combinations of certain words, are all again encountered
(pp. 129; 121; 130; 121; 163s.). In Col. too, a verb is more than once connected directly with a substantive of the same root (p. 164). The
rhythm of genitives is not absent (p. 128). The word πᾶς is used very
frequently (p. 164).

In the matter of thought-rhyming, there are differences. Thought-
rhyming of a paraenetical nature in Col. is found only in the small
paraenetical section Col. 3:18-4:1 which is not even original (p. 152;
154). The rhyming of thought as it occurs in Eph. 1:3-14 and 2:14-18,
is not found in Col. In Eph. such thought-rhyming is based on the
Hebrew parallelismus membrorum.

---

[1] G. Schille first published his research in his stencilled dissertation entitled Liturgisches Gut im Epheserbrief (Göttingen 1952). (Eph. 2:14-18 for example, he treats on
p. 9.) Subsequently, he delivered his investigation in Frühchristliche Hymnen (Berlin
1965). For Eph. 2:14-18, we refer to p. 24ss., for Eph. 2:4-10 to p. 53ss. and for Eph.
1:3-12a to p. 65ss. Comments on the "Zitationspartikeln" are found on pp. 16, 24 and 53s.

However, a Greek parallelism also exists. That type is a parallelism of form.[1] Col. does have thought-rhyming; a thought-rhyming which is partly based on this last-mentioned type of parallelism.

In the sentence Col. 2:8-15, we find a correspondence between two subordinate clauses placed at a distance, with the same thought and corresponding largely in form. The clauses are relative subordinate clauses, beginning with the words ἐν ᾧ καί. These two clauses which are separated by a construction with a participle, are followed by a number of phrases which all tell of an act of salvation by God or Christ and insofar correspond in form, inasmuch as they begin with a participium aoristi (activi or medii) in the nominative singular.[2] A slight correspondence in form between separated sentences is found in Col. 1:3-8.[3] A similar type of thought-rhyming with correspondence in form similar to that of Col. 2:8-15, is found in Col. 1:13-20.[4]

In content matter, the passages Eph. 1:3-14 and 2:14-18, in which the rhyming of thoughts is based exclusively on the Hebrew parallelismus membrorum on the one hand and the passages Col. 1:13-20 and 2:8-15 in which the rhyming of thoughts is partly based on Greek parallelism of form, are closely related. Avowal permeates the whole. All the passages concern acts of salvation of God or Christ and speak of the special significance of Christ. Therefore, thought-rhyming does occur in both epistles under identical circumstances.

---

[1] For this "Parallelismus der Form", see Norden, Antike Kunstprosa II, p. 816.

[2] χαρισάμενος (2:13), ἐξαλείψας (2:14), προσηλώσας (2:14), ἀπεκδυσάμενος (2:15) and θριαμβεύσας (2:15). According to the exegesis of Bultmann (Theologie, p. 179), all these participia concern God's acts of salvation. It is also feasible to regard καὶ αὐτὸ ἦρκεν as the beginning of a new principal sentence of which Christ is the subject, in which case the last three participia refer to acts of Christ.

[3] There are two relative subordinate clauses with a similar beginning (ἣν ἔχετε v. 4 and ἣν προηκούσατε v. 5); two subordinate clauses introduced by καθὼς καὶ ἐν (v. 6); one relative subordinate clause (v. 6); one subordinate clause introduced by καθώς (v. 7) and one relative subordinate clause (v. 7).

[4] There is a series of four separated relative subordinate clauses (1:13, 14, 15 and 18). The second is introduced by ἐν ᾧ and the three others all begin with ὅς. Between the third and the fourth there is much affinity (1:15 ὅς ἐστιν εἰκὼν ... πρωτότοκος κ.τ.λ., 1:18 ὅς ἐστιν ἀρχή, πρωτότοκος). Then there is a series of two subordinate clauses beginning with ὅτι ἐν αὐτῷ (1:16 and 1:19) and a series of two sentences beginning with καὶ αὐτός ἐστιν (1:17 and 1:18). The subordinate clauses beginning with ὅς ἐστιν and the sentences beginning with καὶ αὐτός ἐστιν are about the greatness which Christ has. The sentences introduced by ὅτι ἐν αὐτῷ speak of greatness which God bestows on Christ. The first of each series does not go beyond the creation; the second in each series diverts the attention to the ecclesia, the resurrection and the reconciliation.

The nature of thought-rhyming in the two epistles differs, however. This difference is bridged by the incidence in Eph. of a specimen of the type of rhyme found otherwise only in Col. In the case of that occurrence, in the eulogy, three subordinate clauses are found removed at some distance from each other, each commencing with ἐν ᾧ and all speaking of the salvation the faithful have gained in Christ (p. 135).

As far as grammatical detail and vocabulary are concerned, there is very little to differentiate between the two epistles (pp. 168ss.; 173s.).

All in all, there are but exceedingly slight differences in the style, matters of grammatical detail and vocabulary of Eph. and Col. Curiously enough, this presents no grounds for placing one or other of the epistles at a greater remove from the HP. Percy thought that of the two, Eph. deviates most from the HP.[1] Admittedly, there is the fact of a greater frequency in certain mutual phenomena, in Eph. In Eph., there are more adverbial adjuncts with a preposition and more cumulations of these adjuncts; in Eph., there is a greater incidence of connections between synonyms or words closely related in meaning by means of the genitive and, moreover, more use is made of directly linked verbs and substantives from the same root (pp. 115; 120; 122; 164). Eph. has a stronger tendency than Col. towards articles and uses the connective ἐν αὐτῷ in an odd fashion (pp. 167s.; 107).[2] Furthermore, Col. is closer to the HP than Eph., in that the former has thought progressions which are concurrent with the parallel formulations.[3] The relative subordinate clause introduced by ὅς in Col. 1:13, possesses a symmetrical and dual character; this parallelism goes side by side with the development of the thought. There is also a thought progression in the parallelism of the principal sentence introduced by νῦν in Col. 1:24 and in the binary formulation χαίρων καὶ βλέπων ὑμῶν τὴν τάξιν καὶ στερέωμα in Col. 2:5.

In other respects however, Col. is further removed from the HP. The particles γάρ and δέ occur even more rarely in Col. than in Eph.

---

[1] Die Probleme, p. 185.

[2] If the subject of the participle θριαμβεύσας in Col. 2:15 is Christ, then this is the same kind ἐν αὐτῷ as in Eph. 2:16 after ἀποκτείνας (see p. 170).

[3] Schutz has contrasted the parallelism of Semitic poetry which is lyrical in character and prone to an aria-like pause in thought, with the parallelism of hellenistic-Jewish prose which is recitative in character and usually allows the idea to continue. As an example of the latter, he quotes the passage 1 C. 10:1-4. See the work mentioned p. 161 n. 2 and reference.

(p. 104). Col. has the highest frequency of the preposition $\dot{\epsilon}\nu$[1] and the word $\pi\hat{\alpha}\varsigma$ [2]. Col. also has a higher frequency with regard to the syndetical connection of synonyms or words related in meaning, detailed elaborations and the welding together of adjuncts which are correlative in content and governed by participles (pp. 129; 132). Peculiarities in the use of infinitives, common to both epistles, occur more often in Col. (p. 172). The common tendency to use words constructed of a combination of different words in strongest in Col. and the striking proclivity in Col. to use discomposita, is not manifested in Eph. (p. 173). Thus Mayerhoff and de Zwaan are partly justified when they assert that in language and vocabulary, Eph. has more affinity with the HP.[3]

The opinion of de Wette that the language and style of Eph., in contrast to Col., present many arguments against the epistle's authenticity, may be rejected in its entirety.[4] The correspondence between Eph. and Col. in the matter of grammatical detail and vocabulary, is too great to admit this possibility and the differences between them are not of such a nature that one epistle could be said to be closer to the HP than the other. Often, these difference are merely a question of degree and concern a higher frequency of one or the other peculiarity to be found in both epistles. Both epistles stand in the same position with relation to the HP and everything suggests that both epistles also derive from a common source. We must therefore view them as such and as definitely the work of a single author.[5]

What now, is the relationship of Eph. to the other epistles of the CP minus? None of the other epistles corresponds so consistently with Eph., as Col. Nevertheless, all the stylistic components of Eph. are found again in the other epistles (pp. 103-107; 112; 113; 121s.; 127s. 140s.; 143-149; 152s.; 156ss.; 162-167).

Percy has shown that some of these components are characteristic of the style of the HP and should be regarded as indications of authenticity.[6]

---

1 See p. 114, note 2.

2 See p. 164, note 3.

3 See Chapter I, para. 2 (p. 6) and para. 5 (p. 12).

4 See Chapter I, para. 2 (p. 5).

5 See again Percy, Probleme, p. 240.

6 These components are the cumulations of adjuncts with a preposition (p. 115), cumulations of adjuncts introduced by the same preposition and are of the same or related meaning (p. 120) and the cumulations of genitives (p. 123).

There is still more correspondence between Eph. and the HP.
Thus it became clear to us that particular forms of parallelism which
are found frequently in the HP, also feature in Eph. (p. 129-133).

Paley [1] remarked that in the epistles of Paul, the drift of thought
sometimes wanders away from the main theme because a particular
word which has come up gives rise to an expatiation. Such digressions,
Paley pointed out, also occur in Eph. [2]

Despite all the differences in style between Eph. and R., [3] which
W. Sanday and S. Heallam found, they nevertheless discovered that
"one of the most striking characteristics of St. Paul" which occurs
again and again in R., also figures in Eph. The characteristic in question
is the way in which within an extended framework, small sentences
or equivalent sentence-parts follow in succession. These little sentences
seem to succeed one another like the pieces of an extended telescope.
Each new idea is followed by yet another idea until the central theme
of the whole has been recaptured. Often this process takes place, as it
were, by way of a diversion with a sharp bend at the end. Clear examples of this type of thought pattern are R. 3:21-26 and Eph. 3:1-7.
Furthermore, in R. 1:1-7, 1:18-24; 2:5-16; 5:12-14; 9:22-29 and
15:24-28 as well as in the first three chapters of Eph., sentences have
all been assembled in this characteristic fashion. [4]

Grammatically, there is little difference between Eph. and the HP.
There are a few grammatical details in Eph. which are not found in
the HP (p. 172). Likewise, there is a slight discrepancy with regard to
words and expressions (p. 181). But far stronger than these discrepancies is the affinity. In this respect too, Percy found characteristic
correspondences between Eph. and the HP (p. 181).

The correspondence between Eph. and the HP goes beyond the corres-

---

[1] See p. 5, note 1.

[2] Examples are : the digression in 2 C. 2:15, 16 on the word ὀσμή used in 2 C. 2:14
and the digression in 2 C. 3:14-18 on the word κάλυμμα of 2 C. 3:13. Thus, in Eph. 4:9, 10
an expatiation on the word ἀναβάς from Eph. 4:8 and in Eph. 5:13-15 there is an expatiation on the word φῶς which occurs in Eph. 5:8-11. See Paley, Horae Paulinae, p. 151ss.
and Abbott, Eph.-Col., p. xxis.

[3] W. Sanday and C. Headlam, A Critical and Exegetical Commentary on the Epistle
to the Romans (Edinburgh ⁵1902), p. LV : "We may take Eph. and Rom. as marking
the extreme poles of difference within the Epistles claimed for St. Paul" and p. LV,
note 1 : "The difference between these Epistles on the side we are considering is greater
(e.g.) that between Romans and the Pastorals.".

[4] Op. cit., p. lxs.

pondence in incidental details of style, patterns of thought, words and expressions. In addition, there are a few small sections in the HP which are closely related or even identical in style to Eph. Percy drew attention to the affinity between Eph. and R. 1:8-12; Phil. 1:3-7, 9-11; 2 C. 9:12-15; R. 3:23-26 and 2 C. 1:3, 4.[1]

On the basis of our own research, we can affirmatively state that the style of Eph. is closely linked with that of R. 1; R. 3:21-26 and R. 4:11-5:25 and in furthermore identical to that of R. 1:1-10 and 1 C. 1:1-9. For the rest, there are many points of contact between Eph. and R. in respect of style.

In the Nestle text, R. 1 comprises 78 lines and is thus less than a quarter of Eph. in extent. The specific form of oratio perpetua occurs in this section; the style is neither lively nor mobile. There are few particles or conjunctions.[2] Both rhetorical dialogue and rhetorical questions are missing. The average sentence is almost like the average sentence in Eph. and there are a great many long sentences (pp. 104; 105).

There is a fairly high incidence of cumulations of syntactically superfluous adverbial adjuncts with a preposition.[3] There are many cumulations of genitives.[4] Often, synonyms or words related in meaning are connected by means of a genitive.[5] The elaborative additional descriptions discussed in para. 7, point b and the combinations of adjuncts with participles treated in point d, are frequent.[6]

Thought-rhyming which is akin to the thought-rhyming of the avowal section Eph. 2:14-18, is found in the "penitential sermon" of R. 1:18-31 (pp. 148s.; 157s.). In R. 1:23, there is a rhythm of genitives (p. 128). Adverbial adjuncts introduced by prepositions assume the

---

[1] Die Probleme, p. 245 and p. 245s. note 88. The places mentioned may be augmented by the places treated by Percy on pp. 37s., 41-45.

[2] The frequency of εἰ is 0/78, that of δέ 1/39, that of ὅτι 1/26 and that of ἄρα οὖν 0/78 (see p. 104s. and notes).

[3] 1/9.7. The fact that this frequency is high is evident from p. 120 n. 1. In R. 1:1-10, the frequency is even 1/3.6).

[4] The frequency of all kinds of cumulations is 1/6 and that of cumulations in which the gen. of the pers. pron. is exceptional, 1/15.6. Cf. the frequencies quoted in n. 4 on p. 121. There is nothing special about the frequency of adnominal genitives.

[5] This occurs in R. 1:5, 20 and 23. The frequency of 1/26 is more or less the same as the frequency of 1/24 in Eph.; cf. p. 122 n. 1.

[6] In Eph. we found resp. 3 and 8. In the small section of R. there are resp. 2 (R. 1:1 and 7) and 2 (R. 1-3s. and 27).

function of clausulae (pp. 119; 148). Here too, the recurrence of the same
word and the correspondence between related words, act as a unifying
principle (p. 164). As in Eph. 1:23, the consonant π is used to an aesthetic purpose in R. 1:29, as is the combination $\pi\lambda$ (p. 166). The coincidence
of all these details illuminate that the style of R. 1 is closely related to
that of Eph.

Especially the beginning of R. 1 bears an exceedingly close resemblance to the style of Eph. The very specific form of oratio perpetua
which we have described, is used in the sentence R. 1:1-7. Moreover,
that sentence has a pattern of thought-rhyming which corresponds
totally to that of Eph. 1:3-14 (pp. 140; 145). In both these sentences,
fragments may be characterised by their meaning, Both sentences can
be divided into larger and smaller fragments of a similar pattern
(pp. 143s.; 157). In R. 1:1-7 as well as in Eph. 1:3-14, there are many
fragments with three or more long syllables at the end, a still greater
number ending in a word with the accent on the last syllable and a
few fragments in which long syllables are preponderant (p. 161s.).
In this very section, R. 1:1-7, there is a connection between words
related in meaning, effected through the genitive (1:5): two elaborative
additional descriptions (1:1 and 7) and one combination of adjuncts
ruled by participles (1:3). The importance of the genitive as a stylistic
factor is demonstrated in R. 1:1-4.

In R. 1:1-10 as in Eph. 1:3-14, the prepositions function in the same
way, namely as clausulae (p. 119). Also, there is the same interplay of
prepositions as in Eph. 1:3-14 (p. 117) and cumulations of adjuncts
with prepositions are very frequent (p. 120). Thus we may without
any hesitation talk of a style in the first ten verses of R. 1, which is
identical to the style of Eph. 1:3-14.

In R. 3:21-26, we see the return of various components of the style
of Eph. The sentence is long, occupying almost 14 lines in the Nestle
edition and has the greatest cumulation of adjuncts introduced by
prepositions (p. 119). Thought-rhyming of the same kind as in Eph.
1:3-14 and R. 1:1-7, occurs (pp. 140s.; 144). The element of repetition
is strong here (p. 164). This repetition and the correspondence between
related words form a unifying principle (p. 164). Furthermore, as in
Eph. 1:3-14, there is a re-echoing of similar combinations of words (p.
164).

In the section R. 4:11-5:21, which has a length of 95 in the Nestle
text, the vocative $\dot{\alpha}\delta\epsilon\lambda\phi o\acute{\iota}$, rhetorical dialogue and rhetorical questions
are, as in Eph., not used. In R. 5, many cumulations of adjuncts

introduced by prepositions occur.[1] There is a high frequency of the various cumulations of genitives.[2] The particular form of oratio perpetua previously discussed, occurs in R. 4:16-21 (p. 112). The combination of similar sentence-parts described in para. 7, point c, is found in 4:25 as are in 4:17 the connected adjuncts with a participle described in point d of the same paragraph. In this section there are two long and one very long sentence. The average sentence-length is long.[3] In addition, there are two more striking aspects of correspondence with the style of Eph. in 5:15, there is a connection of two substantives through ἐν which occurs on four occasions in Eph. (p. 114s.) and the strange genitive in R. 4:12, is a pendant of the genitive in Eph. 1:18 (p. 122s.).

In other parts of R., too, we are repeatedly reminded of the style of Eph. Thus, in R. 2:1-6:23, as section which with 300 lines of Nestle is nearly as large as Eph. (338) the vocative ἀδελφοί does not feature even once. In R. 8:18-16:23, a section containing 540 lines, the particle μέν does not occur at all. Therefore, this particle is even rarer in this section than it is in Eph. (p. 104).

In R. 12:9-21, there is some thought-rhyming which corresponds with the though rhyming in Eph. 4:25-6:9 (pp. 152s.; 156s.).

Various components in the style of Eph. are found in R. 15:13-33. There is a low frequency of the conjunction ὅτι (p. 105) and a high frequency of cumulations of adjuncts with a preposition.[4] The average sentence-length is extensive and the frequency of long sentences is high.[5] In R. 15:30, there is an example of the combination of resembling phrases described in para. 7, point c and in R. 15:7, there is an occurrence of the parallelism of a sentence with a modal subordinate clause, as described in para. 7, point f.[6] Isocolism occurs in R. 15:14 being a phenomenon which is often encountered in R. (p. 167).

---

[1] R. 5:1, 5, 9, 11, 16, 16, 18, 18, 21. In the section R. 4: 11-5:21 there are also cumulations in the middle of a group of words which can be regarded as a self-contained whole, e.g. R. 4:18.

[2] The frequency of all kinds of genitives is 1/10.6; of genitives excepting the gen. of a pers. pron. 1/11.8 and that of nominal genitives subject to the same exception 1/47.5. Cf. the frequencies in n. 4 and n. 3 on p. 121. The cumulations are in R. 4:13, 16, 19; 5:2, 10, 14, 17 and 19. The cumulations in 4:11, 12; 5:1, 11 have not been included. Here, a cumulation is always followed by an apposition.

[3] See p. 106 n. 1 and p. 107 n. 1 and n. 2.

[4] 1/10. The cumulations occur in 15:2, 13, 18, 28 and 30. See furthermore p. 120 n. 1.

[5] See p. 106 n. 1 and p. 107 n. 1.

[6] See p. 130 n. 4 and p. 133.

In 1 C. 1:1-9, as in R. 1:1-10, a style can be identified which is
identical to the style of Eph. This section is exceedingly small, being
but 20 lines in length. Not one of the particles εἰ, γάρ, μέν, δέ, διό, (ἄρα
οὖν) occurs there, whilst ὅτι is found but on one occasion (p. 104).
The preposition ἐν occurs frequently.[1] At the end of a sentence and
at the conclusion of the pericope, adverbial adjuncts introduced by
a preposition assume the function of clausulae. The halting of the flow
of words which is the result, is further enhanced by the use of genitives.[2]

Throughout the entire pericope, there is a tendency towards doubling
and parallelism.[3] The special form of oratio perpetua occurs in 1:4-8
(p. 112). Long sentences feature [4] and the word χάρις of 1:3 recurs in
1:4. The construction of a long sentence is supported by the combination of the words εὐχαριστῶ, χάρις and χάρισμα and the correspondence
between these words and the words δοθεῖσα, ἐπλουτίσθητε and
ὑστερεῖσθαι; for this introduces an element of unity into the multitude
of words. There is also a high frequency of the word πᾶς.[5]

We have already come to the conclusion that Eph. and Col. are the
work of the same author. How must we now see the relationship of Eph.
to the HP? In paragraphs 3 and 4 of Chapter V, I demonstrated that
Paul did not work alone in the compilation of his epistles. In the first
place, the other persons mentioned in the praescripts were partly
responsible for the epistles. Besides this, Paul employed a scribe who
wrote the epistle.

This was also true when no co-senders were mentioned in the praescript. It is conceivable that the writer was not always the same scribe
and that the services of various secretaries were used in the writing
of the different epistles.

Therefore, there are a number of people who were involved with

---

[1] The frequency is 1/2. For the frequency in Eph. see p. 114, n. 2.

[2] There are clausulae in 1:8 and 9. For the restraining effect of genitives, cf. p. 126.

[3] The syndetical connection of related words and the combination of resembling
sentence-parts which we treated in para. 7, points a and c, are both present in ἐν παντὶ
λογῷ καὶ πάσῃ γνώσει. The feature described in para. 7, point b. is found in v. 2 and at
the end of v. 9.

[4] In this small part there are only three sentences exceeding a length of seven lines.
See p. 106 n. 1 and p. 107 n. 1.

[5] See para. 11. The frequency of πᾶς is 1/4. The fact that this is a high frequency
may be seen from n. 3 on p. 164.

Paul, in one or the other way, in the writing of his epistles. We would designate him and all these associates collectively as the Pauline circle.

It may be asserted with certainty that someone from this Pauline circle was the author of Eph. The nature and the multitude of corresponding elements in the style of Eph. and that of the HP, eliminate any possibility that the epistle could have been written by anyone outside that circle.

We are strengthened in this certainty by the discovery which we have made in this chapter; namely that long sentences are used in Eph. under the same epistolary circumstances, to treat the same material and under the influence of the same set of associations, as in the other epistles (p. 110). This is further enhanced by the conclusion we reached at the end of Chapter IV, that the author of Eph. must have been witness to the genesis of the HP, even if he was not Paul (p. 70s.).

The many points of agreement between the style of Eph. and that of the HP on which I base my tenet that Eph. must be the work of someone from the Pauline circle, correspond with the general characterisation of the style of Eph. given in para. 15. Therein, we assessed the Greek of Eph. as a Greek which is deficient by the standards of Greek literary prose and the art of ancient literary rhetoric. We spoke of a Jewish-hellenistic style and Semitic inflections. We could also point out that the epistle was not wholly devoid of a literary training or knowledge of Greek rhetoric. We found—be it with failings—the style of the epideictic oration. We are even persuaded that the author would have been capable of writing a somewhat better quality of Greek prose.

Now the fact is that this general characterisation of the style of Eph. is very much in keeping with characterisations of Paul's style coming from authoritative quarters both in antiquity and in our own time. In Origen's opinion, Paul's style was deficient as far as the φράσις (i.e. word-grouping) was concerned and his epistles were scarcely Ἑλληνικός (i.e. correct, with no impurities) with regard to the συνθέσις τῆς λέξεως (i.e. the sentence construction and word-order within the sentences).[1]

Deissmann and Blass-Debrunner find that the Greek of Paul approximates more closely to the Greek of the ordinary man in the

---

[1] See Eust. Hist. Eccl. VI, 25, 11 or Deissmann, L. v. O., p. 54, note 4. For the significance of the technical terms φράσις and συνθέσις, see Lausberg, Handbuch der literarischen Rhetorik, resp. II, p. 881 s. v. and I, para. 911 (p. 455).

street than to literary language, but is clearly elevated above the vulgar level. They were agreed that there is no evidence whatsoever of a classical training as such. However, following the views of Bultmann and J. Weiss, Blass-Debrunner were nevertheless of the opinion that Paul had enjoyed some degree of linguistic and rhetorical education. Deissmann described Paul's prose as a "nicht kunstlose Umgangsprosa eines weitgereisten Groszstädters der römischen Kaiserzeit.".[1]

J. Weiss assumed that Paul had been influenced by the Hebrew parallelism, Old Testament chokma literature and the chokma of Jewish-hellenism.[2] Norden was indefatigable in pointing out oriental and Semitic aspects in Paul's formulations.[3]

There is more to be said on the subject of the relationship of Eph. to the HP. Not only is it certain that somebody from the Pauline circle must have been the author of Eph., but moreover, the nature and abundance of the correspondences, in my view, provide coroborrative support for the assumption the Paul was himself the author of Eph.

Especially in R. we find remarkable affinities with Eph. On the basis of the fact that the praescripts of both epistles mentions Paul alone as the sender, a particularly strong correspondence in style might have been expected (p. 91).

As it is, there is no correspondence in style which runs throughout the entirety of the two epistles. To the contrary, there is on the whole a pronounced difference between R. and Eph. R. has—to quote Bultmann—the style of a diatribe with the rhetorical question and the dialogue. Argument and polemic play a part and the style of the epistle is one of a liveliness and an energetic mood. With respect to all this, Eph. is a different case. For that reason, Sandy and Headlam thought that within the CP, Eph. and R. differed most from each other.[4]

This difference does not however, imply different authorship. Keeping in mind Norden's dictum : "Der Stil war im Alterum nicht der Mensch selbst, sondern ein Gewand, das er nach Belieben Wechseln konnte", (p. 100s.), we may hazard that in R. Paul for most of the time assumed a different guise than in Eph.

---

[1] See A. Deissmann, Paulus (Tübingen 1911), pp. 37s., 54 and L. v. O., p. 54 and Bl.-Debr., p. 3s. "the everyday language, not entirely without aesthetic merit, of a much-travelled citizen of the Roman Empire.".

[2] Beiträge zur Paulinischen Rhetorik (e.g., p. 168).

[3] Agnostos Theos (passim); cf. Radermacher, p. 28.

[4] See p. 196, n. 3.

Besides this difference, there are curious affinities between the two epistles. There is the correspondence enumerated by Sanday and Headlam and the correspondences which we have pointed out (p. 196ss.) These aspects of correspondence—and here I am thinking principally of the correspondence in thought-rhyming and the identical nature of the style in R. 1:1-10 and Eph.—are such that quite incidentally in R., the same author who asserts himself in Eph., stands revealed.

With Col., Eph. has a continuity of style. In both epistles, there is a permanent and unchanging style of writing. They are both written in an epideictic, and intensive, lyrical and poetic style. The style is not identical in the two epistles; there are differences in thought-rhyming. Col. is somewhat more Ἑλληνικός and has thought progressions in parallel formulations. Also, there is a slight difference in vocabulary (p. 192ss.).

We can now put it in such a way that the incidental correspondence between Eph. and R. must be explained by the fact that Paul alone bore the responsibility for these epistles. There were no co-senders. The difference between the two epistles may be attributed to the use of a different trend of writing, the time difference and possibly the use of a different secretary.

The continuous correspondence of style between Eph. and Col. may be explained in terms of a continued use of the same trend of writing, contemporaneousness and the possible use of the same secretary. The difference between the two epistles may ascribed to the fact that in the case of Eph., Paul was solely responsible for the missive whereas in the case of Col., Timotheus was partly responsible for the epistle. (The possible use of a different secretary could also have contributed towards the difference.)

One more question should still be answered. Why is it that in Eph. and Col. the same trend of writing is consistently utilized whereas the other epistles of Paul use a different style?

Percy believes that this different trend in Eph. and Col. has to do with an oriental liturgical-hymnic style. He extablishes that in the other epistles the same style intermittently comes to the fore. This, he finds, occurs in sections which contain prayer, thanksgiving or related expression concerned with God and Christ. He explains the dominant nature of the liturgical- hymnic style in Eph. and Col. by the fact that in these epistles prayer, thanksgiving and the recording of attributes and deeds of God, occupy such an important place.[1]

---

[1] Die Probleme, p. 37-46.

These comments of Percy provide an acceptable answer for the
question posed above. It may be added that this prominence of prayer
and the use of a liturgical-hymnic style in Eph. and Col. is compatible
with the image which Paul presents of himself in R. 15:15, 16.[1]
Furthermore, it should be remarked that the style of the two epistles
is not restricted to oriental liturgical-hymnic aspects; we were also
able to point out a relationship with chokma literature.

The style is a Jewish-hellenistic style which evolved in an environment where more than one language was spoken and in which could be
expressed prayer, giving thanks, the enumeration of God's attributes
and deeds, as well as the religious moral exhortation.[2] The fact that
Paul should have made such extensive use of this style in Eph. may
partly have been the result of the environment in which he found
himself at the time the epistle was written; an environment in which
he was quite concerned with matters of prayer, thanksgiving, avowal
of God and Christ and moral religious exhortation—all questions
which were often treated in the language of the traditional Jewish-
hellenistic style.

Such will have been the case more during the period of imprisonment
in Caesarea than during the imprisonment in Rome. Nearly all the
Jews of Rome spoke only Greek.[3] What is more likely, is a Hebrew
or Aramaic influence on the Greek spoken by the Jewish Christians with
whom Paul could have come into contact in Caesarea.[4] Although
Caesarea was a hellenistic city, Jerusalem and Judea maintained
links with the city because the residence of the Roman procurator
was situated there and because the Jewish metropolis and the Judean
country formed part of the hinterland to this large seaport.

It is conceivable that the traditional Jewish hellenistic style which
must have evolved in a multi-lingual environment, may have also been
known in Caesarea and constituted a familiar medium of expression
for the Christians of hellenistic Jewish origin who lived there.[5]

---

[1] Cf. p. 69.

[2] In Phil. 1:27-30 we are also reminded of the style of Eph, cf. p. 109s. The sentence
is in the nature of a religious-moral exhortation. R. 1:18-31 is similar in character;
here we were very forcibly reminded of the style of Eph. (p. 197s.).

[3] See Deissmann, L.v.O., p. 51.

[4] The city had a predominantly pagan population, Schürer II[4], p. 136s. One of the
rabbis there heard the religious avowal of Deut. 6:4 recited in Greek, Schürer III[4], p. 141.
See also J. N. Sevenster, Do you know Greek? How much Greek could the First Jewish
Christians have known?, Suppl. to Novum Testamentum XIX, 1968, p. 103ss.

[5] Acts 21:8 make it probably that Paul had contact with the Christian community

   Through fellowship with these Christians, through communal prayer,
thanksgiving and giving praise and by communicating with them
as in Eph. 5:19, 20, it is possible that Paul's tendency towards this
style, familiar to him of old, found inspiration. In other epistles,
Paul avails himself in a more original fashion of the common property
which is language. From time to time, we find there an originality
and creativeness which urged von Wilamowitz-Moellendorff to express
his appreciation in an exclamation of enthusiasm.[1] In Eph. (and Col.)
that individualism is far less pronounced; here the apostle said everything in words which others could say with or after him. It would
be unfair to judge this manner of communication by the aesthetic
criteria which may be applied to an individual style of prose.
   The medium of expression used in Eph. is far more closely related
to the non-individual and traditional language of Israel's psalms and
chokma.

We can complete our research into the style, grammar and vocabulary
of Eph. with the following *conclusions*.

   1. The correspondence in style, grammatical detail and vocabulary
is too great between Eph. and Col., to place one epistle at a greater
remove from the HP than the other. Everything corroborates that
the epistles have a common source and must be regarded as the work
of the same author (p. 195). The style of Eph. and Col. is not identical
but there is a continuous affinity of style throughout the two epistles.
Again and again, the same trend of writing is pursued in the two
epistles. If the hypothesis that both epistles are authentic is accepted
as a basic premise, then this continual correspondence may be explained

---

as Caesarea. From Acts. 6:1,5 it can be deduced that Philippus, leader of the community
in Caesarea (Acts. 8:40) was a Ἑλληνιστής. If the traditional Jewish-hellenistic style did
evolve in the Greek-speaking synagogues of Jerusalem, Philippus himself formed a
link between this environment and that of Caesarea. Paul himself was also probably
at home in the same Greek-speaking synagogues in Jerusalem, as was Stefanus (Acts
6:8-8:1), There is also a connection between these synagogues and the Christian community of Antioch which was to assume such importance to Paul; the community at Antioch
was founded by hellenistic Jews, originating from Jerusalem, who had been connected
with Stefanus and Philippus (Acts 11:19-21).
   For the meaning of the term Ἑλληνισταί in Acts 6:1, see J. N. Sevenster, op. cit.
p. 31s. Information on the use of the Greek language in Jerusalem and on a Greek-speaking synagogue in that city, is found in the same work, pp. 32, 143ss. and 131ss.
   [1] See the quotation on p. 88s.

by the constant use of the same tone of address and by the contemporaneousness of the two epistles. The difference between the two epistles
can then be explained on the basis of the fact that for Eph., Paul was
himself entirely responsible whereas in the case of Col., Timotheus was
partly-responsible for the epistle (p. 203).

It cannot be established whether the services of one and the same
secretary were used for both epistles. If it is assumed that this was the
case, it can be assumed that his work has contributed to the affinity in
style. If it is assumed that two different secretaries were used, it is
probable to assume that the slight difference in style and vocabulary
may be partly attributed to them.

2. All the components which together form the style of Eph. may
be found again in the HP. Some of these components are characteristic
of the HP. Also with respect to words and expressions, Eph. here and
there features something which is characteristic of the HP (p. 195ss.).
Therefore it may be assumed that the author of Eph. was a person who
belonged to the Pauline circle. By this circle, we mean Paul and his
associates, including secretaries (p. 200s.).

3. The style of Eph. is identical to that of 1 C. 1:1-9 and that of
R. 1:1-10. Percy showed that there was a correspondence in style between Eph. and some passages form Phil. and 2 C. We ourselves found
a close relationship between the style of Eph. and that of R. 1; 3:21-26
and 4:11-5:25. Besides this, we found many points of contact between
Eph. and R. with regard to the form and manner of expression (p. 196-
200).

Because there is no continuous affinity in style between Eph. and R.,
and because a totally different trend of writing is used through much of
R. (p. 202), it is all the more remarkable that there should be so much
correspondence in style between Eph. and R. Taking as a point of
departure the fact that in the praescripts of Eph. and R. Paul alone
is named as the sender, these remarkable affinities can be explained
on the basis of the assumption that Paul alone bore the responsibility
for both writings.

This explanation is compatible with the fact that Eph. has so much
affinity with precisely that part of R. in which the apostle introduces
himself to the community of Rome and speaks directly about his
person and mission, i.e. R. 1:1-10. It would be conceivable that Paul
would have been especially concerned with this part of his epistle to the
Romans and that he would have allowed his secretary, particularly
in this section, very little freedom of movement in the formulation
of words.

The fact that the style of Eph. is identical to that of 1 C. 1:1-9 and the correspondence in style between Eph. and some passages of Phil. and 2 C. is also in keeping with this explanation. For, in the case of the other epistles, it may be assumed that one is always dealing with authentic words.

Besides the remarkable affinity between Eph. and R., there are also differences. These however, may be ascribed to a possible change of secretary, a difference in time and circumstance and a different manner of writing. In this connection, we refer the reader back to p. 202.

The remarkable correspondence between Eph. and R. could also be explained on the basis of the hypothesis that the secretary who dealt with R., wrote Eph. on his own. But this second explanation lacks one of the advantages of our first explanation. For that explanation was grounded on a certain indicium, namely the fact that in the praescripts of both epistles, only Paul is named as the sender.

Nor is the second explanation directly reconcilable with the identical nature of the styles of Eph. and 1 C. 1:1-9 or the correspondence in style between Eph. and several passages in Phil. and 2 C. Although it may be taken for granted that Paul was himself involved in the writing of those other epistles (the authenticity of 1 and 2 C. and Phil. is generally accepted), it cannot per se be assumed that the same secretary who worked on R. was also employed in the writing of all these epistles.

Less satisfactory even, is the hypothesis that the correspondence between Eph. and R. is due to the fact that yet another member of the Pauline circle, i.e. one of the co-senders of one of the HP, was responsible for Eph. Admittedly, Timotheus is named as co-sender in most of the epistles of the CPminus. (This is also the case with Col.) However, the difficulty is that in precisely R., Timotheus is not the co-sender. Nor is Timotheus a co-sender with respect to 1 C. in which we found a style in 1:1-9 which is identical to that of Eph. (In this epistle, Sosthenes is mentioned in that capacity.) We therefore give preference to the assumption that the remarkable correspondence between Eph. and R. may be explained by the fact that Paul and Paul alone bore the responsibility for both these works. Research into the style of Eph. therefore shows that in all likelihood Paul was the author of Eph.

Throughout the investigations which led to these conclusions, we have availed ourselves of statistical data which naturally did not attain to that standard of exactitude achieved by Morton and his computer analysis. Nevertheless, I choose the results of personal research over and above those of Morton.

I have already rejected the absolute validity of Morton's criterion of authenticity.[1] From our investigation it can be seen that Morton's investigation was not sufficiently comprehensive. His work is confined to sentence-length and the frequency of the words καί, ἐν, αὐτος, εἶναι and δέ. However, other stylistic phenomena, which also lend themselves to objective definition and whose frequency is also open to comparison, are likewise present and should be taken into account. For not only the frequency of such very general words as καὶ, ἐν etc. but also usage of less common words can be characteristic of the style of a speaker or a writer.

Thus the refutation of the authenticity of Eph. by Morton should certainly not be allowed to weigh more heavily than acceptance of the authenticity of Eph. on the strength of the lexicological statistical research undertaken by Grayston and Herdan.[2]

Curiously enough, Morton's research lends force to the theory he so sharply rejected, namely that an amenuensis or a secretary could have influenced the style of Paul's epistles.[3] As it is, he was gradually forced to admit that in the first 150 sentences of what he held to be the authentic R. and in the first part of 2 C., the style does not come up to his own criteria of authenticity and that on the basis of those criteria, some other objections can be raised against R. and 1 and 2 C. These findings may be discounted on the basis of a theory which allows for a certain contribution on the part of co-senders and secretaries in the epistles of Paul.[4]

If Morton continues to reject that kind of theory and if he persists in the one-sidedness of his restricted statistical research, his criticism will have to become even more radical than that of the great Baur whom he held up as his champion and, ultimately, Gal. will be the only epistle left which he will be able to recognise as wholly authentic.

In any event it seems to me that Morton's methods of research will have to be greatly expanded and developed. Not only will it need a

---

[1] See p. 16ss.

[2] See p. 15s.

[3] The Observer, 10 November 1963, "The Rev. A. Q. Morton replies" and Journal of the Royal Statistical Society, Series A, vol. 128, part 2, p. 232.

[4] See note 1, on p. 20.

broad lexocological basis but Morton will also need to acquire more of
an eye for the fact that the same author may have command over more
than a single literary style.[1] It seems in any case to have escaped his
attention that side by side with lively prose which is related to the
diatribe, Paul uses a quite different way of expressing himself when
the subject concerns prayer, thanksgiving or avowal. Morton assesses
the style of Eph. in exactly the same manner as he judges Paul's
ordinary prose. The lyrical, poetical and intensive character of the style
of Eph. has evaded Morton's meticulous but incomplete and mechanical investigation.

One the basis of purely formal correspondences between Eph. and
R., I have already stated my objection to the construction of Goodspeed
and Mitton (p. 71). On the basis of aspects that are less formal within
the strictest sense of the word, renewed objections may be lodged
against their interpretation.

The view held by Goodspeed and Mitton is that the author of Eph.,
having long been familiar with Col. and Phlm., subsequently became
acquainted with R., 1 and 2 C., Gal., Phil. and 1 and 2 Th. He then
absorbed Paul's ideas and decided to produce a work which was to
be in the nature of an introduction to the collected epistles of Paul
and, in addition, to serve as a contemporary version of Paul's thoughts.
To this purpose, the alleged author took smaller and larger groups
of words from Col. in particular, but also from the other epistles of
Paul, converting these into the integrated components of his own
work.[2]

What escaped Goodspeed and Mitton is that the correspondence
between Eph. and the HP goes beyond a correspondence in ideas and
a certain degree of homophony. If this correspondence of ideas and this
use of corresponding expressions and words were to be the only constituents, then this alleged long-standing familiarity with Col. and Phlm.,
the later encounter with the other epistles, the absorption of Paul's

---

[1] Cf. Herdan, Journal, p. 230 on Morton : "The author persistently confuses style
and authorship. The same author may write in a different style at different occasions
and periods, and, on the other hand, different authors may have the same style, if one
defines style, as does Mr. Morton, in terms of the use of a few grammar words only.
In fact rightly understood, even style, let alone authorship, cannot be defined in this
way. It was Yule who first showed how to define it, e.g. in terms of the use of the whole
vocabulary (nours, in his work), and this method has been very much developed in
recent years."

[2] See Chapter I, para. 3.

thoughts and the reproduction of his words could perhaps have served as an adequate explanation for the particular afinity with Col. and the further affinity with the other epistles.

However, in this last chapter we have once again ascertained that the correspondence between Eph. and the HP reaches much farther. It likewise embraces stylistic phenomena. Thus there is a striking correspondence in the use of long sentences (p. 107ss.). Eph. 1:1-14 and R. 1:1-10 both have an interplay of prepositions (p. 117s.).

Corresponding thought-rhyming patterns are found in Eph. 1:3-14; R. 1:1-7 and 3:21-26. Likewise the thought-rhyming in Eph. 2:14-18 is related to that in Phil. 2:5-8 (p. 146ss.). The connection of two sub-stantives through $\dot{\epsilon}\nu$ is found both in Eph. and in R. (p. 114s.). The same peculiar genitive construction appears in both Eph. 1:18 and R. 4:12 (p. 122s.). In various passages in Eph. and in the HP, the genitive constitutes a stylistic factor (p. 127).

None of these phenomena are characteristic of the style of Col. Long sentences there may be in Col.; but the affinity between the long sent-ences of Eph. and other Pauline sentences is by no means restricted to those of Col. (p. 107ss.). In Col., there is but one instance of a rhythm of genitives (p. 128). Col. does not feature the same type of thought-rhyming as Eph. 1:3-14; R. 1:1-7 and 3:21-26. Nor do the other pheno-mena described occur in Col. Therefore, it cannot be alleged that all these characteristics penetrated into the style of Eph. because the author of Eph. was so very familiar with Col. that he could even imitate its style.

Thus the idea of Goodspeed and Mitton that this author, after a relatively short period of intense concentration on the HP should have progressed so far that he could not only imitate the style of Col. but also reproduce certain stylistic idiosyncracies of the other epistles, is highly improbable.

The fact of the matter is that these phenomena did not automatically appear in the text of Eph. because they formed part of the extracts which the author of Eph. borrowed from the HP or reproduced from memory. For the places in which the idiosyncracies of style in question feature in the HP, have for the rest very little or nothing in common with the places in Eph. where they appear.

Thus, Eph. 1:1-14; R. 1:10 and 3:21-26, have no other affinities beyond the occurrence of the general words of greeting in Eph. 1:2 and R. 1:7 and the words $\chi\dot{\alpha}\rho\iota\varsigma$, $\dot{\alpha}\pi o\lambda\acute{\upsilon}\tau\rho\omega\sigma\iota\varsigma$ and $a\hat{\iota}\mu a$ in Eph. 1:6, 7 and R. 3:24, 25. In other places where the above-quoted phenomena appear in the HP, equally little further correspondence will be found with the places where they occur in Eph.[1]

Also a part of the words and expressions which are typical of the HP and which Eph. possesses, are again found in the HP and Eph. in particularly those places which have nothing more in common (p. 181s.).

Therefore, within the framework of the explanation which Goodspeed and Mitton gave for the correspondence between Eph. and the HP. the correspondence in style and vocabulary between Eph. and the HP which remained unremarked by them, could only be explained in terms of imitation. And this is unlikely. Is can scarcely be assumed that a writer, by familiarising himself with a number of epistles, should not only arrive at a partial synthesis of the thoughts and ideas contained in those epistles in a work adapted to the demands of his own time, but that he should also have succeeded in imitating not only the individual style of one of these epistles but a multitude of stylistic characteristics which might feature in all the epistles but this one. The idea that an epistle as Eph., which really does form a complete whole and contains no disparate elements, should have been conceived in such a fashion, deserves no credit whatsoever.

A still odder situation arises if this work of art in alleged to be the work of someone who was in no way concerned with the creation of the other epistles. It is especially unlikely that a non-Jew—for Mitton would have it that the author of Eph. was of pagan origin [2]—should have written this epistle in what was (unremarked by Mitton) a traditional Jewish-hellenistic style, heavily influenced by Hebrew and Aramaic,

A curious fact and one very disfavourable to the thesis of imitation of the HP on the part of the author of Eph., is that in Eph. 4:11, a place which has much in common with 1 C. 12:28 and is therefore in the first place a suitable candidate for literary dependence, the expression $\tau\iota\theta\acute{\epsilon}\nu\alpha\iota$ $\tau\iota\nu\acute{\alpha}$ $\tau\iota$ from 1 C. 12:28 has not been used but, instead, $\delta\iota\delta\acute{o}\nu\alpha\iota$ $\tau\iota\nu\acute{\alpha}$ $\tau\iota$. This discrepancy in not easily reconciled with the theory of literary dependence. But beside this difference, lies a deeper and almost hidden correspondence. The $\delta\iota\delta\acute{o}\nu\alpha\iota$ $\tau\iota\nu\acute{\alpha}$ $\tau\iota$ in Eph. 4:11 is influenced to practically the same extent by a preceding $\check{\epsilon}\delta\omega\kappa\epsilon\nu$ as the $\tau\iota\theta\acute{\epsilon}\nu\alpha\iota$ $\tau\iota\nu\acute{\alpha}$ $\tau\iota$ of 1 C. 12:28 is by a preceding $\check{\epsilon}\theta\epsilon\tau o$ (p. 180). This

---

[1] See Mitton, The Epistle to the Ephesians, p. 280ss., Appendix I.

[2] Op. cit., pp. 262 and 264.

almost imperceptible affinity strongly suggests that Eph. 4:11 in its
context and 1 C. 12:28 in its particular context, are both products of
the same mind.

In any event, it is a fact that until now those who dispute the authenticity of Eph. have used the difference in style between Eph. and the
HP too rashly in support of their contention. This application of the
facts will be justified only when all the correspondence in style between
Eph. and the HP which was demonstrated in this chapter has been allowed to come into its rightful estate.

CHAPTER SEVEN

THE MEANING AND SIGNIFICANCE OF CERTAIN EXPRES-
SIONS WHICH HAVE A COSMIC ASPECT OR ARE
ANTHROPOLOGICAL IN CHARACTER

1. Ἐπουράνιος *the heavenly*

Now that the examination into the formal correspondence between
Eph. and the other epistles comprising the CPminus has been dealt
with, it is time to put the content of our epistle to the test. To begin
with, we shall be studying a number of salient words which have a
cosmic aspect or are anthropological in character.

Whilst doing this, it will often be necessary to consider images and
concepts connected with these words which had other connotations
during the first century. Thus for example, we shall be dealing with
syncreticism and gnosticism.

It would also be impossible to restrict ourselves exclusively to first
century material because to a large extent, these first century images
and concepts are accessible only through the medium of later documents. These, although of a later date, incorporate a considerable
proportion of older material. This is of specific relevance to, for
example, the Greek magical papyri found in Egypt and the Corpus
Hermeticum.

Without doubt, the word ἐπουράνιος is one of the striking words
which has a cosmic implication. It occurs on five occasions, each time
forming part of the expression ἐν τοῖς ἐπουρανίοις.[1] Usually, the
word conveys that something or someone is in heaven. Used in connection with both astronomical phenomena as well as gods, the word
has in the first place a local meaning. This is so in the case of classical
Greek as well as the Greek of the LXX and the hellenistic world.[2]

A qualificatory idea may be attached to the local meaning of the

---

[1] Eph. 1:3, 20; 2:6; 3:10 and 6:12.

[2] Cf. Th. W. V, p. 538s. and Liddell-Scott, s.v. A hellenistic example is found in Deissmann, L. v. O. where, p. 220 line 3041s., the great magical papyrus of the Bibliothèque
Nationale, Paris, is partly reproduced. Here a demon is addressed : καὶ σὺ λάλησον ὁποῖον
ἐὰν ἦς ἐπεουράνιον ἢ ἀέριον εἴτε ἐπίγειον εἴτε ὑπόγειον ἢ καταχθόνιον ... ἐπουράνιος is here
synonymous with ἀέριος as ὑπόγειος is with καταχθόνιος.

word; that which is heavenly is superior. This is true also of the Greek of different periods.[1]

Paul uses the word, together with ἐπίγειος and καταχθόνιος, in the masculine plural in Phil. 2:10 by itself as an indication of locality.[2]

In 1 C. 15:48, it is used in contrast with χοϊκός and there is a clear qualitative differentiation; the category ἐπουράνιος is linked with the categories of πνευματικός, ἀθάνατος, ἄφθαρτος and with the βασιλεία τοῦ θεοῦ.

In a number of places in Eph., as in the case of Phil. 2:10, the masculine plural could likewise be kept in mind and ἐν τοῖς ἐπουρανίοις could be translated as "in the midst of them that are in heaven."[3] One difficulty however, is that the personal meaning of the masculine does not fit in with Eph. 3:10. There is no reason whatsoever to suppose that in this instance the archai and the exousiai are being singled out from amongst a great gathering of heavenly dwellers—denoted by ἐν τοῖς ἐπουρανίοις—as the only group not yet familiar with the wisdom of God.

It is also feasible to regard ἐν τοῖς ἐπουρανίοις as in incomplete expression which should be augmented by τόποις or μέρεσιν. The substantive is quite often omitted in the case of attributed formed by an adjective when the context leaves little doubt as to which substantive is intended. The substantive μέρος in particular, is often missing.

However, it is not always obvious in Eph. which substantive has been omitted. Whenever the substantive μέρος is missing elsewhere, the subject is concerned with the horizontal plane. Here, on the other hand, it appertains to the vertical plane.[4] Moreover, it is odd that,

---

[1] A Pindaric fragment speaks of εὐσεβέων ἐπουράνιοι ψυχαί, Philo of ἐπουρανίοις ἐπιστήμαις (cf. Th. W. V, p. 539 lines 7, 8, 20 and Liddell-Scott, s.v.) and the Codex Alexandrinus in 4 Macc. 11:3 of τῇ ἐπουρανίῳ δίκῃ. To the Hebrew mind, the local difference between heaven and earth can also go side by side with a qualitative difference; cf. Qoh. 5:1 and Is. 55:9. For late Jewish examples, see Meuzelaar, Der Leib des Mesias, p. 103s.

[2] Thus, there is a division of the cosmos into three parts here, as in the Jewish example cited on p. 213 in n. 2. Deissmann, op. cit., p. 223, note 11, speaks of "geläufige jüdische Kategorien" (fluent Jewish categories).

[3] M. Goguel, Introduction du N.T. IV, 2 (Paris 1920), p. 441, note 1 "parmi les êtres célestes".

[4] For the omission of the substantive, particularly μέρος, see Bl.-Debr., para. 241, p. 150s. M. Pope, Of the heavenly places (Exp. T. 1912, p. 365ss.) argues that τοῖς ἐπουρανίοις is neutral and translated this as the heavenly places. To support this, he puts

in spite of the fact that the expression is so frequently used, the substantive is omitted again and again.

Therefore, we think that it would be better to regard the plural (τοῖς) ἐπουρανίοις in the light of a substantiated adjective (with article) constituting a categorical indication of concrete phenomena.[1] A similar plural is found in Phil. 3:19 (τὰ ἐπίγεια) and in Col. 1:16 (τὰ ὁρατὰ καὶ τὰ ἀόρατα).

The expression τὰ ἐπουράνια can be interpreted as the heavenly bodies. In non-biblical Greek, both τὰ ἐπουρανια and τὰ μετέωρα are used to indicate astronomical phenomena.[2] Persons, however, may equally fall under this kind of categorical definition; cf. 1 C. 1:27, 28. Like the categories τὰ ὁρατὰ καὶ τὰ ἀόρατα(Col. 1:16), τὰ ἐπουράνια may embrace not only things but also persons or beings.

In this respect, no exception should be made with regard to the heavenly abodes. According to 2 Macc. 3:39, God has a heavenly abode. He is ὁ τὴν κατοικίαν ἐπουράνιον ἔχων. This abode is equivalent to heaven as such; cf. Deut. 26:15. Other instances of particular heavenly abodes come to mind; cf. Lk. 16:9; John 14:2; 2 C. 5:1.

We may therefore best translate τὰ ἐπουράνια as "the heavenly". This expression encompasses all that is heaven, belongs to heaven and is in heaven. The qualificatory idea attached to the word ἐπουράνιος in 1 C. 15:48, is also common to τὰ ἐπουράνια in Eph. 1:3. Here too, ἐπουράνιος is associated with πνευματικός. In 1:20 and 2:6 the qualificatory thought may also be present but generally when it occurs in Eph., the strictly local meaning of the expression predominates. For that reason it is always connected with the preposition ἐν.

There is no reason whatsoever to regard this expression qua talis as an objection to the authenticity of Eph. The fact that the neuter τὰ ἐπουράνια does not occur in other epistles is an obvious conclusion; in other epistles the concept of heaven is mentioned less.[3]

---

forward the expression ἐν τοῖς ὑψίστοις which, in Mt. 21:9; Mk. 11:10; Lk. 2:14; 19:38, occurs to describe the idea of heaven. As a counter-argument, it may be said that this expression has been taken from the LXX in which its form had already been established; cf. LXX Job 16:19; Ps. 148:1.

[1] Cf. Bl.-Debr., para. 263, p. 165 and Van Veldhuizen, Het taaleigen des N.T., para. 43, page 161.

[2] Cf. Th. W. V, p. 539 line 21, 22; Liddell-Scott s.v. ἐπουράνιος and μετέωρος; and the σώματα ἐπουράνια of 1 C. 15.40 (sun, moon and stars).

[3] R. has 2 times οὐρανός; 1 C. ditto; 2 C. has 3 times οὐρανός (the plural occurs in 5:1 and in 12:2 the concept of a number of heavens); Gal. 1ce; Phil. 1ce; 1 Th. 2 times (once in the plural) and 2 Th. 1ce. Eph. has οὐρανός 4 times in the plural and ἐν τοῖς ἐπουρανίοις 5 times. Col. features οὐρανός 5 times (of which 3 in the plural).

2. Τὰ πάντα

Still more comprehensive than the expression τὰ ἐπουράνια is the expression (τὰ) πάντα which is used repeatedly in Eph. in pronouncements having a direct bearing on God and / or Christ.

The use of the expression τὸ πᾶν or (τὰ) πάντα as a comprehensive expression to embrace all that is created belongs to an extremely ancient philosophical terminology whilst the reduction of "all" or "all things" to a single principle is an equally venerable philosophical tradition.

This reduction of all to a single principle formed the very cornerstone of Stoic philosophy; the concept accentuated the divine character of the all-embracing and all-permeating unity. The same principle provided the foundation to the doctrine of salvation preached by hellenistic mysticism which sought to lead man towards rebirth and apotheosis.

Hellenistic Judaism also became familiar with Stoic concepts; thus it need occasion no surprise when formulations occur in R. 11:36; 1 C. 8:6; Eph. 4:6 and in Col. 1:6s., which are closely related to those of the popular Stoa.[1]

As Dibelius and Bultmann suggested, it must be assumed that in Eph. 4:6 where the utterance is clearly geared to the believers, the cosmological formulation has been given an ecclesiological twist.[2]

As in most cosmological formulations, the various plural forms of πᾶς in Eph. 4:6 are mostly in the neuter gender but this neuter refers to people (cf. 1 C, 1;27, 28) and specifically to the persons indicated in 4:7 by ἡμῶν. They are οἱ ἄνθρωποι (4:8), for whom the formulation represents truth and reality. The neuter plural of πᾶς is used here in the same way as in Gal. 3:22.[3]

Where τὰ πάντα is the direct subject of God's actions in some other formulations in Eph., the expression, in accordance with the philoso-

---

[1] Cf. Norden, Agnostos Theos, p. 240ss.; Clemen, Relig. Erklärung, p. 128; Dib. Gefbr., p. 60; Lietzmann, An die Römer, p. 107; Dupont, Gnosis, p. 335ss.; B. Reicke, Th. W. V, p. 891 lines 1-40 and Mussner, Christus, das All und die Kirche (²1968), p. 29.

[2] Cf. Dibelius l.c. and Bultmann, Theol., p. 74.

[3] Sieffert, Der Brief an die Galater, p. 221 : "Das Neutrum bezeichnet also Personen, welche dadurch unter den Gesichtspunkt der allgemeinen Kategorie gestellt werden, die Gesamtheit" ("The neuter therefore designates people who are thus placed amongst the general category, that of totality"). (The fact that the article is missing from Eph. 4:6 could be the result of an adaptation from current cosmological formulations.)

phical tradition as projected onto Jewish hellenism, must be indicative of the cosmos as a whole. Such is the case with the τὰ πάντα of 1:10 which relates God's intention to gather together all in Christ at the end of time.

There is no reason to restrict this eschatologically redeeming, unifying [1] work of God to the ecclesia. In the μυστήριον of v. 9, the subject concerns the unity of Israel and the nations (cf. 3:4ss.). In the εὐδοκία (ἣν προέθετο) it has to do with the wider perspective which is connected with this μυστήριον and embraces heaven and earth.

Paul expects that the whole of creation (πᾶσα ἡ κτίσις) will be snatched from the jaws of corruption and will partake in immortality when the messianic time has come. Late Jewish apocryphal apocalyptic literature provides us with evidence that in pronouncements of this kind both Paul, Jesus and ancient Christianity must have had in mind something in the nature of a renewed heaven and earth.[2] The fact is that the same breadth of vision in present in Eph. 1:10.

The τὰ πάντα in Eph. 3:9, which is brought into a direct relationship with God by means of the word κτίσας, can be nothing but a comprehensive designation embracing all that is created, in the contemplation of which, as the context dictates, the heavenly reality should not be forgotten.

In Eph. 1:22, the πάντα which has been taken from LXX Ps. 8:7, is probably more limited in meaning; for the πάντα in LXX Ps. 8:7 has a very clearly restricted significance. The beginning of the psalm says that the glory of God is above that of the heavens. However, not only heaven but earth too, is considered in the psalm. When it is said of the ἄνθρωπος or the υἱὸς ἀνθρώπου that he has been given dominion by God over the work of God's hands and that God has put all things under his feet, the interest is diverted to the beasts of the land, the

---

[1] For the redeeming character of unity, see Hanson, The Unity of the Church in the N.T., Colossians and Ephesians, p. 126.

[2] See Schweitzer, Die Mystik des Apostels Paulus, pp. 56, 67, 81. The idea of H. Traub, Th. W. V, p. 157, that all in heaven and earth is gathered together as a body and that Christ is the head of this body, is based on a false interpretation of the expression κεφαλή due to a confusion between the concept of the wordly god and that of the godly anthropos. Nor is it correct when Traub translates ἀνακεφαλαιώσασθαι as "wie in einem Haupt zusammenfassen" ("to gather together in one head"), meaning a head belonging to a body. The word ἀνακεφαλαιώσασθαι which derives not, from κεφαλή but from κεφάλαιον, is obviously a pun on the being κεφαλή of Christ; but still this does not imply the idea that the object belonging to that ἀνακεφαλαιώσασθαι is necessarily a body.

birds of the air and the fish of the sea and the subject particularly concerns the earth where the name of God is excellent.

Despite the fact that it was not the custom during the late Judaic period to apply the exegesis of a word from the Writs too narrowly to the context,[1] one nevertheless gains the impression that much of the original sense of the quotation πάντα ὑπέταξεν ὑπὸ τοὺς πόδας αὐτοῦ has been preserved in Eph.; it would seem that the quotation has been used not so much to illustrate Christ's exaltation over all that is in heaven as his dominion over the earth, over the visible creation, with which man is daily associated. Eph. 1:20-22a more or less evokes the image of the all-present ruler of the world which is found in Is. 66:1 : "the heaven is my throne, and the earth is my footstool".

In 1:22b., however, the word πάντα in the phrase κεφαλὴν ὑπὲρ πάντα is broader in meaning, embracing heaven and earth. He who sits upon the throne of heaven and has the earth for His footstool, is all-surpassing and nothing in heaven or on earth is excluded from his power.

In Eph. 1:11, τὰ πάντα has yet another aspect. In connection with the fact that men have been predestined by God to obtain an inheritance (i.e. eschatological salvation), the text mentions God who worketh "all things" after the counsel of his own will; that is to say, who carries out what He decides, consistently and without defects. ἐνεργεῖν usually stresses the activity of the subject, not the object. Nor is it synonymous with ποιεῖν "to make".[2] Thus in this instance the expression τὰ πάντα is not a comprehensive term for all that has been made by God, the whole of creation as a concrete reality, but a comprehensive term for the sum total of God's design.

In Eph. 1:22b we already saw that Christ was spoken of as a κεφαλὴν ὑπὲρ πάντα. In 4:10 we read that he has ascended above all heavens, that he might fill "all things". In this cosmic context too, τὰ πάντα can represent nothing more or less than a comprehensive expression for all that has been created.

In Eph. 1:23, the predicate [3] τοῦ τὰ πάντα ἐν πᾶσιν πληρουμένου is applied to Christ but would be appropriate for God. τὰ πάντα must have the same meaning. Firstly, there is a close connection with

---

[1] See J. N. Sevenster, "Jezus en de Ebed Jahwe" in Ned. Theol. Tijdschrift 13, 1958, p. 27s.

[2] Cf. the meanings given by Liddell-Scott (s.v. ἐνεργεῖν) and G. Bertram (Th. W. II, p. 649s.).

[3] This is an example of the "hymnische Partizipialstil" discussed on p. 130 in n. 6 and on p. 131 in n. 1.

the κεφαλὴν ὑπερ πάντα in which πάντα also takes into account the whole of creation, secondly there is an analogy with the words ἵνα πληρώσῃ τὰ πάντα in Eph. 4:10 and in the third place πληροῦν is used in popular Stoic language and by Philo in combination with τὰ πάντα in the sense of the entire cosmos.

The ἐν πᾶσιν which follows τὰ πάντα is an intensification, the equivalent of the intensifications which are found in such statements when made by the popular Stoa or Philo. It expresses that Christ will fulfill everything to such an extent that he will permeate all and be present in all. In both the expressions   τὰ πάντα and ἐν πᾶσιν [1] the entirety of all, all that exists, the totality of all that is created is indicated.[2]

Neither immediately preceding nor following Eph. 4:15, is any other πάντα used to indicate either the cosmos or the whole of creation. Nor are heaven or earth mentioned. It is therefore improbable that τὰ πάντα is here intended to signify the cosmos.

Within the direct context however, οἱ πάντες (v. 13) and πᾶν τὸ σῶμα (v. 16) are mentioned. Thus it is obvious that a comprehensive expression has been used here for the whole of the faithful, anticipating the term πᾶν τὸ σῶμα in 4:16.

We find a similar phenomenon in 1 C. 12:19 where τὰ πάντα corresponds with the expression ὅλον τὸ σῶμα in 1 C. 12:17. On the basis of this, there is no reason to adopt Schlier's interpretation of the words τὰ πάντα in Eph. 4:15. The idea that the faithful or the ecclesia will increase the cosmos does not enter into Eph. 4:15.[3] The reflections on the cosmos in Eph. remain within the framework of the other epistles.

3. THE POWERS

The unusual amount of attention devoted to heaven and to the whole of creation in Eph., is combined with a no less striking interest in

---

[1] πᾶσιν is also used as a neuter noun.

[2] For pronouncements of the popular Stoa or Philo in which πάντα incidates the cosmos, see Dupont, Gnosis, p. 463ss. In a number of these prouncements, the intensative διὰ πάντων occurs.

[3] This interpretation is found in Schlier, Eph. p. 205s. Abbott (Eph.-Col., p. 123s.) and Käsemann (Exeg. Versuche u. Besinnungen I, p. 292 line 23s.) regard τὰ πάντα as an accusativus partis or an adverbial accusative with an intransitive αὐξήσωμεν. Reserve should be exercised with respect to this explanation. The examples showing the adverbial use of τὰ πάντα in Liddell-Scott (s.v. πᾶς sub D II. 4) oriignate from older manuscripts.

influential supernatural spirits or powers. The reason for this is that the recipients of the epistle probably lived in an environment where a religious devotion for the cosmos as a whole went side by side with a dread of the influence of miscellaneous cosmic forces and in particular that of heavenly bodies.

The special attention which is given to supernatural powers in Eph., most likely stems from the pastoral motive of preserving the recipients from a relapse into pagan religiosity or a combination of such concepts with those of the Christian religion.[1]

The author of Eph. delivers no direct polemics against pagan or syncretical doctrines. Instead, he propounds his own theme : the Exaltation and the Lordship of Jesus. This central theme lengs organic unity to his pronouncements on heaven, on the totality of creation and on the supernatural powers.

He who has been exalted is the Lord, the kurios. He has dominion over the world and is exalted above alll other powers. This is as it was conceived also by the most ancient Christians. For ancient Christianity. it lay entirely within the framework of reference of Jesus' ascent to heaven and subsequent glorification, to state with emphasis that in the face of the Lord all influential spirits or forces are left powerless.[2]

Eph. creates the impression that a variegated multitude of such forces of energy exists,[3] that some of then are inimically disposed towards the ecclesia and that these will not be in "ὁ αἰὼν ὁ μέλλων", whilst the other part, which is positive in character, will also occupy a place in that coming aeon, under Christ (Eph. 1:21). In my opinion, throughout

---

[1] See De Zwaan, De Efezenbrief van Paulus, pp. 60, 26-34, 53-63. De Zwaan is thinking of a religiosity in which the popularised concepts of the Stoa combine with general astrological beliefs and which also contained certain Persian elements.

[2] The extent to which the central theme of the Exaltation and Lordship of Jesus held the above-mentioned aspects for Paul and ancient Christianity becomes clear in Phil. 2:6-11. With respect to Eph. 6:12, A. Bengel comments : "Quo apertius quisque scripturae liber de oeconomia et gloriae Christi agit, eo apertius rursum de regno contrario tenebrarum". See his Gnomon Novi Testamenti (Stuttgartiae 1891), p. 776. Cf. also R. Ch. Trench, notes on the Parables of our Lord (London, Eightieth Thousand), p. 94 (note 2). Cullmann, Die ersten christlichen Glaubensbekenntnisse, p. 53ss., reveals how closely for ancient Christendom, Christ's might over the powers was connected with the avowal of his Ascension and Exaltation.

[3] For the question to what degree these forces were attributed with a personal character, see H. Berkhof, Christus en de machten (Nijkerk 1952), p. 23ss. and H. Schlier Mächte und Gewalten im Neuen Testament (Quaetiones Disputae 3, Freib. i. Br. 1959) p. 17ss.

the CP minus a like multitude of negative and positive forces are also presumed to exist.[1]

Amongst the host of negative powers (and this applies to Eph. as well as to the CP minus) there is a single predominant figure who, as it were, stands out. Eph. 2:2 speaks of the ἄρχων τῆς ἐξουσίας τοῦ ἀέρος and 2 C. 4:4 of the θεὸς τοῦ αἰῶνος τούτου. In addition, Eph. refers to the διάβολος (Eph. 4:27; 6:11), whilst the CP minus (e.g. 1 C. 5:5) mentions the σατανᾶς. The CP minus does not explain whether or not the god of this world and the Satan are intended to be one and the same figure. Nor does Eph. make clear whether the archon in question and the diabolos are identical characters.[2]

However, it is evident that the diabolos employs the forces of the negative powers and has chosen the ecclesia as his target, whilst the archon under discussion has dominated the pre-Christian lives of the recipients and continues to rule the lives of the unbelievers (Eph. 6:11; 2:2).

In the CP minus, we see the Satan as the great antagonist of believers and apostles. He is able to command over ἄγγελοι. Also it is stated that the god of this world blinds the unbelievers. R. 16:20; 1 C. 5:5; 7:5; 2 C. 2:11; 1 Th. 2:18 illustrate the aforementioned activity of Satan. 2 C. 12:7 speaks of an ἄγγελος σατανᾶ.[3] For the activity of the god of this world amongst the unbelievers, see 2 C. 4:4.

---

[1] The definitive separation of the negative and positive forces will take place at an eschatological judgement of the believers. The believers are the saints who will judge the world and the angels. The conclusion arrived at by Lietzmann and other scholars (cf. Lietzmann, An die Korinther I-II, ³1931, p. 25) that this κρίνειν will deal only with the "fallen angels" and will be nothing short of a damnation, is not to be deduced from 1 C. 6:2ss. κρίνειν can be used in the pregnant sense and mean either to damn or to condemn. The real meaning is to sift, separate or judge. In the context of 1 C. 6:2ss., it concerns a binding pronouncement on certain issues. Therefore, the interpreter should be warned against attaching the pregnant meaning of "to damn" or "to condemn" to the word κρίνειν as used in 1 C. 6:2ss. When, at the eschatological judgement of the saints, a division will be made in the world and between the angels, the negative part will be annihilated. For this element, the κρίνειν will indeed have the effect of a κατακρίνειν. (Elsewhere, namely in 1 C. 2:6; 15:24, an καταργεῖν is mentioned .This verb means to make absolutely of no effect).

[2] Cf. A. J. Visser, "Gnostische" trekken in het denken van Paulus", Vox Theologica 30, no. 1, 1959, p. 22.

[3] The exegesis of Cramer, Stoicheia tou kosmou, p. 110, that in 2 C. 12:7 Paul merely wanted to say that the Satan is in his existence represented by an angel in a metaphorical sense. i.e. by this thorn in the flesh, may be dismissed. The word σκόλοψ, the sharp pointed object, is evidently used metaphorically - it is improbable that the word ἄγγελος should, over and above that, also be metaphorical.

Eph. adds a few new designations to the vocabularly of the CP minus :

1. οἱ κοσμοκράτορες τοῦ σκότους τούτου 6 : 12.

In the other epistles too, the sphere of the believers is contrasted to that of darkness: cf. R. 13:12; 2 C. 6:14 and 1 Th. 5:4, 5. This other area of life of which the believers once formed part but from which they have now been delivered, may also be characterised as ὁ αἰὼν ὁ ἐνεστὼς πονηρός Gal. 1:4.

The negative masters of that area are correspondingly spoken of as οἱ ἄρχοντες τοῦ αἰῶνος τούτου οἱ καταργούμενοι (1 C. 2:6). In the pagan world, the word κοσμοκράτωρ is regarded as a divine predicate.[1]

If the author of Eph. had this in mind, then the expression in Eph. 6:12 conceals the same kind of irony as the ὁ θεὸς τοῦ αἰῶνος τούτου of 2 C. 4:4. The same irony is in evidence in the designation δαιμόνια for the heathen deities in 1 C. 10:20.

2. τὰ πνευματικὰ τῆς πονηρίας 6 : 12.

Here again, the neuter plural forms a comprehensive expression describing the totality of the pneumata who are more closely defined as evil by means of the genitive.[2]

From the addition of these two obviously unfavourable categories to the categories of ἀρχαί and ἐξουσίαι, it emerges that the latter must also be taken in sensu malo. In no instance does it follow as a matter of course that these archai and exousia, unless it is apparent from the context, must be regarded as unfavourable and negative, i.e. that each archon and each exousia in considered to be negative by the author and of the realm of darkness.

I am therefore quite unable to share the view of A. W. Cramer that Eph. conjures up a picture of exclusively demonic world powers, armed and led by Satan, thus differing essentially from the so-called authentic epistles amongst which Cramer numbers Col., with respect to the nature of supernatural spirits of powers.[3]

---

[1] Later on, Christians used the word κοσμοκράτορες for demons; cf. Papyrus Cairo 10263, p. 15 (= P. 13 in K. Preisendanz, Papyri Graecae Magicae II, p. 200s.).

[2] For the neuter plural as a categoric identification of concrete plenomena, see p. 203 and note 7. G. Harder, Th. W. VI, p. 566, speaks of a "Kollektivbegriff" (collective term) and translates : "die Geisterwelt" (spirit world). Cf. also p. 174.

[3] Cramer, Stoicheia tou Kosmou, p. 81ss.

3. ὁ ἄρχων τῆς ἐξουσίας τοῦ ἀέρος 2 : 2.

This indeed, is a highly circumstantial appellation. We have already seen in Chapter VI, paras. 5 and 6, that it is fully in keeping with the style of Eph. that adverbial adjuncts introduced by the same preposition which have a related or similar meaning are joined together or that synonymous or related substantives are connected by means of a genitive. The first component is demonstrated in Eph. 2:2 by the combination of κατὰ τὸν ἄρχοντα τῆς ἐξουσίας τοῦ ἀέρος with the preceding κατὰ τὸν αἰῶνα τοῦ κόσμου τούτου, whilst the second is manifest in the connection of αἰὼν τοῦ κόσμου as well as that of ἄρχων τῆς ἐξουσίας.

In 1 C. 2:6, 8, the matter concerns a plurality of ἄρχοντες, but here in Eph. 2:2, we are concerned with one particular ἄρχων who stands at the head of an ἐξουσία.

What is the meaning of this word ἐξουσία? In connection with this and other similar words, Deissmann drew a parallel with the terminology of oriental courtly style.[1] In Col. (and in 1 C. 15:24), the word is used in the plural form. In the official world of the hellenistic society, the authorities were often designated by the same plural. The singular form, ἐξουσία, could also be used to indicate a group or board of such officials.[2] Thus the idea of a group of ἐξουσίαι must be borne in mind with the ἐξουσία of Eph. 2:2.[3]

These are as it were located in the ἀήρ. The air, the ἀήρ meaning the space which stretches from the earth to the moon, was according to the conceptions of late antiquity the characteristic realm of demons.[4]

The entire body of ἐξουσίαι assembled under this archon and dwelling in the ἀήρ is qualified as a πνεῦμα in the subsequent closer description. In the same way as 2 C. 4:4 talks of the θεὸς τοῦ αἰῶνος τούτου so Eph. 2:2 speaks of a single dominant figure ὁ ἄρχων. And as 1 C. 2:12 relates of the existence of τὸ πνεῦμα τοῦ κόσμου, so Eph. 2:2 mentions τὸ πνεῦμα τὸ νῦν ἐνεργοῦν ἐν τοῖς υἱοῖς τῆς ἀπειθείας. This πνεῦμα has at the same time clearly been conceived as a multitude of πνεύματα.

---

[1] Deissmann, Licht von Osten, p. 311 (Note 4).

[2] Foerster, Th.W. II, p. 560 line 35s. and Liddel-Scott, s. v. II, 2.

[3] Mussner, Christus, das All und die Kirche, p. 19, views the exousia of Eph. 2:2 as. a force (or an army) of demons under the leadership of an archon. Other sholars (e.g Schlier, Eph., p. 102) regard this exousia as a territory or domain.

[4] Cf. Foerster, Th. W. I, p. 165; Visser, "Gnostische" trekken", p. 22 and Schlier, Eph., p. 103.

The belief in a host of evil spirits was also known in academic Jewish Palestinian scriptural circles. Rabbinical literature reveals that these stood under the leadership of a single prince of evil spirits, who was not identical with Satan.[1] The Qumran manuscripts testify to two angels or spirits, contradistinguished as the embodiments of good and evil; likewise, the concept of a multitude of evil spirits, not always distinguishable from the misdemeanours of the individual being, is evident.[2] Paul is aware of a host of πνεύματα (1 C. 12:10; 1 C. 14:12, 33) as well as the πνεῦμα τοῦ κόσμου and the πνεῦμα τοῦ θεοῦ.[3]

Some exegetes have regarded the αἰὼν τοῦ κόσμου τούτου as yet another personalised supternatural spirit or power.[4] If that were indeed the case, then Eph. would be the oldest non-Egyptian document which betrays cognizance of the hellenistic-Egyptian god Aion, who traces his origins from the Persian god of eternity, Zurvan.[5] Moreover, the case would then be that Eph. introduces this god, in passing, as one of the princes of demons; this is highly improbable.

Although this surprising explanation of the words αἰὼν τοῦ κόσμου τούτου could be further supported by regarding the aiones of Eph. 3:9 as personalized beings, the untenability of such an exegesis has been proved by Mussner in his analysis of the text of Eph. 3:9s.[6]

---

[1] E. Sjöberg, Th. W. VI, p. 374 lines 7-24.

[2] Ed. Schweitzer, Th. W. VI, p. 388 lines 20-26 (cf. 1 QS4, 9-11 as quoted in Th. W. VI, p. 551 note 33).

[3] From a grammatical point of view, it is also possible to interpret τοῦ πνεύματος as a closer definition of τοῦ ἀέρος. This is the opinion of Schlier, Eph., p. 104; "Der Luft ist also der Geist der Welt" (the sky is therefore the spirit of the world).

[4] Cf. Schlier, Eph., p. 102; Dib., Gefbr., p. 50.

[5] For the Persian god Zurvan, see Colpe, Die religionsgeschichtliche Schule, Darstellung und Kritik ihres Bildes vom gnostischen Erlösermythus, p. 133 note 5 and p. 209-216.

Cf. O. Weinreich, Aion in Eleusis (Archiv f. Religionswissenschaft, 19er Band), p. 189 for Aion worship in Egypt and also Colpe, op. cit., p. 209-216.

In the Corp. Herm. XI, Aion in described as the highest, the all-embracing divine energy functioning in the cosmos and the δεύτερος θεός. In the magical papyri found in Egypt, Aion is also represented as an energetic force of that nature. Invoked as a deity, he is sometimes distinguished from a higher god. Cf. Papyrus Berlin 5025, line 201 (P.I. in Preisendanz, Papyri Graecae Magicae I, p. 12); P. Bibl. Nat. suppl. gr. 574, line 1205 (P. IV in Preisendanz, op. cit. I, p. 112); P. Leiden J 395, line 71 and line 299 (P. XIII in Preisendanz, op. cit. II, p. 90 and p. 102). Cf. also A. Dieterich (O. Weinreich), Eine Mithrasliturgie (Berlin ³1923) pp. 4,5 and 66 and Reitzenstein, HMR, p. 177.

[6] For the explanation of αἰών and αἰῶνες in Eph. 2:2 and 3:9 as personalized forces, see Chapter I, p. 27 n. 5; Dib. Gefbr., ²1927, pp. 57 and 50 and ³1957, pp. 65 and 67;

A conclusive argument for not interpreting the aion of Eph. 2:2 as a personalized supernatural energy is provided by the meaning of the selfsame word, αἰών, as used in Eph. 1:21. It is not acceptable that the word which, in Eph. 1:21, is an indication of time should, a few lines later, have becomes the name of a prince of demons. The obvious deduction is that the αἰὼν τοῦ κόσμου τούτου of Eph. 2:2 is identical to the αἰὼν οὗτος of Eph. 1:21.

But what does the author in Eph. 2:2 really mean ? The answer must be, more or less the same as is meant by κατὰ σάρκα in the HP. It is not possible to go out of the κόσμος (cf. 1 C. 5:10) but the περιπατεῖν κατὰ τὸν αἰῶνα τοῦ κόσμου τούτου is not fitting for the faithful; for such is the straying path of the unbeliever.

The unbeliever knows no more than the immeasurable duration of this world. Therein lies his limitation. Now and again, O.T. and LXX reveal the limitation in knowledge of the עוֹלָם or αἰών.[1]

Qoh. 3:11 states that God has put the עוֹלָם in the heart of man, but man is nevertheless limited ; for he does not understand God's work ; neither its beginning nor its end.

Sap. 13 speaks of those who are lacking in the knowledge of God and who, in reflecting on the works of creation, are unable to discover the consummate maker. Instead, they mistake fire or wind, sky or constellations, the mighty water or the celestial lights, for gods. They are preoccupied with and search the works of God but cannot, thinks the writer, be excused "For if they were able to know so much, that they could aim at the αἰών ; how did they not sooner find out the Lord thereof ?" (v. 9).

Περιπατεῖν κατὰ τὸν αἰῶνα τοῦ κόσμου τούτου is to exist within a limited awareness, without knowledge of God.[2]

Schlier, Eph., p. 102. Mussner's analysis of Eph. 3:9-11 is found on p. 25s. of Christus, das All und die Kirche.

[1] עוֹלָם is a cognate of עָלַם which really means hidden or incalculable time, which may be either the obscure past or the unimaginable future. Usually, it is best translated as eternity.

[2] Qoh. 3:11 accepts limited awareness as inescapable for man. The author of Sap. 13 regards the limitation in awareness as wrong on the part of heathens; however, he does appreciate those who recognise the beauty of creation and see the forces or elements of creation as gods. Lamentable, in his view, are the heathens who worship idols as gods. The writer of Eph. only sees corruption in the heathens. For him, a limited understanding and the mere awareness of the aeon of this world and attachment to it are inseparable linked with the ἀπείθεια. We hear the intonation of R. 1:18-26 and 1 C. 1:20s.; 3:19;

We have already elsewhere discussed the fact that Eph. uses the appellation ὁ διάβολος instead of the usual ὁ σατανᾶς found in the rest of the CPminus (see above, p. 174)[1].

Col. too, is uncommonly absorbed with supernatural powers. It also contains a designation, i.e. θρόνοι, not found elsewhere in the CP.

In Col. the fact that Christ is exalted over all other powers is expressed by the phrase ὅς ἐστιν ἡ κεφαλὴ πάσης ἀρχῆς καὶ ἐξουσίας in 2:10. Unlike Eph., this superiority in Christ is not—with the exception of the word κεφαλή, which implies a state of high elevation—brought into connection with Christ's exaltation. Col. accounts for this superiority in terms of the creation (1:16s) and the crucifixion (2:15).

The idea of a triumph is explicit in both epistles (Eph. 4:8; Col. 2:15). Bultmann's view that in Eph. too, this triumph represents a victory over the elemental forces, is an acceptable thesis.[2]

Both epistles draw a contrast between the plane of existence of the believers and darkness (τὸ σκότος Eph. 6:12; Col. 1:13). In Col. this darkness is characterized as an ἐξουσία, a controlled territory or realm.[3] We have already observed that in Eph. 2:2, the epithet ἐξουσία occurred as a collective indication for a plurality of powers. Similarly, it is reasonable that ἡ ἐξουσία τοῦ σκότους in Col. 1:13 should be taken to mean a realm governed by a multitude of powers.

Besides 2:15, Col. never expresses in so many words that the superhuman forces could be inimical to Christ or to the believers. There are no battle-cries for a struggle against the powers; nor is there any suggestion of the διάβολος or σατανᾶς or some other personality who controls the negative forces. Col. only warns against the worshipping of supernatural powers (2:18).

Moreover, there is a positive aspect to the allusions to the powers. Christ is the ultimate aim of their creation (1:16). A reconciliation has taken place in the heavenly regions; and in contemplating those recon-

---

7:31. For the author of Eph. too, the σοφία τοῦ κόσμου means folly. Those who do not know that τὸ σχῆμα τοῦ κόσμου is transitory are also ignorant in their attitude to the world.

[1] In 2 Th. 3:3 and Eph. 6:16, the genitive τοῦ πονηροῦ also occurs. Here, as in Mt. 6:13, this genitive could also be a neuter and indicate "die Drangsal der Endzeit" (the anguish of the end of time); cf. Harder. Th. W. VI. p. 561.

[2] Theologie, p. 179.

[3] In Jewish-hellenistic colloquial speech, ἐξουσία is used in the sense of realm or governed territory; cf. Foerster, Th. W. II, p. 361. It is possible that ἐξουσία in Eph. 2:2 has the same meaning; cf. n. 3 on p. 223.

ciled heavenly regions, the forces existing there must also be taken into account (1:20).

Percy has shown that this positive side is not lacking in the HP.[1] No more is it absent from Eph. I already drew attention to the fact that according to Eph. 1:21 such forces will also exist in the αἰὼν ὁ μέλλων. Eph. 1:10 reveals that Eph. proclaims a restoration of order and unity which also extends to the heavenly regions. And even if Eph. does not use the actual word reconciliation, in this connection, it may nevertheless be assumed that the concept of an εἰρήνη in the heavenly regions expressed in Eph. 1:10 is identical to that in Col. 1:20.[2]

4 Πληροῦν and πλήρωμα

Amongst the striking words used in Eph., are the verb πληροῦν (1:23; 3:19; 4:10 and 5:18) and the substantive πλήρωμα (1:10, 23; 3:19; 4:13). In common with the adjective πλήρης, these words could be of cosmic significance for the Greek and the Hellenistic mind.

The original meaning of the adjective πλήρης is full or filled. In addition, it can mean complete or whole.[3] This in its turn, can easily become transformed into the idea of perfect.[4] But the original meaning, particularly, can have cosmic overtones. For the Greek, the world was full of gods.[5] The Stoa knew the principle of a single divinity with which all things were filled.[6] To have fullness was a condition of real being. The antithesis of real or full being could be expressed in terms of emptiness or non-being. Thus, this train of thought also led to the idea of a relationship whereby πλήρης was connected with perfection.[7]

The verb πληροῦν possesses equally a cosmic aspect. The single

---

[1] Die Probleme, p. 102-105.

[2] See also Bultmann, Theologie, p. 502.

[3] Cf. Liddell-Scott, s.v.

[4] Cf. G. Delling, Th. W. VI, p. 283 line 22 and the quotation from the Fragmenta of Aristotle on line 19 : τὸ δὲ πλῆρες τέλειόν ἐστι.

[5] Delling, op. cit., p. 283 lines 12-14.

[6] Dupont, Gnosis, p. 462. See also above. p. 205.

[7] For the antithesis of τὸ πλῆρες and τὸ κενόν, see Dupont, loc. cit. and Delling, op. cit., p. 283 lines 26-31. To Philo, God is πλήρης; all else he sees as κένα and for him,, πλήρης and τέλειος are often synonymous. (Dupont, op. cit., p. 463 and Delling, op. cit., p. 284 lines 5-21). In Asclepius monistic mysticism, both world and godhead are designated as plenus et (resp. atque) perfectus (paras. 30 and 33 ed. Nock-Festugière; cf. Dupont, op. cit., pp. 456 and 459).

divine principle of the Stoa penetrates all and "fills", leaving nothing empty. Variations on this Stoic theme are found in the works of Philo and Hermetic literature.[1]

In the LXX too, the words πλήρης and πληροῦν are not devoid of cosmic significance; this also applies to the verb ἐμπιμπλάναι which is synonymous with πληροῦν. Here, one may read that the earth is full of the mercy of God or is filled with the knowledge of the Lord. There are references to the glory of God which fills the earth and with which the earth is filled. In addition, it is contended that God fills the earth and that the earth is filled with the Spirit of the Lord.[2]

Such affirmations have a certain amount in common with the above-mentioned Stoic dicta, but the implication is different. Unlike the Stoa, these are not concerned with the substance of the earth and are not intended to reduce the whole of reality to a single divine principle. In the LXX such declarations serve to illuminate the greatness of the mercy of God or to draw attention to the omnipresence of God who sees and hears everything.[3]

Only in one place (Sap. 1:7) is there the connotation of some cosmic activity in the filling of the world; the Spirit of the Lord, in filling all, is also the force which contains and gives it permanence.[4]

Another feature worth examining is provided by the soteriological motivation. This is salient whenever the mercy of the Lord which fills the earth is proclaimed or when the knowledge of the Lord with which the earth is filled (Is. 11:9) is raised. This soteriological momentum is equally palpable when Num. 14:21 expounds upon the glory of the Lord with which all the earth is to be filled, since this fulfilment is

---

[1] Hippolytus, Philos. 21, 5 (Diels, Doxographi, p. 571) relates that the Stoa taught πεπληρῶσθαι τὰ πάντα καὶ μηδὲν εἶναι κενά. More material on the Stoa is found in H. Kleinknecht, Th. W. IV, p. 83 line 13ss. For Philo, see Delling, op. cit., p. 287s. Hermetic literature speaks of the ψυχή (C. Herm. XI, 4, ed. Scott) or κόσμος νοητός (C. Herm. XVI, 12 and 17, ed. Scott), which fills the world. For further information on Hermetic and related literature, see Delling, op. cit., p. 286 line 7ss. Extensive data on the concept of the cosmos which is filled, in Dupont, ip. cit., p. 462-466.

[2] Is. 6:3; Ps. 32:5; 118:64; Sir. 42:16; Num. 14:21; Jer. 23:24 and Sap. 1:7.

[3] Jer. 23:24 and Sap. 1:7.

[4] Dupont, op. cit., p. 465, recognises the terminology of the Stoa in Sap. 1:7. Delling, op. cit., p. 287 lines 31-41 points out that the content of Sap. 1:7 is nontheless not Stoically orientated.

op. cit., p. 287 lines 31-41 points out that the content of Sap. 1:7 is nontheless not Stoically not Stoically orientated.

realized through the punitory and salutary acts which God chooses to discharge upon his nation.[1]

To the Hellenistic Jew, the words πλήρης, πληροῦν and ἐμπιμπλάναι in any event conveyed the association of salvation or blessedness. These words, when applied in the LXX to God's nation or to a tribe or members thereof as distinct from the entire earth, frequently imply that God satisfies or bestows through good or blessing. The word πλήρης and its antonym κενός, can even, without further qualification, be used to indicate respectively a condition of blessedness or mortification.[2]

In the LXX the words πλήρης, πληροῦν and ἐμπιμπλάναι may by seen against the background of the words formed from the Hebrew root מלא, under the influence of which they stand. In one of the Qumran manuscripts, the verb מלא is used in an eschatological soteriological connection. A hymn in 1 QM 12, 11 which has bearing on triumph in the eschatological struggle, entreats that God may fill his land with glory and his inheritance (i.e. his nation) with blessing.

In Luk. 1:53, we see the verb ἐμπιμπλάναι and its opposite κενός similarly placed in an eschatological soteriological context.

A word which is even more complicated than πλήρης, πληροῦν or ἐμπιμπλάναι, is the word πλήρωμα. Neither the Stoa nor Philo linked this word with the cosmos but in Hermetic literature, it does have a cosmic aspect.

C. Herm., VI, 1-4, manifests a dualistic tendency; a visible and an invisible world are here contradisposed. The visible world is a πλήρωμα τῆς κακίας; the invisible world an οὐσία πληρεστάτη and a πλήρωμα τοῦ ἀγαθοῦ or a πλήρωμα τοῦ θεοῦ.

C. Herm. XII, 15, evinces a monistic state of mind; the perceptible world is seen as δεύτερος θεός and defined as a πλήρωμα τῆς ζωῆς.

The primary meaning of the word πλήρωμα in such Hermetic passages is "the whole". The world is a whole combination of evil or of life; in contrast, the intelligible world is the whole of the godhead or of good.[3]

With this application of the word πλήρωμα, the idea of fullness also plays a part. The world, which is a whole cumulation of life or of evil,

---

[1] Cf. Delling, Th. W. VI, p. 129 line 5s.

[2] Deut. 33:23; Ru. 1:21; Ps. 80:11; 106:9.

[3] Liddell-Scott, s.v. I, 7, translates "mass, complex". The meaning of "the whole" is closely connected with the idea of the whole number or complement, the sum of total. which are the other meanings of πλήρωμα; cf. Liddell-Scott, s.v., I, 3 and 4.

is of its very nature perceived as full of life or evil. Likewise, the intelligible world which is the whole of the godhead or of good, is seen as something that is full of the godhead or good. When πλήρωμα is qualified in a favourable sense, emphasis is placed on the idea of fullness in the context of the passage.[1] This idea of fullness, when fullness is conceived as favourable, is in its turn once again closely affiliated with the concept of perfection and the reality of being with which the word πλήρης had been imbued by the various philosophical traditions.[2]

In C. Herm. XVI, 3, the word πλήρωμα is not qualified by a succeeding genitive. To the author of this tract, the whole of reality is divine and everything, the perceptible as well as the imperceptible world, is constituted from parts of the godhead (XVI, 19). The word πλήρωμα emphasizes that the whole of creation is no haphazard mass (πλῆθος) but, on the contrary, a unity (XVI, 4). In τὸ πληρωμα, τὰ πάντα and ὁ εἷς are merged; τὸ πλήρωμα and ὁ εἷς have become identical (ἀμφοτέρων ἑνὸς ὄντος). Thanks to τὸ πλήρωμα, the godhead can be both πάντα and εἷς. If the unimaginable, that τὰ πάντα were no longer to be ἕν, were to happen, then το πλήρωμα would be dissolved. In that event, the godhead and the whole world would disintegrate.

The word πλήρωμα in this tract, denotes "the unity in multeity" and expresses the concept of totality. When G. Delling observes that the word is here used in a purely formal context, he is not entirely correct. For the mystically orientated mind of the writer, τὸ πλήρωμα represents a divine reality, the ultimate truth and the very pivot of all that exists.[3]

We find that the gnostics also used the word πλήρωμα. In their case the word conveys a reality, elevated far above the visible and material

---

[1] In C. Herm. VI, 1-4, we already noted the identification of τὸ πλήρωμα του ἀγαθοῦ resp. τοῦ θεοῦ with an οὐσια πληρεστάτη. (Lactantius, Div. Institutiones IV, 6,4, says that the second god or cosmos is πληρέστατος πάντων τῶν ἀγαθῶν. The quotation is from Delling, Th. W. VI, p. 289 line 42.) In C. Herm. XII, 21, after the second god or cosmos has been called πλήρωμα τῆς ζωῆς there is mention of τὴν ὕλην πληρεστάτην οὖσαν ζωῆς. Cf. also the analogous use of πλήρωμα in Philo. In De Praem. et Poen. 65 (ed. Cohn u. Wendland), he calls the soul a πλήρωμα ἀρετῶν. In that case the sould is both πλήρης and οὐδὲν ἐν ἑαυτῇ καταλιποῦσα κενόν.

[2] See p. 227 and note 7.

[3] The πλήρωμα in C. Herm. XVI is discussed by Delling in Th. W. VI, p. 229. The text of the tract may also be read in R. Reitzenstein, Poimandres (Leipzig 1904), p. 349s.

world, which is a mass of unknown spiritual potencies.[1] The gnostics held this pleroma to be attainable and admission to it, the highest form of salvation.[2]

Certain turns of phrase in gnostic writing when treating the pleroma theme are suggestive of a Jewish Hellenistic influence. Thus the Odes of Solomon recount that the son of the Highest has appeared in the pleroma of his Father (41, 13). The 'Gospel of Truth' knows a "coming of the pleroma for them who await the salvation that comes from above" and "a point in time" when "the pleroma is coming".[3]

Pronouncements of this kind recall to mind certain Jewish-Hellenistic formulations. For instance, I am thinking of one of the Greek fragments in the Ethiopian book of Enoch which talks of the descent of God in order to visit the earth with good ($\epsilon\pi\iota\sigma\kappa\epsilon\psi\alpha\sigma\theta\alpha\iota$ $\tau\dot{\eta}\nu$ $\gamma\dot{\eta}\nu$ $\epsilon\pi$ $\dot{\alpha}\gamma\alpha\theta\tilde{\omega}$).[4] A similar account of a visitation from God is also mentioned in 4 Ezra 6 :11-26. In the same way is spoken about the appearance of the Messiah who has until then been kept back by the Highest (4 Ezra 12:32-34).[5] Such Jewish-Hellenistic utterances have also come down to us through the N.T.[6]

The idea of a certain point in time plays an equally important part in the Jewish-Hellenistic pronouncements. In Jewish apocalyptic literature, there are frequent references to the end. The coming of God or the Messiah is connected with this end. For the godless, the end of time

---

[1] From the words in Irenaeus, Adv. Haer. II, 3 and 12,6, it may be deduced that the Valentinians maintained a $\pi\lambda\dot{\eta}\rho\omega\mu\alpha$ which was comprised of thirty $\alpha\dot{\iota}\tilde{\omega}\nu\epsilon\varsigma$ (cf. F. M. M. Sagnard, La Gnose Valentinienne et le temoinage de Saint-Irénée, Paris 1947, pp. 32, 35, 148). In the Excerpta ex Theodoto, par. 32 (W. Völker, Quellen zur Geschichte d. chr. Gnosis, Tübingen 1932, p. 124), the pairs of aeones are themselves in turn $\pi\lambda\eta\rho\dot{\omega}\mu\alpha\tau\alpha$ (cf. Sagnard, op. cit., p. 538). Markos and the Pistis Sophia also speak of a multiplicity of pleromata (H. Leisengang, Die Gnosis, Leipzig², pp. 114, 328s., 339, 345).

[2] Iren., Adv. Haer. I. 7, 1 and I, 21,2 (cf. Sagnard, op. cit., pp. 238s., 265, 421). In the Odes of Solomon 7, 13 and 9,4 (ed. J. Rendel Harris and A. Mingana), the Syrian equivalent of pleroma indicates a state of perfection which is achieved by the gnosis.

[3] The translation is found in J. Zandee, Het Evangelie der waarheid een gnostisch geschrift (Amsterdam 1965), p. 48.

[4] Enoch 25:3 (A. Lods, Le livre d'Hénoch, Fragments grecs, Paris 1892, p. 52).

[5] E. Kautzsch, Die Apokr. u. Pseudepigr. des A.T. II (Tübingen 1900); pp. 365s., 394.

[6] In Rev. 4:8 God is called $\dot{o}$ $\dot{\epsilon}\rho\chi\dot{o}\mu\epsilon\nu\sigma\varsigma$. In Mt. 21:9, the Messiah, the son of David is $\dot{o}$ $\dot{\epsilon}\rho\chi\dot{o}\mu\epsilon\nu\sigma\varsigma$ $\dot{\epsilon}\nu$ $\dot{o}\nu\dot{o}\mu\alpha\tau\iota$ $\kappa\nu\rho\dot{\iota}\sigma\nu$; cf. St. John 11:27 and 1 Tim. 1:15. In Mark 11:10, there is mention of $\dot{\eta}$ $\dot{\epsilon}\rho\chi\sigma\mu\dot{\epsilon}\nu\eta$ $\beta\alpha\sigma\iota\lambda\epsilon\dot{\iota}\alpha$ $\tau\sigma\tilde{\nu}$ $\pi\alpha\tau\rho\dot{o}\varsigma$ $\dot{\eta}\mu\tilde{\omega}\nu$ $\Delta\alpha\nu\dot{\iota}\delta$. Luke 1:78 is reminiscent of Enoch 25:3.

represents only destruction but for the righteous who survive the end, it signifies blessedness.[1]

A well-known Hebrew word to designate this end is קֵץ. In Greek, the word τέλος is most commonly used. On the basis of evidence found in the N.T., this word was taken into an appellation for the coming God or the coming Messiah.[2]

In Hebrew however, the end of time can also be indicated by means of words formed from the root מלא, which have a strong affinity with the words πλήρης and πληροῦν which belonged to the vocabulary of the Greek-speaking Hellenistic Jews.[3] In the Qumran scrolls. various forms of the verb מָלָא are used again and again to indicate the completion or expiration of a certain length of time. In 1 QS the substantive מִילְאָה always defines the end of a period.[4]

The verb πληροῦν and the substantive πλήρωμα derived from it, are similarly used in Greek by Hellenistic Jews.[5] It is therefore a reasonable assumption that the word πλήρωμα was likewise used to describe the eschatological concept of the end.

A number of indications point in this direction. One example occurs in the Odes of Solomon (7, 11) when God is called the pleroma of aeons and their father. In this particular instance, the words in question most certainly assume the context of a gnostic term.

However, it is also probable that these words originally constituted a more general Jewish-Hellenistic term for God or the Messiah and were a variation on the designation ἡ ἀρχὴ καὶ τὸ τέλος which is featured in Rev.[6]

If that is so indeed, then (the equivalent of) πλήρωμα has het implication of the end and (that of) πατήρ that of the beginning. The designa-

---

[1] Cf. 4 Ezra 6:11-26; 12:32-34 and also 13:19s. and 24. In the context of Enoch 25:3 there is a question of τελείωσις μέχρις αἰῶνος (25:4).

[2] See Rev. 21:6 and 22:13 and compare these places with Rev. 1:8.

[3] See above p. 229.

[4] For the verb see 1 QS 7,22; 1 QSd 1,10 and 12; Damasc. 10,1 (cf. 1 QM 6,12). For the substantive מילאת/מילאה K. G. Kuhn, Konkordanz zu den Qumrantexten, Göttingen 1960, p. 122, mentions 1 QS 6, 17-18-21-21; 8,26. In Syrian and Aramaic the words ܫܘܠܡ and סוֹף are respectively found as terms to describe the end (cf. Dalman, Worte Jesu, p. 127).

[5] Cf. Delling, Th. W. VI, p. 287 lines 6-19 and Gal. 4:4.

[6] See above and note 2. (The Syrian equivalent of πλήρωμα (see p. 231, note 2) is ܡܘܠܝܐ).

tion of father of ages, could well trace its source in a Greek translation of the אֲבִי־עַד in Is. 9:5.[1]

A second and clearer sign pointing towards this theory is found in a papyrus dating from the fourth or fifth century A. D. which probably accompanied the dead as an amulet.[2] The burial of the amulet reflected the ancient Egyptian yearning to preserve the body from destruction.

The prayer is partly drived from the ritual of the Christian Church.[3] It contains several component parts which were originally Jewish-Hellenistic formulations. Christ is invoked by the names ὁ βασιλεὺς τοῦ αἰῶνος (line 7) and ὁ θεὸς τοῦ αἰῶνος (line 8) which are also found in the Greek fragments of the book of Enoch.[4]

The "coming" of Christ is much emphasized [5] and, as in Rev. 4:8 (where God is described as due to come), the context brings to mind the thrice holy of Is.6:3.[6]

At the opening of the prayer, Christ is hailed as τὸ πλήρωμα τοῦ αἰῶνος ... χωρούμενο[ν],ὁ ἐλθὼν τῷ κόσμῳ (line 1s.). It would seem that the designation τὸ πλήρωμα τοῦ τοῦ αἰῶνος was originally a Jewish-Hellenistic formulation as were ὁ βασιλεὺς τοῦ αἰῶνος and ὁ θεὸς τοῦ αἰῶνος.

The idea of the end is similarly encountered with respect to the context of the above-mentioned designations from Enoch; on one occasion, this idea is even expressed in terms exceedingly close to the formulation τὸ πλήρωμα. After God has been spoken of as ὁ βασιλεὺς τοῦ αἰῶνος in 25:3, the matter of a τελείωσις μέχρις αἰῶνος is raised in 25:4.

In the papyrus with which we are concerned, the prayer contains the words τὸ πλήρωμα τοῦ αἰῶνος ... χωρούμενον (the coming eternal end), an epithet to describe the coming Messiah. Here thus, we see a

---

[1] Some versions of the LXX have the translation πατὴρ τοῦ μέλλοντος αἰῶνος.

[2] This is the Cairo Papyrus 10263 mentioned in n. 1 on p. 222. The quotations come from the Preisendanz edition in Pap. Gr. Mag. II, p. 200s.

[3] This assumption is based on the reminder of the thrice holy in line 6s., the hailing of Christ as ὁ ἐλθὼν ἐκ δεξιῶν τοῦ πατρός, τὸ ἀρνίον τὸ εὐλογημένον and the supplication ἐλθέ on line 9. The supplication "come", according to Cullmann, was part of the ancient Christian eucharistic ritual. See his Urchristentum und Gottesdienst (Zürich ³1956), p. 16s. The prayer ends with a plea for preservation from demons, lines 15-17. Bousset, Kyrios Christus (Göttingen ⁴1935) repeatedly shows that Christ's domination over demons was made manifest through ritual exorcism (pp. 87s., 226 and 276).

[4] En. 1:3; 25:3 and 5 (ed. Lods pp. 4 and 52).

[5] line 2 and line 9 ὁ ἐλθών and line 8 ἐλθέ.

[6] line 6s.

correspondence between the word πλήρωμα and the word τέλος which was assimilated into a designation for the coming God or Messiah.[1]

It is clear from the correspondence between the designation τὸ πλήρωμα τοῦ αἰῶνος and another designation, τὸ ἔλεος τοῦ αἰῶνος, in the same prayer, as well as from the entire content of this prayer, that the term τὸ πλήρωμα is of soteriological significance. The impression gained is that the expression τοῦ αἰῶνος is always used in the prayer to accentuate the transcendental and godly aspect of the substantive in question and that therefore the pleroma in also designated as godly and transcendental.

With respect to the word πλήρωμα, we are thus confronted with a variety of data.

We have already observed that in Hermetic literature the term possesses a cosmic aspect, being used to indicate both visible and invisible worlds as an entirety of evil or of life and as the whole of the godhead or good. In that context, the word unites the concept of fullness and, when applicable, the notions of perfection and the essence of being.

In one particular instance in Hermetic literature, the word means "the unity in multeity" and exemplifies the final truth, the fulcrum of all existence, which is a godly reality.

Besides, we saw that the word may signify a whole mass of unknown immaterial potencies, elevated far beyond the reality of the visible and material world.

Finally, we found traces which indicated that πλήρωμα was a Jewish-Hellenistic term. In this context the word expresses the eschatological concept of the end and has a soteriological content. The coming God or the coming Messiah could be identified with this coming end by the Hellenistic Jewry.

Certain turns of expression in gnostic writings are reminiscent of this Jewish-Hellenistic term. The term has a cosmic aspect, the end is accompanied by a ἐκδίκησις πάντων (Enoch Gr. frg. 25:4) and an ἐπισκέψασθαι τὴν γῆν ἐπ' ἀγαθῷ (25:3). He who is τὸ πλήρωμα τοῦ αἰῶνος χωρούμενον is also ὁ ἐλθων τῷ κόσμῳ.[2]

Naturally, the word πλήρωμα is related to the words πλήρης, πληροῦν and ἐμπιμπλάναι. To the Hellenistic Jew, the last three suggested an association with the concept of salvation or blessing and sometimes this salvation represented an eschatological advantage.[3]

---

[1] See above p. 232 and note 3.

[2] See the above-mentioned opening of the prayer from Cairo Papyrus 10263.

[3] See above, p. 229.

Now that we have concerned and informed ourselves about the ideas with which the words πληροῦν and πλήρωμα have been elsewhere connected, we may now concentrate on their meaning and content with respect to Eph.

We commence with the word πληροῦν. This word is used on several occasions with Christ as its subject, in which case it has a cosmic aspect. We have already observed that the epistle conveys knowledge of a unifying work by God, embracing heaven and earth (p. 217). The same wide horizons are present in 1:23 and 4:10 with references to the filling of all by Christ. A connection exists between the unifying work of God in 1:10 and this fulfilling in 1:23 and 4:10. Haupt. in explanation of Eph. 1:10, correctly observes that the verb πληροῦν aims to express a "kompendiarische Zusammenfassung vieler einzelnen Dinge in einem" (a summary compilation of many single things in one). For example, he draws attention to the use of the word in R. 13:9 and concludes : "Danach ist der Wille Gottes, in Christo das All zusammenzufassen, so dass in ihm es sich ebenso konzentriert ... wie in dem Liebensgebot die Gesamtheit aller anderen Gebote" (Thus it is God's wish to gather together all in Christ so that it is equally concentrated in him ... as in the command to love the totality of all other commands is contained).[1] The gathering together of all in Christ thus to a certain extent implies the being of the all in Christ. (We say "to a certain extent" because although the word ἀνακεφαλαιώσασθαι places everything in a certain relationship to Christ, it does not merge the all and Christ to establish identical quantities).

Christ's fulfilment of the all corresponds with the idea of the all being in Christ. —Dupont has shown that there was a reciprocity in the philosophical and religious terminology of the Hellenistic period between the fulfilment of all things and to be fulfilled by all things, respectively between the being of the godhead in all things and the being of all things in the godhead.[2]—

We could best interpret this by saying that the unifying work of God (the gathering together of all in Christ) is realized in the fulfilment of all by Christ.

In this process, the exaltation of Christ, his placing at God's own right hand (1:20) is a decisive moment. The exaltation is obviously an accomplished fact. In principle, everything in heaven and on earth

---

[1] Die Gefangenschaftsbriefe, Der Brief a.d, Epheser, p. 21s.

[2] Gnosis, p. (458 and) 459.

has already been brought into the right perspective to Christ (1:21 and 22; see p. 217s.) and brought together in him. However, in effect much is still lacking to complete this. The negative forces (p. 220ss.) which must be fought (6:1ss.) are still active.

The fact that Christ fulfills all brings this incompleteness to an end. This fulfilment stems from that same exaltation. The final clause ἵνα πληρώσῃ τὰ πάντα (4:10) clearly indicates that the fulfilment of all is the aim and result of Christ's exaltation. By its very nature the fulfilment will bring all into the right relationship to Christ. When that has occurred, God's work of unification will have been fully accomplished.

In treating this fulfilment, the author of Eph. uses the customary philosophical and religious terminology of his time. In a formulation as τοῦ τὰ πάντα ἐν πᾶσιν πληρουμένου (1:23), the adverbial adjunct ἐν πᾶσιν constitutes an intensification. This type of intensification is also found elsewhere in dealing with the fulfilment of the all.[1]

What is unusual in this case is that in this formulation the middle voice has been used. However, the N.T. quite frequently uses the middle voice in place of the active form.[2] Perhaps this voice has intentionally been selected in this instance. Under normal circumstances this form denotes that the active person is employed on his own behalf. It is possible that the middle voice in Eph. 1:23 elucidates a similar facet of meaning. The word πλήρωμα precedes the formulation we have quoted. This could give an unjustified impression of the fulfilment of all by means of this pleroma. Behind the use of the middle voice may rest the intention to express that the fulfilment of all is an act behoving Christ alone.

Although the writer of Eph. uses common philosophical and religous terms with regard to this fulfilment, he is a little concerned as the LXX (p. 228) to reduce the total reality to a single godly principle and to make a qualificatory pronouncement on reality. His intention is not to say that τὰ πάντα and Christ merge into one and are identical. Just as God's fulfilment of the earth is a feature of God's greatness

---

[1] Philo, Vita Mos. II238, speaks of God as ὁ πάντα διὰ πάντων πεπληρωκὼς τῆς εὐεργέτιδος ἑαυτοῦ δυνάμεως. The quotation is from Delling, Th. W. VI, p. 288 line 24. From the other quotations cited by Delling in situ (lines 6ss., 14ss. and 24ss.), it is clear that Philo repeatedly adds intensificatory embellishments to the formulation πληροῦν τὰ πάντα. Compare also the quotation from the Orationes of Aelius Aristides in Delling, op. cit., p. 286 line 10.

[2] See Bl-Debr., para. 316.

(p. 228), thus here, in Eph., Christ's fulfilment of all is an aspect of Christ's glory and power. Mussner is right to interpret πληροῦν τὰ πάντα as "das All herrschaftlich durchdringen" (the masterly penetration of all).[1]

Whenever there are references to a godly fulfilment of the earth in the LXX, there is besides the theme of God's greatness and glory, also a soteriological theme (p. 228s.). In Eph. this theme is likewise present; and in view of this, we do not feel that the above-quoted interpretation of Mussner is adequate. The soteriological significance of πληροῦν τὰ πάντα emerges from the correlation of this πληροῦν with the unifying work of God (the ἀνακεφαλαιώσασθαι τὰ πάντα ἐν τῷ Χριστῷ) to which we have already drawn attention. We called this unifying work a work of salvation (p. 217); for, after all, it signifies the end of baleful confusion which will until then exist in the highest reaches of the cosmos.

Furthermore, we may mention the association with the concepts of salvation and blessing which the words πλήρης, πληροῦν and ἐμπιμπλάναι suggested to the Hellenistic Jew (p. 229). Moreover, we recapitulate that in Luke 1:53, the verb's πληροῦν synonym ἐμπιμπλάναι has been placed within an echatological soteriological framework (p. 229).

The Hebrew equivalent of πληροῦν occurs in the same connection in one of the Qumran scrolls (p. 229) where the subject concerns a fulfilling of the land of God. (The word land אֶרֶץ could also have the connotation of the whole earth.)[2]

To the author of Eph., the word πληροῦν likewise prompted an association with salvation and blessing. On both occasions when the word has no bearing on the all and is in the passive voice, it is clearly used in the sense of salvation.

When, in Eph. 3:19, he comes to the last and highest purpose of the apostolic intercession, he uses this πληροῦσθαι. Eph. 5:18 has a reference to the being filled with the pneuma. Also interesting is that in the context of the small sentence ἵνα πληρώσῃ τὰ πάντα, he is concerned with pneumatical endowments.

Therefore, it is desirable to augment Mussner's interpretation and to render πληροῦν τὰ πάντα as : to permeate the whole with his dominion and his blessings. Then, we may understand the fulness in Eph. 1:23 and 4:10 to mean : "Christ's dominion, his exaltation above all

---

[1] Christus, Das All und die Kirche, p. 58s. See also p. 48s.
[2] Cf. H. Sasse, Th. W. I, p. 676 line 28ss.

things is made effective through his fulfilment of the all. But that is
not the entire story. In filling all, the situation of the κένος [88] in which
all things exist, will be brought to an end through his mercy. Christ
who fills all, transforms all into a state of πλήρης.[1]   He fulfils."

Next, we shall study the word πλήρωμα. In Eph. 1:10 the word is
introduced into an indication of time which forms part of the relative
sentence ἣν προέθετο ἐν αὐτῷ εἰς οἰκονομίαν τοῦ πληρώματος τῶν καιρῶν. In the preceding, τὸ μυστήριον τοῦ θελήματος αὐτοῦ (sc. τοῦ
θεοῦ) is mentioned. By means of the adverbial adjunct κατὰ τὴν εὐδοκίαν αὐτοῦ, this mystery is now identified as a benevolence.

It has already been stated that this is dependent on God's will; it is
now more sharply delineated. The mystery in concurrent with God's
goodwill or pleasure.[2] To this is now added that God had resolved
to act upon this goodwill—conceived in terms of what, in His goodwill,
that decision was—at a given time. And it is this that the above-quoted
relative clause proclaims : (the pleasure) which He resolved upon as
an arrangement for the end of all times.[3]

The plural καιροί in the formulation τοῦ πληρώματος τῶν καιρῶν
indicates a number of periods. Jewish-Hellenistic literature was familiar
with the concept that the world exists during the time span of a number
of periods or καιροί and that these will come to an end. The passive
πληροῦσθαι is used to represent this coming to an end.[4] Another idea,

---

[1] See above p. 229.

[2] G. Schrenk, Th. W. II, p. 745 line 5s. : "Auch 1,9 wird τὸ μυστήριον τοῦ θελήματος
durch das κατα την εὐδοκίαν αἰτοῦ in das freie Wohlgefallen gestellt" ("In 1,9, the κατὰ
τὴν εὐδοκίαν αὐτοῦ also places τὸ μυστήριον τοῦ θελήματος within the scope of that
freely given goodwill.)

[3] προτίθεσθαι means to decide or resolve (to do). In the CP the verb generally has
this meaning, also when the matter concerns God (cf. Chr. Maurer, Th. W. VIII, p. 166s.).
For the adjunct ἐν αὐτῷ with προέθετο, see above, p. 170 and for the meaning of οἰκονομία
in Eph. 1:10 ,see p. 175. Michel, Th. W. V, p. 155 line 1s., points out the meanings of
the words measure, arrangement and decree, as featured in papyri. Thus, when we
translate: "(the pleasure) which He resolved upon as an arrangement for the end of times",
we believe that there is an implicit assumption that this arrangement for the end of all
times really will come into effect at the end of all times. A different translation of these
words is found in Reumann, "οἰκονομία-Terms in Paul in comparison with Lucan Heilsgeschichte" N.T. St. 13, p. 164. Reumann sees τοῦ πληρώματος as a genit. object. and para-
phrases εἰς οἰκονομίαν τοῦ πληρώματος τῶν καιρῶν as ἵνα οἰκονομηθῇ τῷ πληρώματι
κ.τ.λ. We, for our part, however, see the adjunct εἰς οἰκονομίαν τοῦ πληρώματος κ.τ.λ.
in terms of a semiticising substitute for the predicative accusative (cf. Bl.-Debr.
para.145 and 157,5).

[4] Tobias 14:5.

also in that literature, is that the eschatological salvation will come to pass when certain destined periods or καιροί have elapsed.[1] In addition, the simple καιρός occurs as a designation for the eschatological concept, the end.[2]

We may take for granted that the formulation τὸ πλήρωμα τῶν καιρῶν is eschatological in character and indicates the conclusion of the present aeon. (With respect to the plural καιροί, two possibilities remain open. It could mean all the periods of this aeon, but it could also have meant a few particular periods which are to precurse the end of this aeon. The very fact that the formulation contains the word καιρός lends an eschatological character to the formulation.)

The stage when all ages of time come to an end, is the stage when all things in heaven and earth are gathered together in Christ. Earlier, we noted that in principle this fusion is accomplished in the exaltation of Christ. However, it will only have achieved full realization when Christ has permeated all things with his dominion and his gifts.

Since the word "pleroma" is part of an eschatological formulation on its first appearance in Eph., it is a foregone conclusion that during the rest of Eph. it will also be of eschatological content. First, we look at Eph. 3:19, which contains the following reference : πληροῦσθαι εἰς πᾶν τὸ πλήρωμα τοῦ θεοῦ. Eph. 5:18 speaks of πληροῦσθαι ἐν πνεύματι. These two formulations differ in meaning. Whereas the adjunct ἐν πνεύματι indicates the fulness that fills, the adjunct εἰς πᾶν τὸ πλήρωμα τοῦ θεοῦ does not identify this fulness but indicates the measure of fulness (p. 171). Nevertheless, this does not detract from the fact it conveys the information required when we seek to know what it is that fills : if the recipients of the epistle are filled to the maximum degree of the pleroma of God, this must mean that that with which they are filled cannot be other than this pleroma. Reviewed in this light, the formulation in Eph. 3:19 corresponds with that in 5:18.

This correspondence suggest that there is also a relationship between the pleroma of 3:19 and the pneuma of 5:18. The affinity between the sentence ἵνα πληρωθῆτε εἰς πᾶν τὸ πλήρωμα τοῦ θεοῦ in 3:19 and the construction κραταιωθῆναι διὰ τοῦ πνεύματος αὐτοῦ in 3:16 lends support to this conjecture. From the adjective πᾶν which is placed in

---

[1] Daniel 12:7.

[2] For the places mentioned in the two preceding notes, see Delling. Th, W. III, p. 460 lines 32-40. For καιρός as a term designating the end, see op. cit., p. 459 line 46-p. 460 line 8.

an anterior position to τὸ πλήρωμα may be deduced that the pleroma is a multiple unit.

If we now take into account that the words πληροῦν and ἐμπιμπλάναι were in the Hellenistic Jewish vocabulary characteristic expressions to convey that God satisfies through good or bestows through blessing (p. 229); and if we furthermore recollect that in Eph. there is a relationship between τὸ πλήρωμα τοῦ θεοῦ and τὸ πνεῦμα, we are justified in the surmise that πᾶν τὸ πλήρωμα τοῦ θεοῦ with which the believers are fulfilled (πληρωθῆτε) is the whole of God's pneumatical gifts.

This theory conforms with the assumption previously stated that the word "pleroma" is of eschatological significance not only in Eph. 1:10 but also throughout the entire episte. God's pneumatical gifts are eschatological gifts.[1] This whole of pneumatical gifts is now bestowed on neither a single believer nor on a group of believers such as the recipients of the epistle; the condition for being fulfilled with the pleroma is maximal community with all the hagioi (3:18), A connection exists between the knowledge of Christ's love, which transcends all knowledge, and being filled with the pleroma in the highest degree (3:19). To comprehend that the ἀγάπη is the greatest gift of the pleroma and a gift which exceeds even the gift of the γνῶσις, would, on the basis of this connection, not constitute a misapprehension concerning the intention of the author.[2]

Using words from the predicate used to describe God in Eph. 1:3, πᾶν το πλήρωμα could be paraphrased as πᾶσα εὐλογία πνευματική.

In effect, we rediscover the Jewish-Hellenistic term for the salvation connected with the end of time, which we reconstructed on pp. 232-234, in this pleroma of Eph. 3:19.

We find that in Eph. 1:23, the word "pleroma" is used as a qualification for the ecclesia. First, the ecclesia is described as σῶμα and subsequently as πλήρωμα.[3] The meaning of the latter word can be

---

[1] See Bultmann, Theol., p. 157 and W. Bieder, Th. W. VI, p. 368 and p. 382 lines 21-34.

[2] This assumption finds supporting evidence in the pericope 4:7-16 which deals with pneumatical gifts. The last word of this pericope is ἀγάπη and with this word the exposition reaches its climax.

[3] C. F. D. Moule, " Fulness' and 'Fill' in the New Testament ", Scottish Journ. of Theology IV, 1951, p. 81, holds τὸ πλήρωμα in Eph. 1:23 to be in apposition to κεφαλήν in 1:22 : "God gave Christ to be head over all things in the Church, which is his body (and to be) the fulness of him (that is God), that filleth all in all". To me, this exegesis seems forced and inspired more by the desire to establish a correspondence between Eph. and Col. than a conclusion based on the text itself.

deduced from its meaning in 3:19. Here too, the entirety of God's pneumatical endowments should be taken into consideration.

Whilst annalysing 3:19 above, we observed that the relationship with all the hagioi was the condition for being filled with all these gifts to the outmost degree. 4:7 and 16 do not especially deal with the pleroma but do expound on the pneumatical gifts, and in so doing, the inter-relationship of the hagioi is presented as conditional for the effectivenes of these gifts. The word used to express this working inter-relationship is "soma". Inasfar as the ecclesia is soma, the gifts function in it and bring about that this soma is developed (cf. also 4:12) or grows.

If in 1:23 the ecclesia is in the first instance called soma, then the word soma makes it possible to subsequently call the ecclesia pleroma. Within the ecclesia, which is soma, the entirety of the pneumatical gifts work to such an extent that the ecclesia itself can be designated as the representative word for the whole of these gifts.

Thus the word pleroma interchanges the meaning of "the whole of the eschatological pneumatical gifts" with "that which is endowed with the whole (gift) of eschatological pneumatical gifts". A transition of this nature corresponds with the character of extreme flexibility which this word possesses both in its capacity as an eschatological term as well as in its general significance.[1]

---

[1] In its eschatological function, the word not only indicates the end but also the God or Messiah who will come at the end. See above, p. 234s. In current contemporary language, the word had a number of meanings : to be sated; the contents; the complement or amplification; the full complement; the great quantity (crowd, mass); the full number; the sum; the full strength (possibly located by a genitive, e.g. the load or crew of a ship; population of a town or the total manpower of an army); the ship, including crew and all; the group or unit (i.e. a group or unit of labourers); the whole (the whole assembly of occupations and the persons engaged in them form the pleroma of a town or the collected kinsmen, in all gradations of relationship, constitute the pleroma of kinship); the totality (i.e. all the characteristics which in combination form the essence of a matter) and the summit or crowning. For these meanings see : J. B. Lightfoot, Saint Paul's Epistle to the Colossians and Philemon (London ²1879), p. 257ss.; Liddell-Scott, s.v. and Delling, Th. W. VI, p. 297s. The transition in meaning which we observed in the above is analogous to the shift in meaning from "the cargo or crew of a ship" to "a ship with crew and all". It is demonstrated in Philo that a type of metonomy, analogous to the last-named transition could occur when the topic in hand dealt with religious or philosophical concepts. Philo uses the formulation πλήρωμα ἀρετῶν (a complement of virtues) as a designation for the soul which is wholly filled with virtues. Similarly, he uses the formulation πλήρωμα καλοκαγαθίας (an entirety of noble virtue) to describe the man who possesses that entirety of noble virtue. See De Praem. et Poen. 65 and De Spec. Leg.

Therefore, the genitive which follows this metonym is not without purpose, it serves to give closer definition and describes the all-fulfilling Christ. The ecclesia is soma only because it is subordinate to Christ, who is the head. The ecclesia is the soma of Christ, τὸ σῶμα αὐτοῦ and only by virtue of the pneumatical gifts of God which Christ bestows upon it, can it be called pleroma. He, the exalted, who fills the universe with his dominion of salvation, is the one and only who makes his soma into a reality, gifted with the whole range of pneaumatical gifts.

In Eph. 4:13 we once again encounter the word πλήρωμα. As before, the genitive (τοῦ Χριστοῦ) following the word evince that the ecclesia will only attain the gifts of God through the medium of Christ. Possibly the word also assumes the function of a metonymic indication for the ecclesia in this instance. If that is so, there is not only in form but also in content a parallel between the adjunct εἰς μέτρον ἡλικίας τοῦ πληρώματος τοῦ Χριστοῦ and the adjunct εἰς οἰκοδομὴν τοῦ σώματος τοῦ Χριστοῦ which occurs in 4:12. In both cases, the words τοῦ πληρώματος τοῦ Χριστοῦ and τοῦ σώματος τοῦ Χριστοῦ would be indicative of the ecclesia.

But the position is not that the context forces us to identify the τὸ πλήρωμα in 4:13 as a metonymic indication for the ecclesia. Perhaps the word should be interpreted in the light of its more original meaning, as the whole of the pneumatical eschatological gifts. What is clear, in any case, is that the gifts are destined for the ecclesia.

Another aspect which here becomes clear is that for the author of Eph. the concept of pleroma has the implication of perfection and maturity. Namely, he speaks of a degree of maturity[1] which belongs to the pleroma which Christ bestows. This statement serves to elucidate the preceding one: "a perfect man". A connection between the idea of perfection and πλήρωμα is quite usual; the relationship between the substantive and the adjective πλήρης, which can mean perfect, is the immediate cause of that connection.[2]

Similarly, the idea of perfection led to the idea of stature of matu-

---

I, 272 in the Cohn-Wendland edition. We have already encountered a similar type of metonomy (above, p. 229) in Hermetic literature, where the cosmos is called a πλήρωμα τῆς κακίας or τῆς ζωῆς.

[1] For ἡλικία see J. Schneider, Th. W. II, p. 943ss.

[2] See above p. 227. Cf. also Pallis, To the Romans, ad. R. 11:13 : "τελῶ and πληρῶ with their derivates are synonymous.".

rity.[1] In Philo too, the ideas of perfection and maturity go side by side.[2] Although the ecclesia is filled to such an extent by pneumatical gifts that in 1:23 and, apparently, in 4:13, it is called τὸ πλήρωμα, the full complement of believers have not yet achieved that measure of perfection and maturity which is the property of the pleroma.

Following this, the matter of false doctrines and of being νήπιος is brought up.[3] In order to reach this required state of perfection and maturity, it is necessary that the ecclesia become a full body [4] and that this body of Christ may be increased and grow. The body can only draw the power to do this from Christ himself who ensures that each part partakes of his gifts.[5]

With this, we have attended to each occurrence of the word πλήρωμα in Eph. In this epistle, it does not have obvious cosmic connotations. However, in Eph. 1:23 and 4:10, the word πληροῦν does have this aspect. The character of πλήρωμα is one of eschatological significance. Although we found that the words is variable in meaning, the idea of "the end" was never lost. In 1:10, the word was even used as a designation for this end; elsewhere it indicated the whole range of gifts associated with the end. This last-mentioned sense of the word was also retained in 1:23 where it took on the function of a metonymic indication for the ecclesia.

Our investigation into the words πληροῦν and πλήρωμα, affords us some insight into the eschatology of the epistle. As far as the author is concerned, the period in which the ecclesia flourishes is the end of all times. For him, the great event of the end of all times is the gathering together of all things, the culmination of God's work of unifying salvation, in Christ. Since the ecclesia is itself the evidence, this work of unifying salvation upon which God had previously resolved, is now carried into effect (2:14).

With respect to this unifying work, there is a question of a μυστήριον

---

[1] The word τέλειος can also mean : adult (cf. Delling, Th. W. VIII, p. 69 line 44ss.).

[2] Schneider, op. cit., p. 69 line 50s. and p. 72 lines 36-38.

[3] To be νήπιος or παιδίον is the typical contrast to being ἀνὴρ τέλειος (cf. Schneider, op cit., p. 69 line 45ss.). For the connection between the expression τέλειος with insight and (highest) knowledge, see Schneider. op. cit., p. 70 line 25ss., p. 71 lines 30ss. and 26ss. For ἀνὴρ τέλειος see also para. 6, point c.

[4] We have in mind the unity which is stressed in the preceding and the working together and being joined of all parts of the body, mentioned in 4:16.

[5] This emerges from the adjunct ἐξ οὗ in 4:16 which refers to Christ and the adjunct κατ' ἐνέργειαν ἐν μέτρῳ ἑνὸς ἑκάστου μέρους which is connected with 4:7.

and an οἰκονομία τοῦ πληρώματος τῶν καιρῶν (1:9, 10). The disposition of this mystery becomes known through the ecclesia (3:9-11). The ecclesia which makes known the disposition of this mystery is enabled to do this through the death and resurrection of Christ by which the ecclesia itself was formed (2:11-19) and through the gifts of revelation bestowed by the exalted Christ.

So probably, the end of all times commences with the death and resurrection of Christ. God's unifying work is consummated because Christ permeates all things with his dominion and blessings (p. 235). The work will have been completed when the negative forces have ceased their activity and when everything is in the right relationship to Christ (p. 225).

Christ's fulfilment of all things goes side by side with the ecclesia being filled with the pneuma and all the pneumatical eschatological gifts (p. 239s.). The maximum degree of fulness is still to be achieved (3:9). Through the power and gifts of Christ, the ecclesia must grow towards him to become the habitation of God (4:16; 2:22). Thus there is also a future for the church. The ecclesia is an eschatological force, treading the path towards an objective which beckons.

In Col. the word πλήρωμα is used twice; in 1:19 and in 2:9. Since the adjective πᾶν precedes the substantive on both occasions, the pleroma must in these places too be assumed to represent a multiple entity. Col. 2:9 states that all this fulness dwells in Christ.[1] Similarly,

---

[1] In Col. 2:9 σωματικῶς cannot have a direct bearing on the body of Christ, despite the view of Abbott, Eph.-Col., p. 249. κατοικεῖν σωματικῶς does not mean dwelling in a soma but living as a soma. Haupt, Gefbr., p. 83, quite correctly translates: "in Art eines Leibes" ("in the manner of a body"). But it is overdone to interpret this rendering, as he does, as "in Art eines einheitlichen Organismus" ("in the manner of a single organnism"). Preferable to this would be, bearing in mind 2:17 as Meuzelaar, Der Leib des Messias, p. 139, has done, "leibhaft" ("corporeal") but not "schattenhaft" ("shadowlike") as he suggests. In that light, it would be possible to take into account the astrological term σωματικῶς which means the opposite to "in aspect" (see Liddell-Scott, s.v. σωματικῶς sub 2). To me however, it seems more desirable with respect to σωματικῶς to remember the meaning of σῶμα in the sense of "the body or whole of a thing" or "the whole body or frame of a thing"; "a body of writings" as found in Liddell-Scott, s.v. σῶμα sub IV. In that case, the κατοικεῖν σωματικῶς states that the pleroma does not disperse itself (not σποράδην) but dwells somewhere in its totality. See the example quoted by Liddell-Scott, s.v. σωματικῶς sub 3. These statements about a totality dwelling somewhere in its totality seem tautologous. In reality, however, this superfluous formulation is not without sense; the idea that the pleroma could exist in part somewhere outside of Christ, is radically refuted.

in 1:9, the whole of the pleroma is said to be in Christ. Therefore, the pleroma is inseparable from Christ.

In 1:9, the reconciliation of all things is ascribed to the pleroma, indicating that God, in this reconciliation through the pleroma and the dwelling of the pleroma in Christ, is the active agent. [1]

In 2:9, the words $\pi\hat{a}\nu$ $\tau\grave{o}$ $\pi\lambda\acute{\eta}\rho\omega\mu a$ havebeen augmented by the genitive $\tau\hat{\eta}s$ $\theta\epsilon\acute{o}\tau\eta\tau os$. If we consult the Pastor of Hermes for an explanation for this genitive, we find that it has a reason. This work, with its many Jewish allusions, uses the word $\theta\epsilon\acute{o}\tau\eta s$ as a categoric designation for God and everything relating to God. Its genitive characterises the pneuma of the Christian prophets and the strength of that pneuma which has been given them through the power of the pneuma of God.[2]

Instead of interpreting the formulation $\pi\hat{a}\nu$ $\tau\grave{o}$ $\pi\lambda\acute{\eta}\rho\omega\mu a$ $\tau\hat{\eta}s$ $\theta\epsilon\acute{o}\tau\eta\tau os$ in a philosophical sense, meaning the whole complex of characteristics comprising the essence of the godhead,[3] I would prefer to think of a totality, godly in nature and bestowed upon man by virtue of God, just as the pneuma in the Pastor is godly in nature and a gift to the prophets. To this totality must be attributed all the treasures of wisdom and knowledge which are latent in Christ and to which the mystery of God appertains (2:3).

The Christ in whom these treasures lie concealed, is an eschatological personification, reminiscent of the Son of man in the Ethiopian book of Enoch who unveils all treasures that are hid. Even the name he bears in 1:13 (the son of his, i.e. God's, love) calls to mind the appellation "chosen" which the Son of man bears in Enoch.[4]

---

[1] The most obvious exegesis of 1:19 and 20 is that $\pi\hat{a}\nu$ $\tau\grave{o}$ $\pi\lambda\acute{\eta}\rho\omega\mu a$ is the subject of $\epsilon\grave{v}\delta\acute{o}\kappa\eta\sigma\epsilon\nu$ and both infinitives which are dependent on this $\epsilon\grave{v}\delta\acute{o}\kappa\eta\sigma\epsilon\nu$. Any other exegesis is contrived. $\pi\hat{a}\nu$ $\tau\grave{o}$ $\pi\lambda\acute{\eta}\rho\omega\mu a$ is used here as a metonymic indication for God. Nevertheless, there is a certain brevity in the sentence of the kind found in a metaphor or allegorical representation, cf. Lausberg, Handbuch para. 558 and 895. The intended meaning is that it has pleased God that the whole of the pleroma should dwell in Christ, reconciliating all things with God through the medium of Christ.

[2] For Jewish allusions in the Pastor, see Vielhauer in Hennecke, Neutestamentliche Apokryphen II[3], p. 454. In Herm. m. X, 1,4 $\theta\epsilon\acute{o}\tau\eta s$ is found as a categorical indication. In m. XI, 5, 10 and 14, the genitive $\tau\hat{\eta}s$ $\theta\epsilon\acute{o}\tau\eta\tau os$ characterises the pneuma which speaks through the prophets and the power of this pneuma, given as it were from above, through the power of the spirit of God.

[3] For philosophical formulations of this kind, see Delling, Th. W. VI, p. 300 lines 29-34 and Liddell-Scott, s.v. 6.

[4] See Enoch 46:3-6 and 51:3 and compare En. 48:4 with Col. 1:27 (cf. also G. Seven-

We may therefore regard the pleroma in Col. as an eschatological reality. It is in this reality that the believers have a share.

2:2 speaks of πᾶν πλοῦτος τῆς πληροφορίας τῆς συνέσεως. Clearly, this formulation anticipates the formulation πάντες οἱ θησαυροὶ τῆς σοφίας καὶ γνώσεως ἀπόκρυφοι which follows in 2:3. We have already expressed our conviction that all these riches of wisdom and knowledge are part of the godly pleroma which dwells in Christ. If this opinion is correct, the "riches of ... understanding" mentioned in 2:2 also belong to this pleroma. There is a strong possibility that the genitive τῆς πληροφορίας more or less seeks to make this clear.

In non-biblical literature, the rare word πληροφορία signifies "certainty".[1] The verb πληροφορεῖν however, is closely related to πληροῦν.[2] Therefore it is arguable that πληροφορία in Col. 2:2 is closely connected in meaning with the general meaning of πλήρωμα, "full measure" or "fulness".[3] If that is the case, then the formulation in 2:2 may be translated as "all the richness of the completeness of understanding" and moreover, the word πληροφορία would suggest the pleroma implicit in 2:3 and 1:19 and actually mentioned in 2:9.

The believers who are referred to in 2:1, do not yet possess all the riches of understanding which are the property of the pleroma, the condition is that they be joined in love as behoves the body of Christ, which is the ecclesia. Only thus will they come closer to this treasure.[4]

Besides the word πλήρωμα, we encounter the passive form of the verb πληροῦν on two occasions in Col. Both times, the being filled means the receiving of salvation which is part of the pleroma. Col. 1:9 speaks of a being filled with the knowledge of God's will in all wisdom and spiritual understanding. There is a connection here with the riches of understanding and the treasures of wisdom and knowledge of 2:2 and 3 which, in our opinion, are part of the pleroma. The πνευματικῇ

---

ster, De Christologie van het N.T., Amsterdam 1946, p. 81s.). The references to the treasures of wisdom and knowledge are also reminiscent of LXX Is. 33:5 and 6,

[1] See Liddell-Scott s.v.; Bauer, Wörterbuch z. N.T., s.v. and Delling, Th. W. VI. p. 309 lines 1-5.

[2] See Delling, op. cit., p. 307 line 27ss.; Liddell-Scott s.v. and Bauer, op. cit. s.v.

[3] Delling, op. cit., p. 309 line 17s. : "tautologisch mit πλοῦτος, von der Überfulle ... des Glaubenserkennens" ("tautology with πλοῦτος, of the plenitude ... of the religious knowledge"). Bauer, op. cit., s.v. : "Aber mindestens Kol. 2,2. Hb. 6,11. 10,22. 1 Kl. 42,3 ist auch die Bed. d. Fülle möglich" ("but at least in Col. 2:2; Heb. 6:11; 10:22 and in 1 Kl. 42:3, it could also have the meaning "fulness")".

[4] The συμβιβασθένες which precedes the formulation εἰς πᾶν πλοῦτοσ κ.τ.λ. in 2:2, corresponds with συμβιβαζόμενεν in 2:19.

which is adjunctive to συνέσει, is clear proof that the pleroma embraces pneumatological properties.

Col. 2:9 contains a reference to being fulfilled by or in or with Christ in whom the pleroma dwells; it is obvious that being filled is a benificial state. (If the adjunct ἐν Χριστῷ is not intended to convey that which fills, the alternative is the same absolute use of πεπληρωμένος as we encounter in Jewish-Hellenistic literature in the adjective πλήρης in its positive sense (p. 229).) The beneficial state in question cannot mean anything else but participation in the benefit of the pleroma that dwells in Christ.

Finally, Col. 4:12 gives rise to the conviction that for the author of Col., the pleroma has the implication of perfection. 4:12 recapitulates statements made in two earlier places i.e. 1:9 and 2 : 1ss. In 1:9, there is an intercession for knowledge of God's will. (This knowledge belongs to the pleroma.) 2:1ss. relates on the struggle in behalf of the addressees and other believers, that they may receive all the riches of full understanding. (This riches also belongs to the pleroma.) The recapitulation in 4:12 declares perfection to be the aim of prayer and the objective of the struggle.[1]

Thus we observe that there is much in common between Eph. and Col. respecting the words πληροῦν and πλήρωμα whilst, nevertheless, both epistles retain a certain degree of originality in their use. In Eph. the emphasis is on the identification of the pleroma with the ecclesia whilst in Col. the words are tend to establish the identify the pleroma with God or Christ.

The fact that the expression τὸ πλήρωμα τῶν καιρῶν in addition occurs in Eph. has the result of placing a stronger accent on the eschatological character of the pleroma in this epistle. In Col. however, greater stress falls on the aspects of wisdom, knowledge and understanding. These gifts or treasures as such feature less prominently in Eph. although in essence they form a definite part of the pleroma. After all, the measure of maturity which is inherent in the pleroma, implies ascendancy over all heresy (Eph. 4:14).

Love comes to the fore in Eph. (3:17, 19; 4:15). However, on closer examination, it becomes clear that in Col. agape is in no way a less important aspect of the pleroma. In Col. 2:2, love and understanding

---

[1] The πεπληροφορημένοι following upon τέλειοι is an allusion to the τῆς πληροφορίας in 2:2 and means either to be filled with assurance or to be completely filled, sc. with the understanding mentioned in 2:2. The adjunct ἐν παντὶ θελήματι may be connected with σταθῆτε but not with τέλειοι καὶ πεπληφορημένοι.

go together. We have already established that the idea of perfection
is connected with the pleroma; in Col. 3:14 it is made clear that love
is essential to the attainment of perfection.

The concepts which are connected with the word pleroma in Eph.
and the HP are more closely inter-related than has often been thought.
In view of our present investigation into the authenticity of Eph.,
we think that it is of direct consequence to evince this close inter-relationship. This affinity is established in the strictly eschatological
character which the expression "pleroma" possesses both in Eph. as
well as in the HP. In Gal. 4:4 as in Eph. 1:10, this eschatological character is particularly striking. Furthermore, both these passages have
to do with the Jewish-Hellenistic term of reference; i.e. the end.[1]

In Gal. 4:4, the word has a double meaning. Within the framework
of the parable of the heir which is used in Gal. 4:1ss., the word simply
means the end of an arranged period of time; in truth, however, the
matter in question refers to the eschatological end, the end of this age.

The particular event which marks this end, is that God sends his
Son. This again, is immediately connected with the sending of the
pneuma. In essence therefore, the pleroma in Gal. 4:4 is as full of benefit
as the pleroma in Eph. 1:10. A feature worth noting is that Gal. 4:4
draws the same association between the word "pleroma" and the concept of maturity which we have already encountered in Eph. 4:13.

In R. 11:12, the word is used as a counterfoil to the words παράπτωμα
and ἥττημα, which describe the lamentable circumstances which befell
that part of Israel which God abandoned to its obduracy and depra-
vity.[2] Their pleroma will come when God's reconciliation takes the
place of his rejection. But, like the renewed grafting of the broken
branches, described in subsequent verses in the form of a parable,
this pleroma is of the future. According to R. 11:26, the pleroma will
come with the advent of the deliverer and may, as intimated in 11:15,
be prized as life from the dead.

The redeeming advent of God or the Messiah was known to Hellenistic Jews who conceived the "end" as the time of this advent (p. 220).

---

[1] See p. 232 and note 5.

[2] The words παράπτωμα and ἥττημα respectively mean stumble and overthrow;
one has the impression however, that they can describe not only an action or event but
also a situation. In 1 Cl. 56,1 there is a reference to τῶν ἔν τινι παραπτώματι ὑπαρχόντων.
In LXX Is. 31:8. ἥττημα is a rendering of the word מס (forced labour) and evidently
conveys the idea of a deplorable situation. In 1 C. 6:7, ἥττημα describes the position of a
loser.

For this branch of Judaism the concept of life from the dead was connected with this end. Therefore, the concept of pleroma as manifested in R. 11:12, must be regarded as an eschatological concept. Clearly, it is a state of being full and complete which awaits obdurate Israel. This state of being full and complete may be associated with ideas of salvation and blessing and the notion of perfection.[1]

When this pleroma has come, the line of division which now runs through Israel will be eradicated; there will no longer be one part of Israel that is obdurate and another part that is not obdurate. The whole of Israel will be saved (R. 11:25, 26). This pleroma is anticipated by the work of Paul himself. First of all, he fulfils the gospel (i.e. reveals the gospel for what it is, R. 15:19; cf. Col. 1:25) in the orbis terrarum (R. 15:19, 24, 28).[2] Then $\tau\grave{o}$ $\pi\lambda\acute{\eta}\rho\omega\mu\alpha$ $\tau\hat{\omega}\nu$ $\grave{\epsilon}\theta\nu\hat{\omega}\nu$ will come ($\epsilon\grave{\iota}\sigma\acute{\epsilon}\lambda\theta\eta$).[3] And only when this pleroma has come, will there be no hardening in part of Israel (R. 11:25). On the basis of these indications, the coming pleroma of the nations must also be interpreted as an eschatological concept. In my view, the primary meaning of the word would seem to be that of the end.

Jewish apocalyptic literature is familiar with the concept that God has abandoned Israel to the Gentiles, that Sion or Jerusalem will be saved when the times of the Gentiles are "fulfilled" and that God will come at the end of this age to exercise his wrath on them.[4] Everything surrounding the eschatological advent of God or the Messiah could be designated as the end (p. 221). There was however, a dual aspect to this coming; for heathens and the ungodly it was terrible whilst for the righteous of Israel it was a beneficial event (p. 221). It is therefore understandable that in describing the end for Israel, the conception was one of salvation and blessing whilst a simultaneous designation for the end of the heathens implied wraht and judgement.

---

[1] See p. 228s. and cf. B. Murmelstein, "Adam, ein Beitrag zur Messiaslehre", WKZM 35, 1928, p. 254. Murmelstein quotes Exodus rabba XXX, 3, in which the concept of "full" is combined with the day of the Messiah who will prepare an end to death.

[2] Cf. Lohmeyer, Grundlagen paulinischer Theologie, pp. 165, 207 and 208.

[3] This $\epsilon\grave{\iota}\sigma\epsilon\lambda\theta\epsilon\hat{\iota}\nu$ in R. 11:25 does, however, suggest entering in the $\beta\alpha\sigma\iota\lambda\epsilon\acute{\iota}\alpha$. Nevertheless, this verb is never used in the CP in that context. Invariably the verb $\kappa\lambda\eta\rho\rho\nuo\mu\epsilon\hat{\iota}\nu$ is used (1 C. 6:9, 10; 15:50; Gal. 5:21). The $\epsilon\grave{\iota}\sigma\epsilon\lambda\theta\epsilon\hat{\iota}\nu$ of R. 11:25 bears an affinity to the $\pi\alpha\rho\epsilon\iota\sigma\hat{\eta}\lambda\theta\epsilon\nu$ of R. 5:20 and has the same meaning as the $\grave{\epsilon}\lambda\theta\epsilon\hat{\iota}\nu$ in R. 3:8; 7:9; 1 C. 4:5; 11:26; 13:10; Gal. 3:19, 25; 4:4 the fact that in R. 11:25 does not stop at the simple $\grave{\epsilon}\lambda\theta\epsilon\hat{\iota}\nu$ but gives $\epsilon\grave{\iota}\sigma\epsilon\lambda\theta\epsilon\hat{\iota}\nu$ conforms to the Koine tendency to make use of compound words; cf. Radermacher, p. 31. and Bl.-Debr., para. 116,1.

[4] See 4 Ezra 5:28; 6:18 and Luke 21:24 ($\check{\alpha}\chi\rho\iota$ $o\grave{\mathring{v}}$ $\pi\lambda\eta\rho\omega\theta\hat{\omega}\sigma\iota\nu$ $\kappa\alpha\iota\rho o\grave{\iota}$ $\grave{\epsilon}\theta\nu\hat{\omega}\nu$).

In the case of R. 11:25, the question of the end or the pleroma of the heathens arises; but here this end means a redeeming end. The end signifies a state of fulness and completeness even for the other nations. This particular concept, that there is such a thing as an eschatological salvation for the nations or all the inhabitants of the earth, is only encountered on a few occasions in Jewish apocalyptic literature.[1]

If our deductions are correct, the meaning of the word "pleroma" in R. 11:12 and 25 is not synonymous with the meanings it expresses in Eph. 1:23; 3:19 and 4:19; yet the connection between these different aspects of the word is close. In all the places mentioned as well as in Gal. 4:4 and Eph. 1:10, the word constitutes an eschatological concept.

The word makes one more appearance in Romans, i.e. in R. 15:29. In my view, the word in this context is identical in meaning with the meanings it has in Eph. 1:23; 3:19 and 4:13. R. 15:29 relates that the apostle, who is travelling through the world to preach the gospel, will, when he comes to the community in Rome, come $\dot{\epsilon}\nu$ $\pi\lambda\dot{\eta}\rho\omega\mu\alpha\tau\iota$ $\epsilon\dot{\upsilon}\lambda o\gamma\dot{\iota}\alpha s$ $X\rho\iota\sigma\tau o\hat{\upsilon}$. The phrasing of R. 15:29 gives the impression that it is by no means a self-evident fact for the apostle that his arrival will be an $\dot{\epsilon}\nu$ $\pi\lambda\dot{\eta}\rho\omega\mu\alpha\tau\iota$ $\epsilon\dot{\upsilon}\lambda o\gamma\dot{\iota}\alpha s$ $X\rho\iota\sigma\tau o\hat{\upsilon}$ coming. Paul, however, is possessed of the certain and prophetic conviction that he will be able to come in such a way.[2]

The context in which this is expressed, deals with unity and community between Christian converts from paganism and the hagioi in Jerusalem, and a communal striving on the part of the Christians in Rome with the apostle, to seal this unity and community, in prayer. This reinforcement of the ties between the Christian converts and the hagioi in Jerusalem will make it possible for the apostle to arrive in Rome with joy and there, together with the Christians, enjoy rest and refreshment (15:32).

It stands to reason that this joy and rest belong to the $\pi\lambda\dot{\eta}\rho\omega\mu\alpha$ $\epsilon\dot{\upsilon}\lambda o\gamma\dot{\iota}\alpha s$ $X\rho\iota\sigma\tau o\hat{\upsilon}$. The confirmation of unity between the Christian converts and those in Jerusalem will result in the apostle's coming with the pleroma. In R., joy is envisaged as an eschatological pneumatical gift (14:17; 15:13; cf. Gal. 5:22). In other places, it is clear that

---

[1] See 4 Ezra 6:26 and W. Bousset-H. Gressmann, Die Religion des Judentums im späthellenischen Zeitalter ([4]1966 ,Hndbch NT 21), p. 234, note 3.

[2] The pleonasm $\dot{\epsilon}\rho\chi\dot{o}\mu\epsilon\nu os$ ... $\dot{\epsilon}\lambda\epsilon\dot{\upsilon}\sigma o\mu\alpha\iota$ intensifies the statement (cf. Lausberg. Handbuch, para. 503). $o\hat{\iota}\delta\alpha$ is also used to introduce a declaration in a speech of Paul in Acts 20:25 and 29. In both these places it is unmistakeably clear that we are concerned with the prophetic declarations of the apostle.

the state of rest forms part of eschatological salvation.[1] Thus, there are ample grounds for treating this πλήρωμα εὐλογίας Χριστοῦ as a whole range of blessings bestowed by Christ. These blessings are pneumatical eschatological gifts. They are bestowed provided there is an internal communion between the believers.

All these observations correspond with our findings in Eph. R. 15:29 just expresses in stronger terms that the apostle has a very special relationship with this pleroma. This does not mean to say that he can dispose over it; it is not his instrument. Rather the converse, that he is the instrument of the pleroma, is true. Yet, when he comes ἐν πληρώματι, all those around him find refreshment in the gifts of the pleroma. Something of this nature is also discernible in Eph. In Eph. 3:9, the intercession of the apostle is one contributory factor towards the attainment of the pleroma for the addressees.

A pleroma of this kind is also found outside the CP. In John 1:16, we read about a pleroma embracing the grace and truth of God which has manifested itself in Jesus Christ. The contrast drawn between Moses and Jesus Christ and between the law and this grace and truth lend an eschatological aspect to this pleroma. The designation μονογενής which is applied to Christ in this context, has affinities with the messianic designation ὁ ἀγαπητός, thereby reinforcing this aspect.[2]

Beyond this however, there are no direct indications that for the author, this word had immediate associations with the eschatological concept of the end. He uses the word because, in 1:14, he has described the glory of the only begotten son and because he has depicted this glory as the state of being full ⟨πλήρης⟩ of grace and truth.

We are reminded more forcibly of the Pauline pleroma in Ignatian literature. Although the word has no overt eschatological aspect, it is nevertheless clear that it serves to indicate a whole host of blessings. In the praescript of his letter to the Ephesians, Ignatius addresses himself to the ecclesia of Ephesus as τῇ εὐλογημένῃ ἐν μεγέθει θεοῦ πατρὸς πληρώματι.

The adjunct ἐν μεγέθει describes the respect in which the ecclesia is blessed, namely in the greatest and most powerful way, as might be expected from God.[3] The adjunct θεοῦ πατρὸς πληρώματι indi-

---

[1] See Rev. 14:13; Hebr. 4:10s. and Matt. 11:29. In R. 15:32, the word συναναπαύσωμαι is used; elsewhere, respectively ἀναπαήσονται, κατάπαυσις and ἀνάπαυσις.

[2] For this affinity see F. Büchsel, Th. W. IV, p. 747.

[3] Liddell-Scott, s.v. II, gives the following meanings for μέγεθος : greatness, magnitude, might, power. Bauer, Wörterbuch, s.v., has the following remarks in respect to

cates the medium through which this blessedness is bestowed. This pleroma would thus appear to be a whole number of godly blessings.

In the praescript of the letter sent to Tralles, Ignatius addresses the Trallian ecclesia with the following relative clause : ἣν καὶ ἀσπάζομαι ἐν τῷ πληρώματι ἐν ἀποστολικῷ χαρακτῆρι. The final three words may be translated as : "in the way that is characteristic for the apostles".[1] Probably, the word pleroma refers to the gifts of salvation which were always wished on the recipients in the greeting at the beginning of an apostolic missive.[2] Almost certainly, similar words were also spoken when an apostle, such as, for example, Paul, addressed a community and opened his speech with a greeting. Charis and eirene thus, are vital components of this pleroma.[3]

At this juncture, we would like to establish some *results of our investigation* into the word πλήρωμα as it appears in Eph. We ascertain that we arrived at an opinion that diverges from that of Hoekstra, Pfleiderer and Schmiedel who all refuted the homogeneity of the concept of pleroma as set forth in Eph. and Col. (p. 23). We have seen, despite the fact that both epistles treat the subject in an individual manner, that the pleroma in question is one and the same.

As we see it, our interpretation of the concept has the advantage that it allows the connotation "the end" which hallmarks the word "pleroma" at the beginning (1:10) of Eph. to be sustained throughout the remainder of the epistle.

Another important factor in our opinion is that the designation "pleroma" for the ecclesia is elucidated when, taking into account our interpretation, the pleroma is seen as the whole spectrum of eschatological gifts. Because Christ fills it with all these gifts, the ecclesia is indicated by the metonymic designation τὸ πλήρωμα. The sense

---

the words that are quoted : "ἐν μεγέθει gehört zwar grammatisch nicht zu θεοῦ, das durch das folgende πληρώματι gebunden ist, beschreibt aber doch irgendwie Wesen u. Art Gottes" (although grammatically ἐν μεγέθει does not belong to θεοῦ which is linked to the succeeding πληρώματι, it nevertheless somehow describes the nature and way of God").

[1] Thus Bauer, Wörterbuch, s.v. χαρακτήρ. Funk, Patres Apostolici I, p. 242, interprets the adjunct as de more apostolorum.

[2] Funk, l.c. : "... eam (sc. l. vocum πληρώματι) de gratiae plenitudine interpretamur, quam Ignatius Trallianis deprecatur de more apostolorum ......cf. Rom .1,7; I Cor. 1,3; II Cor. 1,2; Gal. 1,3 etc.".

[3] The χάρις and the εἰρήνη are not only mentioned in the greeting at the beginning of Pauline epistles but also in those of 1 Pt. (1:2) and 2 Pt. (1:2). In the greeting of Jude (2), ἔλεος, εἰρήνη and ἀγάπη occur.

of the words "the whole of eschatological pneumatical gifts" here means "that which is gifted with all of the eschatological pneumatical gifts".[1]

Schlier holds that Paul, the author of Eph. and Col., borrowed and refashioned the pleroma concept from an early form of gnosticism.[2] Dupont, on the other hand, discerns in Eph. and Col. a literary dependence on the cosmological theories of the vulgarized Stoa. The term "pleroma" itself, he also attributes to the Stoa.[3] In Dupont's view, Paul took the word from the vocabulary of the Stoa but transformed its meaning, remoulding it in an original fashion from a cosmological designation into an ecclesiological term.[4]

Meuzelaar, however, sought a quite different explanation for the word which he defined in terms of rabbinical literature and the concept of completeness or perfection.[5]

We are persuaded that the word "pleroma" functioned in more than one sense. The fact is that the word has a pleasant sound.[6] This

---

[1] Our interpretation of Eph. 1:23 comes close to that of H. Berkhof, De katholiciteit der kerk (Nijkerk 1962), p. 57 and H. Ridderbos, Paulus, Ontwerp van zijn theologie (Kampen 1966), p. 463. They spoke resp. of "het gebied, waarover de heerschappij wordt uitgeoefend, het domein of dominium" ("the sphere in which ht domination is enforced, the domain or dominion") and of "het door Hem d.w.z. Christus vervulde (gebied of dominium)" ("that (sphere or domain) which is filled by Him, i.e. Christ"). To my mind the connotation of domain or dominion with respect to the word "pleroma" is open to doubt. The thesis presented by Mussner (see p. 237 and note 1) is not sufficiently convincing to link the verb πληροῦν with "domination" so irrevocably that this connection dictates that the word πλήρωμα should automatically lead to the idea of "dominion" or "domain". When Ridderbos, l.c., for the rest describes the pleroma in Eph. as "een pneumatische realiteit, die verstaan moet worden tegen de achtergrond en in het licht van Christus alomvattende macht" ("a pneumatical reality which schould be understood against the background and in the light of Christ's all-embracing might"), we are able to agree with him. Mussner too, op. cit., p. 59, associates the word "pleroma" in Eph. 1:23 with a pneumatical reality and speaks of "die pneumatischen Lebenskräfte Christi" ("the pneumatical life forces of Christ"), observing : "Insofern besteht zwischen "Pleroma" und "Pneuma" eine "enge Verwantschaft" (Wikenhauser, Die Kirche, S. 190), wenn auch beide Begriffe nicht identisch sind" ("Thus far, there is a "close relationship" between "pleroma" and "pneuma", even if the two concepts are not identical"). Berkhof, l.c. disputes this, arguing that in the context of the word "pleroma" in Eph. 1:23, there is no question of the powers of the Spirit; our reply to this is that the text preceding the word "pleroma" in 4:13 does ennumerate Christ's pneumatical gifts, i.e. 4:7-11.

[2] Eph., p. 98.

[3] Gnosis, p. 471-474.

[4] Der Leib des Messias, p. 132.

[5] Der Leib des Messias, p. 132.

[6] The Greeks regarded the combination πλ as mellifluent. 1 C. 15:39 evinces a perference for the sounds η and ω. Thus, for example, the word πλήρωμα was selected

could explain why so many people of diverse spiritual convictions has a preference for the word.

The word was by no means a term specific to the Stoa (p. 229). As a cosmological term, we first encounter it in syncretical Hermetic literature which was partially under the influence of the vulgarized form of the Soa, In one particular Hermetic tract, τὸ πλήρωμα denotes a divine reality, the ultimate truth and the very pivot of all that exists (p. 230.).

The Gnostics who, like the authors of the Hermetic writings, based themselves on syncretism and certain vulgarized philosophical traditions, turned the word into a designation for the highest form of salvation and it became one of their favourite terms (p. 230s.).

In our opinion the Hellenistic Jews also appropriated the word as their own and, despite the fact that their conception of salvation was quite different, they nevertheless used the selfsame word for their ultimate and highest salvation (p. 232ss.). We also believe that the Jewish-Hellenistic conception of the pleroma sometimes influenced the gnostic manner of dealing with the gnostic pleroma (p. 231ss.).

It could be asserted with confidence that the word τὸ πλήρωμα was vaguely fashionable during the late Hellenistic period.[1] In popular parlance, it meant some kind of ultimate divine reality or highest form of salvation. The differences lay therein that the content of this salvation wan not the same for all.

As it is used in Eph. (and Col),. the word traces its meaning back to the language of Jewish Hellenism where it assumes the meaning of "the end". We found a late but conclusive sign of this in Cairo Papyrus 10263 (p. 233s.).

We find ourselves in full agreement with H. Ridderbos that the conttent of Eph. and Col. is too far removed from the syncretic literature of the Hellenistic "Umwelt" (environment) to ratify an explanation of the term in the two epistles on that basis.[2] When a gnostic work such as the Gospel of Truth sometimes comes close to Eph. (and Col.) in statements featuring the pleroma, this is due to its Jewish-Hellenistic phraseology (p. 231).

Schlier apparently identifies the combination of πλήρωμα and πληροῦν in Eph. 1:23 and 3:19 as gnostic terminology and has it that

---

rather than the word τέλος which has a related meaning but ends in a σ which was less popular. See p. 165 and note 1.

[1] For the theory that πλήρωμα was a fashionable word, see Berkhof, op. cit., p. 51s.

[2] Op. cit., p. 439 note 96.

this signifies absorption into the pleroma.[1] My research however, has only led me to the discovery of one single (equivalent of) this combination in the so-called Apocryphon of Jacobus.[2] And this Apocryphon can scarcely, after all, be called a gnostic writing. Quite often ideas are therein expressed which are reminiscent of ideas found in the CP. To speak of a Pauline influence in the case of this work would be more apposite than to surmise a gnostic influence in Eph. 1:23 and 3:19.[3]

The proposition put forward by Meuzelaar does not reach out far enough. Statements on the pleroma in Eph. and Col. would be somewhat colourless and flat if the word conveyed the exclusive meaning of completeness or perfection. Furthermore, the concept of completeness or perfection was never so central to rabbinical theology that it would clarify its predominant character in Eph. and Col.

The word "pleroma" did not acquire the meaning of completeness or perfection through the medium of a Hebrew or Aramaic influence. By virtue of its relationship with $\pi\lambda\acute{\eta}\rho\eta\varsigma$, $\pi\lambda\acute{\eta}\rho\omega\mu\alpha$ had of old been traditionally associated with the concept of perfection (pp. 227, 230). Far closer to the Hebrew equivalent of the pleroma than the idea of perfection or completeness, is the meaning "the end".[4]

A striking element in the places Meuzelaar cites from rabbinical literature is that whenever the Hebrew equivalent has the connotation of completeness or perfection, an eschatological aspect comes to the fore. When that occurs, the context relates to a state of perfection which existed in the beginning of the creation. Moreover, it is a rabbinical thought, explicitly stated in one of those places, that this perfec-

---

[1] Op. cit., pp. 97 and 176.

[2] Hennecke I³, at the bottom of p. 247.

[3] For the non-gnostic character of this work, see W. C. van Unnik, Openbaringen uit Egyptisch zand (De vondsten bij Nag-Hammadi, Den Haag 1958), p. 75 and H.-Ch. Puech in Hennecke I³, p. 249. For its affinity with Pauline literature, see Van Unnik, loc. cit. Van Unnik does not think a direct influence from Paul very likely.

[4] In the places quoted by Meuzelaar, the concepts of maturity, perfection or completeness are contiguous to derivates from the root מלא. It is however not favourable to his explanation that in Hebrew substantives derived from this stem were not usually connected with the idea of perfection. Aramaic and Syrian substantives from the same root were also not associated with perfection in any imputant sense. See J. Levy, Chaldäisches Wörterbuch über den Targumim II, 1868. s.v. מלא; J. Levy-H. L. Fischer, Neuhebr. und chaldäisches Wörterbuch über die Talmud und Midraschim III, 1883, s.v.; M. Jastrow, A Dictionary of the Targumim, The Talmud Babli and Yerushalmi and the Midrashis Literature II (London 1903), s.v. See above, p. 232 and note 4 for the word meaning the end, which is connected with the root מלא.

tion which existed in the beginning will come to pass once again in the days of the Messiah.[1]

All these factors strengthen our view that the Jewish-Hellenistic word "pleroma" should be interpreted in the light of an eschatological concept.[2] We attach great importance to the fact the we also found affinities with the HP in respect of this word. Until now, that emphasis has always been on the difference in meaning of the word in Eph. and Col. and as it is used elsewhere in the Pauline epistles.[3] This assess-

---

[1] We refer to the commentary on Gen. 2:4 in Genesis rabba XII, 6 which Meuzelaar quotes. The same idea is present in the statement from Exodus rabba XXX, 3 mentioned above, p. 249 n. 1. Meuzelaar himself (p. 133) draws attention to the image of the Massiah as the second Adam which is connected with the concept of completeness.

[2] By pleroma, we understand a whole range of pneumatical gifts in Eph. and Col. The concept that the pleroma is bestowed is also found in Meuzelaar (op. cit., p. 139 ad Eph. 3:19). In addition, he includes the concept of the pleroma as a whole number of attributes. Echoing L. Deimel (Leib Christi, Freiburg i. B. 1940, p. 146) he says that perfection is "eine rein qualitative Fülle rein geistiger Güter" ("a purely qualitative plenitude of purely spiritual attributes"). The difference of this with our interpretation is, however, that attributes which constitute part of the pleroma are seen not so much as pneumatical gifts as predominantly moral qualities on the part of the believers. Meuzelaar emulates Deimel when the latter interprets this "Fülle rein geistiger Güter" ("plenitude of purely spiritual attributes") as a "Fülle der sittlichen Reife und Tatkraft" ("plenitude in moral maturity and energy"); Deimel, op. cit., p. 149. The quotations are from Meuzelaar, op. cit., p. 140s.

[3] E.g., Schlier, Eph., p. 97 and Mitton, The Epistle to the Ephesians, p. 94ss. (cf. also Berkhof, op. cit., p. 44). Even scholars who do not accentuate the difference give a different interpretation to the word in Eph. than that propounded by R. Delling, Th. W. VI, p. 330ss. : "das ... Erfüllte" ("the ... that which has been filled") in 1:23: "die ganze Fülle, die Gott gibt" ("the whole fulness which God bestows") in 3:19; "das Vollmasz" ("the full measure") in 4:13; but, in R., "dass vollzählig werden "("becoming complete") in 11:12; "die Gesammtheit" (the totality") in 11:25 and "die Fülle der Reichtum" ("the fulness of riches") in 15:29. Mussner, bases himself on the connotation "die Göttliche Lebensfülle" ("the divine fulness of life") in Eph.; cf. op. cit., p. 60s. In R. however, he gives the following definitions : "$\pi\lambda\acute{\eta}\rho\omega\sigma\iota s$" (i.e. the fulfilling of the divine will) in 11:12; "Vollzahl" ("full number") in 11:25; "Vollendung" ("perfection") in 13:10 and "Fülle" ("fulness") in 15:29; cf. op. cit., p. 54. Ridderbos interprets the word as "het door Christus vervulde (gebied of dominium)" ("that (sphere or domain) which is filled by Christ") in Eph. 1:13 and translates it in Eph. 3:18 and 4:13 with "volheid" ("fulness"); cf. op. cit., p. 436. In R.11:12 and 11:25 the word is translated as "vol getal" ("full number"). He also renders it here as "volheid" ("fulness") and acknowledges its eschatological significance. Ridderbos believes that the theme concerns 'het onweerhoudende, het volle aandeel van Israël in de komende verlossing" ("that' which cannot be withheld, the full participation of Israel in the coming salvation") and of "een volle inbreng" ("a full yield") which the Gentiles will bring to the nation of God. See op. cit., p. 399ss. Meuzelaar, op. cit., p. 140, note 3 adopts a different point of view

ment was based on R.[1] However, we think that we managed to establish that in R. 11:12 and 25 we are as much concerned with an eschatological concept as in Eph.

The $\tau\grave{o}$ $\pi\lambda\acute{\eta}\rho\omega\mu\alpha$ $\alpha\grave{v}\tau\hat{\omega}\nu$ in R. 11:12 is a state of fulness or perfection that awaits Israel at the end. Here, in this context, the matter concerns an eschatological salvation. This applies also to R. 11:25 where $\tau\grave{o}$ $\pi\lambda\acute{\eta}\rho\omega\mu\alpha$ $\tau\hat{\omega}\nu$ $\grave{\epsilon}\theta\nu\hat{\omega}\nu$ means the end of the pagans and has the same implication of an eschatological salvation.[2]

In R. 15:29 we found the identical pleroma of Eph. When we wanted to describe the pleroma in Eph., we selected the words of Eph. 1:3 $\pi\hat{\alpha}\sigma\alpha$ $\epsilon\grave{v}\lambda o\gamma\acute{\iota}\alpha$ $\pi\nu\epsilon\upsilon\mu\alpha\tau\iota\kappa\acute{\eta}$ (p. 240). If we were to periphrase the formulation $\grave{\epsilon}\nu$ $\pi\lambda\eta\rho\acute{\omega}\mu\alpha\tau\iota$ $\epsilon\grave{v}\lambda o\gamma\acute{\iota}\alpha\varsigma$ $X\rho\iota\sigma\tauo\hat{v}$, we could with impunity avail ourselves of the formulation of Eph. 1:3 and write $\grave{\epsilon}\nu$ $\pi\acute{\alpha}\sigma\eta$ $\epsilon\grave{v}\lambda o\gamma\acute{\iota}\alpha$ $\pi\nu\epsilon\upsilon\mu\alpha\tau\iota\kappa\hat{\eta}$ $X\rho\iota\sigma\tauo\hat{v}$.

A point of interest is that we not only discovered a close relationship with regard to the word "pleroma" itself in Eph. and the HP but that we also found a congruence in the complex of thoughts and ideas that are interwoven with this word. Thus we found that in the context of Eph. 3:19, internal fellowship between the faithful is a condition for full participation in the pleroma (p. 240). This idea is also expressed in Eph. 1:23 (p. 241).

The context of R. 15:29 evinces the same idea (p. 250). R. 11 was found to contain related ideas. We read in that chapter that the pleroma as far as it affects Israel, means the end of the line of division separating Israel, moreover, this pleroma cannot be effective unless it also takes place for the nations (p. 249).

The correspondence goes further. We refer to the significance of the apostle with relation to the pleroma. In Eph. 3:19, there is the factor of the apostle's intercession. In R. 15:29, we find a special relationship between the apostle and the pleroma (p. 250; see also p. 251). In addition, there is a similar association between the word and the idea of maturity in Gal. 4:4 and Eph. 4:13 (pp. 243, 248).

Lastly, we direct our attention to R. 13:10, where $\pi\lambda\acute{\eta}\rho\omega\mu\alpha$ occurs

---

and sees a correlation between Eph. and R. 11:12-25, maintaining that in R., as in Eph., the issue is one of moral perfection.

[1] The correspondence in meaning between the word in Gal. 4:4 and in Eph. 1:10 is obvious.

[2] For Ridderbos, the $\pi\lambda\acute{\eta}\rho\omega\mu\alpha$ in R. 11:12 and 25 has the character of an eschatological state of perfection. (See p. 256 note 1.) The eschatological significance of the word in Eph. is not pointed out by him.

once again. Within this particular context, the word is not an eschatological term and does not, as far as we are able to judge, imply the idea
of the end or the salvation that will come at the end. However, in
view of the significance which the exegesis of people like Paul, versed
in the Scriptures, could attach to all kinds of correspondences,[1] it is
worth noting that here, in R. 13:10, the pleroma is the agape; Eph.
taught us to regard the agape as the highest gift of the pleroma as
described there (p. 240),

A few more questions should be asked. An investigation into the
words πληροῦν and πλήρωμα gave us an insight into the eschatology
of Eph. The question is : to what extent does this eschatology correspond with that of the HP ?

Eph. lacks those moments of apocalyptic drama which we from time
to time encounter in the HP. There is no question of an archangel's
call (1 Th. 4:16) or the sound of a trumpet (1 C. 15:32; 1 Th. 4:16).
The raising of the dead, as treated in 1 C. 15 and the παρουσία τοῦ κυρίου
which is repeatedly mentioned in 1 Th. (2:19; 3:13; 4:15 and 5:23)
are reflected only in the hymn quoted in 5:14. Eph. has no references
to standing before the judgment seat of God (R. 14:10) or to appear-
ing before the judgment seat of Christ (2 C. 5:10). Once, in passing,
the coming of the wrath of God in mentioned (Eph. 5:6).

However, this moderation in the use of eschatological pronouncements by no means signifies that the eschatological structure in Eph.
is essentially different from that in the HP. If it is correct to say that
the end of time begins with the death and resurrection of Christ (p. 244),
then in Eph. the era in which the apostle and the faithful are living
is evaluated in the same way as it is in the HP. One need only recall
1 C. 10:11.

The possibility offered by Gal. 4:4 of connecting the end of time with
the birth of Jesus must not lead us into the temptation to place the
emphasis on that birth. In the HP the turning point of all time is the
death and resurrection of Christ (2 C. 5:14-17). The birth of Jesus is
in the first instance the condition for his death (2 C. 8:9). That birth
is a coming under the law and this coming reaches its climax in the
ἐξαγοράζειν (Gal. 4:5) that is enacted on the cross (Gal. 3:13).

The end not only coincides with the sending of the Son but also
with the υἱοθεσία (to be made a son or sons) and the sending of the
Spirit of the Son (Gal. 4:4-6). This our criterion is the resurrection rather

---

[1] See Bousset, Die Religion des Judentums, p. 160s.

than the birth. When considering the expression "sending" of the Son", it should not be overlooked that it is through the resurrection that the fact that Jesus Christ is the Son of God is established (R. 1:4). Eph. therefore essentially has the some structure in its eschatology as the HP. The present is evaluated in the same way.

If we search the content of the eschatology of Eph., we remark that the basic premise lies in the exaltation of Christ and that he is kurios. The exalted kurios is central to this epistle. Organically connected with this central theme is the particular attention devoted to heaven and all creation as well as the equally remarkable interest vested in influential supernatural spirits or forces (p. 220).

The author recognises a correlation between the salvation of the faithful and the cessation of the baleful chaos which exists up to the highest reaches of the cosmos. God's unifying work of salvation is the most momentuous event of the end of time. Christ is the very centre of this unifying salvation which is designated as "the gathering together of all things in Christ" (p. 239).

This is accomplished because the exalted Christ permeates all things with his dominion and his blessings (p. 239). These blessings must be conceived in terms of the changes in the cosmos through which the above-mentioned chaos will be brought to an end. Unity within the ecclesia is evidence that God's unifying work has already become a reality (p. 243). This work will have been completed only when the negative forces have ceased to be active and when all things are in the right relationship with Christ (p. 235s. and p. 244).

We have said that the unifying work of God finds consummation when Christ permeates all things with his dominion and benediction. Christ's fulfilment of all things goes side by side with a fulfilment of the ecclesia. Christ not only permeates the universe with his dominion and blessings but he also fulfils the ecclesia. For the universe these blessings take the form of cosmic changes. For the ecclesia, it means being filled with the pneuma. The blessings bestowed on the ecclesia are the eschatological pneumatical gifts or the pleroma (p. 244).

It will still take some time until God's unifying work is finished; the moment when the negative forces are no longer active and the cosmos is completely permeated by Christ's blessings is not yet at hand. Similarly, a maximum degree of fulness in the pleroma is still in the future for the ecclesia. Completion and perfection have still to be realized (p. 243).

Although it is not possible to point out exact places in the HP where thoughts of this nature are combined and developed in the same way, narrow scrutiny nevertheless reveals that such ideas are by no means absent. In the HP too, we find the concept that the all—which owes its existence to the one creative God (R. 11:36; 1 C, 8:6; 11:12)—will be restored to the right relationship with God. (εἰς αὐτὸν τὰ πάντα R. 11:36). This relationship is one of subordination in which God is ὁ ὑποτάξας τὰ πάντα (1 C. 15:28). There will be unity, then. God will be πάντα ἐν πᾶσιν.[1] This situation of unity which evolves through subjection cannot be regarded otherwise than as a redeeming and perfect situation.[2]

The HP does not speak of a fulfilment of all things through Christ. In Eph. this fulfilment is an intermediary process. After all, God's unifying work is accomplished through the fulfilling of all things by Christ, i.e. by his permeation of all things with his dominion and blessings. And even if the HP does not use the word in this connection, a similar intermediary activity on the part of Christ does play a part. Until the moment when the redeeming and perfect situation of unity in God, described in 1 C. 15:28, has been achieved, Christ is God's "representative".[3] Only because he, Christ, realizes his dominion and neutralizes supernatural forces (1 C. 15:24, 25), can the time come when God may be all in all.

As in Eph. (1:20-22), Christ is able to exercise his dominion and draw all forces into the right relationship to himself because he is exalted on high and sits in heaven at God's right hand (Phil. 2:9; R. 8:34) and because God has already, by way of a task, put all things under him (1 C. 15:27).[4]

One of the formulations in the HP with πάντα which have been borrowed from current contemporary philosophical terminology, very obvi-

---

[1] Hanson, The Unity of the Church in the N.T., p. 100 ad 1 C. 15:28 : "Consequently, eschatological unity implies, that everything—the Church, humanity, the entire cosmos—will be comprised into a unity in God, who will be "all in all'."

[2] Dupont, Gnosis, p. 343s. : "L'achèvement de toutes choses est affirmé dans une formule d'un étonnant vigeur dans 1 Cor. 15:28".

[3] Hanson, l.c. : "This implies that Christ, having hitherto represented God, will cease to be His representative".

[4] Cf. C. F. G. Heinrici, Der erste Brief an die Korinther (Kritisch-Exegetischer Kommentar ü. d. N.T. V, [8]1896), p. 472 on 1 C. 15:27; "Das ὑπέταξεν Gottes stellt die Aufgabe, das ὑποτέτακται Christi bezeugt ihre Vollendung" ("The ὑπέταξεν of God sets the task and the ὑποτέτακται of Christ bears witness to its accomplishment").

ously assigns to Christ the role of an intermediary : δι' οὗ τὰ πάντα (1 C. 8:6).[1]

It is striking that the formulation ἐξ οὗ τὰ πάντα which refers to God in the above-mentioned passage, is not followed by καὶ εἰς αὐτον τὰ πάντα as in R. 11:36, but by καὶ ἡμεῖς εἰς αὐτον. In my judgment, this modification (which, incidentally, reminds us of the ecclesiological turn which is given to the cosmological formulation πάντα in Eph. 4:6 (p. 216) serves to express that the faithful are already in the right eschatological relationship to God. (This idea would tally with R. 5:1.)

Everything and all has yet obviously not arrived at this relationship. What it has attained is the intermediary agency of the one κύριος Jesus Christ (1 C. 8:6).

The faithful are also familiar with the intercessionary activities of Christ (ἡμεῖς δι' αυτοῦ), thanks to which they are υἱοὶ θεοῦ and have already arrived at unity (Gal. 3:26 and 28).

This υἱοὶ θεοῦ has still to become manifest (R. 8:19). Also the unity of Israel and the faithful Gentiles will have to be reinforced still more (R. 8:29-32). The result will be that no division-line will run through Israel (p. 249) and that the ecclesia will no longer be threatened by dissent (1 C. 1:12). There will be no more "in part" ; knowledge in part or prophesy in part. All that is "in part" will be done away. Only the perfect and complete will remain and love or charity will reign supreme (1 C. 13:8-13). In this passage we are reminded of the maximum measure of fulfilment in the pleroma which is mentioned in Eph. 3:19.[2]

One day, all will have achieved the right eschatological relationship to God. When Paul is thinking of the total realization of unity between Israel and the Gentiles who have believed and the full revelation and manifestation of the wisdom and choosing love of God, he uses the formula εἰς αὐτὸν τὰ πάντα (R. 11:36).[3]

---

[1] For the resemblance between 1 C. 8:6 and philosophical utterances, see Dupont, op. cit., p. 335ss.; for the meaning of the preposition διά in 1 C. 8:6, op. cit., p. 342 note 2.

[2] 1 C. 13 also deals with pneumatical endowments. The ἀγάπη is as supreme as in Eph. 3:19.

[3] The --ἐξ αἰτοῦ καὶ δι' αὐτοῦ καὶ εἰς αὐτὸν τὰ πάντα of R. 11:36 is a cosmological formula in keeping with the general philosophical terminology of the day, here used is connection with God's soteriological activities—as described in 11:32—and the unfathomable wisdom of God—praised in 11:33ss. In view of the fact that the words εἰς αὐτὸν τὰ πάντα do occur in R. 11:36, in contrast to 1 C. 8:6 where they do not, a connection may be drawn between the soteriological activities of God which, in context, reveal his unfathomable wisdom.

When the faithful have been utterly and completely revealed as υἱοὶ θεοῦ, a universal salvation for the whole of creation, which will to be delivered from all destructive agencies, will take place (R. 8:19ss). A truth which as yet exists only for the faithful (ἡμεῖς εἰς αὐτόν) will then, when that time has come, be a reality for the whole of creation (εἰς αὐτὸν τὰ πάντα).

And finally, we come to this. We drew attention to the absence of moments of apocalyptic high drama in the eschatology of Eph. However, the HP also contains eschatological pronouncements that are devoid of this element of drama. When 1 C. 13 speaks so succinctly about ὅταν δὲ ἔλθῃ τὸ τέλειον (10) and ὅτε γέγονα ἀνήρ (11) and Phil. 3:12 of τετελείωμαι, it seems almost as if a future, which can be attained by way of a harmonious development of growth, is under discussion. 2 C. 5:1 momentarily suggests the possibility of a glory which will fall to the share of the believer, immediately after his individual death. Nevertheless, despite this calm, such places do not lack the eschatological drama of parousia and the raising of the dead with all that surrounds the event.

For example, the οἰκία ἀχειροποίητος αἰώνιος ἐν τοῖς οὐρανοῖς can be noto her body than the σῶμα πνευματικόν of 1 C. 15:44.

A number of factors in Eph. lead us to assume that although there is no apocalyptic high drama in its eschatological pronouncements, this by no means implies that the reality of this drama is rejected. The fact that this, in truth, is not so, may be deduced from the comment of days that are evil (5:16), the exhortation to wrestle against the evil forces (6:10ss.) and the summons to watchfulness (6:18). For these are words of undoubted apocalyptic vividness.

5. THE FOUR DIMENSIONS

We find the following four-fold formulation in Eph. 3:18 : τὸ πλάτος καὶ μῆκος καὶ ὕψος καὶ βάθος. This enumeration has a cosmological aspect. A world, comprised of four spheres, was an idea familiar to the ancient cultures of Mesopotamia.[1] The number four, as is also manifest from the O.T., represented totality.[2]

Four cosmic magnitudes form the sum total of creation in Ps. 103:11,

---

[1] See Schlier, Th. W. I, p. 515; J. Hehn, "Siebenzahl und Sabbath" in Leipziger Semitische St., Bd. II, 1907 p. 13s. and Dupont, Gnosis, p. 478.

[2] See Zimmerli, Ezechiel, p. 53.

12 as well as in Ps. 107:3. In the first case, heaven, earth, east and west are named; in the latter, east, west, north and sea. An ancient Semitic conception identifies the high mountain, the divine dwelling-place, with the north. The antithesis to this mountain in the north, consisted of the chaotic forces of the primaeval water.[1]

Job 11:8, 9 speaks of the highness of heaven, the deepness of hell, the length of the earth and the breadth of the sea. Ps. 139:8, 9 suggests that there exists no place where God can be evaded. He is present in the heights of heaven as well as in the depths of the realm of the dead, in the sunrise of the east and in the uttermost sea of the west.[2]

See against the background of such concepts, it becomes probable that the quadruple formulation of Eph. 3:18 is in reality indicative of the four immeasurable dimensions which, according to ancient geocentric cosmological theories, defined the frontiers of the cosmos.[3]

The formulation occurs not only in Eph. 3:18 but in an almost identical shape in a papyrus dating from the fourth century A.D.[4] In the papyrus in question the syncretism manifest in the context of the formulation has a Jewish component.[5] The formulation is part of a rite to invoke a manifestation of a godly kurios. The divinity will make an appearance when the dwelling-place of the all-ruling god Albalal (ὁ οἶκος τοῦ παντοκράτορος θεοῦ Ἀλβαλαλ) is opened and when φῶς, πλάτος, βάθος, μῆκος, ὕψος, αὐγή may be "seen".

It would seem that the four dimension named are the dimensions of the light-giving and shining dwelling of the pantocrator. He who utters the incantation, must be able to see this dwelling in the midst of a fire before him. In all likelihood, this dwelling represents the empy-

---

[1] See Kraus, Psalmen, p. 342ss.

[2] Cf. Kraus, op. cit., p. 919.

[3] Not only the quadruple but also three-fold formulations are found; cf. Schlier Eph., p. 172. The latter could have bearing on a heavenly city conceived of as a cube in which case a depth-dimension would not be relevant since the idea of a nether world does not fit in whith this cube-concept.

[4] This is the papyrus mentioned in n. 2, p. 213 (N. 574 de Supplément grec de la Bibliothèque nationale, Paris = Pap. IV in Preisendanz, Pap. Graec. Magicae). The passage in question (line 959ss.) is extensively quoted in Dupont, Gnosis, p. 478 and in a more abbreviated form in Dibelius, Gefbr., p. 58 and Schlier, Eph., p. 173. Earlier, Reitzenstein had already compared the enumeration πλάτος βάθος, μῆκος, ὕψος in the papyrus with the almost identical one in Eph. 3:18 (cf. above, Chapter I, p. 27 n. 5). For the dating of the papyrus, see Preisendanz, op. cit., p. 64 or Dupont, op. cit., p. 497 note 1.

[5] Cf. the designation Ἰάω Σαβαώθ which occurs, in the context of the repeated enumeration.

rean, the inaccessible fire which—according to ancient cosmological conceptions—lies beyond the last and furthest region of heaven and encircles the cosmos.[1] The cosmos is contained within the four immeasurable dimensions of this empyrean.[2]

The naming of the four immeasurable dimensions in Eph. 3:18, could well be an allusion to the fact that Christ fills all things.[3] One could even endorse the view of Schlier that through this formulation, Christ is indicated as "weltumfassender Anthropos" ("world-embracing anthropos").[4]

A more plausible explanation is that the naming of these four immeasurable dimensions evokes the idea of a divine transcendence. When Job 11:8, 9 speaks of the heights of heaven, of hell that is deep, of the earth which is long and the sea which is broad, the intention is to underline God's transcendence. In this instance, this has specific reference to the actions of God which are unfathomable to man and the exercise of a wisdom far beyond human comprehension.[5]

---

[1] For the ancient conception of the cosmos, see de Zwaan, De Efezenbrief van Paulus, p. 54.

[2] Because the conception of the cosmos admitted the idea of depth and an underworld, this prayer could refer to the light-giving dwelling of the pantocrator.

[3] Cf. Dupont, op. cit., 9.497 : "Les quatres dimensions doives évoquer tout l'univers mais plus spécialement les espaces célestes." Furthermore, Dupont regards the enumeration not so much as a reference to Christ's filling all as an indication to the "sphères dans lesquelles le Christ a été exalté, et où les chrétiens, à sa suite, doivent être revêtus de gloire" (l.c.). Dibelius, l.c. holds that the enumeration pertains to heaven or the heavenly city which represents salvation. For this interpretation, see also Sclier, op. cit., p. 172s. However, unlike the empyrean, there can be no question of the $\beta\acute{\alpha}\theta o\varsigma$ in connection with the heavenly city. The latter can only be on high; cf. Rev. 21:10. The same objections may also be raised against Dupont's view. Ancient cosmology and astronomy could speak of the $\beta\acute{\alpha}\theta o\varsigma$ of heaven; cf. Lietzmann, An die Römer, p. 89. But in Eph., as in the HP, salvation is not situated in this $\beta\acute{\alpha}\theta o\varsigma$, i.e. the region of heaven below the horizon, whence the stars rise. Salvation lies upwards.

[4] Schlier, op. cit., p. 173. This view finds corroboration in rabbinical conceptions regarding the immense size of Adam's body; cf. Schenke Der Gott, "Mensch" in der Gnosis, p. 127ss. and Meuzelaar, Der Leib des Messias, p. 132 note 5. What is not acceptable is that Schlier wants to see the concept of the Cross, which embraces the world, behind Eph. 3:18. It is conceivable that speculations about divine anthropos are older than Eph. To infer that such speculations were already connected with the idea of a world-embracing cross, is a rash hypothesis. Besides, in Eph. 3:18 and 19, the author has in mind not especially Jesus, who is on the cross, but more the exalted Christ. It is also not right that Schlier—as it would seem—identifies the pregnant terms of left and right in the example he quotes from Act. Andr., with the conceptions of length and breadth.

[5] Cf. F. Horst, Hiob (Bibl. Komm. At XV), p. 169s.

In the Wisdom of Jesus Sirach, the opening words of the book(1:1-8) deal with the transcendental wisdom of God. To make its transcendental character quite clear, this wisdom is compared with the height of heaven, the breadth of the earth and the depth of the deep. Subsequently, the book discloses that God makes this wisdom rule over every people and nation and that it has its dwellingplace in Israel (24:3-12). This wisdom reveals itself to man through the law of Moses (24:23). In all this, wisdom remains transcendental and inexhaustible. This last is again expressed through the medium of an analogy; the wisdom which shows itself in the law is compared with the sea and the great deep (24:29).

The construction in Eph. 3:18 is an infinitive construction and parallel with the following infinitive construction in 3:19. Therefore, the four immeasurable dimensions must be connected with the object of the parallel infinitive γνῶναι : τὴν ὑπερβάλλουσαν τῆς γνώσεως ἀγάπην τοῦ Χριστοῦ.

This love of Christ, which is greater in value than the pneumatical gift of knowledge, is transcendental and unending. That which is said of God's actions in Job. 11:8 [1] and of God's wisdom in Sirach 1:1-8 and 24:29, is equally true of Christ's love.

The ecclesia has a share in this transcendental love. It can comprehend and know this love. Unity between the faithful amongst each other (see p. 240) and to be rooted and grounded in faith (3:17) is the condition for this comprehension and knowledge. It is not possible to know this love of Christ without living by it.

The statement on the divinely transcendental and unending nature of the love of Christ is not far removed from the affirmations found in R. 8:39. R. 8:39 declares that no influence or event can separate the faithful from the love of God, which is in Christ. This accords with the transcendental and unending character of the love in Christ as described in Eph. 1 C. 13:8 states that charity, or love, never ends. This aspect of a never-ending existence can easily be reconciled with the conception of an endless extension into space.[2]

---

[1] This was maintained by Grotius. See his Annotationes in N.T., ad Eph. 3:18 : "est allusio ad locum Iob. 11:7".

[2] E.g. see how the word עוֹלָם in post-biblical Hebrew came to mean "world" and how "never-ending time" blends in meening with "world" in the words αἰών and saeculum (cf. Sasse, Th. W. I, p. 206s.). In Sirach 1:1-8 when the nature of wisdom is discussed, there is not only a question of cosmic dimensions but also of the eternal nature of wisdom.

The last point in this connection to which we would like to draw attention, is that the use of the word βάθος in the four-fold enumeration of Eph. 3:18 has something in common with the same word as used in R. 11:33 or 1 C. 2:10. In both cases, it serves to illustrate the transcendental character of the wisdom of God and the knowledge of God (which is the love that chooses) or the actions of God (which flow from his hidden wisdom).

6. ANTHROPOLOGICAL DESIGNATIONS

In our introductory chapter, we mentioned that adherents of the religio-historicalschool believed they had uncovered certain mythic data in Eph.[1] Eph. was found to contain traces of the gnostic redeemer myth. Indications to suggest this were deduced from the designations καινὸς ἄνθρωπος, παλαιὸς ἄνθρωπος, ἔσω ἄνθρωπος, ἀνὴρ τέλειος, κεφαλή, σῶμα and μέλος.

We shall investigate these terms in the following section.

As we ascertained earlier, the constructions of the religio-historical school have recently come under attack.[2] This school of thought (and this applies specifically to Reitzenstein) sought to trace the origins of the myth in ancient Persia.[3]

Colpe has clearly demonstrated that neither the doctrine of Zarathustra nor later movements founded upon his doctrine included a divine archetype who resembles the divine anthropos of the gnostic myth. In his view, it is dubious whether the figure of Gayomart (i.e. mortal life), whom the historical theologians wanted to equate with the anthropos, originally had any cosmogonic function and whether he was at all conceived of in terms of a macro-anthropos. Thus Colpe refutes any idea that late Jewish or gnostic conceptions appertaining to the archetype had their foundation in the figure of Gayomart.[4]

When the descriptions "Erlösermythus" (redeemer myth) and "Anthroposmythus" or "Urmenschmythus" (anthropos or archetype

---

[1] See Chapter I, para. 6 (p. 26ss.).

[2] See p. 33s.

[3] Cf. Colpe, Die religionsgeschichtliche Schule, p. 33 and P. Pokorný, Der Epheserbrief und die Gnosis, Die Bedeutung des Haupt-Glieder-Gedankens in der entstehenden Kirche (Berlin 1965), p. 35.

[4] Die religionsgeschichtliche Schule, p. 140-170 (especially p. 156 and p. 169). Schenke, Der Gott "Mensch" in der Gnosis, p. 17s., also gives little credence to the notion that Gayomart originally represented the "Weltgott" (universal god). See also, Pokorný, op. cit., p. 35.

myth) are regarded as synonymous, Colpe has no objections. The redeemer myth is often concerned with some kind of archetypal man or the idea of a spiritualised macrocosm. He does, however, object when the terms "archetype" and "redeemer" as such are put down as synonyms.

For in gnosticism, the redeemer is by no means invariably indicated as the archetype: quite different designations where frequently used for the former.[1] Colpe shows that in Manichaeism the archetype, as far as salvation is concerned, merely occupies a place amongst other redeeming powers. As such, he does not at all feature in the central position which Reitzenstein assigned to him.[2]

It is therefore not correct to speak repeatedly of the redeemed redeemer; the myth does not use this term. Nor is the saviour qua talis salvatus. The term defines but a single one of the many stages through which the redeemer passes.

There is also a stage of the salvator salvandus. This last-named, is more characteristic of gnosticism and could be used as a criterion for determining the distinct premises of gnosticism within the syncretic framework of later antiquity.[3]

We feel that Colpe's criticism is justified and that particularly his comments on the "gnostische Erlösermythus", as sketched by Bultmann, deserves serious consideration. Colpe values Bultmann's methodologic model as an intelligent synthesis of the various conceptions found in different systems. Its value is evident from the fact that to a large extent the model corresponds with the Manichaean system. However, Colpe warns against the grave error which would be entailed in projecting this model into the past and regarding it as a reconstruction of a myth; a myth which evolved "in grauer Vorzeit" (in the grey mists of pre-history), "irgendwo im fernen weiten Orient" (somewhere in the far distant Orient), which then wandered through "Raum und Zeit" (time and space) leaving trances and fragments wherever it went.[4]

---

[1] Op. cit., p. 171.

[2] Op. cit., p. 115-117. For the place of the archetype in Manichaean cosmogony, see Schenke, op. cit., p. 108ss.

[3] Op. cit., p. 188-191.

[4] Op. cit., p. 191. Schenke, op. cit., p. 19ss. gives a lucid account of how Bousset and Reitzenstein envisaged the evolution and history of the myth. He also gives the theories of C. H. Kraeling, H. Gressmann and G. Widengren who followed either Bousset and Reitzenstein, making corrections and modifications in their own work, op. cit., p. 25ss. (and p. 145ss.).

In Colpe's view it is incorrect to interpret against the background of the endresult, seen as a genetic explanation, all conceptions found to have been current around the beginning of our era which subsequently amalgamated to form a single movement. A more responsible attitude with respect to historical veracity was, in Colpe's opinion, called for.

One year after the appearance of Colpe's great stydy, a work by Schenke was published in which a certain complex of these conceptions was investigated in a manner compatible with the demands of history.[1]

Schenke, in this book, describes the evolution of the gnostic conception of the heavenly anthropos (or Adam, resp. Adamas) in whose being the Gnostic has a share. His assumption is that somewhere around the beginning of our era, Judaism was intensely preoccupied with the biblical Word of Gen. 1:26s.[2] All specimens of later rabbinical speculation on these texts corroborate this impression.

Schenke believes that he has found irrefutable evidence for his theory in Philo's—not derivative but original—speculations on the nature of the first heavenly man and the first earthly man which are based on this Word from Gen. It was not only Philo who, inspired by the *Weltanschauung* of the Stoa, developed his conception of the heavenly and earthly (first) anthropos from Gen. 1:26s.[3] Similarly, a Jewish and/or Samaritan gnosis developed its conception, with its own premises, of a divine anthropos who is identical with the deepest core of man, from the same text.[4]

Originally, this conception had nothing to do with the image of the macro-anthropos or the "Allgott" ("Weltgott").[5] Nor was it connected with the kingly first man from paradise.[6] Although these three conceptions were sometimes linked during the pre-Manichaean period, this according to Schenke, was of an incidental nature. Only with Manichaeism did a real synthesis take place.

Despite the interresting affinities, the scholar should not be tempted to see Manichaesm as the source of the Pauline conception because

---

[1] Der Gott "Mensch" in der Gnosis. The complete titles of the works of Colpe and Schenke is found respectively on p. 27, n. 5 and p. 33, n. 3 (in para. 6 of Chapter I).

[2] See op. cit., p. 64s.; p. 71; p. 134; p. 121 and p. 155.

[3] Op. cit., p. 122-124.

[4] Op. cit., p. 69-71.

[5] Op. cit., pp. 153, 17 and 19.

[6] Op. cit., pp. 153 and 151s. (Schenke makes a connection between the king of paradise and the preexistent son of man of Jewish apocalyptic literature.)

a great chronological time-gap lies between Manichaean doctrine and the Pauline conception of the body of Christ.

However, Schenke does admit the possibility of a point of contact between the ancient conception of the "Allgott" and the Pauline concept of the body of Christ and particularly so in the case of this concept as expressed in Eph. and Col. Given that that is so, the idea that Christ is Lord of the world developed into the idea that he was the "Allgott"; as such he was seen as the head of the world and the world as his body. Subsequently, this cosmological conception—perhaps under the influence of the thought of Christ as the second Adam and founding father of a new race of men—acquired an anthropological aspect and definition whereby the world was seen in terms of humanity, of lost humanity.[1]

When Schenke draws this kind of connection between the concept of the "Allgott" or macro-anthropos and the concept of the body of Christ as evinced in Eph., he is to a certain extent in agreement with the ideas which Colpe developed in an earlier essay.[2]

In this essay, Colpe combines a number of the ideas of Philo. One of these, that the logos permeates and rules the cosmos, is well known. In Philo, the $\kappa\epsilon\phi\alpha\lambda\dot{\eta}$ could designate the logos of all things. Both logos and cosmos are sometimes called the son of God. Consequently, Colpe asserts that Philo regarded not only the logos but also the cosmos as an anthropos. Furthermore, he thought Philo could contemplate the cosmos in a light so spiritualized that for him it was coincidental with the immanent logos or anthropos. The logos on the other hand, he was considered to have evaluated independently, regarding it as an almost transcendental magnitude or an "oberen oder himmlischen Anthropos oder Verwalter" ("higher or heavenly anthropos or administrator"). Yet, Colpe thought, Philo at the same time conceived this "himmlische Verwalter" in terms of the head or guiding part of the macro-anthropos who is the cosmos. Colpe now wishes to propound this "Philonic" speculation, in place of the redeemer-myth, as a solution to explain Eph.

It seems to me as if Colpe had discovered more content than there is, in reality to be found in Philo. Philo may well contemplate the cosmos as the greatest body, embracing a multitude of other bodies

---

[1] Op. cit., p. 153-156.

[2] "Zur Leib-Christi-Vorstellung im Epheserbrief", Festschrift für J. Jeremias (BZNW 26, Berlin 1960), p. 172-187.

(De plantatione 7); that is a philosophical conception. He can speak of the cosmos as the son of God, using this image to express the idea of the creation. Moreover, he sees the world as the visible manifestation of the logos.[1] However, all this does not constitute the conception of the macro-anthropos. Philo is aware of the concept and knows how to make use of it inasfar as he regards the world as the visible expression of the logos. For the rest, however, Philo rejects this concept.[2]

It is the logos which occupies the central place in Philo's philosophical contemplations. When he uses the word "anthropos" in its non-original sense, he is in the first place thinking of the logos. That which intrigues Philo is not the man-cosmos relationship but that of man-logos. This relationship he sees as the interplay between "Urbild" and "Abbild" ("original" and "reproduction"). Logos and man stand confronted as οὐράνιος ἄνθρωπος and γήινος ἄνθρωπος In this relationship, the characteristics of man which are like and correspond with those of the logos, are in his capacity for thought and knowledge; the physical element does not come into this. The νοῦς of man is the εἰκών of the logos which is completely νοῦς.[3]

Philo's conception of the logos diverged from the more popular Stoic trend in that he continued to assert the transcendental nature of God and the reality of the creation. He does, however, remain within the framework of Stoic philosophy. To help convey the idea that the logos guides and rules all, he also uses the word κεφαλή.[4]

---

[1] For the sonship aspect of logos and cosmos, see Schweizer, Th. W. VIII, p. 356 lines 27-29 and p. 347 lines 7-15. From the designation Philo assigns to God, πατὴρ τοῦ κόσμου, it is clear that the idea of the creation plays a part in the sonship of the cosmos; De spec. legibus I, 96: De ebrietate 30 and De vita Mosis II, 134. In the context of the last-mentioned, Philo obviously intends the cosmos by the expression τελειοτάτῳ τὴν ἀρετὴν υἱῷ (cf. B. Badt in a note in the German translation in the Cohn-Wendland edition). His formulation is such, however, that the logos must involuntarily come to mind (cf. the explanation attached to the Greek text in the same edition).

[2] Cf. the following places : De. migr. Abrahami 220 and Quis rerum div. heres sit 155. In Schenke, op. cit., p. 122-124, see the antithesis οὐρανιος ἄνθρωπος and γήινος ἄνθρωπος.

[3] See Schenke, op. cit., p. 122-124. The antithesis οὐράνιος ἄνθρωπος and γήινος ἄνθρωπος is found in Legum allegoriae I, para. 31 and 88 (cf. also Reitzenstein, IEM, p. 105).

[4] For the logos as κεφαλή, see Quaestiones in Ex. 117. Philo also used the words ἀρχή, πρεσβύτατος υἱός or πρωτόγονος to indicate the dominant position of the logos in relation to all (De confusione linguarum 146, 147 and 62). The meanings of these words, as evinced by the information under κεφαλή, can also be connected with this word in Jewish Hellenistic Gr.

But this does not imply that Philo has before him the image of the macro-anthropos with the logos and cosmos as its head and body.[1] What this designation could mean is that for Philo the logos assumed the aspect of a divine or higher reality. In the contemporary Stoic and philosophical scene, the conception that the all-permeating logos dwells especially in the higher or heavenly echelons, was sufficiently known.[2] Therefore, a related philosophy from Philo would not be unexpected.[3] We have already observed that he was known to call the logos "οὐράνιος ἄνθρωπος". This suggests that the designation κεφαλή is equally likely to have been indicative of some highest region in the hierachy of the heavens.[4] However, this designation does not embrace the concept of the macro-anthropos.[5]

---

[1] The argument of Quaestiones in Ex. 117 has no reference to the symbolism of the body. The garments of the highpriest are only allegorical; they are invested with a cosmic symbolism. An interposition mentions that the logos is the κεφαλή of all things. However, the head is not included in the symbolism; it is the highpriest himself who is the symbolic figure. He symbolises the logos. In Flavius Josephus. Antiquitates III, 7,7 a cosmic symbolism is attributed to the tabernacle and the garment of the highpriest. There also, the head of the highpriest has no symbolic function but the πῖλος (hat) which symbolises heaven, does.

[2] The seat of the νοῦς in the human body was considered to be the head. The characteristic seat of the logos in the cosmos was in heaven. See Dupont, Gnosis, p. 337 note 1 and Schweitzer. Th. W. VII, p. 1035 line 38 and p. 1036 lines 8-10.

[3] That which comes to mind is the statement in De opificio mundi, 82, on man as a small heaven. In this work, the principles of art, science and virtue man has within himself are compared to the stars.

[4] In De somniis I, 144, he compares both the cosmos and the psyche of man with a ladder. The bottom of the ladder represents earth and the top (κεφαλή), heaven. For Philo's estimation of the οὐρανός see Traub, Th. W. V., p. 500s.

[5] We are confirmed in this view by the fact that in the passage quoted in the previous note which deals with the cosmos and the human psyche, the word κεφαλή indicates the top of a ladder with no allusions to the image of the marco-anthropos. The Procopius version of Philo's Quaest. in Ex. 117 which Schlier quotes (cf. Schweizer, Th. W. VII, p. 1051 note 340) is too dubious to warrant the drawing of conclusions on Philo's conceptions concerning the macro-anthropos. W. L. Knox, in his article entitled "Parallels to the N.T. Use of σῶμα" (JThSt 39, July 1938, n. 155, p. 243-246), also wrote about the relationship between κεφαλή and σῶμα in Philo. He attempted to show that Philo regarded the highpriest as the kephale of a soma which is the nation of Israel, because the highpriest had a cosmic significance. In my opinion, however, Knox did not succeed in proving that Philo saw the highpriest as the kephale of the soma of Israel. Nor is it correct that for Philo himself, the highpriest had a commic significance. His garments had cosmic meaning. The priest himself represented the logos (cf. De fuga et inventione para. 108-112 in which the following statement occurs : "In him should be seen not a man but the divine logos who assumes the world like a garment".). Knox propounds that the popular

The work of E. Brandenburger intersects with the researches of Schenke and Colpe. It is his tenet that the Gnostic doctrine of the heavenly anthropos anticipates Philo and was, moreover, in its earlier forms already known in Jewish Hellenistic circles during his lifetime. Brandenburger maintains that the doctrine originated in a convergence between certain Jewish Hellenistic groups and their pagan Hellenistic environment. His ratiocination is based on the fact that Hellenistic Jews participated in the Hellenistic mystery religions, allowed themselves to be initiated into the mysteries and were also involved in various syncretical movements.[1]

Furthermore, he thinks that Judaism during the immediate pre-Christian period linked the figure of Adam with certain cosmological ideas.[2] On the basis of this he finds it probable that either or during the actual period or slightly after, the speculations concerning the heavenly anthropos and those concerning the heavenly macro-anthropos conjoined to infiltrate the mental environment of a heretical and gnostically inclined Judaism.[3] Brandenburger wants to explain Eph. 4:8-10 and 1:20ss. and the Pauline conception of the σῶμα Χριστοῦ in terms of this combination.[4]

In this connection, we would like to observe that it is impossible to demonstrate a clear link between the conception of the cosmos as a macro-anthropos and the figure of Adam during the period of Judaism immediately prior to the Christian era. Nor are we convinced that speculations on the heavenly anthropos and macro-anthropos become fused by a heretical and gnostic Judaism. We therefore prefer to keep

---

Stoa, which was influenced by the Hellenistic religions, not only called the divine, fiery principle of reason the ψυχή or νοῦς of the cosmos but also had the designation κεφαλή to describe it. This has remained unproven. What was, as we have already observed in note 2, true is that heaven was conceived as the special domain of the logos, as in man the nous is situated in the head. In De fuga et inventione, l.c., we are reminded of this conception. Philo there regards the head of the highpriest, who symbolises the logos, pre-eminently suitable as an example with which to demonstrate the excellence of the divine logos. The anointing of the head of the highpriest exemplifies the fact that the logos shines with a sparkling light and the diadem is a token of the dominion which is the property of the logos.

[1] E. Brandenburger, Adam und Christus, Exegetisch-religionsgeschichtliche Untersuchung zu Römer, 5, 12-21 (1 Kor. 15), (Wissenschaftl. Monographien zum A. u. N.T. VII, Neukirchen 1962), p. 129, 130 and p. 129s. note 2.

[2] Op. cit., p. 78 note 2.

[3] Op. cit., p. 153 (cf. p. 139 and p. 78 note 2).

[4] Op. cit., p. 153 and p. 152 note 5.

to Schenke's point of view which we have set out (p. 268), holding that a convergence of that nature is not to be discerned until the advent of Manichaeism. What we are prepared to accept is that long before that, there were already incidental and little thought-out combinations of elements which belonged to three different schools of conception (i.e. the anthropos; the "Allgott" and the king of paradise).

Yet another solution has been put forward by P. Pokorný.[1] From the so-called "Naassenerpredigt" and Hermetic literature he has reconstructed a Gnostic doctrine on the anthropos which was not influenced by Christianity. Apparently this doctrine, which was rooted in an altered form of Jewish Hellenistic conceptions of the anthropos, was in circulation about eighty years after Christ in the western part of Asia Minor. Pokorný sees this doctrine in the light of a contrasting background to what he considers to be the non-authentic Eph. Eph. in fact had so many points in common with this Gnostic movement that a later Christian Gnostic was prompted to furnish an old Gnostic work, which contained the precepts of the movement in question, with quotations from Eph. His view is that the end-product of this Christianized redaction of the older Gnostic tract which originated in Asia Minor became what is known as the Sermon of the Naasenes.[2]

Pokorný regarded as an important component of that Gnostic movement as it was known in c. A.D. 80, a general tendency to depreciate the value of the ordinary human body, a longing to abandon this body and to merge into a non-individual abstract body. In Eph. this ideal gives way to the idea that the faithful are taken into the concrete body of the ecclesia.[3] The conception of the ecclesia as the body of Christ, the author of Eph. was to have borrowed from Paul.[4]

Pokorný not only manages to reconstruct the doctrine of certain Gnostics living in the western regions of Asia Minor around A.D. 80, but he also presents as if it were a hypothesis essential for the explanation of Eph., a reconstruction of the way an initiate was adopted into their circle, including all the cultic elements attendant upon such an initiation.[5]

We have certain reservations against Pokorný's conclusions. A priori, we do not feel compelled at all to draw a strong line of demarca-

---

[1] See the work mentioned above, p. 266 n. 4.

[2] Op. cit., p. 51-58.

[3] Op. cit., p. 69s.

[4] Op. cit., pp. 50, 69s. and 81.

[5] Op. cit., pp. (89)- 110.

tion between statements contained in Eph. and conceptions resulting
from a gnosticised Jewish Hellenism. But we do feel that it is going
too far when Pokorný presents us with the Hippolytus rendering of
a Naasene tract which has so patently been influenced by Eph., and
then proceeds unequivocally to assert the secondary nature of Eph.
with respect to the original redaction of the Gnostic piece. In addition,
we find his reconstruction of the initiation liturgy somewhat reckless.
However, our most serious objection is that Pokorný's reason for
arriving at such an advanced date for Eph. is due to the fact that he
places the doctrines of his Gnostics at so late a stage. For there is
absolutely no cause whatsoever to allocate the one particular tenet of
their creed which provides the basis of Pokorný's argument, to as
late a period as the eighties of the first century. Corresponding ideas,
i.e. a sense of depreciated value with regard to the ordinary human
body, the desire to be released from that body and the longing to merge
into a higher, non-material and non-personalized reality, can be found
as early as in the work of Philo.[1]

Pokorný's study bears the following subtitle : "Die Bedeutung des
Haupt-Glieder-Gedankens in der entstehenden Kirche" ("The Significance of the head-member idea in the developing Church"). Indeed,
he does explain how the alleged author of Eph., who substituted the
idea of incorporation into the church for the Gnostic idea of incorporation into an abstract body, came to his conception of the head and the
members. Pokorný thinks that the author of Eph. borrowed the designation of Christ as the head form much older Christian Hellenistic
hymns and that we are here dealing with an Old Testament and ancient
Christian Hellenistic idea.[2]

We do not deem it necessary to look for references in Christian Hellenistic hymns and are persuaded that the author of Eph., when he designates Christ as κεφαλή, takes this word from the contemporary everyday Hellenistic vocabulary, hence drawing on Old Testament and
Semitic associations.[3] Referring for endorsement to the original ancient
Christian hymn which, he claims, underlies Col. 1:16-18, Pokorný
attempts to propagate the thesis that in hymns of this kind the word
κεφαλή characterises Christ as a cosmic authority.[4] The element of
qualitative novelty which the author of Eph. introduced was that he

---

[1] See Brandenburger, op. cit., p. 120 and the references to Philo terein given.

[2] Op. cit., p. 69s.

[3] See under κεφαλή

[4] Op. cit., p. 68.

had made the connection between the head-theme and the ecclesia to which, as a reaction to Gnosticism, he had applied the Pauline concept of the σῶμα Χριστοῦ.[1]

In our opinion, the motivation which prompted the author of Eph. to call Christ "head" was founded on Old Testament themes. The fact that he was able to link the conception of the head with the community, envisaged as σῶμα, which is the ecclesia, is due to the character of the Hellenistic idiom of the day.[2] If our position on this is correct, no objection against the authenticity of Eph. could he raised from the religio-historical point of view. At this juncture it is therefore called for that we try to corroborate our position by means of detailed research into the anthropological data present in Eph. Our investigation follows.

a. Κεφαλή

From ancient Greek civilisation, Hellenism adopted the idea that the head is the guiding organ of the human organism and the seat of his capacity for awareness, the νοῦς. Hellenistic Judaism also took over this idea.[3] To the (biblical) Hebrew as well as the Greek way of thinking, the head was the crux of existence and the focus of man's personal life.[4]

Furthermore, the ancient and widely held conception of the world as a macroanthropos was familiar to the Hellenism of the first century after Christ.[5] Within the framework of this conception, the head was equated with heaven. This was an obvious deduction; in the general consciousness, head and heaven—even when leaving aside the conception of the macro-anthropos—had the common attribute of being high and elevated.[6]

---

[1] Op. cit., p. 69.

[2] See under κεφαλή.

[3] See Schlier, Th. W. III, p. 673 line 21ss., Behm, Th. W. IV, p. 954 line 12; I.J. du Plessis, Christus als hoofd van kerk en kosmos, p. 4 and above p. 271 n. 2.

[4] Life is identical with the head. Misfortune falls on someone's head. Greek examples are given in Schlier, loc. cit., rr. 42-50. Hebrew examples are found in 1 Ch. 12:19; 1 S. 28:2; Jos. 2:19; Ez. 9:10; 11:21; 16:43.

[5] See Käsemann, Leib und Leib Christi, p. 59s. and p. 60 notes 1 and 2; also Philo, Quis rer. div. her. sit, 155.

[6] See Schlier, op. cit., p. 675 lines 39-47 and lines 30-35; above p. 271 and note 2 and furthermore the identification of κεφαλή with οὐρανός which underlies the discussion of heavenly bodies (φωστῆρες) in the later vulgarised Stoa (Epiphanius, Adv. haereses I, 5, 1 of H. Diels, Doxographi Graeci, p. 587, quoted by Dupont, Gnosis, p. 442 and note.).

It should here be mentioned that in connection with the macro-anthropos conception, the head was not conceived as of special significance; it was not contradistinguished with the body.[1] In the philosophy which was currently popular during the Hellenistic era, the cosmos was often represented as a body with different parts. In this case too, the head was not thought of as a part or member of the body which played any particular role.[2] The image served merely to illustrate unity within the cosmos.

Not only the cosmos but also a more limited entity could be defined in terms of a body, i.e. a human community, a nation or a state. Sometimes the analogy assumed the shape of a comparison with the human body and had a moralising tendency.[3] Because the body—and not of necessity the human body exclusively—was regarded as the typical example of the association of many parts within a single whole, in the Latin of this period, the word "corpus" came to be a metaphor for a college, a group, a nation or a state. In the edicts of Augustus published in Greek, the word σῶμα was used in exactly the same way.[4]

When Livy wants to identify the leader of such a corpus, he chooses the word "caput" in the following metaphor : "corpori valido caput deerat.". We find Plutarch, probably following a Latin saying, using the word κεφαλή in a precisely analogous situation.[5]

Philo sees the head as the governing organ of living creatures—certainly not thinking of the human body only—and the seat of the faculties which inspire the parts of the body. He uses the word κεφαλή to indicate a king who is exalted over other kings, to describe a man superior amongst other human beings or a nation which is above other nations of the world.[6]

In Philo the word is also used as a designation for the logos. Philo probably uses it in this case to express that he regards the logos as a heavenly reality. A head is high and exalted (p. 271). However, the designation "head of all things" brings to bear especially the idea

---

[1] Cf. Schlier, op. cit., p. 766 lines 1-3.

[2] Cf. Schlier, op. cit., p. 91.

[3] Cf. Schlier, l.c.; Dupont, Gnosis, p. 436 and Meuzelaar, Der Leib des Messias, p. 2.

[4] See Schlier, l.c. and Dupont, l.c.

[5] See Dupont, p. 444s.

[6] See the quotation from De praem. et poenis, 125 in Schlier, Th. W. III, p. 675 line 5ss. or Dupont, Gnosis, p. 446 (cf. Schweizer, Th. W. III, p. 1025 line 10ss) and the quotation from De vita Mosis II, 30 in the article by Knox mentioned above, p. 271 n. 5.

of giving leadership and ruling. The Hebrew influence contributed to the connection made between this thought and the word κεφαλή.

It is an illuminating fact that in this respect Philo not only calls the logos "head of all things" but also uses the following words to describe it : ἀρχή, πρεσβύτατος υἱός or πρωτόγονος.[1] Being a Jewish Hellenist, Philo was well able to equate and associate expressions such as leader, beginning, oldest or firstborn son with the word κεφαλή.

The connotation "the beginning" had been attached to the word since long previously.[2] This meaning was enhanced by influences from the Hebrew. The Hebrew equivalent of kephale, ראש, not only indicates that which is highest, such as the head of a man or animal or the top of a mountain, but also that which goes in front, i.e. the first thing, the first person and the beginning.[3] (The othersinvolved would then be implicit in this first thing or person.)[4]

Both the idea of height and elevation and the idea of precedence led to an association between the word ראש and the idea of leadership. That which is highly placed is, after all, the most important thing which dominates.[5] He who goes in advance and is the first, leads. Thus we find the word also used to describe the head of a family or tribe, for the most important city of kingdom or for the commander of an army.

Gradually, by degrees, the word assumed the sense of leader, chief or administrator.[6] The association with the idea of first-born which

---

[1] See p. 270 n. 4.

[2] See Schlier, Th. W. III, p. 675 line 7ss. and Liddell-Scott, s.v. sub II d.

[3] An example would be the apex of a formation or group (2 Ch. 13:12; Am. 6:7;) and the commencement of a set period of time (Jg. 7:19, a nightwatch; Ez. 20:1, a year and in Ex. 12:2, the months of the year).

[4] ראש is the beginning of the tributary of a river and the tributary itself (Gen. 2:10) or the beginning of one of the smaller groups which divide a larger whole and that group as such (Jg. 7:16, 20; 9:34, 37, 43 and 1 S. 11:11).

[5] This is clear from Is. 2:2 and also from the metaphor of Is. 9:13 in which the branch of the palm, which is high, is contrasted with the rush in the low marsh. The same is evident from the other part of the same metaphor in Is. 9:13 and that of Dtn. 28:13,44 in which the head, which raises itself, is contrasted with the tail. When Philo in De. praem et poenis 125 speaks of a man or nation as the kephale of the human race, it is a continuation of this metaphor.

[6] In Thr. 1:5, "to be a head" means to dominate. The monarch and highpriest Johannes Hyrcanus designated himself ראש חבר היהודים on coins (Schürer, Gesch. d. j. V. I, p. 269). In rabbinical literature also, ראש appears in the sense of chief or leader. The ראש הכנסת is in charge of divine services and is probably the administrator of the building. The leader of a section of priests is a ראש. (See Schlier, l.c., line 21s.

the word must have had from ancient times may have promoted this. Just as the beginning or the first (רֹאשׁ) could imply the rest, so the power of all was thought to be concentrated in the first-born (בְּכֹר).[1] Very often the head of a family or tribe or the commander of an army (רֹאשׁ) would have been a first-born (בְּכֹר) son. The two words were equal in strength and meaning. When in Ex, 4:22 and Ps. 89:28 Israel and the anointed king are called בְּכֹר, and when in Ps. 18:44 the anointed king[2] is designated as a רֹאשׁ amongst nations, we are presented with similar statements.

Schlier has conclusively proved that the different redactions of the LXX evince that for Jewish Hellenists the idea of leadership was certainly associated with the word κεφαλή. The various editions show that the words κεφαλή, ἡγούμενος, ἄρχων and ἀρχηγός correspond in meaning. However, with this meaning of the word κεφαλή there is never any suggestion that those who are led by this head constitute a body appurtenant to this head.[3] On surveying these data, we may conclude that to a Jewish Hellenist of the first century, the following notions could be attached to the word.

1. The head is the guiding organ within the human organism, the seat of the capacity of awareness and the crux of existence. It the place in which the powers which inspire the different parts of the body are situated.

2. The head suggests the idea of heaven. The conception of the macro-anthropos equates heaven with the head. Also when this conception is not directly envisaged, a correspondence between heaven and the head is nevertheless recognised.

3. The head is elevated on high in both the litteral and figurative sense. It rises above the rest and is superior.

4. The head is the beginning with which the remainder can be included and in which the power of the whole can be concentrated. (κεφαλή,

---

and Schürer, Gesch. d. j. V, II, pp. 511, 512 and 290). The Syrian ܪܝܫ has in conjunction with some combinations, clearly the meaning "head" and "ruler" (cf. Payne Smith, A compendious Syriac Dictionary, s.v.).

[1] See Gen. 49:3; Deut. 21:17 and Meuzelaar, Der Leib des Messias, p. 117.

[2] Cf. Kraus, Psalmen, p. 149 on Ps. 18:44 : "Hier wird das in den Königspsalmen geläufige Thema "Weltherrschaft des Gesalbten Jahwes" angeschlagen" ("This touches upon a theme which occurs frequently in the royal psalms. i.e. dominion over the world by Jahwe's anointed").

[3] Schlier, op. cit., p. 674 line 32ss.

ἀρχή, πρεσβύτατος υἱός or πρωτόγονος are closely affiliated expressions.)

5. In a comparison, the head can represent the leading figure amongst a unit of people which is represented as a body.

6. The word κεφαλή can directly mean master or ruler even without the implication of a body.

The correctness of these conclusions is endorsed if we study a number of writings more recent than Philo or the LXX and partly influenced by Christianity.

Thus we read in Test. Seb. 9 : Split not yourselves in two heads for everything made by the Lord has a single head. This statement is a combination of the fourth and fifth of the above ideas. The word "kephale" is a metaphorical designation for a leader (fifth notion) and, in addition, an indication for leader as well as the group he leads (fourth notion). A new element introduced is that the head is seen as the principle upon which the unity of the body depends.

The Apocalypsis Sedrach emphatically expounds on the correspondence between the human head and heaven.[1]

A heterogeneous and somewhat garbled passage in the Corpus Hermeticum gives the impression that the head was identified with a globular and perfect spiritual world.[2]

In Gnostic literature, all kinds of statements are combined in a curious fashion with the word "kephale". The word is connected to a strong degree with the notion of being high, elevated and superior. Also the idea of leader, master or ruler predominates. An example of this is found in the so-called Sermon of the Naasenes which contains an analogy between the human head and the κορυφή or πετρή, which is ὁ ἀχαρακτήριστος ἐγκέφαλος or ὁ ἀρχάνθρωπος ἄνωθεν Ἀδάμας. The Adamas from above has come down as χαρακτηριστικὸς ἐγκέφαλος into the (human) head of the Gnostic whose ἔσω ἄνθρωπος he has become. Thus this Adamas became εἰς κεφαλὴν γωνίας (cf. LXX Ps. 117:22).[3]

Another element which may be combined with these conceptions is the sacrament for the dead which was practised by the Markosians.

---

[1] See Schweizer, Th. W. VIII, p. 1047 line 23ss.

[2] C.H.X, 10b.

[3] Hippolytus, Refutatio omnium haeresium V, 8,13 κορυφή and (ὁ ἀχαρακτήριστος ἐγκέφαλος) V, 7,35 and 36 (πετρή, ὁ ἀρχάνθρωπος ἄνωθεν Ἀδάμας, ὁ χαρακτηριστικὸς ἐγκέφαλος, ὁ ἔσω ἄνθρωπος and ὁ εἰς κεφαλὴν γεγενημένος γωνίας). The texts may be found in Völker, Quellen zur Geschichte der christilichen Gnosis, pp. 19 and 16.

Their custom was to anoint the head of the dead with oil so that no archont or power could get a grip on them and so the invisible pneumatical ἔσω ἄνθρωπος was able to ascent.[1] Moreover, these statements also involve a Gnostic realization of the conception that the head is the seat of the nous and the centre of life.

With the Valentinians and the Basilidians, we encounter the notion of leadership with the word which they used in association with the words ἀρχή or κύριος when the demiurge is called κεφαλή, ἀρχή and κύριος. The Basilidians had the appellation κεφαλὴ τοῦ κόσμου for the great archon.[2]

The notions of being high and ruling go together in the Acta Thomae and in the Syrian Odes of Solomon.[3] The head is featured as the place of elevation. Thus, to sit on the head or to stand on the top of a mountain signifies that a particular figure rules and permeates everything. In one of the said Odes, head and feet are contrasted as ruler and that which is ruled. Here also, the head is symbolic of the elevated factor. Furthermore, the head is associated with the beginning.[4]

Besides these, we find additional and new conceptions. In the Odes of Solomon, the head is depicted as the place whence the revelation of wisdom or the intimation of redeeming knowledge are emanated.[5]

---

[1] See Leisegang, Die Gnosis, p. 348s.

[2] The demiurge as κεφαλή, ἀρχή and κύριος in Irenaeus, Adversus haereses I, 5, 3 (Völker, op. cit., p. 108 line 27s.). The great archon described as ἡ κεφαλὴ τοῦ κόσμου in Hippolytus, Refutatio VII, 23, 3 and 27,9 (Völker, op. cit., pp. 50 and 56).

[3] In the Acta Thomae 6 (in Hennecke, Apokr. II³, p. 311) a maiden who is a heavenly world of light is described partly in terms of a building. Her bridegroom, the king, sits on her cranium and rests upon her head. This does not indicate that the king is the head of the maiden and she his body as Schlier, Th. W. III p. 677, thinks. In Od. Sal. 24:1 (Hennecke, op. cit., p. 605) the dove sits upon the head of Christ and, precisely the other way round, Christ is called the head of the dove. In the first instance, the sitting on the head must be interpreted as a situation of elevation; it represents the same as the standing on the top in Od. Sal. 33:3 (Hennecke, op. cit., p. 613). In both cases, we have to do with something which rules and penetrates all. The dove which sits on the head, sings. Its voice is heard and the immense influence of this voice holds sway everywhere (Od. Sal. 24). Similarly, the voice of him who stands on the top, carries to the very ends of the earth (Od. Sal. 33).

[4] Od. Sal. 23 (Hennecke, op. cit., p. 604s.). At the head (i.e. beginning) of a heavenly letter may be seen the head, the ruler who takes possession of all things (line 18s.). The wheel which receives the missive and becomes the token of it, makes the head descend to the feet, i.e. to that which is governed by the head (line 16).

[5] The dove which sits on the head makes its voice heard (see note 3). The implication of this is that the Lord (Christ) makes his progression known and that people are roused to awareness (Od. Sal. 24, 13s.). The voice of him who stands on the top (see note

The same idea is evinced in one of the Coptic manuscripts collated in the Codex of Jung, namely the Apokryphon Iacobi.[1]

In the Sermon of the Naassenes, we saw a special relationship between the word κεφαλή and a particular ἄνθρωπος, i.e. the ἀρχάνθρωπος ἄνωθεν 'Αδάμας.

Another aspect we sometimes encounter is when a head is conceived as a personified energy and stands in a relationship with a body formed by men. We have already observed that Plutarch—probably under the Latin influence—spoke of the ruler of a nation as the head of a body. Likewise, Gnostic literature can also place a head against the whole number of Gnostics endowed with spirit. This conception of all the pneumatologically gifted as a body remains within the mainstream of popular philosophy in which the cosmos was spoken of as a body or a living organism and the people were compared to the members of this body. It is apparent from Livy's account of Menenius Agrippa and from the material in R. 12 and 1 C. 12 that a community of nations or a whole mass of people could also be compared to a body or living organism (p. 266). Philo compared humanity or the whole number of the nations of the earth with a body (p. 276).

Now we see that in Gnostic literature, the spiritual or elect ones are designated as members. In a similar trend, the Gospel of Truth, the second tract in the Jung Codex, refers to those who possess the gnosis as the members of the Father of all.[2] The Acta Ioannis, call the man who has arrived at gnosis, "a member of the one who has descended".[3] These terms can scarcely be interpreted otherwise than the spiritual together form a body. It is not made clear how this body belongs to the Father of all or to the one who has descended.

One of the Odes of Solomon also designates those who partake in the gnosis as members. Although not stated explicitly, it may be assu-

---

3) calls for conversion and heed to the teaching of the redeeming knowledge (Od. Sal. 33,6, 10, 11 and 13). The head which was mentioned in note 4, is a head which reveals itself (Od. 13, 18).

[1] The reader learns that since the decapitation of John the Baptist, all prophecy has come to an end because prophecy always emanates from the head. Van Unnik, Openbaring uit Egyptisch zand, p. 73.

[2] Cod. Jung 18, 29b-40. See Pokorný, Der Epheserbrief und die Gnosis, p. 66 and Zandee, Het Evangelie der Waarheid een gnostisch geschrift, p. 61. The "members of the Father of all" could also be interpreted as aeons; that would make little difference since the aeons are the prototype pneumatological beings (cf. Zandee, op. cit., p. 62).

[3] Acta Ioannis 100. See Pokorný, op. cit., p. 65 and Hennecke, Apokr. II[3] p. 158.

med that they collectively also form a body. Now however, it becomes clear in which way this body belongs to another. For this body has a head. The single one who is redeemed and who reveals the gnosis (Christ) has become the head and those who collect around him have become members.[1]

The fourth tract in the Jung Codex, the so-called Treatise on the three natures, contains not only the designation "members" and "head" but also a comparison "with the human body and the denomination "body". Unfortunately, the complete contents and translation of this tract have not yet been published and we must use whatever scattered data are available.

The first piece of information in this tract is provided by a comparison between all, i.e. the whole number of aeons, and a human body which, without being segregated, is devided into members of members first members and last members, down to the very smallest member. These aeons, which may be compared to members, have been raised up by God. This raising up coincides with an unfolding in which the Father (God) unfolds himself. Together, the aeons form the one aeon of truth which is a single one, yet multiple. They generate the "image and likeness" of the Father.[2] This first item displays a correlation with the popular philosophy which envisaged the cosmos as a living organism. However, the tract yields more; we are also reminded of the Gnostic, Markos, who depicts the great aeon from whom all other aeons spring, as a maiden, "Truth", who is a female macro-anthropos.[3] In addition, the reference to the "image and likeness" of the Father recall for us the haeretical Jewish speculations on the first man.

A further number of data are presented by statements on the perfect human and his members. The perfect man had descended and returned to the place whence he descended after the redemption had been preached and he had received the gnosis. He returned into the unity. In a mysterious manner, this perfect man is all things. The elect are his members. Through teaching, they too can once again be taken into the pleroma.[4]

The thrid item of information is the following declaration : "The spiritual race ... has, when his head appeared, hurried towards him

---

[1] Od. Sal. 17, 14-16. see Pokorný, op. cit., p. 66 and Hennecke, op. cit., p. 598.

[2] Jung, Codex, 73, 16-74, 18. See Zandee, op. cit., p. 64. The image and likeness are treated in Jung Codex 70, 25-37. See Zandee, op. cit. p. 62.

[3] See Leisegang, Die Gnosis, p. 329ss.

[4] See Brandenburger, Adam und Christus, p. 80.

and formed a body for his head.".[1] It is probable that there was some identification between the perfect man and this head. A reasonable assumption is that the body which is formed by the elect, is conceived as a large human body and there is also a (mystical) common identity between the one great aeon of truth and the macro-anthropos who is formed from the spiritual kind and his head.

In the Excerpta ex Theodoto, the conception of the macro-anthropos and the term head are possibly also united in some statements. Christ is called πρωτότοκος. He is εἰκών of the pleroma and has ascended into the pleroma and in so doing has, as κεφαλή, also lifted up the body of Jesus. We do not yet see the conception of the macro-anthropos in this raising up of Jesus. But there exists a mystical relationship between this body of Jesus and the ecclesia. Christ is also κεφαλή of spiritual ones or σπέρματα who are the ecclesia. He is head of τὸ σπέρμα and Jesus is the shoulders of the sperma.[2] Behind such expressions obviously lies concealed a conception of the macro-anthropos who is composed of Christ, Jesus and the spiritual

Having acquainted ourselves above (p. 278s.) with six different notions which a first century Jewish Hellenist could associate with the word κεφαλή, we can now establish also that Christian Gnostics of a later period associated the same ideas with this word. The concept of the head was very important to them. For the Christian Gnostics the word κεφαλή was moreover connected with the idea of revelation and the unfolding of gnosis. Furthermore, the word implied a certain soteriological notion. On the basis of the idea that the elect form a body or living organism and by combining this with a speculation concerning the great aeon who is a macro-anthropos, they saw the kephale as the one who collects those about to be saved around him through the revelation of gnosis and thus enables them to share in the salvation due to him. Both the word κεφαλή as such[3] and the idea that the spirituals ones form a single body or form part of a macro-anthropos were connected with speculations on the first man by these Christian Gnostics.

It cannot be stated with certainty to what extent the now concep-

---

[1] See G. Quispel - H.-Ch. Puech, Op zoek naar het Evangelie der Waarheid (Nijkerk), p. 43.

[2] Clement of Alexandria, Exc. ex Theod., para. 33,2 and para. 42,1 and 2. See Völker, Quellen zur Geschichte d. chr. Gnosis, p. 124 and p. 127.

[3] As in the Sermon of the Naasenes; cf. above, pp. 279, 281. See also the connection between kephale and the first man in note 3 on p. 286.

tions which we encountered in literature written after the first century were known by the first century or before. The data in the younger literature could be traditional. However, one thing is clear; the concept of kephale was of great significance for the Christian Gnostics.

This significance is not dependent on function in the conception of the macro-anthropos. In general, an analogy had always been recognised between the human head and heaven. The head originally had no particular strength in the macro-anthropos conception. Texts exist "in which the head is scarecely or not at all mentioned whilst the body, however, is all the more prominently featured".[1] On the other hand, if we take into account that in Gnostic texts the head is sometimes of such importance "that a closer description of the body is more often than not neglected",[1] we are led to deduce that the concept must have had its own history and that this may easily be of greater antiquity than Christian Gnosticism. If we furthermore consider that a Semitic influence served to enhance the scope of the word, then Hellenistic Judaism would be the first quarter to search for the important developments affecting this history.

Whenever the head-aspect is stressed in the macro-anthropos conception, as, for example, we observed was the case with the Treatise on the three natures, we are not dealing with the original version of this conception. Whilst the original macro-anthropos is a "summing-up of the world as such", the conception in its later form is a "summing-up of the world of souls".[2] Our theory is that when so much emphasis is placed on the head of the macro-anthropos, who is a world of souls, a point has been reached where the significance of the term "head" as well as the macro-anthropos conception have both arrived at a late stage in their particular historical developments.

It seems to us eminently possible that the combination of the two terms "kephale" and "soma" in Eph. and Col. anteceded this stage and contributed to the later development when the macro-anthropos began to envisage in terms of a world of souls and the head of the macro-anthropos head began to be the subject of so much discussion. In fact, this is not only possible but becomes probable when we see that those statements in the Excerpta ex Theodota which are found to deal with the conception of a macro-anthropos with Christ as its head, reveal a strong dependence on Eph. and Col. Thus, we shall regard the combina-

---

[1] See Käsemann, Leib und Leib Christi, p. 74.
[2] See Käsemann, op. cit., p. 69.

tion of the terms "kephale" and "soma" in Eph. and Col. as an original phenomenon.[1]

The sense of the term "soma" is the same as in 1 C. 12 and R. 12. Within the conceptual framework of popular contemporary philosophy, a single mass of people was envisaged as a living organism. Such is the case in 1 C. 12 and in R. 12 and, also, in Eph. and Col. But in Eph. and Col., the term "soma" is combined with the term "kephale" which must already have had considerable significance in Hellenistic Judaism before Eph, and Col. were written.

In Hellenistic Judaism, however, the comparison which speaks of head and body is applied to a whole mass of people when it appertains a dominant figure and a mass of people. This is borne out by the fact that Plutarch, under the influence of Latin, could speak metaphorically about a ruler and a nation as the head and body. Thus it is understandable that the author of Eph. (and Col.) combined the two terms "soma" and "kephale". In so doing, he remained within the framework of his culture and his time.

However, we must not seek for the macro-anthropos conception in this combined soma and kephale. There is nothing to indicate that the Christ, called the kephale, and the ecclesia, called the soma, are together regarded as a single anthropos. Although the epistle does express the idea that $\pi\epsilon\rho\iota\tau o\mu\eta$ and $\dot{\alpha}\kappa\rho o\beta\upsilon\sigma\tau\iota\alpha$ together become $\epsilon\dot{\iota}s$ $\kappa\alpha\iota\nu\dot{o}s$ $\ddot{\alpha}\nu\theta\rho\omega\pi os$, it does not express, as Schlier thought, that Christ-kephale, together with the (redeemed) soma is the (redeemed) anthropos.[2]

---

[1] Pokorný, op. cit., p. 68s., holds that the combination of the terms "kephale" and "soma" should be attributed to Christian Hellenistic communities. Referring to Schille, Frühchristliche Hymnen, he argues that older Hellenistic Christian hymns are found particularly in Col. In these hymns, Christ is presented as a cosmic authority by the designation "head"; the cosmos, he maintained, was represented by a body (cf. also Schille, op. cit., p. 82). In Pokorný's view, the original aspect in Eph. and Col. is the application of the combined terms head and body to Christ and the church instead of Christ and the cosmos. This explanation is not satisfactory. Pokorný fails to appreciate that in ancient times there was no particular emphasis on the head of the macro-anthropos and, moreover, he fails to make clear how it come about that the head suddenly became so important in these Christian Hellenistic hymns.

[2] In Th. W. III, p. 676, Schlier describes how in Gnosticism the kephale is on the one hand the saviour of the archetype (the fallen body) and, on the other, part of the redeemed archetype. On p. 697 he says that statements on head and body in Eph. and Col. follow the pattern of thought of the Gnostic redeemer myth : "Und zwar ist mit der Bezeichnung Christi als Hauptes der Kirche von diesem Hintergrund aus einmal die

The first time we encounter a macro-anthropos conception in which the head is emphasized, is in the works of the later Christian Gnostics, where the head, together with the members of the body, forms a macro-anthropos. This literature, without mentioning the word "body", can expound on a relationship between head and members. In Eph. and Col. this is not the case-despite our hymn-books. The two epistles contain no references whatsoever to the head and the members or to members belonging to a head.[1]

As in the philosophical comparison between a society and an organism, the members are members of a body. In 1 C. 12 and R. 12, this is also the case. Now, in Eph. and Col., that body is brought into connexion with a head. This relationship, as Meuzelaar has so rightly pointed out, is an indirect relationship.[2] Christ is not kephale of the soma which is the ecclesia in Eph. and Col.; he is kephale of the ecclesia and it is the ecclesia which can be regarded as his soma. However, even leaving aside that ecclesia which is soma, he is notwithstanding kephale.

The expression "kephale" did not need to be qualified through the espression "soma" to be significant. In itself, the word was sufficiently meaningful for Hellenistic Jews, being connected with the associations mentioned on p. 278s. There is a possibility that the idea of a kephale as the source of redeeming revelation already previously existed and that the identities of a kephale and the first man were equated.[3]

Christ is designated by the word κεφαλή as a heavenly and superior being in Eph. 1:22. Previously, in 1 :20,he has been spoken of as sitting in heavenly places and being exalted over all cosmic forces, whilst in the preceding part of 1:22, there is a reference to his dominion over the

---

Einheit zwischen Christus und der Kirche hervorgehoben"(For, in the light of this background, the designation of Christ as head of the church at the same time draws attention to the unity between Christ and the church).

[1] Illuminating are the following passages in Eph : ὅτι μέλη ἐσμὲν τοῦ σώματος αὐτοῦ in 5:29 and ὅτι ἐσμὲν ἀλλήλων μέλη in 4:25.

[2] Op. cit., p. 122-124.

[3] The association between the term "kephale" and the terms "revelation" and "first man' could well be older than the works encountered on p. 279ss. In Quaest. in Ex. 117, Philo calls the logos the kephale of all things. Elsewhere he indicates the dominant position of the logos by means of the related designations ἀρχή, πρεσβύτατος υἱός πρωτόγονος. See above, p. 270 n. 4. Philo connects pronouncements on the logos, which is πρωτόγονος and πρεσβύτατος υἱός, with the first man. See Brandenburger ,Adam und Christus, p. 118-131. It is possible that for Philo there was already an association between the term "kephale" and the first man.

earthly reality of creation.[1] These statements lead up to the subsequent description of Christ as κεφαλὴ ὑπὲρ πάντα. The adjunct ὑπὲρ πάντα brings to bear that this κεφαλή exceeds the measure of all (heavenly and earthly) things. The preposition ὑπέρ with the accusative has the same meaning as the ὑπέρ in the ὑπὲρ δύναμιν of 2C. 1:8.[2]

Philo, refering to the significance of the head in a organism, cites Philadelphus, who in excellence (ἤκμασεν =) exceeded the other Ptolemies as the head of kings.[3] In Eph. 1:22, Christ is likewise called the head which excels over all, whilst the context more or less raises the image of the omnipresent ruler of the world.[4] However, there is a qualification involved; Philo may use the designation of kephale of all things for the logos[5], whereas the author of Eph. calls Christ the kephale above all things. The latter expression is less forceful and the author, as in Eph. 4:6, probably intended to assign ultimate and absolute dominion to God.

With regard to God, Christ occupies a secondary position. He sits at his right hand and he is exalted above all cosmic forces because it is God who has placed him so highly and he commands over the earth because God has put this under him.

Although the author in his use of the designation "kephale" was following Hellenistic Jewish traditions, some conceptions which he associates with the terms may be regarded as original.

The thought expressed in Eph. 4:11 could be an extension of the Hellenistic Jewish tradition. In this verse it is stated of the highly exalted Christ who, in 4:15, is once again named the kephale, that he has given apostles, prophets, evengelists, pastors and teachers. All these categories are most narrowly connected with the transmission of the revealed knowledge of the mystery (3:5), the word of truth (1:13) and the teaching (4:21) of the truth. Thus, this idea lies within the framework of a kephale who is the source of redeeming revelations, a conception which was perhaps already part of Hellenistic Judaism.

Different is the case of the descending and ascending of the kephale Christ, which is not part of any Hellenistic Jewish tradition. We have to take into account the possibility that in Hellenistic Judaism an

---

[1] See p. 217s.

[2] Liddell-Scott, s.v. sub B II gives the following translations for ὑπέρ with the accusative : above, exceeding, beyond.

[3] De vita Mosis II, 30; cf. p. 276 and note 6.

[4] See p. 218.

[5] See p. 270 and note 4.

identification was made between a kephale and the first man and that speculations on descending and ascending were connected with this first man.[1] In Eph. also, a certain identification may be supposed between the kephale, Christ and a particular human being and there is quite clearly a question of descending and ascending. Yet this does not link up with the conception of a descending and ascending anthropos. For Eph. does not accentuate that the anthropos is kephale nor, in fact, is this even expressed.

Psalm 8, from which the words καὶ πάντα ὑπέταξεν ὑπο τοὺς πόδας αὐτοῦ are quoted to precede the designation κεφαλή in Eph. 1:22, speaks of a ἄνθρωπος or υἱὸς ἀνθρώπου. But whether or not Christ is the anthropos does not enter into discussion in the context of Eph. 1:22. This question is of equally little relevance when 4:8-10 treats the subject of the descension and ascension of Christ. Schlier is consequently totally mistaken when he thinks that the author (Paul) a priori interpreted the verse from Psalm 68 (LXX 67) which he quotes in 4:8 in the light of the ascension "des (zuvor) herabgekommenen Menschensohn-(Urmenschen) Erlösers".[2] "of the (previously)descended Son of Man-(first man) Redeemer".

The author of Eph. 1:22 speaks of Christ as the kephale on the basis of the ancient Christian kerugma set forth in 1:20 and also to be found in R. 8:34. It is the light of this kerugma that he a priori sees the words from Psalm 68 in 4:8 and subsequently again, in Eph. 4:15, refers to Christ as kephale. The form in which Paul was familiar with this kerugma, spoke not only of an ascension but also of a previous humiliation. This is the kerugma of the Son of God who was sent out, was made of a woman, made under the law (Gal. 4:4); who sprung from the seed of David (R. 1:3); who, though he was rich, became poor (2 C. 8:9); of Him who lowered himself and in the form of a servant became equal to men, humbled himself and became obedient unto death; who was afterward exalted by God (Phil. 2:7-9); and declared to be the Son of God with power according to the spirit of holiness, by the resurrection from the dead (R. 1:4).

It is this kerugma that underlies Eph. 4:8-10. The elements of humili-

---

[1] Philo knows of a return (in essence, a rising uip) of the true or inner man; cf. Brandenburger. op. cit., p. 120 and p. 129s. For the connection between the expressions κεφαλή, (ἀρχ)ἄνθρωπος, descending and ascending, in the so-called Sermon of the Naässenes, see above, p. 279 and Branderburger, op. cit., p. 83ss.

[2] Eph., p. 192.

ation and being anthropos are there, but they are of a different character than the speculations ascribed to a (heretical) Hellenistic Judaism. Here there is no question of a man who descends but of the Son of God who "becomes" a man. And if the author of Eph. in quoting Psalm 68 in 1:22 was thinking, without saying so, that this Psalm speaks of a ἄνθρωπος or υἱὸς ἀνθρώπου, the image before him will not have been that of a descended man but of the Son of God, who became ἄνθρωπος. After having become a human being and after his humiliation the Son of God became υἱὸς θεοῦ ἐν δυνάμει (R. 1:4) and exalted (Phil. 2:9). God made him both Lord and Christ (Acts 2:36).

In designating Christ "kephale", the author of Eph. is guided by these concepts of the old Christian kerugma.[1] Christ, for him, is ὁ ἠγαπημένος (1:6). As can be deduced from LXX Is. 44:2; Col. 3:12; 1 Th. 1:4; 2 Th. 2;13: R. 9:13 and 9:25, this word is alsmost synonymous with ὁ ἐκλεκτός and a variation on the designation ἀγαπητός which is so frequently used to describe the messianic dignity of Jesus in the synoptic gospels.

These designations, ἠγαπημένος and ἀγαπητός, probably trace their origin in the Hebrew words בָּחוּר (cf. Psalm 89:20) and בָּחִיר (cf. Psalm 89:4) which the first community understood as messianic predicates· In Eph. 1:6, the word ἠγαπημένος is also a messianic predicate, implying the idea of Jesus being the Son of God. (In the synoptic gospels, the designation ἀγαπητός is repeatedly connected with the designation υἱός μου. In LXX Gen. 22:2, 12 and 16, the word corresponds with יָחִיד, only "son".[2] A similar desgination occurs in Col. 1:13 : ὁ υἱὸς τῆς ἀγάπης αὐτοῦ.) It is a word evocative of exaltation and the wielding of power. We are reminded Ps. 89:4 and 20 in this context. However, the word does not exclude the idea of suffering and humiliation; ὁ ἀγαπητός also denotes the suffering servant of God spoken of in the quotation from Is. 42 in Mat. 12:18.

For the author of Eph., the designation "kephale" has precisely such a bias and he employs it to suggest the idea of exaltation and the wielding of divine power. The words κεφαλὴ τῶν πάντων could well have been used in a translation of 1 Chr. 29:11 which approximated more closely to the masoretic text than the LXX did, rendering more strongly the idea of the dominion of God which is conveyed in the original text. In LXX Ps. 109:7 ,the difficult words διὰ τοῦτο ὑψώσει

---

[1] Cf. Bultmann, Theologie, p. 28.

[2] Cf. Sevenster, De Christologie van het N.T., p. 101s.

κεφαλήν could easily have lent themselves to the interpretation, by a non-academic exegetical mind, of the appointment of the Messiah as kephale after the messianic struggle. There must have been a close association for the author of Eph. between this psalm and the eighth psalm from which he quotes in Eph. 1:22.

A statement which corresponds to this quotation, occurs in LXX Ps. 109:1, which also speaks of subjection beneath the feet of the ruler who sits at God's right hand. As far as the conception that exaltation and the state of kephale are preceded by a phase of descent and suffering is concerned, this the author or the evironment which determined his vocabulary, could find in the eighteenth psalm (LXX Ps. 17).

This psalm, too, must for the author have been closely connected with the eighth psalm from which he quotes. It speaks of submission under the feet of God's anointed (ὑπο τοὺς πόδας μου, ὑποκάτω μου and ὑπ' ἐμέ LXX Ps. 17:39, 40 and 48) and there are references to exaltation and to becoming kephale ἐπι τὰ ὑψηλὰ ἱστῶν με and καταστήσεις με εἰς κεφαλὴν ἐθνῶν 17:34 and 44). However, this exaltation is to take place only after falling into the snares of death and the cords of Sheol (cf. ὠδινες θανάτου, ὠδῖνες ᾅδου and ἐξ ὑδάτων πολλῶν 17:5, 6 and 17).

The designation "kephale", just as the designations ἠγαπημένος or ἀγαπητός, is a messianic predicate that presupposes humiliation and sorrow. This suffering is of soteriological significance. In fact, the designation κεφαλὴ τῆς ἐκκλησίας corresponds with the designation σωτὴρ τοῦ σώματος in Eph. 5:23 which anticipates the statement in 5:25-27 on the soteriological significance which the death of Christ has for the ecclesia.[1]

To be kephale represents, qua talis, rulership. The kephale surpasses all things and is elevated beyond all other powers. This in itself must already constitute an advantage for the ecclesia. In any event, her enemies (6:12) are impotent in the face of this kephale. Moreover, like the suffering which went before it, this state of being kelpale and practising dominion serves to enhance the ecclesia.

But there is more to this aspect. Christ is not, in short, just kephale

---

[1] The designation σωτήρ is an eschatological predicate forming part of the ancient Christian kerugma. See Bultmann, Theologie, p. 81s. and Foerster, Th. W. VII, p. 101ss. For commentary on the soteriotological significance of Christ's death in Eph. 5:25-37, see K. Romaniuk, "L'origine des formules pauliniennes "Le Christ s'est livré pour nous", "Le Christ nous a aimés et s'est livré pour nous" " in Novum Testamentum, V, 1962, p. 55ss.

but the situation is also that God has given him who is κεφαλὴ ὑπὲρ πάντα, to the ecclesia to be its kephale (1:22).[1] Because God has given Christ to the ecclesia to be its kephale, the ecclesia may be the body of Christ.[2] The ecclesia, which is the body, must be built up and must grow (2:21s.). Christ, the kephela, endows the ecclesia with all the categories necessary to carry out and realize the revelation of redemption (p. 287). This provision contributes towards the establishment of the body and promotes the growth of the entire movement. Ultimately, through this, all the faithful will achieve unity, perfection and maturity.

The building-up and the growth of the body as well as coherence between all parts and the individual functioning of each of these parts, are all due to the kephale, Christ. Eph. 4:12-16 expresses this in clear terms. The idea of a coordination between many parts, each working properly, thus ensuring the effectiveness of the whole, hinges on the metaphoric designation "soma" which is here in Eph. assigned to the ecclesia.

Within the framework of the contemporary popular philosophy, the image of the body provided an ideal epitome of unity and cohesion. (p. 276). In Eph., the unusual element lies therein that the body metaphor is given an association with the term "kephale". At this point, the Jewish-Hellenistic idea of the head as the beginning which comprehends the other elements and as the focus of the collective strength, comes into its own. As in Test. Sab. 9, the head is now seen in terms of the principle on which the unity of the body depends.[3] The whole somatic character of the ecclesia is made dependent on Christ, who is the kephale and only in relation to him is the ecclesia enabled to be a body.

Christ is not the only figure to be designated "kephale" in Eph.

---

[1] See Schlier, p. 89 : "Der Satz ist sehr knapp formuliert. Eigentlich sind in ihm zwei Aussagen enthalten. Denn zunächst wird wiederholt, dass Christus das Haupt "Über alles" ist ... Dann aber wird auch gesagt dasz er der Kirche als Haupt ist gegeben." (The sentence is very succinctly formulatid and really contains two statements. First of all, it reaffirms that Christ is the head "over all things", going on to state that he has been given to the church as head.) I.J. du Plessis, in Christus als hooft van kerk en kosmos, p. 71, gives a somewhat different interpretation to the sentence. Nevertheless, he too thinks that Christ is here seen as the head of all creation as well as the head of the church.

[2] Cf. I.J. du Plessis, op. cit., p. 73 : "Die feit dat sij sij lichaam is, is alleen moontlik, omdat Hij haar Hoof is ..." ("The fact that it is his body is only possible because he is its head ...").

[3] See the fourth association listed on p. 278 and the quotation on p. 279.

Man is also thus described. Man, the husband, is κεφαλὴ τῆς γυναικός (5:23). The women to whom this passage of the epistle is addressed, are urged to submit to their husbands. When in this instance, the husband is designated as "kephale" of the wife, the word is not as loaded in meaning as when it is used as a predicate of Christ. Nevertheless, this designation as it is here applied to the husband, clearly derives its context from the predicate relating to Christ and there is some correspondence between Christ's situation as kephale and that of the man who is the husband.

We have already indicated that with respect to the designation "kephale" in relation to Christ, we see an affinity between Eph. and Col. It is clear from the corresponding designations πρωτότοκος and ἀρχή which we found in Col. 1:15 and 18, that the term "kephale" must have had a previous history in Hellenistic Judaism. Above (p. 277), we pointed out that the words κεφαλή, ἀρχή and πρωτόγονος are related terms. The same applies to the word πρωτότοκος which is synonymous with the word πρωτόγονος.

Now we ask whether there is also an affinity between Eph. and 1 C. 11. In 1 C. 11, an even higher form of kephale is described than in Eph. God himself is called kephale in 1 C. 11:3. This is in keeping with the O.T.; in 1 Chr. 29:11, God is head (ראשׁ) over all things. In 1 C. 11:3, the sentence κεφαλὴ δὲ τοῦ Χριστοῦ ὁ θεός evinces God's superiority with regard to Christ. 1 C. 15:27, 28, expresses this idea of God's elevation at its most elaborate. It is our opinion that the same is conveyed in Eph. (p. 287).

Furthermore, 1 C. 11, like Eph., knows Christ as kephale. Christ, in 1 C. 11:3 is essentially the kephale of all who believe. The passage presents him as the kephale of each man. That does not mean that women do not fall under the rule of Christ; this would be in contradiction to other texts in the same epistle. In this connection we are thinking particularly of 1 C. 3:23 and 7:10s. Also, it would clash with Gal. 3:28.[1] Christ is only called the kephale of every man because the author

---

[1] Οὐκ ἔνι ἄρσεν καὶ θῆλυ, This equality of man and woman within the scope of Christ's presence is also treated within the pericope under discussion. According to the pericope, the differential between man and woman has been laid down at the creation. It is to man that creation gave superiority. Wherever the κύριος is present, this superiority gives way to solidarity (1 C. 11:11). Besides, the innate superiority of man at the time of the creation is already mitigated by the method of birth (ὁ ἀνὴρ διὰ τῆς γυναικός) and a common dependence on God (τὰ δὲ πάντα ἐκ τοῦ θεοῦ 1 C. 11:12).

wishes to pre-empt any form of self-overestimation on the part of man—
for in the same text (11:3) the man is named the kephale of the woman.

Continued, the theme treats this difference between man and woman
whereby the man is the woman's kephale. The affirmation παντὸς
ἀνδρὸς ἡ κεφαλὴ ὁ Χριστός ἐστιν which precedes the statement
κεφαλὴ δὲ γυναικὸς ὁ ἀνήρ precludes any possibility that man should
unrestrainedly consider himself as kephale; his position as kephale
is limited by Christ's position as kephale which, in turn, is limited
by God's position as kephale.

This affirmation κεφαλὴ δὲ τοῦ Χριστοῦ ὁ θεός is not superfluous
since it illuminates how Christ is himself kephale. The position of Christ
as kephale goes together with obedience and subordination to God and
the purpose of that last statement is that the man, as kephale, should
take as his example Christ, who is also kephale. As in Eph., the designation "kephale" in this pericope derives its content, in relation to a man,
from the predicate as applied to Christ and there is an association
between Christ's position as kephale and that of a man.

A difference exists between Eph. 5 and 1 C. 11 in that the latter
is only concerned with the question as to how a many and a woman
should behave in the public gatherings of the community whereas
Eph. 5 seeks to lay down rules of conduct in marital and family life.
Thus, with reference to the term "kephale", although there is a remarkable affinity between Eph. and 1 C. 11, the difference in bias between
Eph. 5 and 1 C. 11, obviates any far-reaching correspondence.

b. Σῶμα and μέλος

Käsemann and Schweizer have provided us with extensive information on the meanings of the word σῶμα during the classical and Hellenistic periods.[1] I should like to devote some attention to a few of these.
The word can be used to indicate the complete person or personality
and can more or less replace the function of the reflexive pronoun.[2]
When the subject has to do with the taking of a vote or count, the word
is used in the same way as we use "person".[3]

As others before him, Plato recognised a contradistinction between
body and soul. The soul is locked in the body from which it may be

---

[1] See Käsemann, Leib und Leib Christi, p. 23-50 and Schweizer, Th. W. VIII,
p. 1025-1027.

[2] Schweizer, op. cit., pp. 1026 1.10ss., 1029 1.29, 1030 1. 11ss. and 1040 1.11ss.
In the CP, σῶμα is also used instead of the refl. pron. : R. 12:1; 1 C. 13:3.

[3] Schweizer, op. cit., p. 1030 1.13s., 16s. and p. 1040 1.8ss.

separated and which it may leave.[1] Plato was also familiar with ἄψυχα
σώματα. The inorganic materials with which the artist works, are such
σώματα.[2] For the Stoa, both soul and the godhead constituted a
soma and all kinds of concepts which we regard as abstract, were
represented in terms of somata.[3] Yet again, other scholars find that
the characteristic feature of a soma is the fact that it is a palpable
thing.[4]

We furthermore observe that the word is used in connection with
any number which could be regarded as a unit; groups, colleges, an
army, the population of a city or a popular assembly (ἐκκλησία)
may be represented as somata.[5]

We have already remarked (p. 276) that the organism of the body
functioned as the epitome of a unit composed of many interlinked
and connecting parts. Both cosmos and human community were envisaged and represented in terms of a body, during the Hellenistic period.

Hellenistic Judaism gave no new content to the word "soma" which
is relevant to the interpretation of Eph and conformed with Hellenistic
anthropology which differentiated between the soul and the body.[6]
We also notice this in rabbinical literature where the equivalent for
"body" is the word גוף. In Jewish Aramaic, this word also acquired
the meanings "person", "essence" or "main substance" and "self".[7]

In Gnostic literature that was influenced by Christianity, we found
the comparison of the whole number of aeons with a human body.
We saw that this corresponds with the popular philosophy which saw
the cosmos in terms of a living organism and we were in addition
reminded of the ancient and widespread conception of the macro-
anthropos (p. 281s.).

---

[1] Id., op. cit., p. 1026-1028 and Käsemann, op. cit., p. 26ss.

[2] Schweizer, op. cit., p. 1028 1.5s. and note 38.

[3] Id., op. cit., p. 1032s. and p. 1040 1.15ss.

[4] Id., op. cit., p. 1034 1.24ss. and Liddell-Scott, s.v. sub III, 2.

[5] A literary composition is an σῶμα as is a collection of evidence; see Schweizer,
op. cit., p. 1038 1,1ss. and Liddell-Scott, s.v. sub IV τὸ σῶμα τῆς πίστεως(cf. also Schweizer, op. cit., p. 1039 1.23ss.). For σῶμα as a group, an ἐκκλησία, etc., see Schweizer, op. cit.,
pp. 1033 1.35ss., 1034 1.1ss. and 1037 1.38ss. Cf. further the verb σωματοποιεῖν for which
Liddell-Scott, s.v. sub II gives : organize as a body (e.g. τὸ ἔθνος σωματοποιεῖν), make
into a whole. Schweizer, op. cit., p. 1037s. :"σωματοποιεῖν wird die Bildung eines Trupps
von Anhängern genannt" (a formation of a group of retainers in called σωματοποιεῖν).

[6] See Schweizer, op. cit., p. 1043-1054 and Käsemann, p. 16-18.

[7] See Käsemann, op. cit., p. 19-22; R. Meyer, Th. W. VII, p. 115-118 and Dalman,
Jesus-Jeschua, p. 129ss. and id. Neuhebr. Handwörterbuch z. Targum, Talmud und
Midrasch, s.v.

Furthermore, this literature made us aware of a new macro-anthropos conception in which not the world as such but rather the world of souls, all the spiritual, are envisaged as a human body (p. 284). In the Excerpta ex Theodoto, we remarked on a mystic relationsihp between the body of Jesus and the ecclesia (p. 283) and thought that we detected there in a certain dependence on Eph. and Col. (p. 284). The tract generally known as the Treatise on the three natures, speaks of a pneumatical race which forms a body for his head (p. 282s.). A Pauline influence may also be assumed in the case of this work. This in fact, becomes quite clear in the following sentence : "until the members of the body of the ecclesia form a unity... manifesting themselves as "ein ganzheitlicher (?) Leib."[1]

A Pauline influence may likewise be assumed in the case of the Stoic philosopher, Pantaenus, whom Clement of Alexandria quotes. Converted to Christianity, this philosopher's conceptions bordered on the periphery of Gnosticism. Pantaenus speaks of the ecclesia as a body, embodied in the sun. This body is formed from individuals from the same race; these are $\phi\omega\tau\epsilon\iota\nu o\iota$. Some are the head, others the eyes, ears, breast or feet that have been placed in the sun.[2] Despite the fact, that such pronouncements derive partly from non-Christian traditions, they cannot explain the term $\sigma\hat{\omega}\mu a$ as used in the Pauline works, being themselves directly or indirectly dependent on Pauline influences.

With regard to the word $\mu\epsilon\lambda o\varsigma,$ we have the following comment. The word corresponds with the substantive $\mu\epsilon\rho o\varsigma$ which may also be used as an appellation for a part of a body. Both Plato and Philo regarded these two words as synonyms. Later, Marcus Aurelius differentiated between them.[3]

In the eyes of popular Stoic philosophy, the cosmos was one vast organism of which man was a harmonious cooperative member ($\mu\epsilon\lambda o\varsigma,$ membrum).[4] Seneca called this entire great complex a god; to him, human beings were the socii and membra of this god.[5]

---

[1] G. Quispel, "Der gnostischen Anthropos und die Jüdische Tradition" in Eranos-Jahrbuch XXII/1953 (Zürich 1954), p. 227. (Trans. : "wholeful(?) body.)

[2] Eclogae propheticae 56, 1-3. The quotation may be found in Käsemann, op. cit., p. 80. See also Schweizer, op. cit., p. 1089 and Meuzelaar, Der Leib des Messias, p. 166.

[3] See J. Horst, Th. W. IV, p. 560 1.13ss. and Note 2; J. Schneider, Th. W. IV, p. 599; J. Horst, op. cit., p. 562s. and p. 561 1.5ss.

[4] Dupont, Gnosis, p. 432-436.

[5] Seneca Ep. 90, 30 : "Totum hoc quo continemur, et unum est et deus : et socii eius sumus et membra". The quotation in Dupont, op. cit., p. 434.

Human society was also envisaged as a body or organism and in moral comparisons the members of a community were equated with parts of the body (p. 276). Whenever the ancient macro-anthropos conception came to the fore, the parts of the cosmos were regarded as physical members.[1] There is a convergence between the philosophical image of the cosmos as an organism and the ancient conception of the macro-anthropos when, in the Treatise on the Three Natures, there is a comparison between the aeons and limbs (p. 282s.).

Finally, we are presented with the newer form of the macro-anthropos conception as held by the Gnostics according to which all those, who have "knowledge", represented a human body, whilst the individuals form the limbs and members of this body. These members are scattered and must be gathered or established.[2] (A similar vision is found in Pantaenus and Porphyrius.[3])

This gathering can be a gathering round a head.[4] In onther works, we read of a soul which collects or gathers its members.[5] When the matter concerns the gathering around a head, we are dealing with a conflation of the macro-antropos conception, which has its own background, and the term "kephale" which developed independently. We date this conflation later than Eph. and Col. (p. 284s.)

The image of the gathering together of scattered members or limbs, is not limited and bound to the expression "kephale" and traces its origins far back in the ancient past. Thus we may recall an "alten kosmoginischen Mythus, der erzählt, wie ein Gott oder Riese stibrt und aus seinen Teilen die Welt entsteht"[6] or the ancient Thracian legend

---

[1] This conception makes a comeback in the work of the Gnostic, Markos; see p. 282.

[2] In the fragment of the Gospel of Philippus, preserved by Epiphanius, the soul of a salvandus says at the ἄνοδος : συνέλεξα τὰ μέλη τὰ διεσκορπισμένα (Hennecke I³, p. 195). In a Gnostic prayer given by Käsemann, op. cit., p. 78 and J. Horst, op. cit., p. 561 1.34, the following plea is uttered : "save all my members which since the creation of the world ... are scattered and gather them together and take them into the light". In the Odes of Solomon 6:15, these about to be saved who drink of the water of life are "limbs which raise themselves". This is a reference to Is. 53:3 (Hebr. 12:12) and the conception of the gathering together of the scattered limbs may be discounted.

[3] For Pantaenus, see above and for Porphyrius, Epistola ad Marcellum caput 10, Hennecke I³, p. 196s.

[4] See p. 282s.

[5] See the first two examples quoted in note 2.

[6] This is from Schenke; see his Der Gott "Mensch" in der Gnosis, p. 17. (Trans. The old cosmogonic Myth which relates how a god or giant dies and the world is created from his parts.)

of Zagreus which explains a ritual act.[1] At a later stage, this myth took on an anthropological and cosmogonic character.[2]

Another myth we should take into account in this connection, is the Egyptian chthonian myth of Isis and Osiris. The Dionysus-Zagreus myth was about a διαμελισμός, a tearing to pieces. The Isis and Osiris myth which the Orphicists, Herodotus and other Greeks identified with Dionysus, contained the additional element of Isis gathering together the scattered pieces of the body of Osiris which then sprung to life again.[3]

When Plutarch relates the myth of Isis, who assembles together the fourteen parts of the body of Osiris, he talks of the logos which is united in the heart of the myste who is being initiated into the mysteries of Isis.[4] The thirteenth tract of the Corpus Hermeticum deals with the rebirth which takes place when the logos is reconstituted, limb by limb, by ten divine forces in the heart of the one reborn.[5]

In the Coptic work which is known as "Unbekanntes altgnostisches Werk" (an old Gnostic work of unknown authorship), the process of gathering together the limbs is called "die Einsammlung der Zerstreung Israëls" ("the gathering together of Israel dispersed").[6] This has probably been borrowed from Judaism and suggests that syncretical Hellenistic Judaism became familiar with the concept of gathering together the scattered members. Late rabbinical literature tells that pieces from limbs of Adam were removed and scattered.[7] However, there is no reason to assume on the basis of this that the concept of collecting the

---

[1] See E. Rohde. Psyche, Seelencult und Unsterblichkeitsglaube der Griechen (Tübingen, [10]1925), II, p. 117s.

[2] Amongst the Orphicists, the myth was expanded : the Titans who devoured Zagreus, were struck by the thunder of Zeus. It is from their ashes that the human race evoled. Perhaps the cosmological aspect is already inherent in the Orphicists : "durch Frevel verliert sich das eine Gotteswesen in die Vielheit der Gestalten dieser Welt" (through wickedness the one godly being is lost amongst the multiplicity of beings in this world). see Rohde, op. cit., p. 118s.

[3] See K.H.E. de Jong, Das antike Mystrienwesen in religionsgeschichtlicher, ethnologischer und psychologischer Beleuchtung (Leiden 1919), pp. 29, 77, 99ss.

[4] See Reitzenstein, HMR, p. 49 (cf. for the myth in Plutarch, J. Zandee, Egyptische tempels en goden (Kampen 1965), p. 121ss.).

[5] See Reitzenstein, op. cit., p. 49. For the connection between the Corpus Hermeticus and ancient Egyptian esoteric doctrines, see De Jong, op. cit., p. 101.

[6] The quotation comes from Käsemann, op. cit., p. 78.

[7] See Murmelstein, "Adam, ein Beitrag zur Messiaslehre", p. 263. Murmelstein gives a late Jewish legend concerning Adam who, at first ,was as great as the world but later became smaller because God took pieces from his limbs. Adam had to carry these

scattered limbs did not penetrate further into Judaism, beyond this peripheral syncretical Hellenistic Jewish fringe.[1]

Eph. repeadedly uses the words "soma" and "melos" to indicate respectively the ecclesia and the believers. When the ecclesia is described in some detail as the body of Christ, in 1:23, this is done which some emphasis. The word σῶμα corresponds—purely formally—with the words τοὺς πόδας and κεφαλὴν which precede and lend some relief to the word σῶμα.[2]

A warning in 4:25 is motivated by the words ὅτι ἐσμὲν ἀλλήλων μέλη. The reader gains the impression that the author took for granted and as generally known, the fact that the faithful are members in relation to each other. Also the causal subordinate clause ὅτι μέλη ἐσμὲν τοῦ σώματος αὐτοῦ in 5:30 has the character of a remark made in passing, stating the obvious.

4:12 and 16, in connection with the pneumatical gifts and the categories of those who, by virtue of these, serve the ministry,[3] speaks of increase of the ecclesia, here designated as "soma". In 4:16 this soma is at length compared to an organism and depicted as sum total of parts effectively working together. Here the term "melos" is no longer used to indicate the faithful; for in the rhetorical passage, the author uses another word, namely the synonymous word μέρος.[4]

The word "soma" in 2:16 and 4:4 is deserving of especial attention. 2:15 states how Christ made two groups into one new man; the two groups which were earlier described as ἀκροβυστία and περιτομή or as τὰ ἀμφότερα, the author now calls τοὺς δύο in 2:15 and τοὺς ἀμφοτέρους in 2:16. He does this not in order to give each group the character of a person or individual but on account of the correspondence with the expression εἷς καινὸς ἄνθρωπος in 2:15. The word ἕνα in the group of words εἰς ἕνα καινὸν ἄνθρωπον, accentuated that there is no difference. Both groups form the "one new man" who is distinguished by unity and knows of no differences.[5]

---

pieces to all parts of the earth and everywhere the pieces fell, they were transformed into matter to populate the earth with the descendants of Adam. It is possible that the story is of much greater antiquity than Murmelstein's quotation and that there is a connection between this and the Gnostic prayer quoted above, p. 296 n. 2.

[1] Cf. again Reitzenstein, HMR, p. 270-75 (and Käsemann, op. cit., p. 76s.).

[2] See p. 163.

[3] See p. 287.

[4] For the synonymity of these words, see p. 295.

[5] εἷς can be used emphatically in which case it means "einer und derselbe" (one

Now, 2:16 goes on to say that Christ reconciles both groups with God in one body, by means of the cross. The ἑνί in the words ἐν ἑνὶ σώματι also brings the view to bear that there exists no difference for the two groups; for both, the reconciliation took place within one and the same body and this happened through the cross.

The words ἐν ἑνὶ σώματι are an adverbial adjunct of the verb ἀποκαταλλάξῃ. Similarly, for example, the words ἐν τῷ Χριστῷ in 2 C. 5:19 are an adverbial adjunct of the participle καταλλάσσων and the words ἐν τῷ σώματί μου in Ph. 1:20 an abverbial adjunct of the verb μεγαλυνθήσεται. We are therefore unable to agree with Percy that Eph. 2:16 expresses the thought that both groups were contained in the crucified body of Christ.[1] If that were the case, the words ἐν ἑνὶ σώματι would have to form an adverbial adjunct belonging to the substantive ἀμφοτέρους. Despite this, Percy at the same time also recognises these words as adverbial adjuncts of ἀποκαταλλάξῃ. This becomes obvious when he interprets the word σῶμα of Eph. 2:16 as "den Leib ..., in welchem die Versöhnung der beiden Menschengruppen mit Gott als Ereignis stattfand".[2]

The explication is as follows; after the words ἐν ἑνὶ σώματι have identified the place where the reconciliation took place, the adverbial adjunct διὰ τοῦ σταυροῦ indicates the method by which the reconciliation came about. In the same way, in the example mentioned from Ph. 1:20, the adverbial adjunct of location is followed by the words εἴτε διὰ ζωῆς εἴτε διὰ θανάτου explain the two methods or ways in which the μεγαλυνθήσεται can become a reality. The adverbial adjunct διὰ τοῦ σταυροῦ expresses with sufficient clarity that the one body can be no other body than the body of Christ, that was crucified.[3] Meuzelaar, however, thinks that the word ἑνὶ with σώματι in 2:16 proves that the body here intended is that of the body of the ecclesia, consisting of Jews and Gentiles, which is so often mentioned elsewhere in the epistle.

Meuzelaar refers to Col. 3:15; R. 12:6; 1 C. 10:17 and 12:13, in which

---

and the same man) or "ein einziger" (one sigle man). See Bauer, Wörterbuch z. N.T., s.v. sub 2a and 2b. Liddell-Scott, gives the following meanings s.v. 2 and 2b: the same; possessing unity. For an analysis of the term καινὸς ἄνθρωπος,see p. 325ss.

[1] Probleme, pp. 109, 281, 289, 317 and 382.

[2] Op. cit., p. 281 ("the body... wherein the reconciliation of both groups with God took place").

[3] The view that the soma of 2: 16 is the body of the crucified is found in the work of many exegetes; cf. Schweizer, Th. W. VII, p. 1075; Percy, op. cit., p. 281 and Schlier, Eph., p. 135 and the authors mentioned by him.

the expression ἓν σῶμα is used each time for the ecclesia. The omission of a genitive αὐτοῦ to follow σώματι in 2:16, reinforces his view that the body indicated is not that of Christ himself.[1] Now it is true that the words ἓν σῶμα in the above-mentioned places in Col. and the HP refer on each occasion to community amongst the faithful. But that is no conclusive reason to ascribe the same meaning to these words in Eph. 2:16. In our view, the indications presented by the context outweigh the importance of their meaning in those other passages. (Besides, in the present investigation, we have to beware against forcing the affinities between Eph. and the HP.)

Furthermore, we are unable to share the view of Meuzelaar that the word σῶμα in Eph. 2:16 could only then be interpreted to mean Christ's own body if it were followed by the possessive αὐτοῦ. The mere fact that Christ happens to be the subject of the sentence renders an adjunct to express that this one body is no other body than the body of Christ, unnecessary after the words ἐν ἑνὶ σώματι.

We would in addition like to observe that 2:18 states that the two groups (ἀκροβυστία and περιτομή) have access to the Father in one spirit. Like the words ἕνα in 2:15 and ἑνί in 2:16, the word ἑνί in 2:18 intends to say that there is no difference between the two groups.

In form, there is a strong affinity between the words οἱ ἀμφότεροι ἐν ἑνὶ πνεύματι in 2:18 and the words τοὺς ἀμφοτέρους ἐν ἑνὶ σώματι in 2:16. This gives rise to the assumption that there is also an inner connection between verses 16 and 18. This is indeed the case. The strain of 2:18 provides an enhancement to what has been said in 2:16. The two groups have been reconciled in one and the same body with God, through the cross, and have gained access to the Father in one and the same spirit. From a reconciliation with God in the one body, flows forth access to the Father in the one spirit. They who have a relationship to the body of Christ which was crucified have, in consequence of this, also a relationship to the hagion pneuma.

Let us now examine the word as it occurs in 4:4. In this verse, an enumeration of concepts all characterised by the number one, opens with the words ἓν σῶμα καὶ ἓν πνεῦμα. This enumeration is intended to strengthen an exhortation to preserve unity through the bond of peace. This unity is a unity of a pneumatical nature. Unity exists because all the faithful participate in one and the same spirit.[2] The

---

[1] Op. cit., p. 56 note 5. In this note, the word ἐν is derogatively printed as ἐν).

[2] τὴν ἑνότητα τοῦ πνεύματος. Hanson, The Unity of the Church, p. 148, observes that the genitive in question is a genitivus qualitatis and translates it as "the spiritual unity". He adds : "The Christians are a unity since they are all partakers of the Spirit".

words καὶ ἓν πνεῦμα in 4:4 and the declaration on the gift that is given to each believer in 4:7, all bear witness that the unity of the pneuma to which the exhortation in 4:3 alludes, must be interpreted in this way.

In 4:4 the author lets the words ἓν σῶμα precede the καὶ ἓν πνεῦμα.[1] By doing this, he gives the impression that he is only enabled to speak of the ἓν πνεῦμα because the reality of the ἓν σῶμα already exists. For him, the concept ἓν σῶμα logically obviously precedes the concept ἓν πνεῦμα. It is because the faithful are joined in one body, they are also connected by one spirit.

It is usually assumed that ἓν σῶμα in 4:4 is an indication for the ecclesia.[2] Ultimately, that is true. If, however, one asserts that the author is only thinking of the organism of which the faithful are members or parts when he uses the word σῶμα,[3] this ignores the finer points of his trend of thought. To hold that the author exclusively envisages the organism of the ecclesia with the ἓν σῶμα of 4:4, contradicts the logical sequence of the concepts σῶμα and πνεῦμα. Logically, the pneuma precedes the organism of the ecllesia; Because the same spirit works in the faithful, they mutually form a single body or organism.

The reverse, namely that the faithful partake in one and the same spirit because they belong to the same body or organism, is not the case. On the contrary; 4:12 and 16 can talk of a σῶμα and of the μέρη and of a building up and increase of this σῶμα because the pneumatical gifts are there, also the people whose edification is mentioned in 2:22 are built up ἐν πνεύματι. As far as the categories of people who serve the building up of the soma is concerned (4:11, 12). they are in essence and relevance totally determined in terms of the pneumatical gifts.[4]

The reason that the author, who regards the pneuma as the consituent

---

[1] We are in agreement with Hanson, op. cit., p. 51, who thinks that the enumeration of concepts, all characterised by the number one, although possessed of features resembling an acclamation, is rhetorical in character: "It is argumentative, didactic, parenetic. In other words, it is a diatribe, not an acclamation".

[2] Abboth, Eph.-Col., p. 107; Haupt, Der Brief an die Epheser, p. 29; Hanson, op. cit., p. 152; F.W. Grosheide, De Brief van Paulus aan de Efeziërs (Kampen 1960), p. 63; Meuzelaar, op. cit., pp. 56 and 170 and Schlier, Eph., p. 186.

[3] Haupt, l.c.: "die Vorstellung des Einheitlichen Organismus" (the conception of the single organism). See also Meuzelaar, op. cit., p. 170. Grosheide is unclear with regard to ἓν πνεῦμα as an organism (Grosheide, l.c.).

[4] On the other hand, the state of being truly σῶμα, of close cooperation and community between the faithful, is again the condition for maximum fulfilment with the pneumatical gifts. See above, p. 240s.

factor of the organism of the ecclesia, nevertheless places the words
ἓν σῶμα first and gives priority to the concept of σῶμα, must be attributed to the fact that in dealing with the words ἓν σῶμα he is at the
same time thinking back to the crucified body of which he spoke in 2:16.

Indeed, what other explanation could there be? In 2:16, he has described that body which was crucified in precisely the same words,
ἓν σῶμα. Moreover, this crucified body, quote logically, precedes the
pneuma that constitutes the body of the ecclesia. By virtue of the fact
that they are connected with the body which was killed on the cross,
the faithful have been endowed with pneumatical gifts. Eph. 1 affirms
this; the ἐν ᾧ ἔχομεν τὴν ἀπολύτρωσιν διὰ τοῦ αἵματος αὐτοῦ of
1:7 precedes the ἐν ᾧ καὶ ... ἐσφραγίσθητε τῷ πνεύματι τῆς ἐπαγγελίας τῷ ἁγίῳ of 1:13.

When discussing the ἓν σῶμα of 2:16, Schlier speaks of a "Doppeldeutigkeit" (ambiguity) which is reflected in the opinions of exegetes
who have traditionally divided on the matter. In 2:16, the ἓν σῶμα is
the body of the crucified. Yet a number of exegetes thought it referred
to the body of the ecclesia and, in the opinion of Schlier, not unjustifi-
ably so since the ambiguity is a real and not apparent one.[1]

Thus we find two varieties of soma in Eph : the soma which is the
ecclesia (a combination of closely coordinated members or parts) and
the body which was suspended on the cross. Now it could be that,
in the mind of the author, the two concepts become mingled. For him,
the word "soma" had a dual meaning. When speaking of the body
of the crucified Christ in 2:16, he is thinking of the body that is the
ecclesia. If, on the other hand, he is concerned with the body that is
the ecclesia, he is again thinking of the body on the cross.

Our impression was that it was normal for the author to think of the
faithful as members of each other(ἀλλήλων μέλη 4:25) and to speak of
the members of a body (μέλη τοῦ σώματος αὐτοῦ 5:30). We have already touched on this, above (p. 298). In any event, he did not take the
term μέλος as a designation for the faithful man from the metaphor
in 4:16; for there he chose to use the synonym μέρος.

The ease with which the author uses the unusual adjective σύσσωμος,
in the sense of "also belonging to the σῶμα"[2] (3:6) again suggests that
he was quite accustomed to the word "soma" as a metaphoric designation for a certain community.

---

[1] Schlier, Eph., p. 135.

[2] For the rarity of the word σύσσωμος, see Schweizer, Th. W. VII, p. 1078 and
note 514. For the meaning of the word, see Bauer, Wörterbuch z. N.T., s.v.

We therefore find ourself supporting Meuzelaar's theory [1] that it is possible that the conception of all the faithful as a single body and the designation for the faithful as members ($\mu\epsilon\lambda\eta$) as used in this epistle, is based on Hellenistic Jewish idiomatic language. It is our view that the author, when he calls the ccelesia a body, is ruled by a Hellenistic Jewish tradition where-by the nation of Israel is compared to a body. For we also find this analogy in Philo.[2] Probably, this comparison was so often applied to Israel in Hellenistic Judaism that it gradually was taken into rabbinical Judaism.[3]

The frequency of this analogy as applied to Israel may have been one of the reasons which led the syncretical Hellensistic Jews to associate the conception of the scattered members with the idea of the gathering together of a scattered Israel.[4]

The assumption that the author, in calling the ecclesia "soma", was conforming to a Hellenistic Jewish practice of comparing Israel with a soma gains in strength when we note that in 2:12 he supposes that the converted pagans will in the future partake in Israel's privileged position.[5] It would seem that he more or less identifies the ecclesia with Israel.

Another idea which would follow the trend of a Hellenistic Jewish tradition is the idea that the faithful who have been converted from paganism, are $\sigma\acute{v}\sigma\sigma\omega\mu o\iota$ (i.e. also part of the body). As a matter of fact, we find that Philo expresses the idea that Jews and proselytes form a single unit which he then compares with an organism or a body.[6]

---

[1] Op. cit., p. 66.

[2] Philo, De specialibus legibus, 131 : "The activity of the highpriest is so directed that people of all ages and from all part of the nation, as if belonging to a single body, are gathered together into one and the same community and strive for peace and obedience through the law.".

[3] Rabbinical Judaism also compared Israel to a body. A rabbinical utterance, probably dating from the second century, states that the nation of Israel is a single body and a single soul. This declaration is ascribed to rabbi Simon ben Jochai (cf. Hanson, The Unity of the Church, p. 146. note 1).

[4] See the quotation from the "Unbekannte altgnostische Werk" on p. 297 and the comments on that page.

[5] For exegesis of Eph. 2:12, see Strathmann, Th. W. VI, p. 534s.

[6] De virtutibus 103 : "The law-giver orders the people to love the proselytes ... so that in the divided parts a single living being appears to be encompassed, since common feeling unites and, as it were, makes them grow towards one another". Purely for purposes of style, this pronouncement uses $\dot{\epsilon}\nu$ $\zeta\tilde{\omega}ov$ instead of $\dot{\epsilon}\nu$ $\sigma\tilde{\omega}\mu\alpha$ (cf. the article by Knox mentioned above, p. 271 n. 5 and also Meuzelaar, op. cit., p. 66 and note 2).

However, the case is not that the author merely followed the Jewish tradition of comparing Israel to an organism and then simply applied this to the ecclesia. He has his own and original thoughts. The metaphor of the body and the members is not just a useful metaphor for explaining a certain aspect of the ecclesia; for the author it expresses the essence of the ecclesia. In the eyes of the writer of Eph., the ecclesia is a body with many limbs which, if it did not earnestly desire to be soma, would betray the grace-given truth and its God-given estate. Similarly, the individual believers would also betray the truth and their God-given state if they refused to be closely cooperating μέλη or μέρη.

Other new aspects are the special relationship of this soma of the ecclesia with the soma of Christ, which was killed on the Cross, and the total bond of this soma of the ecclesia with Christ. The special relationship with the crucified body is evinced by the fact that the author can, as it were, embrace both somata at a single glace. We saw before that the author, when in 2:16 and 4:5 he is discussing each of the somata, is at the same time thinking of the other.

This absolute bond between the soma of the ecclesia and Christ is evinced by the words ἐξ οὗ with which the comparison in 4:16 is introduced, by the genitives which follow the designation σῶμα in 1:23, 4:12 and 5:30 and by the predicate σωτὴρ τοῦ σώματος that is applied to Christ in 5:30.

Instead of a bond with Christ, one might even speak of an indentification with Christ. Although the ecclesia is not in a position to equate itself with Christ, Christ, in his love for it, places it in a position equal to himself.

This is made clear when in 5:22-33 the relationship between man and woman is placed against the background of the relationship between Christ and the ecclesia. 5:29 states that Christ nourishes and cherishes the ecclesia. In contemplating this, one may think of the sustaining love which Christ bears the ecclesia in the present.[1]

---

[1] The ἀγαπᾶν in Eph. 5.25ss. of which Christ is the subject encompasses the past and the present. Insofar as this ἀγαπᾶν expresses itself in the ἑαυτὸν παρέδωκεν (5:25) it is bound by the fact of Christ's death. Inasfar as the ἀγαπᾶν is concerned with the purpose of this death, i.e. the αὐτὴν ἁγιάσῃ (scil. τὴν ἐκκλησίαν) and παραστήσῃ ... ἔνδοξον τὴν ἐκκλησίαν (5:26,27) it manifests it self in the present. For that reason the abbreviated subordinate clause καθὼς καὶ ὁ Χριστὸς τὴν ἐκκλησίαν may be augmented by the words τρέφει καὶ θάλπει from the preceding principal sentence and it is unnecessary to transpose these forms into forms of the aorist and to think of a completed or accomplished act.

Christ devotes his care to the ecclesia because the faithful are members of his body (ὅτι μέλη ἐσμεν τοῦ σώματος αὐτοῦ 5:30). This
caring love of the present is linked with Christ's surrender of himself
which took place in the past through his death (5:25). Through this
surrender he has made the ecclesia into his body and the faithful
have become members of his body.[1] When Christ gave himself for
the ecclesia, he and the ecclesia became εἰς σάρκα μίαν (5:31, 32).
As a result of that, Christ has become kephale of the ecclesia and the
ecclesia which is soma, has become the soma of Christ. Thus when
Christ nourishes and cherishes the community, he is nourishing and
cherishing his own body and his own flesh.

For the ecclesia to be the soma of Christ means that it is saved.
The head of the ecclesia is the saviour of the body (5:23). By his death
the ecclesia does not only become his body, but is also saved.[2] He
died so that he might make her sanctified (ἀγία) and glorious (ἔνδοξος)
as is said in 5:26s.

His humiliation was followed by his exaltation. Now, he is the
heavenly ruler.[3] And the ecclesia, because she is his body, shares in
his glory. His resurrection is her resurrection and his exaltation is her
exaltation (2:6). God has blessed her in Christ in heavenly places with
all spiritual blessings (1:3). On each of the faithful Christ has bestowed
the grace that is the pneumatical gift (4:7). From Christ the body
draws the strength to grow (4:16). Thus—although not expressed in
so many words—the state of being εἰς σάρκα μίαν which became a
reality with the death of Christ, develops into a state of being εἰς ἕν
πνεῦμα.[4]

---

[1] This could be expressed more succinctly : by delivering up his body, Christ has
made the ecclesia his body. This idea is not encountered expressis verbis in Eph. 5:25ss.;
however, it could be implicit. The words ἑαυτὸν παρέδωκεν in 5:25 could equally well
have been : τὸ σῶμα αὐτοῦ παρέδωκεν. In Greek, the reflexive form and σῶμα are interchangeable (see p. 293) and one of the meanings of the Aramaic word for body—as we
saw on p. 294—is "self". We believe that the Greek of Eph. has been somewhat influenced
by Aramaic (cf. p. 188). One of the reasons why the author does not put the assiciations
of the word ἑαυτόν with τὸ σῶμα αὐτοῦ could be that for him the words ἑαυτὸν παρέδωκεν
formed an established formula (cf. Romaniuk, "L'origine des formules pauliniennes
"Le Christ s'est livré pour nous", "Le Christ nous a aimés et s'est livré pour nous" in
Novum Testamentum V, 1962, p. 55ss.)

[2] See p. 290 and note 1.

[3] Cf. p. 289s.

[4] Taking into consideration how the author of 1 C. 15:45 deduces from the ἐγένετο ὁ
πρῶτος ἄνθρωπος Ἀδὰμ εἰς ψυχὴν ζῶσαν of Gen. 2:7 that the last Adam was made a

On the part of the ecclesia, this being $\epsilon is\ \dot{\epsilon}v\ \pi v \epsilon \hat{v} \mu a$ is realized through obedience (5:24) and growing towards Him who is kephale (4:15).

This close relationship between Christ and the ecclesia, which the author derives from Gen. 2:24, he transforms into a paradigm for marriage. Although his ideas on marriage may, in fact, have affected his view on the relationship between Christ and the ecclesia, he does not in principle explain the Christ-ecclesia relationship on the basis of the marriage pattern; on the contrary, the reverse is true and he frames his ethical directives for marriage by analogy with the relationship between Christ and the ecclesia.

A very important factor which comes into play in the love which Christ bears the ecclesia, is the sacrament of baptism, mentioned in 5:26. As is made clear by the $\dot{\epsilon}v\ \beta \acute{a}\pi \tau \iota \sigma \mu a$ of 4:5, the author recognises but one baptism and that is the baptism in which all the faithful partake. And, because there is but one baptism and because the ecclesia is a unity ($\dot{\epsilon}v\ \sigma \hat{\omega} \mu a$), he can, in 5:26, speak of baptism as a single event that embraces the entire ecclesia.

Baptism is described as a sanctifying or cleansing act of Christ. But it also has a positively active function; it is, after all, the purpose of Christ's death that the ecclesia should become not merely spotless, without wrinkle and without blemish, but also glorious and holy. In 5:26s., the negative aspect of baptism is inseparable from the positive. The words $\dot{a}\gamma \acute{\iota}a$ and $\ddot{a}\mu \omega \mu os$ are mentioned in one breath. Christ's act of cleansing, of which baptism is the embodiment, is indissoluble from that activity which makes the ecclesia holy and glorious. Thus the words $\dot{a}\gamma \iota \acute{a}\sigma \eta$ and $\kappa a\theta a\rho \acute{\iota}\sigma as$ are linked most closely in 5:26.

We may picture this as follows : through the sacrament of baptism, Christ bestows part of his death and the cleansing of the ecclesia, which is what he intended by his death and moreover gives the glory and sanctity to the ecclesia which was also the purpose of his death. There is but one baptism for the whole ecclesia which is a unity. Each believer who undergoes baptism partakes both in the baptism of Christ, the cleansing of the ecclesia and the sanctification and glorification of the ecclesia. He is part of the unity ($\mu \acute{\epsilon}\lambda os\ \tau o\hat{v}\ \sigma \acute{\omega} \mu a\tau os$) and partakes in the cleansing and holiness of it all.

---

life-giving spirit ($\acute{o}\ \ddot{\epsilon}\sigma \chi a\tau os\ \text{'}A\delta a\mu\ \epsilon is\ \pi v \epsilon \hat{v} \mu a\ \zeta \omega o\pi o\iota o\hat{v}v$), it would not be going too far to assume that the author of Eph., who sees Christ in the Adam of Gen. 2:24 and the ecclesia in the woman, similarly deduces from the $\epsilon is\ \sigma \acute{a}\rho \kappa a\ \mu \acute{\iota}av$ that Christ and the ecclesia are $\epsilon is\ \dot{\epsilon}v\ \pi v \epsilon \hat{v} \mu a$.

In Col. the ecclesia is also soma. In this epistle, the individual believer is not designated as melos. However, the soma of the ecclesia is here compared to an organism (2:19). When ἐν σῶμα comes under discussion, it is solely the body of the ecclesia, which is a unity of many (3:15), that is intended. The ambiguity which surrounds the expression ἐν σῶμα in Eph., is not found here. The body of Christ which died on the Cross is distinguished as τὸ σῶμα τῆς σαρκὸς αὐτοῦ (1:22) from the ecclesia, which is τὸ σῶμα αὐτοῦ (1:24).

We find the same total bond of the soma of the ecclesia with Christ which we also found in Eph. (1:18, 24; 2:19). The difference is that the nature of this relationship is not described in as much detail as in Eph. Christ, who is κεφαλή over all cosmic powers (2:10), is in 1:18 also named simply κεφαλὴ τοῦ σώματος τῆς ἐκκλησίας.

This brevity makes it seem as if this kephale and this soma are together seen as a single organism; but this is not really the case. When Christ is designated "kephale", this is a Jewish-Hellenistic appellation' as we have already established (p. 292). It is only for the sake of a play on words that the whole ecclesia (the πάντες, of which this kephale is the head and the first) is referred to as soma. There are no implications concerning an organic connection between a head and a body; there is merely an association with this connection. This is the first time that the word occurs in Col. When the word is first used in Eph., a similar association is present, the word being made to correspond with the words τοὺς πόδας and κεφαλήν which come some distance before (p. 298). In Col. 2:19, where the ecclesia is compared to a developing body, there is once again a combination with the term "kephale"; nevertheless there is no idea of an organism formed by a head and a body. If that were the case, we would, like Meuzelaar, expect a relative feminine form after κεφαλή.[1]

Col. 1:24 vaguely reminds us of an idea found in Eph., namely that Christ has become one flesh with the ecclesia through his sorrows and death. To be precise, the text speaks of the suffering of Paul for the sake of the recipients of the epistle. Through this suffering, Paul, for the sake of the soma of Christ (the ecclesia), fills up that which was lacking in the afflictions of Christ. From this we may deduce that the writer sees Christ's suffering in the flesh as a suffering for the sake of his body (the ecclesia).

When we examine some of the thoughts expressed in the HP, we

---

[1] See op. cit., p. 122.

do discover a close relationship with the thoughts that are connected with the words "soma" and "melos" in Eph. For example, the idea that the faithful are ἕν σῶμα is encountered in 1 C. 10:17. In speaking of this one body, i.e. the faithful, the author is thinking of the crucified body. The faithful are a single body because they all partake in the one bread that was broken and shared at the Lord's Supper and which gives a share in the crucified body of Christ. And when, in 1 C. 11:29 he speaks of not discerning the body that was crucified, the strong implication of this is that he still has in mind the contempt for the ecclesia, to which he refers in 1 C. 11:22.[1] Therefore, it is clear that the ecclesia, which is soma, has the same special relationship with the soma of Christ, which was murdered on the Cross, as described in Eph.

The total bond of the soma of the ecclesia with Christ which is evident in Eph., is equally powerful in the HP. R. 12:5 provides clear grounds for this assertion. In 1 C. 12:12 it is expressed particularly strongly; the words οὕτως καὶ ὁ Χριστός link the one body (of many members) so closely with Christ that Christ is in effect identified with this body. As in Eph., one might speak of an identity between the soma of the ecclesia and Christ.[2]

Although the words "soma" and "melos" are not directly named, the HP nevertheless contains pronounced parallels to the idea, expressed in Eph., that Christ, by delivering himself up to death, has made the ecclesia his body. Indubitably present, is the idea that through Christ's surrender of himself, the faithful have become his own. Because the Son of God loved him and gave himself for him, Paul considers himself to belong to Christ (Gal. 2:20). Paul himself and the other believers do not belong to themselves but have been bought with a price (1 C. 6:10).

Becoming εἰς σάρκα μίαν in Eph. 5:31, corresponds with God sending his own Son in the likeness of sinful flesh in R. 8:3.

Whereas the relationship between Christ and the ecclesia forms a paradigm for marriage in Eph., R. 7:1-6 explains Christ's relationship with the faithful by analogy with the marriage law. In Eph. 5:32, the τὴν γυναῖκα from Gen. 2:24 is interpreted as τὴν ἐκκλησίαν. R. 7:1-6, on the other hand, draws a comparison between the faithful and a woman in terms of her position in marriage according to Mosaic law.

In the HP, the attachment of the faithful to Christ, which came

---

[1] J. de Zwaan, Paulus als geestelijk hervormer (Amsterdam 1932), p. 133, even holds that τὸ σῶμα in 1 C. 11:29 means nothing else but "the new community" i.e. the ecclesia.

[2] For this identity in 1 C. 12:12, see G. Sevenster, De Christologie van het N.T., p. 185.

about through his death, represents salvation. This salvation is a
form of death; the faithful partake in the death of Christ (2 C. 5:14).
Eph. does not say this in so many words but concedes the point in the
statement on putting aside the old man, which we shall presently
deal with on p. 327ss.

In the HP, the faithful have died by law (R. 7:4; Gal. 2:19), are dead
to sin (R. 6:11) and crucified for the world (Gal. 6:14). The fact that
the death of Christ has abolished the rule of the law for the faithful
is also stated in Eph. 2:15.

The salvation which is bestowed on the faithful because they have
been bound to Christ through his death, has a dual nature in the HP.
It is on the one hand a dying with Christ and, on the other, a living
with Christ (2 C. 5:15; R. 6:8). On this point too, similar thoughts are
evinced in the HP and in Eph. As in Eph. 1:19s. and 2:6s., the faithful
have a share in his resurrection (R. 8:11) and partake of his glory
(R. 8:30).

If the heavenly ruler in whose glory the ecclesia shares, is designated
κεφαλή (cf. 286s., 290, 305) in Eph., in R. 8:29 he is given the related
appellation πρωτότοκος ἐν πολλοῖς ἀδελφοῖς.[1] As in Eph., the participation in the resurrection and glorification of Christ which the faithful
have by grace of their bond with Christ through his death, implies
endownemt with the pneuma and the spiritual gifts (R. 8:2 and 11).

Whenever the pneuma and the pneumatical gifts come under discussion, all the faithful are by repetition characterised as a soma with
many members (R. 12:3-5; 1 C. 12:12, 13). When Christ died for the
faithful and became at one with them, they were σάρξ (R. 8:3; 7:5);
now they are μέλη of Christ. This being a melos of Christ concerns
their whole person. The believer is also a melos of Christ in terms of
being a soma. In contemplating his body, he may also be regarded
as a melos.

Even after the death of Christ, the believer is still sarx. The μέλη of
Christ may be made μέλη of a πόρνη, a believer and a πόρνη are then
εἰς σάρκα μίαν. However, the aim is to be ἐν πνεῦμα with the κύριος.
This is possible because the soma of a believer is the temple of the hagion
pneuma (1 C. 6:15-20). The true substance of the soma which embraces
all the faithful, is also pneumatical in nature. Despite the fact that
the faithful, and thus also the soma, were sarx when Christ, in dying,
bound himself to them and to the soma, and despite the fact that the

---

[1] Cf. p. 292.

category "sarx" still applies to them, the constituent factor in the soma is the single pneuma and the μέλη are only μέλη by virtue of the pneumatical gifts. 1 C. 12:12, 13 and R. 12:3-6 are unequivocal in this respect. Most certainly, the true substance of μέλη and σῶμα is a pneumatical one.

We are here concerned with exactly the same thoughts as we encountered in Eph. (p. 301s. and p. 305). A particularly salient feature is that the transition from the εἰς σάρκα μίαν to a εἰς ἓν πνεῦμα which we deduce in Eph. (p. 305s.) can also be traced in the HP. We again encounter this transition if we place the ἐν ὁμοιώματι σαρκὸς ἁμαρτίας of R. 8:3 beside the ἓν πνεῦμα of 1 C. 6:17 (which has the εἰς σάρκα μίαν as its backgound in a different way).

More evidence that the ideas connected with soma and melos also occur in the HP is found when the sacrament of baptism is discussed in the HP. In Eph., the author takes as his point of departure that there is but a single baptism for the entire ecclesia; he sees baptism as a single act of Christ which embraces the whole ecclesia which is ἓν σῶμα. The same idea, namely that there is but one baptism for all who believe, likewise forms the background for 1 C. 1:13. There is a strong consciousness that all who have been baptised form a unity (Gal. 3:28; 1 C. 1:13) or a ἓν σῶμα (1 C. 12:13). It is obvious that baptism constitutes a single act, enfolding all the ecclesia. A close connection exists between the event of all the Israelistes passing through the sea and that of baptism (1 C. 10:2).

In the same way as in Eph. 5:26 baptism expresses the love of Christ, who gave himself for the ecclesia, in 1 C. 1:13 it expresses the love of Christ who was crucified for the sake of the faithful.[1]

Furthermore, baptism in the HP has a similar negative and positive aspect as was found to be the case in Eph. (p. 306); it is a cleansing sacrament through Christ (ἀπελούσασθε 1 C. 6:11). To be baptised is to partake in Christ's death. (R. 6:31)

The negative aspect cannot be divorced from the positive. The ἀπελούσασθε of 1 C. 6:11 is immediately succeeded by ἡγιάσθητε. To take part in the death of Christ cannot be separated from a share in his resurrection (R. 6:5).

We have one more reflection to make on the subject of a comparison between Eph. and the HP with regard to the use of the term "soma".

---

[1] The answer to the question raised in 1 C. 1:13 must be answered as follows : Χριστὸς ἐσταυρώθη ὑπὲρ ἡμῶν καὶ εἰς τὸ ὄνομα Χριστοῦ ἐβαπτίσθημεν. The connection between the σταυρωθῆναι and the ἀγαπᾶν of Christ is clear form Gal. 2:19, 20.

The total bond connecting the soma of the ecclesia with Christ which we found expressed in both quarters, cannot be explained on the basis of one of Percy's recontructions : namely, that the ecclesia is no other soma but the soma which died on the cross and rose up again on the third day.[1] Hence, Percy deduces from Eph. 2:16 that with the crucifixion of Christ, both groups are encompassed by the crucified body. This exegesis was found to be unacceptable earlier on in the present work (p. 299).

In Percy's view, the same kind of thought is evinced by 1 C. 12:13 ; he interprets the words $\epsilon i s$ $\epsilon \nu$ $\sigma \hat{\omega} \mu a$ $\epsilon \beta a \pi \tau i \sigma \theta \eta \mu \epsilon \nu$ to mean that a candidate for baptism is genuinely incorporated in the body of Christ which died on the cross.[2]

Our opinion is that the adjunct introduced by $\epsilon i s$ with the verb $\beta a \pi \tau i \zeta \epsilon \iota \nu$ is not such a definite indication of locality but more an indication of the matter or person with which contact is established through the $\beta a \pi \tau i \zeta \epsilon \iota \nu$. This point is elucidated when 1 C. 10:2—by analogy with the $\epsilon i s$ $X \rho \iota \sigma \tau \grave{o} \nu$ $\beta a \pi \tau \iota \sigma \theta \hat{\eta} \nu a \iota$. (Gal. 3 : 24; R. 6 : 3) - speaks of a $\epsilon i s$ $M \omega \nu \sigma \hat{\eta} \nu$ $\beta a \pi \tau i \sigma a \sigma \theta a \iota$[3] In any event, the context of 1 C. 12:13 leaves no doubt but that the matter concerns not the crucified body but the ecclesia.[4]

Percy thinks that for Paul all men were already contained within the first progenitor, Adam, when he brought death upon his descendants. Therefore, precisely in the same way, all the believers were enclosed within their substitute, Christ, when he died and rose up from death.[5] The conclusion, thinks Percy, is that the body of the ecclesia is not other than the body of the crucified and risen Christ; it is identical with Christ himself.

We can find no corroboration for this interpretation in Eph. 2:16 and in 1 C. 12:13 which, in our mind, is not subtle enough. The conception of representation which Percy associates with this hypothesis seems to us more appropriate in connection with the ecclesia and Christ, since part of the conception of representation entails a unity between the representative and the represented. Whatever is inflicted on the representative is also done to those he represents.

---

[1] Der Leib Christi, p. 44.

[2] Op. cit., p. 13 and p. 28.

[3] See also Oepke, Th. W. I, p. 537 1.21ss.

[4] See also Hanson, The Unity of the Chruch is the N.T., p. 76.

[5] Op. cit., p. 38.

Within the close affiliation between the ecclesia and Christ as described in Eph. and the HP, the concept of personification also has a role.
A group can be personified as a person. There may also be an almost
imperceptible transition from group to person and visa versa. Furthermore, the same word can sometimes be construed as referring to a
person and sometimes to a group.[1]

We are in full agreement if such conceptions are comprehended under
the heading of "a corporative personality"; however, it is going too
far if this term in addition covers the conception that a group is
incorporated in the body of its representative and if this definition
of a corporative personality proposes to explain the close concurrence
between the soma of the ecclesia and Christ in Eph. and the HP.[2]

1 C. 15:22 and R. 5:12ss. bear witness to a bond between Adam and
all humanity. This bond exists because Adam is the progenitor of all
men and not because all men are comprised in Adam; that all men
die is attributable not to the fact that they are all incorporated in him
but to his action.

Of course it is possible that Paul thought that all men were incorporated in the body of Adam when he committed his sin—but if this
is indeed so, it is not indicated by the text. In 1 C. 15:22, all die $\dot{\epsilon}\nu\ \tau\hat{\omega}$
'Αδάμ. This $\dot{\epsilon}\nu\ \tau\hat{\omega}$ 'Αδάμ must not be purely understood as an adverbial adjunct of locality.

The fact is that a certain vagueness is inherent in the Koine
preposition $\dot{\epsilon}\nu$. J. H. Moulton described this preposition as "a
maid-of-all-work".[3] As far as the preposition $\dot{\epsilon}\nu$ followed by an indication of person is concerned, A. Oepke is not able to say more than that
in general $\dot{\epsilon}\nu$ is used "zur Bezeichnung der engen Zusammengehörigkeit
eines Besitzes, einer Eigenschaft oder eines Vorgangs mit der betr.

---

[1] Personification is found in the O.T. when Israel is presented as Jeshurun or
God's son (Deut. 32:15; 33:5; Is. 44:2 or Hos. 11:1). We are confronted by an imperceptible transition from group to person and vice versa when the "Son of man" of Dan. 7:13, 14
turns out, in Dan. 7:18, to be a nation and when the "servant of the Lord" in Is. 41-53
sometimes clearly means a collective noun whereas at other times it is strongly described
in terms of an individual (cf. Cullmann, Die Christologie des N.T., p. 53 and O. Eisfeldt,
Einleitung i.d. A.T., Tübingen 1934, p. 381s.). Thus the $\tau\grave{o}\ \sigma\pi\acute{\epsilon}\rho\mu\alpha$ of Abraham in R.
4:13, 16 and Gal. 3:19 is also a unit of (two groups of) people, whilst in Gal. 3:16 it applies
to a single person. I. J. du Plessis is quite correct to speak of interaction. (See Christus
als hoof van kerk en kosmos, p. 25. In a footnote he quotes the term "oscillation" used
by A. R. Johnson.)

[2] See also p. 322.

[3] See N. Turner, Grammatical insights into the N.T. (Edinburgh 1965), p. 155.

Person".[1] In Blass-Debrunner, the following observation may be read : "Äuszerst unbestimmeter Deutung ist auch das ἐν Χριστῷ (κυρίῳ)...".[2]

When the preposition is partly used in its local sense in the sentence ὥσπερ γὰρ ἐν τῷ Ἀδὰμ πάντες ἀποθνῄσκουσιν, it is important to remember that the adverbial adjunct belongs to the verb. The preposition does not primarily indicate the locality of all men but only relates the dying of all men to a particular place.

To us it seems as if the intention is not so much to assert that the death of all men occurs in Adam but that the preposition is merely used to indicate the place where their death first assumed the proportions of an inevitable fact.

Just as in 1 C. 15:22 and R. 5:12ss. a bond is described between Adam and all men, there is also a bond between Christ and the faithful. The interrelationship between Christ and the faithful cannot be based on the idea that all the faithful are contained in Christ.

It is possible that Paul did have the conception that all the faithful are incorporated in Christ. However, this has by no means been proved. And even if he really did have this conception in mind, there must have been yet a deeper explanation for the bond between the faithful and Christ. Although incorporation in the body of Christ could constitute an aspect of this bond, it is not the reason for it.

As far as Adam is concerned, the reason for his bond with all men lies in the fact that he is their progenitor. The bond between Christ and the faithful may be compared to that bond but requires another explanation. What then, is this explanation, we may ask.

To make the bald statement that Christ is here envisaged as the progenitor of the faithful would be a violation of the text. But how otherwise should the mutual dependence between Christ and the faithful be explained ? In the first place, it may find elucidation through the eschatological conception framed by A. Schweitzer : "die der vorherbestimmten Zusammenhörigkeit der zum messianischen Reich Erwählten untereinander und mit der Messias ...".[3]

As far as this "vorbestimmte Zusammenhörigkeit" (predestined

---

[1] Th. W. II, p. 535 1.27ss. (Trans. : 1 "to describe affiliation of a property ,a quality or an occurrence with respect to the person in question". 2 "a highly ambiguous indication is also found in the ἐν Χριστῷ (κυρίῳ) ...".

[2] Bl.-Debr., p. 141 para. 219,4.

[3] Die Mystik des Apostels Paulus, p. 102.(Trans. : "the predestined inter-belonging which exists amongst those elected to the messianic kingdom themselves and between them and the Messiah ...")

mutual belonging) is concerned, this finds realization through the death
of Christ on the cross; for it is through this death on the cross that the
faithful become the possession and "$\gamma\upsilon\nu\dot{\eta}$" of Christ. We can see this
in R. Through the body that was crucified on the cross— $\delta\iota\dot{\alpha}$ $\tau o\hat{\upsilon}$
$\sigma\dot{\omega}\mu\alpha\tau o\varsigma$ $X\rho\iota\sigma\tau o\hat{\upsilon}$ [1]—they have been (made) dead to the law and can
become the property and "$\gamma\upsilon\nu\dot{\eta}$" of Christ (R. 7:4). It is frequently made
clear that Paul regards the faithful as the possession of Christ. (Cf. for
this the $o\hat{\upsilon}\tau o\varsigma$ $o\dot{\upsilon}\kappa$ $\ddot{\epsilon}\sigma\tau\iota\nu$ $\alpha\dot{\upsilon}\tau o\hat{\upsilon}$ of R. 8:9, the $o\dot{\iota}$ $\tau o\hat{\upsilon}$ $X\rho\iota\sigma\tau o\hat{\upsilon}$ of 1 C.
15:23 and the $\epsilon\dot{\iota}$ $\delta\dot{\epsilon}$ $\dot{\upsilon}\mu\epsilon\hat{\iota}\varsigma$ $X\rho\iota\sigma\tau o\hat{\upsilon}$ of Gal. 3:19.) They, as we saw on
p. 308, have been bougth with the price of his death. In Eph., it is
equally apparent from 5:25 and 5:31, 32, how the ecclesia was affiliated
to Christ through his death as his "$\gamma\upsilon\nu\dot{\eta}$" (p. 243).

Both R. 8:29, 30 and Eph. 1:4 put into words how this mutual belonging on the part of Christ and the faithful is rooted in God's counsel
and his predestined purpose. It is on account of this "vorbestimmte"
(predestined) and in time, realized "Zusammenhörigkeit" (mutual
belonging) that Christ and the faithful are bound to one another.
The conception of an assimilation into Christ occurs neither in the
HP nor in Eph.

We must therefore not assume that it is the locality of the faithful
which is being determined when Eph. so frequently refers to things
which happen "$\dot{\epsilon}\nu$ $X\rho\iota\sigma\tau\hat{\omega}$" to the faithful (Eph. 1:3; 2:6; 2:13).
Whenever the preposition $\dot{\epsilon}\nu$ assumes its local sense in the sentences
in question, the event is defined in local terms; i.e. in that case it is
stated that Christ is the place where a certain event has taken place
or where a certain event has become an irrevocable fact. It that case,
the $\dot{\epsilon}\nu$ $X\rho\iota\sigma\tau\hat{\omega}$ expresses no more than the $\dot{\epsilon}\nu$ $\tau\hat{\omega}$ $'A\delta\alpha\mu$ and the
analogous $\dot{\epsilon}\nu$ $\tau\hat{\omega}$ $X\rho\iota\sigma\tau\hat{\omega}$ of 1 C. 15:22.[2]

Finally, we would like to turn our attention towards the fact that the
growth and building or increase of the soma of the ecclesia is treated
in Eph. (4:12, 16). A discussion of the growth of the body is in
keeping with a teleological theme that is encountered from time to
time in the HP and in Eph. In these works the reader senses a longing to
achieve a state of ripeness in understanding and ripeness in a moral
aspect, a total uninamity with the will of God and a true state of
freedom. This is what the apostle Paul desires for himself and to which

---

[1] If Percy's construction of the assimilation of the faithful into the body of Christ
were as decisive as he believes, the text should have read : $\dot{\epsilon}\nu$ $\tau\hat{\omega}$ $\sigma\dot{\omega}\mu\alpha\tau\iota$ $X\rho\iota\sigma\tau o\hat{\upsilon}$.

[2] See above.

the faithful are exhorted. We are hereby, for instance, thinking of Phil. 3:12; 1 C. 14:20 and Gal. 4:19.

This longing for perfection is no individualistic asperation; the point of issue is not that the individual or as many single persons as possible should attain this perfection but that the faithful should together achieve the goal of their objective. Texts such as 2 C. 11:2; 1 Th. 2:19 and Eph. 4:13; 5:27 leave open no doubts in this respect.

To depict the progress of all the faithful towards this perfection, the author of Eph. employs side by side with the metaphor of the attainment to manhood (εἰς ἄνδρα τέλειον, εἰς μέτρον ἡλικίας) in 4:13, the metaphor of growth in 4:15, 16.

There is an association between the latter metaphor and the metaphor of planting which is found in Ps. 80:9, 16; Is. 60:21; 61:3. Ps. 80 draws the connection between the metaphor of planting and that of growth. After the planting of the vine that is Israel has been described in v. 9, verses 10-12 describe the wondrous growth of the vine which developed as a result of God's care. The image of planting the vine is coincidental with that of its growth. Subsequently, in v. 18, this first image is recapitulated and combined with a metaphor to illustrate the attainment to manhood. The vine, Israel, which was planted by God and which grew is, at the same time, the son who was reared by God.

By analogy, Eph. 4:13, 15, 16 combines the of image of coming to full stature (meaning the attainment to manhood and maturity) with that of growth.[1] Both metaphors, that of planting and that of growth, are found in the Jewish literature of the day.[2]

In 1 C. 3, the planting and growth metaphor is associated with that of child-rearing. The analogy with the bringing-up of children is found in 1 C. 3:1-4. Planting and growth are treated in 1 C. 3:6-9.

Besides dealing with the themes of maturation and growth, Eph. goes on to discuss the subject of building—and this in direct combination with the metaphor of growth. Thus "all that is built" in Eph. 2:21, grows. And after Eph. 4:12 has concentrated on the building of the body of the ecclesia, Eph. 4:16, by direct association, deals with the building and growth of the body of the eccleasia.

---

[1] For the combination νήπιος - ἀνὴρ τέλειος see the following section of this paragraph, p. 319ss.

[2] For the metaphor of planting and growth, see 1 QH 7,19 (cf. A.S. v.d. Woude, De Dankpsalmen, Amsterdam 1957, p. 44), For the child-rearing image, see H. Braun, Qumran und das N.T. I (Tübingen 1966), p. 218.

This combination of building and growth also shows an affinity with the O.T. in which the combined metaphors of planting and building are often found.[1] Moreover, the Qumran scrolls and the Odes of Solomon testify that this ancient O.T. metaphor of building and planting was to retain its significance for Judaism into far later times.[2]

In 1 C. 3:6-9, the metaphors of planting, growing and building are found togehter. The expression θεοῦ γεώργιον which is placed in direct sequence with the expression θεοῦ οἰκοδομή in 1 C. 3:9, recapitulates the planting and growth theme. Both expressions in this connection, refer to the entire corpus of all the faithful.

We therefore find that there is a strong degree of correspondence between Eph. 4:12-16 and 1 C. 3:1-9. In both we find a convergence of three traditional images, i.e. that of the increase in size of children, that of growth and that of building. As in the case of Eph., the metaphors of growth and of building are closely connected in these passages.

A striking feature is the fact that in Eph., the building of the ecclesia is discussed as though it concerned the building up of a body. Here, we are probably confronted with a traditional Jewish conception of an allegorical nature.

When terms relating to the building of people or the building of Israel are used in the O.T., this building always refers to the granting of lasting prosperity of happiness.[3] However, it may also apply to building in a more literal sense. In Jer. 31:4, the nation of Israel is addressed as a virgin. The following promise is made to this virgin : "Again I will build thee, and thou shalt be built, O virgin of Israel". Here we therefore have an example of building in both the literal and the metaphorical sense of the word.

The woman of which Gen. 2:21ss. speaks, evolves because God constructed her from a rib which He took from Adam. In this example, the fashioning or building of the woman is conceived as a construction in the realistic sense. The word as used in Gen. 2:22 tallies with the comparison between a woman and a building which is to some extent applied to the bride of the Song of Solomon (Cant. 7:4; 8:9, 10).

It is quite possible that in speaking of the building of the body of the ecclesia, the author of Eph. intends this building to mean the

---

[1] See Michel, Th. W. V, p. 139.

[2] See 1 QS 11,8 and 8,5s. In the Odes of Solomon 38,16, the laying of foundations and planting go together (cf. Hennecke II³, p. 169).

[3] See Jer. 42:10; Mal. 3:15; Ps. 28:5 and cf. Dupont, Gnosis, p. 242.

granting of lasting prosperity for the church, at the same time having in mind the analogy between a woman and a building.

After all, in Eph. 4:15, Christ is called "kephale". This same word is also applied to the man who is a husband (1 C. 11:3; Eph. 5:23). Now we find in Eph. 5:23, as in Eph. 4:15, 16, the designation "kephale" for Christ and "soma" for the ecclesia. Moreover, the word "gune" from Gen. 2:24 is declared to be of application to the ecclesia in the context of Eph. 4:23.

Therefore there is a possibility that in Eph. 4:16 the ecclesia is also envisaged as the gune from Gen. 2:24 of whom it is stated in Gen.: 2:22 that God made her and that this image of the gune conjoined in the mind of the author with the image of the bride as a building in the Song of Solomon.

Throughout the first century, Jewish exegetes were preoccupied with allegorical speculations on the Song of Solomon.[1] Similar reflections on the wife of the first man were probably also current. We have already observed that intense speculations concerning the first man were current around the beginning of our era (p. 268). Later Gnostic data give the impression that the wife of the first man was equally an object of speculation.[2]

A plausible theory would be that this Jewish field of concentration surrounding the wife of the first man aquired certain features from an allegorical exegesis of passages in the Song of Solomon in which the bride is compared to a building. We see the same development with respect to wisdom; in Hellenistic Judaism, much reflection was given to the subject of wisdom and wisdom was conceived in the shape of a bride.[3]

In a hymn to wisdom which has been preserved in the Acts of Thomas, there is a passage which bears a Jewish complexion. Wisdom,

---

[1] See, Joach. Jeremias in Th. W. IV, p. 1095 1.1ss. and note 28.

[2] In one of the Coptic Gnostic manuscripts found at Nag-Hammadi, "The Hypostasis of the archons" we find a doctrine based on Gen. 1:26 and 2:7 concerning the creation of man. The same manuscript also mentions a spiritual female figure, the mother of the living (cf. Gen. 3:20) who is the image of Adam. For these pronouncements, see : Schenke, Der Gott "Mensch" in der Gnosis, p. 61 and 62. Probably, Jewish heretical speculations on the first man, Adam, and his wife, Eve, were partly responsible for providing a source for the gnostic doctrinal tendency of this work.

[3] For these speculations in Hellenistic Judaism, see : U. Wilckens, Th. W. VII, p. 498ss. From Quispels's investigations, we deduce that these speculations continued into Gnosticism. For example, see his article "Gnosticism and the New Testament" in Vigiliae Christianae 19 (1965), p. 74-77.

who is hailed as a bride in this hymn, is compared to a building in
this passage in a fashion highly reminiscent of the Song of Solomon.[1]
It is thus possible that in speculating on the wife of the first man, this
woman, in imitation of the Song of Solomon, may have been evisaged
as a bride and compared to a building.

We are persuaded that in his symbolical explanation of Gen. 2:24,
the author of Eph. who sees the wife of the first man as the ecclesia
and describes this ecclesia as a body which is being built in Eph. 4:12,
16, merely avails himself of images which had already previously been
used in allegorical exegeses of Gen. 2:24 and were partly derived from
the Song of Solomon. The emphatic ἐγὼ δὲ λέγω in Eph. 5:32 furthermore leads us to observe that in his allegorical exegesis of Gen.
2:24, the author comes to different conclusions from the exegetes who
preceded him.

His ideas are distinguished from others of his time and later, by
their sobriety. The comparison to a building is not depicted in flowery
terms and the woman or bride is not acclaimed.[2] The image of the
woman or bride as an edifice is applied to the image of the ecclesia
as a soma with a clear matter of factness. For a Jewish Hellenist of the
first century, it was not difficult to expound on the body as a building.[3]

One further has the impression that the speculations of Hellenistic
Judaism, rooted in allegorical exegesis, were more than a compendium

---

[1] Acta Thomae ˊ6 (p. 280). See Hennecke II³, p. 311. In this hymn, the virgin is
a place of rest for the king. This in itself already suggests a building. Subsequently, when
the neck of the virgin is likened to a stairway, we are forcibly reminced of Cant. 4:4 and 7:4.
The passage has a Jewish character. God is described as the first master builder of the
world; certain rabbinical sources speak of God as the master builder of the world;
cf. Michel, Th. W. V, p. 139. For the treatment of wisdom in the Acta Thomae, see also
Wilckens, op. cit., p. 513.

[2] We find speculations dating from a later period in the hymn mentioned in note 1
and in Herm. s.9 in which the πύργος whose edification is so closely described, is depicted
as a woman and bride. The motif of the maidens who surround her is part of the metaphor
of the bride and marriage; cf. Ps. 45;15: Cant. 2:2,7; 5:8, 16 and Acta Thomae 7 (p. 110;
Hennecke II³, p. 311). We may assume that the poetical character and extensiveness
of the speculations in Acta Thomae 6 and Herm. s.9 are traditional and within the
framework of the first century.

[3] The Greek word σῶμα has many meaning (see above p. 293s.). Due to this ambiguity,
it lends itself more easily to the metaphor of building than our word, body. The Hebrew
word for build (בָּנָה) also has an ambiguity which makes for an easier combination with
the image of a body (see above p. 316). In a metaphor, Philo uses the word οἰκοδομεῖν in
connection with the body : the rest of the body is built on the heart (Leg. all. 2,6, see

of ideas on wisdom and the conception of the bride in the Song of Solomon and on a similar fusion of the wife of the first man and the bride in the Song of Solomon; it seems that these speculations were also centred around a direct combination of the concept of wisdom and the wife of the first man.[1] In Eph. 3:10 we see a relationship between the ecclesia and wisdom. By means of the ecclesia, the manifold wisdom of God becomes known in "the heavenly" (ἐν τοῖς ἐπουρανίοις). In treating this theme the author, for whom the ecclesia is the wife in Gen. 2:24, may once more be drawing upon traditional material. If this is true, Eph. 3:10 echoes the connection between wisdom and the wife of the first man, which was devised by a Hellenistic Judaism entranched in allegory.

c. Ἀνὴρ τέλειος

Schlier believes that the words ἀνὴρ τέλειος in Eph. 4:13 refer to Christ. In his opinion, the verse in question does not embrace the

---

Michel, Th. W. V, p. 140). Van der Woude holds that in 1 QS4, 20ss. the body is referred to as "the edifice". See Tweemaandelijks bulletin der theologische radiocolleges (N.C. R.V.), 3e jg. nr. 3, mei 1961, p. 24.

[1] In the Coptic Gnostic work, "The Apocryphon of John" (which has come down to together with the work mentioned in n. 2 p. 317, "The Hypostasis etc."), the spirit, through which man has the power to move, is the force of the mother of the demiurge. This mother is wisdom or sophia (see Schenke, op. cit., pp. 35, 36 and 66). This work moreover mentions the Holy Spirit who is the mother of the living (see Schenke, op. cit., p. 62). This last designation once again reminds us of the designation for the wife of the first man which we find in Gen. 3:20. This gnostic affirmation leads us to think that the allegorically-rooted Hellenistic Jewish speculations concerning the wife of the first man and wisdom drew a direct connection between the two, giving them the common designation "the spirit". The spirit is also the motivating force which enables the newly-created man to move in "The Essence etc.". This is probably the same spirit which, somewhat later, was called the spiritual woman, the mother of the living and the image of Adam (see Schenke, op. cit., p. 61 and p. 62). The designation "spiritual woman" is reminiscent of wisdom as depicted in Hellenistic Judaism (see the theories of Wilckens mentioned in n. 3 p. 317). In the Wisdom of Solomon, wisdom is not only envisaged as a woman and bride (see the places quoted in Wilckens, 1. c., note 211) but also given the qualificatory epithet of spirit (πνεῦμα), see Sap. Sal. 7:7 and 22). Schenke is justified to assert (op. cit., p. 67) that the sophia is not an anthropogonic but a cosmogonic principle. However, this did not deter Hellenistic Judaism to combine speculations rooted in allegorical exegesis on wisdom with the wife of the first man. The logos is a cosmic principle. Nevertheless, Philo draws a concurrence between the logos and the first man, for him, logos and man stand confronted as οὐράνιος and γήϊνος ἄνθρωπος (see above, p. 270). Therefore, speculations on the first man and his wife left room for the in essence cosmic principle of the sophia. Sap. Sal. 10:1 speaks of the first man's concern for wisdom.

idea that the faithful must grow into a perfect man but that the faithful must draw near to Christ who is the head of the body. Only then will the faithful, who are the body, form the whole Christ together with him who is the head.[1]

In essence, Schlier sees a macro-anthropos conception behind Eph. 4:13. However, the perfect human being does sometimes occur within the macro-anthropos terminology. An example of this is found in one of the Nag-Hammadi manuscripts.[2] But the appellation perfect *man* is not excessively closely bound to this conception since it possesses a different bias and differentiates itself to an important degree from the designation perfect human being.

To Philo, who described the cosmos as a τελεώτατος ἄνθρωπος,[2] a ἀνὴρ τέλειος meant the man who was permeated with the rules of the Torah and lived according to its precepts.[3] In the Epistle of James, the ἀνὴρ τέλειος is presented as the antithesis of the ἀνὴρ δίψυχος (3:2 and 1:8). This man has no doubts, not only hears the words, but is also active for the law of freedom and stumble not even in speaking. For the Stoa, he who is a master in all moral accomplishment and

---

[1] Eph., p. 200-202.

[2] The macro-anthropos conception which Schlier applies to Eph. 4:13 is the conception in its later form as discussed on p. 284 of the present work. The same applies to the Nag-Hammadi manuscript in question. The manuscript, known as The Treatise on the Three Natures, contains the designation the perfect human being, which plays a part in the later form of the conception. See above, p. 282s. On the subject of this perfect human being, Zandee has the following observation : "The perfect human being is also known to the Jewish Gnostic movements. He represents the preexistent heavenly Adam according to whose prototype spiritual people must be patterned." (The Gospel of truth, p. 83). On one occasion, Philo describes the cosmos which he sees as the visible manifestation of the logos, as a great and perfect human being. (De migr. Abr. 220; cf. p. 270 and note 2 above.) In this case, the macro-anthropos conception does not come into play. The Ophites used the designation τέλειος ἄνθρωπος. In the so-called Sermon of the Naassenes, the τέλειος ἄνθρωπος is a macro-anthropos. (Actually, it speaks of great Oceanus who flows forth from his middle. In this connection, cf. the statements on the macro-anthropos quoted by Schlier in Th. W. III, p. 675 1s.41 and 47.) The τέλειος ἄνθρωπος of this document is also the ἄνω Ἀδάμας and, in addition, the individual salvandus who must ascend. See Hipp. Ref. V, 8, 20 and 21 and V, 7, 7 (Völker, Quellen zur Geschichte d. chr. Gnosis, p. 20 and 21). In an exposition on the Sethians, the logos whose example the salvandi must follow, is called τέλειος ἄνθρωπος (Hipp. Ref. V, 19, 18-22. Quotations found in Leisegang, Die Gnosis, p. 155 and Colpe, Die religiongesch. Schule, p. 184 and 185).

[3] Delling, Th. W. VIII, p. 72 line 26s. For the idea of perfection in Philo, see further P. J. du Plessis, Τέλειος, The Idea of Perfection in the N.T., p. 115ss.

"possesses all ἀρετάς", may be called τέλειος.[1] Both in classical philosophy and in Philo perfection has a certain intellectual aspect.[2]

In addition, the word τέλειος can also mean adult.[3] The word ἀνήρ in itself is already closely related to the idea of maturity. It occurs in this sense in a passage of the Sermon of the Naassenes in which both the macro-anthropos and the salvandus are described as τέλειος ἄνθρωπος. The condition for the rebirth of the salvandus here is to be mature, to be ἀνήρ. But a direct association between the concept of being ἀνήρ and the macro-anthropos conception cannot be deduced from this.[4]

Manichaean documents have a counterpart term for the whole expression ἀνὴρ τέλειος. For the Manichaeans, the perfect man is a figure who bears the world, fills all creation and provides an intermediate "port of call" for the soul of the salvandus, on its way to the kingdom of light. Colpe thinks that the Manichaean term has been derived from Eph. 4:13.[5] However, this later item of information does not help us to gain an understanding of the words ἀνὴρ τέλειος in Eph.

In order to gain this insight, we are in the first place forced to rely on the context which needs some other interpretations than that of Schlier. He draws a direct connection between the words καταντήσωμεν ... εἰς ἄνδρα τέλειον (4:13) and αὐξήσωμεν εἰς αὐτὸν τὰ πάντα, ὅς ἐστιν ἡ κεφαλή (4:15) from which he concludes that the ἀνὴρ τέλειος represents no other than Christ-kephale. However, he totally ignores the direct parallelism between the adjunct εἰς ἄνδρα τελειον and the adjunct εἰς τὴν ἑνότητα τῆς πίστεως καὶ τῆς ἐπιγνώσεως τοῦ υἱοῦ τοῦ θεοῦ which immediately precedes it. He interprets the word πλήρωμα 4 : 13 in a spatial sense and then, as if the adjunct εἰς τὴν ἑνότητα κ.τ.λ. were not there, goes on to apply the verb καταντᾶν to this πλήρωμα. Schlier assumes that the verb implies the spatial motion, i.e. the "durchschreiten" (traversing) of this πλήρωμα. He completely divorces the word ἡλικία from its connotation of age, assigning to it the meaning of "Grösze" (size).[6] Through this process, he arrives at the conception

---

[1] Delling, Th. W. VIII, p. 71 line 21.

[2] Cf. Delling, op. cit., p. 70 line 25ss. and line 41 and p. 71 line 29ss. For Philo, see also P. J. du Plessis, l.c.

[3] See p. 242s. and notes 1 and 2 on p. 243.

[4] Hipp. Ref. V, 8, 19-21 (Völker, op. cit., p. 19s.).

[5] For the perfect man in Manichean literature, see Käsemann, Leib und Leib Christi, p. 71 and Colpe, Die religiongesch. Schule, p. 103 and note 9.

[6] In the papyri, the word is generally used in the sense of age. It can also indicate the length of a body but does not simply mean "Grösze" (stature-size); cf. P. J. du Plessis, τέλειος, p. 189 and Liddell-Scott, s.v.

that the faithful, on their path towards Christ-kephale, "durch-schreiten" (traverse) the pleroma in its full measure (the measure of its size).[1]

We, on the other hand, think that the words εἰς ἄνδρα τέλειον, εἰς μέτρον ἡλικίας τοῦ πληρώματος τοῦ Χριστοῦ should be translated as : "to a perfect man, to the full measure of maturity which is the property of the pleroma of Christ". These words formulate a common aim which applies to the faithful communally and cannot be achieved by the individual.[2]

This aim has a number of facets. The facet of maturity is one of these. It is not only indicated by the words μέτρον ἡλικιάς and the word ἀνήρ; the word τέλειος also contributes in its description. In addition, the word τέλειος also means "perfect" which must be construed to mean a perfection in morals and in understanding. This maturity and this perfection in the moral sense and understanding are the antithesis of being νήπιος which goes side by side with moral inferiority and heresy.[3]

The common aim (εἰς ἄνδρα τέλειον κ.τ.λ.) is inseparably inter-twined with another aim which is formulated in the immediately preceding adjunct, εἰς τὴν ἑνότητα τῆς πίστεως καὶ τῆς ἐπιγνώσεως κ.τ.λ., i.e. one and the same faith with one and the same knowledge of the Son of God. When the aim described in the previous adjunct has been achieved, the aim expressed in the words εἰς ἄνδρα τέλειον κ.τ.λ. will also have been gained.

How are we to envisage the attaining of the last-mentioned goal ? Hanson speaks of "the Church, the Body of Christ ... attaining its complete size".[4] P.J. du Plessis similarly thinks that the church, as the body of Christ, must become a ἀνὴρ τέλειος.[5] However, it is not very likely that the ecclesia of Eph. 4:13, which is the γυνή of Gen. 2:24 in Eph. 5:31s., should be so unequivocally regarded as ἀνήρ of Eph. 4:13. It seems to us that Hanson is in this instance too liberal in applying the conception of the "corporate personality".

Granted that the ἀνὴρ τέλειος is not a goal that each of the faithful may achieve individually and that this may only be communally

---

[1] L.c.

[2] Cf. p. 243 with note 4 and p. 315 above.

[3] Mussner (op. cit., p. 61 n. 105) quotes an excellent parallel, from the works of Philo (De sobr. 9), to the ἀνὴρ τέλειος and νήπιος antithesis in Eph. 4: 13, 14.

[4] The Unity of the Church, p. 159.

[5] L.c.

achieved; it is, however, carrying exegesis too far when the words
μέχρι καταντήσωμεν οἱ πάντες ... εἰς ἄνδρα τέλειον are in fact translated as "until we all together ... become a single perfect man".

The three adjuncts belonging to the verb κατανταν, all introduced by
εἰς, are indicative of purpose. But this does not mean that καταντήσωμεν
means "to become". Each time, the matter concerns an aim that must
be realized. The ἀνὴρ τέλειος is also an objective which must be
attained communally.

Furthermore, it would be wise to remember that both the goal
of the single faith and the one knowledge which comes before the goal
of the perfect man, as well as the goal of maturity, are abstract in
nature. It might therefore be expected that the words ἀνὴρ τέλειος
also have an abstract meaning.

To support our argument that we are here concerned with abstrac-
tions, we postulate that the writer of the epistle in a Jewish Hellenist
and perhaps influenced by a Hebrew idiom which does not distinguish
sharply between the concrete and the abstract. A second argument
is that the abstract expressions ἡ ἀνδρεία and τὸ ἀνδρεῖον were less
suitable for indicating what the author intended, than the concrete
ἀνήρ which was more generally used to characterise man in a full stage
of development.[1]

We therefore propose that the words ἀνὴρ τέλειος indicate the state
of the perfect man. The attainment of this state entails that the faithful
are no longer νήπιοι. They must achieve this state together. Although
this does not mean that they must together become a single perfect
man but it does imply that all must be "perfect men". This transition
from being νήπιος to becomming ἀνήρ is simultaneous with building
up the body of Christ (4:12) and the growth of the whole (τὰ πάντα)
or the body towards Christ-kephale (4:15).

We may assume that the development of the faithful towards
being ἀνὴρ τέλειος is a matter of becoming like Christ and the image of

---

[1] For Hebrew idiom, see p. 337 n. 3 The substantive ἡ ἀνδρεία means manhood in
the sense of courage, power and endurance. (In a negative sense, it can mean brutality.)
The meaning "manly age", is rare. In the plural form, the word means courageous
deeds. The substantiated neuter τὸ ἀνδρεῖον is synonymous with ἡ ἀνδρεία in the sense
of manly courage. The plural τὰ ἀνδρεῖα is synonymous with αἱ ἀνδρεῖαι. See Liddell-
Scott, s.v. ἀνδρεία and ἀνδρεῖος and Bauer, Greichisch-Deutsches Wörterbuch, s.v.
ἀνδρεῖος. The substantive ἀνήρ indicates the man who has attained the age of a man and
who is distinguished from children, youths and old men. See Liddell-Scott, s.v. sub III
and Oepke, Th. W.I, p. 363 lines 8-11. See also p. 337 n. 3

Christ. Three combined factors support this assertion. Achieving the state of being a perfect man is the same thing as attainment of the knowledge of the Son of God (4:13). Reaching the state of being a perfect man goes side by side with the growth of the body of the ecclesia towards Christ-kephale. The Son of God or Christ-kephale, according to the author, is himself also indicated as ἀνήρ in Gen. 2:24.

By using more words, the author could have expressed the idea that the faithful must together become ἄνδρες τέλειοι more clearly than he does. In my opinion he has deliberately chosen this pregnant formulation in order to retain the idea that only through the faith and through knowledge of Christ the Son of God, who is the true ἀνὴρ τέλειος, can the faithful be ἄνδρες τέλειοι.

The fact that there were women amongst those faithful did not prompt him to express himself differently. We notice the same feature in the epistle to the Romans. When the subject concerns being like the Son of God, only the sons of God and the many brothers of the firstborn are mentioned (R. 8:19, 29).

A connection exists between Eph. 4:13 and Gal. 4:19. We have already commented on a common teleological motif (p. 315) in these passages. In both places the faithful are compared to children who must still undergo development. In Eph. 4 there are more people guiding this development. Amongst these are the apostles. Gal. 4 speaks only of the apostle Paul. He is worried about this development and experiences again the travails of birth for the recipients of the epistle who have been instructed and won over to the faith by him and are therefore addressed as "his" children.

The goal of the desired development could be maturity in 1 C. 14:20 as well as in Eph. 4:13. Here, in Gal. 4, something is stated of which Eph. 4 contains only a hint. The point is that all the faithful, by virtue of their close bond with Christ, will begin to resemble him. He must find shape in them. This statement is in turn closely related to Eph. 3:17 in which, concerning the apostle Paul, the addressees are told of a prayer in which he pleads on their behalf that Christ may dwell in their hearts by faith.

If one considers, besides this, the νήπιος — ἀνήρ antithesis and the concurrence between being ἀνήρ, the coming of τὸ τέλειον and the perfect ἐπίγνωσις in 1 C. 13:10, it may be asserted that in the above-mentioned places Eph. displays a distinct affinity in thought-matter with the HP and is governed by the same associations as prevail in the HP.

In Col. 1:28, 29 a related idea in found. The text deals with the efforts of the apostle Paul on behalf of those in whom the gospel has found acceptance,[1] that each of them might be perfect in Christ. As in Eph. 4:13, the issue is that all the faithful may become perfect. The attainment of that perfection is also there declared to be only in Christ. In Col. 3:14 it is made quite clear that this perfection can and must only achieved in community.

d. Ἔσω ἄνθρωπος, παλαιὸς ἄνθρωπος and καινὸς ἄνδρωπος

The expression ὁ ἔσω ἄνθρωπος in Eph. 3:16 is a designation for the invisible inner part of man which can be strengthened through the hagion pneuma. Another expression for this inner spirituality is (ὁ νοῦς or) τὸ πνεῦμα τοῦ νοός to which 4:23 alludes.[2] Instead of strengthening the believer's inner self however, 4:23 talks of a renewal. Both instances concern an almost identical working of the hagion pneuma.

Already by the time of Plato a certain facet of man's innermost self could be expressed as it is here in 4:16.[3] Hellenistic Judaism which was familiar with the concept of an antithesis between the soul and the body [4] use corresponding terms and combined these with speculations on Gen. 1:26s. This is clear from the work of Philo [5] and can also

---

[1] The struggles and endeavours of the apostle are in this epistle directed at the eccle- sia in 1:24 and especially at the fiathful mentioned in 2:1.

[2] For the eegsexis of the dative τῷ πνεύματι τοῦ νοὸς ὑμῶν in 4:23, see Abbott, Eph.-Col. p. 137, Percy, Probleme, p. 196; Schlier, Eph., p. 220 and Schweizer, Th. W. VI, p. 443 note 773. In my view this is a dativus relationis and we are confromted with a combination through the genitive of two (synonymous or) related words in meaning. (Reitzenstein has deomnstrated, HMR, p. 337s., that the words πνεῦμα and νοῦς can be synonymous in Paul.)

[3] See Joach. Jeremias, Th. W.I, p. 366 line 17ss.

[4] See Käsemann, Leib und Leib Christi, p. 18.

[5] Philo, who envisages a relationship between his cosmic principle of the nous or logos and the nous or logos of man (see above, p. 270), develops the conception on the basis of Gen. 1:26 of the οὐράνιος ἄνθρωπος or the logos or nous who governs all creation (De conf. ling. 41, 62, 146, 148; Leg. all. 31; cf. Reitzenstein, HMR p. 347; Colpe, Zur Leib Christi Vorstellung, p. 181; Schenke, Der Gott "Mensch", p. 122ss. and Branden- burger, Adam und Christus, p. 122s.) and the conception of the anthropos who is like this logos, is more than individual, more than sexual and is the logos or nous of the individual man (De opf. mundi 69 and 72-75). To this nous who represents for him the essence of man, he assigns the designation of the true man or the man within the human being (see Jeremias, l.c. and cf. Schenke, op. cit., p. 122).

be construed from Hermetic literature,[1] a certain work by Zosimos,[2] the Sermon of the Naassenes [3] and the Apocryphon of John.[4]

In Philo and all the Gnostic and syncretical works mentioned above, we find the conception that the inner man must relinquish the body and ascend to a heavenly place or world where he rightly belongs by virtue of his association (resp. identification) with some divine principle such as the logos, the nous, the heavenly anthropos or the heavenly light.

We have not been able to ascertain that the term $\dot{o}$ $\ddot{\epsilon}\sigma\omega$ $\ddot{a}\nu\theta\rho\omega\pi os$ was used in the popular philosophy of the beginning of our era. We therefore surmise that the author of Eph. borrowed the designation from Hellenistic Judaism. Nothing he writes, however, suggests that he himself associated it with speculations on Gen. 1:26; his work provides no evidence that he believes the inner man to be qua talis connected with some divine principle.

With relation to or within [5] the inner man the believer is given strength by the pneuma (3:16). The dwelling of Christ in the hearts of the faithful goes together with this being strengthened through the pneuma (3:17). From the fact that those two statements stand combined, we may infer that the designation $\dot{o}$ $\ddot{\epsilon}\sigma\omega$ $\ddot{a}\nu\theta\rho\omega\pi os$ and the word $\dot{\eta}$ $\kappa a\rho\delta\dot{\iota}a$ can be used equally to describe the invisible innermost part of man. Neither Christ nor the pneuma can be regarded as identical

---

[1] In C.H. I para. 15, 18 and 21 $\dot{o}$ $o\dot{v}\sigma\iota\dot{\omega}\delta\eta s$ $\ddot{a}\nu\theta\rho\omega\pi os$ or $\dot{o}$ $\ddot{\epsilon}\nu\nu ovs$ $\ddot{a}\nu\theta\rho\omega\pi os$ who dwells in the empirical human, is essentially more than individual, androgynous and connected with and like the androgynous godhead Nous, is named. (See Jeremias, l.c.; Schenke, op. cit., p. 44-48 and Brandenburger, op. cit., p. 93-95.) In C.H. XIII para 7, $\dot{o}$ $\dot{\epsilon}\nu\delta\iota\dot{a}\theta\epsilon\tau os$ $\ddot{a}\nu\theta\rho\omega\pi os$, who is entrapped in the prison of the body, is related to and like the Logos, is mentioned. (See Reitzenstein, HMR p. 49 and Jeremias, l.c.)

[2] The manuscript by Zosimos which is quoted by Jeremias (l.c.); Schenke (op. cit., p. 52ss.) and Brandenburger (op. cit., p. 81-83), approximates closely to the first Hermetic tract which was evidently written under a Jewish influence. This work relates of a heavenly archetypal man who succumbs to the temptation of assuming an earthly body. The body is the $\gamma\dot{\eta}\iota\nu os$ or $\sigma\dot{a}\rho\kappa\iota\nu os$ 'A$\delta\dot{a}\mu$. The fallen anthropos, $\dot{o}$ $\ddot{\epsilon}\sigma\omega$ $\ddot{a}\nu\theta\rho\omega\pi os$, is confined in the jail which is Adam, who is $\dot{o}$ $\ddot{\epsilon}\xi\omega$ $\ddot{a}\nu\theta\rho\omega\pi os$.

[3] This also refers to a $\ddot{a}\nu\omega$ $\ddot{a}\nu\theta\rho\omega\pi os$ ('A$\delta\dot{a}\mu as$) who becomes $\dot{o}$ $\dot{\epsilon}\nu\tau a\sigma\sigma\dot{o}\mu\epsilon\nu os$ 'A$\delta\dot{a}\mu as$ or $\dot{o}$ $\ddot{\epsilon}\sigma\omega$ $\ddot{a}\nu\theta\rho\omega\pi os$ (Hipp. Ref. 7,6 and 7,36; cf. Völker, Quellen, p. 12 and p. 16 and Schenke, op. cit., p. 57s.).

[4] For this Apocryphon work see Hennecke I[3], p. 229ss. and Schenke, op. cit., p. 34-37. Here too, we find a man (spiritual man) who is incarcerated in a mortal body. See Hennecke, op. cit., p. 237 (middle of the page) and p. 229 (top of the page).

[5] The preposition $\epsilon\dot{\iota}s$ in 3:17 is used either to replace $\pi\rho\dot{o}s$ or $\dot{\epsilon}\nu$ (with the dative); cf. Bl.-Debr., para. 207,1 and 205.

or related to this inner man. The fact of the matter is that the faith is the specific preoccupation of this inner being, that the pneuma exerts an effect upon it and that it is in this field that the influence of Christ works. The thoughts which we find expressed in 3:16 as well as 4:23 correspond wholly in character to those of R. 10:10; 12:2; 2 C. 1:22; 4:6; Gal. 2:20; 4:6; Phil. 4:7 and Col. 3:11, 15.

The designation ὁ ἔσω ἄνθρωπος also occurs in the HP. One instance is in R. 7:22 where the word ὁ νοῦς is used to the same purpose. This text describes the inner man in his helplessness. From that which follows, it appears that this inner man needs the life-giving action of the pneuma (R. 8:11) As in Eph., it is again God who makes the pneuma work in the faithful. But the pneuma does not work on the strength of relating. It is a gift.

In R. this working of the pneuma is directly connected with the resurrection of Christ (8:11). When Eph. 3:16 and 1:19 are subjected to a comparison, it can be observed that there too, the strengthening power of the pneuma is associated with the resurrection. Eph. 3:16 speaks of the mighty strengthening power of the pneuma as a gift from God; Eph. 1:19 associates the exceeding greatness of the power of God on the believers with the raising of Christ from the dead.

We likewise encounter the designation ὁ ἔσω ἄνθρωπος in 2 C. 4:16. The designation ὁ ἔξω ἄνθρωπος is its conterpart here. 2 C. 4:16 yields as little evidence as R. 7:22 that the designation involves any speculation on Gen. 1:26 as far as the author is concerned. The context indicates that the renewal of the inner man should be attributed to the pneuma and that the renewing force of the pneuma is connected with the resurrection of Christ. Again, the pneuma does not work because of inner man's relationship with it but by virtue of God who bestows the pneuma (4:13, 14).

In Eph. 4:22 the designation ὁ παλαιὸς ἄνθρωπος occurs and in 4:24 the designation ὁ καινὸς ἄνθρωπος. These two designations in 4:22 and 24 are respectively connected with the infinitives ἀποθέσθαι and ἐνδύσασθαι, which suggest the discarding and donning of clothing or armour.

We now propose to examine the background to this reference to putting off the old man and putting on the new man.

When Aristotle gives an exposition of the Pythagorean doctrine of the transmigration of the soul, he speaks of the soul which puts on a body.[1]

---

[1] Aristotle, De anima, I, 3, p. 407, 623; cf. Oepke, Th. W. II, p. 319 line 40s.

The Book of Job associates the idea that man in his exterior appearance is a work of wonder fashioned by God with the notion of being clad.[1]

Philo compares the inner being of man with the logos and the human body with the cosmos. He speaks of the logos, which puts on the cosmos, and the soul of man which assumes the body.[2]

The seventh Hermetic tract quite explicitly talks of the body as a garment; it is a ἐχθρὸς χιτών and τὸ τῆς ἀγνωσίας ὕφασμα that have been donned.[3]

In the above-mentioned work by Zosimos, it is the inner man who puts on or assumes the body which is here called the outher man or the γήινος or σάρκινος Adam.[4]

In the afore-mentioned examples from Greek literature, we invariably find that the middle voice of the verb ἐνδύειν is used. The same verb also occurs in LXX Job. 10:11. However, in that particular instance, the active voice is used since the narrative relates that God has clothed man.

Besides the conception that man has put on his body as if it were a garment, we also meet the idea that this garment can be put aside. Although Philo may appreciate the body as a work of God and as a holy temple for the soul, his ideal is, nevertheless, that the soul or spirit of man should disengage itself from the influences of the body. Philo describes this liberation as stripping off the body.[5]

In Hermetic literature, conceptions are found which are affiliated to these trends of thought. An aspect which is missing there, is the positive appreciation of Philo for the body. The Hermetic ideal is that the mortal body is dissolved and surrendered to transformation until the visible form disappears. After that, on his way to the eighth region of heaven, the no longer physical human being can be liberated from the bad qualities which he has accumulated under the influence of the planets. Elsewhere, the tract teaches that man must tear off the garment that is the body.[6]

---

[1] Job. 10:11 (for the conception that the exterior appearance of man is a work of wonder wrought by God or an apparel made by his hands cf. Ps. 119:73 and 139:13, 15).

[2] See De opif. mundi 134 and De fuga et inventione para. 108-112 (see p. 271 n. 5).

[3] C.H. VII, 2.

[4] See Reitzenstein, Poimandres, p. 103 and Brandenburger, Adam und Christus, p. 81ss.

[5] See Käsemann, Leib und Leib Christi, p. 53-55 and Brandenburger, op. cit., p. 120.

[6] Resp. C.H. I, 24 and 25 and C.H. VII, 2. In C.H. I, 25, one reads that man, after his ἄνοδος through the seven regions of heaven is γυμνωθείς ἀπὸ τῆς ἁρμονίας ἐνεργημάτων

The Sermon of the Naassenes describes the ascent or rebirth as a βαλεῖν τὰ ἐνδύματα, i.e. casting aside the clothes.[1]

It is in conformity with these conceptions on stripping off the body, tearing off its garment and casting aside the clothes ,that the ideal state should be envisaged as one of bodilessness or nakedness. Thus Philo, in Legum alleg., II, para. 59, speaks of a state of being γυμνός and ἀσώματος. The no longer bodily man whom we meet in Hermetic literature, is "denuded" of bad qualities.[2] Zosimus refers to a return to the non-human estate.[3]

Both the conception of discarding garments as well as the ideal nakedness are themes which were derived from a Hellenistic Judaism which either framed these conceptions by its own initiative or otherwise took them over from some other source to integrate them with their own existing speculations.

We arrive at this conclusion by observing that the Gnostics and the Encratites again and again connect the conceptions in question with the coats of skins mentioned in Gen. 3:21 [4] and the circumstance related in Gen. 2:25, that the man and his wife were naked and not ashamed. The concept of sexlessness which people associated with the concept of nakedness, also fits in whith Hellenistic Jewish speculations on the nature of the first man.[5]

(Scott translates : "having been stripped of all that was wrought upon him by the structure of heavens".) For C.H. I, see also Brandenburger, op. cit., p. 94s. For the Jewish influences on this tract, cf. Schenke, Der Gott "Mensch", p. 47.

[1] Hipp., Refutatio, V, 8,44 (Völker, Quellen, p. 23).

[2] See note 6 p. 328.

[3] See Reitzenstein, Poimandres, p. 103s. and Brandenburger, op. cit., p. 82.

[4] Probably Job. 10:11 (LXX δέρμα ... με ἐνέδυσας) was partly responsible for the fact that Gen. 3:21 (LXX χιτῶνας δερματίνους ... ἐνέδυσεν αὐτους) was interpreted to apply to the human body. The conception of the body as a garment (ἐχθρὸς χιτών C.H. VII, 2) especially, was probably derived from Hellenistic Judaism.

[5] The nakedness of Gen. 2:25, the treading with the feet upon the cast-off robe of shame and the sexlessness in the case of Cassianus (Clem. Alex., Strom.' III, 91ss., see Hennecke I[3], p. 110s.). In the Gospel of Thomas, logion 3, there is a similar instance of undressing and not being ashamed, upon which the clothes are trampled with the feet (see R. Schippers, Het evangelie van Thomas, Apocriefe woorden van Jezus (Kampen 1960), p. 29 and 35s.). The undressing and trampling of the clothes is regarded as a "childish" matter. It is clear from logion 21 and 22 that this childishness should suggest sexlesness (the logia 22 and 37 also in Hennecke, I[3], p. 215). In the Coptic Dialogue of the Redeemer (fifth writing in the first codex of Nag-Hammadi), we find the following : blessed wilst thou be when thou goest wholly naked. This work is Encratic in tendency (Hennecke I[3], p. 174). A Coptic papyrus, found at Deir el-Bala'zah, combines the ideas

Instead of the ideal nakedness, the discarding of the body or garment can also be succeeded by a transference to another body. In one of the Hermetic tracts it is written that when the former bodily form has disappeared, the reborn assumes an immaterial form and is transmuted into an (invisible) non-mortal body.[1]

Such a transition can also be couched in terms of donning a new garment. The O.T. frequently uses the metaphor of the garment when the theme involves abstract concepts relating to the soul, ethical qualities or circumstances of salvation or calamity. In these cases, such expression are used in combination with the word meaning to put on clothes (לָבַשׁ LXX ἐνδύειν).[2]

In 1 QS 4, 7s., eschatological salvation is described as "a crown of glory and a robe of honour in the eternal light".[3] Hellenistic Jews, Christian writers and Gnostics alike, conceived a particular type of garment as characteristic of a preexistent or future state of salvation and would speak of the transition to that state as the putting on or being clothed with a robe.[4]

The possibility is not ruled out that non-Jewish influences also contributed to this image of a preexistent or future state of salvation

---

of nakedness and sinlessness in a context which mentions Adam and paradise (Hennecke I³, p. 244s.). The theme, based on Gen. 3:21, of discarding the coats of skin also occurs in the Exc. ex Theodoto para. 55 (see W. Bauer in Hennecke II³, p. 607 note 1). In the place in the Sermon of the Naassenes which is mentioned in n. 1 p. 329, the βαλεῖν τὰ ἐνδύματα is associated with sexlessness, i.e. the state of being simultaneously both man and woman, as also mentioned in logion 22 of the Gospel of Thomas.

[1] C.H. XIII, 3, cf. Reitzenstein, HMR, p. 48.

[2] Cf. Is. 61:10 and see Oepke, Th. W. II, p. 320 line 5ss.

[3] Cf. Brongers, De Gedragsregels, p. 69.

[4] Od. Sol. 25,8 talks of being wrapped in the robe of the spirit. In the Acta Thomae, in the so-called Hymn of the Pearl, the son of the king has to change his contemptible, unclean robe for his former (double) glorious robe (cf. Hennecke II³, p. 349ss. and Leisegang, Die Gnosis, p. 366ss.). See also Käsemann, Leib und Leib Christi, p. 87ss., in which an example from Philo, De somniis I, para. 224s. is given. In the Ethiopian book of Enoch 62:15-16 and the Slavic Enoch 22:8s., the donning of a robe of glory or garments of glory also occurs. (Slav. En. 22:8s. is guoted by Brandenburger, Adam und Christus, p. 115.) In the Revelation to John, there are frequent references to white raiment (Rev. 3:4, 5; 3:18; 4:4; 6:11; 7:9, 13). In the Gospel of Truth and the Apocryphon Iacobi it is resp. said of Jesus that in his preexistence he was clothed with eternal life and that after death he put on immortality and after his exaltation, he unclothed in order to clothe himself anew (Hennecke I³, resp. p. 163 and p. 248). In a manner reminiscent of the O.T. combination of the word meaning to clothe with certain concepts, Od. Sol. 13, 3; 23, 3 and 30, 3 speak of putting on the holiness of the Lord, putting on joy and love and putting on the name of the Highest.

in terms of a garment.[1] But it is certain that the direct source of all these references to the assumption of a robe of salvation in Hellenistic Jewish, Christian and Gnostic works, can be traced to Jewish speculations on the glory of Adam before his fall.[2] It is probable that contemplations on Psalm 8 and "the son of man" also grew to be linked with those speculations on the glory of Adam.[3]

---

[1] See Brandenburger for the views of G. Widengren on the Iranian Vohu Manah-robe (op. cit., p. 117 note 1)and the reference to the comments on the "Syrische Sprachdenken" (the Syrian logical process, which is determined by linguistic associations) of A. Adam in Colpe, Die religiongesch. Schule, p. 178 note 1.

[2] In the opinion of Van der Woude, 1 QH 17, 15 and 1 QS 4, 23 evince the thought that certain people will inherit the glory that was Adam's (De Dankpsalmen, pp. 74, 100). See also Damasc. 3,20 (cf. Brongers, op. cit., p. 28). In Od. Sal. 25, the garment of the spirit is the opposite of the skins worn by Adam after his fall. The transient rags which stand contrasted to the immortality Jesus assumes after his death in the Gospel of Truth (see n. 4 p. 330), are in all probability the same garments with which the fallen Adam was clothed. Quispel, "Gnosticism and the N.T.", p. 72, remarks on the Jewish character of the combination of the conception of the preexistence of the soul with the glorious robe, in the Hymn of the Pearl (see n. 4 p. 330). Also the robe of glory mentioned in the Eth. En. (see n. 4 p. 330) reminds us of the story of Adam's expulsion from paradise; for it represents a robe of life and is the opposite of clothes which age. The garments of glory in the Slav. En. (see n. 4 p. 330) are likewise reminiscent of a return to paradise. See the commentary in Bousset-Gressman, Die Religion des Judentums, pp. 200, 284 and 498 or Slav. En. 22:8. For rabbinical data on the glory of Adam before the fall, see Schenke, Der Gott "Mensch", p. 127ss. A magical heretical-Jewish or syncretic prayer talks of a return by Adam to his earlier glory and how Adam is greeted again by his former heavenly μορφή and πνεῦμα. In this prayer Adam is addressed as God himself (see Brandenburger, Adam und Christus, p. 77s. and cf. Quispel, "Der gnostische Anthropos und die Jüdische Tradition", p. 215 and 216 and note 37ss. and Quispel-Peuch, Op zoek naar het evangelie der waarheid, p. 46s.

[3] Psalm 8 speaks of the glory which God the Creator has bestowed on man. It is an obvious deduction that this man. crowned with honour and glory, should have been thought of as Adam, before the fall. In v. 5, however, Psalm 8 speaks of man also as בֶּן־אָדָם. In Hellenistic Judaism, the בֶּן־אָדָם of Psalm 8 could have been identified with the בַּר אֱנָשׁ of Da. 7:13. In any event, a connection was seen in Hellenistic Judaïsm between the glory of Adam of which the salvandi will partake and the glory of the son of men. Enoch, who goes to heaven, may be regarded as the type of salvandus who will gain a share in the glory of paradise (see Eth. En. 62,15 and Slav. En. 22,8 and cf. Brandenburger, op. cit., p. 115). He is acclaimed as the son of man, (Eth. En. 71:14 and 16). Participation in the glory of Adam and consorting with the son of men are equal and interchangeable concepts in Hellenistic-Jewish apocalypticism. 4 Ezra 14:14 speaks of discarding the burden of humanity and the extinguishing of weak nature. Against this we do not find, as is usual in cases of this kind, the glory of Adam but sojourn with the son of God and his companions till the end of time (4 Ezra 14:9). This son of God. however, is the man or human (4:Ezra 13:32 and 12). He is identical with the son of man

Our opinion is that the above-mentioned Hellenistic Jewish speculations on the clothes of skin from Gen. 3:21 and on the glory of Adam
before the fall, also form the background against which the expressions
"putting off the old man" and "putting on the new man" were conceived.

Perhaps similar formulations had already been shaped within the
terminology of Hellenistic Judaism; we find a related phrase, "putting
on the perfect man" in two Gnostic works, both dealing with the creation of man.[1]

In 4 Ezra 4:14 we read an item of advice, formulated in terms very
close to the expression in Eph. 4:22 : "cast off the burden of humanity,
take off the weakness of nature.".[2] In Eph. 4:22, it is made clear that
the old man was manifest in the previous way of life of the faithful and
that he was subject to corruption because of his deceitful lusts.[3] If we
take into account the wider implication of the context, we become
aware that the path of the old man towards perdition was the cause that
the faithful were formerly dead in sins (2:5) and that the lusts and desires of the flesh (2:3) were part of the nature of this old kind of man.

---

from Da. 7:13. (This is apparent when 4 Ezra 13:2 and 3 are compared with Da. 7:2,3).
In 1 QS 4, eschatological properties mentioned are the glory of man (4,23) and a crown
of glory and a mantle of honour in the eternal light (4,7). We have already seen that Van
der Woude believes that 4,23 deals, in fact, with Adam's glory (note 2). It seems to
me that the crown of glory and the mantle of honnour in 4,7 are, on the basis of Rev.
14:14 and 1:13, traditional attributes of the son of men. (The crown of glory could derive
from Psalm 8:6.) If this explanation of 1 QS 4,23 and 4,7 is correct, then Palestinian
Judaism also put the glory of Adam and the glory of the son of man on one level. In
addition, we would observe that it is precisely that combination of the glory of Adam
and the glory of the son of man which could have brought about that the ideal nakedness
of Adam gave way for the glorious robe. The son of man, as he features in Hellenistic
Jewish apocalyptic literature, is always clothed.

[1] In the Apocryphon of Ioannis 64, 17-65, 16, the putting on of the perfect human
being is associated with ascent to the world of the light (Branderburger, op. cit., p. 93).
This ascent implies a stake in the glory of the world of the light which is the world of the
highest God, the God "human being". Next to this God "human being" is the son of
men (cf. Schenke, op. cit., p. 35). In the Gospel of Maria (see Hennecke I³, p. 254), the
putting on of the perfect human being is also mentioned; however, the mythological
background to the expression as it occurs in the Ap. Ioannis is not evinced in this Gospel,
where it merely serves as an ethical directive (cf. Brandenburger, op. cit., p. 93). This
work also deals with the creation of man. Another statement it contains is that the son
of men is within men (see Hennecke I³, p. 253 and p. 252).

[2] Cf. Kautzsch, Die Apokryphen und Pseudepigraphen des AT II, p. 399.

[3] For the meaning of the preposition κατά in 4:22, see Radermacher, Neutestamentliche Grammatik, p. 139.

It is therefore self-evident that the word ἀποθέσθαι should have been used to describe a severance of the affinity with the old man.

The middle voice ἀποτίθεσθαι (used in the litteral sense for the discarding of clothing or armour) is used in the figurative sense to press the disengagement from certain impulses and practises. In the same way as ῥίπτειν, it may have a person or, rather, a person performing a certain function as its object to convey that the person is relinquishing a property or function which he held until that time. For example, a person may cease to be a spectator or soldier.[1] Thus, in our case, we are concerned with a cessation of the old man.

If we now turn to the corresponding Hellenistic Jewish, Christian, Hermetic and Gnostic formulations we have quoted, we find the following correlation : in all of them the metaphor of discarding clothes is used to convey a changed mode of existence. Here, in Eph., however, this image is used in a less plastic sense; there is no explicit mention of casting (or tearing) off clothes. Furthermore, there is the difference that that which is spoken of as a garment, is not the body or human nature as such.

Even if we must look to Hellenistic Jewish speculations for the origins of the expression "putting off the old man", there is no doubt that the author of the expression had detached himself from them. He imbued the term with a new content and did not adhere to the movement which was to lead to the plastic mythology and dualism of the Gnostics.

The expression "putting on the new man" is even more evocative of its derivation from Hellenistic Jewish speculations on the first man than the corresponding expression. "putting off the old man". The words τὸν ... ἄνθρωπον τὸν κατὰ θεὸν κτισθέντα point unmistakeably to Gen. 1:26s.[2]

---

[1] ἀποτίθεσθαι as used for the relinquishing of certain practices is found, e.g. in 4:24 Other instances of ἀποτίθεσθαι in combination with impulses and practices are quoted in Bauer, Wörterbuch z. N.T., s.v. Liddell-Scott, s.v. cites an example from Euripides, Iphigenia Aulidensis 558, where Aphrodite is put on a par with sexual desire : ἀποτίθες-θαι τάν Ἀφροδίταν. Examples of ἀποτίθεσθαι and ῥίπτειν with a person in a particular capacity as the object, in Bauer, l.c. and Oepke, Th. W. II, p. 320 line 1 : ἀποθέμενος τὸν θεατὴν ἀγωνιστὴς γενέσθαι (Maximus Tyr. 1,4th cease being a spectator and becoming a wrestler) and ῥίψας στρατιώτην ἐνέδυ τὸν σοφιστήν (Lib. Ep. 1048,4 he ceased to be a soldier and became a philosopher).

[2] κατά can be an indication for correspondence and resemblance, e.g. 1 Pt. 1:15 and Gal. 4:28. As is the case in these examples, the author is not concerned with a resemblance in appearance or exterior in Eph. 4:24. Whilst the affinity in 1 Pt. 1:15 lies in being ἅγιος, so in Eph. 4:24 it rests in being δίκαιος and ὅσιος.

At the same time, we are aware of a certain remove from these Hellenistic Jewish speculations and from Gnosis. The word κτισθέντα has already been stamped by the use of the word κτίζειν in 2:10 and 15. It does more than merely refer to an act of God in the creation of the world; in this context, it particularly refers to an act of God in Christ (2:10) or an act of Christ himself (2:15).

The stringent formulation τὸν κατὰ θεὸν κτισθέντα makes no allowances for the idea that this new man shares an identity or is connected with Adam before the fall.[1] The δικαιοσύνη and ὁσιότης which make the new man like God are the δικαιοσύνη and ὁσιότης of the truth (ἀλήθεια). The ἀλήθεια is bound with Jesus (4:21) and comes to man through the εὐαγγέλιον τῆς σωτηρίας (1:13).

Although this new man is presented as a new garment through the infinitive ἐνδύσασθαι, the author does not, expressis verbis, talk of a new garment in the way we observed that the Hellenistic Jewish and Gnostic and Christian writers did. The infinitive may evoke the metaphor of the garment but in actual fact it does no more than express acquisition or receiving.

We are herein confronted with the same figurative use of the words denoting the assumption of clothing which we found in the Hebrew O.T. and in the LXX.[2] But because that which is acquired or received is the new man, the acquiring and receiving in Eph. 4:24 is tantamount to : the act of becoming.[3]

Qualities which are essential to this new man are those of the δικαιοσύνη and the ὁσιότης through which God is pleased and finds the new man acceptable. There is nothing in the text to suggest that the person who puts on the new man has already attained a state of salvation or glory. In this respect Eph. 4:24 differentiates itself from sources in which the new garment represents a preexistent or future salvation.[4]

---

[1] Had the formulation run as follows : κατ' εἰκόνα θεοῦ there would still be some leeway. If Adam were regarded as the εἰκών of God, the formulation could refer to him and mean : like him who is the image of God. This happens, mutatis mutandis, in Philo who envisages the logos as the image of God (see Schenke, Der Gott "Mensch", p. 122).

[2] See above, p. 330 and note 2. Cf. also Ps. 132:9 (LXX 131:9). The putting on of the new man, in whom righteousness is essential, stands closely related to being clothed in righteousness, as in the psalm in question.

[3] In this sense the active form of ἐνέδυ, which was quoted from the works of Libanius in note 1 p. 333 occurs.

[4] In the majority of the literature quoted p. 330 n. 1 and p. 331 n. 2, the garment is the symbol of preexistent or future salvation or the direct condition for this salvation. See also examples given by Käsemann, Leib und Leib Christi, p. 88s. were the garment is the salvation which becomes the share of the salvandus.

Eph. 4:24 no more evinces a bodily aspect than does Eph. 4:22. Pokorný holds that the author of Eph. is negatively reacting to a Gnostic trend of thought which contrasts the mortal body, which the salvandus must relinquish, to a heavenly, immortal body into which the salvandus must grow. Instead of the dissolution of the earthly body and transmutation into a heavenly, immaterial body, the author of Eph., according to Pokorný ,was arguing an incorporation into the body of the ecclesia. This incorporation, which was to urge people towards a communal activity in the world, the author put in the fore-front of importance.[1]

If Pokorný's theses is correct, we might have expected to find some symptoms of this negative reaction on the part of the author in Eph. 4:22-24. After all, Gnostic mythology does call the mortal body which must be dissolved, a garment, which must be put aside [2] and the immortal, heavenly body, a robe which must be gained.[3]

If the author had really been attempting to refute a Gnosis familiar with such conceptions, he would surely have been thinking of the Gnostic conception of a garment of repudiation and a garment of aspiration when he formulated the expressions he uses in 4:22-24. We may safely assume that if that had indeed been the case, he would have adopted a polemical tenor in speaking of putting off the old and putting on the new man. Nor is it likely that his repudiation of the Gnostic ideal of the dissolution of the earthly body and metempsy-chosis into a heavenly body would have been restricted to speaking of the ecclesia as a soma.

The chances exist that during the lifetime of the author there were already many who followed the trend which arrived at the plastic mythology and dualism of Gnosticism by way of Hellenistic Jewish speculations. We have been unable to find any evidence that the author of Eph. entered upon any form of recusal or discussion against those many or a section of them. All we can see is that he himself did not take that path. His way led elsewhere.

This was already manifest from the way he talked of the inner man. In this respect, he is set aside from those other ways of thinking. The inner man, as the author of Eph. conceives him, evinces no resemblance to a figure from a heavenly world of light. From the way he uses the

---

[1] Der Epheserbrief und die Gnosis, pp. 57 and 69s.

[2] See above, p. 328s.

[3] See above, p. 329 and cf. Reitzenstein who draws attention to the heavenly robe as the symbol of the haevenly body (HMR, pp. 179, 263 and 353).

metaphor of the clothes which are discarded and assumed, this is also clear. The metaphor is not drawn sharply and in detail; there is only a suggestion and that is not connected with the conception of a disposable earthly body and the antithetical heavenly body. What it does relate to is two different ways of being. The old man is the believer in his previous mode of being; a human being who is deceived by the desires of the flesh and in the process of corruption. The new man is the believer in his new mode of existence; a human being who lives on the basis of truth, in the image of God and and is pleasing unto Him.

For the believer the fact that he has rejected the old man and embraced the new man is a fact of reality. The aoristic infinitives in 4:22 and 24 give a secondary suggestion of instant accomplishment and characterise the action as having taken place in the past.[1] They do not (indirectly) record a demand on the faithful.[2] The sentence of 4:20-24 has the motivating force of an admonition but is not, in fact, either an admonition or a command. It is presumed in the sentence that when Christ was divulged to the addressees and they were taught about him, they became aware that they had put off the old man and put on the new man.

This act of having put aside the old man and put on the new is truth $\dot{\epsilon}\nu$ $\tau\hat{\omega}$ $\text{'}I\eta\sigma o\hat{v}$; only when people have been instructed "as the truth is in Jesus" have they "learned $\tau\dot{o}\nu$ $X\rho\iota\sigma\tau\dot{o}\nu$" in the right way. In 4:21 the author links to this $\dot{\epsilon}\nu$ $\tau\hat{\omega}$ $\text{'}I\eta\sigma o\hat{v}$ not only the proclamation of Christ but also the fact of having put off the old man and put on the new.

The name $\dot{o}$ $\text{'}I\eta\sigma o\hat{v}s$ is here stated with emphasis. W. Foerster has remarked that Paul has the death and resurrection of Jesus strongly in mind in the case of most places when he uses only the single name Jesus.[3] Evidently, the author of Eph. 4:21 also had the death and resurrection of Jesus in mind and it is for this reason that he speaks so emphatically of $\dot{\epsilon}\nu$ $\tau\hat{\omega}$ $\text{'}I\eta\sigma o\hat{v}$. If this is correct, then the only proclama-

---

[1] Cf. Burton-de Zwaan, Syntaxis der wijzen en tijden i.h. Gr. N.T., para. 116; K. Brugmann-A. Thumb, Griech. Gramm. (Handbuch Klan. Alt. Wissenschaft) ⁴1913, p. 600 para. 587; R. Kühner-B. Gerth, Ausführliche Grammatik d. griech. Sprache II, Satzlehre, ³1998, para. 389,3, note 5 and W. W. Goodwin, Syntax of the Moods and Tenses of the Greek Verb, 1897, para. 116, 117.

[2] Thus Schlier, Eph., p. 217 : "Der Jesus Christus, den sie gelernt haben, fordert ein 'Ablegen' " (The Jesus Christ of whom they have learnt, demands a "putting off' ") and p. 219 : "dasz gefordert ist, den neuen Menschen anzuziehen ..." ("that it has been commanded to put on the new man ...").

[3] Th. W. III, p. 298.

tion of Christ which he considers legitimate is the one which acknowledges him as the crucified and resurrected Jesus. The author also saw
an association of the most intimate kind between the act of having put
off the old man and put on the new and the death and resurrection
of Christ.

On a complete par with this having put off the old man and put on the
new, is a renewal in the spirit of understanding.[1] Expressed by means
of an infinitivus praesentis, this renewal is not a completed action but
one which is still being enacted in the present. This too, is connected
with the death and resurrection of Jesus.

The designation καινὸς ἄνθρωπος also occurs in Eph. 2:15, being
preceded by the numeral εἷς. As in Eph. 4:24, the designation characterises the new state of existence of the faithful. Formerly, there were
two groups of which the one could be characterised by the word ἀκροβυσ-
τια (foreskin or uncircumsicion) and the other by the word περιτομή
(circumcision). Now, all can be characterised as "the new man".
The preceding numeral stresses that there is no longer any question
of differences in this new man.[2]

The designation which we encounter here, in 2:15, is the same which
occurs in 4:24. In the context of 2:15, the creation of this new man is
attributed to the crucified Christ. That corroborates our interpretation
of the word κτισθέντα and the designation ὁ ᾿Ιησοῦς in 4:24 and 21
(above).

Although essentially the same, the designation καινὸς ἄνθρωπος is
used differently in the two places, as a result of which the connotation
varies slightly. In 4:24, the new man is especially the new kind of
existence which the believer wins. In 2:15, the connection gives a
collective meaning to the term.[3] Here the term, above all, designates

---

[1] See above, p. 325 and note 2.

[2] See above, p. 298 and note 5.

[3] The Greek word ἄνθρωπος is flexible and allows fine distinctions. Liddell-Scott,
s.v. 1 and 2 quotes some examples of the meaning it can have : "man, both as a generic
term and of individuals" and "the ideal man, humanity". Philo on one occasion uses
τὸν ἄνθρωπον for τὸ γένος (De opif. mundi 76, see Brandenburger, Adam und Christus,
p. 119, note 1). Hebrew idiom and thought-patterns, which had a considerable influence
on the author of Eph., since he was a Jewish Hellenist also allowed for such gradations
in meaning. S. Wibbing, Die Tugend und Lasterkatalogen im N.T. (Beihefte z. Zeitschr. f.
d. neutest. Wissenschaft 25, Berlin 1959), p. 88, gives the following meanings for אָדָם :
man and humanity. The word has the second meaning in 1 QS 11,9 (cf. Brongers, De

all the faithful together, who all have a new kind of existence and thus
form a new kind of humanity.

If we now turn our attention to similar pronouncements in Col.,
it becomes obvious that there is no question of slavish imitation with
respect to either one or the other epistle. Both epistles evince originality. In place of the word ἀποθέσθαι in Eph., we find that Col. uses
the word ἀπεκδυσάμενοι (3:9). Whilst Eph. only speaks of putting off or
aside the old man, Col. also speaks of putting τὸ σῶμα τῆς σαρκός
(2:11).

This putting off the body of the flesh is a death (3:3) which has already
taken place for the faithful and was followed by a raising-up from the
dead. Col. describes this as an invisible circumcision or the circumcision
of Christ. To be raised up from the dead is to be raised up with Christ.
The faithful have been given this dying, burial and awakening with
Christ through the sacrament of baptism. For the faithful, this death
with Christ is the motivating force to kill the earthly members (τὰ μέλη
τὰ ἐπὶ τῆς γῆς) which consist of various reprehensible proclivities and
activities.

One might argue that the expression "putting off the body" in Col.
2:11, is somewhat closer in approach to the rejection of the human
body we find in Hermetic literature and the Sermon of the Naassenes,[1]
than to the expression "putting off the old man". On second thoughts,
however, this is not so. There is still a great gap between the Gnostic
conception of the body and the expression in Col. 2:11. The Gnostic
conception could be described as follows : "σῶμα ist hier Exponent
der Materie, diese aber das widergöttliche Prinzip slechthin".[2] Since
the body is nothing but matter, it is just worthless. Col. 2:11 speaks
of τὸ σῶμα τῆς σαρκός. In other words, the body is not entirely to be
rejected : it is worthless only in as much as it is σάρξ and exclusively
qualified as such.

The mind (ὁ νοῦς), as the precious, immaterial component, cannot
be subtracted from this body. Col. 2:18 makes clear that this mind
may equally be qualified in terms of the flesh and may equally well

---

Gedragsregels, p. 88). Klein, Der älteste chr. Katechismus und die jüdischen Propaganda-
Literatur, p. 166, relates that rabbi Ben Asai in Sifra Kedoschim P. 4 interprets "of man"
in Gen. 5:1 as : "of all men in their unity and sameness".

[1] See above, p. 328s. Cf. also Käsemann, Leib und Leib Christi, A III para. 2, Der
"Körper" in der Gnosis (p. 56s.).

[2] Käsemann, op. cit., p. 58. Trans. : σῶμα here is the exponent of matter, but quite
plainly the ungodly principle."

be subject to rejection. In that case, the members of men are earthly members and may be equated with the reprehensible proclivities and activities with which they are connected (3:5).

In Col. 3:9, 10 we find that the same thought is expressed as in Eph. 4:22-24 but formulated in a different way. The text is just as definite as Eph. 4:24 that those who have put on the new man have not reached a state of salvation or glory (p. 334). In Eph., the accomplished fact of having put off the old man and put on the new, goes together with a renewal which is still continuing in the present (p. 337). In Col., this continuous renewal is directly associated with the concept of the new man. The essential factor for the new man is to be renewed in knowledge; this knowledge concerns the understanding of God's will and His purposes of salvation, as a comparison with 1:9 and 2:2 presently reveals.

The new man is a man in the image of God. The words κατ' εἰκόνα τοῦ κτίσαντος αὐτοῦ as the formulation τὸν κατὰ θεὸν κτισθέντα in Eph. 4:24, harks back to Gen. 1:26s. (p. 333). Both convey that the new man corresponds to or is like the image of his creator.[1] Unlike Jewish Hellenistic conception, where this is sometimes the case, this image refers not to Adam but to Christ, who, according to Col. 1:15, is εἰκὼν τοῦ θεοῦ.

The new man of Eph., is the same in 4:24 and 2:15. We observed that the term "new man" forms a collective designation in Eph. 2:15 (p. 337). This collective idea is also present in Col., where it is immediately associated with the putting on of the new man.

We find several formulations not only in Col. but also in the HP which are reminiscent of the pericope Eph. 4:22-24. The formulation ὁ παλαιὸς ἄνθρωπος also appears in R. 6:6, which reads ὁ παλαιὸς ἡμῶν ἄνθρωπος συνεσταυρώθη. The preceding words τοῦτο γινώσκοντες, ὅτι lead us to assume that the apostle, in speaking about the old man, takes for granted that the recipients understand what he is talking about, on the basis of previous instruction. From 6:12, it may be deduced that this previous instruction referred to, is baptism. Eph. 4:22-24 also alludes to instruction which the recipients appear to have received on a previous occasion.

In R. 6:6, as in Eph. 4:24, the designation the old man is of application to the former way of live of the faithful. We read in Eph. that the old man was subject to corruption because of his deceitful lusts.

---

[1] For κατά as an indication for correspondence or resemblance, see p. 333 n. 2.

This statement should be seen in combination with the death in sins which was their earlier condition (p. 332).

The reference to the old man in R. 6:6, should also be viewed in the perspective of a state of being dead through sin. But now (6:11), the faithful are dead to sin and alive to God. That which can be said of Christ, "θάνατος αὐτοῦ οὐκέτι κυριεύει" (6:9), is now also true of them. Thus, we may surmise that their former mode of existence was a live governed by death, or dead to God, and was a life of sin. This assumption is borne out by a preceding passage (R. 5:17) in which there is, espressis verbis, mention of the reign of death and the fact that later on, R. 7:10 talks of their having been dead.

It seems to us that all of R. 5:12-7:24 appertains to the idea of the old man and that this idea was central to the theology of Paul and his circle.

In R. 6:6, as in Eph. 4:22-24, the faithful have finished with the old man by grace of the death of Christ. R. does not speak of putting on the new man. On the other hand, it strikes us as an obvious conclusion that in the teaching to which, in our opinion, the apostle refers in R. 6:2, ὁ καινὸς ἄνθρωπος as the opposite number to the old man, must have played a part.

Besides, R. 6:4 talks of a newness of life (καινότης ζωῆς). It would seem that this καινότης has been bestowed on the faithful and that it is God's intention that they should also follow in its path. They who partake in this newness of life are, as 2 C. 5:17 and Gal. 6:15 put it, a new creature (καινὴ κτίσις).

The term "put on" also occurs in Gal.; the baptized have "put on" Christ (3:27). To have put on the new man entails (in Eph. and Col.) that the faithful have become new men. In Gal., the putting on of Christ should not be interpreted to mean that the faithful have become Christ. There is no question of Χριστὸς εἶναι. For there is but the Χριστοῦ εἶναι. See Gal. 3:29.

Just as the "new man" has a collective connotation in Eph. 2:15 and Col. 3:9s, the references in the HP to a new mode of existence for the faithful also have a collective implication. In Eph. 2:15, the εἰς καινὸς ἄνθρωπος has brought about the end of the περιτομή — ἀκρο-βυστία controversy. Similarly, the καινὴ κτίσις of Gal. 6:15 means that this contradisposition is no longer valid. The act of having put on Christ in Gal. 3:28 implies unity and betokens the same consequences as the act of having put on the new man in Col. 3:10.

We have already remarked that the contemporary notion of the ideal of nakedness is absent from Eph. 4:22-24. It is therefore striking that in 2 C. 5:3, 4 an aversion to that ideal nakedness comes to the fore. 2 C. 5:3 evinces a burning desire to be clothed (ἐνδυσάμενοι) and not to be found naked. This state of being ἐνδυσάμενοι would appear to be a condition for receiving the οἰκίαν ἀχειροποίητον αἰώνιον ἐν τοῖς οὐρανοῖς (5:1).

ἐνδυσάμενοι are they who have received τὸν ἀρραβῶνα τοῦ πνεύματος (5:5). We take it that this state of being ἐνδυσάμενοι is a state of having put on Christ or—what is in effect the same thing—the new man. For whoever has put on Christ is of Christ (Gal. 3:27, 29). And being of Christ comprehends having received and partaking of the pneuma (R. 8:9). He who has not got the pneuma and who has not put on Christ and does not belong to Him, will be found naked. To the mind of the apostle, such a nakedness seems horrendous.

7. CONSPECTUS

In the process of investigating a number of the more salient terms found in Eph., as set out above, we discovered that a substantial part of the content of the epistle was revealed. The author took the most ancient Christian kerugma as his point of departure (p. 288s.). The very central theme of his epistle is the exaltation and dominion of Jesus (p. 220).

He calls the exalted Lord by the name κεφαλή. This word could have made him think of heaven. In any event, it implied the notion of that which is superior. The concept of leadership and dominion could both be connected with the word. For the author, a Jewish Hellenist, it may have been closely associated with the terms ἀρχή, πρεσβύτατος υἱός or πρωτόγονος. In connection with this word, he may also have been thinking of the idea of a beginning, in which the other things it entailed was included and in which the concentrated power of the whole was vested (p. 277ss.).

Perhaps the author was even already acquainted with the conception, which is elsewhere evinced in the literature of a later date, of the head as the source of revelation; maybe it is for this reason that in Eph. 4:15 he designates Christ "kephale" anew, after he has spoken in 4:11, about the different groups of people whom Christ has given to serve the revelation (p. 287). However, as the case may be, the author uses this designation primarily to convey the notion of Christ's exaltation and dominion.

The ancient Christian kerugma which Paul transmits, was not only concerned with an exaltation but also with humiliation. It is the kerugma of the Son of God who became a man and humbled himself. To the mind of the author of Eph., the exaltation must accordingly come after the humiliation. The designation "kephale" wich he uses has an affinity with the designation ὁ ἠγαπημένος which he also employs, as well as with other designations equivalent to that, such as ὁ ἀγαπητός, ὁ ἐκλεκτός and ὁ υἱός μου ὁ ἀγαπητός. The name "kephale" leaves as wide a margin for the idea of suffering and humiliation as any of those; in fact, it is one of the messianic predicates that presuppose suffering and humiliation. What is manifest in the epistle is that the suffering implied by the predicate "kephale" is considered to be of soteriological importance (p. 288ss.).

The epistle frequently speaks of the whole of creation, of the heavenly and of supernatural powers. The term "the heavenly" (τὰ ἐπουράνια encompasses all that is heaven, belongs to heaven and is in heaven (p. 215). It is possible that the amount of attention the author devotes to all these cosmic forces, emanates from a pastoral motivation. In the pagan environment of his readers, the whole of the cosmos was probably worshipped and fear of the various cosmic forces, and particularly of the heavenly bodies, was widespread. Obviously, the author wanted to preserve his readers against a relapse into such beliefs. However, he did not engage in any direct polemics against pagan or syncretical doctrines.[1]

Edicts on all things, on the heavenly and on the supernatural forces flow forth from the central theme of the epistle in a meaningful progression (p. 220). In the first place, these desclarations proclaim that Christ-kephale exceeds all and that nothing in heaven or on earth is above the power of his dominion (p. 218).

In addition, the edicts on the cosmic forces are given an immediate connection with the workings and dealings of Christ-kephale. Although his exaltation has, in principle, caused all that is in heaven and on earth to be in the right rellationship to him, in reality this order is still far from complete. Negative forces are still active and at large. For this reason, the exaltation of Christ is succeeded by his fulfilment of all things. This, in effect, will draw everything into the right perspective with relation to him. And thus, an end will come to the baleful confusion which still prevails throughout the whole of creation.

---

[1] Cf. Grosheide, De brief van Paulus aan de Efeziërs, p. 7. For scholars who read a refutation of Gnosticism into Eph., see p. 349 n. 1.

It was God's purpose to bring this confusion to an end at the end or fulness of times and to comprehend everything in Christ. The activity of Christ-kephale is a realization of this eschatological plan of God (pp. 217, 235s.). There is delineated in the HP a similar work of redeeming mediation on the part of Christ with respect to all things (p. 260s.).

Although there are a few designations for supernatural forces in Eph. which do not occur elsewhere in the CPmin, by and large the epistle does not give these supernatural forces a different treatment from the other epistles. In this connection we repudiated the view of Cramer who saw a major difference between Eph. and the so-called authentic epistles on this issue (p. 222).

The cosmological attitudes evinced in the epistle likewise remain within the framework of the other epistles. Schlier was unjustified in finding the thought in 4:15 that the ecclesia will bring the cosmos to increase (p. 219). Although, as in R. 8:21, there is a connection in this epistle between the salvation of the whole of creation and the salvation of those who believe, the situation is not that the ecclesia itself effects the salvation of all things. It is Christ himself who permeates all things with his dominion and his gifts of blessing. He, not the ecclesia, fulfils all things (p. 236). When Schlier wants to see the ecclesia as the representative of Christ with respect to the world,[1] he fails to render adequately the thoughts of the author of Eph. But there is a connection between the salvation of the ecclesia and the salvation of all things; this we shall be dealing with in the following chapter on the subject of the ecclesia.

The ecclesia is given particular prominence in the epistle. The author cannot divorce from the focal kephale, humbled and exalted, the eschatological people who belong to this eschatological figure.[2]

Being kephale presupposes suffering and death. Through his suffering and death, Christ has made the ecclesia his undisputed own. He, the kephale, from whose rule nothing in heaven or on earth is exempt, is in a special sense the kephale of the ecclesia (pp. 291s., 605).

Through his death, the ecclesia has not only become Christ's own but has also been saved. He died to make the ecclesia holy and glorious.

---

[1] Cf. e.g. Eph., p. 94 : "der 'Leib' ... die Erscheinungsform und die Repräsentation des 'Hauptes' im Kosmos ...". ("the 'body' ... the manifestation and the representative of the 'head' in the cosmos ...").

[2] For the conception of a belonging together of the Messiah and the messianic people, which also occurs in the HP, see Schweitzer, Die Mysitk des Apostels Paulus, p. 102-105.

His resurrection is the resurrection of the ecclesia and his exaltation is the exaltation of the ecclesia (p. 305).

Christ is able to bestow spiritual gifts because he has been exalted. These gifts, he bestows on the ecclesia. With his death and resurrection the end of ages commences. The gifts he lavishes on his eschatological people are part of the whole sum of God's eschatological spiritual gifts which the author designates by the Jewish Hellenistic term "pleroma"—a term which originally meant the "end" and grew to be a designation for the salvation of the end of time.

In the words of Eph. 1:3, this salvation may be described as $\pi\hat{a}\sigma a$ $\epsilon\hat{v}\lambda o\gamma\hat{i}a$ $\pi\nu\epsilon\upsilon\mu\alpha\tau\iota\kappa\hat{\eta}$ (p. 240). This whole complement of eschatological gifts, of which charity is the highest, works to such an extent in the ecclesia that the term pleroma can be used to designate the ecclesia itself (p. 241).

The maximum degree of fulfilment with the pneuma and the totality of the spiritual eschatological gifts has still to take place for the ecclesia. For the ecclesia, there is a future. The ecclesia is an eschatological potential on the path towards a goal (pp. 234, 314s.). This aim, the utmost of fulfilment with the complete gifts, can only be attained if the ecclesia makes the fullest use of the gifts which have already been given and if it lives according to the highest gift of all, that of love.

By working through the gifts bestowed and by living in love, the ecclesia demonstrates that it is soma (body). As a metaphor for a certain community, the word "soma" had long been familiar to the author. There was probably an existing Hellenistic Jewish tradition whereby Israel was compared to a soma.

This analogy, the author applies to the eschatological, messianic people, which is the ecclesia, by identifying them with the Israel of yore to whom God gave his promises and privileges. Furthermore, he takes it as a matter of course that the faithful are members of this body and regard each other as members.

However, he uses this metaphor not only in order to illuminate a particular aspect of the ecclesia but also to define its essence. The ecclesia is not only like a body; it is, when properly contemplated, a body. If the ecclesia and the faithful neglect to behave like a body and members, they are betraying the truth and the God-given salvation.

Without Christ the ecclesia and the faithful could not possibly be body and members. Not only does the ecclesia demonstrate by using the gifts of Christ that it is the body of Christ, but it is also true that it can only be body by virtue of these gifts. It is from Christ alone that the body draws the strength to grow (p. 302-305).

For the ecclesia, which is soma, the great condition for existence is the fact that it is subordinate to Christ, who is kephale (p. 242). As a soma, it is utterly and absolutely bound to Christ.

A special relationship exists between the soma of the ecclesia and the soma of Christ that was killed on the cross. The author is able to comprehend both bodies at a glance. When Christ gave himself or his body for the ecclesia, he and the ecclesia became one flesh and since then, the ecclesia has been the body of Christ. In turn, Christ's cherishing and nourishing the ecclesia is a cherishing and nourishing of his own flesh.

In his love, Christ puts the ecclesia on one level with himself. There is, in this respect, a common identity between Christ and the ecclesia. It is important for the ecclesia that it should foster this identity; in obeying Christ-kephale, it grows closer towards him. In this way, the ecclesia, with whom he became one flesh and whom he now cherishes and nourishes as his own flesh, can become one in spirit with him (p. 304s.).

The affinity between Christ-kephale and the ecclesia ensures that there is a connection between the salvation of the ecclesia and the salvation of all things. Christ's position with regard to the supernatural forces and his activity with respect to all things are first and foremost to the advantage of the ecclesia. The unifying work of God which, through the medium of Christ, finds accomplishment and embraces heaven and earth, has already found realization in the ecclesia (p. 259). It is through the ecclesia that a unity has already come into existence and it is for the ecclesia that the formula $\epsilon \hat{\iota}s \ \theta \epsilon \grave{o}s \ \kappa \alpha \grave{\iota} \ \pi \alpha \tau \grave{\eta} \rho \ \pi \acute{\alpha} \nu \tau \omega \nu$, $\acute{o} \ \epsilon \pi \grave{\iota} \ \pi \acute{\alpha} \nu \tau \omega \nu \ \kappa \alpha \grave{\iota} \ \delta \iota \grave{\alpha} \ \pi \acute{\alpha} \nu \tau \omega \nu \ \kappa \alpha \grave{\iota} \ \epsilon \nu \ \pi \hat{\alpha} \sigma \iota \nu$, which will one day freely apply to the whole cosmos, is already valid (p. 216).

Amongst mankind, the ecclesia does not have an exclusive position. The gifts which Christ has bestowed on men, he has given to the faithful, and these serve the increase of the body of Christ which is the ecclesia. Nevertheless, these gifts are gifts that have been bestowed on mankind. The fact that they have been given to the faithful and serve the building of the ecclesia does not mean that they are restricted in meaning and destiny.

The ecclesia must not regard itself as a exclusive group but as the new humanity, created by the crucified Christ. Christ has welded the category of "uncircumcision" and the category of "circumcision" together in a new humanity.

Schlier, quite incorrectly, envisaged the ecclesia as Christ's representative in its relation to the world (pp. 219, 343). We see the ecclesia presented, no less than the world, as the object of the activity of Christ. The world is not the work-object of the ecclesia. Together with the world, the ecclesia is the object of God's work of salvation. Only when this primary fact has been taken to heart is it allowable to observe that within this world, the ecclesia has a salutary significance provided it obeys Christ and makes use of his gifts.

In that capacity, the ecclesia is a manifestation of the wisdom of God and reveals this wisdom to the supernatural powers (3:10). It may be expected from the faithful that they will struggle against all negative supernatural powers, protected by the armour of God (6:10ss.). For it is amongst them that the gifts which Christ bestows on men are found. They are light in the Lord and through the light are the works of darkness made manifest (5:8ss.).

Our research into a number of salient words in Eph. brought us to an understanding of this epistle that diverges from various interpretations we have quoted. Thus, with respect to the word "pleroma", we were able to agree neither with Schlier, who attributes the word to an early form of Gnosticism, nor with Dupont, who believes that the word derives from the vocabulary of the Stoa. We also rejected the interpretation of Meuzelaar who refers the word to the expression for completeness or perfection in rabbinical literature (p. 253-256).

We were equally unable to agree with Schlier in respect of the formulation concerning the four dimensions in Eph. 3:18. He maintains that Christ is here described as "weltumfassender Antropos" ("world-embracing anthropos"). In our opinion, it is more probable that here, in a Jewish and Hellenistic Jewish manner, the idea of a divine transcendence is being evoked; the text is speaking about the transcendental and infinite nature of the love of Christ (p. 264ss.).

On the interpretation of Eph. 4:8, we also parted company with Schlier. He maintains that the author of the epistle himself saw the verse he quoted from Psalm 68 in the light of the ἄνοδος of the original archetypal man or salvator who came down to earth. We, on the other hand, would hold that he saw in the words of that verse the ancient Christian kerugma of the Son of God who humbled himself, became man, and was then exalted (p. 288).

In the interpretation of the expressions kephale and soma, we diverged from many others. We disagreed with Schlier who—as has just emerged once again—is constantly coming up with his "orientalisch-gnostische Urmensch-Erlöser-Mythus" ("oriental-gnostic myth about the archetypal man who is the redeemer"), that great reconstruction by the school which advocates the religio-historical approach[1]. Nor do we find ourselves at one with Colpe, Schenke, Brandenburger and Pokorný, whose work no longer proceeds from the hypothesis that such a myth ever existed in very ancient times. The criticism which Colpe and Schenke level at the great construction of the religio-historical school is well-founded. Less sound, in our view, is the tendency on the part of Colpe, Schenke and Brandenburger to discover the macro-anthropos conception in the expressions kephale and soma (pp. 266-275). On this point we concur with Meuzelaar who has rightly argued that there subsists only and indirect relationship in Eph. (and Col.) between the two expressions kephale and soma (p. 286). With him, we would regard the expression soma as an expression in its own right.

In Eph. (and Col.) the word soma is definitely not possessed of a cosmic aspect. Nor is it the case that in Eph. (and Col.) we have to do with an ecclesiological reinterpretation of an originally cosmological notion.[2] Underlying these epistles is not the conception of the cosmos, which is a body with Christ for its head, but the traditional metaphor by which a community is designated as a body (302s.). On this point we are in agreement with Meuzelaar.

However, we do not agree with him that the author, when he talks of the ecclesia as soma, is merely applying a traditional metaphor and doing nothing but fitting the image of the organism to the ecclesia (p. 304). We do not construe the expression ἓν σῶμα in Eph. 2:16 as a designation for the ecclesia; moreover, we also hold that the same expression, when it appears in 4:4, is more than a simple designation for the ecclesia (p. 299ss.).

To our mind, the author, in the first-mentioned place, means the crucified body whilst at the same time thinking of the ecclesia, whereas in the second instance, whilst meaning the ecclesia, he again has the crucified body in mind (p. 302) : For him, there is a very special relationship between the soma of the ecclesia and the crucified body (p. 304).

But this does not mean that we arrange ourselves with Percy, in whose opinion the idea is expressed in Eph. 2:16 that the group of the circumcised and the group of the uncircumcised were contained within the crucified body of Christ, and who believes that for Paul the soma of the ecclesia is none other than the crucified and resurrected

---

[1] see e.g. his Eph., p. 92.

[2] For the view that we have to do with just such a situation, see also Dibelius, Gefbr. pp. 64 and 27 and Schweizer, Th. W. VII, p. 1072ss.

body of Christ (pp. 299, 311ss.). In our opinion, Percy places too
much weight, in his interpretation of Paul, on the idea of the corporative personality (p. 312).

There is a certain identity shared between Christ and the soma of
the ecclesia, but we must exercise the utmost circumspection in discussing it. This identity is not dependent on the idea, that by virtue
of the concept of the corporative personality, the soma of the ecclesia
is no other soma than the crucified and risen body of Christ; nor does
it depend on the view "dasz in dem Leibe Christi am Kreuz ... virtuell
und potentiell die Kirche da ist", as Schlier maintains.[1] This identity
rests, in our reasoning, on the "vorherbestimmte Zusammenhörigkeit"
of the eschatological messianic people and the Messiah, which has found
realization through the death of Christ.[2] The identity exists in that
Christ in his love makes the ecclesia equal to himself and cares for it
as his body. Only so far is it identical with him (p. 304).

With the "perfect man" of Eph. 4:13, the macro-anthropos conception—here mooted by Schlier—comes to the fore once again, as
does the "corporate personality" in the form expounded by Hanson
and P.J. du Plessis (pp. 320, 322). We feel differently about this,
preferring to think that the expression $\dot{a}\nu\dot{\eta}\rho$ $\tau\acute{\epsilon}\lambda\epsilon\iota os$ is abstract in
meaning, that it indicates the state of being the perfect man which
must be the communal aim of all believers and that it implies a likeness
to Christ (p. 323s.).

Repeatedly, during the course of our investigation, it has been
brought home to us that Eph. must not be interpreted in the light
of a Gnostic background. Thus, for instance, we find no relationship
in the expression $\dot{o}$ $\ddot{\epsilon}\sigma\omega$ $\ddot{a}\nu\theta\rho\omega\pi os$ between this inner man and a
manifestation from a heavely world of light (p. 326). The way the
author talks of the old and the new man goes back to Hellenistic
Jewish speculations on the nature of the first man; but the author
gave his own content to these expressions and was not tempted down
the path which led from these speculations towards the mythology
and dualism of Gnosis (p. 333-335).

We came to the conclusion that the expressions "the old man" and
"the new man" were concepts that were central to the theology of
Paul and his circle and which had a place in their teaching with respect
to baptism. We believe that Eph. has to do with the same concepts.

---

[1] Eph., p. 135. ("that the church is virtually and potentially present in the body of
Christ on the cross. ..."). Incidentally, we are on his side when he draws attention to
the ambiguity or the "Doppeldeutigkeit" of the expression in 2:16. See above, p. 302.

[2] See p. 313.

For the rest we have not been able to discover that Eph. served to refute certain Gnostic doctrines. Pokorný, on the other hand, hypothesizes such a refutation as the initial premise of his interpretation of the notion of soma in Eph.[1] The fact is, however, that we found no traces of polemics against such doctrines, even on precisely those occasions when they might confidently have been expected (p. 335).

We have been investigating the words studied in this Chapter with a view to testing the contents of the epistle with respect to its Pauline character. We believe that we have shown that no valid religio-historical objections could be raised against the authenticity of our epistle. The thoughts in Eph. correspond with those of the HP. Eph. is not distinguished from the HP by any obvious influences from definitely syncretical and Gnostic quarters. Again and again, we discovered when treating the various words, a far-reaching correspondence of the thoughts connected with them, on the one hand, and the ideas encountered in the epistles of generally-acknowledged authenticity, on the other. It would not be viable to recapitulate all of these points of affinity; time after time, we found striking points of similarity in thoughts. This correspondence and relationship strengthens our conviction that the mind which gave birth to Eph. is that self-same spirit which holds such masterly sway over the homologoumena.[2]

---

[1] Before Pokorný, Holtzmann, Maurer and Coguel had already put forward that Gnostic influences find refutation in Eph. See our Chapter I, para. 6.

[2] For this correspondence, see pp. 248-251, 257-262, 265s., 288, 292s., 308-314, 324, 327, 339ss. Cf. also pp. 221, 225, 285, 343.

CHAPTER EIGHT

A CLOSER ENQUIRY INTO THE ECCLESIOLOGICAL
CONTENT OF THE EPISTLE

In the course of the previous chapter, our investigation frequently touched upon the subject of the ecclesia (pp. 216s.; 240-244; 252s.; 259; 286; 290s; 304-306; 313-317; 322-324; 343ss.). As a result, we were able to establish that a great deal of attention is devoted to the ecclesia in this particular epistle (p. 343).

Yet, this does not signify that the kerugma has been reduced to a mere message of the church, nor does it mean that the theme of the epistle is solely concerned with the doctrine and characteristics of the church.

This was Käsemann's view on Eph. According to him, there is a diametrical contrast between the HP and Eph. whenever the question of the church as the body of Christ arises. Whereas, Käsemann maintains, in the HP the ecclesia is always defined in christological terms, in Eph. the christology is always interpreted from the ecclesiological point of view. In fact, it could be asserted of Eph. that : "Nur der Christusleib läszt erkennen, wer Christus ist".[1]

However, we are inclined towards a different opinion. The kerugma of Eph. has the same basic premise as that of the HP (p. 288; 341s.). The exaltation and dominion of Jesus is at the core of the thoughts of the author of Eph. (p. 220).

There is a direct connection between this theme and the many pronouncements in the epistle on the nature of all things, the upper regions and the supernatural forces. All serve to express the fact that Jesus occupies the highest place and rules as lord (p. 220, p. 259).

A similar connection exists between the central theme and the extensive interest devoted to the ecclesia. He, who has been exalted and exercises dominion, is the Messiah.[2] In the Jewish tradition there is

---

[1] "Das Interpretationsproblem des Epheserbriefes", p. 254s. See also above. p. 29. Trans. : "Only the body of Christ can reveal who Christ is".

[2] Both the designation κεφαλή and the appellation ἠγαπημένος are messianic predicates (see above, p. 289). J. H. Roberts, Die opbou van die kerk volgens die Efese-brief (diss. Kampen 1963), p. 46 note 1, holds that the title Χριστός in Eph. has a clear messianic definitiveness and he also draws attention to the messianic character of the word ἐλθών in 2:17 ("die Messias as ὁ ἐρχόμενος "i.e. "the Messiah as ὁ ἐρχόμενος !").

a conception that there is a messianic people who belong to the Messiah. Thus Ps. Sal. 17:26 speaks of a holy nation which will be brought together by the Messiah. A connection existed between this conception and the idea of predestination. Schweitzer is, in fact, quite justified, when he talks of "die vorherbestimmte Zusammengehörigkeit der zum messianischen Erwählten untereinander und mit dem Messias" (p. 313). It seems to us that the author of Eph. was not only familiar with this tradition but that he based himself upon it.

Furthermore, we take it that the author found additional evidence for this mutual involvement between the Messiah and the messianic people in Ps. 110 (LXX Ps. 109). As far as he was concerned, there was a common element in this psalm and in the eighth psalm which he quotes in Eph. 1:22 (p. 288). Moreover, from Mat. 24:41ss. and texts parallel to it, it appears that there was a Jewish tradition of giving a messianic interpretation to the hundred and tenth psalm.[1]

In Eph. 1:20, Christ is envisaged as the one who is described in Ps. 110:1 (LXX Ps. 109:1). This is in accordance with the ancient Christian kerugma and it is similarly expressed in R. 8:34 and Col. 3:1.[2] It is possible that, just as the last verse of this psalm could have suggested to the author that Christ is kephale (p. 289s.), the third verse could, to his way of thinking, have referred to the interrelationship between Christ-kephale and the messianic people.[3] In our opinion, "die vorherbestimmte Zusammengehörigkeit" of the Messiah and the messianic people is reflected in the words of Eph. 1:4.

As we understand it, this predestined reflexive relationship between the Messiah and his people has, in the eyes of the author of Eph., found realization through the death of Jesus on the cross (p. 313s.). Since his basic tenet involved this relationship between the exalted master and his messianic people, it is inevitable that the author's reflections on the exaltation should have gone hand in hand with reflections on the ecclesia. To discuss Christ-kephale without mentioning the ecclesia would have been unthinkable to him.

In stating that the christology of Eph. is interpreted almost exclusively from the viewpoint of the church, Käsemann exaggerates. Christ

---

[1] Cf. Grundmann, Th. W. II, p. 38 and N. H. Ridderbos, "Het lied van den Priesterkoning" in Vox Theologica, 15 jg. n. 6, 1944, p. 99.

[2] Cf. A. Vis, "Is Ps. CX een Messiaanse Psalm ?", in Vox Theologica, 15 jg. n. 4/5, 1944, p. 91.

[3] The Masoretic text of Ps. 110:3 speaks of the "people" of the priest-king, whilst in LXX Ps. 110:3 there is a reference to the "saints".

is kephale not only over the ecclesia but over all creation and over all
forces (1:20-23).[1] Christ fills not only the ecclesia with his al gifts but
he permeates all things with his blessed dominion (p. 259). Therefore,
the christology of the epistle is by no means exclusively ecclesiological.

However, it is true that the epistle stresses the particularly close
relationship between Christ and the ecclesia. In a sense, we were even
able to talk in terms of a shared identity (p. 304). The fact of it is that
in Eph. the ecclesiological aspect is an inseperable complement to the
christology of the epistle.

We furthermore maintain that, on the whole, the balance between
christology and ecclesiology is no different in the HP.[2] In the HP
epistles we likewise encounter an interbelonging of the Messiah and
his people, which is anchored in predestination.[3] This is manifest for
example, in R. 8:29 where Christ is called πρωτότοκος ἐν πολλοῖς
ἀδελφοῖς within the context of predestination.[4] Again and again, we
find described a close affiliation between Christ and the ecclesia.

On occasions when the dominion of Christ is the topic of discussion,
all things created and the forces are also dealt with (1 C. 15:24-27 and
Phil. 2:9-11). The title κύριος can be used without further qualification,
can have a universal connotation, but is often qualified by the genitive
ἡμῶν. When this is the case, it expresses the bond between Christ and
the ecclesia.

In texts such as 1 C. 3:23; 12:12 and 15:22 and 23, this bond is very
palpable. In 1 C. 3:23, which also concerns the cosmos and the powers,
the formulation ὑμεῖς δὲ Χριστοῦ draws a close connection between
Christ and the ecclesia. 1 C. 12:12 evinces the same identification between Christ and the ecclesia as described in Eph.[5] Christ and the eccle-

---

[1] Cf. p. 289s.

[2] Schmidt likewise sees no essential difference between Eph. and the HP in the matter
of the christology-ecclesiology relationship; for him this relationship takes the form of
identicalness. ("Jedenfalls ist Christologie gleich Ekklesiologie und umgekehrt"—in
any event, christology is at the same time ecclesiology and visa versa".) This he finds true
not only of Eph. but also of the HP (Th. W. III, p. 512 line 23s. and op. cit., p. 515 line
19ss) In his view the only distinction between the ecclesiology of Eph. and Col. and the
HP is that of a "gnostisch-mythologische Begriffssprache" (some Gnostic-mythological
terms of reference") op. cit., (p. 515, line 7ss.).

[3] See Schweitzer, Die Mystik des Apostels Paulus, p. 102-105.

[4] This designation has an affinity to the designation κεφαλη; cf. above, p. 277s.; 292.

[5] We have already explained our interpretation of how Eph. describes the identity
between Christ and the ecclesia on p. 345s. In our opinion, the statement by Schmid
quoted in note 2 lacks in definition.

sia (the latter here defined as πάντες and οἱ τοῦ Χριστοῦ), being represented as closely linked.

However, there is one striking difference between Eph. and the HP on the subject of the ecclesia. Eph. frequently talks of the ecclesia in general whereas the epistles of the HP tend to deal with the ecclesia in a specifically local situation. Nevertheless, this does not mean that our epistle falls outside the main conceptual framework of the HP; the latter does, after all, sometimes talk of "die Gesammtgemeinde ("the wider community") and the ecclesia is, be it rarely, discussed in terms which have a significance beyond the local.[1]

When we were dealing with the expressions pleroma (pp. 239ss.; 344), soma (pp. 304ss.; 313-319; 344-348), the new man (pp. 337ss.; 348s.) and the metaphors of building, growth and maturity (pp. 314-319; 322ss.), we were presented with a great deal of ecclesiological material. If we are now to embark upon some deeper exploration of this material, it will be necessary to give some more attention to those statements pertaining to building.

We shall in the first instance set about this by looking at the passage Eph. 2:19-22. The preceding verses have alluded to the "access" which exists for the two united groups of circumcised and uncircumcised. The word προσαγωγή itself had its origins in ritual.[2] Gentiles did not have "access" to the temple in Jerusalem; they were not permitted into the court of the Israelites. Only those whom God had chosen might "approach" and dwell in his courts to find satisfaction in the goodness of his house.[3] If a gentile wanted to partake of these advantages, he had to have himself circumcised and become a proselyte.[4]

For the author of Eph., all this has changed. The uncircumcised are no longer excluded from the polity of Israel and the covenants of

---

[1] See Schweitzer, op. cit., p. 104ss.

[2] Cf. Schmidt, Th. W. I, p. 131 line 31ss. and B. Gärtner, The Temple and the Community in Qumran and the New Testament (Cambridge 1965), p. 61.

[3] See Ps. 65:5 which deals with the privileges of those who may partake in the ritual of the temple. F. Baethgen, Die Psalmen, ²1897 (Handkomment. z. AT II, 2), p. 191 and Kraus, Psalmen I, p. 451, maintain that Ps. 65:5 applied not only to priests and the levitical personnel of the temple but to all who took part in the ritual. See also Ps. 15:1; 23:6 and 27:4.

[4] The pi'el-root of קרב which is used in Ps. 65:5 also occurs in rabbinical texts dealing with the acceptance of gentiles as proselytes, in which case "cause to approach" means acceptance of a proselyte. See W. C. van Unnik, De verlossing 1 Petrus 1:18-19 en het probleem van den eersten Petrusbrief, 1942 (Med. Ned. Akad, van Wet., afd. Lett. Nieuwe Reeks, Deel 5, No. 1) and Meuzelaar, Der Leib des Messias, p. 60.

promise (2:12), but have a share in the privileged relationship which Israel has with God, as a result of that promise. In Eph., the circumcised adherents to the faith are called "saints" [1] and the gentiles who have turned towards the faith are "fellow-citizens with the saints".[2]

Since both groups stand under the influence of one and the same pneuma, they both have "access" to the Father. They, who were formerly heathens, may now also dwell in the presence of God and be satisfied with the goodness of the house of God. The author, in accordance with Is. 56:3-8, calls them οἰκεῖοι τοῦ θεοῦ.[3]

The author of Eph. no longer applies the ritually defined terms of "access" (2:18) and "household of God" (2:19) to the holy precincts of Jerusalem.

In the eschatology of late Judaism, the expectation of a new temple, to be built or brought about by God, was a familiar concept.[4] Furthermore, this late Judaism believed in the concept of a heavenly Jerusalem and a heavenly temple.[5] This belief was current long before 70 B.C.

When the Ethiopian book of Enoch speaks of the new temple which will be brought by God, this temple is called a house, with the idea that God and the Israelites—the latter being depicted as sheep—will dwell in that house. There is also an idea that the gentiles will become converted and will gather in that house.[6]

Elsewhere in this particular book, is there talk of dwellings for the righteous or chosen, in heaven, with the angels, which will be there at the end. This conception is linked with that of "the chosen one", i.e. the Messiah, who, together with the righteous, hass a dwelling-place in heaven under God's wing.[7]

Therefore, we need not be surprised when the author of Eph. no longer connects the term "access" and the conception of dwelling in the

---

[1] In 1:15 and 2:19 ,the designation "saints" also applies to the faithful.

[2] See Strathmann, Th. W. VI, p. 534s.

[3] See Mussner, Christus, das All und die Kirche, p. 1...

[4] Jub. 1:28; Eth. En. 90:28 (Kautzsch, Apokr. u. Pseudipigr. II, resp. p. 41 and p. 297). Bousset, Die Religion des Judentums, p. 12s. places both Ju. and Hen. 85-90 in the period of the Maccabees. For the expectation of the new temple in late Judaism, see also Strack-Billerbeck IV 2, p. 884ss.; Ph. Vielhauer, Oikodome, Das Bild vom Bau in der christlichen Literatur vom N.T. bis Clemens Alexandrinus (Karlsruhe-Durlach 1940), p.20s. and Gärtner, op. cit., p. 20s.

[5] See Schrenk, Th. W. III, p. 239s. See also H. Wenschkewitz, Die Spiritualisierung der Kultusbegriffe Tempel, Priester und Opfer im N.T., Angelos Beiheft 4, ,1932, p.46s.

[6] Eth. En. 90:29-36, See Kautzsch, op. cit., p. 297 with the footnote of G. Beer.

[7] Eth. En. 39:4, 5; 41:2 and Eth. En. 39:6, 7 (Kautzsch, op. cit., p. 259s.).

house of God with the temple of Jerusalem. His "access" refers to the association with God which is part of the temple of the new age. To be in God's house or in the presence of God is part of the eschatological salvation. As we saw in Enoch, the heathens are also included in this salvation.

When this book talks of the chosen dwelling with the Messiah under God's wings, there is an element of transcendentalism. The place in which Enoch envisages the dwelling(s) is at the end of heaven.[1] In Eph. 2:18, this transcendendal aspect is probably also present. "Access" and dwelling in the household of God may be regarded in the nature of a heavenly reality.

If this is so, it is in agreement with the fact that God has blessed the faithful with all kinds of heavenly blessings and has given them a place with Christ in heaven (1:3; 2:6). Similarly, the polity which is the heritage of the circumcised and in which the uncircumcised believers will share as συμπολῖται τῶν ἁγιων, will become a heavenly reality. The term "hagioi" imparts an affinity with the angels to the circumcised believers.[2]

The conceptions in the book of Enoch regarding the righteous who dwell in heaven together with the angels and the Messiah, may be seen as a fitting beckground to the formulation "fellow-citizens of the saints" and members of "the household of God". The hagioi, to whom is due the polity and who are of God's household, are the eschatological people of God or the messianic people who belong to the Messiah.

A new qualification now follows the term οἰκεῖοι τοῦ θεοῦ, introduced by the participle ἐποικοδομηθέντες. For the author, the fact that the word οἶκος or οἰκία can be found again in the substantive οἰκεῖοι and the participle ἐποικοδομηθέντες, has the same strength as a strictly logical connection.

This new qualification has been borrowed from the allegory of building and is developed in a number of statements which all have a bearing on the notion of building. We have on a previous occasion remarked on the teleological theme which is common to the allegory of growth and maturity; the same theme is found in the metaphor of building (p. 316).[3]

---

[1] Eth. En. 39:3 (Kautzsch, op. cit., p. 259).

[2] See O. Procksch, Th. W. I, p. 111.

[3] For this allegory as used in the CP and the rest of the N.T., see Vielhauer, op. cit., p. 56ss. and especially p. 120-122 as well as Dupont, Gnosis, p. 237ss.

It is the faithful who are being built. They are being built upon the foundation of the apostles and the prophets. In rabbinical literature we also encounter the conception of a building the foundations of which consist of persons. Ph. Vielhauer takes this conception to be of great antiquity.[1]

One of the Qumran manuscripts, the Manual of Discipline, mentions the foundation of truth upon which Israel or the community or the council of the community is founded.[2]

In the light of this information, it appears likely that the expression "built upon the foundation of the apostles and prophets" derives from a Jewish figure of speech.

We assume that the apostles and prophets were envisaged as foundations by virtue of their specific activity, which consisted of revealing the message entrusted to them. They were regarded as a foundation on the basis of what they had to say and said, rather than for their personal attributes.

The prophets mentioned in 2:20 could be the O.T. prophets. In support of this assumption, M. Barth argues : "... dennoch zeight die überwiegende Mehrheit der neutestamentlichen Bücher, dasz das Evangelium vom Jesus, dem Messias, ohne das Alte Testament, d.h. ohne Zeugnisse von Israëls Erwählung, Leben, Gottesdienst gar nicht verkündet werden kann.".[3]

However, in 3:5 and 4:11, there is renewed talk of prophets. In these places, they are again mentioned in one breath with the apostles. It is evident that the author quite definitely has the prophets of the New Testament era in mind here. An obvious deduction must be that these same prophets should be borne in mind in connection with 2:20, since it would be fairly inexplicable if there were no correspondence within such as short span as from 2:20 to 3:5.

Therefore, taking for granted that both pronouncements pertain to the same source of reference, we are able to define the message which has been entrusted to the apostles and prophets, which gives

---

[1] Op. cit., p. 18. Braun, Qumran u. d. N.T. I, p. 187, believes that in 1 QH 2,20 a person is being envisaged as a foundation in an analogous fashion.

[2] See 1 QS 5,5; 9,3 and 8,4-10 (Brongers, De gedragsregels, pp. 71, 81 and 79ss.), and Braun, op. cit., pp. 186ss. and 217.

[3] Israel und die Kirche im Brief des Paulus an die Epheser, Theologische Existenz Heute 75, 1959, p. 36. (Trans. : "... nevertheless, the overwhelming majority of New Testament books show that the gospel of Jesus, of the Messiah, cannot be revealed at all without the testimony of the O.T., i.e. without the evidence of Israel's election by God, Israel's life and Israel's religion.)

them the function of a foundation, in greater detail. The content of the message is intimately related to the mystery mentioned in 3:5.[1]

According to the subsequent words in 2:20, Jesus Christ is the ἀκρογωνιαῖος in the building of the faithful on the foundation of apostles and prophets.

The meaning of this word is a matter of some controversy. The question is whether the stone intended is the stone which puts the final touch to a building, a cornice-stone, or whether it means the stone at the base of a building, a corner-stone, which is of vital importance to the foundations to and the whole structure of the building.

We would in this matter opt in favour of the latter exegesis, proved to our satisfaction by J. H. Roberts.[2] It is abundantly clear that the akrogoniaios is considered of paramount importance in Eph. 2:20. For that reason, we think that the corner-stone would be more significant than a cornice-stone, in the type of building envisaged by the author.

J. Jeremias strenuously defended the first point of view and maintained that the stone refers to a stone which crowns an edifice, holding that this was a Jewish figure of speech which traces back to the O.T.[3] However, our acquaintance with Jewish metaphor would suggest that "corner-stone" is the operative interpretation.

An analogous case, written in a contemporaneous language, is found in 1 QS 8, 4-10; there the stone definitely means a corner-stone which must prove guarantee that the foundations will be steady.[4] In the Pirqe Rabbi Eliezer, an exegesis of Ps. 118:22 shows that the author is thinking in terms of a stone which is placed at the base of an edifice.[5]

---

[1] The fact that the author interrupts the next complete sentence with a digression on τὸ μυστήριον τοῦ Χριστοῦ, lends strength to this interpretation of the foundation mentioned in 2:20. In Hebrew and Aramaic, there is also a connection between the word for foundation and the word for secret. The words יָסַד (settle), מוּסָד (foundation) and the word סוֹד (secret), are related in form (cf. Gärtner, op. cit., p. 69). In view of the Jewish character of the formulation in 2:20 and by reason of the Semitic influences in Eph. on which we have already remarked we are persuaded that it is legitimate to attach significance to this affinity.

[2] For the arguments and Roberts' own exegesis, see Die opbou van die kerk volgens die Efese-brief, p. 60-66.

[3] Cf. Th. W. I, p. 792 and IV, p. 275-283.

[4] See Brongers, De Gedragsregels, p. 79s. Cf. also Braun, Qumran u. das N.T. I, p. 47s., in which there in reference to O. Betz, "Felsenmann und Felsengemeinde (= Felsenmann)" in ZNW 48, 1957, p. 50-54 and also Gärtner, op. cit., p. 64.

[5] See Strack-Billerbeck I, p. 875s. Amongst quotations from Pirqe R. El. 24, there is the following : "und legt man denn nicht jeden auserlesenen u. kostbaren Stein nur

In the case in hand, there is a clearcut sequence. First of all, the author of Eph. discusses the fact that the faithful are in the process of being built up, and he points out the necessity, in this building, of a relationship with the words of the apostles and prophets and with the allpowerful position of Christ. Then, in 2:21, a statement on the aim of this building follows; by virtue of the relationship with Christ, all that is being built is welded together to grow into a temple which is holy in him.[1]

Here the author has combined the two metaphors of growth and building—a combination we have already discussed (p. 316s.). By means of the word συναρμολογουμένη, he emphasizes the fact that this objective can only be achieved through cooperation and fellowship.

In 4:12 the necessity for communal striving is similarly stressed when ἀνὴρ τέλειος is described as the aim. The idea of cooperation and an inner bond is intrinsic to the conception of the body which plays such an important part in our epistle.

In the passage with which we are at present dealing, in 2:21, this idea is interwoven with the theme of coexistence between the circumcised and the uncircumcised—a prominent issue in Eph. 2. This theme is once again brought to bear in 2:22.[2]

Moreover, it there becomes clear that the building of the temple is guided by the pneuma. God builds the faithful through the pneuma and it is through the pneuma that He wishes to dwell in them, as his temple.[3]

The temple of this passage is the new temple which was expected in

---

an die Ecken des Hauses ?" ("and does one not lay each choice and precious stone only at the corners of the house ?").

[1] We will translate the words πᾶσα οἰκοδομή by a circumlocution, i.e. "all that is being built". The verses 2:20-22 do not describe an object but a particular event and its objective. As is evident from the verbal forms ἐποικοδομηθέντες, and συναρμολογουμένη, αὔξει and συνοικοδομεῖσθε, they are dynamic in character. οἰκοδομή is also a word which in the first place suggests the action of building; cf. Michel, Th. W. V. p. 147 line 39s. The primary meaning is "die Bautätigkeit" ("the activity of building"), "den Akt des Bauens" ("the act of building"). In 2:22, the word is not meant to convey the idea of a "fertiges Gebäude" ("a completed building"). Irrespectively of whether the text is read as πᾶσα οἰκοδομή or as πᾶσα ἡ οἰκοδομή, there is neither the implication of various concrete buildings nor of a single large edifice or building.

[2] Just as the conception that people are built, the idea that they who do not belong to Israel are being built together with Israel can be deduced from the O.T. For this see Jer. 12:12 and cf. also Meuzelaar, Der Leib des Messias, p. 127ss. and Dupont, Gnosis, p. 237ss.

[3] For the exegesis of Eph. 2:22, see Roberts, op. cit., p. 109-113.

late Jewish eschatology.[1] The author represents this temple as a building comprised of people. In fact, he has spiritualized the concept of the heavenly eschatological temple.

During the period when Eph. was written, there was a current Hellenistic Jewish tendency to explain terms which were rooted in Jewish ritual on the basis of allegory. This conformed with the Hellenistic trend originating in the Stoa, of attributing a spiritual meaning to formulations derived from ritual.[2]

However, an explanation based on Hellenistic Jewish linguistic practises fails to shed an adequate light on the imagery of Eph. 2:21s. The collective aspect in our text is not in keeping with the individualistic character with which Stoic philosophy and the contemplations of Philo endowed the spiritualized sacred terminology.[3]

The conception of a temple, built of many people, developed not in Hellenistic but in Palestinian Judaism. B. Gärtner has proved that criticism of the ritual of the Jerusalem priesthood culminated in the community of Qumran regarding itself as the temple of God and regarding an observance of the law by its members as the true cult.

The writings of the sect evince not only the expectation of future glory for the temple of Jerusalem but also some eschatological passages which make no mention whatsoever of such a restoration. In the latter passages, the new eschatological temple is described in purely spiritual terms which apply only to the community and a rightful way of life in the law.[4]

The following designations corroborrate that the community regarded itself as a temple : sanctuary in Aäron, sanctuary for Israel and temple of men.[5] The community is also depicted as a temple, in formulations

---

[1] See p. 354 and note 4.

[2] Wenschkewitz, op. cit. passim and especially pp. 19, 113 and 113s. note 3; Strathmann, Th. W. IV, p. 229 and Michel, Th. W. IV, p. 891 note 25 and p. 894 line 17s.

[3] Wenschkewitz, op. cit., p. 112 : "Weder in der Stoa noch bei Philo treffen wir diesen Gedanken, denn hier war alles auf den Einzelnen ... eingestellt" ("neither in the Stoa nor in Philo do we encounter this idea, for there everything was envisaged in terms of the individual").

[4] Op. cit., passim. See especially p. 18-20. The results of Gärtner's research outdated the view held by Wenschkewitz "dasz im Spätjudentum Palästinas Versuche zur Spiritualisierung des Tempelbegriffes nicht nachweisbar sind ..." ("that there is no evidence for any attempts to spiritualize the language of the temple during late Palestinian Judaism"); see Wenschkewitz, op. cit., p. 113s. note 3.

[5] See Gärtner, op. cit., pp. 23 and 26 (quoting 1 QS 5,5ss. and 8,4ss.) and p. 34 (quoting 4QFlor. 1,6 and giving a commentary on the words מִקְדַּשׁ אָדָם).

containing the word "house". Thus, the sect is e.g. the house of truth in Israel; the house of perfection and truth in Israel or the house of the community for Israel.[1]

In the manuscript known as the Florelegium, the community is given the qualification of a house built by God, a place where the saints (i.e., the angels) are and above which God shall be seen (i.e., where God will be present).[2]

This description recalls to mind Eph. 2:19-21 which also speaks of building and in which the enlightened gentiles are called the fellow-citizens of the saints and the household of God. Although the saints in Eph. are not angels but Israelites, the expression undoubtedly has something to do with angels (p. 355). The Florelegium also devotes some thought to the gentiles; we read that they may never enter the house in which the angels dwell.[3] The contrast brings our pericope into a particularly strong relief.

As is the case with Eph. 2:21, the writings of the sect combine the conception of a spiritual temple not only with the idea of building but also with the idea of growth. In our opinion, this association goes back to the O.T. We are hereby thinking of such places as Ex. 15:17 [4] and Ps. 92:13.[5] It is of such texts that the community was probably thinking when denoting itself as a planting of the Lord and connecting the terms "temple" and "house" with the idea of vegetation.[6]

---

[1] Cf. Gärtner, op. cit., pp. 23 and 29 and 1 QS 5,5ss.; 8,5ss. and 9,5ss. (see Brongers, De Gedragsregels, resp. pp. 71, 80 and 82).

[2] See Gärtner, op. cit., p. 32s.

[3] See Gärtner, op. cit., pp. 32 and 62. The Florelegium uses, inter alia, the words מַמְזֵר and בֶּן נֵכָר to describe foreigners and uncircumcised persons.

[4] In the Florelegium, this text is combined with an edict on the eschatological house; see Gärtner, op. cit., p. 31.

[5] The name Lebanon appears in this. The Lebanon is used to describe the council of the community in one of the Qumran scrolls. In later Jewish texts, the name Lebanon is often used to indicate the temple. Following the theory of G. Vermès, Gärtner talks of a certain exegetical tradition whereby the word Lebanon can be used as a designation for the Messiah, for kings of the future or, more often even, the temple or the temple of the messianic era. See Gärtner, op. cit., p. 43s.; cf. also 1 QP Hab. 12,1ss. (Van der Woude, Bijbelcommentaren en Bijbelse verhalen, pp. 39 and 45).

[6] See 1 QH 6,15ss.; 8,4ss. and 20ss. (Van der Woude, De Dankpsalmen, pp. 39ss. and 46ss.); 1 QS 8,5 and 11;5ss. (Brongers, De Gedragsregels, pp. 79 and 88) and Gärtner, op. cit., p. 28. It is possible that in the Florelegium the community is indicated by the words "shoot of David" and that it is also regarded as the fallen hut or tabernacle of David, mentioned in Amos 9:11, which will be raised up again and will appear to save Israel. It is in this sense that Gärtner (op. cit., p. 35-42) interprets the passage in question in the Florelegium. (The passage is found in Van der Woude, Bijbelcommentaren en Bijbelse verhalen, p. 85.)

The correspondence between the conception of the temple in Eph.
2:19-22 and the statements in the Qumran scrolls would seem to point
to Palestine as the source of the image. There is no reason to suppose
that the formulations in Eph. have been directly borrowed from the
writings of the sect. In the pericope, there is no trace of that criticism of
the priests of Jerusalem and their ritual which forced the leaders of
Qumran to regard their community as a temple.[1]

On the contrary, we detect something of the Hellenistic Jew in the
author Eph.; a Jew who was less involved with the rituals of Jerusalem
than his compatriots who lived there and who therefore felt free to
give a spiritual connotation to various sacral terms.[2]

In any event, the fact of it is, that observations on the temple in
Eph. (as, indeed, corresponding statements in the CP) were influenced
to a far greater degree by Judaism than R. Wenschkewitz supposed
possible.[3]

The overtly Jewish character of the pericope causes us to reject
the "Iranisch-gnostische" (Iranian-gnostic) interpretation of Vielhauer.[4]
We are unable to discover either the mythical figure of a divine anthropos, the substitution of a building for a person as in Manichaeism or
the Mandaean conception of a heavenly edifice into which the salvandi
may gain admission ("eingebaut", i.e. "built in ").[5]

Nor is it an argument to say that because the concept of the growing
anthropos was so well known, the word "grows" in 2:21 suggests the
mythical anthropos. The passage does not describe a heavenly edifice;
verses 20, 21 and 22 are dynamic in character and deal with an actual
event. In the first instance, the word οἰκοδομή evokes the idea of, the
act of building and the expression πᾶσα οἰκοδομή describes not the

---

[1] Cf. Braun, op. cit., p. 217.

[2] See p. 359 n. 2.

[3] We are referring to the study mentioned in n. 5 on p. 354. In Wenschkewitz's
opinion the spiritualisation of the concept of the temple in the CP was mainly attributable
to the use of spiritualised ritual terms in Hellenism and Judaism contributed little to the
conception as found in the CP. Wenschkewitz based his theories on an assumption which
was invalidated by the discovery of the Qumran scrolls and subsequent research; cf.
above, p. 359 n. 4.

[4] Cf. Hanson, The Unity of the Church, p. 130: "This thought is impossible on account of the conception of the Church as a ναός, which does not have its foundation in
Gnostic but in Israelite-Jewish speculations". (Hanson refutes the Gnostic interpretation of Schlier which is the basis of Vielhauer's arguments.)

[5] Vielhauer, op. cit., pp. 128s. and 142s.

product (or products) of that which is being built but the faithful, who are the object of building.[1]

Although the temple in question does constitute a heavenly reality, it does not represent the heavenly building of the Gnostics but the temple expected in late Jewish eschatology. This identification of the ecclesia with the eschatological temple was a basic component of the ancient Christian kerugma, manifest, for example, in the naturalness with which 1 Pt. 4:17 and 1 Tim. 3:15 refer to the community as the "house of God".[2] That kerugma was connected with the kind of Palestinian Jewish thinking revealed in the writings of Qumran.[3]

In connection with the problem surrounding the authenticity of Eph., it is pertinent to take note of the correspondence which exists between Eph. 2:19-22 on the one hand and 1 C. 3:9, 16, 17 and 2 C. 6:16-18 on the other.

In 1 C. 3, verses 10-15 inclusive form a long parenthesis. After the word οἰκοδομή in v. 9, the author embarks upon a spontaneous expatiation, allegorically expanding upon the word, and it is not until v. 16 that he returns to his starting-point.[4] Thus, the expressions θεοῦ γεώργιον, θεοῦ οἰκοδομή (in v. 9) and ναὸς θεοῦ (in v. 16) are closely affiliated.

Once again, we see the already familiar combination of the words for building and temple with a word pertaining to vegetable matter. The words οὐκ οἴδατε in v. 16 imply that the author is alluding to some form of instruction which the faithful have received on a previous

---

[1] See above, p. 358 n. 1.

[2] Cf. Michel, Th. W. V, p. 129 line 29s. : "Man wird wohl sagen dürfen, dasz dieser Traditionsstoff festgefügtes urschristliches κήρυγμα ist" ("one may say that this traditional material is basic ancient Christian κήρυγμα"). Mussner, Christus, das All und die Kirche", p. 115, similarly observes : "Der Eph. 2:20-22 vorgetragen Kirchenbegriff vom pneumatischen Gottestempel gehört also zu einer Tradition, die sich ... durch das ganze N.T. hindurchzieht" ("the ecclesiological conception of the pneumatological temple of God as presented in Eph. 2:20-22, thus forms part of a tradition which is maintained... throughout the entire N.T.").

[3] This is proved by Gärtner's analyses of 2 C. 6:14-7:1; 1 C. 3:16, 17; Eph. 2:18-22; 1 Tm. 3:15; 1 Pt. 2:3-6 and Heb. 12:18-24 (op. cit., p. 47-98). Cf. his observation : "... the infiltration of Qumran traditions must have taken place at a very early date, or it would not be represented in such divergent traditions as Paul, 1 Peter and Hebrews" (p. 122). Since this does not fall within the scope of the present work, we shall leave aside the question whether Gärtner does not draw too direct a connection between the relevant texts and the Qumran manuscripts.

[4] Paley has described this phenomenon as "the going off at a word"; cf. Abbott, Eph.-Col., p. xxii.

occasion.[1] It would seem that it was probably part of Paul's teaching to tell the faithful that the ecclesia was God's building, temple and planting. (A warning that the temple should not be defiled through dissidence follows in v. 17.)

In 2 C. 6:16-18, the ecclesia and the temple are likewise identified. The context exhorts against contamination of the temple in terms strongly reminiscent of pronouncements found in the Qumran works.[2] The thought expressed in v. 18, that the faithful are the sons and daughters of God, corresponds with the qualification members "the household of God" in Eph. 2:19.

When the allegory of building in Eph. 2:19-20 concerns the subject of the foundation, it has less affinity with the HP than the rest of the passage. Whereas, in Eph. 2:20, it is the apostles and prophets who are described as the foundation, in 1 C. 3:11, 12, it is Christ who is the foundation.

However, undue importance should not be attached to this discrepancy since the somewhat random [3] allegorical digression of 1 C. 3:10-15 was almost certainly formulated ad hoc. No less attention should be paid to the points which do correspond. In Eph., the apostles and prophets, in their capacity of a foundation, are defined in terms of Christ who is the corner-stone. They function as a foundation because they spread the gospel. In the HP it is also the proclamation of the gospel which is involved when the metaphor of the foundation is introduced. The first revelation of the gospel, through which people are turned towards the faith and Christ, is called the laying down of the foundations in 1 C. 3:10-15 and, as apparent from the words "another man's foundations" in R. 15:20, is regarded as the basic work.

The most probable explanation for the divergence between Eph. and the HP in this respect is that the kerugma which formed the background to Eph. 2:19-22; 1 C. 3:9-17 and R. 15:20, did not entail a fixed conception of the foundation. In the Qumran scrolls, the words denoting foundation also have a flexible meaning.[4]

Besides the passage Eph. 2:19-22, the expression "building" appears

---

[1] For the meaning of these and corresponding words and expressions, see D. Plooy, Studies in the Testimony Book, 1932 (Verh. Kon. Akad, van Wet., afd. Lett. Nieuwe Reeks, deel 33, no. 2), p. 24 and Gärtner, op. cit., p. 57.

[2] Cf. Gärtner, op. cit., p. 49ss. and Braun, Qumran und das N.T. I, p. 201-203.

[3] Cf. Vielhauer, op. cit., p. 83s.

[4] See 1 QS 5,5ss.; 8,5 and 9:1ss. (Brongers, De Gedragsregels, pp. 71, 79s. and 81); cf. Braun, op. cit., I, p. 187 and Gärtner, op. cit., p. 68s.

in Eph. 4:12, 16 and 29. The last-mentioned offers little of outstanding interest; edification is mentioned in connection with words the faithful utter and occurs of necessity. From 4:30 and 5:18, 19, it becomes obvious that this is to be interpreted as spiritual speech. We are therefore strongly reminded of 1 C. 14:26, with the provision that there is no assumption of the question of glossolalia.[1]

What does emerge from all this is that in building the faithful obtain grace through each other. The ecclesia is built when, by virtue of inter-community, grace is bestowed. The spiritual word is the vehicle of grace.

An interesting feature of Eph. 4:12 and 16 is that these texts speak of building the body of Christ. However, this is in keeping with the nature of the matter. The author's conception of building is denuded of all individualism; as we have just seen from 4:29 and, earlier on, from 2:21 (p. 358), building presupposes fellowship and cooperation. Moreover, this is of advantage on all counts. It is therefore significant when 4:12 and 16 expound on "the edifying of the body of Christ".

Although it occurs nowhere else in the CP, the content of the expression is in perfect harmony with the concept of oikodome as evinced in the HP, as Vielhauer so rightly observed.[2]

We are unwilling to accept the religio-historical explication which Vielhauer gives; the "iranisch-gnostische" ("Iranian-gnostic") principles seem to underlie Eph. 4:12 and 16 no more than they do Eph. 2:20-22.

(The substitution of a term denoting building for a person, as in Manichaeism, provides an equally inadequate solution for the term "the edification of the body of Christ" as the combination of this substitution with yet another which occurs in Manichaeism, i.e. that of the salvator and his body.[3]

---

[1] For the correspondence with 1 C. 14:26, cf. Vielhauer, op. cit., p. 144. Within the CP the glossolalist aspect is mentioned only in 1 C.

[2] Vielhauer, op. cit., p. 142 : "Mit dieser Formel 'Bau des Leibes Christi' hat der Eph.—auf den sachlichen theologischen Gehalt gesehen—auch die eigentliche Intention des paulinischen Oikodome-Begriffes zu ihrem schärfsten Ausdruck gebracht" ("With the formula "edification of the body of Christ", Eph.—from the point of view of actual theological content—has most potently expressed the real point of the Pauline oikodome-concept").

[3] Cf. the criticism of Colpe and Schenke on interpretations of this nature, based on Manichaeism. See above, p. 266-269. Furthermore, in dealing with the expressions soma and kephale, we have already indicated that the Gnostic soma-kephale pattern as described by Schlier and Käsemann does not explain the use of the term soma in Eph.

This figure of speech can in the first place by explained on the basis of the highly meaningful connection between the expressions oikodome and soma, to which we have already drawn attention. Other factors to be taken into account are a traditional Jewish conception, allegorical in character, which we have attempted to elucidate as well as the identification of the expressions for body and building which, as already mentioned,[1] came readily to mind for a Jewish Hellenist.)

As Vielhauer sees it, the difference in the expression oikodome in the HP and in Eph. can be traced back to the background as reconstructed by the religio-historical school.[2] In the opinion of K. L. Schmidt, the only difference between the ecclesiology of the HP and that of Eph. is the use of a "gnostisch-mythologische Begriffssprache" ("gnostic-mythological terms of reference")[3].

We have been unable to find such a gnostic terminology either in the conceptions governing building and growth nor in the various expressions relating to the ecclesia, to which we devoted our previous chapter.

We reaffirm that in our view the author of Eph. is not motivated by the trend which led, by way of Hellenistic Jewish speculations, to the later dualism and plastic mythology of Gnosticism.[4] His only convergence with Gnosticism lies therein that his mind was rooted in Jewish traditions and Hellenistic Jewish speculations and that he sometimes makes use of the same expressions. To ascribe to the author of Eph. a Gnostic way of thinking and talking is to do him an injustice and it is fruitless to continue in pursuit of a Gnostic background to Eph. which can serve to enhance an argument against the authenticity of the epistle.

In our study of the allegory of building, we ascertained that the ecclesia is envisaged as the spiritualised, new (eschatological) temple. As a result, the ecclesia acquires the complexion of a spiritual cult. This aspect comes out with some frequency.

In 5:2 the fact that Christ loved the addressees is presented as an example to them, whereby the act of his love is described as an offering

---

(cf. p. 285). Vielhauer speculates entirely on the basis of this construction (cf. op. cit., p. 132).

[1] See above, p. 316-319 and particularly note 3 on p. 318.

[2] Op. cit., p. 142.

[3] See above, p. 353 n. 2.

[4] See above, pp. 333, 348.

and sacrifice. Although the terminology used does not exclude the bloody nature of this sacrifice, it does not stress it.

In order to characterise the act of Christ as a sacrifice, it was not strictly necessary to add the qualification εἰς ὀσμὴν εὐωδίας to the words προσφορὰν καὶ θυσίαν τῷ θεῷ. Nevertheless, this adjunct comes at the end with some emphasis. The fact is, that to a Hellenistic Jewish mind, these word readily lent themselves to a figurative use, indicating a wise way of life which is pleasing to God or characterising the bloodless celestial ritual.[1]

Probably, the author of Eph. wishes to make clear with this adjunct that the imitation of Christ's love, which he exhorts, is as pleasing to God as the sacrifice of Christ.

Indeed, one has the impression that in reality he also sees the description of the sacrifice, which he attaches to the example, as relevant to the imitation. His intention seems to be that to walk in love, according to the example of Christ, is not only pleasing to God but it is also, as that love of Christ, to be regarded in the light of a sacrifice. To describe the sacrifice of Christ he has terefore made use of a terminology which does not accentuate the bloody character of that sacrifice and even ends towards a spiritual meaning.

A ritual aspect could also be inherent to the expression ἔργον διακονίας in 4:12. There exists a difference of opinion with respect to the grammatical coherency of the three adjuncts introduced by a preposition of which this forms a part.[2]

In our opinion, these three adjuncts are not coordinated.[3] The adjunct εἰς ἔργον διακονίας is dependent on the adjunct πρὸς τὸν καταρτισμὸν τῶν ἁγίων. The third adjunct, εἰς οἰκοδομὴν τοῦ σώματος τοῦ Χριστοῦ expresses that the building of the body of Christ is realized both by the καταρτισμὸς τῶν ἁγίων as well as the directly resulting ἔργον διακονίας.

Haupt is quite correct in associating the phrase πρὸς τὸν καταρτισμὸν τῶν ἁγίων εἰς ἔργον διακονίας with v. 7 in which it is stated that Christ has given grace to each believer according to a certain measure. He

---

[1] See Wenschkewitz, op. cit., pp. 19 and 45ss. which deal with Jub. 2:22, Apoc. Mos. 33 (erroneously quoted by W. as Vita Adae et Evae 33) and Test. Levi 3. For ὀσμή and εὐωδία as Hellenistic-Jewish characterisations for wisdom and the wise, see A. Stumpff, Th. W. II, p. 808. line 40s. and p. 809 lines 1-8.

[2] See Haupt, Die Gefangenschaftsbriefe, p. 140ss.; Abbott, Eph. -Col.,p. 119; Vielhauer, op. cit., p. 131; Hanson, The Unity of the Church, p. 156 and Schlier, Der Eph., p. 198s.

[3] See above p. 113.

writes : "Die im Vorigen genannten Apostel, Propheten u.s.w. sind von Christo darum gegeben, um die gesammte Gemeinde (τῶν ἁγίων) instand zu setzen, ihre Aufgabe der Diakonie zu lösen ... und zwar zo, dass, wie V. 16 abschliessend sagt, die Gesammtgemeinde in dem Masse sich auferbaut, in welchem jedes einzelne Glied die ihm speziell gegebene Aufgabe löst.".[1]

But what, then, is the precise meaning of the words ἔργον διακονίας ?

Abbott, Hanson and Schlier, who quite incorrectly connect the expression διακονία with the apostles, prophets, etc. mentioned in v. 11, respectively hold the word to mean "official service"; a "ministry" to which the apostles etc. have been appointed by Christ, or a "Dienst" ("service") which is based on a permanent mandate which the kurios has enjoined upon those who have been delegated.[2]

It would appear that these scholars cannot conceive that the expression ἔργον διακονίας may merely mean that a man is of use or service to Christ or his fellow-believers; in their eyes, the expression clearly has a official character.

In our judgement, the word διακονία delineates service to Christ and the helping of fellow-believers, whilst the expression ἔργον διακονίας in addition conveys the idea of one or another public task. What we ask ourselves in this context, is why, without any preliminaries, the life of the believers is here characterised as a life of service.

Now it seems to us that the word ἔργον is tantamount to a task or a function which is being completed or exercised.[3] We furthermore observe that Flavius Josephus sometimes uses the word διακονεῖσθαι to describe the fulfilling of the office of priesthood and that he assesses this office as much a service to God as a service to men.[4]

H. W. Beyer records that the word διακονεῖν is totally foreign to the LXX. However, he also relates that during the period of N.T. formation, the word primarily had the connotation of "to fulfil religious and ritual duties".[5]

---

[1] See op. cit., p. 143s. Trans. : "The afore-mentioned apostles, prophets, etc., have been given by Christ so that the whole community (τῶν ἁγίων) is able to fulfil its task in the diaconate ... and that in the way explicitly stated in v. 16, ... i.e. that the whole community builds itself up in proportion to the degree in which each single individual absolves his special task.".

[2] See the places quoted in note 2 on p. 366.

[3] Cf. Liddell-Scott, s.v. IV.

[4] Cf. the examples quoted by H. W. Beyer, Th. W II, p. 83 lines 5-7.

[5] Op. cit., p. 82 lines 38-40 and p. 81 lines 13-15.

The fact that Flavius Josephus uses διακονεῖσθαι where the transla-
tors of the LXX would have selected an alternative word, leads to
the assumption that Hellenistic Jews of his time represented O.T.
expressions in which the words עָבַד and עֲבֹדָה occur, with formulations
containing the words διακονεῖσθαι and διακονία.

As has already been observed, Palestinian Judaism was familiar
with spiritualised versions of ritual terms. The term עֲבֹדָה also lent itself to such a transformation. After the destruction of the temple
of Jerusalem, rabbinical Judaism often equated the study of the law
and living according to the law with the עֲבֹדָה or temple service.[1]

It is our impression that the Hellenistic-Jewish author of Eph. who,
in 2:18-22 ,had already applied a spiritualised meaning to the term
προσαγωγή, and who was preoccupied with the conception of a
spiritual temple, was thinking of the spiritual ritual which belonged
to the spiritual temple when he used the words ἔργον διακονίας in
4:12. We hold that the formulation hearks back to the expression
מְלֶאכֶת עֲבוֹדָה which remains extant in 1 Ch. 9:13. In Eph., the spiritual
"service- task" consists of the mutual help or service (ἐπιχορηγία) for
the sake of Christ's will, of which the faithful are capable, according to
4:16 (and 4:7), by virtue of the grace given to each.

For the problem of the authenticity of Eph., it is important to establish whether the life of the faithful in the HP bears the same ritual
aspect.

In Phil. 2:17, it is depicted as a sacrifice and a priestly duty.[2] The
Christians of Rome are urged towards a spiritualised sacrifice and a
spiritual service (R. 12:1) and perhaps even represented as priestly
servants of God (R. 13:6).[3]

It could be that the word diakonia in R. 12:7 has the same bearing
as the word in Eph. 4:12, in which case it should be interpreted as
referring to the spiritualised ritual.[4]

---

[1] For עֲבֹדָה denoting temple service, see Num .4:23, 35; Ex. 30:16; 35:24; 1 Ch. 9:13
and 28:14. For the spiritualisation of this term in rabbinical Judaism, see Meyer, Th. W.
IV, p. 231s. Gärtner, op. cit., p. 45s., maintains that this spiritualisation of the עֲבֹדָה
in fact already existed amongst the community at Qumran.

[2] Cf. Strathmann, Th. W. IV, p. 234 line 32ss. and Haupt, Die Gefangenschaftsbriefe,
p. 104.

[3] See J. A. C. van Leeuwen and D. Jacobs, De brief aan de Romeinen (Kampen ²1939),
p. 252.

[4] In general, the word διακονία in the HP relates to the activity of specific persons.
This is also the case when the word appears for the first time (in the accusative) in

One of the typical characteristic features of the ecclesiology of Eph. is the particular concern evinced for the unity of the community. This idea of unity has been worked out more consistently in our epistle than in any other.

As, for example, the implications of the expression oikodome [1] and the importance of the conception of the body [2] are set forth more lucidly in Eph. than in many a homologoumenon, so as the unity of the ecclesia is also promoted more forcefully than in any other epistle.

The unity theme comes to the forefront again and again as part of the conception of the soma as a whole organism constituted of closely cooperating parts. However, it is more than just part of that conception. For the author, the idea of this unity is of fundemental significance to all his thinking and is in essence determined by his belief in the unity of God.

In 4:6 he declares this faith in an avowal which bears the stamp of Hellenistic Judaism.[3] He knows the single God as the father of all. Therefore, the present state of confusion and dividedness in all things must not persist. God has resolved. before the beginning of ages, to gather together the universe in Christ.

The glorified Christ makes this plan into a reality. He fills all things with his dominion and the blessings of his kingdom (pp. 217; 236s.; 239; 243s.). This fulfilment means unification.

If God is the father of all things, He is also the father of all men. The second category is definitely envisaged when the word "all" is used (p. 216). It is not for nothing that 3:5 states that this conusel was formerly unknown to the ctegory of man (sons of men). Men too, must become one; for God desires a new humanity (2:15).

This unity of men exists in the ecclesia. The faithful are one body (4:4). Because they have a relationship with the one crucified body, they can be nothing but a single and undivided body (p. 298s.).

Spiritual gifts enable them to achieve such a unity (4:7, 8). Christ, who fills all things with the blessings of his dominion, fulfils the ecclesia,

---

R. 12:7. But it becomes clear in the same place that this word, as the words πίστις, ἁπλότης, σπουδή and ἱλαρότης can be one of the fundamental characteristics of the lives of all the faithful. When used for the second time in R. 12:7 (in the dative), it is as comprehensive as in Eph. 4:12.

[1] See p. 364 and note 2.

[2] Chapter VII, para. 5b. describes the great importance of the conception of the soma in Eph. We also showed that ideas connected with this concept are not lacking in the HP.

[3] Cf. above. p. 364 and note 2. See also Hanson, op. cit., p. 58.

which is his body, with the pneuma and the spiritual gifts (pp. 241s., 291). In this way the promise which Israel received, becomes fact.

Also those who were strangers to this promise (2:12) obtain a share in it through the gospel. They may also belong to the body (3:6). When Christ created the new humanity, he made the group of circumcised and the group of uncircimcised into a single, renewed humanity (2:14, 15).[1]

The unity of the ecclesia encompasses humanity. The gifts with which Christ fills the ecclesia are gifts to men (4:8). In the unity of the ecclesia, the all-embracing unifying work of God has already found its embodiement (p. 345).

Although the unity of the ecclesia does not occupy as prominent a place in the HP as it does in Eph., it is nevertheless taught in a corresponding manner. In the HP we also find this idea side by side with the conception of the body (R. 12:4ss. and 1 C. 12:12ss.). The expression "new creature" in 2 C. 5:14, 15 and 17 places the unity of the faithful against the background of the salutary activity of an all-encompassing God.[2]

The implication of God's eschatological work is the cessation of the division between the two groups of circumcised and uncircumcised (Gal. 6:15, 16).[3] Nations too, have a stake in the salvation promised to Israel (R. 15:8-12 and Gal. 3:29). Those who have a share in the salvation of the messianic peace promised to Israel, are a new humanity (R. 5:1, 12-21).[4]

Eph. 2:14-17 deals with a certain facet of the unity of the ecclesia; it stresses the end of the schism between the circumcised and the uncircumcised and expresses in no uncertain terms that the ecclesia is the new humanity.

At this juncture, it seems important to us to establish that the material at hand does not constitute a convergence of mythological and Gnostic factors, alien to the HP, thereby adopting a different stand from Schlier and Schille.[5]

---

[1] See p. 337 above.

[2] For the cosmic aspect of the expression καινὴ κτίσις, see H. Ridderbos, Paulus, p. 41s.

[3] Cf. H. Ridderbos, op. cit., p. 316.

[4] For peace as the salvation promised to Israel, falling to the share of both circumcised and uncircumcised, see Gal. 5:15. For the new humanity, cf. also 1 C. 15:22 and 49.

[5] Cf. Schlier, Der Eph., p. 122-133; Schille, Liturgisches Gut im Eph., p. 5-9 and id., Frühchristiliche Hymnen, p. 27-30.

It is our view that the passage presents no other elements besides an assimilation of Jewish thoughts and O.T. references. Thus, the phrase "for he is our peace" in Eph. 2:14, is a reiteration of Mi. 5:5. Apparently, contemporary opinion dictated that the Messiah is the one designated as "peace". (In old rabbinical texts, the same appellation is used. This was in conformity with Is. 9:6.)[1]

Various features of Eph. 2:14-22, i.e. the thoughts concerning the unification of two groups, the peace of the messianic era and the conceptions governing the foundation and the house of God, can also be found in Ez. 37:15-28. (Although the expression "foundation" is not found in the Masoretic version of the text, judging by the "et fundabo eos" in the Vulgate Ez. 27:26, it has from ancient times onwards been found in this place from time to time.)

This parallelism between Eph. 2:14-22 and Ez. 37:15-28, leads us to assume that the statement "who has made both one" in 2:14 is a reference to Ez. 37:17 and 22.

Noteworthy enough, the same section of Ez. 37:15-28 also plays a part in 2 C. 6:16, Ez. 37:27 being one of the quotations on which the author bases his declarations about the ecclesia as a temple.

The image of the division wall which forms an enclosure ($\tau\grave{o}$ $\mu\epsilon\sigma\acute{o}\tau o\iota$-$\chi o\nu$ $\tau o\hat{v}$ $\phi\rho\alpha\gamma\mu o\hat{v}$) is Jewish. The metaphor of the enclosure was current in Hellenistic and rabbinical Judaism wilst the Qumran scrolls repeatedly mention a wall. The law of Moses and the way of life which was based upon it, were as a protection for the nation of Israel.[2]

In using the words $\tau\grave{o}$ $\mu\epsilon\sigma\acute{o}\tau o\iota\chi o\nu$ $\tau o\hat{v}$ $\phi\rho\alpha\gamma\mu o\hat{v}$, the author of Eph. must have had the law of Moses and all that appertains to it in mind, but with this he deals later. In Eph. 2:14, he merely intimates that an irrevocable difference previously existed between Jews and gentiles and that this has been brought to an end by Christ.[3]

The following words in 2:15, namely $\tau\grave{\eta}\nu$ $\check{\epsilon}\chi\theta\rho\alpha\nu$ $\dot{\epsilon}\nu$ $\tau\hat{\eta}$ $\sigma\alpha\rho\kappa\grave{\iota}$ $\alpha\dot{v}\tauo\hat{v}$,

---

[1] Cf. Str.-B., III, p. 587. According to Mi. 5:5; Ez. 34:25; 37:26 and Zech. 9:10, peace is the salvation of the messianic era.

[2] For the image of partition in Hellenistic and rabbinical Judaism, see Mussner, Christus, das All und die Kirche, p. 81ss. and Str.-B. III, op. 127 and 588). In Damasc. 4,12; 4,19; 8:12. and 1 QS 8,7 (cf. Brongers, De Gedragsregels, pp. 28, 29, 34 and 79) a wall is mentioned. It would seem that this wall is not virtuous if the law is not faithfully observed with respect to its doctrine and a life compatible with it; when the law is well taught, the wall is good and firm.

[3] The word $\mu\epsilon\sigma\acute{o}\tau o\iota\chi o\nu$ or $\mu\epsilon\sigma\acute{o}\tau o\iota\chi o\varsigma$ is rare; an exemple of figurative use in which the word applies to a diametrical antithesis is found in C. Schneider, Th. W. IV, p. 629 line 15ss.

form a vital interpretative issue.[1] Whilst engaged upon our study of the style of the epistle, we found that together with the words τὸν νόμον τῶν ἐντολῶν ἐν δόγμασιν, they form a complete whole.[2] The words τὴν ἔχθραν ἐν τῇ σαρκὶ αὐτοῦ καταργήσας belong together and indicate that Christ was able to unite the two groups of Jews and gentiles and could dissolve the great difference between these two because he put enmity to an end in his flesh.

The formulation τὸν νόμον τῶν ἐντολῶν ἐν δόγμασιν has been added to the word τὴν ἔχθραν as a corollary.[3] The annihilation of enmity also constituted an abolition of the law. By virtue of this dissolution, both groups could become one and find reconciliation with God.[4]

Having made an end to enmity, Christ became the king of Zech. 9:9, 10 who "comes" and shall "speak peace unto the nations". The peace of which he speaks is the peace for "the far" and "the near", which was prophecied in Is. 57:19.

We hold that the author is here presenting a review of Jewish messianic expectations. The peace mentioned in the passage, is the messianic salvation which comes from God and which implies a new relationship with God. The enmity mentioned, in the antithesis of this peace and consists of an unredeemed confusion.

In this passage, a new element is integrated into such Jewish expectations, viz. the concurrence and unity of Jew and pagan. For the pagan too, there is a messianic salvation; in unity with the Jew, he shares in the new relationship with God.

The state of enmity which is terminated, is contrary to peace partly because it goes hand in hand with opposition and discord between Jew and pagan. This enmity is fostered by the law which engenders a wrong relationship with God and promotes division and strife between Jews and pagans. The law has a dual action; it not only keeps the Jew apart from God but it also brings about a schism between Jew and gentile.[5]

---

[1] Cf. Abbott, Eph.-Col., p. 61ss. and Haupt, Die Gefangenschaftsbriefe, p. 78ss.

[2] See above, pp. 128, 139 (166). We assume that in dealing with the formulation τὸν νόμον τῶν ἐντολῶν ἐν δόγμασιν we have before us an example of an idiosyncracy sometimes found in Eph., whereby two substantives are linked by ἐν. For this peculiarity, see p. 114s.

[3] J. Moffat, The New Testament, a New Translation (London, new edition revised), p. 284 translates : "in his own flesh he put an end to the feud of the Law with its code of commands".

[4] For the exegesis cf. p. 289s. above.

[5] See Foerster, Th. W. II, p. 413s.

The train of thought evinced in Eph. 2:14-17, corresponds with ideas in the HP. Again and again, the HP epistles proclaim that the great difference between Jew and pagan has found resolution in Christ (Gal. 3:28; R. 10:12; 1 C. 7:19 and Gal. 5:6). The end of this schism is directly linked with the death of Christ.

As a result of the law on which the Jew is dependent and to which he looks for guidance, there is discord between Jews and gentiles (R. 2: 17-24). Christ represents the end of the law. Rignteousness according to the rule of the law has been replaced by the avowal of Christ as Lord, the belief that God has raised him and the invocation of the name of the Lord (R. 10:4-13).

Jew and pagan have an equal share in the salvation which is in Jesus Christ. The dispensation laid down by the law has now been replaced by the ministry of reconciliation (R. 3:24, 25; 4:25; 1 C. 3:1-18; Gal. 4:21-31). This reconciliation exists by virtue of Christ's death.

In the HP, the unblessed relationship with God which was brought to an end through the reconciliation, is also characterised as a state of enmity (R. 5:10; 8:7). This enmity is identical with sin. Sin is the result of the law and the commandment (R. 7:7ss.; R. 8:2-7).

The new relationship of salvation with God, is peace (R. 5:1). Unlike Eph. 2:14-17, the expressions "enemy" and "peace" are not applied to the inter-relationship between the circumcised and the uncircumcised. However, it is clear that enmity of God is concomitant with enmity towards fellow-men (R. 3:10-18; Gal. 5:20) and that peace with God has the implication of a peaceful relationship with all fellow-men (R. 3:17, 18; Gal. 5:22; 1 C. 7:15; 14:33 and 2 C. 13:11).

It is noteworthy that there is a particularly strong link between R. and Eph. 2:14-17. Expressions such as "enmity", "peace", "reconciliation with God" and the notion of the law as a negative influence are all found in both Eph. 2:14-17 and R. 5 (5:1, 10, 13 and 18).

The term "access" which follows in Eph. 2:18, likewise has its counterpart in R. 5 (namely in R. 5:13). In addition, the idea expressed in Eph. 2:14-17 and the adjacent verses, that Israel possesses certain spiritual prerogatives and that the gentiles will be saved together with Israel, is also present in R. 9:1-4, 24-29 and 11:25-36.

On the basis of the above, we may therefore assert that over and above the points of formal correspondence we found between Eph. and R. (pp. 64, 197ss., 206s.), there exists also a close association with respect to thought-matter.

Furthermore, it may be remarked that the correspondence in content between Eph. 2:14-17 and the HP has another remarkable aspect. Statements in these epistles which are akin to Eph. 2:14-17, are often so placed and formulated within an avowal, that they have the character of a sententia or decider. In this connection, we are thinking of Gal. 3:28; R. 10:12; 1 C. 7:19; Gal. 5:6; R. 8:7; 10:4; 1 C. 15:22; Gal. 3:28 and 6:15.

Such places give the impression that Paul and the possible co-senders of the epistles are alluding to principal truths of which the recipients are already aware.

The correspondence between Eph. 2:14-17 and these statements concerning fundamental truths, leads us to believe that this passage more or less provides an example of the kind of basic teaching which Paul and his associates gave to new converts, which would form a framework for future reference.

This assumption conforms with our theory that Eph. is an authentic Pauline writing, addressed to persons but recently converted to the revelation of the gospel.

Another point to which we would like to draw attention is that in the use of O.T. material, as, for example, the expression "who has made both one" or v. 17. the method used to explain O.T. words is the same as that identified by H. J. Schoeps in the case of R. Prophecies which in fact speak of re-acceptance for the rejected nation of Israel, are interpreted in such a way that they refer to a common vocation for Jews and gentiles.[1]

But the passage Eph. 2:14-17 differs from R. in one respect : the idea justification through the faith is missing from Eph. Although the declaration on abolishing or nullifying the law is reminiscent of the edict in R. 10; 4, the notion of justification is lacking. This is also the case elsewhere in Eph.

Eph. is totally in keeping with the pivotal profession with which Paul proclaims his gospel in R. 1:16. "To the Jew first, and also to the Greek" could be regarded as the theme of Eph. The words "for by grace you have been saved through faith" (Eph. 2:8) echo Paul's words "for it is the power of God unto salvation to every one who believes". However, the term "righteousness" which occurs in R. 1:17, does not occur in Eph. 2.

This absence of the doctrine of justification through the faith could

---

[1] See his Paulus, Die Theologie des Apostels im Lichte der Jüdischen Religionsgeschichte, p. 247s.

be explained on the basis of the hypothesis that Eph. is not authentic. Nevertheless, such an explanation would need to be questioned on several counts.

It is, after all, a fact that extensive homologoumena exist which occasionally betray a familiarity with this notion, yet lack the salient formulations of R. and Gal. and omit to draw the direct connection between the conceptions of righteousness and faith. Here we are thinking of 1 and 2 C. and particularly 1 C. 1:30; 6:11 and 2 C. 5:21; 3:9 and 11:5. Moreover, there is the homologoumenon 1 Th. which does not even evince a familiarity with the notion to this extent.

On the other hand, there are post-Pauline works which are certainly less closely associated with the HP than Eph.; yet these contain certain formulations which show that their authors were aware that the notion of justification through the faith is part of the Pauline heritage. In this connection, we are thinking of Barn. 13:7; 1 Cl. 31:2; 32:4; Ign., Phld. 8:2; 2 Cl. 11:1 and Pol., Phil. 8:1.

A wholly implausible explanation to account for this absence of the idea of justification through the faith in Eph., is the hypothesis reasoned by Mitton, on the basis of the epistle's inauthenticity.

The theory of Mitton is that the author of the epistle, an admirer of Paul, was writing for gentiles and, being himself gentile, knew that references to justification and the law were meaningless to readers not versed in the traditions of the synagogue. However, this theory is not acceptable to us for the following reasons.[1]

In the course of this study, we have had frequent opportunity to observe that the author of this epistle must have been a Hellenistic Jew. For example, in Eph. 2:11-19, he uses a munber of terms which are in keeping with the kind of teaching practised in the Hellenistic synagogeus. Moreover, in the case of Eph. 2:12-19, it is even a reasonable proposition that he is keeping to the words traditionally used in these synagogues for former pagans who had been entirely converted to Judaism.[2] In 2:15, there is an unmistakeable reference to the law.

---

[1] For Mitton, see above, p. 8s.

[2] See Str.-B. III, p. 585s. for ἐγγύς and μακράν. In Hellenistic Judaism, the words πάροικος and προσήλυτος were used promiscuously; if the distinction between the circumcised and the uncircumsiced was being stressed, they tended to use the term προσήλυτος for the former and πάροικος for the latter; cf. Meyer, Th. W. V, p. 848s.; K. Lake in Jackson-Lake V, p. 83s.; Meuzelaar, Der Leib des Messias, p. 62, note 1 and Klein, Der älteste christliche Katechismus, p. 172. For the term προσαγωγή with reference to proselytes, see bove, p. 353 note 4 and for the notion that proselytes were taken into a community

There seems to be no reason why an author who was quite content to have used terms such as these, should specifically have shrunk back from using the term justification.

Our feelings on the matter take a different bent. It seems to us that the idea of justification through the faith is one of the most characteristic element throughont the theology of Paul; those who takes the understating of this aspect as the basis for interpreting his theology, have lost track of the essential Paul.

However, sometimes Paul would draw attention to the central truths of the kerugma without especially mentioning this aspect of justification. This occurs, for example, in 1 C. 15:3, 4; 1:23, 24 and 2:2. Similarly, in Eph. he again enumerates the main themes of the kerugma without drawing special attention to justification through the faith.

One subject he does deal with in extenso in Eph., is a matter of deep personal concern in his theology and the very guiding principle behind all Paul's work. We refer, of course, to Paul's mission amongst the pagans and their share in the salvation of Christ, which is also described at length in Gal. 1:15-2:10. In all probability, this aspect' was of overwhelming fundamental importance to Paul, overriding all others.

The idea of justification through the faith is directly connected with this mission amongst the pagans and the revelation of their share in the salvation of Christ. However, in this context it has a more or less secondary function, serving to illuminate how it is possible that the pagans may partake in salvation.

Paul only enters upon discussions and debates on the law and justification through the faith in R. and Gal. There is a reason for this. He wished to establish firmly that principle on which he expounds so extensively in Gal. 1:15-2:10.

If it was unnecessary to defend that principle, such discussions could be left aside. However, that does not imply that the ideas expressed in such polemics were then forgotten or that there was a change in the train of thought.

We are therefore totally at odds with Schlier who believes that Eph. 2:14 b c and 15 a are examples of an "Uminterpretation" (reinterpretation) of material which hails from a quite different background than the "paulinisch-jüdischen Gesetzesdebatte".[1]

---

household, see Meuzelaar, op. cit., p. 63 (note 4). The references to proselytes which van Unnik, op. cit., p. 72ss. collected in Philo, bear witness to the interest evinced in them in the Hellenistic synagogue and gives the impression that words were also addressed to them at their conversion.

[1] "Pauline-Jewish controversies about the law"; cf. Schlier, Der Eph., p. 126.

The unity of the ecclesia which is so characteristic an aspect of the ecclesiology of Eph. is closely related to the mystery which is also repeatedly mentioned in Eph. (1:9; 3:4; 9; 6:19). This mystery is connected with the all-encompassing unifying work of God. This work of God finds realization in the unity of the ecclesia. The fact that the gentiles also form part of the one body of Christ which is the ecclesia, is of cardinal significance in the mystery.[1]

The term "mystery" has a certain Jewish character. In the LXX and the Book of Daniel, the word μυστήριον appears as a translation of the Aramaic רָז and denotes a secret plan of God or a detail of such a plan. A secret of this kind is revealed in an indirect fashion, i.e. in a dream of by a number of words in an unintelligible script. Only God or a person who has been inspired by the spirit of God may unveil the meaning of the secret or mystery.[2]

Similar mysteries were known to the writers of Hellenistic Jewish apocalyptic literature.[3] In the Qumran scrolls, where they play a role of considerable importance, they are indicated through the words רָז and סוֹד.[4]

J. van der Ploeg had the following to say about mysteries in the biblical commentaries of the Qumran community : "De Leeraar der gerechtigheid was er zich van bewust, dat hij van God openbaringen had ontvangen omtrent "geheimen", die tevoren verborgen waren. God had hun zelfs "alle geheimen van zijn dienaren de profeten" meegedeeld ... het zijn goddelijke raadsbesluiten door de woorden der profeten aangeduid en nu door openbaring daarin duidelijk geworden aan de ingewijde. God heeft van het begin af zijn plan met de wereld vastgesteld nog voor de dingen geschapen waren ...".[5] Rabbinical literature also speaks of mysteries.[6]

---

[1] For this train of reasoning, see above, p. 369s.

[2] See J. de Zwaan, Paulus als geestelijke hervormer (Amsterdam 1932), p. 126s. and G. Bornkamm, Th. W. IV, p. 821.

[3] See Eth. En. 61:5 and Bornkamm, l.c.

[4] Cf. Kuhn, "Der Eph. im Lichte der Qumrantexte", p. 336.

[5] Cf.v.d. Ploeg, Vondsten in de woestijn van Juda, De Rollen van de Dode Zee(²1957), p. 109s. See also v.d. Woude, Bijbelcommentaren enz., p. 10. Trans. : "The Teacher of righteousness was aware that he had received revelations from God concerning "mysteries" which had formerly been hidden. God had even "revealed all the secrets of his servants the prophets" ... these are divine resolutions, intimated by the words of the prophets which have now become clear to the intitiated through revelation. God has from the beginning, before things were created, resolved on his plan for the world ..."

[6] Cf. Str.-B. I, p. 695s. In this literature, the words רָז and סוֹד, מִסְתָּרִין, מִסְטְרִין or סֵתֶר are used for this term.

For Judaism, the word had a number of aspects. A secret can be eschatological in nature—this is first encountered in the Book of Daniel.[1] There is also a cosmic (or cosmogonic) aspect to the word. Creation is full of secrets and possesses invisible forces and cosmic spaces which are a secret.[2] The two aspects go together when unknown changes in the cosmos are revealed which will take place in the unknown, now revealed, end of time.[3]

In addition, the notion of the principle or foundation can also be associated with the term "secret". Words which are connected with the term "secret" can sometimes have a double meaning in the Qumran texts; they simultaneously serve to draw attention to the mystery which has been entrusted to the community and to the character of a foundation which is the attribute of the community. The community is a foundation because a secret revelation has been unveiled for them.[4]

The expression "mystery" in Eph. fits within the framework of such Jewish conceptions. Eschatological in nature, the term at the same has a cosmic character. The context concerns an age-old godly plan that was probably determined before the beginning of the world. This secret resolve had already been intimated by the O.T. prophets and in the books of the law. That explains why the author, when dealing with the unity of the ecclesia in Eph. 2:14 and 17, looks to Ez. 37:17, 27; Zech. 9:10 and Is. 57:19 (p. 371s.) and gives an explication of Gen. 2:24 in Eph. 5:32.

Indeed, in the last-mentioned place, he even writes that Gen. 2:24 is a great mystery. (In this instance the word $\mu\nu\sigma\tau\acute{\eta}\rho\iota\sigma\nu$ means : a veiled intimation of a hidden plan. The plan in question is a detail of the great

---

[1] Bornkamm, l.c. : "$\mu\nu\sigma\tau\acute{\eta}\rho\iota\sigma\nu$ hat bei Daniel zum erstenmal den für die weitere Geschichte des Begriffes bedeutsamen Sinn eines eschatologischen Begriffes" ("It is in Daniel that the word $\mu\nu\sigma\tau\acute{\eta}\rho\iota\sigma\nu$ first has significance as an eschatological term as far as the subsequent history of the term is concerned.") Cf. further Kuhn, l.c. : "Sachlich sind die "Geheimnisse" in den Qumrantexten solche der Schöpfung und des eschatologischen Zeitplanes" ("In actual fact, the 'secrets' in the Qumran texts are those (secrets) of creation and the eschatological time scheme"). In rabbinical literature, the term "secret" can also be used in an eschatological context; e.g. "the end", i.e. the beginning of the messianic era (cf. above, p. 232) is designated as "the secret of God" (see Str.-B. I, p. 659s.).

[2] For this aspect of Jewish apocalyptic literature, see Bornkamm, Th. W. IV, p. 821s.; for the Qumran texts, see Kuhn's comment quoted in note 1 above and for rabbinical references, see Bornkamm, op. cit., p. 823 and Str.-B., l.c. including the references there given.

[3] See Bornkamm, op. cit., p. 822 lines 8 and 9 Eth. En. 80 and 91.

[4] See Gärtner, op. cit., p. 69.

plan which has already frequently been mentioned. This concerns the unification of Christ and the ecclesia through which the ecclesia becomes the body of Christ.)

Through the pneuma the content of the great resolution of God has been revealed to certain persons, i.e. to Christ's prophets and apostles (3:5). They, in turn, may reveal it to others. Paul himself has received a command to reveal it. The apostles and prophets to whom the essence of the mystery has been entrusted constitute a foundation for that construction of God which is the ecclesia.[1]

The conception of such a hidden plan is also present in R. 11:33ss. and 1 C. 2:7. In the latter, the term "mystery" is actually used. God has revealed the mystery to Paul and Apollos through the pneuma.[2]

The term "mystery" also occurs in R. 11:25 and 1 C. 15:51. In these places, the reader has the impression that the mystery refers to plans of a lesser scope. If this deduction is correct, it becomes increasingly likely that both in the HP as well as in Eph., there is a basic assumption of a great divine decision, the details of which are formed by more limited plans.

Furthermore, there are indications that the great resolution of Eph. is identical with the one discussed in the HP. R. 8:34 and 1 C. 15:20-28 lead one to think that Christ, the one who died, rose again and was exalted, also stands at the centre of this divine scheme.

The election or choice dealt with in R. 8:18-39 may be regarded as an intrinsic part of the predestined plan. As in Eph. 1:4, 5 the choice in this instance concerns adoption, as of children (R. 8:23) and, as in Eph.,[3] this refers primarily to Israel. The word $\pi\rho o\acute{\epsilon}\gamma\nu\omega$ in R. 8:29 applies to the same foreknowledge as that mentioned in R. 11:2. The object of this elective knowledge is Israel. The adoption as sons (R. 8:23) and the doxa (R. 8:18 and 23), represent according to R. 8:4, the blessings of salvation which are the due heritage of Israel.

Both in the HP as well as in Eph., the cardinal feature in the great plan of God is the wondrous fact that the uncircumcised may share

---

[1] See Eph. 2:20 and the exegesis of this place on p. 363. In 1 QS it is not only the entire community which is regarded as a foundation; the notion is also applied to a smaller circle i.e. to the council of the community; cf. p. 356 and note 2 above.

[2] See 1 C. 2:10. In our opinion, the pronoun in the 1st. pers. plur. in 1 C. 2:6, 10 and 4:1 refers to Paul and Apollos; cf. 1 C. 4:6. In the adjunct $\epsilon\grave{i}s$ $\delta\acute{o}\xi a\nu$ $\acute{\eta}\mu\hat{\omega}\nu$ (2:7), the pronoun has a generalized meaning and indicates the faithful. There, it probably had something to do with a formula which had already been coined in another connection.

[3] The chosen mentioned in Eph. 1:4 are according to the qualification $\tau o\grave{v}s$ $\pi\rho o\epsilon\lambda\pi\iota\kappa\acute{o}\tau as$ in 1:12, representatives of Israel.

in Israel's privileged position of salvation. Eph. 3:6 states that they
too, may belong to the body of Christ. Undoubtedly, this body is the
Israel which has become the property of Christ.[1]

R. 11:16-24 depicts the faithful who are converts from paganism
as branches which have been grafted onto the noble olive tree. This
olive tree may also be taken to mean the Israel which belongs to Christ.

However, there is one great difference between R. and Eph. in the
respect of the problem of Israel's lack of faith. Whereas the matter
is completely ignored in Eph., Paul is intensively preoccupied with
it in R.[2] In this connection, it would be legitimate to ask whether this
discrepancy between Eph. and R. could be ascribed to the inauthenticity of the former.

Furthermore, there is the additional aspect that Eph., unlike the
first chapters of R., Gal. and Phil. 3:2 and 3, does not dicsuss circumcision and living according to the law. Eph. contains no polemics against
those of Paul's opponents who wanted to force the pagan converts to
have themselves circumcised and to observe certain practices pertaining to the law.

In the opinion of Pfleiderer, Eph. and the HP were written in totally
different circumstances. Whereas Paul defended Christian converts
from paganism, he claims that the author of Eph. fought against
neglect of the Jewish Christians and advocated a continued unanimity
of purpose with them. Besides this, according to Pfleiderer, Eph. is
distinguished from the HP by virtue of an entirely different view of
the prerogatives of Israel.[3]

However, Pfleiderer's interpretation does not take the facts correctly
into account. It would require a preconceived idea that Eph. is inauthentic and tendentious to discover in it a plea for more appreciation
of the Jewish Christians. Without such a prejudice, Eph. must in
the first place be regarded as a work designed to praise the great
mercy of God which enables gentiles to partake in the privilege of
Israel. In essence, the unity between Jew and pagan are contemplated
in identical terms in Eph. and the HP.

Another assertion which needs to be refuted is that the author of
Eph. ascribes different prerogatives to Israel than Paul. does The
covenants of promise in Eph. 2:12 correspond with the covenants and

---

[1] See p. 303s.
[2] Cf. R. 11:2, 5, 7, 13-25, 28, 29 and 31.
[3] See Chatper I. para, 6.

promises (or promise, depending on the version) of R. 9:4. Similarly, the polity of Israel as described in Eph. 2:12 is at one with the nature of the privilege of being Israelite, a subject also treated in R. 9:4.

Goodspeed and Mitton subscribe to the view that Eph. evolved in a post-Pauline era. On the basis of the fact that Eph. contains no expostulations on circumcision and Jewish customs, they argue that by the time of the author of Eph., efforts were no longer being made to win pagan converts to Christianity over to circumcision and practises dictated by the law.

Mitton maintains that by the time when Eph. was written, it was already generally acknowledged that the uncircumcised deserved an equal position in the Church as Jewish converts. Goodspeed, on the other hand, maintains that in the days of Eph., Jewish Christians were no longer of any account and that the Church consisted exclusively of uncircumcised members.[1]

A point which should, be borne in mind is that it was an absolute certainty for Paul that the circumcised and the uncircumcised belonged equally to the ecclesia. In practise, this view was accepted by the communities in Antioch and elsewhere. Therefore, it is not difficult to imagine why Paul should have kept quiet, in an epistle, about the problem of Israel's lack of faith or refrained from polemics against the opponents who wanted to force non-Jewish Christians into circumcision and a life conforming to the law. He probably only argued against his opponents when an acute contingency presented itself.

In the case of R., the Christians there were more exposed to Israel's unbelief. It seems plausible that the disapproving attitude of the many Jews who lived in the city provided a source of doubt to the Christian community of Rome. This may have been one of the reasons why Paul deals so explicitly with this factor in his epistle to this particular community.

We think it perfectly feasible that Paul should give full treatment to the content of the faith without involving the problem of Israel's unbelief and entering upon discussions about circumcision and the observance of Jewish practises. For this reason we hold that silence on this problem and lack of discussion of this kind need not necessarily be taken as an argument against the authenticity of Eph.

---

[1] See Mitton, The Epistle to the Ephesians, p. 16 and Goodspeed, The Key to Ephesians, p. V.

We also think that the section Eph. 2:11-22 shows that the doctrine in favour of circumcision and life by the law, so strongly contested by Paul, has by no means been lost to sight in this epistle. Indeed, a closer examination of this section can only lead to amazement over Goodspeed's assessment: "There is no room for any Jewish Christianity in the picture. Christianity a gentile religion".[1]

Quite apart from the differences we have just observed, there is much correspondence on the issue of the relationship between Israel and non-Israel in Eph. and the HP. This correspondence is one of the factors which suggest that the great, hidden decision of God which is treated in Eph., also forms an underlying assumption throughout the HP.

Other indications of this kind exist. Thus, in Eph., this decision of God is partly cosmic in character. God had not only decided that the gentiles should share in Israel's privilege but it was also his resolve to gather together all things in Christ (1:10). When R. 8:21-23 talks of the fact that Israel is chosen, the same cosmic aspect emerges; for when the awaited adoption transpires, the whole of creation is involved.

1 C. 15 deals with the eschata. The use of the word "mystery" in v. 51, places these eschata within the scope of God's hidden counsel. Verses 24 and 28 leave no doubt that the eschatological acts of God embrace the entire cosmos and are unifying. Here, therefore, is another affinity with Eph., since in both 1 C. (15:24-28) and Eph. (3:10), God's eschatological activity clearly affects the supernatural forces.

In 1 C. 2., there is also a connection between the mystery and the supernatural forces. As in Eph. 3:10, the wisdom of God which expresses itself in the mystery is previously unknown to these supernatural powers.[2]

1 C. 2:8, 9 expresses the thought that if the archons had known of it, the crucifixion of Christ would have been prevented. Apparently, their power has ended or been curtailed with the death of Jesus which they could not have foreseen. It seems to us as if their power was especially affected because former worshippers of idols or devils (1 C. 10:19, 20) had, thanks to the death and resurrection of Jesus,

---

[1] See l.c.

[2] For the view that the archons mentioned in 1 C. 2:6 are cosmic forces, see Delling, Th. W. I, p. 488 and Lietzmann, An die Korinther I-II, 1931, p. 12s. For Eph. 3:10, see above, p. 319.

been delivered from the present evil world (Gal. 1:4) to inherit the glory of Him who is the King of Glory.[1]

If this glory is truly the share of the faithful, the might of the archons has come to an end and they must give definite way before the dominion of Christ. When that has evented, God's unifying work will have found accomplishment.[2]

Eph. corresponds with these details. Here too, the mystery represents glory for the faithful.[3] The struggle of the powers against the ecclesia (6:12) proves that the rulers of darkness feel threatened and diminished.

Col. once again reveals the common characteristics of the mystery as described in Eph. and 1 C. 2. The implication of the mystery is doxa for the faithful (Col. 1:27) and the death of Christ represents defeat and overthrow for the principalities and powers (Col. 2:15).

Here, in Col., we find a further and very special affinity with Eph. Namely, it is very clear from Col., too, that the mystery is intended to effect the participation of the gentiles in the glory of Christ (Col. 1:27).

All these data persuade us that the great resolve of God is known in Eph. as well as in the HP and in Col.[4] The mystery is the foundation of the ecclesiology of all these epistles.

---

[1] The adjunct εἰς δόξαν ἡμῶν of 2:7 which refers to those who love God (2:9) and not only to the bringers of the kerugma (cf. p. 379 n. 2), refers to this future glory of the faithful.

[2] See 1 C. 15:24-28 and 43.

[3] See Eph. 1:18; 3:13.

[4] In the above, we have not attempted to consider the question whether a relationship exists between the term μυστήριον in Eph. and the Hellenistic mystery cults. On this point we agree with Bornkamm that "Aufs Ganze gesehen, ist μυστήριον ein im N.T. seltener Begriff, der nirgends Beziehungen zu den Mysterienkultus erkennen läszt" ("on the whole μυστήριον is a term rarely used in the N.T. which in no way evinces any connection with the mystery cults"), in Th. W. IV, p. 831. O. Casel, on the other hand, thought he could indicate the influence of these cults in the language of the epistles of Paul, specifically in Col. and Eph. (see J. Plooy, De mysterieleer van O. Casel, diss. Leiden 1964, p. 150). His view was contested by K. Prümm and Chr. Mohrmann (see Plooy, op. cit., p. 151-153). Plooy is also unable to share Casel's view (op. cit., p. 153 and 157). In our opinion, the word μυστήριον has been given a particular content when used in Eph., Col. and the HP; in the Hellenistic world, the word had a familar ring to assure it of a welcome reception. The Hellenistic world had taken the word from the mystery religions and knew it as a designation for that liberating and deepest metaphysical knowledge which is the goal of philosophy. However, in Eph., Col. and the HP, the word does not refer to the deepest reality but bears upon God's liberating activity. In Gnosticism, the word was used to describe revelations concerning some divine metaphysical drama. What is lacking here, is the conception of the redeeming intervention of God and the notion that this redeeming activity has found realization in the concrete, histo-

From it we learn that God has on purpose selected through Israel which is historic, the ecclesia which consists of Jews and gentiles, and called it to Him.[1] We also come to realize that the glory which is lavished on the ecclesia, is inextricably linked with the salvation which awaits the whole of creation.

The death and resurrection of Christ means the following things : it releases Israel from the law of commandments and ordinations and binds it to Christ; it delivers the gentiles from the power of evil forces and causes them to belong to the liberated Israel which is the body of Christ; it is the end of all senseless confusion in creation and represents the beginning of the new universal unity. Such insights ultimately serve to strengthen the case for the authenticity of Eph. (and Col.).

Our study of the ecclesiological content of Eph. would not be complete without some further observations on the composition of the ecclesia and certain groups wiich the author of the epistle considered of special importance to the well-being of the ecclesia. For it should be mentioned that some scholars see differences with the HP in the matter of the composition of these groups which are detrimental to the authenticity of Eph.

Amongst these, H. von Capmenhausen, for example, thought that Eph. 4:7 and 16 diverge slightly from the HP. It was his view that it is in these texts explicitly and for the first time stated that each member of the community receives charis or charisma. Although the authentic epistles hinted as such, definite statements never occurred.[2]

In our opinion, however, the perception of the faithful as a whole has been conceived in the same spirit in both Eph. 4:7 and 16 and the HP. When 1 C. 12:6, after some comments on the nature of the diversity of gifts, administrations and operations, states that the same God

---

rical appearance of Christ, his suffering, death and resurrection. In the Pauline epistles: the word μυστήριον has a "noetic" aspect and relevance to the history of salvation Plooy (op. cit., p. 157 and 159) is in our opinion misguided when he objects to the noetic character of the term. We also object to his interpretation of μυστήριον in the CP as the hidden, salutary reality of the kingdom of God and his idea that according to Paul, observance of the sacrament ensures complete participation in this salutary reality. In this respect, he adheres too closely to Casel and quite erroneously argues a formal connection with the Hellenistic mysteries and their mystical physical soteriology (cf. op. cit., p. 160).

[1] Cf. H. Ridderbos, p. 402.

[2] Kirchliches Amt und geistliche Vollmacht in den ersten drei Jahrhunderte (Tübingen 1953), p. 63 note 2.

"works all in all", this surely represents a no less positive and universal declaration than the words of Eph. 4:7 and 16.

By the same token, R. 12:3-16 presents all demonstrations of faith in the light of the grace given to all. This pericope forms a unit and must be seen as a whole; it is incorrect to introduce a cesura near the end of the eighth verse, thus assigning the charismata to only some categories.[1]

With respect to Eph. 4:11. Von Campenhausen thought there was a flagrant dispcrepancy with the HP and particularly with 1 C. 12:28. The category of pastors mentioned in Eph. 4:11 does not, in his view, conform with the organization of the communities as known to Paul. Instead, he holds that the pastors in question are no other than the elders who, in continuation of Jewish practise, were acknowledged in the non-Pauline, Jewis Christian communities as the custodians of tradition and the accredited leading group. Von Campenhausen postulates that the elders in Eph. aquired the designation "pastors" during the post-apostolic era when their authority and influence had grown to such an extent that they were entrusted with safeguarding the faith of the communities against the encroachment of the heresies of Gnosticism.[2]

Unlike Von Campenhausen, we are by no means convinced that the structure of the Jewish Christian communities of the apostolic period differed all that much from that of the Pauline communities. A factor we would like to take into account in any event, is the possibility that the influences of Hellenistic Judaism and the traditions of the Helleni-

---

[1] In corroboration we refer to a lecture given by Käsemann, entitled "Amt und Gemeinde im Neuen Testament", published in Exegetische Versuchungen und Besinnungen I (p. 109-134), with special reference to p. 117s. Käsemann also sees the HP and Eph. as conceptually homogeneous. Besides, Van Campenhausen's own characterisation of the community described in Paul ("ein einheitlicher, lebendiger Kosmos freier geistlicher Gaben, die einander dienen und ergänzen, deren Träger sich aber niemals übereinander erheben oder gegeneinander verschlieszen können" Trans. : "A world which is alive and unified, where undisturbed spiritual gifts are held by people who use them to help and augment each other and who never try to outdo or become alienated from each other", p. 69), is completely in harmony with the content of Eph. 4:7 and 16. If he differentiates between the HP and Eph. in the place quoted in the last footnote, this is probably due not so much to thorough deliberation as to a certain predisposition regarding the authenticity of Eph. One very often has the impression that theologians who are convinced of the inauthenticity of Eph., more or less automatically point to differences between the HP and Eph. (and Col.) when dealing with topics of N.T. theology.

[2] Op. cit., p. 83-88.

stic synagogue may have left their mark on the latter type of community.

Another point to be considered is that it is almost inevitable that the organisation of these communities must have undergone some development, even in Paul's time. Von Campenhausen himself is prepared to admit that this may account for the fact that bishops and deacons are not mentioned until Phil., which is a late epistle.[1] We think that the designation "pastors" in Eph. could be explained along similar lines.

It is curious that Von Campenhausen believes that these pastors really belong to communities of a later date, consisting of a small upper echelon of authoritarian figures and the larger mass of ordinary members of the community whose relationship with the former was one of unquestioning, childlike obedience. He argues that these later communities had lost the Pauline unity of the organically homogeneous charismata which encompassed the whole of a community. By this time, it could no longer be said that within these communities every action originated from spiritual gift.[2]

The trouble with Von Campenhausen's theory is that, for the rest, nothing else in Eph. suggests two levels, an upper and a lower, of this kind; on the contrary, there is much stress on mutual obedience and the universality of the charisma. Indeed, on the strength of the above-quoted opinions held by Von Campenhausen, this aspect of universality in Eph. is even augmented.

As a result, we are unable to share his views on the pastors of Eph. 4:11. Our impression is that the words τοὺς δὲ ποιμένας καὶ διδασ-κάλους probably relate to one and the same activity, within the ecclesia, i.e. that of teaching the Christian way of life.[3]

In the late period of Judaism, the term "pastor" was quite often connected with the idea of giving leadership or ruling. If it is this idea Eph. 4:11 wants to convey, Von Campenhausen is justified in regarding the pastors as authoritarian personages. However, during the same period there was yet another notion which was associated equally strongly with the term; it also pertained to the teaching of a way of life based on the explication of the law.[4]

---

[1] Op. cit., p. 74.

[2] Cf. op. cit., pp. 73, 80, 81, 86-89.

[3] For διδάσκειν as ethical teaching, see Rengstorf, Th. W. II, p. 149 lines 17-33.

[4] See Str.-B. II, p. 537; J. Jeremias, Th. W. VI, p. 488 lines 13-17 and for the meaning of teacher in particular, see the Syrian Apocalypse of Baruch 77, 13-16 (R. H. Charles,

With respect to Eph. 4:11, it is the second of these notions which should be borne in mind. In the present case we are not concerned with a Christian version of Jewish leaders and potentates but with a certain form of teaching adapted to the requirements of Christianity. Like the Jewish teachers, their Christian counterparts were there to shed a light of understanding on the question of how life should be lived.

The close connection between the words ποιμένας and διδασκάλους in Eph. 4:11 is evidence that the work of these pastors consisted of instructing the community. The word ποιμήν is by way of being a metaphor rather than directly indicative of a specific function.[1] It is for that reason that ποιμένας is given a more precise definition by the διδασκάλους which follows.

This double indication for those engaged in teaching is intended to embrace all those able, by virtue of the gift of the pneuma, to give instruction to the communities.[2] The persons who are described as προϊστάμενοι in 1 Th. 5:12 are probably also included amongst the categories indicated by this double designation.[3]

When summing-up those who are of especial value to the ecclesia, Eph. 4:11 mentions exclusively those categories concerned with the revelation of the gospel and teaching. After all, it is on account of their insight into the mystery and the revelation they have experienced, that the apostles and prophets are called the foundation in Eph. 2:20 (p. 379). Eph. never, in so many words, talks of administrative matters.

In connection with the faithful generally, Eph. only mentions a spiritual way of speaking and singing (4:29s. and 5:18ss.). We are not told about any other charismatic activities. The fact that the author

---

The apokrypha and Pseudepigrapha of the O.T. II, Oxford 1913, p. 521). In the same place in Baruch, the pastors are also envisaged as lamps which illuminate. The metaphor accentuates their pedagogic function and that of disseminating knowledge.

[1] Cf. J. Jeremias, op. cit., p. 497 lines 7-12.

[2] It does not serve the present purpose to discuss the question whether the words ποιμένας and διδασκάλους in Eph. 4:11 refer to two different functions or two forms of the same (cf. Abbott, Eph.-Col., p. 118; Haupt, Die Gefangenschaftsbriefe, p. 145 and Schlier, Der Eph., p. 197). The double designation means all those, by whatever name, who are engaged in teaching and who do not belong to the previously mentioned categories of apostles, prophets and evangelists.

[3] It is clear from the context that they also taught. We count them amongst the pastors and teachers on the basis of this teaching. Käsemann looks to the charisma of rulership to explain the correspondence between the προϊστάμενοι and the ποιμένες, op. cit., p. 114.

of Eph. displays such a particular interest in the spoken word does not mean that he fails to see or acknowledge other spiritual channels. There is room for a rich amplitude of charismata within the definitions of Eph. 4:7 and 16. But it is clear that the spoken word through which Christ sends out his servants, which is inspired by the pneuma, is for the author of this epistles of paramount importance.

Although we read about a more variegated selection of charismata in the HP, the spoken word nevertheless occupies a position of primary significance. In 1 C. 12:28, a number of different charismata and talents are listed. However, these are only recorded after an enumeration which resembles Eph. 4:11, naming the categories which serve through the spoken word. The adverbs $\pi\rho\hat{\omega}\tau o\nu$, $\delta\epsilon\acute{u}\tau\epsilon\rho o\nu$ and $\tau\rho\acute{\iota}\tau o\nu$ accentuate with some emphasis that the apostles, prophets and teachers. come before other gifts and charismata.

2 C. 5:19 and 20, when speaking about the word of reconciliation, also bear witness to the overriding importance of the spoken word. Taking all this into consideration, it would be unjust to assume merely on the basis of Eph. 4:11, that the epistle dates from a post-apostolic stage of the church.[1]

In fact, the very reticence on administrative activities within the ecclesia seems out of character with so late a date. A reasonable supposition would be that the activity of leading persons, able to assume authority, might by now have been expected to increase in importance for the life of the communities, especially during the decades immediately after the era of the apostles.[2]

---

[1] Cf. J. Alizon, Etude sur le Prophétisme Chrétien depuis les Origines jusqu'a l'An 150 (1911), p. 40s. : "Il ne parait donc pas évident, quelle que soit l'opinion que l'on ait sur l'attribution de cette lettre à Paul, qu'il faille chercher dans l'Épître aux Éphésiens un stade plus avancé, où l'aspiration tendrait à se canaliser, et les dons à devenir des emplois. Il faudrait alors tirer les mêmes conclusions de la liste donnée par 1 Cor. 12, 27-28. Les renseignements qui nous sont donnés sont trop incomplets pour permettre de noter avec netteté une évolution. Il se peut qu'à Ephèse les manifestations de l'Esprit aient été moins riches et moins spontanées (il n'y est pas question de glossolalie), mais c'est en tout cas aller trop loin que de reconnaître dans cette situation un état commun à toutes les Eglises, l'indication que l'ère de l'inspiration libre est près de sa fin."

[2] Cf. Heussi, Kompendium der Kirchengeschichte, par. 10c (p. 36). Käsemann maintains that an intensive absorption in the administration and organisation of the local communities is typical of the Pauline communities of the generation immediately after Paul. He believes that the evidence for this is to be found in the works of Luke and the Pastoral epistles. See p. 127ss. of the essay quoted above, p. 385 and his essay "Paulus und der Frühkatholizismus" in Exeg. Vers. u. Bes., II, p. 249s.

The term $\epsilon\mathring{u}\alpha\gamma\gamma\epsilon\lambda\iota\sigma\tau\mathring{\eta}s$ which is used in Eph. 4:11, occurs nowhere else in the CP minus.

Another argument for attributing a late date to Eph. is as follows. The epithet ἅγιος which is applied to the apostles in Eph. 3:5, is alleged to be expressive of the veneration in which a later generation held the great figures of the past.

Moreover, this is supposed to be an idealized picture of Paul's situation, viz. that the other prophets and apostles are unreservedly backing up his judgement that the uncircumcised are entitled to a place in the ecclesia, equal to that of the Jews. This, despite the evidence of Gal. 2:1-14 that other apostles accepted Paul's view with reluctance, that Peter, in an unfortunate moment, disassociated himself from it and that even the apostle Barnabas [1] was "carried away".[2]

We believe that the epithet "hagioi" in Eph. 3:5 has been misinterpreted. In Pauline literature, the word ἅγιος often corresponds with the words ἐκλεκτός or κλητός. Even in Eph. 3:5, the word has the connotation of chosen and called.[3] It is connected with the word ἀπόστολος and also applies to the word προφήτης which comes later.[4]

When Paul speaks of his task to reveal the gospel amongst the pagans in Gal. 1:15 and 16, he writes that God had singled him out from his mother's womb and called him by His grace. Similar associations come to bear in Eph. 3:5 which states that the apostles and prophets who realize that the uncircumcised should partake fully in the grace of Christ, did not gain this understanding by themselves but that it was revealed to them.

The word "hagioi" conveys that these apostles and prophets have been called by God and thus stresses the fact that they are not acting from independent motivations. Furthermore, the author, by using this

---

It is also found in Acts 21:8 and 2 Tm. 4:5 but not in the Christian literature which in order of time immediately succeeds the N.T. Thus we think that the word in Eph. 4:11 owes its origins to the terminology of the earliest Christianity and not to a later period. We additionally refer to G. Friedrich, Th W. II, p. 735 and D. Y. Hadidian, "tous de euangelistas in 4,11" in The Catholic Biblical Quarterly 28, 1966, p. 317ss. We do not share the opinion of Hadidian that the word euangelistes specially indicates a "gospel writer" as opposed to a "preacher of the gospel".

[1] For the qualification apostle, see 1 C. 9:5,6.

[2] See Chapter I, para. 6 (p. 24) and Holtzmann, Lehrbuch, p. 274; Abbott, op. cit., p. 82; Haupt, op. cit., p. 100s. and Alizon, op. cit., p. 40.

[3] Cf. Haupt, op. cit., p. 101 : "Ἅγιος ist dem P. Wechselbegriff mit ἐκλεκτός". See also Procksch, Th. W. I, p. 108.

[4] The author is not in agreement with the translation of Eph. 3:5 in the Nieuwe Vertaling van het Nederlandsch Bijbelgenootschap. For the exegesis of Eph. 3:5, see Percy, Die Probleme, pp. 335, 336. 345ss.

word, wants to make clear that he is aware that other apostles and prophets also exist: people who may call themselves apostles and prophets but who stubbornly refuse to acknowledge that salvation is also due to the gentile.

Thus it need not necessarily be that Eph. 3:5 suggests that all prophets and apostles are unanimously and without reservation in agreement with Paul's views on missionary work amongst the pagans. The word hagioi has the effect of limiting the number of apostles and prophets who shared the opinion of Paul.

If this restrictive function of the word is taken into account, it becomes an acceptable proposition that Eph. 3:5 was not in conflict with the historical state of affairs. To us it seems highly likely that during a period which came after the events related in Gal. 2:11-14, Paul's conception had come to be recognised in an ever wider circle with increasing conviction.

But even before that, Paul had already won considerable support for his work. We read of positive reactions amongst the communities of Judea (Gal. 1:23, 24), of an encouraging attitude on the part of respected people in Jerusalem and even of a formal agreement between on the one hand, James, Peter and John and, on the other, Paul and Barnabas (Gal. 2:7-10).

It seems to us as if the increased sympathy for Paul's work was in no small measure the result of support from the prophets who had had their own revelation. Maybe it is for this reason that Eph. 3:5 so explicitly mentions the prophets and that they are qualified as a co-foundation in Eph. 2:20.

In the same way as the word "hagioi" of Eph. 3:5 is connected and has affinity with the phrase "separated me from my mother's womb and called me" in Gal. 1:15, the word "foundation in Eph. 2:20 is related to the term "pillars" which is used in Gal. 2:9 to describe the leaders of the Jerusalem communities who came to an understanding with Paul and Barnabas.[1]

Such points of close affinity between Eph. 3:5 and Gal. 1:23, 24 and Eph. 2:20 and Gal. 2:9 cannot merely be ascribed to some literary dependence and must be regarded as symptomatic of a kindred or identical mind at work.

A small difference between Eph. 3:5 and Gal. 1:23, 24 is that unlike

---

[1] The architectural terms στῦλος (Gal. 2:9) and θεμέλιος (Eph. 2:20) have the same background and strength, as is demonstrated by the Qumran works and 1 Tm. 3:15 (cf. Gärtner, op. cit., p. 68ss.).

the Gal. text, Eph. makes no allusion to the agreement with the communities. Thus, it is interesting to note that a statement of a fairly
generalised nature in Col. 1:26ss. amplifies Eph. 3:5. Col. 1:26ss.
relates that God has manifested the mystery to the saints. The implication is that not only the communities within Judea but also those
outside agreed with Paul.

Unlike Eph. 2:20 and 3:5, Col. fails to mention that the apostles
and prophets were the more immediate recipients of this revelation.
However, there are no real discrepancies between the accounts found
in Gal., Eph. and Col. After the time when the position was as described
in Gal. 1:23, 24, circumstances only continued to improve for the better
from Paul's point of view. Col. and Eph. both illustrate facets of this
favourable development.

We would now like to go over some *results* which this chapter of
our study has yielded. We came to the conclusion that the character
of the epistle is not determined by its ecclesiological but by its christological aspect. The ecclesiology constitues an inseperable complement
to the christology of the writer. In principle, the relationship of christology to ecclesiology is the same in Eph. as in the HP (p. 351s.).

A major part of ecclesiological edicts in the epistle concern the
notions of building and growth, the term "temple" and other expressions
which have liturgical connotations. We arrived at the decision that
the "iranisch-gnostische" interpretation of the notion of building
(and those of growth and temple) which Vielhauer applied to our epistle
should be rejected.

The term "oikodome" has the same associations in Eph. as in the
HP (p. 362ss.). When Eph. proclaims that God is building the faithful
into a temple through the pneuma, this means the new temple, the
temple expected and awaited in late Jewish eschatology (p. 358s.).

This temple is a spiritualized temple. Other terms which derived
from ritual and liturgy were also given a spiritual inclination. Judging
from data in the Qumran scrolls to which Gärtner first drew attention,
the spiritualization of all such terms in Eph. and the HP owed a far
greater debt to Judaism than had previously been supposed by Wenschkewitz (p. 359ss.).

From information in 1 and 2 C., it seems likely that when teaching
new converts, Paul and his associates made a special point of telling
them that it was the whole of the faithful whom God was building
into his temple (p. 362). This was part of their very basic teaching.

In this connection, the apostle and those around him made use of a traditional association between the terms for planting, building and temple. We find the same combinated in the Qumran manuscripts. The combination of the notions of building, growth and temple in Eph. (p. 360) corresponds with this practise. However, Eph. distingui- shes itself from 1 and 2 C. in that it emphasizes the fact that the uncir- cumcised are included and part of the temple which is being built.

Not only do the faithful form a spiritual temple; their life acquires a ritual aspect. The services and aid which the faithful extend to each other by virtue of the grace given to each, are seen as a spiritual ritual which is appropriate to the spiritual temple. In the HP, adherence to a rightful path in life by the faithful is also envisaged as a ritual activity (p. 368).

The motifs of building, growth, temple and other ritual notions, are discussed side by side with the eschatological, heavenly attributes which are due to the faithful (p. 354s.). In all this, the author is con- stantly looking towards the future (p. 355). This teleological aspect is in our opinion no less characteristic for his ecclesiology than the prominence given to the concept of the body.

An equally typical feature of the work of the author is the attention devoted to the unity of the ecclesia. This idea of unity is one of funda- mental significance to his way of thinking and is defined by his belief in the unity of God (p. 369). He not only conceives of the faithful as a single and undivided body, but he also speaks of the circumcised and the uncircumcised, united in Christ, as the one and only new humanity (p. 369). Although the subject of the unity of the ecclesia is not develo- ped as much in the HP as in Eph., it is nevertheless very much there (p. 372s.).

We examined the passage Eph. 2:14-17 with special attention. We were unable to detect the Gnostic and mythological material which Schlier and Schille thought they had discovered; instead, we found striking resemblances with the HP, particularly with R. and more specifically with R. 5 (p. 370ss.). There seems to be some evidence to suggest that in contemplating this passage, we are, in fact, looking at an example of the sort of teaching which Paul and his associates gave to new converts and to which they could revert in the future (p. 374). Moreover, we noticed that the method here used to explain O.T. references corresponds to R.

This specimen of basic teaching does not treat the doctrine of righte- ousness through the faith. In the HP there is some indication that

Paul sometimes presented the central truths of the kerugma without necessarily drawing special attention to this element (p. 375ss.).

The idea of the unity of the ecclesia is intertwined with a certain mystery. This mystery is in keeping with the conceptual world of Judaism in the same way that the mysteries which are mentioned in the HP are also Jewish in complexion (p. 377ss.).

We came to the conclusion that both the HP and Eph. contain the underlying assumption of some great mystery or decision (p. 383s.). Part of the plan entailed by this decision was that the gentiles should share in salvation and the fact that they too were encluded in the election of Israel (p. 384).

This last and highly important element is expounded in R. but not in 1 C. Nor is the mystery directly associated with the unity of the ecclesia in 1 C. 2, as is the case in Eph. All the same, these is an essential connection between the mystery of Eph. and that of 1 C. 2 (p. 382s.). The mystery featured in Col. evinces this selfsame relationship and, moreover, has a bearing on the salvation of the pagans (p. 383).

Unlike Von Campenhausen, it is our opinion that the structure of the ecclesia, as described in Eph., is identical to that of the HP and that it is the same categories which are considered to be of special importance to the ecclesia. Apart from this enumeration, the epistle makes no further allusion to the administrative activities involved, nor is there a compilation of the different charismata.

Eph. gives priority to the message ordained by Christ and the pneumatically inspired word. The HP evinces the same priority. The fact that the epistle is silent on the administrative side of the running of the community and does not contain an exhaustive register, is no evidence that the epistle originates from the post-apostolic period.

The view of Holtzmann (and others) that the epithet ἅγιος in 3:5 betrays the fact that the apostles (and prophets) are sacrosanct figures of the past to the author, must stand refuted. The epithet, in this particular case, has a different function (p. 389s.).

When we read, in Eph. 3:5, that God has by revelation made known the mystery to his apostles and prophets, this is not in contradiction to the situation as described in Gal. All it means is that circumstances have since developed to the advantage of Paul and his creed (p. 390s.).

CHAPTER NINE

THE PARAENESIS

The paraenesis occupies a major portion of Eph. Although there have been sholars who aver that there is a difference in the paraenetical material of Eph. and the HP,[1] this is not of sufficient importance to constitute a serious objection against the authenticity of the epistle.

An interesting question are the so-called "Laster- und Tugendkataloge" (Eph. 4:2, 31, 32; 5:3, 4). These are also found in the HP (R. 1:29-32; 13:13; 1 C. 5:10; 6:10; Gal. 5:19-22). Such catalogues of good and evil are a general cultural phenomenon, fairly frequent in Hellenistic literature and also found in the works of Hellenistic Jewish authors and the Qumran manuscripts.[2]

The notions listed in Eph. derive from a mixed background and it is in the heterogeneous character of the paraeneses that Eph. and the HP correspond. It was W. Schrage who proved that there are many non-Christian themes and influences in the paraenetical material of these epistles. In order to trace these influences, it is important to look beyond the immediate confines of Palestinian and Hellenistic Judaism and also cast a reflective eye towards Hellenistic popular philosophy and a number of formal and material elements of classical Greek ethic which were generally accepted.[3]

The fact of it is that these same cultural tendencies can be detected

---

[1] Cf. Percy, Die Probleme, p. 134s., p. 343-355 and Bultmann, Theologie, pp. 526, 530, 536, 554s. and 564.

[2] See Bultmann, Der Stil der paulinischen Predigt, pp. 19 and 71; B. S. Easton, "New Testament Ethical Lists" in JBL, vol. 51, 1932, p. 1ss. and p. 9ss.; A. Vögtle, Die Tugend- und Lasterkataloge im N.T. (NTA 16, 4-5, Münster 1936); E. Kamlah, Die Form der katalogischen Paränese im N.T. (Wissensch. Untersuch. z. N.T. 7, Tübingen 1964). Cf. also Str.-B. III, p. 75. Kamlah's view is interesting; he maintains that amongst the non-Christian forms which are connected with the N.T. tradition of lists, there are a number of types which can be traced back to the cosmology of Iran and originate in the six Amesha Spenta of Mazdaism. When drawing a connection between, on the one hand, Iranian cosmology and, on the other, both the doctrine of the two spirits in 1 QS 3,17ss. and the rabbinical psychology of the two "Triebe" (drives), Kamlah does not do so without justification (p. 49-53; see also Schweizer, TH. W. VII, p. 387ss. and Bertram, Th. W. V, p. 943 lines 12-15).

[3] W. Schrage, Die konkreten Einzelgebote in der paulinischen Paränese, Ein Beitrag zur neutestamentlichen Ethik (Gütersloh 1961), p. 197-200.

in Eph. Terms such as βλασφημία, εὐτραπελεία, θυμός, ὀργή πικρία and πλεονεξία (Eph. 4:31 ; 5:3, 4) would not have been surprising from the mouth of a Hellenistic orator. The words ἃ οὐκ ἀνῆκεν in Eph. 5:4, in common with the expression τὰ μὴ καθήκοντα in R. 1:28, have some affinity with the idiom of ancient Greek and, specifically, Stoic ethics.[1]

Notions such as ἀκαθαρσία, ἀσέλγεια and πορνεία (Eph. 5:3 ; 4:19), typify the stricter attitudes of Hellenistic Judaism.[2] Furthermore, as in the HP, words occur in Eph. which, as was demonstrated so ably by S. Wibbing,[3] represent an equivalent to the indications used in Palestinian Judaism and particulary in the Qumran community, for the various virtues and failings.

This does not complete the number of affinities between the paraenesis of Eph. and that of the HP. In all these epistles, moral exhortation is determined by the same eschatological conceptions. These exhortations are based on the assumption that a great change has taken place. The pneuma is part of this new situation. The faithful have received the pneuma. The great change has not yet been completed but will be, soon, when the wrath of God will become apparent but definitive salvation will also occur. Those who continue to be guilty of evil, will have no share in the coming salvation.

The theme of the pneuma appears in Gal. 5:18-23 and Eph. 4:3, 30. The idea of the coming wrath of God is important in the catalogues of Eph. 5:5, 6 and Gal. 5:18-23.[4] In R. 13:11-14 and Eph. 4:30, the salvation element is in the foreground. 1 C. 6:9, 10 and Gal. 5:21 as well as Eph. 5:5 give warning that those who commit certain sins will not have part in the salvation to come.

The three last-mentioned places all make use of a corresponding terminology. 1 C. and Gal. speak of sinners who "shall not inherit the kingdom of God", whilst Eph. states that no man such as that "has any inheritance in the kingdom of Christ and of God".

It is striking that the warning in each of the three epistles is introduced by a similar type of formulation. 1 C. 6:9 has the rhetorical question:

---

[1] In Stoic ethics the apposite is τὸ καθῆκον and the opposite τὸ παρὰ τὸ καθῆκον cf. Schlier, Th. W. III, p. 440s.

[2] For ἀκαθαρσία see F. Hauck, Th. W. III, p. 431 line 30ss. and for the other terms Str.-B. III, p. 75.

[3] Die Tugend- und Lasterkataloge im N.T. (Beiheft z. ZNW 25, Berlin 1959, p. 91-114.

[4] The eschatological wrath of God is frequently mentioned in the HP (R. 2:5, 8 ; 3:5 ; 5:9 ; 9:22 ; 1 Th. 1:10) and it is the law which operates on wrath. The formulation "Against such there is no law" (Gal. 5:23) consequently aims at the absence of wrath.

"Do you not know ... ?". In Gal. 5:21 the apodictic declaration "I warn you, as I warned before ..." precedes the warning, whilst Eph. assures "You know very well ...".[1]

Furthermore. the remark "Let no man lead you astray with words" appears in the context of the exhortation, whilst 1 C. similarly warns : "Be not deceived" (6:10).

Thus we remark that the HP and Eph. not only contain the same eschatological theme pertaining to the coming salvation which eludes the hardened sinner but that there is, moreover, a striking affinity as regards the way this theme is treated and expressed. On the basis of this correspondence, we believe it would not be reasonable to ascribe the authorship of the epistle to anyone other than a member of Paul's associates and fellow-workers. Therefore, unless Paul himself was the author, it must certainly have been written by somebody within his immediate circle.

As we come to examine the underlying eschatological beliefs in the paraneses of the HP and Eph., we find ourselves increasingly confirmed in that opinion. Throughout the whole of this paraenetical material, these assumptions rest on the conception of the two aeons described in Jewish apocalyptic works (resp. two series of aeons).[2] The faithful already form part of the new age. This idea found, for example, in Gal. 1:4, finds repeated expression in Eph. in the most vivid of terms.[3]

At the very core of all eschatological expectation is the coming of the kurios who whill bring to light all that is hidden in darkness. The words of 1 C. 4:5 tell of this coming and this revelation. Eph. 5:13, 14 is preoccupied with the same idea.

When the kurios comes, it will be "the day of the Lord" (1 Th. 5:2), but the new age can, as a whole, also be represented as "the day" (R. 13:12).[4] The designation used in Eph. is "the day of redemption".[5]

Eph. 5:11 anticipate the unmasking which will be the order of the

---

[1] For the formula ἴστε γινώσκοντες, see above, p. 179 with notes 4 and 5.

[2] Cf. Sasse, Th. W. I, pp. 206, 207 and 205 line 29ss. In Eph., this conception is encountered in 1:21 and 2:7.

[3] Here we are thinking of Eph. 2:19; 1:3; 2:6. See above, p. 354s. In addition, there is the expression τέκνα φωτός (Eph. 5:8), which corresponds with the designation υἱοὶ φωτός and υἱοὶ ἡμέρας in 1 Th. 5:5.

[4] Cf. Ev. Lövestam, Spiritual Wakefulness in the N.T. (Lunds universitets årsskrift N.F. Avd. 1 Bd. 55 no. 3), p. 46-49.

[5] Eph. 4:30. This designation probably derives from Jewish apocalyptic writings (cf. En. 51:2 and the other Jewish texts quoted in Str.-B. II, p. 256 with reference to Luke 21:28).

day when the kurios arrives to reveal all. This anticipation takes form in that the faithful are already exposing sinful practices. Such a trend of thought is, without doubt, fully consistent with ideas found in the HP.[1]

To counterbalance this kind of advance action—geared to an event timed to coincide with the arrival of the kurios—stands the fact that it will later not be possible to accomplish things which should be done now. It is for that reason that the faithful are urged, in Gal. 6:10, to do good as long as the opportunity lasts. In Eph. 5:16, they are analogously exhorted to "redeeming the time", i.e. to take advantage of the opportunity.[2]

One notion which is central to the paraeneses of the HP and Eph., is that the way of life of those who belong to the new age must be diametrically opposed to their former habits (R. 6:17-22; 8:2, 4, 13; 12:2; 1 C. 3:3; Eph. 2:1-; 4:17ss.). In exemplifying these different ways of life, both the HP and Eph. avail themselves of a number of ideas and conceptions which come from late Judaism.

One of these conceptions is that of the eschatological struggle which occupies an important place in late Judaic literature and is mentioned, for example, in the Qumran manuscripts.[3] The work in question relates

---

[1] In R. 1:18, one finds that the conception of the coming wrath is already revealed (cf. the explication of G. Bornkamm, Das Ende des Gesetzes, Paulusstudien, Gesammelte Aufsätze Bd I, München 1958, p. 32s.). 2 C. 6:17 evinces the idea that the faithful who are the eschatological temple must prove this by separating themselves from the unbelievers. In 1 C. 5:12, 13 it is demanded that the faithful must judge those within their circle who engage in wicked practices and eject them from their midst. The "children of disobedience" mentioned in Eph. 5:6 and 11, whose sins must be unmasked and punished, were probably people who numbered themselves amongst the faithful.

[2] The expression also features in Col. 4:5. The only corresponding expression ($\kappa\alpha\iota\rho\grave{o}\nu$ $\grave{\epsilon}\xi\alpha\gamma\rho\rho\acute{a}\zeta\epsilon\iota\nu$) is found in Dan. (LXX and Theodition) 2:8. In Eph. 5:16 (and Col. 4:5) the meaning is different from Dan. 2:8. Admittedly, the words are in Dan. 2:8 connected with the idea that a turning-point has been reached, that times will change and that the critical situation will come to an end (Dan. 2:9); this idea is also present in Eph. People are living in the bad days which precede the great end of all times. 1 C. 7:26 describes these days of evil as "the present distress". For the faithful, these days are an incentive to walk the path of wisdom and redeem the time. Unlike, Dan. 2:8, the point at issue is not to win time but to make use of all possible opportunities to do good. For this last meaning of the expression, see Büchsel, Th. W. I, p. 128. (Schlier, Der Eph., holds (p. 244) that the meaning is : to use the time available, in spite of the fact that evil forces dominate these days, in such a way that it tuns out to be God's good time for good decisions. Apparently, Schlier wants to do justice to the meaning of saving and freeing which the word $\grave{\epsilon}\xi\alpha\gamma\rho\rho\acute{a}\zeta\epsilon\iota\nu$ can have.)

[3] See O. Bauernfeind, Th. W. VII, p. 511s. and Kuhn, Th. W. V. p. 297s.

of a war between the sons of light and the sons of Belial or the children of darkness. The cosmic powers are also involved in this fight. Before battle, the priest addresses the hosts of the good side with the words : "Be strong and stout of heart and be men of strength".[1]

In conformity with the O.T. and Greek idiom, a figurative use was made in late Judaic literature, of terms relating to arms and armour. The O.T. knows God a as warrior at arms.[2]

In Is. 59:17ss., divine attributes or deeds are depicted as the armour or weapons clothing God. God himself can also be a weapon to defend the faithful, as in Ps. 3:3, where he is called a shield. Similarly, a particular quality of God is described as a shield or buckler for the faithful in Ps. 91:4.

Greek philosophers and comic writers would sometimes indicate abstract concepts with words denoting armour.[3] Thus, the Hellenistic Jewish author of the Sapientia Salomonis speaks, like Is. 59:17ss., of God assuming certain divine properties as his armour. He also represents certain natural phenomena as weapons with which God arms the cosmos to join with Him against his enemies (Sap. 5:17ss.).

In other late Jewish literature, it is the faithful themselves who fight with divine arms. Their armour conists of real weapons which have been provided by God or are, in some mystical fashion, identical with weapons handled by God himself.[4]

Another conception is that of the spiritual sword. For example, the strength to resist temptation which comes from prayer, is described as a sword given by God.[5] Philo sees the logos as a weapon or armour which has been given to man.[6]

Whenever the antithesis between the old and the new may of life is made the HP use such late Jewish material. R. and 1 Th. both convey the thought that in the eschatological struggle which is being enacted, it is possible to be either on the good or the bad side. It is the duty of

---

[1] 1 QM 15,7, see Lövestam, op. cit., p. 15.

[2] For God as a warrior, see e.g. Ex. 15:3; Is. 34:2ss.; 42:13; 63:5, 6. The armour of God is mentioned in Ps. 7:13ss.; 35:2, 3; Ez. 21:9ss.; Hab. 3:9.

[3] See Oepke, Th. W. V, p. 293 lines 10-19.

[4] Thus, in Test. XII Levi 5,3, Levi receives a shield and a sword from an angel to wreak vengeance in Sichem (Oepke, op. cit., p. 297). An inscription identifies the spears of the warriors in the eschatological struggle in 1 QM 6, 2 and 3 with the weapons of God (cf. Brongers, De Rol van de strijd, p. 39 and p. 90 notes 3-5).

[5] In Test. XII Jos. 6,2 Joseph receives this sword (cf. Oepke, l.c., line 20ss.);

[6] See Oepke, op. cit., p. 293 lines 36-41 and p. 297 lines 36-42.

the faithful to adhere to the good side and to assume the armour of light, i.e. the breastplate of faith and love and the helmet of salvation.[1]

Sometimes, instead of the armour of light, the armour of righteousness or weapons which are not of the flesh are mentioned. This connection between the image of armour and the concept of righteousness is also drawn in the O.T. and in late Jewish literature.[2]

There is a warning in 1 C. 16:13 which is the equivalent of the summons which precede the last battle of 1 QM 15,7 when the clarion-call of the priest evokes the battle-cry of 2 Sam. 13:28 ("be courageous and be valiant"). The caution in 1 C. 16:13, is at the same time an exhortation to fight; words as "quit you like men, be strong", are reminiscent of the battle-cries of old which resound through Deut. 31:6, 7, 23; Jos. 1:6; 10:25 and Ps. 31:25.

It is of considerable significance that the exhortation to the struggle should occur in the tiny paraenetical section of 1 C. 16:13, 14. Although, in concrete terms, quite concerned about the life conduct of the addressees and willing to discuss certain ethical questions in some detail, Paul has omitted from 1 C. the type of general parenesis which usually occupies such a prominent place in other epistles.[3] He give to understand that Timothy will in person deliver this general paraenesis before the Corinthians (4:17).

The warnings of 1 C. 16:13, 14 are the only general exhortations in the epistle. Therefore, it might have been expected that these also would have some elements of the type of paraenetical teaching which Paul gave wherever he went. And indeed, this is the case.

The fact that the exhortation to let charity rule over all, as in 1 C. 16:14, is quintessential to Paul's paraenesis, needs no further corroboration. It is self-evident, therefore, that the appeal of 1 C. 16:13 presents us with an essential part of his teaching. Thus we can see how important the concept of the eschatological struggle was to Paul.

---

[1] Underlying R. 6:13, is the idea of a transference from the bad camp to the good. R. 13:12 and 1 Th. 5:8 speak of putting on armour.

[2] The armour of righteousness, like the non-carnal weapons, are wielded by Paul himself (2 C. 6:7; 10:4). In Is. 59:17 and Sap. 5:18, the breastplate of righteousness is mentioned. When R. 6:13 speaks of the instruments of righteousness, this pertains to all the faithful. The instruments or weapons are the members of their body previously instruments of unrighteousness.

[3] For the content of 1 C. see above, p. 59. Schrage, op. cit., pp. 42ss. and 117ss. correctly draws attention to the existence of this type of general Pauline paraenesis which is not aimed at a concrete situation.

We see both men and supernatural forces as the protagonists and enemies in this fight.[1]

In Eph. 6:10-18, the late Judaic metaphor of battle and armour has the same function as in the various HP pronouncements. The term "the armour of God" conveys that the activities and properties which are characterised as arms, have been bestowed by God and are not inherent to man.[2] This idea is also evinced in 2 C. 10:3, 4 which states that the war is not conducted with the flesh but with weapons that are not carnal; i.e. are spiritual.

This is also the case in 2 C. 6:6, 7 where the armour in question quite clearly does not relate to the natural aspect of man but to qualities or gifts, worked and bestowed by God. These are arms which are synonymous with purity, knowledge, the ability to be longsuffering, with kindness, the Holy Spirit, love, the word of truth and the power of God. The concepts described in Eph. 6:14-17 are of the same kind as the qualities and gifts listed in 2 C. 6.

Each of the abstract concepts in Eph. 6:14-17 is vividly characterised as a certain piece of armoury. The same procedure is followed in 1 Th. 5:8. Judging by Sap. 5:17ss., this is a traditional method of representation which was used as early as Is. 59:17.

In observing this convention, both Eph. 6:17 and 1 Th. 5:8 preserve the association between the notion of blessedness (or salvation) and the helmet, which already occurs in Is. 59:17.[3] In addition Eph. 6:14 also draws the analogy between a breastplate and righteousness which is similary found in Is. 59:17 and Sap. 5:18.

When this terminology is employed in the HP, righteousness, is not connected with a separate weapon; "weapons of righteousness" is the term used in these epistles.[4]

In 1 Th. 5:8, the breastplate is identified with faith and love. Thus, the metaphor of the breastplate and helmet from Is. 59:7 is here applied to the triple concept of faith, hope and charity which is also encountered in 1 C. 13:13.

---

[1] Human opponents are found in Phil. 1:27, 28 and 2 C. 10:3-6. Demonic opponents must be presumed in 1 C. 10:12, 13 (cf. Lietzmann, An die Korinther, p. 47 on 1 C. 10:13). The context of R. 6:14 suggests that the struggle is against the dominion of death. In 1 C. 15:25, 26, death and other supernatural forces are the enemies of Christ and the faithful. Satan is the great opponent in R. 16:20.

[2] Eph. 6:11 and 13. The word armour ($\pi\alpha\nuο\pi\lambda\acute{\iota}\alpha$) also appears in the allegory of Sap. 5:17.

[3] See Oepke, Th. W. V, p. 315.

[4] See p. 399 note 2.

Eph. 6:14 and 17 show an additional correspondence with Is. 11:5 and 4 in the allegory of the girdle and the sword. However, one has the impression that in Eph. the metaphor of the armour has been adapted to conform slightly more with the traditional allegory than is the case with the HP.

As in 1 C. 16:13, we encounter a rallying-call in Eph. 6:10. But here the exhortation is at a somewhat further remove from the battle-cry : "be strong and of good courage" of Deut. 31:6, 7 and 23 and Jos. 1:6; 10:24 than the "quit you like men, be strong" of 1 C. 16:13.

As the antagonists, a host of superhuman powers are named in Eph. 6:12.

We thus ascertain that in the HP and Eph. we are dealing with identical conceptions of the final struggle and the same allegory of weaponry. Nevertheless, the passage Eph. 6:10-18 is possessed of an individual character and shows subtle differences from analogous texts in the HP. This idiosyncratic character and the small divergences entailed, forbid us to define this passage in terms of borrowing from the HP. Rather than attribute the affinities to derivation, we are persuaded that a single author was responsible for the whole body of work in question. Moreover, this was an author who was perfectly at home with the traditional material pertaining to war and armour and was able to deploy it at his discretion.

Other constituents involved in the complex of traditional conceptions to which we alluded on p. 397, are the metaphors of sleeping, awakening and watchfulness.[1]

Philo combines the conception of awakening with that of standing upright. He does not, in this context, speak of waging war.[2]

Paul uses this same combination, but is thinking of war. Both the notion of awakening [3] and that of standing [4] have a military connotation. The exhortation to watch (wake) and stand in 1 C. 16:13 is part of the battle-call.

The word πίστις occurs in this exhortation. The word is connected with the call to stand fast and is, on the whole, of central significance to the context. Elsewhere, as in 1 C. 10:12, Paul associates the notion of standing fast with resistance to the demonic temptations which can treachrously and unexpectedly lead to the downfall of the believer.[5]

---

[1] For these metaphors see Lövestam, op. cit., pp. 6, 25ss., 35ss. and 40ss.

[2] De Somniis II, 160-162, cf. Lövestam, op. cit., p. 36.

[3] See R. 13:11 and 12.

[4] See the στήκετε in Phil. 1:27 and the ἑστάναι in 1 C. 10:12.

[5] See p. 400, note 1.

In Eph. the lives of those who belong to the new age is also characterised by the associated notions of waking, standing and fighting. The
three metaphors are found together in Eph. 6:10-18.

Here, unlike 1 C. 16:13, the faith is not particularly linked with the
notion of standing; in 6:16, it is depicted as a shield. As a result of the
preceding adjunct "above all" and the subsequent description which
attributes a particular value to this shield of faith, the faith has the
same pivotal significance which it has in 1 C. 16:13.

In 6:13, the exhortation to continue to stand after the task has been
fulfilled is of the same kind as the warning "let any one who thinks
he stands take heed lest he fall" in 1 C. 10:12.

The notion of not sleeping or watching is brought into play in 6:18
and connected with perseverance in prayer. This same association
between watching and prayer, which is found in the literature of the
old Israel and the Qumran community[1], is also taken for granted in
1 Th. 5:10. (Perseverance in prayer is linked with the state of being
awake or on the watch in the same way in Col. 4:2 as in Eph. 6:18).

A figure of speech which is inseparable from the metaphor of armour
is that of the robe. When God is envisaged as a warrior arrayed in arms
in Is. 59:17, his clothing and armour are mentioned in one breath.
The king who is described in Ps. 45:3-10 bears a sword and clothing. The
son of man, as represented in Jewish apocalyptic literature, is dressed
in a glorious fashion.[2] He is also seen as the kingly conqueror who brings
destruction upon the ungodly rulers and deceivers.[3]

The Hellenistic Jewish writers used the idea of clothing and unclo-
thing to illustrate a radical change in the human condition as a result
of speculations on the glory of Adam before the fall and the clothes
that he wore, made of skin.

Such speculations on the glory of Adam gradually merged with
reflections on Psalm 8 and the "son of men".[4] It is in this way that
the conception of a warlike nation, which shares in the regal dignity
of the son of men and will inherit the glory of Adam, evolved.[5]

---

[1] See Lövestam, op. cit., p. 64 and 65.

[2] See note 3 on p. 331s.

[3] Cf. Colpe, Th. W. VIII, p. 427 lines 9-16 and Rev. 1:(12-) 16.

[4] See above, p. 331.

[5] The notion that there is a holy people which belongs to the son of men can be found
in Dan. 7:13, 25 and 27. The members of the Qumran community probably regarded
themselves as that holy people of saints mentioned in Dan. 7:27. (See Gärtner, op. cit.,
p. 128.) They may well also have hoped for the glory of Adam (see p. 331, notes 2 and 3).
In Hellenistic Jewish apocalyptic literature the two conceptions of participation in

Thus it is scarcely suprising that this conception should also have played a part when the metaphors of clothing and armour were used in late Judaism. When Paul uses this sort of imagery to characterise the way of the old and the new ages, this conception froms the background. (However, Paul is different in that he does not talk of the glory of Adam before the fall but of Christ, the last Adam, and the glory of the new creation.[1])

The paraenetical passage in which Paul illustrates the old and the new ways of life using these metaphors, is R. 13:12-14. The words he uses are ἀποτίθεσθαι and ἐνδύεσθαι. In the paraenesis of Eph., i.e. in 4:25; 6:11 and 14, the same words are used to describe the old and the new life.

The conception which we suspected in Pauls' writing, is very manifest here, in Eph., in 2:6; 4:22-24 and 6:10-18.[2] It is also obvious in Col. 3:9 where it is immediately connected with the words ἀποτίθεσθαι and ἐνδύεσθαι which form part of the paraenesis in resp. 3:8 and 3:12. An element which is, however absent in Col. is the struggle.

Finally, we would like to draw attention to the antithesis of light and darkness. Although by no means specifically Jewish, this antithesis was very familar to Judaism.[3] In fact, it occupies a prominent place amongst the complex of traditional concepts and conceptions which we mentioned on p. 397.

The members of the Qumran community conceived of themselves as the sons of light and their enemies as the children of darkness.[4] For them, the last battle was in essence a battle between light and darkness.

Paul was aware of the fact that Jews who were true to the law saw themselves as representing light whereas the pagans walked in darkness (R. 2:19). He calls the faithful "the children of light" (1 Th. 5:5), whilst, as far as he is concerned, the life of those who are of the old

the glory of Adam and dwelling with the son of men are interchangeable (see note 3, p. 331). The concept of the son of men can sometimes become welded together with that of the Messiah (see Colpe, op. cit., p. 432s.). The Messiah is a warrior who belongs with a warrior people. This applies, for example, to Ps. 110 which may be interpreted in a messianic light. As a result of this conflation, the militant character of the eschatological nation of God becomes even more pronounced.

[1] See 1 C. 15:45, 53s.; Gal. 3:27; 6:15 and 2 C. 5:17 and cf. p. 339s. above.

[2] For Eph. 4:22-24, see above, p. 327ss.

[3] See Lövestam, op. cit., p. 13ss.; Wibbing, op. cit., p. 37 and p. 72 note 130; H. Conzelmann, Th. W. VII, p. 433s. and Braun, Qumran u. d. N.T. I, p. 18ss.

[4] See p. 397s. and note 3.

aeon belongs to darkness and they accordingly walk in darkness
(1 Th. 5:4, 5). The words "armour of light" (R. 13:12) makes clear that
Paul saw the eschatological struggle as one between light and darkness.

For Paul, darkness and light are the essence of the old and the new
ages. The old aeon is the darkness or night which is already far advanced.
The new one is the light or day which is at hand (1 Th. 5:2, 5). The
darkness is determined by Belial—a correspondence with the Qumran
community (p. 398). The light is epitomized by Christ (2 C. 6:14, 15;
R. 13: 12-14). It shines in the hearts of the faithful (2 C. 4:6).

In Eph., the antithesis of light and darkness is presented in a similar
way, i.e. the essence of the old aeon is darkness. The designation
ὁ αἰὼν οὗτος (6:12) corresponds with the expression ὁ σκότος οὗτος
Those who belong to the new age may be characterised as darkness
(5:8) and they are, as in R. 13:12, surrounded by the works of darkness.
Their opposites may be described as light or the children of light and
their way of life should be concomitant which light (5:8).

Light challenges the darkness (5:13). Darkness is personified by the
diabolos (6:11) and light by Christ, the kurios (5:8, 14). The light is
the light of the dawning day (5:14). The light is already aflame in the
hearts of believers (1:18).

(In Col., less prominence is given to this antithesis, although darkness
and light are likewise contrasted as the esssential properties of the old
and the new ages. The faithful have been translated from the darkness
to the light (1:12, 13). However, the conception is not given a paraenetical bearing.)

One fact that does emerge from all these items of information, is
that the HP and Eph. (and Col.) were drawing upon the same conceptual
world and spiritual sources. Elsewhere in ancient Christian literature
we, also encounter elements of this complex of traditional concepts and
conceptions. In 1 Pt. 5:8, 9 and Jam. 4:7, we meet the concept of the
warlike confrontation. In Pastor Hermae, mand. XII, 1 and 2, the
image of battle coincides with the metaphors of clothing and armour.
In 1 Pt. 1:13; 2:1 and Jam. 1:21, there are allusions to clothing in the
figurative sense of the word. An exhortation to wakefulness or vigilance
occurs in 1 Pt. 5:8, whilst 1 Pt. 5:9 talks of steadfastness or diligence
in the faith.

However, not a single one of these three works evinces as consistent
an affinity with the HP as Eph. in respect of the application of these
notions. Although the author of 1 Pt. is familiar with the light—darkness antithesis (2:9), he fails to connect this with the struggle. None

of the works in question convey the idea that the faithful have been committed to the struggle because they already belong to the new age and already form a new humanity or creation. There is no suggestion anywhere that the believer is part of a world or aeon of light which is wholly governed by Christ. The struggle is given a more personalised aspect and is presented in terms of direct conflict with the devil (1 Pt. 5:8; Jam. 4:7) and against evil desire (mand. XII, 1 and 2).

Although mentioned, armour is given a less plastic treatment in mand. XII, 1 and 2 than in either the HP or Eph. The ἀποτίθισθαι — ἐνδύεσθαι antithesis is not found when the metaphors of armour or clothing are used. The first word, ἀποτίθεσθαι, only occurs in 1 Pt. 2:1 and Jam 1:21, whilst ἐνδύεσθαι features but once, in mand. XII, 1, 1.

In its use of traditional Jewish material, Eph. displays far more affinity with the HP than with any of the three above-mentioned works. To be precise, it may even be asserted that traditional material is used and applied in the same way in Eph. and the HP. We feel that this correspondence, which is significant and far-reaching in its implications, is an important argument for the authenticity of the epistle.

There are some points of divergence between Eph. and the HP. Thus, the latter epistles make no allusion to the imitation of God, the subject of Eph. 5:1, although they do have references to the appropriateness of following the example of Paul. Whatever the truth concerning the circumstances surrounding Eph. may be, Paul was not personally known to its recipients and therefore an exhortation to follow his example would have been slightly pointless.

On registering the frequency of HP statements which urge adherence to Paul's example (i.e. 1 C. 4:16; 11:1; Gal. 4:12; Ph. 3:17; 4:9; 1 Th. 1:6; 2 Th. 3:19), it begins to seem as if this concept of imitation was a favoured theme, almost indispensible to the Pauline paraenesis. The apostle's intention thereby, was not to arouse respect and admiration for his personal life conduct but to promote that obedience in the faith ordained by God, which he taught not only in word but also in deed.[1]

If Eph. is assumed to be authentic, one might say that Paul's predilection for the imitation-theme encouraged him to use God directly here since circumstances did not warrant that he could use his own life as an example.

---

[1] Cf. Schrage, op. cit., p. 132s.

In Jewish Hellenism, there existed an ethically similarly orientated conception of the imitation of God.[1] Targum Jer. I also presents God's compassion as an example to man.[2] Luke 6:36 offers a comparable logion. By analogy, the prayer which Jesus gave to his followers teaches forgiveness in relation to the Divine forgiveness (Matt. 6:12; Luke 11:4). When Eph. 4:32-5:2 speaks of the imitation of God, it bespeaks the dual conceptions of God's tenderheartedness and love which, in Luke 6:35, 36, are mentioned in relation to the example of God, as well as the notion of forgiveness which is similarly applied in Matt. 6:12 and Luke 11:4.[3]

An agreement of this nature between the words of Eph. 4:32-5:2 and the words of Jesus[4] as recorded by the first Palestinian Christians leads us to the following supposition; namely, that the notion of Imitatio Dei, as expounded in this section of Eph., conformed with the idiom of some Christian Jewish-Hellenistic circle which was closely affiliated with the earliest Aramaic-speaking Christian groups.

In what is known as the "Haustafel" (Eph. 5:22-6:9), we encounter another exclusive feature, i.e. pronouncements on marriage which give a quite different impression than the type of advice given in 1 C.7.

Haustafeln figure only in Eph. and in Col.—nowhere in the HP. We believe that they trace their origin to a certain series of moral exhortations composed by a Jewish-Hellenistic preacher or writer. Furthermore, it is conceivable that of the codes given in Eph. and Col. one is depedent on the other in which case Eph. is probably later version (see above, p. 155).

Neither of the two Haustafeln in Eph. and Col. furnish any evidence contrary to the authenticity of the two respective epistles; enumerations of virtues, sins and other traditional themes occur within HP paraeneses in an integrated form. Why, therefore, should there be any reason to rule out the possibility that this conventional pattern

---

[1] See Michaelis, Th. W. IV, p. 666 line 1ss.

[2] See Dalman, Worte Jesu. p. 342.

[3] Both the εὔσπλαγχνοι of Eph. 4:32 and the οἰκτίρμονες of Luke 6:36 may be seen as equivalent to the word רַחֲמָנִין which occurs in Targum Jer. I and which perhaps provided the background to the word οἰκτίρμονες in Luke 6:36 (cf. Dalman, op. cit., pp. 342, 167 and Köster, Th. W. VII, p. 552).

[4] If there were variations in connection with the word for forgiveness amongst the earliest Aramaic-speaking Christians (cf. Dalman, op. cit., p. 335-337), something of this remains in the ἀφιέναι or Matt. 6:12 and the χαρίζεσθαι of Eph. 4:32.

of injunctions concerning family life should be interwoven with the paraenetical material of an authentic epistle ?[1]

However, in dealing with the comparisons between Christ and the ecclesia which are interwoven with exhortations aimed at the state of marriage, we are faced with a problem since this introduces an entirely new element into the familiar scheme. It has, in the past, been argued that these comparisons are irreconcilable with 1 C. 7 since they bear witness to an evaluation of marriage which was totally alien to Paul.[2]

It is our opinion that there is a certain question which should be asked before raising the issue of whether or not Paul would have been capable of speaking about marriage in the manner described in Eph. It is this : could Paul have conceptualised the relationship between Christ and the ecclesia as it is described in Eph. ? For, after all, to the author of Eph. the relationship between Christ and the ecclesia takes precedence over marriage. The primary consideration was, for him, the fusion between Christ and the ecclesia; mortal marriage is of secondary consequence and it derives its norms from that first and foremost union between Christ and the ecclesia (see above, p. 306). Now we have already seen that the conception of the union between Christ and the ecclesia as envisaged in Eph. is in keeping with data found in the HP (p. 308).

Bultmann and his shool are in error when they see the unity of Christ and the ecclesia, as described in Eph., as analogous with the Gnostic suzugia.[3] Notions of the reconstitution of a once-disrupted unity of a male-female principle (against the background of a dualistic *Weltanschauung*), play no part in Eph. The issues at stake in Eph. are the humiliation of the Son of God who became a man, who realized the union with his people previously ordained by God and who now allows this people to partake of his exaltation and glory. In our view, this conception is in keeping with Paul's thoughts.

Could it be that his mind may also have entertained the notion that the unity between Christ and the ecclesia sets the standard for the

---

[1] Cf. Schrage, op. cit., p. 198s. R. 13:7 is a typical HP enumeration, displaying a formal correspondence with 1 Pt. 2:17 which, in turn, evinces an affinity with the Haustafel, for the enumeration of 1 Pt. 2:17 is followed, in 2:18, by a rudimentary Haustafel.

[2] See above, p. 24 and Käsemann, RGG II, (³1958), p. 518s.

[3] See Bultmann, Theologie, p. 182, Käsemann, loc. cit. and the works quoted in Mussner, Christus, das All und die Kirche (1968), p. 158 note 386. For the Gnostic suzugia, see Mussner, op. cit., p. 163; Delling, Th. W. VI, p. 300 and id. Th. W. VII. p. 750.

marriages of the faithful? In order to find a satisfactory answer to this question, we must examine the pronouncements in the HP which pertain to marriage.

1 C. 7 reveals that as far as Paul is concerned, marriage, under the eschatological circumstances, may not, in fact, be the most desirable state for the faithful. He believes that the unmarried are in a position to devote themselves wholeheartedly to the work of the Lord and are exempt from certain difficulties. But a special charisma is needed for the self-control which the unwed state demands and those who are not endowed with this particular gift should not wish to be unmarried.

Both in Judaism and the popular Stoa, marriage was regarded as a duty. [1] That Paul was the last to break with this general conception is clear from 1 C. 7:2 and 1 Th. 4:4.[2] Nor is it perchance that he names the divine decree protecting marriage as the first of a series of prohibitions in R. 13:9.

Paul may admit that, under the eschatological conditions prevailing, marriage is not the ideal way of life. Yet, he does not hesitate to put that other modus vivendi which, for so many believers, is the rule, in the light of the salvation through which, by virtue of the faith, they are saved.

There is to some degree a correlation with the state of enslavement; the apostle is decidedly unwilling, as such, to regard it as desirable. Nevertheless, he sees the life of the believer who is a slave as filled with the salvation of the kurios (1 C. 7:21, 22).

For slavery or marriage, there are no revolutionary consequences when the apostle places these two forms of life in a soteriological framework. In so doing, he does not release the slave from obedience and bondage to his master, nor does he cease to demand that woman be subordinate and obedient to the man (1 C. 7:20, 21; 11:8, 9; 14:34, 35).

All the same, a change has taken place. The slave is a slave in a new sense of the word. Freed by the kurios, the slave is no longer the slave of men and the believer who owns a slave is no longer his unrestricted master (1 C. 7:22, 23). Equally, the man is no longer the undisputed master or head of the woman: he is her head and lord in the same way as Christ is the head and Lord of the faithful.

---

[1] See Schrage, op. cit., p. 144 note 14 and Weidinger, Die Haustafeln, p. 32s.

[2] We are following Maurer's interpretation of 1 Th. 4:3-6. See Th. W. VII, p. 361-363, 365-368. For the marriage obligation in 1 Th. 4:4, see op. cit., p. 367 lines 25-31.

The driving force behind this dominion of Christ is mercy and an unquenchable thirst for power is unthinkable in this situation.[1] Although the subordination of woman to man, established at the creation, comes into full play where the mercy of God reigns through Christ, this new phase of existence for the faithful, i.e. being "in the Lord", does imply a union whereby the subordination of the woman and the dominance of the man is transcended. Both of them must come to realize that they are equally unable to do without each other (1 C. 11:8-12).

This new situation demands that the believer must win his wife and live with her in honour and sanctity. In view of the fact that the man is the head and lord of the woman who aids and serves him, the sanctification must come from his side. God, from whom all things come, the creation as well as the blessedness of Christ, is the one who makes this sanctification possible through the agency of the Holy Spirit.[2]

The (sexual) obligations which man and woman bear towards one another in marriage apply without reservation to religious men and woman (1 C. 7:3, 4). Although entitled to lend additional strength to prayer though temporary withholding, this is only proper by mutual consent. In fact, since as partakers in salvation they are constantly exposed to the temptations of the devil, it is wrong for them to live in prolonged abstinence (1 C. 7:5).

Having regard to all such considerations, we maintain that it could well be Paul himself who laid down the directives for marriage amongst the faithful in Eph. 5:22-33 as based on the relationship between Christ and the ecclesia. It seems to us that Eph. 5:22-33 deals explicitly and in detail with a subject at which the HP merely hints.

Thus the passage Eph. 5:25, 26 which sets up Christ, who gave himself for the sanctification of the ecclesia, as an example to man in

---

[1] 1 C. 11:3. For the restrictive meaning of the last sentence : "and the head of Christ is God", see p. 233s, above. The fact that the relationship between man and woman is placed within the framework of God's works of mercy in Christ in 1 C. 11:3, becomes clear through the τὰ δὲ πάντα ἐκ τοῦ θεοῦ in v. 12.

[2] For the meaning of σκεῦος κτᾶσθαι in 1 Th. 4:4 see Delling, loc. cit. For ἁγιασμός (1 Th. 4:4) as the nomen actionis, see Proksch, Th. W. I, p. 114 line 44-p. 115 line 6. The τὰ δὲ πάντα ἐκ τοῦ θεοῦ of 1 C. 11:12 entails that the creation and the blessedness of Christ both emanate from God. The words ὁ ἀνὴρ διὰ τῆς γυναικός convey that in the new situation, the woman is also the instrument or σκεῦος of the man. For the hagion pneuma as the principle of sanctification, see 1 Th. 4:8.

his loving capacity, highlights the notion expressed in 1 Th. 4:4 that
in winning and living with his wife man must take responsibility for
sanctifying the union. The subordination of woman and the dominance
of man is here more sharply aligned with the new situation of the faithful than in 1 C. 11:3, 8-12.

In Eph., Christ as the head is presented as the whole background
to the man in his position as head. This represents a difference with
1 C. 11:3, 8-12 in which the man's position as head is described as
also hairing been settled at the time of the creation. There is yet another
difference, namely that in Eph., sexual relations between couples are
discussed less openly and directly than in 1 C. 7 and 1 Th. 4:4, 5.

However, these divergences should not be exaggerated. When Paul
deals with sexual intercourse and remaining unmarried in 1 C. 7, he
does this in response to a communication which specially concerned
such matters. Furthermore, in 1 C. 14:34, he also relates the subordination of woman directly to the eclesia and itsorder rather than—or
at the most, obliquely—to the creation. There are certainly no grounds
for asserting that Eph. introduces a conceptual world which is essentially at odds with that of the HP.

Bultmann thought that there was a discernable gap between the
paraeneses of the HP and that of Eph. He thought that in Eph., the
church was well on the way to a religious moralism. Although aware
of a glorious future to come, the present is envisaged as the time of
salvation in Eph. This salvation is incorporated in the ecclesia and
the consciousness of belonging to the ecclesia imbues the faithful with
the necessary strength to live a pious life on the basis of brotherly love
which fits within the framework of a civic existence (on the lines of the
Haustafel). Bultmann goes on to say that the paradox of the unity
of the indicative and the imperative which is found in the HP is greatly
diminished in Eph.[1]

We cannot support this view of Bultmann's. In this chapter, we have
indicated that the paraenesis of Eph. is motivated by the same eschatological conceptions as those which govern the HP paraeneses. If there
are certain directives in the paraenesis of Eph. which could concievably
be reconciled with a religious moralism and the ethics of civic decency,
this is by no means contrary to the eschatological background of the
epistle. After all, in 1 and 2 Th., in which the eschatological aspect
is much stressed, there are also exhortations to a regular industrious

---

[1] See the references given on p. 394 note 1.

life which would be admirably in keeping with this type of ethic and moralism (1 Th. 4:11, 12; 2 Th. 3:6-12).

In our opinion, the unity of the indicative and the imperative is evinced just as strongly in Eph. as in the HP. This is particularly salient when, in Eph. 4:22-24, the preceding exhortations and, in truth, also the subsequent paraenesis are both motivated by a recapitulation i.e. the teaching about putting off the old man and putting on the new man, which has become a certainty through the death and resurrection of Jesus (see above, p. 336). The consciousness of the faithful, that they must and can begin a new life, is the result of not so much an awareness of belonging to the ecclesia as the knowledge of this truth (whereby a being renewed in the pneuma is implicit).[1]

According to Bultmann and Percy, another difference with the HP is that the paraenesis, partly on account of the different lists cataloguing sins and virtues, is fairly "katechismusartig" (catechism-like).[2] Moreover, Percy adds, the paraenesis has an "algemein gehaltene Art" (generalised bearing) and not, as R. (12:3ss.), Gal. (6) and 1 Th. (5:12ss.) a genuine "Gemeindeethik" or community ethic.[3]

Now, as Percy himself observes, not all the HP evince an ethic which has a special bearing on community life. Is so far as it is not explicitly stated (Eph. 4:29; 5:18-21), this type of ethic is discounted by the reflections expressed in Eph. 4:3-16.

The "algemein gehaltene Art" or general tendency of the paraenesis of Eph. is no argument against its authenticity. Schrage's study reveals that the HP paraeneses frequently have this character and that, in the past, the Pauline exhortation has often and unjustly been conceived of in terms of an actual concrete situation.[4]

With some reservations, we are prepared to accept the definition "katechismusartig". In so doing, we are not thinking of some ancient Christian catechism, the historicity of which has yet to be proved, but of the paraenesis to which 1 C. 4:17 alludes. It seems to us that Paul and his associates knew of a fundamental paraenesis in their teaching. Although this paraenesis did not consist of a definite number of fixed maxims, it nevertheless had a certain content which again and again assumed form in like formulations.

---

[1] Cf. Percy, op. cit., p. 355. Percy also refuset Bultmann's remark that in Eph. the flesh is no longer discussed in a Pauline spirit (Bultmann, op. cit., p. 556).

[2] Percy, op. cit., p. 134 and Bultmann, op. cit., p. 566s.

[3] Op. cit., p. 354.

[4] Op. cit., p. 117ss.

Whenever their gospel found response and led to conversion, they would teach this basic paraenesis which could then be used for future reference.

It seems likely that Eph. introduces some of this fundamental paraenetical material. In any event, this would be in character with an epistle which, after all, aims to establish an initial contact between Paul and communities which were not founded by him and which he has not visited. In addition, it explains why one particular element of this fundamental paraenesis, i.e. the eschatological struggle, is given such thorough treatment (see above, p. 397ss.); Whereas other epistles allude to the topic in passing, Eph. sets out to deal with it specifically.

Thus, we maintain that the paraenesis of Eph. does not essentially differ from those of the HP. Whatever differences exist are outweighed by the striking affinities which we have described in this chapter.

CHAPTER TEN

THE FRAGMENTAL AFFINITY WITH COL. AND OTHER EPISTLES

As follows from the opening chapter, the fragmental affinity between Eph. and Col. may be regarded as the greatest difficulty in the critical historical study of Eph.[1] Points of concurrence occur as follows :

Eph.	and Col.		Eph.	and Col.
1:1-3	1:1-3		4:2-4	3:12-14
1:4	1:22		4:15,16	2:19
1:7	1:14		4:22,24,25	3:8-10
1:10	1:16		4:31	3:8
1:10	1:20		4:32	3:13
1:13	1:5			
1:15	1:4		Eph. 5:3	and Col. 3:5
1:15,16	1:9		5:6	3:6
1:18	1:27		5:15,16	4:5
1:19,20	2:12		5:19-22	3:16-18
1:21	1:16		5:23	1:18
1:22,23	1:17-19		5:24,25	3:18,19
			5:27	1:22
Eph. 2:1	and Col. 2:13		5:28	3:19
2:5	2:13			
2:10	1:10		Eph. 6:1	and Col. 3:20
			6:5-9	3:22-4:1
Eph. 3:2	and Col. 1:25		6:19,20	4:3,4
3:7-9	1:25-27		6:21,22	4:7,8
3:19	2:9,10			

In the above, we have listed exclusively those parallel places in which three corresponding words—separated only by short intervals—are found. Different forms of verbs from the same root have been chassified as identical. We have also equated totally or partly concurrent designations indicating the person of Jesus Christ. A number of small words which are in general quite common have been omitted altogether.[2]

---

[1] Chapter I para. 2 (p. 4ss.).

[2] These are :
— all preposition except κατενώπιον which is rare;
— all relative pronouns :
— all pronomina possessiva and genitive forms of the pronomina personalia used as such;

We observed these criteria in the interests of the objectivity of our investigation and now affirm that nowhere in the CP is there more a correspondence between two epistles with regard to words than between Eph. and Col.

Going by the hypothesis that one of the two epistles is dependent on the other in a literary respect, a study of the parallel places occurring in the two epistles does not result in a satisfactory outcome.

Sometimes the data at hand would indicate the priority of Eph. An example of such an instance is the parallelism between Eph. 1:4 and Col. 1:22. In Eph., the parallel words occur in organic cohesion with the context which deals with the elected choice. The words in question are also firmly grounded within the entire epistle. As it is, we see the words ἅγιος καὶ ἄμωμος repeated in Eph. 5:27 where we also encounter the conjunctive παραστήσῃ of which the infinitive παραστῆσαι in Col. 1:22, reminds us. It seems more probable that Col. 1:22 should reflect Eph. 1:4 and 5:27 rather than that the contents of Col. 1:22 should be spread over verses 1:4 and 5:27 in Eph.[1]

The parallelism between Eph. 1:7 and Col. 1:14 also suggests the priority of Eph. in view of the fact that in Eph. (as distinct from Col.) the words could not be omitted without affecting the pericope as a whole. In this part of Eph. the word ἀπολύτρωσις is firmly corroborated by the reiteration in Eph. 1:14.

With respect to the correspondence between Eph. 4:15, 16 and Col. 2:19, the priority of Eph. is likewise a feasible proposition. In Col., we see a lucid whole; it emerges clearly that heresy conflicts with the growth of the body of Christ. The growth of this body is discussed very comprehensibly. In Eph., we are concerned with the same idea

---

— all   forms or the verb εἶναι;

— the conjunctions ἵνα, ὅτι, καί, τε, οὖν, γάρ, and ἀλλά;

— the particles οὐ, μή, μέν and δέ.

[1] Holdzmann, Kritik der Eph. und Kolosserbriefe, p. 47 argues the priority of Eph. in connection with the parallelism between Eph. 1:4 and Col. 1:22 : he finds the relationship of the words in Col. which correspond with those in Eph. quite uneasy in context. In Holtzmann's view it is more probable that the word ἀνέγκλητος was added in Col. instead of being omitted from Eph., in view of the tendency of both epistles to heap up similar words. He thinks, op. cit., p. 46, that we are confronted with a process whereby a writer reads an already completed work in parts which he then reproduces in a shortened form. The same applies to the following parallel places, he maintains : Eph. 1:6,7—Col. 1:13, 14; Eph. 3:3,5, 9-Col. 1:26; 2:2; Eph. 3:17, 18; 4:16; 2:20-Col. 1:23; 2:2,7; Eph. 4:16-Col. 2:19; Eph. 4:22, 23, 24-Col. 3:9, 10; Eph. 5:19-Col. 3:16. In all these cases he opts for the priority of Eph. (op. cit., p. 48-55).

but the language is laboured and circumlocutory. Therefore, it is not difficult to imagine that the less successful formulations of Eph. were the original ones and those of Col. the second and improved version. Besides this, it should be taken into account the verses Eph. 4:15, 16 are very closely interwoved with their context through the notion of unity which comes into play here as well as the places (4:1-13) immediately before.[1]

Then there are other instances which would plead for the priority of Col.[2] As is evident from our earlier observations (p. 155) this may be surmised of the parallelisms between Eph. 5:24, 25-Col. 3:18, 19; Eph. 5:28-Col. 3:19; Eph. 6:1-Col. 3:20 and Eph. 6:5-9-Col. 3:22-4:1.

The fragments which are alike in Eph. 4:2-4 and Col. 3:12-15 could suggest the priority of either one or the other of the epistles. The word σύνδεσμος occurs in both. In the case of Col., one should probably bear in mind a bond which binds people together, creating a close community or society.[3] The meaning of the word as it occurs in the LXX, i.e. "an alliance" and the classical connotation of "that which binds together or bond of union" would tend to support this exegesis.[4] Moreover, the notion of a bond which brings people together would be in keeping with the sentences which come after 3:15 and pertain to the peace of Christ and the one body. The genitive τῆς τελειότητος which follows the word σύνδεσμος is a genitivus qualitatis which accentuates the positive bias of the word.[5]

Both its context and the adjunction τῆς εἰρήνης in Eph. 4:3 instantly explain that the word signifies a bond which unifies people as a close

---

[1] Cf. also Holtzmann, op. cit., p. 52.

[2] N. A. Dahl. "Der Epheserbrief und der verlorene, erste Brief des Paulus an die Korinther" in Abraham, unser Vater/Juden und Christen im Gespräch über die Bibel/Festschrift für Otto Michel zum 60. Geburtstag, herausg. van O. Betz, M. Hengel u. P. Schmidt (1963), p. 71 finds indications suggesting priority both in Eph. and in Col. He remarks on a return to the older theories of Holtzmann and Mayerhoff (see above, p. 6 and p. 5 n. 6) in some contemporary commentaries, resp. those of Ch. Masson (Commentaire du Nouveau Testament IX, Paris 1953 and X, Paris 1950) and F. C. Synge (Ephesians, 1941 and Philippians and Colossians 1951).

[3] The context does not suggest that in Col. 3:14 love is qualified as a bond which links the virtues named in 3:12. For this eminently refutable exegesis and objections against it, see Percy, Die Probleme, p. 406s.

[4] See G. Fitzer, Th. W. VII, p. 856 and Liddell-Scott, s.v. and cf. the meaning of the word in Ep. Arist. 205 (see Fitzer, l.c. and Kautsch, Die Apokr. und Pseudep. II, p. 267).

[5] In LXX Is. 58:6; 3 Bas. 14:24 and Acts 8:23 the word is used in a bad sense. The possible equivalent סוד found in1 QH I, 22 also has a negative meaning (see Fischer, l.c., note 6).

community or society. Since the word is less clear in meaning in Col.
4:13[1] and since the expression "bond of peace" is somewhat akin to
the state of perfection which is already mentioned earlier on in Col. 1:29,
there is sufficient reason to attribute a priority to Col. in the case of the
parallelism between Eph. 4:2-4 and Col. 3:12-15.

However, a number of counter-arguments can be brought forward.
If one considers that in Eph. it is peace which is the subject of a bond
whereas in Col. it is love, the dependence of Eph. becomes a lesser
proposition. On top of this, there is the fact that the notions of the
unity of the spirit and the bond of peace in Eph. 4:3 are closely and
organically related with the series of concepts named in Eph. 4:4-6,
each of which is characterised by the numeral one.This enumeration
has certainly not been borrowed from Col.

Again, on seeing how the lines "humbleness of mind, meekness,
longsuffering : Forbearing one another and forgiving one another ...
even as the Lord forgave you" have ther parallel in formulations distri-
buted over two places in Eph. (4:2 and 4:32), the priority of Eph.
seems reasonable. After all, it would scarcely be credible if the words
were first grouped together in Col., only to be separated and spread
over different places in Eph.

As for the hypothesis that either of the epistles has a literary dependence on the other, there exists no convincing evidence in this respect
in any of the places discussed above. The only indication of this kind
can be found in Eph. 6:21, 22 and Col. 4:7 where the text is largely
similar. In fact, this concurence is highly remarkable.

The praescripts of the two epistles (Eph. 1:1-3 and Col. 1:1-3) also
evince a far-reaching correspondence in vocabulary but this does not
occasion us undue surprise. The praescripts of Pauline epistles are
formal in character and when subjected to comparison may yield
a number of mutual or common features.

However, there are no declarations in any other two epistles which
are as alike as that found in both Eph. 6:21, 22 and Col. 4:7. There
can be no solution but that this should be attributed to a literary
dependence of some kind. (In the final analysis, however, the possibility
should be left open that this may not be a case of direct literary dependence and that in this particular instance the material in Eph. and
Col. may have been drawn from a common source. Furthermore, it

---

[1] It has even been suggested that the author of Eph. had failed to comprehend Col.
3:14 : cf. the references in Percy, op. cit., p. 407 note 87. In view of the many facets wich
the word σύνδεσμος possesses, this was a somewhat precipitate conclusion.

should not be overlooked that this correspondence may have been intentional. In real letters, a statement of this nature may be somewhat official in aspect, being designed to give an accreditation to the messenger who delivers the document. With respect to two letters which were dispatched at the same time and meant to be read in the same places (Col. 4:16), it could be that the verbal affinity between the two declarations served to inspire trust in the messenger (and the letters themselves) who was supposed to read them out.)

This specific correspondence between Eph. 6:21, 22 and Col. 4:7 is the only direct piece of evidence to support the thesis which argues a literary interdependence for the two epistles. For the rest, no other parallel fragments contain such unambiguous indications.

As for arguments for or against the priority of either epistles, the position is more or less the same. Using the hypothesis of a literary dependence as a working base in the preceding, we discovered as many data in favour of the priority of Eph. as against it.

Eph. 6:21, 22 and Col. 4:7 reveal nothing to show which of the two epistles is secondary in character. Many sholars have thought that the words καὶ ὑμεῖς in 6:21 betray that the author of Eph. was in this instance thinking of the text of Col. 4:7.[1] But the fact is that we are here confronted with a Greek linguistic idiosyncracy. The little word καί used in front of the personal pronoun expresses that the knowledge of which the recipient is sensible agrees with the state of affairs as known to the informant.[2]

Other parallel places reveal no more in the way of convincing evidence for the priority of either of the two epistles. Eph. 1:10 - Col. 1:16 and Eph. 1-10 : Col. 1:20 merely show that the author of Eph. was not completely lacking in originality.

The greatest degree of correspondence in these places occurs between Eph. 1:10 and Col. 1:20, where ideas are closely connected.[3] Nevertheless, each of the two epistles has its own formulation. The correspondence rests on the words πάντα, οὐρανοί and γῆ. The words evince "a dichotomic division of cosmos common to Judaism".[4] The same words are also responsible for the correspondence between Eph. 1:10 and Col. 1:16 and also have a place in Eph. 3:15.

In our opinion the affinity between Eph. 1:13 and Col. 1:5 depends

---

[1] See Percy, op. cit., p. 389 note 47.

[2] According to Percy, op. cit., p. 390 who refers to A. Wifstrand.

[3] See Hanson, The Unity of the Church, p. 126.

[4] See Hanson, l. cit.

on a style of expression which had already become traditional. The
same applies which regard to Eph. 1:15 and Col. 1:4. The double indication for the word which is preached in Eph. 1:13 and the dual indication
for the spiritual wealth of the addressees in Eph. 1:15 are wholly in
keeping with the style of Eph. 1:3-23 which tends so much towards
parallelism.

It is almost certain that the fragments Eph. 1:15, 16 and Col. 1:9
contain traditional turns of phrase which account for the particularly
strong resemblance between the two epistles in these places. The traditional character of the expression emerges clearly from our study of
the disposition of Eph. (p. 47ss.). Formulations of the same type also
occur in R. 1:8-10. Yet is it striking that in the two small sections of
Eph. 1:13-18 and Col. 1:8-10 the epistles should share so many traditional sayings. It is our impression that the language of Eph. 1:15, 16 is
slightly more laboured than that of Col.[1]

The correspondence between Eph. 1:18 and Col. 1:27 is not very
pronounced and may be ascribed to the fact that the same style is
used.

In Eph. 1:19, 20 and Col. 1:16, we encounter the same basic Christian
avowal.[2]

Eph. 1:21 and Col. 1:16 both contain a reference to supernatural
powers as a result of which there is some resemblance. However,
the situation is by no means that the description of these supernatural
powers is identical.

The fragments Eph. 1:22, 23 and 5:23 and Col. 1:18 all express the
notion that Christ is kephale of the ecclesia which is in turn the body
of Christ. This is the extent to which these places correspond, the explanation being that all three concern a common theologoumenon.

Granted that there exists some additional correspondence between
Eph. 1:22, 23 and the context of Col. 1:18, there is no immediate cause
to argue in terms of literary dependence. For example, the word πάντα
features in both Eph. 1:22 and Col. 1:17. In both cases it is used to
convey the superiority of Christ. But the fact that the notion is differently formulated in each instance counts against the likelihood of
interdependence in this connection. Eph. 1:23 and Col. 19 correspond
by virtue of the word πλήρωμα but two such entirely different shades
of the term are involved that any interdependence is almost ruled out.

---

[1] Some scholars have objected to the διὰ τοῦτο κἀγώ; in this connection, see Percy,
op. cit., p. 386-389.

[2] See Bultmann, Theologie, p. 83s.

The similarity between Eph. 2:1 and Col. 2:13 could be due to derivation one way or the other. If that is indeed the case, it is our impression that the somewhat laborious constructions of Eph. could well be the original. Nevertheless, it should be said that the expressions καὶ ὑμεῖς or καὶ ὑμᾶς are often employed in Eph. and Col. when the narrative seeks to point out that the addressees are included in the salvation of Christ or should alter their way of life (Eph. 1:13; 2:1; 2:5, 22; 5:33 and Col. 1:21; 2:13; 3:8).

Therefore, we feel that the similarity between Eph. 2:1 and 5 and Col. 2:13 is the result not so much of interdependence as of a stereotype phraseology.

The correspondence between Eph. 2:10 and Col. 1:10 is so insignificant that it scarcely required comment.

On the other hand, the fragments Eph. 3:2, 7-9 and Col. 1:25-27 have much in common. In the first place, we recognise corresponding ideas and conceptions.[1] However, if these fragments are taken at face value, i.e. statements by the apostle Paul about himself, this conformity may be sufficiently explained by the assumption that the two epistles were written within a short space of time under the same conditions.

If there is some literary interdependence between Eph. and Col., much of the available evidence would favour the priority of Eph. It is a fact that the pericope Eph. 3:2-9 forms an integral part of the epistle, serving as a consolidating link. The pronouncements on the mystery have already been introduced in the course of the eulogy (1:3-14) and the unusual connotation of the word οἰκονομία in 3:9 already occurs in 1:10.[2] Furthermore, the verb γνωρίζειν is not only used in this pericope but is elsewhere also associated with the term "mystery" (1:9; 3:10; 6:19).

Some scholars have thought that the description τοῖς ἁγίοις ἀποστόλοις αὐτοῦ καὶ προφήταις in Eph. 3:5 is a maladroit version of the words τοῖς ἁγίοις αὐτοῦ in Col. 1:26, but this view conflicts with our exegesis of the description in question.[3]

There is a remarkable degree of parallelism between Eph. 3:19 and Col. 2:9, 10. The expression πᾶν τὸ πλήρωμα as well as some form of the passive πληροῦσθαι occur in both places. Essentially, the same

---

[1] For the correspondence of the οἰκονομία in Eph. 3:2 and Col. 1:25 see above, p. 175 and for the affinity between the two epistles in connection with the mystery, see p. 383

[2] See above, p. 175.

[3] For this view, see Percy, op. cit., p. 336 and his references in note 94. For our exegesis, see above, p. 389ss.

idea is being expressed; yet the formulations are different and indivi
dual.

We are also aware of this independence in formulations concerning
the traditional theme of putting off the old man and putting on the
new. In both epistles this theme is firmly defined in christological
terms; in both epistles it dominates the paraenesis and in both epistles
it is linked with a warning against falsehood. In this connection, see
the paralellisms between Eph. 4:22, 24, 25 - Col. 3:8-10 and Eph. 4:31 -
Col. 3:8.

Despite the many aspects of correspondence in thought-matter and
vocabulary, there is a considerable amount of variation in the actual
formulations. Thus, for instance, the arguments are presented more
compactly and easily in Col. This could be interpreted as evidence
for the secondary character of places such as Col. 3:8-10. In Eph. 5:3 -
Col. 3:5 and Eph. 5:6 - Col. 3:6 the paralellism in ideas and words goes
side by side with an independence in the way these are expressed.

With respect to the paralellism between Eph. 5:15, 16 and Col. 4:5,
the situation is different again; the exhortation in Eph. is more
extensive than the terse advice given in Col. 4:5. In fact, the caution
of Col. with the adjunct πρὸς τοὺς ἔξω could be seen as a summing-up
of Eph. 5:15, 16 and the preceding verse which also pertains to relations
with non-Christians. However, Eph. 5:11, 15, 16 could equally well
be regarded as paraphrase and commentary on Col. 4:5.

There is extensive paralellism between Eph. 5:19-22 and Col. 3:16-18.
In the past, the exhortation of Eph. has sometimes been viewed as
an unsuccessful version of that in Col. It was argued that in Col. 3:16
the words ψαλμοῖς ὕμνοις ᾠδαῖς πνευματικαῖς belonged to the ᾄδοντες
which comes later and that the author of Eph. had erroneously separated them.[1]

It has also been thought that whereas Col. urges that all talk and
action should happen "in the name of the Lord Jesus", the author of
Eph. had inadvertently combined the adjunct "in the name of our
Lord Jesus Christ" with giving thanks.[2] Moreover, it was argued that
the fact that the commoditive dative τῷ θεῷ in Col. 3:16 corresponds
with a like dative, i.e. τῷ κυρίῳ in Eph. 5:19, indicates that Eph. was

---

[1] Thus in Cramer, Stoicheia tou kosmou, p. 106 note 6. Cf. also Percy, op. cit., p.395
and note 66.

[2] Mitton, The Epistle to the Ephesians, pp. 80 and 253.

written at a later date by which time the figure of the kurios had become central to the cult.[1]

In addition, it was held that the author of Eph. had borrowed the word ὑποτάσσεσθαι from Col. 3:18 to introduce the exhortation ὑποτασσόμενοι ἀλλήλοις ἐν φόβῳ Χριστοῦ with which the "Haustafel" opens. As it is, this is a misapplication since there is no question of a general reciprocal submission in the "Haustafel".[2]

We do not share these reservations with respect to Eph. 5:19-22. It seems to us more likely that those exegetes who maintain this have not fully comprehended the structure of Col. 3:16 rather than that some imitator misinterpreted or misunderstood the passage in question. The section ὁ λόγος τοῦ Χριστοῦ ἐνοικείτω ἐν ὑμῖν πλουσίως ἐν πάσῃ σοφίᾳ is a self-contained unit which is rounded-off by an adverbial adjunct introduced by ἐν. This not unusual since such adjuncts are constantly used in Col. to complete a sentence.[3] The next section, beginning with διδάσκοντες and correspondingly concluded by the adjunct ἐν τῇ χάριτι is also complete in itself and closely connected with the preceding. The point is that it draws the psalms, hymns and spiritual songs which are named closely together under the heading of "the word of Christ" and accentuates their enlightening character. After all, in Col. 4:16, the words ᾄδοντες ἐν ταῖς καρδίαις ὑμῶν τῷ θεῷ which indicate the ritual singificance of the songs, are used to end the final sentence.

The second sentence, διδάσκοντες ... ἐν τῇ χάριτι, in Eph. 5:19, corresponds with that series of words which opens with λαλοῦντες and and ends in ᾠδαῖς πνευματικαῖς. These words are closely linked with the preceding exhortation πληροῦσθε ἐν πνεύματι of Eph. 5:18

As in Col. 3:16 (and 1 C. 14:26) the doctrinal nature of the songs is brought out except that here, in Eph., they are not presented in relation to "the word of Christ" as a common denominator. There is a great deal of emphasis (as in 1 C. 14:1 and 15) on the spiritual aspect of the songs and the ritual character is expressed through the words ᾄδοντες καὶ ψάλλοντες τῇ καρδίᾳ ὑμῶν τῷ κυρίῳ, which are strongly reminiscent of the sentence ᾄδοντες ἐν καρδίαις ὑμῶν τῷ θεῷ in Col. 3:16.

To make a distinction between the dative τῷ κυρίῳ in Eph. 5:19 and the dative τῷ θεῷ in Col. 3:16 is a misconception; to regard Eph.

---

[1] See Percy, op. cit., p. 417 and his references in note 3.

[2] See Percy, op. cit., p. 405 and the references he gives in note 80.

[3] See above, p. 114.

on the basis of this, as connected with a later ritual form is equally wrong. It is a well-known fact that the designations for God and Christ are interchangeable in a number of HP texts and that it emerges time and time again in these epistles to what extent Paul is conscious of meeting God in Jesus Christ.

Christ also takes the place of God for Paul, when it comes to prayer or praising God.[1] In Paul's eyes the avowal of Jesus as Lord is the criterion for every word that is inspired by the pneuma and the great purpose of God's work of salvation (1 C. 21:3 and Phil. 2:10).

Therefore, there is no reason to object to the fact that the christocentric character of the songs in question is expressed by means of the dative $\tau \hat{\omega}$ $\kappa \nu \rho i \omega$ in Eph. 5:19; it should be realized that the same type of songs have also been christologically conceived in Col. 3:16, since they are there designated as "the word of Christ". In the light of Col. 1:28, this word of Christ may be understood as the word which has Christ as content.

Nor can we see why the exhortation "giving thanks always for all things unto God and the Father in the name of our Lord Jesus Christ" (Eph. 5:20) should have been the work of a thoughtless imitator, basing himself on "and whatsoever you do in word or deed, do all in the name of the Lord Jesus, giving thanks to God and the Father by him" (Col. 3:17). We canot see a greater difference between these two sets of instructions than between 1 Th. 5:18 and 1 C. 10:31. Moreover, in our opinion the exhortation $\pi \epsilon \rho \iota \sigma \sigma \epsilon \dot{\nu} o \nu \tau \epsilon \varsigma$ $\dot{\epsilon} \nu$ $\epsilon \dot{\nu} \chi \alpha \rho \iota \sigma \tau i \alpha$ in Col. 2:7 has much correspondence with Eph. 5:19.

We furthermore observe that the exhortation "submitting yourselves one to another in the fear of Christ" is not intended to be an introduction to the "Haustafel". It forms the logical and grammatical conclusion of a number of exhortation which apply to the whole of the community. The reciprocal pronoun, $\dot{\alpha} \lambda \lambda \dot{\eta} \lambda o \iota \varsigma$, has the same general significance (i.e. relating to the entire community) as the pronouns $\dot{\alpha} \lambda \lambda \dot{\eta} \lambda \omega \nu$ in Eph. 4:25; $\dot{\epsilon} \alpha \nu \tau o \hat{\imath} \varsigma$ in Eph. 5:19; $\dot{\alpha} \lambda \lambda \dot{\eta} \lambda o \nu \varsigma$ in 1 Th. 5:11; $\dot{\epsilon} \alpha \nu \tau o \hat{\imath} \varsigma$ in 1 Th. 5:13 and the expression $\epsilon \hat{\imath} \varsigma$ $\tau \dot{o} \nu$ $\ddot{\epsilon} \nu \alpha$ in 1 Th. 5:11 which takes the place of the reciprocal.

Following these exhortations which are pertinent to the entire community in the same degree, there are a number of exhortations which pertain to certain very specific relationships in which the faithful may be involved. The latter occur in what is known as the "Haustafel".

---

[1] See G. Sevenster, De Christologie v. h. N.T., p. 144s.

After these, in 6:10, there are again a number of directives which affect all the faithful equally, i.e. the exhortation to struggle against the evil forces.

This pattern of thought has some affinity with the paraenesis of R. In R. 12:1 and 2, the apostle urges the faithful to a spiritual priesthood. In R. 12:3-21, he enumerates a number of exhortations which concern all and in which the element of reciprocity plays a part.

Then, in R. 13:1-7, he deals with special relationships which the faithful can have with others outside the communities. In this connection he mentions the paying of dues and the rendering of respect and honour.

He then, in R. 13:8-10, comes back to inter-relationships after which, in R. 13:11-14, he makes an exhortation to the spiritual struggle in a manner which is closely related to R. 12;1 and 2.

Both in the paranesis of R. 12 and 13 as well as in that of Eph. 5:14-6:18, there is a somewhat circular movement in the thought-process. At the conclusion of the paraenesis is Eph. we also find ourselves back at the point of departure. The themes of awakening, the eschatological situation and liturgy are discussed in Eph. 5:14-19 as well as in Eph. 6:13-18.

Eph. 5:21, 22 has a feature in common with R. 13:7, 8. In the latter, there is an unexpected transition from exhortations which relate to the authorities and the fiscal administration to a general exhortation to love which has already been mentioned earlier. Similarly, in Eph. 5:21, 22, the generalised exhortations suddenly give way to pronouncements which pertain to family life. In both these instances there is some connection between the different trends of thought. The link, in R. 13:7, 8, is provided by the terms "dues" and "owe" which respectively occur in v. 7 (ὀφειλάς) and v. 8 (ὀφείλετε), whilst the relevant notion in Eph. 5:21, 22 is the submission and fear of Christ.

However, the notion "submit" is so inherent to the first exhortation of the traditional Haustafel that the author does not repeat it after 5:21 and 5:22 but makes use of an ellipse—and quite justifiably, since a repetition would not have had the dramatic effect of the successive ὀφειλάς and ὀφείλετε in R. 13:7, 8. But he does come back to the φόβος Χριστοῦ in 5:21 by means of the expression ὡς τῷ κυρίῳ. The significance of this is that the author is placing the traditional material of the Haustafel within the new framework of the fear of Christ.

If we now come back to our original point, i.e. the paralellism between Eph. 5:19-22 and Col. 3:16-18, we find that in spite of the considerable correspondence in words and ideas, there is neverheless an important element of independence discernible in the two epistles. In Col., the whole piece is firmly anchored in the phrase διδάσκουντες καὶ νουθε-τοῦντες which also occurs in 1:28. The originality of Eph. rests on the emphasis given to the working of the pneuma and the unusual manner in which the Haustafel is linked with the preceding section.

As with last-mentioned parallel, the concurrence between Eph. 6:19 and Col. 4:3, 4 has sometimes been ascribed to the fact that the author of Eph. had merely produced a bad imitation of Col.[1] The most common assumption was that the door which is open or about to be opened in 1 C. 16:9; 2 C. 2:12 and Col. 4:3 represents God's given access to the hearts of men (i.e. the possibility of successful missionary work).

Although this interpretation could be reconciled with Acts 16:4 it cannot be deduced from it since, on the one hand, the characteristic word θύρα is missing from Acts and, on the other, the so dominant word καρδία in Acts is absent in the CP places in question.

In rabbinical writings, the expression "open a door" can be used in the sense of giving a chance or possibility. The idea did not entail receptiviness to religious propaganda or successful missionary work; usually it pertained to a God-given opportunity for prayer or the chance of conversion or penance.[2]

It seems quite likely that the rabbinical expression goes back to a sacred terminology in which the door as such represents the point of contact between the divine and the human spheres.[3] Man approaches the godhead by means of the door or, otherwise, the godly salvation or knowledge comes to man through such a door.

There is another factor which should be taken into account. In the O.T. psalms there are frequent references to speech through the mouth or lips as, for example, in the prayer : "O Lord, open thou my lips; and my mouth shall shew forth thy praise" (Ps. 51:17).[4] Under these circumstances, it is not hard to conceive how the Jewish notions govern-ing the accessgiving door between the human and the divine realms, the door which opens to the godhead and the gifts of the godhead,

---

[1] Cf. Percy, op. cit., p. 392ss. and see his references in notes 58 and 59.

[2] See Str.-B. III, p. 484s.

[3] See H. de Nie, "De geopende deur" in Vox Theologica, 10e jg. nr. 6, juni 1939, p. 188ss.

[4] Cf. also the converse prayer; "Set a watch, O Lord, before my mouth; keep watch over the door of my lips" in Ps. 141:3.

gradually fused or gave way to the notion of the mouth or lips, opened by God.

Therefore, we think that the rabbinical term "opening a door" is not only rooted in a generalised sacred terminology but is also based on the O.T. idea that the word of man can be inspired by God who can open his lips or mouth. In rabbinical literature, this word especially implies praying to God or turning to God and doing penance.

This kind of fusion of ideas emerges clearly from Barn. 16:9. Opening the door is in this instance, sacred terminology. When God opens the door to the faithful, He leads them into his eternal temple (which, incidentally, is in man when God dwells in the faithful). The open door is emphatically equated with the mouth; the opening of this door goes side by side with the inspired word. (I.e., God prophesies through the faithful.) It is also associated with penance and conversion. Barn. 16:10 subsequently deals with the relation of the man who wants to be saved and the preacher of the gospel. There is an observation to the effect that the salvandus must not look to him who reveals but to Him who dwells in the bringer of the word and from whose (human) mouth His (divine) words emanate.

References to the door which is open or about to be opened in 1 C. 16:9, 2; 2 C. 2:12 and Col. 4:3 are probably also associated with the notion of the mouth which God has opened or is about to open and the speaking or revealing of the gospel through a God-inspired speech. This would be in keeping with the conceptions of this image in Judaism and as envisaged by the author of Barn.

In Col. 4:3, the contents of Paul's prayer of intercession is that God may open the door of the word so that Paul may speak the mystery of Christ in the appropriate fashion. That which comes through the door is hereby the God-given word ὁ λόγος, whilst the mouth is the door for the inspired word θύρα τοῦ λόγου.[1] The formulation ἀνοίξῃ

---

[1] Herm. von Soden, Die Briefe a.d. Kolosser, Epheser, Philemon u. die Pastoralbriefe, a.l. (see Percy, loc, cit., note 60), holds that Col. 4:3 refers to a door which gives access to the word. De Nie associates it whit the power of God which is released and used by Paul in the revelation of the gospel (op. cit., p. 192). Thus, these authorities also connect Col. 4:3 with the idea of inspiration. Our point of view diverges, since we regard the door as an indication for the mouth. Our strongest evidence is that of Barn. 16:9. Lohmeyer saw "the door of the word" as a metaphor for the mouth of Paul and refers to Ps. 141:3 (see Percy, l.c., note 62). Percy's argument against this interpretation is that, if it were correct, the article would come before θύρα. In Col. 4:3, however, the mouth is not conceived as the door or organ of all speech but as the gateway for the inspired word which is identical to the word mentioned in 1:15, 25 and 3:16. The article before λόγος is ana-

ἡμῖν θύραν τοῦ λογοῦ signifies that God opens the door which is Paul's mouth and makes him speak through his inspiration.

In Eph. 6:19, there is no actual reference to the door but the opening of Paul's mouth is directly mentioned.[1] The meaning of the subordinate clause ἵνα μοι δοθῇ λόγος ἐν ἀνοίξει τοῦ στόματός μου, is identical to the corresponding clause, ἵνα ὁ θεὸς ἀνοίξῃ ἡμῖν θύραν τοῦ λόγου in Col. Therefore, if Eph. 6:19 is indeed a reproduction of Col. 4:3, the author has interpreted the words of Col. correctly. In that event, it would be equally viable to regard Col. 4:3 as a correct reading of Eph. 6:19.

If we argue along the lines of erroneous contemporary exegeses, Col. 4:3 presents us with the more difficult material. This could imply the priority of Col. Yet, it should also be excogitated that for the author of Eph., a contemporary of the author of Col. and one who lived in the same spiritual climate, the words would not have presented any problem. Hence, the language difficulty can be eliminated as a serious argument for the priority of Col.

At this stage, we have discussed all the corresponding fragments of Eph. and Col. Leaving aside Eph. 6:21, 22 and Col. 4:7, we may state with impunity that we found no evidence for literary interdependence between the two epistles. Nevertheless, we have constantly taken this hypothesis into account and have searched for possible signs indicating the priority of either one or the other epistle. These we were unable to find.

Moreover, what evidence was found, pointed towards the priority of Eph. Or at least, most of it did, although there were no conclusive indications.

We therefore maintain that it serves no further purpose to continue looking for the possibility of some kind of literary interdependence between the two epistles. For the same reason, we also reject the likelihood of some source of mutual dependence.[2] Consequently, we shall look elsewhere to explain the extraordinary number of parallels between Eph. and Col., whilst considering the following factors.

---

phoric and emphatic; cf. Bl.-Debr. para. 252,1 and Van Veldhuizen, Het taaleigen des N.T., p. 152,153. An article of this kind would not be suitably placed in front of θύρα.

[1] ἄνοιξις is a nomen actionis.

[2] This is the hypothesis of Holtzmann (see above, Chapter I, para. 2, p. 6). In the first place, he reckoned with the priority of Col. However, in our view, the (feeble) indications for the priority of Eph., are more numerous than those which indicate the priority of Col.

A certain number of parallel fragments are distinguished by the fact that they also form part of a corresponding element in the disposition of the epistles. In addition, these have the same sequence. We shall proceed to list these in such a way that the parallelism in question emerges as clearly as possible.

Eph. 1:1-3, praescript and opening of the eulogy,[1] "Paul, an apostle of Jesus Christ by the will of God, to the saints ... and ... faithful in Jesus Christ : grace be to you, and peace, from God, our Father ... God ... Father of our Lord Jesus Christ".

Col. 1:1-3, praescript and opening of the thanksgiving,[2] "Paul, an apostle of Jesus Christ by the will of God ... to the saints and faithful ... in Christ : grace be nuto you, and peace, from God our Father ... God the Father of our Lord Jesus".

Eph. 1:15, thanksgiving, "after I heard of the faith in the Lord Jesus which is yours, and love unto all the saints".

Col. 1:4, thaksgiving, "since we heard of your faith in Christ Jesus, and of the love ... to all the saints".

Eph. 1:15, 16, thanksgiving with transition to the intercession, "for this cause I also since I heard ... do not cease to ... for you".

Col. 1:9, beginning of intercession, "for this cause we also since we heard ... do not cease to ... for you".

Eph. 1:21, intercession (avowal-section), "all principality ... power ... dominion".

Col. 1:16, intercession (avowal-section), "all things ... dominions ... principalities ... powers".

Eph. 1:22, 23, intercession (avowal-section), "all things ... and Him ... head ... all things to the church ... is his body, the fulness ... all ... all".

Col. 1:17-19, intercession (avowal-section), "all things ... all things ... and He is the head of the body, the church ... all ... all fulness".

Eph. 3:2, statement concerning the sender, "the ministry ... of God which is given me for you".

Col. 1:25, statment concerning the sender, "the ministry of God which is given me for you".

Eph. 3:7-9, statement concerning the sender, "whereof I was made a minister ... of God given to me ... saints ... Gentiles ... riches ... ministry ... the mystery hidden for ages".

---

[1] For the disposition of the epistles and their elements, see Chapter III and IV.

[2] For the relationship between the eulogy and the thanksgiving, see above, p. 47ss.

Col. 1:25-27, statement concerning the sender, "whereof I am made a minister ... the ministery of God ... given to me ... the mystery hidden for ages ... saints ... riches ... the Gentiles".

Eph. 4:15, 15, paraenesis (following exhortation against heresy), " "grow ... from whom the whole body ... knit together ... joint ... makes the increase".

Col. 2:19, paraenesis (following exhortation against heresy), "the Head, from whom the whole body ... joint ... knit together ... increases with the increase".

Eph. 4:22, 24, 25, paraenesis (important theme), "that you have put away ... the old man ... and that you have put on the new (καινόν) man ... has been created ... putting away".

Col. 3:8-10, paraenesis (important theme), "put away ... having put off the old man ... and put on the new (νέον) man, which is renewed (ἀνακαινούμενον) ... created".

Eph. 4:32, paraenesis, "forgiving one another even as ... in Christ has forgiven you".

Col. 3:13, paraenesis, "forgiving one another ... even as the Lord has forgiven you".

Eph. 5:19-22, paraenesis (completing general exhortations and commencement of Haustafel, "one another in psalms and hymns and spiritual songs, singing ... in your heart ... giving thanks ... for everything in the name of ... Lord Jesus Christ to God the Father, submitting ... wives ... your own husbands ... the Lord".

Col. 3:16-18, paraenesis (completing the general exhortations and commencement of Haustafel, "one another in psalms and hymns and spiritual songs ... singing with your hearts to God ... whatever ... everything ... in the name of the Lord Jesus, giving thanks to God, the Father ... wives, submit to your husbands ... the Lord".

Eph. 5:24, 25, paraenesis (Haustafel), "is subject ... wives to their husbands ... husbands, love your wives".

Col. 3:18, 19, paraenesis (Haustafel), "wives, be subject to your husbands ... husbands, love your wives".

Eph. 5:28, paraenesis (Haustafel), "husbands ... love their own wives".

Col. 3:19, paraenesis (Haustafel), "husbands, love your wives".

Eph. 6:1, paraenesis (Haustafel), "Children, obey your parents in the Lord for this is".

Col. 3:20, paraenesis (Haustafel), "Children, obey (your) parents ... for this is ... in the Lord".

Eph. 6:5-9, paraenesis (Haustafel), "servants, be obedient to them that are your masters according to the flesh ... in singleness of your heart, as unto Christ; not with eyeservice as menpleasers ... servants of Christ ... from the heart ... doing service as (to) the Lord and not (to) men : knowing that ... receive of the Lord ... slave ... masters ... knowing that ... your Master is in heaven ... is no respect of persons".

Col. 3:22-4:1, paraenesis (Haustafel), "servants, obey ... your masters according to the flesh; not with eyeservice, as menpleasers ... in singleness of heart ... the Lord ... heartily ... as (to) the Lord and not (to) men; knowing that from the Lord ... serve the Lord Christ... shall receive of the Lord and (there is) no respect of persons ... masters ... your slaves ..., knowing that ... Master in heaven".

Eph. 6:19, 20, plea for intercession, "that ... utterance ... to proclaim the mystery ... that ... as I ought to speak".

Col. 4:3, 4, plea for intercession, "that ... utterance to declare the mystery ... that ... as I ought to speak".

Eph. 6:21, 22, reference to the bringer of the epistle, "... my affairs ... Tychicus, a beloved brother and faithful minister in the Lord, will tell you everything, whom I have sent unto you for the same purpose, that you may know our affairs, and that he may comfort your hearts".

Col. 4:7, 8, reference to the bringer of the epistle, "all about my affair Tychicus, a beloved brother and faithful minister and fellowservant in the Lord, will tell you, whom I have sent unto you for the same purpose, that you may know our affairs, and that he may comfort your hearts".

These fragments reveal, as it were, the patterns of the two epistles. Even if we limit ourselves to this particular selection, there is no reason to accept the hypothesis of a direct literary interdependence. The criteria which apply to the whole number of corresponding fragments may also be applied to this selection. There are too few indications for the priority of either one or the other epistle.

Since the selected fragments have elucidated the pattern of the two epistles, we feel that we are now in a position to bring forward a different and better hypothesis. In our opinion, both epistles are based on a third piece of documentation and the above-mentioned common words are the remnants of the original work.

The number of common words at our disposal are not sufficient to make a complete reconstruction of the original source. All we can do, is to establish its somewhat sketchy pattern. Nor would it serve any purpose to promote this hypothetical original manuscript to the status of an original Pauline epistle which was converted, by one or more imitators, into two inauthentic epistles, i.e. Eph. and Col. We do not command over enough material to support such a claim and prefer to maintain the idea of a blueprint which preceded the two epistles.

Admittedly, there is no known example of such a blueprint in antiquity, but, as we have already observed, the epistles of Paul were of an extraordinary length (see above, p. 93). We are therefore prepared to think that the process of their composition was equally exceptional and that a written draught could have been a step in their production.[1]

Some of the parallelisms between Eph. and Col. (i.e., those listed above), are explained by our hypothetical common blueprint. However, an explanation must also be found to explain the remaining fragments. On the basis of the hypothesis that both Eph. and Col. are authentic, we would suggest that, besides the blueprint, there was yet another common source. This source was the Pauline circle to which, apart from Paul himself (the sender of Eph. and Col.) and Timotheus (the co-sender of Col.), the secretary or secretaries who put the epistles to paper, also belonged.[2]

Parallelisms which cannot be explained on the basis of the blueprint-hypothesis, could be due to the fact that they are couched in traditional terms or contain professions of avowal which were familiar to Paul and his circle. We are thinking, for instance, of a phrase such as "to present ... holy and without blame before him" (which features completely or in part in Eph. 1:4; 5:27 and Col. 1:22 the avowal "in whom we have redemption, the forgiveness" (Eph. 1:7 and Col. 1:14) or the traditionally twofold Jewish arrangement of the creation (Eph. 1:10 and Col. 1:16 and 20),[3] an already by that time traditional indication for the word that is preached (Eph. 1:13 and Col. 1:5),[4] a basic communal avowal of the first Christians (Eph. 1:19, 20 and Col. 2:12)[5] as well as the stereotype language to which we have (see above, p. 419) drawn attention (Eph. 2:1, 5 and Col. 2:13).

---

[1] One reservation must be kept in mind with this hypothesis; the mnemotechniques of Paul and his associates were different from those of a 20th century person. Possibly, the blueprint for Eph. and Col. was not on paper but nevertheless, due to an ancient Jewish talent for mnemonics, laid down firmly.

[2] For the responsibility of the senders Paul and Timotheus, see Chapter V, para 3 and for the secretary or secretaries, see Chapter V, para 4 and Chapter VI, para. 16.

[3] See above, p. 417.

[4] See above, p. 417s.

[5] See above, p. 418 and note 2

The common material of Eph. 4:2-4 and Col. 3:12-15, we would also evaluate from the point of view of some readily available source.[1] Traditional material is found in Eph. 4:13 and Col. 3:8 which fits in with the theme of putting off the old man and putting on the new (found in the context of both places).[2] Similarly, the two places Eph. 5:3 and Col. 3:5 both contain the traditional material of a catalogue of vices whilst Eph. 5:6 and Col. 3:6 evince a traditional exhortation which is well in keeping with such a catalogue.

If, on the strength of Eph. 6:21, 22; Col. 4:3, 4; Eph. 3:1; 4:1 and Col. 1:24, it is agreed that both epistles were written during the same period in Paul's life, our hypothetical blueprint and the thesis that traditional material, well-known to the Pauline circle, was used, is sufficient explanation to account for the correspondence in words in the two epistles. The reason that Eph. (an epistle of Paul which was scripted by a secretary) and Col. (an epistle of Paul and Timotheus, also put to paper by a secretary—perhaps even the one who wrote Eph.) turned out to be similar productions based on the same draught, is due to the fact that they were written more or less simultaneously and to the contact which existed between the various people involved in the work.

Another fact which should be taken into account is that a certain period elapsed between the time when the originals were written and the date of the earliest manuscripts we have of these epistles. During this period, the epistles were read out in public, in services, on countless occasions and were for that purpose copied out again and again.[3] In our view it could well be that in the course of that interim, two epistles which were so alike could easily have been adapted even more so that pieces of Eph. were taken to elucidate or embellish Col., for example, and visa versa.

---

[1] See above, p. 415s.

[2] For the traditional character of the "Laster- und Tugendkataloge", see above, p. 394. The enumerations of sins in Eph. 4:31 and Col. 3:8 are resp. connected with the notions of taking away or taking off . So there is an anology with the old man who is put off or aside. Cf. above, p. 327ss. and p. 403. Kamlah maintains that the catalogues of sins and virtues have their roots or "Sitz ins Leben" in a fundamental paraenesis which was directly or indirectly associated with baptism. He also ascribes the image of putting off the old man putting on the new to this paranesis (op. cit., p. 33-38). For the connection between the image of the old and the new man with baptism, see also above, p. 338.

[3] Cf. the remark of J. S. Semler, quoted in Schweitzer, Geschichte der Paulinischen Forschung, p. 5.

At this juncture, we should make clear a point which could otherwise be open to misunderstapdings; the blueprint theory we have put forward did not determine the actual finished product to the extent one would expect in the case of a modern letter. Despite the common pattern which is the foundation of both epistles, each has its own character. Thus Eph. concentrates more on the ecclesia and draws attention to the unity of Jew and Gentile. Col. is more or less directed against heresy. The expression "pleroma" has a slightly differnt tendency in the two epistles (see above, p. 247s.).

There exists, as we have already established, another problem; namely that more than any other homologoumenon, Eph. has a strong fragmentary correspondence with the other epistles of Paul.[1]

A Eph.	Col.	R.	1 C.	2 C.	Phlm.	
1:1			1:1			
1:2		1:7	1:3		3	Gl. 1:3
1:1,2						Phil. 1:1, 2;
						1 Th. 1:1;
						2 Th. 1:1, 2
1:3		15:6				
1:1-3	1:1-3			1:1-3		
1:13, 14				1:22		
1:15, 16	1:9	1:8-10			4,5	
1:21	1:16		15:24			
1:22			15:27			
2:20, 21			3:9-12			
3:2	1:25		3:10			
3:3-6		16:25, 26				
3:8-10	1:25-27	16:25, 26				
3:9, 10			2:7			
3:11, 12		5:1, 2				
3:21		16:27				
4:1						1 Th. 2:12
4:6			8:6			
4:11			12:28, 29			
4:15, 16	2:19		11:3			
4:28			4:12			1 Th. 4:11, 12
5:2						Phil. 4:18
						Gl. 2:20
5:5			5:11			
			6:9, 10			
5:10		12:2				

---

[1] See Chapter I, para. 4.

5:13		14:24			
5:20					Phil. 1:3, 4
5:23	1:18	11:3			
5:25					Gl. 2:20
5:31		6:16			
6:8			5:10		
6:18					Phil. 4:6
6:23	1:7	1:3	1:2	3	Gl. 1:3; 2 Th. 1:2

B Col.	R.	1 C.	2 C.	Phlm.	
1:1	1:1			1	Gl. 1:1
1:2	1:7				Gl. 1:3; Phil, 1:1, 2
1:1, 2		1:1-3			
1:3	15:6				
1:1-3			1:1-3		1 Th. 1:1, 2
1:4		13:13			
1:1-4					2 Th. 1:1-3
1:2-4				3-5	
1:8	15:30				
1:10					1 Th. 2:12
1:26		1:7			
1:26, 27	16:25, 26				
1:27	9:23				
3:11					Gl. 3:28
3:12, 13					Gl. 5:22
4:18		16:21			

C Phil.	R.	1 C.	2 C.		
1:1, 2					Eph. 1:1, 2; Col. 1:1, 2
1:2	1:7	1:3	1:2	Gl. 1:2; 2 Th. 1:2	
1:3				Phlm. 4	
1:3, 4					Eph. 5:20
1:9				Phlm. 4-6	Col. 1:9
1:11					Eph. 1:12
1:17	2:8				
1:27					Eph. 1:4
2:2			13:11		
2:11	16:11				
3:1			13:11		
3:9	1:17; 3:21				
4:2	15:5				
4:9	15:33		13:11		
4:18					Eph. 5:2
4:20	16:27				
4:23	16:20			Gl. 6:18	

The extent of this correspondence emerges from the survey of parallelisms (see, survey A) in which we have reserved a column for Col.[1] as well as for the large epistles R., 1 and 2 C. and for Phlm. which is contemporaneous with Eph.

Survey B. reveals that Col. has far fewer parallelisms with the other epistles.

Col. is smaller than Eph. In the Nestle edition, Eph. contains 338 lines and Col. a mere 222. Therefore, it might have been expected that Col. has two thirds of the number of parallels Eph. has with the HP. However, that is not the case. The determining factor is that Eph. has a particularly large number of parallelisms with 1 C. In fact, if this last-mentioned factor is not taken into account, the fragmentary correspondence between Eph. and the HP is not at all out of the ordinary.

Our survey of the parallelisms (see survey C) between Phil. which numbers 320 lines and the other epistles addressed to communities, confirms this view.

Hence, the problem presented by the many parallelisms which exist between Eph. and the HP may be reduced to the problem presented by the many parallelisms between Eph. and 1 C. If we now examine the corresponding fragments of Eph. and 1 C., it is quite clear that there is no question of literary dependence since the incidental affinities are far too few.

With respect to the parallelisms of Eph. 1:21- 1C. 15:24 and Eph. 1:22-1 C. 15:27, we are concerned with a common theologoumenon which resulted in a certain concurence in formulation because some supernatural powers are mentioned and because a word from the O.T. is quoted which forms the basis of this theologoumenon.

In Eph. 2:20, 21 and 1 C. 3:9-12, the same words are used because both places deal with the allegory of building.

Eph. 3:2 and 1 C. 3:10 confront us with stereotype expressions. There is little likelihood that an imitator who depended on 1 C. would have spread various words of 1 C. 3:9-12 over Eph. 2:12. In the case of Eph. 3:9, 10 and 1 C, 2:7. the possibility of dependence on the latter is not excluded. But in that case, it could equally well be that R. 16:25,

---

[1] If there are also affinities with Col. besides the affinities with one or more of the other epistles, the parallel places in Col. are also indicated.

26 as well as Col. 1:26 are dependent on 1 C. 2:7. In our opinion, the best solution is that all these places are independent formulations of the same conception. Eph. 4:6 and 1 C. 8:6 are stereotype phrases. We have already confuted the idea of a literary dependence in connection with Eph. 4:11 and 1 C. 12:28, 29 (see above, p. 211s.). Our investigation into the title given to Christ in Eph., κεφαλή, did not lead us to conclude that the author had borrowed this appllation from 1 C. 11:3, because there is too little correspondence between 1 C. 11:3 and all the places in which the word occurs in Eph. Therefore, we attach little faith to the possibility of a dependence on 1 C. 11:3 in the case of Eph. 4:15, 16. The words of Eph. 5:23 which correspond with those of 1 C. 11:3 have also not been borrowed from the latter but are most probably fixed terms.

Judging by the correspondence presented by 1 C. 4:12 and some manuscript versions of 1 Th. 4:11, the expression fo working with one's own hands has a stereotype character. This sufficiently explains the use of a similar formulation in Eph. 4:28.

In Eph. 5:5; 1 C. 5:11; 6:9 and 10, we are dealing with some fundemental paraenetical material. Fairly obvious combinations of words are used in the different contexts of Eph. 5:13 and 1 C. 14:24. In Eph. 5:23 and 1 C. 6:16, the correspondence is due to an O.T. quotation. Although the train of thought is different, the same underlying assumptions govern both places.

If we were to examine the parallelism between Eph. and the other homolougomena, we would discover the same phenomena, since the correspondence in those cases is also rooted in the use of stereotype language and traditional material.

For example, we find the same derivative ritual terminology deployed in the same way but in different contexts in Eph. 5:2 and Phil. 4:18. Eph. 5:2 resembles Gal. 2:20 because a certain phrase occurs in both instances. This phrase is part of the Christian avowal which had already assumed a settled form.

We therefore have no hesitation in rejecting the theory of Goodspeed which seeks to explain the corresponding fragments in Eph. and the HP chiefly on the basis of literary dependence.[1] The construction of Mitton we find equally unacceptable. In his view, the author of Eph. never, at any time, formed part of the Pauline circle and the correspon-

---

[1] The key to Ephesians, p. XIII (cf. also Chapter I, para. 4).

dence between this work and the HP was by Mitton ascribed to a mne-
monic process.[1]

Since the author of Eph. was so able to cope with traditional material
and stereotype phraseology which also occurs in the HP, we surmise
that all these formulations belonged to his spiritual heritage of which
he could dispose with facility. There is absolutely no evidence to suggest
that we are dealing with a person from a later period whose command
of such expressions was solely the result of reading and re-reading the
HP.

More objections could be raised against the postulations of Goodspeed and Mitton. We would again bring forward the affinities in style
between Eph. and the HP; affinities which can be explained neither
on the basis of immitation of Col. nor by the style of passages in the
HP which evince parallelism with fragments in Eph.[2] Furthermore,
there is the unaccountable affinity in thoughts and manner repeated
attention in Chapters VII-IX.

The extent to which the coincidence in style and contents escaped
these two scholars in Eph. and the HP. emerges when they declare
with such ease that the author of Eph. was either no Jew [3] or probably
no Jew.[4] They made no allowances whatsoever for the Jewish Hellenistic character of the epistle and the testimony of its so unmistakeable relationship with Judaism.

In addition, the cornerstone of their theories is the dependence of
Eph. on an authentic Col. We have demonstrated that more indications
can be found which argue the priority of Eph. (see above, p. 426). Nor
does the close affinity in disposition between Eph. and R. suggest any
dependence on the part of Eph. on Col. (see above, p. 71). (As for the
fact that many scholars attach as much doubt to the authenticity of
Col. as that of Eph.—this passes without comment on the part of Goodspeed and Mitton.)

We believe that the corresponding fragments in Eph. and the HP
originate in the fact that those who drew up Eph. drew on and had acces
to the same spiritual inheritance as those who took part in the writing
of the HP.[5] Eph. and the HP are products of the same circle. The

---

[1] Cf. Chapter I, para. 4.

[2] See above, p. 210-212.

[3] Goodspeed, The Key to Ephesians, p. V.

[4] Mitton, The Epistle to the Ephesians, p. 262.

[5] Dahl, op. cit., p. 74ss. comes to a similar conclusion. He thinks that the epistle
was probably written or dicated by a pupil of Paul.

dominant figure in this circle was Paul. It is Paul, therefore, whom we may call the author of all these epistles.

There is one particular aspect of Eph. which may explain why this epistle contains so very may fragments which are reminiscent of the HP and especially of 1 C. The epistle is addressed to presons who are new converts and have not as yet been in personal contact with Paul. Unlike the HP epistles, he does not enter in detail upon certain problems, nor does he express himself so explicitly on the subject of heresy as in Col. The epistle is more general in character and tends towards a fundamental sort of teaching.[1] For that reason it contains such an extensive amount of traditional material and stereotype phraseology which likewise makes an appearance in the other epistles

Since a fair number of topics are handled in 1 C, which is large—more, even, than in R. which is longer—a great deal of such material is also found there. That is the reason for the special correspondence with this epistle.

We shall not concern ourselves with the correspondence between our epistle and 1 Pt. and James. In our opinion, this is not decisive to the authenticity of Eph.[2] and we attribute it to the fact that the elements of the kerugma and Christian paraenesis used in these epistles were not only the spiritual properby of Paul and his associates but that were the common possession of an altogether far more extended ancient Christian circle.

---

[1] Cf. above, pp. 374, 411s. See also Dahl, op. cit., p. 73s.

[2] Cf. Chapter I, para. 4.

IN CONCLUSION

Let us, now that we have come to the end of this investigation, turn to summarizing our conclusions.

To begin with, the outward testimony suggests that the Epistle to the Ephesians was written prior to the year A.D. 96 (p. 44). In its formal aspects, the epistle conforms to ancient epistolary standards (p. 55).

The disposition of Eph. diverges from that of the HP in its combined eulogy and eucharistia formulation and in the length of the prayers. Nevertheless, there are a number of utterances in these other epistles which could well account for this departure from the norm. Apart from this, the disposition of Eph. is so typically Pauline and so close to R. that we have no alternative but to assume that the author was closely involved in the creation of all the HP and particularly with the writing of R. (p. 71).

The difficulty presented by the corrupted praescript is surmounted if we consider the possible erasure of two place names; if this is done, the praescript falls into line with the rest of the HP. As it is, there seems to be justification to surmise that the names of Hierapolis and Laodicea were originally quoted in the praescript.

If the epistle in authentic, the fact that Paul is the only sender named can be satisfactorily accounted for. As in R., the apostle, making his first direct contact with Christians amongst whom he has not yet worked personally, approaches them alone, in the full consciousness of a unique and prophetic mission.

In the case of epistles where others, besides Paul, are mentioned as senders, we must reckon with a contribution on the part of these co-senders. In the light of the common factor linking R. and Eph., any differences and similarities between them must be weithed seriously when coming to an assessment of the authenticity of Eph. Nor must it in this connection be forgotten that all the epistles may, to a certain extent, have been coloured by whatever scribe actually put the missive to paper.

The greetings or blessings at the end of Eph. are not obviously similar to those in the other epistles. However, the more deep-seated affinities in this section do furnish a positive indication for the authenticity of the epistle (p. 98).

A correspondence in style, grammatical detail and vocabulary between Col. and Eph. makes us think that the two are the work of the same hand. There are a few differences from Col. but this must be ascribed to the fact that the latter was written together with Timotheus. Then, again, there is the factor that the same scribe need not necessarily have been employed on the two occasions.

The writing of Eph. and Col. is stamped with the same very specific hallmark; this owes a certain debt to Semitic influences and probably evolved in a bilingual Palestinian milieu. It could well be that contact with the Christians living in Caesarea stimulated Paul, to whom this style was by no means alien, to cultivate it intensively in Eph, and Col.

Various components of this style, so manifest in Eph., can also be detected in the HP and some, moreover, are characteristic of it. An identical style is used in 1 C. 1:1-9 and in R. 1:1-10. In point of style, Eph. has many features in common with R. A number of passages in 2 C. and Phil. bear a like affinity.

The correspondence in style which exists between Eph. on the one and and the HP—especially R.—on the other, leads us to presume that despite some pronounced differences, Paul must have been the author of Eph. (p. 205ss.).

Our investigation into some of the more striking words used in Eph. resulted in a view of the epistle which conflicts with the interpretations and hypotheses put forward by others. As far as we are concerned, we were unable to make out the traces of any early forms of Gnosticism or even arguments to refute them. We found ourselves hesitant with respect to Meuzelaar's rabbinic interpretation and extremely cautious over attaching exaggerated significance to the notion of the "corporate personality".

It is our contention that the author of Eph. is again and again guided by Jewish and Hellenistic Jewish conceptions and ways of thinking. There is a marked distinction from the HP in that the author by repetition deals with the ecclesia as a general concept and never with the ecclesia in an exclusively local context.

Furthermore, whilst looking at such striking words as well as on closer scrutiny of the ecclesiological content of the epistle, we were able to discover a substantial correspondence with ideas found in the HP (p. 349; 391ss·). In the chapter dealing with the eccesiological material of the epistle for example, we pinpointed a frequent use of the metaphor of building or edification. In this connexion, we were forced to refute any suggestion of an "Iranian Gnostic" interpretation and found, on the contrary, a similarity with Palestinian Jewish patterns of thought which are also manifest in the Qumran scrolls (p. 359; 365).

The paraenesis of Eph. bears a distinct resemblance to the equivalent sections in the HP and, like them, displays both Jewish, Greek and Hellenistic aspects. Eph. and the HP make identical use of a complex of traditions which were the peculiar property of late Judaism. In all likelihood, Eph. contains some basic paraenetical material which may explain the fact that the concept of the struggle is given such thorough and exhaustive treatment (p. 411s.).

After acquainting ourselves with the fragmental points of agreement between Eph., Col. and the HP, we parted company with the theories of Goodspeed and Mitton and the idea of literary interdependence. We feel that the most acceptable proposition is to assume the existence of a common "draft" which provided the basis for both Eph. and Col. We hope we successfully indicated the vestigial remnants of this draft in the two epistles.

All other affinity between Eph. and Eph. and the HP is due to the fact that all these epistles drew on a certain stock of stereotype expressions and traditional material which formed part and parcel of the intellectual heritage and equipment of Paul and his associates. Since Eph. and Col. came into being at more or less the same time, there is an especially large number of such coincidental expressions in these two epistles.

Yet, Eph. also shares many correspondences of this kind with the HP. In our opinion, this is due to the generalized tenor of the epistle and to the fundamental nature of the doctrine it propounds.

Taking all these factors into account, we arrive at the final conclusions that it is not only plausible but even probable that Paul was the author of Eph. It seems to us that the epistle must have been written during the period of imprisonment at Caesarea.[1]

This investigation should be seen as part of the controversy surrounding the historical problem of the authenticity of Eph. The author sincerely hopes that, as the debate continues, his study will serve to prevent the affinities between Eph. and the epistles generally regarded as authentic from being dismissed too lightheartedly. Moreover, he hopes that scholars of the future will not be over-hasty in construing discrepancies between the thoughts and ideas encompassed within this epistle and the thoughts and ideas of that apostle who must surely rank amongst the greatest of all prophets.

---

[1] Our reasons for citing Caesarea in particular are given on p. 204s.

INDEX LOCORUM

O.T. (HEBR. TEXT)

LXX

N.T.

APOSTOLIC FATHERS

PHILO

PSEUDEPIGRAPHA OF THE O.T.

QUMRAN

SYNCRETISM AND GNOSIS

INDEX OF AUTHORS

Italicized numbers indicate pages on which full titles are to be found